The Discourses

Volume One

Letter from the General Editor

The Library of Arabic Literature makes available Arabic editions and English translations of significant works of Arabic literature, with an emphasis on the seventh to nineteenth centuries. The Library of Arabic Literature thus includes texts from the pre-Islamic era to the cusp of the modern period, and encompasses a wide range of genres, including poetry, poetics, fiction, religion, philosophy, law, science, travel writing, history, and historiography.

Books in the series are edited and translated by internationally recognized scholars. They are published as hardcovers in parallel-text format with Arabic and English on facing pages, as English-only paperbacks, and as downloadable Arabic editions. For some texts, the series also publishes separate scholarly editions with full critical apparatus.

The Library encourages scholars to produce authoritative Arabic editions, accompanied by modern, lucid English translations, with the ultimate goal of introducing Arabic's rich literary heritage to a general audience of readers as well as to scholars and students.

The Library of Arabic Literature is supported by a grant from the New York University Abu Dhabi Institute and is published by NYU Press.

Philip F. Kennedy
General Editor, Library of Arabic Literature

المحاضرات

أبو عليّ الحسن اليوسيّ

المجلّد الأوّل

LIBRARY OF المكتبة ARABIC العربية LITERATURE

The Discourses

Reflections on History, Sufism, Theology, and Literature

Volume One

Al-Ḥasan al-Yūsī

Edited and translated by
Justin Stearns

Volume editors
Philip F. Kennedy
Shawkat M. Toorawa

NEW YORK UNIVERSITY PRESS
New York

NEW YORK UNIVERSITY PRESS
New York

Library of Congress Cataloging-in-Publication Data

Names: Yūsī, al-Ḥasan ibn Masʿūd, 1630 or 1631-1691, author. | Stearns, Justin, 1974- editor translator. | Yūsī, al-Ḥasan ibn Masʿūd, 1630 or 1631-1691. Muḥāḍarāt fī al-adab wa-al-lughah. English. | Yūsī, al-Ḥasan ibn Masʿūd, 1630 or 1631-1691. Muḥāḍarāt fī al-adab wa-al-lughah.
Title: The discourses : reflections on history, Sufism, theology, and literature / Al-Ḥasan Al-Yūsī ; edited and translated by Justin Stearns.
Other titles: Title on Arabic added t.p.: [Muḥāḍarāt]
Description: New York : New York University Press, 2021. | Includes bibliographical references and indexes. | In English and Arabic. |
Summary: "The Discourses offers rich insight into the varied intellectual interests of an ambitious and gifted Moroccan scholar, covering subjects as diverse as genealogy, theology, Sufism, history, and social mores. In addition to representing the author's intellectual interests, The Discourses also includes numerous autobiographical anecdotes, which offer valuable insight into the history of Morocco, including the transition from the Saadian to the Alaouite dynasty, which occurred during al-Yusi's lifetime. Translated into English for the first time, The Discourses offers readers access to the intellectual landscape of the early modern Muslim world through an author who speaks openly and frankly about his personal life and his relationships with his country's rulers, scholars, and commoners"-- Provided by publisher.
Identifiers: LCCN 2019040230 (print) | LCCN 2019040231 (ebook) | ISBN 9780814764572 (cloth) | ISBN 9780814789292 (ebook) | ISBN 9780814764831 (ebook)
Classification: LCC AC106 .Y8713 2021 (print) | LCC AC106 (ebook) | DDC 892.7/44--dc23
LC record available at https://lccn.loc.gov/2019040230

LC ebook record available at https://lccn.loc.gov/2019040231New York University Press books are printed on acid-free paper,
and their binding materials are chosen for strength and durability.

Series design by Titus Nemeth.

Typeset in Tasmeem, using DecoType Naskh and Emiri.

Typesetting and digitization by Stuart Brown.

Manufactured in the United States of America
c10 9 8 7 6 5 4 3 2 1

Table of Contents

For Anahita, Clio, and Makeda

Acknowledgments

This translation has been a labor of love—a project that has inspired me with joy even as my conviction grew that my abilities were entirely insufficient for the task. That I have been able to bring it to this point has everything to do with the support I received. While it may be a common trope to claim that a given work is really the product of the effort of a host of friends and colleagues, in this case the claim is valid in more ways than one. None of the following is responsible for any of this book's failings and all deserve more credit than I am able to give here.

My thanks go first to the Library of Arabic Literature (LAL) family, beginning with Philip Kennedy, who initially encouraged me to submit a proposal and subsequently had the dubious pleasure of being paired with me as my initial editor. Phil significantly improved my first efforts, patiently corrected my belabored attempts to parse the poetry included in *The Discourses*, and provided steady emotional support throughout. I am grateful to the anonymous external reviewer for suggestions and revisions, and for pushing me to make my introduction and the text more approachable. I am aware that I was not able to address all of the concerns raised. I also owe a tremendous amount to the efforts of the initially anonymous executive reviewer, Shawkat Toorawa, who went over every line of the book, rewrote many sentences, corrected numerous errors of translation and style, and simply made it a better work overall. I am additionally grateful to the cartographer, Martin Grosch, for his beautiful and accurate maps, and to Rana Siblini for her careful attention to voweling the Arabic poetry. When it came to the final stages of editing, Stuart Brown and Keith Miller did truly impressive work in catching numerous discrepancies and errors—their careful reading has made the text clearer and more elegant. Through this entire process, Chip Rossetti, LAL's editorial director, has guided the translation through its various stages with careful attention and good humor. My debt to all of them is profound.

Many years ago, while carrying out my doctoral research in the Consejo Superior de Investigaciones Científicas (back when it was still in the heart of Madrid), Maribel Fierro placed a copy of *The Discourses* in my hands, telling me it was always worth having a look at what al-Yūsī had to say. For that initial suggestion and her ongoing support and friendship I am deeply grateful.

At New York University Abu Dhabi (NYUAD), my colleague Maurice Pomerantz, who, although on the LAL board, was not officially affiliated with this project, may well have felt that he was, considering the number of times I knocked on his door with questions that he invariably answered with grace and insight. I am deeply grateful to him for his support and friendship, and also to my other colleagues who have listened to me ramble on about al-Yūsī's *Discourses*, and who have offered occasional suggestions. These include Nora Barakat, Laila Familiar, Maya Kesrouany, Erin Pettigrew, Nathalie Peutz, and Dris Suleimani. Then there are the LAL fellows who have come through NYUAD over the past few years. I was fortunate enough to discuss translation from the Arabic in general with them, and occasionally, in our intermittent seminars, my attempts to translate *The Discourses*. This group included Michael Cooperson, Robert Hoyland, Marcel Kurpershoek, Joseph Lowry (who also suffered through the pages of the first draft I submitted to LAL), Bilal Orfali, Dwight Reynolds, Mohammed Rustom, and Sophia Vasalou. I should add to them LAL's executive editors, Shawkat Toorawa and James Montgomery, from whose repeated visits to Abu Dhabi and the lectures and classes they gave during them I learned a great deal. Together with Phil, LAL's general editor, both Shawkat and James have done the fields of Arabic literature and Middle East history a tremendous service. It has been a privilege to be a witness to their ongoing efforts.

There is a world beyond the office, and it is the one where I have spent the most important and rewarding moments in the past eight years since I first conceived of undertaking this translation. That world has been made magical by my family: my amazing and accomplished wife, Nathalie Peutz, and my remarkable children, Mattheus, Anahita, Clio, and Makeda. It is in the hours of roughhousing; playing at the park; driving to and from school; playing chess, cribbage, and card games; debating books and movie plots; finding lost toys; teaching bike riding; and building sandcastles at the beach—between tantrums and laughter, with many, many hugs—that they continue to teach me to unfold the love they create within me. From further afield in space, but not in spirit, I have been sustained by my parents, Bev and Steve; my mother-in-law, Beverly; my brother, Jason; his wife, Lusungu; and my nephews, Baye and Masha. I haven't seen enough of them in these past years and I hope that the coming ones will remedy that somewhat. My love to all of them.

My daughters joined us six years ago almost to the day as I write these words. This book, which has been growing up alongside them, is for them. Count it as a gift, not quite at the level of chocolate-chip pancakes, but one also made with love.

Introduction

In 1084/1685, at the age of roughly fifty-four, and after a long and distinguished career during which he had become arguably the most influential and well-known intellectual figure of his generation in Morocco, al-Ḥasan al-Yūsī, an Amazigh scholar from the Middle Atlas, began writing a collection of essays on a wide variety of subjects. Completed three years later and gathered in a book titled *The Discourses on Language and Literature* (*al-Muḥāḍarāt fī l-adab wa-l-lughah*), they offer rich insights into the varied intellectual interests of an ambitious and gifted eleventh/seventeenth-century Moroccan scholar, covering subjects as diverse as genealogy, theology, Sufism, literature, and sociology. The book is not only representative of the author's intellectual interests—some of which, including the fields of logic and epistemology, received short shrift—but also includes numerous autobiographical anecdotes, passages about the recent history of Morocco that al-Yūsī had lived through, and passages about the people he had met and the places to which he had traveled. Today, *The Discourses* presents the reader with the rare opportunity of gaining access to the intellectual landscape of the early modern Muslim world through an author who speaks openly and frankly about his personal life and his relationships with rulers, scholars, and commoners. Morocco's complicated history during al-Yūsī's lifetime heightens the value of the work even as it requires the contemporary reader to acquire an overview of the general features of Moroccan political history.[1]

Al-Yūsī's life spanned the gap between the two dynasties that have governed Morocco from the sixteenth century AD until today, the Saʿdis (927–1069/1521–1659) and the ʿAlawites (1075/1664–present), both of which managed to preserve Morocco's independence from the expanding power of the Ottoman Empire. These two dynasties claimed descent from the Prophet Muhammad, implicitly affirming their Arab origins, unlike the Almoravids, Almohads, and Merinids, the major Amazigh dynasties that had ruled Morocco from the eleventh through the fifteenth centuries. Beginning with the death of the Saʿdis' strongest and most famous ruler, Aḥmad al-Manṣūr, in the plague of 1012/1603, the Saʿdis' control over Morocco splintered and regional leaders launched varyingly successful bids for power to preserve or contest Saʿdi rule before the dynasty's last ruler died in Marrakesh in 1659. During most of these five decades, much of Morocco was outside the control of the descendants of al-Manṣūr as they fought with each other and with a variety of rebels. One such rebel was the messianic Ibn Abī Maḥallī (d. 1022/1613), of whose career al-Yūsī offers an incisive critique in *The Discourses*. More lasting opposition to the Saʿdis was presented by a number of Sufi orders, predominantly those at Dilāʾ in the Middle Atlas, where al-Yūsī lived, studied, and taught for fifteen years, and Iligh in the Anti-Atlas, where Sīdī ʿAlī of Tazeroualt (d. 1070/1659–60) built his own political center in the 1040–50s/1630–40s before being eclipsed by the rising power of Dilāʾ in the 1050s/1650s. The importance of these political centers was equaled by the rising importance of other orders as centers of learning and scholarship, such as the Ḥamziyyah-ʿAyyāshiyyah in the High Atlas and the Nāṣiriyyah in the Darʿah Valley in the south of Morocco.[2] This was in a century when the traditional urban centers of learning at Fez and Marrakesh were overtaken, if not eclipsed, or at the very least reduced to just two among many sites of intellectual production. It was also a century when the political, economic, and intellectual contribution of what has been called "Saharan Morocco"[3]—those areas lying south of the High Atlas—played a much greater role than they had in the previous several centuries, or would in subsequent ones.

Under the Saʿdis in the sixteenth century, Moroccan rulers had extended their control of the Saharan trade routes, which in previous centuries carried travelers as well as merchants trading in gold, salt, and slaves. This expansion had culminated in Aḥmad al-Manṣūr's sending of an expedition composed largely of Moriscos and Christian converts equipped with firearms to conquer the West African Songhay Empire in 999/1591. This conquest brought the cities of Timbuktu and Gao under Moroccan control, but one that only lasted a few decades in any meaningful sense.[4] The strengthening of the political ties between West Africa and Morocco's urban centers north of the Atlas resulted in the trade route in the south of Morocco gaining in importance and realigning from Sijilmāsah in the Tifilalt region to the Darʿah Valley, farther west, where the Nāṣirī order was founded in the seventeenth century at Tamgrūt, south of Zagora. Although both the Saʿdi and the ʿAlawite dynasties came to power north of the Atlas and are remembered today for their imperial projects in Meknes, Fez, and Marrakesh, both began in the Tifilalt and then moved north.

Al-Yūsī's education was shaped foundationally by his stay at Tamgrūt and his long relationship with Abū ʿAbd Allāh Maḥammad ibn Nāṣir (d. 1085/1674) who first inducted him into the Shādhilī order of Sufism. To understand Morocco in the seventeenth century, and the political and intellectual nature of the world that al-Yūsī moved through and wrote about, we need to grasp this orientation toward the south. Doing so not only corrects the modern-day marginalization of this part of Morocco, it also cautions us against judging Morocco to be at the intellectual margins of the Muslim world in the early modern period. As Khaled El-Rouayheb has persuasively argued in a recent book, it was precisely during the seventeenth century that the Arab Ottoman lands—and Egypt and Syria in particular—experienced an intellectual revival due to an influx of scholars from the so-called geographical margins: The importance of Moroccan scholarship in fact reached far beyond its borders, into the central Ottoman territories to the East.[5]

The lands under Ottoman rule play only a minor role in *The Discourses*, due no doubt in part to al-Yūsī not having traveled east before composing it; he did perform the pilgrimage to Mecca in the years before his death, but subsequently barely interacted with the scholars in Egypt and in the Hijaz. The one extended episode of *The Discourses* that is set in Egypt details a meeting between the leader of the Dilāʾ lodge, Abū ʿAbd Allāh Maḥammad al-Ḥājj (d. 1082/1671), and the famed author of the history of al-Andalus, Abū ʿAbbās Aḥmad ibn Muḥammad al-Maqqarī (d. 1041/1632), who had previously lived in Fez for many years. Besides this and what Maḥammad al-Ḥājj related to al-Yūsī of al-Maqqarī's own experiences in Egypt, discussion of the contemporary eastern Mediterranean—as opposed to during the Abbasid period—is completely absent.

The world al-Yūsī describes also almost entirely ignores Morocco's northern neighbors, Spain and Portugal. This omission is especially striking considering the establishment of Christian European enclaves on the Moroccan coast in the sixteenth to seventeenth centuries and the mass expulsion of Moriscos from Spain in 1018–23/1609–14, many of whom found their way to Morocco, settling in the north of the country, including in Salé, Rabat's sister city. It was in Salé, during the first decades of al-Yūsī's life, that an independent pirate state emerged, composed in large part of former Moriscos and Christian converts to Islam.[6] This is in stark contrast to mentions of these events in the works of such figures as the Morisco Aḥmad al-Ḥajarī (d. after 1051/1641–42) and to the careers of the Jewish Pallache family, whose members in this period were almost constantly involved in economic and political affairs with European powers.[7] Al-Yūsī's interests, on the contrary, and thus also the content of *The Discourses,* are focused on Morocco's internal history, and its intellectual and spiritual landscapes.

The author

Al-Ḥasan al-Yūsī was born into the Amazigh tribe of the Aït Yūsī in 1040–41/1631 in the Fezāz region of the Middle Atlas of Morocco. His mother died early in his life, a loss he describes in his *Fahrasah*, or account of his studies, as having a great impact on him, leading him to focus on his studies and to ask his father to send him away to further his learning.[8] His father sent him south, where he studied first in Marrakesh, Sijilmāsah, and Tarundant, and then, much more importantly, in the Darʿah Valley south of Zagora at Tamgrūt, where he studied with Abū ʿAbd Allāh Maḥammad ibn Nāsir, the founder of the Nāsiriyyah branch of the Shādhilī order. That Sufi order and its branches, together with the Qādirī order, have dominated the social and intellectual landscape of Morocco from the seventh/thirteenth century until today. [9]

Al-Yūsī returned to the Middle Atlas and settled at the Dilā' *zāwiyah,* or lodge, which was in the process of becoming the central political power in northern Morocco. He was based at the Dilā' lodge for fifteen years, during which time he married, had children, and solidified his status as a major scholar. In 1079/1668, Rashīd ibn al-Sharīf (d. 1082/1672), the first ruler of the rising ʿAlawite dynasty, defeated the Dilā'iyyah, razed their lodge, and brought al-Yūsī and other scholars to Fez. Al-Yūsī enjoyed generally good relations with the first two rulers of the new ʿAlawite dynasty, but he deeply mourned the destruction of the Dilā' lodge and wrote a long poem lamenting its demise.

For the next decade and a half, al-Yūsī moved between teaching in Fez, Tetouan, and Marrakesh. In 1095/1684, he was sent by the second ʿAlawite ruler, Moulay Ismāʿīl, to live near the ruins of the Dilā' lodge, where he spent three years. It was here, where he had been happiest years before, that he wrote *The Discourses,* and it was also from here that he wrote a letter to Moulay Ismāʿīl admonishing him publicly for some of his policies, including his disarming of several major tribes.[10] Notwithstanding this critical letter (which added substantially to its author's fame), and a subsequent exchange with the ruler, al-Yūsī seems to have remained on favorable terms with the ruling family.[11] In 1101/1690, he undertook the pilgrimage to Mecca with Moulay Ismāʿīl's son al-Muʿtaṣim.[12]

In 1102/1691, shortly after his return from the east, al-Yūsī died in his hometown of Tamzīzīt and was buried there. His body was later moved to a tomb near Sefrou. His influence in Morocco was substantial, not only through his many written works, but also because some of his many students spread his teachings east to Egypt and the Levant.[13]

A work and its intellectual context

The Discourses does not fall easily within any given genre. In it, al-Yūsī moves seamlessly from history to poetry, from Sufism to personal anecdote, from grammar to theology. For the modern reader, especially one who has not read widely in Islamic intellectual history, *The Discourses* therefore poses a variety of challenges, not the least of which is understanding why al-Yūsī cared about the things he did. A brief and necessarily insufficient survey of the major intellectual trends of his time will be useful.

Al-Yūsī belonged to the Shādhilī Sufi order—named after its putative founder, Abū l-Ḥasan al-Shādhilī (d. 656/1258)—which had been revived in Morocco by al-Jazūlī (d. 869/1465) in the ninth/fifteenth century; to the Ashʿarī school of theology, which had been introduced in the Maghrib in the fifth/eleventh century; and to the Sunni Mālikī school of jurisprudence, which had dominated the Muslim West since the same period.[14] Whereas these affiliations may be distinct, al-Yūsī hardly experienced them that way. In seventeenth-century Morocco, and throughout the premodern Muslim world, the study and practice of jurisprudence and theology—not to mention logic, medicine, and grammar—were carried out by scholars who were to varying degrees associated with Sufi orders. These scholars brought the focus of these orders on disciplining the desires of the body and on cultivating an awareness of the immanence of the Divine to their understanding of how to organize society and interpret the natural world. This understanding of Sufism as a coherent method to interpret and synthesize jurisprudence and theology had arguably first reached Morocco with al-Ghazālī's (d. 505/1111) *Revival of the Religious Sciences* (*Iḥyāʾ ʿulūm al-dīn*) in the sixth/twelfth century, an arrival often associated with Ibn Tūmart's Almohad movement, and one mentioned in passing in *The Discourses* itself. The extent to which a scholar should focus on mystical as opposed to more worldly scholarship was a personal issue for al-Yūsī, and in a striking anecdote in *The Definitive Collection of Rulings Regarding the Sciences* (*al-Qānūn fī aḥkām al-ʿilm*)—his book on knowledge, teaching, and studying—he reflected on his own desire to turn his back on his social responsibilities and devote himself to spiritual practice:

> In the time that I kept company with our teacher, the exemplar Abū ʿAbd Allāh ibn Nāṣir, Exalted God have mercy on him, my ego incited me to occupy myself solely with religious devotion, to travel only for spiritual purposes, and to give up teaching. He did not agree with this, so I asked him one day, "Which is better, knowledge or mystical understanding?" "Mystical understanding," he replied, and I said, "Why then do we not busy ourselves with those things that bring it about?" And he replied, "Mystical understanding is an allotment, and whoever it has been allotted to will receive it. In our time, I have not seen anything better than teaching knowledge."
>
> I spent some time in Fez in the days of Rashīd ibn al-Sharīf. I taught and was well compensated for doing so. I would ride to his court, eat his food, and dress like the others, but I became troubled by this state of affairs and planned to flee and travel the world, leaving my family in the care of their Great and Mighty Creator. I mentioned this to our teacher Abū Muḥammad ʿAbd al-Qādir ibn ʿAlī al-Fāsī, and he said to me, "If this took place in the proper fashion, it would be possible, but I am afraid that you would do it out of vain desire and therefore find doing so to be without profit." Because of this, I gave up my plan. What he was referring to is the fact that if the worshipper moves toward Exalted God, then he is a worshipper of Exalted God, who will then help him and care for him. But if he moves due to his ego then he is a worshipper of his ego, and he will give himself over to it and will perish along with it.[15]

Al-Yūsī uses this anecdote as an occasion to stress the importance of having a teacher to guide one through complicated matters, and consoles himself by noting that while abandoning one's family to focus on God may have been appropriate for al-Ghazālī and al-Shādhilī, both the mystic and the scholar have roles to play, and while the former is nobler, the latter is of greater use to God.

A number of Moroccan Sufi saints appear in *The Discourses*, including those who brazenly rejected religious rituals and are remembered principally for their ecstatic sayings.[16] Al-Yūsī was profoundly devoted to his spiritual teachers and, from what we can tell from his writings, to developing his own spiritual practice, but he was also deeply critical of those Sufis who demonstrated a desire for political power or social authority. This is perhaps unsurprising given the political unrest of his time. Yet, in his analysis of the dangers of the ego, al-Yūsī not only critiques such prominent cases as the rebel Ibn Abī Maḥallī (d. 1022/1613), who had messianic pretensions, he also criticizes the more systemic abuses within Sufi communities, notably those leaders who mislead their followers or deceive them in hopes of temporal gain and social prestige. It needs to be emphasized that al-Yūsī's conservatism was one of principled critique and not of conformity. His suspicion of Sufis who sought temporal power was balanced by his sense that a person of principle, such as himself, ought to hold authority to account. This impulse runs through both *The Discourses* and the letters he wrote in the last years of his life to the ruler Moulay Ismāʿīl calling on him to live up to the example of rule offered by the four righteous caliphs who succeeded the Prophet Muḥammad.[17] Similarly, his critique of abuses should not distract from his discussion of the numerous prominent Sufis who appear in the pages of *The Discourses*, presenting a far-flung interconnected web of spiritual devotion to God that united the Baghdad of the third/ninth century with the Cairo of the ninth/fifteenth century and the Morocco of the five hundred years preceding al-Yūsī himself.

On the theological front, the reader of *The Discourses* will repeatedly encounter the doctrine of occasionalism, central to the Ashʿarī school to which al-Yūsī belonged, which holds that God is the only causative agent of everything that occurs (this doctrine could easily be associated with the imperative to place one's trust in God, which is prominent within Sufi circles, but also often found outside them). Proponents of Ashʿarism, which included to varying degrees the vast majority of Mālikī jurists in North and West Africa in the eleventh/seventeenth century, saw occasionalism as an elaboration of a belief in the unity and oneness of God and opposed it to the belief in secondary or natural causation that they attributed to philosophers.[18] Al-Yūsī's repeated engagement with occasionalism, particularly in the section of *The Discourses* where he discusses contagion, deserves close reading for numerous reasons, among them his willingness to criticize an unspecified group of Sufis for going too far in their interpretation of the principle: They ignored the fact that God's habit of making things happen in specific ways can be relied upon with confidence.[19] There is for our author no tension between the regularity of natural processes and God's status as sole actor. Al-Yūsī moves effortlessly between natural and moral worlds when he compares God being the original cause of the transmission of disease with man's ego (and not Satan) being the original cause of his sins. For al-Yūsī, a correct understanding of causality is vital for the discerning scholar who wishes to understand the external and internal worlds.

In terms of jurisprudence, al-Yūsī's Mālikī background is comparatively irrelevant in comparison with the broader historical, literary, theological, and spiritual concerns that run through the entire work. This is not necessarily curious, but in a work that ranges so broadly it is worth noting that the author was not invested in exploring his interests in law (or logic, for that matter), although he adopts a highly logical approach to many of the themes he discusses.

A final aspect of *The Discourses* that may surprise readers new to premodern Islamic literature is its relentlessly classical nature. By classical I mean the author's use of a canon of poetry, political history, and literary anecdotes that have little to do directly with Morocco in the seventeenth century, but that deeply reflect al-Yūsī's education and self-understanding. Much of the poetry he quotes is by Arab poets of the sixth through twelfth centuries from the Arabian Peninsula, Iraq and the Levant, preponderantly pre- or early Islamic. Similarly, he retells or quotes numerous accounts from the lives of the Prophet Muḥammad, his Companions, and the first four caliphs, as well as scattered anecdotes from the Umayyad and Abbasid caliphates. In doing so, al-Yūsī not only demonstrates that an Amazigh scholar from the Middle Atlas had fully absorbed the classical Arabic literary heritage—after all, this had been happening for centuries—but he also weaves Morocco's contemporary political and spiritual landscape into this much earlier Eastern narrative. Thus, the hubris of the first ʿAlawite ruler, al-Rashīd, is compared to that of a Buyid ruler of fourth/tenth century Baghdad, and prominent Sufis of his own day are juxtaposed with Junayd (d. 298/910) and Sarī al-Saqaṭī (d. 253/867), Sufis of the classical period. The desire to reach into the past to find stories and anecdotes with purported moral and pedagogical benefit is not limited to the East, however, and al-Yūsī has a biting passage on the misguided nature of the sixth/twelfth century messianic Amazigh Almohad movement that united the Iberian Peninsula with sub-Saharan West Africa and reshaped the intellectual and political landscapes of the Muslim West in the succeeding centuries. It is this desire and ability to include episodes from Morocco itself that gives *The Discourses*' classicism a local touch, although it bears remarking that al-Yūsī includes material from only as far back as the Almoravids in the fifth/eleventh century, mentioning the Arab Muslim conqueror of North Africa, ʿUqbah ibn Nāfiʿ (d. 63/683), only briefly in passing.

The place of *The Discourses* within al-Yūsī's body of work

Al-Yūsī was a prolific author with broad interests, writing major works on literature, logic, legal theory, theology, epistemology, and Sufism, along with a variety of shorter treatises, legal opinions, and poems. For this period, we have historical chronicles, travel accounts, biographical dictionaries, works of Sufism, collections of poetry, works on medicine, and works addressing the compartmentalization of knowledge, but nothing that draws on all of these and does so interspersed with personal anecdotes, reflections, and samples of the author's poetry. *The Discourses* is unique within al-Yūsī's output and within the general literary production of early modern Morocco. It is also clearly a work of an author's mature years: Al-Yūsī refers several times to his earlier works, and relies on several of them in *The Discourses*. For example, toward the end of *The Discourses* he draws at length on his large collection of sayings and proverbs, *Flowers from the Greatest Proverbs and Sayings* (*Zahr al-akam fī-l-amthāl wa-l-ḥikam*), compiled early in his career. He also describes the circumstances that led him to compose a substantial treatise on the unity of God, *The Well of Knowledge for the Commoners and Elect Concerning the Profession of Faith* (*Mashrab al-ʿāmm wa-l-khāṣṣ min kalimat al-ikhlāṣ*). Other aspects of his intellectual production, especially his work on legal theory, *The Shining Moons of Commentary on the Choicest Collection of Legal Theory* (*Budur al-lawāmiʿ fī sharḥ jamʿ al-jawāmiʿ fī uṣūl al-fiqh*), a commentary on a work of the famous Shāfiʿī jurist Tāj al-Dīn ʿAbd al-Wahhāb al-Subkī (d. 771/1370), barely register in *The Discourses*.[20] His other major theological work, a commentary on the popular and widespread creed of the influential Ashʿarī theologian (and logician) al-Sanūsī (d. 895/1490), *Al-Yūsī's Marginal Glosses on the Longer Creed of al-Sanūsī* (*Ḥawāshī al-Yūsī ʿalā sharḥ kubrā al-Sanūsī*), contains passages that take up occasionalism in a manner similar to *The Discourses*.

Today, we must be wary of praising *The Discourses* by contrasting it with what Jacques Berque and Muḥammad Ḥajjī, giants of scholarship on Morocco in the second half of the last century, termed a stale culture of commentary and general intellectual decline. Current scholarship on Islamic intellectual history now argues strongly against the idea of early modern scholarly production as largely derivative. Khaled El-Rouayheb, for instance, has persuasively demonstrated in particular the intellectual vibrancy of Morocco during al-Yūsī's life. Yet *The Discourses* nevertheless appears exceptional in its composition and breadth, and as a window on many aspects of seventeenth-century Moroccan life that are otherwise omitted from the available sources—keeping in mind that we do not yet have a complete picture, as much of the scholarship of this century has not yet been edited.

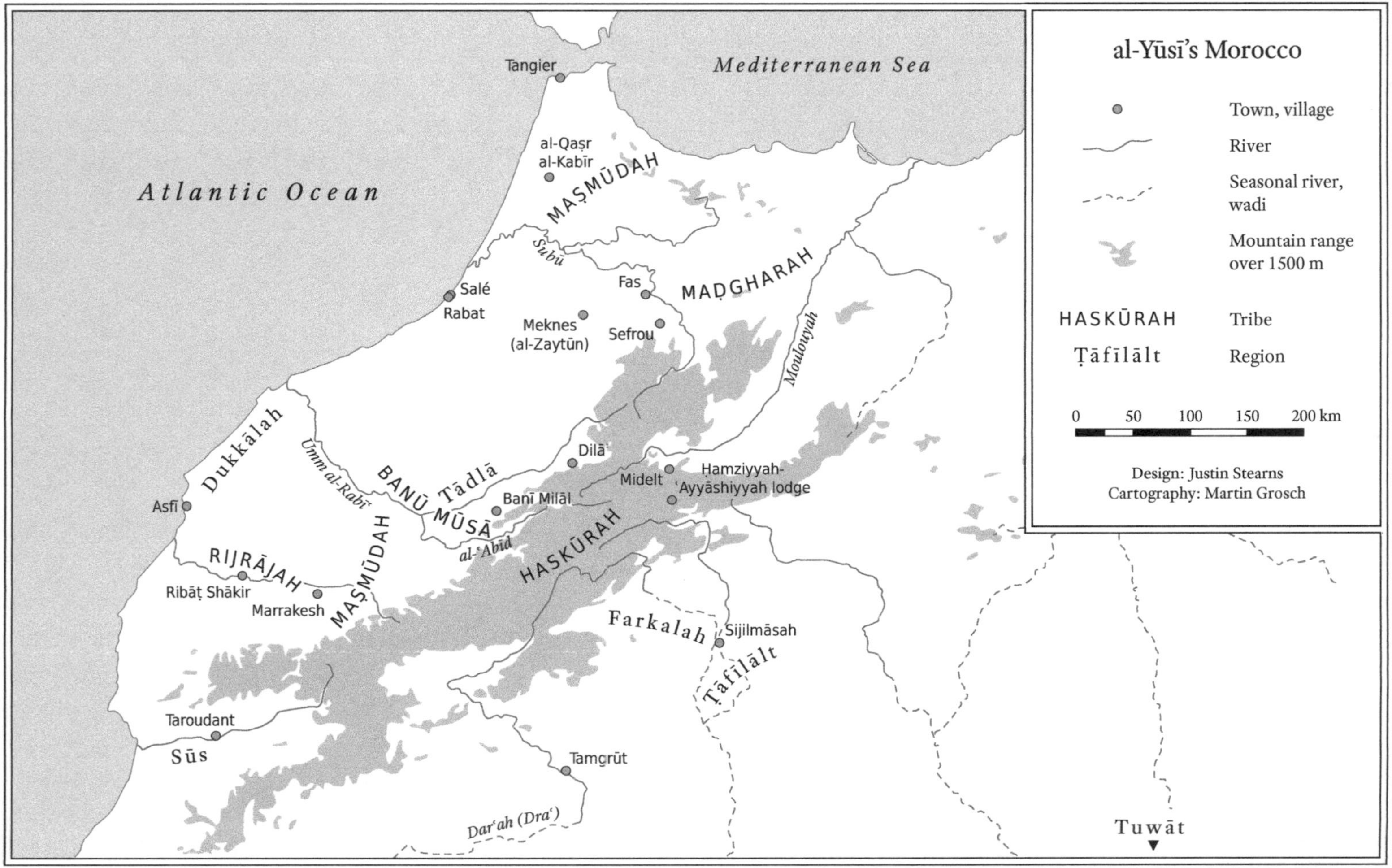
al-Yūsī's Morocco
Town, village
River
Seasonal river, wadi
Mountain range over 1500 m
HASKŪRAH
Tribe
Ṭāfīlālt
Region
0 50 100 150 200 km
Design: Justin Stearns
Cartography: Martin Grosch
Atlantic Ocean
Mediterranean Sea
Tangier
al-Qaṣr al-Kabīr
MAṢMŪDAH
Subū
Salé
Rabat
Fas
MAḌGHARAH
Meknes (al-Zaytūn)
Sefrou
Moulouyah
Dukkālah
Umm al-Rabīʿ
BANŪ MŪSĀ
Tādlā
Dilāʾ
Midelt
Hamziyyah-ʿAyyāshiyyah lodge
Asfī
Banī Milāl
al-ʿAbīd
HASKŪRAH
RIJRĀJAH
Ribāṭ Shākir
Marrakesh
MAṢMŪDAH
Farkalah
Sijilmāsah
Ṭāfīlālt
Taroudant
Sūs
Tamgrūt
Darʿah (Draʿ)
Tuwāt

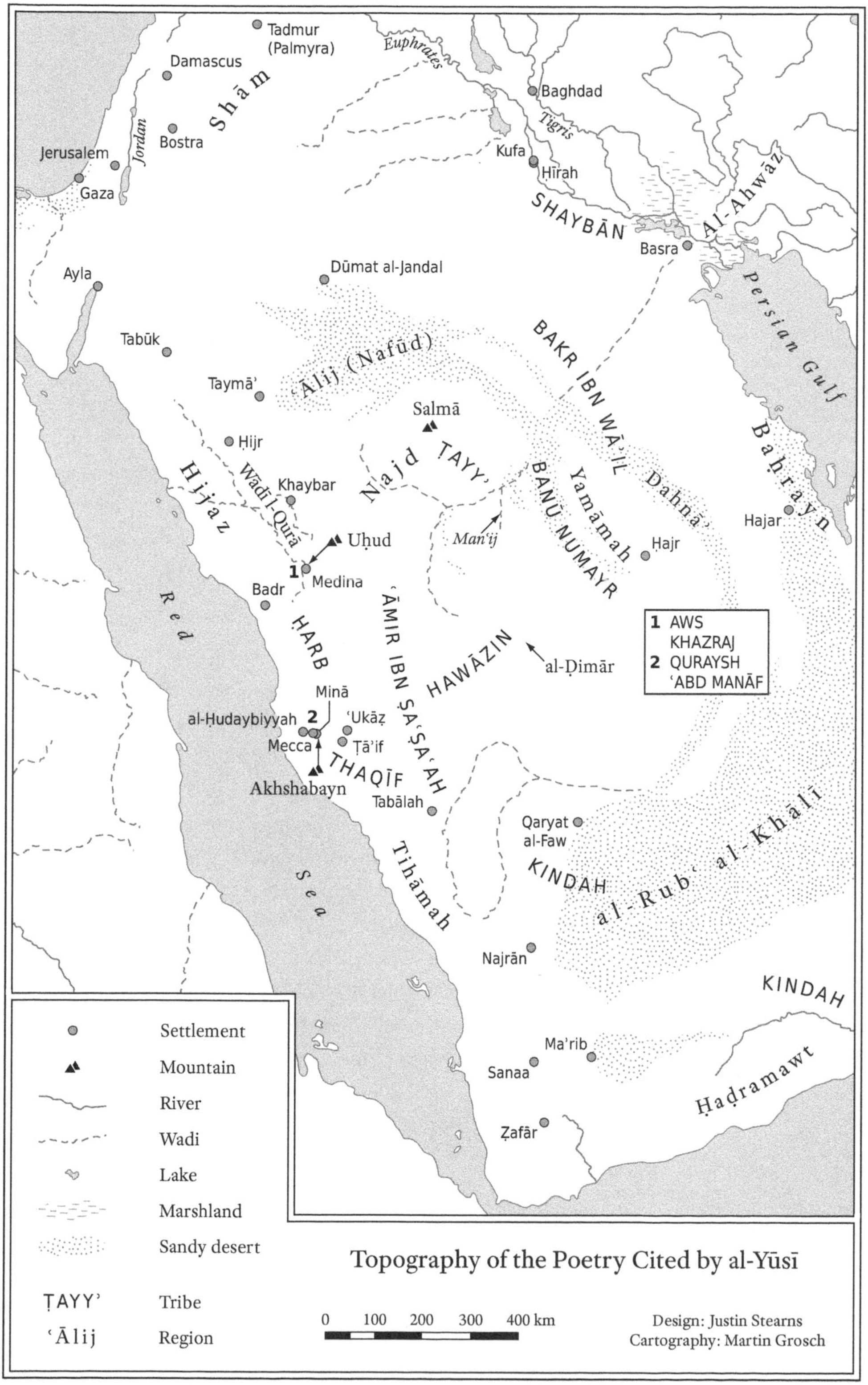

Topography of the Poetry Cited by al-Yūsī

Note on the Text

Al-Yūsī shared many of the prejudices of his age. *The Discourses*, like virtually every other book of its period, was written by a man for an audience of men.[21] For al-Yūsī, women's voices are marginal at best and he includes occasional misogynistic comments and anecdotes. Similarly, the work contains anti-Jewish asides as well as negative comments on same-sex acts between men. As translator, I am aware that al-Yūsī's prejudices contribute to widely held prejudices regarding Islamic societies. While each reader will have to wrestle with passages he or she may find offensive or problematic, I hope the historical and literary richness of *The Discourses* emerges from these pages, as well as the tensions and complexities of the society that produced the author and his work.

Questions of Translation

The Discourses presents the translator with numerous problems, beginning with the sheer quantity of poetry—both quoted and the author's own—which is difficult to effectively render into a different language. I have translated the poetry as best I could, often leaning on the advice of those far more competent in this area than myself. This poetry is followed in difficulty by the author's detailed criticism of word choice and comments on wordplay. As for geographical terms, I have translated Maghrib as Morocco, as it is almost always restricted in *The Discourses* to an area generally equal to the current borders of the nation-state of Morocco, even though the term can refer to all of North Africa west of Egypt. I have rendered the term *bilād al-qibla* (literally "land in the direction of Mecca") as "land to the south," as Moroccan scholars used it to refer the south of their country.[22] For the technical vocabulary of the many disciplines the book deals with, including theology, linguistics, and above all Sufism, I have again leaned on the work of prior scholars. The term *nafs*, for example, I at times translate as "soul," but more often as "ego," depending on the context. The latter carries certain modern connotations, but it is also more precise in conveying the fact that al-Yūsī is discussing that part of the self that contains the base, lower, selfish desires. Another difficult term is *ghaybah*, familiar to students of Shiʿism as referring to a state of occultation, usually of the twelfth Imam, in which a figure of spiritual power is present in this world but is inaccessible to his followers. Al-Yūsī, however, uses the term to refer to the trance state experienced by an adept during a listening session (or *samāʿ*, another term with a different meaning than it has in Egypt or the Levant).[23] *Ghaybah* in the sense it is found here is close to the spiritual ecstasy elsewhere referred to as *wajd* (and related *tawājud*). Terms used to describe scholars or figures of spiritual authority are somewhat more straightforward, such as *mawlā* (master), *ustādh* (teacher), *imām* (leader, exemplar), *ṣāliḥ* (devout), and *fāḍil* (distinguished). *Sayyid* is complicated in that it can refer both to a prominent figure or leader of the Muslim community, as when al-Yūsī uses it to refer to Bilāl ibn Rabāḥ, or to a descendant of the Prophet, such as the members of the Saʿdi and ʿAlawite dynasties (although he generally refers to such descendants as *sharīf*, pl. *ashrāf*). In the above cases and with the following terms related to Sufism, I have tried to be as consistent as possible: *ahl al-ṭarīq* (People of the Path), *maqām* (station (on the spiritual path)), *ʿārif* (gnostic), *faqīr* (devotee), *murābit* (ascetic), *wālī* pl. *awliyāʾ* (Friend of God), *murīd* (disciple), and *zāwiyah* (lodge), as well as less familiar ones such as *mamlakah* (temporal realm). Because LAL strives for an accessible and uncluttered presentation of its translations, I have commented minimally on these choices in the footnotes themselves while leaving as few of these terms in the original Arabic as possible. One of these is *shaykh*, which I have preserved in English as shaykh, both because of the precise connotations of the word and the fact that it is now found in English-language dictionaries. Finally, when al-Yūsī refers to the indigenous inhabitants of Morocco—an ethnic group to which he himself belongs—he does so with two terms: *barbar*, which I have kept as Berber, and *ʿajam*, a term meaning non-Arabic speaker that in the Mediterranean East would signify Persian, but which I have translated here as Amazigh. I chose to do so not so much as a nod to the contemporary politics of Amazigh identity in Morocco today, but in recognition of the degree to which the term Berber was a creation of Medieval Arabic historiography.[24]

The structure of the text

The printed Arabic edition of *The Discourses* breaks up the text into essays that run from a few paragraphs to over fifty pages. This division, along with the titles that precede the individual sections, gives the text a clear structure and makes its component parts more digestible for the reader, but it has no parallel in the manuscripts themselves. Most manuscripts use the phrase "Everything is God's to command" (*Li-llāh al-amr min qabl wa-min baʿd*) to signal the close of a given section or subject, though the phrase is not used uniformly in the manuscript tradition, to which I have tried to remain faithful. I have accordingly omitted the section breaks and the subheadings, which are not to be found in the Arabic at all. The result is a less-defined text that drifts more or less seamlessly between one subject and the next, but I believe that this decision results in a reading experience closer to the original organization.

The manuscripts and Arabic text

In establishing the Arabic edition, I relied extensively on (A) the printed 1982 edition of Muḥammad Ḥajjī and Aḥmad al-Sharqāwī (Dar al-Gharb al-Islami, Rabat). This remains the edition of *The Discourses* that any serious student of the text will want to turn to first. Their text was based on the following three manuscripts:

1. Number 32 (ج), in a collection titled *Diwān al-Yūsī*, in the Moroccan National Library in Rabat (al-Khizānah al-ʿĀmmah). It dates from around fifty years after the death of the author in 1102/1691. Due to its clarity and precision, this was the primary text they used for their edition.
2. Number 2329 (ك), also in the Moroccan National Library in Rabat (al-Khizānah al-ʿĀmmah). This manuscript is approximately a decade older than the previous one, and contains additional material, but due to the scribe's frequent copying errors, Ḥajjī and Sharqāwī used the previous one as their base.
3. A private manuscript from the library of the writer, poet, and historian ʿAbdallāh Muḥammad ibn Aḥmad Akansūs (d. 1294/1877), which they chiefly consulted for Akansūs's marginal corrections and comments on the manuscript. The editors also referred to (B) the previous 1976 printed edition (Rabat: Maṭbuʿat Dār al-Maghrib li-l-Ta'līf wa-l-Tarjamah wa-l-Nashr), edited by Ḥajjī and based on National Library number 2329 *kāf*, which had been lithographed and published in Fez in 1317/1899–1900.

I have used their edited text as the basis for my own edition and have benefited greatly from the editors' footnotes and comments on the text. In my edition, their text is referred to as (م).

In addition, I have consulted two further complete copies in the possession of the King ʿAbd al-ʿAziz Foundation in Casablanca, Morocco:

4. Number 367 was copied in 1157/1744–45. It was originally owned by Muḥammad al-ʿĀbid al-Fāsī. I refer to it as (ط).
5. Number 1/001, copied in 1202/1787–88. In general, this manuscript, which is written in a much tighter and smaller hand than number 367, contains more mistakes and omissions than the former. Most egregiously, there are several places where the copier has omitted several pages of text without noting the omission. Despite these errors and omissions, this copy contained numerous readings of interest. I refer to it as (ق).

I am very grateful to Mohamed Kadiri for his help in acquiring copies of these two manuscripts and for discussing the manuscript presence of *The Discourses* in Moroccan libraries in general.

The text of Ḥajjī and al-Sharqāwī is excellent, which should come as no surprise considering that Muḥammad Ḥajjī was among the most prominent and gifted Moroccan historians to have worked on sixteenth- and seventeenth-century Moroccan history. Comparing their text with the other two manuscripts led to few corrections of the text per se, though it did more frequently reveal interesting minor variants in the textual reception of *The Discourses.* I have indicated only those places where ط and ق offered a more likely reading than that provided by م—this is very rare—or where they included a plausible or interesting variant. I did not indicate in my text places where ق and ط had omissions or what I considered to be variants of little interest, though I plan to make available an edition with a more extensive apparatus.

Finally, in the very last stages of the preparation of this work, I was able to consult ʿAbd al-Jawwād al-Saqqāṭ's recent edition of al-Yūsī's *Diwān,* which proved to be of great interest and which also revealed variant readings of those of al-Yūsī's own poems that he included in *The Discourses.*

Notes to the Introduction

1 The best biography of al-Yūsī is Berque, *Al-Yousi*. See also Honerkamp, "Al-Ḥasan ibn Masʿūd al-Yūsī." However, both need to be supplemented by El-Rouayheb, *Islamic Intellectual History in the Seventeenth Century*, in which he discusses al-Yūsī at length in chapter 6, 204–34.

2 On the Nāṣiriyyah, see Gutelius, "Between God and Man," and especially Hammoudi, "Sainteté, pouvoir et societé."

3 I take the term from the title of the magisterial two-volume study of Jacques-Meunié, *Le Maroc saharien*.

4 See Saad, *Social History of Timbuktu*, 174–96.

5 El-Rouayheb, *Islamic Intellectual History*.

6 For the pirate community of Salé, see the eccentric Wilson, *Pirate Utopias*; Maziane, *Salé et ces corsaires*; and the study of maritime technology transfer in Staples, "Intersections."

7 On Aḥmad al-Ḥajarī's life, see Wiegers, "A Life between Europe and the Maghrib." On the Pallache family, see García-Arenal and Wiegers, *A Man of Three Worlds: Samuel Pallache*.

8 See al-Yūsī, *Fahrasat al-Yūsī*, 111, and the valuable studies by Gretchen Head: "Moroccan Autobiography," 111–66, and "Space, Identity, and Exile in Seventeenth-Century Morocco."

9 The indispensable study of Sufism in Morocco is Cornell, *Realm of the Saint*. The spread of the Shādhilī order is discussed at 146–54. For a recent study of al-Yūsī's poem in praise of Ibn Nāṣir, see Reichmuth, "The Praise of a Sufi Master as a Literary Event." I am grateful to Professor Reichmuth for having shared this chapter before it was published.

10 For a detailed discussion of this "short letter" (*al-risālah al-saghīrah*), see Munson, *Religion and Power in Morocco*, 27–31, and for the context in which al-Yūsī was sent to Dilāʾ, see al-Madgharī, *al-Faqīh Abū ʿAlī al-Yūsī*, 149–51, and Head, "Space, Identity, and Exile," 238–39.

11 See Geertz, *Islam Observed*, 29–35, and Munson's incisive criticism of Geertz in *Religion and Power in Morocco*, 32–34. Geertz's impressions of al-Yūsī, largely based on Jacques Berque's biography, doubtlessly in part shaped the work of his student Paul Rabinow,

who carried out fieldwork among al-Yūsī's descendants in the early 1970s, as described in his influential *Reflections on Fieldwork in Morocco*.

12 For al-Yūsī having accompanied Moulay Ismāʿīl's son al-Muʿtaṣim on the pilgrimage, see al-Zayānī (ed. and trans. O. Houdas), *Le Maroc de 1631 à 1812*, 42 (Arabic text 22), and Ibn Zaydan, *al-Manzaʿ al-laṭīf fī mafākhir al-mawlā Ismāʿīl ibn al-Sharīf*, 165.

13 On al-Yūsī's influence in the East, see El-Rouayheb, "Opening the Gate of Verification," especially 269–71.

14 On al-Jazūlī and the history of Sufism in Morocco in the eleventh to sixteenth centuries in general, see Cornell, *Realm of the Saint*.

15 Al-Yūsī, *al-Qānūn*, 452–53.

16 For a discussion of saints who flouted social convention in premodern Fez, see Kugle, *Sufis and Saints' Bodies*, chapter 2.

17 These letters have been edited and commented on by al-Qiblī, *Rasāʾil Abī ʿAlī al-Ḥasan ibn Masʿūd al-Yūsī*, 1, 125–246.

18 For an overview of the arrival and spread of Ashʿarism in the Maghrib, see Serrano Ruano, "Later Ashʿarism in the Islamic West," 515–33, and Iḥnāna, *Taṭawwur al-madhhab al-Ashʿarī*.

19 I have written about this at greater length in Stearns, "'All Beneficial Knowledge is Revealed.'"

20 For a detailed list of all of al-Yūsī's works, see Honerkamp, "Al-Ḥasan ibn Masʿūd al-Yūsī."

21 My point here is not that women did not read or partake in scholarly activity in the premodern period—there are numerous examples to the contrary—but that virtually all authors construed their readers as male. For an overview of one area of scholarship in which women were active in the premodern Muslim world, see Sayeed, *Women and the Transmission of Religious Knowledge*.

22 Geographically, of course, this makes little sense, as Mecca is almost due east of Morocco. The usage may be linked to the fact that some early mosques in al-Andalus and North Africa were built facing south instead of being oriented toward Mecca. For the debate between Andalusī and Moroccan scholars on this issue between the twelfth and seventeenth centuries, see Rius Piniés, *La alquibla en al-Andalus y al-Magrib al-Aqṣà*, 23–25.

23 I have been guided here by the translation and commentary in Cornell, *The Way of Abū Madyan*, 80.

24 I have been influenced here by the discussion in Rouighi, "The Andalusi Origins of the Berbers?"

المحاضرات

المجلّد الأوّل

The Discourses

Volume One

بِسْمِ ٱللَّٰهِ ٱلرَّحْمَٰنِ ٱلرَّحِيمِ

الحمد لله الذي أنزل من سماء رحمته غيثًا نافعًا فأنبت به في قلوب عباده زهرًا ناضرًا ١٫١
وثمرًا يانعًا. [بسيط]

زَهْرٌ مِنَ ٱلْعِلْمِ وَٱلْعِرْفَانِ مُؤْتَلِقٌ   فِي ٱلطِّرْسِ وَٱلنَّفْسِ يَسْتَهْدِي بِأَلْوَانِ
وَثَمَرٍ يَجْتَنِيهِ ٱلْأَذْكِيَاءُ بِتَشْ   مِيرٍ وَلَا يَجْتَنِيهِ ٱلْفَدْمُ وَٱلْوَانِي
لِلّٰهِ دَرُّ كِرَامٍ فَازَ فَائِزُهُمْ   قُدْمًا بِحَلَبِ دُرُورٍ مِنْهُ مِلْبَانِ
وَبِٱبْتِنَاءِ مَبَانٍ مِنْهُ سَامِيَةٍ   لَا يَبْتَنِي مِثْلَهَا فِي دَهْرِهِ ٱلْبَانِي
هَذَا هُوَ ٱلْمَجْدُ فِي ٱلدَّارَيْنِ وَٱلشَّرَفُ ال   مَحْضُ ٱلَّذِي مَا بِهِ فِي فَضْلِ ثَانِ
فَٱعْكِفْ عَلَيْهِ مَعَ ٱلْآنَاءِ مُعْتَنِيًا   وَلَا يَكُنْ لَكَ عَنْ تِطْلَابِهِ ثَانِ
وَاعْلَمْ بِأَنَّكَ لَنْ تَحْظَى بِصَهْوَتِهِ[1]   حَتَّى تَجُوزَ ٱلْمَدَى فِي كُلِّ مِيدَانِ
مَا لَمْ تَسُحِّ[2] عَلَيْهِ كُلَّمَا شَجَرَ   يُرْجَى ٱلْجَنِيُّ مِنْهُ أَرْضِي وَعَيْدَانِ
وَتَبْذُلُ ٱلنَّفْسَ بَعْدَ ٱلْمَالِ مُطَّرِحًا   لِكُلِّ تَرْفِيهِ أَرْوَاحٍ وَأَبْدَانِ
وَتَغْتَرِبُ بُرْهَةً فِي كُلِّ آلِفَةٍ   مِنْ ذَاتِ قُرْبَى وَأَوْطَانٍ وَإِخْوَانِ

والصلاة والسلام على سيّدنا ومولانا محمّد ينبوع الأحكام والحكم ومجموع شيم ٢٫١
الفضائل وفضائل الشيم وعلى آله ذوي المجد والكرم وصحبه بحور العلوم ونجوم الظلم.

أمّا بعد فإنّ الدهر أبو العجائب وينبوع الغرائب وفي المثل الدّهر حبلى لا يدري ما تلد. وقال الشاعر: [خفيف]

وَٱللَّيَالِي كَمَا عَلِمْتَ حَبَالَى   مُقْرِبَاتٍ يَلِدْنَ كُلَّ عَجِيبَهْ

---

١ ط: بصفوته. ٢ ط: تسنم.

In the name of the Compassionate, the Merciful:

Praise God who sent down His mercy from heaven as a beneficial succor to mankind. With it, He nourished blossoming flowers and ripe fruits in the hearts of His worshippers. 1.1

A flower of knowledge and insight sparkles
on paper—the soul of man seeks guidance from its colors.
The intelligent, never the dull-witted or feeble,
gather its fruit by exercising their minds—
Those nobles who succeeded in the past with God's help,
milkers of the heaviest milch camels,
Builders of the highest structures,
the like of which no architect ever built.
This is the glory of this world and the next,
pure nobility that has no equal.
Devote yourself to knowledge assiduously;
hold nothing equal to seeking it.
Know that you will not attain its summit
until you have reached the limit of every subject.
What you do not find on the tree
harvest on the ground, fallen from branches.
Sacrifice yourself and your possessions,
reject all physical and spiritual pleasure,
Leave all that you know for a time,
your relatives, your homelands, your brethren.

God bless and keep our lord and master Muḥammad, source of all rulings and wisdom, in whom virtue and character are united; and bless and keep his family, glorious and noble, and his Companions, oceans of knowledge and stars in the darkness. 1.2

To proceed: Time is the progenitor of marvels, the source of wonders. There is a saying: "Time is a pregnant woman, who gives birth to unknown things." As a poet has said:

As you know, the nights are like heavily pregnant women
who give birth to every marvel.

وقال طرفة: [طويل]

سَتُبْدِي لَكَ ٱلْأَيَّامُ مَا كُنْتَ جَاهِلاً وَيَأْتِيكَ بِٱلْأَخْبَارِ مَنْ لَمْ تُزَوِّدِ

وإنّ للعاقل على مرور الجديدين علماً جديداً حيث انتهى فهمه كما له عيش حيث ٣،١
تهدي ساقه قدمه. وكنت قلت في نحو ذلك: [هزج]

أَرَانِي حَيْثُمَا أَخْطُ أَجِدْ مَا لَمْ أَجِدْ قَطّ
وَإِنَّ ٱلدَّهْرَ حُبْلَى كُلَّ مَا حِينَ لَهُ سِقْطُ
لَقَدْ سَايَرْتُهُ طِفْلاً إِلَى أَنْ مَسَّنِي وَخَطُ
فَلَمْ يَنْفَكَّ يَشْتَدُّ عَلَى ٱلْمَرْءِ وَيَشْتَطُّ
وَلَمْ يَأْلُ إِذَا ٱسْتَعْلَى يَوْمَ ٱلْهَوْنِ أَوْ يَسْطُو[1]
لَهُ فِي كُلِّ أُذْنٍ مِنْ بَنِي أَبْنَائِهِ قُرْطُ
وَفِي كُلِّ قَذَالٍ وَسْ مَةٌ بِالنَّارِ أَوْ شَرْطُ
وَقَدْ يَحْنُو وَيَسْتَأْنِي وَقَدْ يَحْبُو لِمَنْ يَعْطُو
سَمَاءُ دِيمَةٍ تَأْتِي بِزَهْرٍ زَهْرُهَا رُقْطُ
فَحُمْرٌ وَمُصْفَرٌ[2] وَمَوْفُورٌ وَمُنْقَطُّ
وَمَجْدُودٌ وَمَحْرُومٌ وَمُسْتَعْمَلٌ وَمُنْحَطّ
وَمُنْقَادٌ وَمُعْوَجٌّ وَكَزُّ ٱلخَلْقِ أَوْ سَبْطُ
قَضَاءٌ مُبْرَمٌ مِمَّنْ إِلَيْهِ ٱلْحَلُّ وَٱلرَّبْطُ
إِلَهٌ أَمْرُهُ الأَمْرُ وَمِنْهُ ٱلرَّفْعُ وَٱلْحَطّ

١ ق: ولم يأل إذا الله تعالى يسوم الهؤلا وبسط. ٢ ط: محيض ومسود.

And as Ṭarafah said:

The days will reveal to you what you did not know,
  one you did not task will bring you unexpected news.

The one who understands the passing of day and night finds new knowledge at the limits of his understanding, just as he finds sustenance wherever his feet lead him. I composed the following on this subject: 1.3

I find at every step
  what I never found before.
Time is pregnant and
  never miscarries when due.
As a child, I carried on heedlessly
  until touched by old age.
Time always wrongs man,
  and treats him harshly.
On the day when humiliation overpowers you
  it does not hold back its attack.
It has hung an earring on the ear
  of each and every child,
And on the back of each head a mark
  cut or branded.
It may have pity and wait,
  it may incline to one it favors.
A sky of constant rain makes
  speckled flowers bloom.
Red and yellow
  whole and broken
Straight and bent
  precious and worthless
Pliant and bending
  thorny and lank.
This is our inescapable fate
  from One who loosens and binds.
It is all God's to command.
  He raises us high and brings us low.

وَمِنْهُ ٱلْيُسْرُ وَٱلْعُسْرُ وَمِنْهُ ٱلْقَبْضُ وَٱلْبَسْطُ
لَـهُ فِي كُلِّ مَا يَوْمٍ شُـؤُونٌ مِنْـهُ تَخْتَطُّ
وَذُو ٱلْفَـهْـمِ لَـهُ عِلْمٌ جَدِيدٌ حَيْثُمَا يَخْطُو
فَفَكِّرْ وَاعْتَبِرْ تَعْلَمْ عُلُومًا دُونَهَا ٱلضَّبْطُ
وَتُدْرِكْ غَيْرَ مَا فِي ٱلصُّحُـ ـفِ يَوْمًا خَلَدَ ٱلْخَطُّ
وَسَلِّمْ وَارْضَ بِالْمَقْدُو رِ لَا يَذْهَبْ بِكَ ٱلسُّخُطُ
وَلَا تَبْرَمْ إِذَا ٱلْمَوْلَى يَشُدُّ ٱلْحَبْلَ أَوْ يَمْطُو
فَمَا تَرْجُو مِنَ ٱلرِّضْوَا نِ أَنْ تَرْضَى لَهُ شَرْطُ

١،٢ وإنّي قد اتّفقت لي سفرة بان بها عنّي الأهل شغلاً وتأنيساً وزايلني العلم تصنيفاً وتدريساً. فأخذت أرسم في هذا المجموع بعض ما حضرني في الوِطاب ممّا أحال فيه أو حان له إرطاب وسمّيته المحاضرات ليوافق اسمه مسمّاه ويتّضح عند ذكره معمّاه. وفي المثل خير العلم ما حوضر به وإنّما أذكر فيه فوائد وطرفاً وقصائد ونتفاً وذلك ممّا اتّفق لي في أيّام الدهر من ملح أو لغيري ممّا ينتقى ويستملح ولا أذكر نادرة فيها معنى شريف إلّا شرحته ولا لطيفاً إلّا وشحته وذلك هو لباب الكتاب وفائدة الخطاب والله الملهم للصواب.

٢،٢ وقد أذكر بعض ما صورته هزل يستهجن وفيه سرّ[١] يستحسن وكما أنّ المقصود من الأشجار ثمارها فالمطلوب من الأخبار أسرارها. وإنّما حملني على الأخذ فيه أمور منها التفادي من البطالة التي هي مدرجة الجهالة والضلالة ومنها إفادة جاهل

١ ق: بر.

From Him comes ease and distress,
  difficulty and relief.
Every day, all affairs
  are arranged by Him.
He who possesses understanding gains new knowledge
  in whatever he undertakes.
Ponder, reflect, and you will learn
  sciences leading to good judgment.
You will discern the eternal script
  that is not found in books.
Accept what has been decreed and be content,
  and you will not be overwhelmed with bitterness.
Do not be grieved if the Master
  tightens or loosens the rope.
What you desire from the Angel of Paradise[1]
  is conditional on your pleasing him.

When I stumbled upon a volume containing both serious and diverting works of the brethren, I became absorbed by the study of knowledge and its composition. I began to set down in this collection some of what I had in milk skins—what had changed in them and what had thickened—and I called it *The Discourses*, so that it would be properly titled and so that its meaning would be clear if any obscure part were mentioned. As the saying goes, "The best knowledge is shared." Indeed, in it I recount useful and choice matters, poetry, and witty anecdotes, recounting what I have experienced in my life as well as what others have selected and collected. I mention no anecdote noble in meaning without commenting on it, nor an amusing story without elaborating on it. This is the essence in this book that I write, wherein there is benefit and insight—truly, it is God who inspires us to what is right. 2.1

I might mention things that have the appearance of jest, and that might be thought better kept at bay. But there are hidden purposes that none will gainsay. Just as the purpose of trees is to bear fruit, so the points of the accounts I relate have their purposes. Indeed, I have been motivated to include such accounts by a number of factors, including guarding oneself from idleness, which leads to ignorance and error; benefiting the ignorant and instructing 2.2

أو تنبيه غافل ومنها تخليد المحفوظ لئلاّ ينسى. وتفصيله نوعًا وجنسًا ومنها استمطار علم جديد عند الاشتغال بالتقييد. فإنّ العلم كالماء نبّاع وبعضه للبعض تبّاع وما هو في قلب ذكي الفؤاد إلّا كما قال امرؤ القيس عند وصف الجواد: [طويل]

يَجُمُّ عَلَى ٱلسَّاقَيْنِ بَعْدَ كَلَالِهِ   جُمُومَ عُيُونِ ٱلْحِسْيِ بَعْدَ ٱلْمَخِيضِ

٣،٢ ومنها تعليل النفس ببعض الأنس فإنّ النفس ترتاح للأحماض وتستشفي بروحه من الإمضاض. ولا سيّما مثلي ممّن ترامت به الأقطار وتباعدت عنه الأوطان والأوطار. وقلت في ذلك: [طويل]

سَلَا هَلْ سَلَا عَنْ أَهْلِهِ قَلْبُ مَعْنِيِّ   بِرَيْبِ ٱلْهَوَى وَٱلْبَيْنِ عَنْ جِيرَةِ ٱلْحَيِّ
وَهَلْ ذٰلِكَ ٱلْوَجْدُ ٱلَّذِي قَدْ حَشَا ٱلْحَشَا   مُقِيمٌ عَلَى أَدْيَانِهِ غَيْرُ مَكْفِيِّ
وَهَلْ قَلْبُهُ يَوْمَ ٱلنَّوَى مُتَقَلِّبٌ   تَقَلُّبَ مَفْؤُودِ ٱللَّظَى سَاعَةَ ٱلشَّيِّ
وَهَلْ بِنَوَى ٱلْأَحْبَابِ مُشْفٍ عَلَى ٱلتَّوَى[1]   وَلَيْسَ بِوَصْلٍ مِنْ حَبِيبٍ بِمُشْفِيِّ
وَهَلْ أَعْشَبَتْ تِلْكَ ٱلشِّعَابُ وَأَمْرَعَتْ   فَجَاجُ مَرَاعِيهَا بِعَهْدٍ وَوَسْمِيِّ
وَهَلْ أُقْحُوَانُ ٱلْجِزْعِ فَاحَ وَنَدُّهُ   بِعُرْفٍ تَهَادَاهُ ٱلشَّمَائِلُ مِسْكِيِّ
وَهَلْ تَالِكَ ٱلْأَزْهَارُ تَهْتَزُّ نَضْرَةً   بِكُلِّ جَمِيلٍ فِي ٱلْخَمِيلَةِ مَوْلِيِّ
وَكُلُّ مَجُودٍ فِي ٱلنُّجُودِ تَنَاوَحَتْ   عَلَيْهِ ٱلرِّيَاحُ مِنْ جَنُوبِيِّ وَشَرْقِيِّ
إِذَا مَا ٱلسَّحَابُ ٱلْغُرُّ عَاطَيْنَهَا ٱلْحَيَا   تَمَايَلْنَ نَشْوَى مِنْ مُدَامٍ شَبَامِيِّ
وَإِنْ صَافَحَتْهَا بَعْدَ وَهْنٍ يَدُ ٱلصَّبَا   فَنَمَتْ[2] بِأَذْكَى مِنْ عَبِيرٍ وَأَلْوِيِّ
فَمَا شِئْتَ فِيهَا مِنْ يَوَاقِيتَ تَجْتَلِي   وَمِنْ كَوْكَبٍ يُعْشِي ٱلنَّوَاظِرَ دُرِّيِّ

١ ق: الثوى. ٢ نتابع ملاحظات المحقّقين ونقرأ "فنمت" بدلاً من "تنمت" وهو في النص (أنظر إلى المحاضرات، ص١٣).

the heedless; and, finally, preserving knowledge so it is not forgotten. The book is arranged by topic and theme. One theme is seeking after new knowledge through the process of writing. Knowledge, like water, gushes out of the source and a little of it leads to more. In one who has a wise heart, knowledge is no different from what Imru' al-Qays said when he described a swift horse:

Exhausted, he urges his legs to run farther
like deep well water swelling up after being struck.

Another theme is healing the soul with good company, for the soul relaxes through merriment and takes comfort from torment. This is especially true for someone like myself, banished by countries and separated from homelands and yearnings. On this subject I composed the following: 2.3

Can a heart suffering from the uncertainty of fleeting desires
and separation from home ever be consoled of the loss of those dear?
Is this love, which had long filled the heart
waiting for its debts to be repaid, never to be satisfied?
On the day of separation, his heart writhes
like the heart of the flame when it is ready to be seared.
Can a doctor cure lovers of their illness
when he is always absent from their tryst?
Have the mountain passes grown verdant and
the pastures become green after spring rains?
Does the lily of the valley waft sweetly,
its scent like fragrant musk from the northern winds?
Do these flowers tremble in full bloom
in the thicket with every welcome downfall?
Every heavy rain on mountain roads
is accompanied by howling winds from the south and east.
When the bright clouds give the branches life
they sway, drunk on Shibāmī wine.
When the favor of the east wind greets them after a lull,
the trees grow fragrant with a sharp, bitter smell.
Hyacinths emerge in abundance,
glowing stars that blind the sight.

وَمِنْ بُسُطٍ تَزْرِي ٱبْتِهَاجًا بِمَفْرَشٍ   أَعَدَّتْ بَنُو سَاسَانَ لِلْبَسْطِ مَوْشِيِّ
وَهَلْ لِسُلَيْمَى مِنْ ثَوَاءٍ بِدَارِهَا   سَقَى ٱللهُ تِلْكَ ٱلدَّارَ أَطْيَبَ مَا رِيِّ
وَحَيًّا مُحَيَّاهَا ٱلْوَسِيمَ وَإِنْ لَوَتْ   غَرِيمًا تَقَاضَى وَصْلَهَا طُولَ مَا لِيِّ
وَحَيًّا زَمَانًا لَاحَ لِلْوَصْلِ بَيْنَنَا   تَبَاشِيرَ كَٱلصُّبْحِ ٱلْمُنِيرِ عَلَى رَيِّ
زَمَانُ[1] دِيَارِ ٱلْحَيِّ دَانٍ مَزَارُهَا   وَنَحْنُ عَلَى عَهْدٍ مِنَ ٱلْوُدِّ مَرْعِيِّ
نَعِمْنَا بِإِينَاسِ ٱلْبُرُوقِ مِنَ ٱلْحِمَى   أَنِيسًا وَإِنْ لَمْ نَحْظَ مِنْهُ بِإِنْسِيِّ
وَنَسْمَةُ أَرْوَاحِ ٱلصَّبَا وَهُبُوبُهَا   عَلَيْنَا نُمُومًا مِنْ صِبَاهَا بِمَطْوِيِّ
وَتِنْشَاقِ آسٍ بِالأَجَارِعِ تَعْتَلِي   بِنَفْحَتِهِ لِلْمُسْتَهَامِينَ عِطْرِيِّ
وَكُنَّا عَلَى أَنَّا كَأَنَّا بِوَصْلِهَا   نُغَادَى بِكَأْسٍ مُطْمَئِنِّينَ خَمْرِيِّ
وَنَرْتَعُ فِي رَوْضِ ٱلْمُنَى وَنَنَالُ مَا   نَشَاءُ وَلَا نَرْتَاعُ مِنْ بَيْنِ مَهْوِيِّ
وَعِشْنَا زَمَانًا لَا نُعَانِي صَبَابَةً   وَلَا نَتَبَاكَى مِنْ سُلَيْمَى وَلَا مَيِّ
وَلَا نَتَشَكَّى مِنْ صُدُودٍ وَلَا صَدًى   وَلَا وَجْدٍ مَفْؤُودِ ٱلْجَوَانِحِ مَبْرِيِّ
لَيَالِيَ كَانَ الشَّمْلُ[2] مُنْضَبِطَ ٱلْكِلَى   وَحَبْلُ التَّوَالِي مُحْصَدٌ غَيْرُ مَفْرِيِّ
فَلَمْ تَلْبَثِ ٱلْأَقْدَارُ أَنْ مَدَّدَتْ بِنَا   عِنَانًا إِلَى شَحْطِ النَّوَى غَيْرَ مَثْنِيِّ
فَحَالَتْ مَوَامٍ دُونَهَا ذَاتِ مَنْزَعٍ   وَدَيْنُ التَّدَانِي قَدْ غَدَا غَيْرَ مَقْضِيِّ
وَكَانَ ٱلَّذِي خِفْنَا يَكُونُ مِنَ النَّوَى   وَصِرْنَا لِأَمْرٍ مُذْ أَحَايِينَ مَخْشِيِّ
عَلَى أَنَّ فَضْلَ اللهِ مَا ٱنْفَكَّ هَامِرًا   عَلَيْنَا وَلُطْفٌ دَائِمٌ غَيْرُ مَزْوِيِّ
فَلَا تَغْتَرِرْ بِالدَّهْرِ يَلْقَاكَ بِشْرُهُ   فَإِنَّ وَرَاءَ ٱلْبِشْرِ طَعْنَ الرُّدَيْنِيِّ

١ زيادة: (لَاحَ لِلْوَصْلِ بَيْنَنَا تَبَاشِيرَ كَٱلصُّبْحِ ٱلْمُنِيرِ عَلَى رَيِّ زَمَانُ) من م، ط. ٢ ط: الوصل.

You delight at such a verdant spread,
as if the Banū Sāsān had laid out their embroidered carpets.
Is Sulaymā home?
May God pour the best rain on her house!
God preserve her beautiful face!
When she looks at a rival, my long connection with her is lost.
God preserve the blessed time of our tryst
that was the morning light reflecting off the dew.
The time is near when we will visit our neighbors,
joined in sustaining bonds of love.
At the sanctuary, we enjoyed the hopes that lightning brought
together, not blessed by the presence of anyone else.
The east wind gusts upon us with its breeze,
bringing whispers of her passion folded within it.
A desperate man feels longing for the high stony ground,
a perfumed scent for lost souls.
We moaned as if in her company:
Content, we drank a cup of morning wine.
We revel now in the garden of desires and obtain our wishes
not fearing separation from our love.
Living for a time, not suffering from the pangs of those in love
nor pretending to cry for Sulaymā or Mayy.
We did not complain of rejection or thirst,
nor of the heart's acute passion.
Nights of union, sound and healthy
when the rope of companionship was strong, not fraying.
Fate wasted no time in reining us in
and leading us directly to the shores of separation.
Deserts now intentionally came between us;
the promise of closeness was no longer fulfilled.
And the separation we feared came about:
We reached a point we had dreaded for ages.
Yet the grace of God has continued to flow over us,
His perpetual kindness unceasing.
Do not be fooled by the good tidings Time sends you—
behind the joys are the piercing spears of Rudaynah.[2]

وَلا تَأْمَنَنْ مِنْ هَوْلِهِ إِنَّ رِيحَهُ   تَهُبُّ إِذَا هَبَّتْ عَصُوفًا بِلُجِّيِّ
وَلا تَغْتَبِطْ مِنْ حَظِّهِ بِمُنَوَّلِ   وَلَوْ تَاجَ مُلْكٍ فَوْقَ أَشْمَخِ كُرْسِيِّ
فَمَا حَالَةٌ مِنْهُ تَدُومُ عَلَى ٱمْرِئٍ   وَلَوْ خَالَ جَهْلًا أَنَّهُ غَيْرُ مَذْهِيِّ
وَمَا هُوَ إِلَّا مِثْلُ دُولَابِ زَارِعٍ   فَعُلْوِيُّهُ يَعْتَاضُ حَتْمًا بِسُفْلِيِّ
فَكَمْ أَنْزَلَتْ نَسْرَ السَّمَاءِ صُرُوفُهُ   وَحَلَّتْ بِبِنْتِ ٱلْمَاءِ دَارَةَ عُلْوِيِّ
وَكَمْ ضَعْضَعَتْ مُلْكًا وَأَفْنَتْ مَمَالِكًا   وَكَمْ عَادَ عَانِي رَيْبِهَا غَيْرَ مَفْدِيِّ
وَكَمْ زَيَّلَتْ بَيْنَ ٱلْمُحِبِّينَ فَٱغْتَدَى   دَمُ الصَّبِّ مِنْ فَتْكِ ٱلْهَوَى غَيْرَ مَوْدِيِّ
قَضَاءٌ مِنَ ٱلْمَوْلَى لَهُ كُلَّ سَاعَةٍ   تَصَرُّفُ[1] مُخْتَارٍ وَإِنْجَازُ مَقْضِيِّ
فَأَعْلِقْ بِهِ أَشْطَانَ قَلْبِكَ وَٱعْتَمِدْ   عَلَيْهِ تَنَلْ رُشْدًا وَتَنْجُ مِنَ ٱلْغَيِّ
وَقِفْ أَبَدًا فِي بَابِهِ مُتَأَدِّبًا   مُنِيبًا بِسَعْيٍ عِنْدَ مَوْلَاكَ مَرْضِيِّ
قَنُوعًا رَضُوًا بِٱلْقَضَاءِ مُسَلِّمًا   بِقَلْبٍ عَلَى التَّوْحِيدِ وَالصِّدْقِ مَحْنِيِّ
فَذَالِكَ ٱلَّذِي يَرْقَى بِهِ لِمَنَازِلَ   بِهَا كُلُّ صِدِّيقٍ حَوَى ٱلْفَضْلَ رَبِّيِّ
وَإِنْ كُنْتَ لَمْ تُسْعِدْكَ فِي ذٰلِكَ ٱلْقُوَى   فَزَاحِمْ بِمُسْطَاعٍ مَعَ ٱلْحُبِّ وَٱلزِّيِّ
فَإِنَّ جَلِيسَ ٱلْقَوْمِ مَا إِنْ يَنَالُهُ   شَقَاءٌ وَمَنْ عَنْ حُبِّهِمِ غَيْرُ مَرْمِيِّ
وَمَنْ قَدْ حَكَاهُمْ فَهْوَ مِنْهُمْ وَكُلُّ ذَا   أَتَى فِي حَدِيثٍ عَنْ ذَوِي الصِّدْقِ مَرْوِيِّ
وَكُلُّ ٱمْرِئٍ يَوْمًا سَيُجْزَى بِمَا أَتَى   مِنَ ٱلْخَيْرِ بَلْ يُجْزَى عَلَى كُلِّ مَنْوِيِّ

لِلّٰهِ الأمر من قبل ومن بعد.

[1] ق: يصرف.

Do not feel you are safe from its power—when its wind blows
like tempests from the deepest ocean.
Do not take joy in the changing allotments of fate,
even in a king's crown on a lofty throne.
No such state persists for man
even if he ignorantly imagines he will not be struck.
Fate is like the tilling wheel of the farmer—
the upper part inevitably replaces the lower.
How often its vicissitudes dispatch heaven's eagle
and seize the egret from its high roost!
How often these vicissitudes raze possessions and destroy kingdoms!
How often one experiences affliction without being saved!
How many lovers she scattered, though they had consumed
the blood of undying love, kindling vain desire.
It is all decreed by the Master to whom belongs in every hour
the choice and fulfillment of ordained actions.
Fasten your heart to His decree and depend upon Him.
You will receive right guidance and will be rescued from error.
Stand respectfully at His door, eternally,
and strive to please your Master.
Content and satisfied, submitting to what has been decreed
with a heart inclining to sincerity and faith in God's Oneness.
The one guided upward by Him will live in a place
where every friend is devout and pious.
If you have not been given the power to do this,
then, through love and grace, find someone who has.
The one who sits among the people will not be afflicted by hardship
or excluded from their love—
The one who follows their example is counted among them.
All of this is found in the hadith on reliable authority.
Every person will be rewarded for the good they have done
and be recompensed for every good intention.

Everything is God's to command.

قد جرت عادة من ألّف بل من كتب رسالة أن يتسمّى في كتابه ليعرف وفي معروفيته فوائد منها في كلامه أن يعرف مذهبه أو مطلبه ليتمكّن[١] جوابه أو يشهد له أو[٢] عليه. ومن أهمّها أن يعلم هل يوثق بنقله وعقله[٣] ويقتدى به في أصله فإنّ كلام الحجّة حجّة وإنّما يعرف كونه حجّة ومرتبته من العلم بشهادة أهل العلم وذلك في ثلاثة أشياء أحدها التصريح بذلك مشافهة أو في ترجمته ولذلك صنّفت طبقات أهل العلم وأعتني بتراجمهم. ثانيها عدّه مع العلماء عند ذكرهم في مذهب أو وفاق أو خلاف أو حكاية كلامه فيما يحكى من كلام العلماء أو مذهبه أو نحو ذلك وهو كالتصريح. ثالثها الأخذ عنه أو إقراء تصانيفه أو شرحها أو تقليده أو نحو ذلك. ١،٣

وإنما يحصل له ذلك من ثلاثة أشياء أحدها سماع كلامه مشافهة. ثانيها مطالعة تصانيفه والوقوف على تحريره وتحصيله أو سماع فتاويه وآرائه وكلامه بنقل الغير له كما وقع للصحابة رضي الله عنهم. ثالثها شهادة الغير له كما مرّ وهلمّ جرّا. وبعد حصول مطلق المرتبة من العلم تحصل خصوصيّات المراتب بشهادة من هو أهل لذلك بها بمشافهة أو في ترجمة أو اقتداء الأكابر به أو ترجيحه على غيره أو نحو ذلك. ومنها في خارج أن تعرف مرتبته كما مرّ أو يتعرّض لدعاء داع أو ثناء مثن بخير ومحبة وودّ وغير ذلك. فرأيت أن أتسمّى في هذا المجموع وأضيف إلى ذلك ما اتّفق لي من كنية وما أدركت من نسب بعد أن تعلم أنّ الاسم العلم ثلاثة اسم وكنية ولقب. ٢،٣

١ م، ق: او يتمكن. ٢ م، ق: و. ٣ سقط من م.

It has become customary that anyone who composes a work, or even writes an epistle, names himself in his book so that he be known. There are several merits to his being identified. One benefit is that readers may learn the doctrine the author espouses or the point he intends to make from his writings, so that they might respond to him or testify in his favor or against him. Among the most important benefits is that one may learn whether he can be trusted as a transmitter of texts, whether his reason is sound, and whether one should adopt his fundamental principles: for the words of an authority are themselves authoritative. His status as an authority and his rank in learning may be deduced only through the testimony of scholars, which consists of three types of evidence. The first is an explicit statement, either delivered orally or presented in a biographical entry devoted to him. For this reason, biographical dictionaries recording the generations of scholars have been compiled, and pains have been taken to collect scholars' biographical entries. The second type is to count him among scholars when they are mentioned as belonging to a particular doctrine or as parties to agreement or disagreement over a particular issue, and to cite his pronouncements together with the statements of other scholars, or to refer to his doctrine and the like. This is similar to an explicit statement. The third type is evidence that scholars have studied under him, assigned his books to be read, commented upon them, followed his opinion, and the like. 3.1

For his part, the author gains renown from three things: One is that people hear what he has said. The second is that people read his books and study his writings and scholarship, or they listen to his legal opinions and relate his views while others transmit his speech, such as occurred with the Prophet's Companions, God be pleased with them. The third consists of others testifying in his favor, as mentioned above, and so on. Once you know someone's general rank of learning, you can gain insight into the specifics of his ranking through the testimony of those who are specialized in the field—this testimony can be oral, found in a biography, deduced from major scholars emulating him, or from their preferring him over someone else, and other similar indications. Another merit of naming the author is that others, as mentioned before, will know his rank, and thus he will in turn receive the blessings of well-wishers or the praise, generosity, friendship, and affection of his supporters. Therefore, I decided to name myself in this collection of essays, to include the teknonyms I have acquired, and what I have learned of ancestry, based on the understanding that names are of three types: given name, teknonym, and moniker. 3.2

أمّا الاسم فهو من حيث هو ما أريد به من تعيين المسمّى لا يعطى مدحاً ولا ذمّاً لصلاحية كلّ اسم لكلّ مسمّى عند المحقّقين ولكن إذا كان منقولاً فكثيرًا ما يلاحظ فيه زيادة على تعيين المسمّى مدلوله الأوّل الحقيقيّ أو المجازيّ فيشعر بمقتضاه إشعارًا. ومن هذا وقع التفاؤل والتطيّر بالأسماء وكان صلّى الله عليه وسلّم يحبّ الفأل الحسن ويقول إذا أبردتم إليّ بريدًا فأبردوه حسن الوجه حسن الاسم. ٣،٣

وكان صلّى الله عليه وسلّم يغيّر من الأسماء ما لا يرضى فسأل عن اسم ماء فقيل له: بيسان وماؤه ملح فقال بل هو نعمان وماؤه عذب فكان كذلك وجاءه رجل فقال ما اسمك؟ فقال غاوي بن عبد العزّى. فقال صلّى الله عليه وسلّم بل أنت راشد بن عبد ربه وجاءه آخر فقال ما اسمك؟ فقال حزن فقال بل أنت سهل فقال الرجل ما كنت لأغيّر اسماً سمّاني به أبي وكان الإمام سعيد المسيّب رضي الله عنه والرجل من أجداده يقول فما زالت الحزونة فينا. فانظر كيف حكم مدلول اللفظ الأوّل وقال صلّى الله عليه وسلّم يوم الحديبيّة حين أقبل سهيل من ناحية قريش سهل عليكم أمركم. ومن هذا قوله صلّى الله عليه وسلّم أسلم سالمها الله وغفار غفر الله لها وعصيّة عصت الله ورسوله. وقال أمير المؤمنين عمر رضي الله عنه وقد سأل عن اسم رجل استعمله أو أراد أن يستعمله فقيل له هو خبيئة بن كناز هو يخبأ وأبوه يكنز لا حاجة لنا به. وبدّل صلّى الله عليه وسلّم اسم[١] برّة بنت أبي سلمة بدرّة فرارًا من التزكية التي يعطيها اللفظ. وقال مولانا عليّ كرّم الله وجهه[٢] أنا الذي سمّتني أمي حَيْدره. ٤،٣

١ سقط من م. ٢ ق: رضي الله عنه.

The given name designates first and foremost a certain individual, without any blame or praise being implied, in accordance with what the scholars might believe is suitable to the person. Yet, when the given name is pronounced, one often perceives a supplement to the designation of the person—its primary literal or metaphorical signification—and one is left with a corresponding impression. Here lie the origins of seeing good and bad omens in names, and the Prophet, God bless and keep him, loved good omens. He used to say, "If you send me a messenger, let it be someone who has a pleasant face and an auspicious name." 3.3

The Prophet, God bless and keep him, used to change those names he was not happy with. He asked about the name of a well and was told that it was Bīsān, meaning "calamity," and that its water was salty. "Its name is now Naʿmān, 'blessing,'" he responded, "and its water is sweet." And true enough, that is how it turned out. A man came to the Prophet, who asked, "What is your name?" "Ghāwī ibn ʿAbd al-ʿUzzā, 'Tempter, son of the worshipper of al-ʿUzzā,'" replied the man. The Prophet, God bless and keep him, responded with, "Your name is now Rāshid ibn ʿAbd Rabbihi, 'Rightly Guided, son of the worshipper of his Lord.'" Another man came to the Prophet, who asked, "What is your name?" "Ḥazn, 'Rough,'" the man replied, and the Prophet said, "It is now Sahl, 'Smooth.'" But the man said, "I'm not going to change the name my father gave me!" This man was an ancestor of the exemplar Saʿīd ibn al-Musayyab, God be pleased with him, who said, "And roughness is still within us." Consider how defining the promising first significance of the name was! The Prophet, God bless and keep him, said on the day of al-Ḥudaybiyyah, when Suhayl approached him on behalf of the Quraysh, "May things go well for you." This is the origin of the Prophet, God bless and keep him, saying, "May God be reconciled with Aslam, 'Soundest,' and forgive Ghifār, 'Forgiven,' whereas ʿUṣayyah, 'Disobedient,' has disobeyed God and His Prophet."[3] The Commander of the Faithful, ʿUmar,[4] God be pleased with him, once asked about a man he had employed or wanted to employ. He was told, "His name is Khabīʾah ibn Kannāz, 'Hider, son of Hoarder.'" "He hides and his father hoards," said ʿUmar. "We have no need of him." The Prophet, God bless and keep him, changed the name of Abū Salamah's daughter from Barrah, "Pious," to Durrah, "Pearl," in order to avoid the aura of self-righteousness the name lent her. Our leader ʿAlī, "Exalted," God honor his countenance, said, "I am the one whom my mother named Ḥaydarah, 'Lion.'" 3.4

٣،٥ وقال الحريريّ في المقامات على لسان الغلام أمّا أمّي فاسمها برّة وهي كاسمها برّة. وقالت اليهود يوم خيبر لمولانا عليّ كرّم الله وجهه وقد تقدّم بالراية فتسمّى لهم: علوتم وربّ الكعبة. وقالت العرب في أمثالها إنّما سمّيت هانئاً لتهْنأ.

٣،٦ وقال الأخطل في كعب بن جعيل: [متقارب]

وَسُمِّيتَ كَعْباً بِشَرِّ ٱلْعِظَامِ وَكَانَ أَبُوكَ يُسَمَّى ٱلْجُعَلِ
وَإِنَّ مَكَانَكَ مِنْ وَائِلٍ مَكَانُ ٱلْقُرَادِ مِنَ ٱسْتِ ٱلْجَمَلِ

٣،٧ وكان بعض الرؤساء القيسيّة أحضر جفاناً من طعام وكان بالحضرة بعض مَلاسين بكر بن وائل فأراد القيسيّ أن يعبث به. فقال له هل رأى بكر بن وائل قطّ مثل هذه الجفان؟ فقال ما رآها ولا رآها أيضاً قطّ عيلان يعني جدّه هو. ولو رآها ما قيل له عيلان بل شبعان.

٣،٨ وقالت هند بنت النعمان بن بشير تهجو زوجها الفيض بن أبي عقيل: [بسيط]

سُمِّيتَ فَيْضاً وَمَا شَيْءٌ تَفِيضُ بِهِ إِلَّا سُلَاحُكَ بَيْنَ ٱلْبَابِ وَالدَّارِ

٣،٩ وقال الآخر: [طويل]

وَلِلْحَرْبِ سُمِّينَا فَكُنَّا مُحَارِبًا إِذَا مَا ٱلْقَنَا أَمْسَى مِنَ الطَّعْنِ أَحْمَرَا

٣،١٠ وممّا ينخرط في هذا السلك أنّ بعض الملوك عزل وزيراً له اسمه الياقوت. فحلف الملك ليستوزن أوّل من يلقى فخرج فلقي رجلاً أعرابيّاً فاستوزره. فإذا هو من أعقل الناس وأنجبهم.[١] فلمّا رأى الوزير الأوّل ذلك كتب إلى الملك: [خفيف]

١ ط: أنجحهم.

In his *Assemblies*, al-Ḥarīrī said through the voice of a young man, "My mother's name is Barrah and she is pious, like her name."[5] On the day of Khaybar the Jews said to our leader ʿAlī, God be content with him, when he had already approached with the standard and told them his name: "By the lord of the Kaaba, you have reached great heights." The Arabs have been known to say something similar to this: "Surely you have been named Hāniʾ, 'Delight,' so that you may be happy." 3.5

Al-Akhṭal said about Kaʿb ibn Juʿayl: 3.6

You were named Kaʿb, "Ankle," after the worst of bones,
your father was named al-Juʿal, "Dung Beetle,"
And you are among the Wāʾil tribe,
like a tick on a camel's anus.

One of the leaders of the Qays brought some dishes of food to a gathering. One of the eloquent companions of Bakr ibn Wāʾil was present. The Qaysī wanted to have some fun with him, so he said, "Has Bakr ibn Wāʾil ever seen anything like these dishes?" The Qaysī continued, "He has not, nor has ʿAylān"—referring to Bakr ibn Wāʾil's ancestor. "If he had, he wouldn't have been called ʿAylān, 'Poor,' but Shabʿān, 'Satiated.'" 3.7

Hind bint al-Nuʿmān ibn Bashīr[6] mocked her husband, al-Fayḍ ibn Abī ʿAqīl: 3.8

You were named Fayḍ, "Flood," yet nothing pours from you
but diarrhea between the privy and the house.

Someone else said: 3.9

We were named after Ḥarb (war), and so we became warriors,
Our spears red with blood from piercing the enemy.

On this subject is the story of the king who dismissed his vizier, named al-Yāqūt, "Sapphire," and swore to replace him with the first person he came upon. He went out and met a Bedouin man, and appointed him. He turned out to be one of the smartest and noblest people. When the first vizier saw this, he wrote to the king: 3.10

أَحْكَمَ ٱلنَّسْجَ كُلُّ مَنْ حَاكَ لٰكِنْ نَسْجَ دَاوُودَ لَيْسَ كَٱلعَنْكَبُوتِ
أَلْقِنِي فِي لَظًى فَإِنْ غَيَّرَتْنِي فَتَيَقَّنْ أَنْ لَسْتُ بِٱلْيَاقُوتِ

يشير إلى أنّ الياقوت المعروف لا يفسد بالنار.

١١،٣ فأجاب الآخر: [خفيف]

نَسْجُ دَاوُودَ مَا حَمَى صَاحِبَ ٱلغَا رِ وَكَانَ ٱلْفَخَارُ لِلْعَنْكَبُوتِ
وَفِرَاخُ السَّمَنْدِ فِي لَهَبِ النَّا رِ أَزَالَتْ فَضِيلَةَ ٱلْيَاقُوتِ

أشار إلى السمندل وهو دويبة في ناحية الهند تتّخذ من جلودها المناديل. وتلقى في النار فلا تزداد إلّا نضارة وحسناً ولا تحترق والله على كلّ شيء قدير إلى غير هذا ممّا لا ينحصر ولو تتبّعناه لطال.

١٢،٣ وأمّا الكنية واللقب فيعتبران بوجهين الأوّل نفس إطلاق الكنية واللقب وهما في هذا مختلفان. فإنّ الكنية الأكثر فيها إذا لم تكن اسماً أن يراد بها التعظيم. وينبغي أن يعلم أنّ الناس باعتبارها ثلاثة أصناف صنف لا يكنّى لحقارته وهو معلوم من أنّ الحقارة أمر إضافيّ فربّ حقير يكون له من يراه بعين التعظيم فيكنّيه. والمقصود أنّ الحقير من حيث هو حقير لا يكنّى إلّا هزءاً أو تمليحاً. وصنف لا ينبغي أن يكنّى لاستغنائه عنها وترفّعه عن مقتضاها. ومن ثمّ لا يكنّى الأنبياء عليهم الصلاة والسلام لأنّهم أرفع من ذلك حتّى إنّهم أشرفت رفعتهم على أسمائهم فشرفت. فإذا ذكروا بها كانت أرفع من الكنى في حقّ غيرهم.

١٣،٣ وللملوك وسائر أكابر الناس نصيب من هذا المعنى. وصنف متوسّط بين هذين وهو الذي يكنّى تعظيماً ثمّ إن كان التعظيم مطلوباً ككنية أهل العلم والدين ومن يحسن شرعاً تعظيمه فحسن. وكذا اكتناء المرء بنفسه إن كان تحدثاً بالنعمة أو تبرّكاً بالكنية

Everyone who can make fabric can weave,
yet the weaving of David is not like that of the spider.[7]
Cast me into the flame, and if it changes me
know well that I am not a sapphire.

In this last line he referred to the fact that the sapphire we are familiar with is not harmed by fire.

The king replied: 3.11

The weaving of David did not protect the one in the cave.[8]
The glory was the spider's.
The young of the salamander, playing in the fire,
put an end to the superiority of the sapphire.

Here he was referring to the salamander, which is an animal in India, from the skin of which kerchiefs are made. When they are thrown into the fire, salamanders increase in luster and beauty and do not burn. God is capable of everything, of countless other things, and it would take too long to list them.

The teknonym and the moniker can be considered from two angles. The 3.12 first is the act of giving them: In this the two are distinct. The teknonym, when it is not an actual given name, is most often intended as glorification. There are effectively three types of people. The first does not have a teknonym because of his baseness. Baseness is, admittedly, relative, and there are base people whom some deem worthy of glorification and being given a teknonym. What is important is that one who is base should not be given a teknonym except in mockery or in jest. There is a second type of person who does not need to be given a teknonym, and that is the person who is by his nature superior to the connotations it brings with it. Thus, prophets, blessings and peace upon them, are not given teknonyms, for they are so far above such practice that their eminence towers over their names, conferring honor upon them. If prophets are given teknonyms, these are more elevated than the teknonyms of others.

The situation is somewhat the same with kings and other prominent fig- 3.13 ures. There is a third type of person, who falls between these two: The kind who is given a teknonym for the purpose of glorification. If the glorification is appropriate, as with the teknonym of people who are knowledgeable in religion, and those whose glorification is sanctioned by revelation, then the practice is fine. It is similar with a person who gives himself a teknonym: If he does

باعتبار من صدرت عنه أو نحو ذلك من المقاصد الجميلة فحسن وإلّا فن الشهوات النفسانيّة. فما كان تكبّرًا أو تعظيمًا لمن لا يجوز تعظيمه بغير ضرورة ونحو ذلك فحرام. وإلّا فمباح وليس من هذا الباب ما يقصده به مجرّد الإخبار فقط كقولك جاء أبي أو أبو فلان هذا أي والده. ولا ما يقصد به معناه على وجه التفاؤل مثلًا نحو أبي الخير وأمّ السعد. وأمّا اللقب فيقصد به كلّ من المدح والذمّ وغير ذلك والحكم كالذي قبله.

١٤،٣ الوجه الثاني النظر إلى مدلولهما الأصليّ وهما في ذلك كما مرّ في الاسم بل ذلك هنا أولى لأنّ الأصل فيه أوضح. ولبعضهم في ذلك: [وافر]

أَتَيْتُ أَبَا ٱلْمَحَاسِنِ كَيْ أَرَاهُ   بِشَوْقٍ كَادَ يَجْذِبُنِي إِلَيْهِ
فَلَمَّا أَنْ أَتَيْتُ رَأَيْتُ فَرْدًا   وَلَمْ أَرَ مِنْ بَنِيهِ ابْنًا لَدَيْهِ

يريد أنّ لفظه ينبئ عن كون المحاسن لازمة له لزوم الأولاد لأبيهم ثمّ إنّها لم يجدها عنده. وكذا يقال في أبي المكارم وأبي الفضل وأبي البخت وجمال الدين وشمس الأئمّة. والأصل في جميع هذا أنّ المستحسن في العقول وإن لم يكن لازمًا خلافًا لمن زعم ذلك أن يطابق الاسم المسمّى أي مدلوله الأصليّ حتّى يصير الاسم كأنّه وصف مشتقّ لموصوف بمعناه. فإن لم يكن كذلك فإنّ التسمية خطأ وكأنّ الاسم لا مسمّى له. ومن هذا جرت العادة بتخيّر الاسم عند التسمية وكذا عند الملاقاة كقصّة البريد السابقة. أمّا التخيّر عند التسمية فلفائدتين إحداهما التلذّذ بسماعه وتجمّل المسمّى

so to confer a blessing or to receive one, doing so out of consideration for the one the teknonym is coined for, or out of a similar noble aim, then it is well and good. In cases other than this that involve selfish motivations, including the putting on of airs, or unnecessarily glorifying someone who does not deserve it, and the like, this is proscribed. In cases other than this, it is permitted. It is not forbidden when what is intended is simply to impart information, such as your saying, "My father and the father of so-and-so came." This use of the teknonym merely signifies his progenitor. Nor is it forbidden if the teknonym carries a good omen, such as Father of Goodness and Mother of Happiness. As for the moniker, people can intend it to confer praise, blame, and other qualities. The protocol regarding it is as with the teknonym.

A second aspect involves looking at the original significance of either the teknonym or the moniker—in this, what applies to the name applies similarly, save that here it is more appropriate to look into their original signification, for the origin of the meaning in this case is clearer. Someone composed the following lines about this: 3.14

Drawn by desire I came
   to the "Father of Virtues" to behold him.
When I arrived, I found him alone
   and did not see a single one of his offspring.

The author intends his wording to refer to the virtues being attached to their "father" as children are to their parents, and to indicate that he did not find him possessing these qualities. The same can be said of "Father of Generous Acts," "Father of Virtue," "Father of Luck," "Beauty of Religion," and "Sun of the Exemplars." With all of these, it is the case that what is being described as good is a mental abstraction and is not inherent in its object. This is quite different from the name being congruent with what is named—the original signified object—to the point that the name is a derivation of the described object. If it does not resemble it, then the designation was mistaken and the name has no meaning. On account of this, it became habitual to choose an auspicious name, as is also the case when meeting someone—for example, in the above-mentioned story of the messenger. There are two benefits in seeking auspiciousness when giving names: One of them is the pleasure that comes when the name is heard—the adorning of the named object. The second lies

بذلك. الثانية التفاؤل بأن يصدق معناه وذلك على حسب ما يريده وللناس أغراض تختلف.

١٥،٣ وقد قيل لبعض العرب لم تسمّون عبيدكم نافعاً ومرزوقاً وأولادكم حرباً ومرّة. فقال إنّا نسمّي أولادنا لأعدائنا ونسمّي عبيدنا لأنفسنا. أي فلا فرق بين فائدة النفع وفائدة الدفع وحلاوتهما بل الدفع أهمّ.

١٦،٣ وكان وادي السباع في بلاد العرب وفيه قال قائلهم: [طويل]

مَرَرْتُ عَلَى وَادِي السِّبَاعِ وَلا أَرَى كَوَادِي السِّبَاعِ حِينَ تُبْصِرُ وَادِيَا
أَشُدُّ بِهِ رَكْبَا أَتَوْهُ تَئِيَّةً وَأَخْوَفُ إِلّا مَا وَقَى اللهُ سَارِيَا

قيل سبب تسميته أنّ امرأة من العرب كانت نزلته ولها عدّة أولاد فوجدها رجل يوماً وحدها فهمّ بها. فقامت تصيح بأولادها وتقول يا ليث يا نمر يا أسد يا كذا وهي أسماؤهم. فأقبلوا إليها يشتدّون فانطلق الرجل وهو يقول هذا وادي السباع.

١٧،٣ أمّا التخيّر عند الملاقاة والمعاملة فلفائدتين أيضاً إحداهما التلذّذ والتفاؤل. الثانية رجاء أن يكون قد طابق فيوجد معناه ويكون حسن الاسم دالّاً على حسن المسمّى كما تقرّر في الفراسة الحكميّة من أن حسن الخَلق دليل على حسن الخُلق. وفي الحديث اطلبوا الخير عند حسان الوجوه على وجه. ولم يبعث الله تعالى نبياً إلّا حسن الوجه حسن الاسم. وفي كلام العامّة الاسم يدلّ على المسمّى.

١٨،٣ ومن التفاؤل الصادق والرجاء الواقع ما وقع لعبد المطّلب في تسمية نبيّنا صلّى الله عليه وسلّم حيث سمّاه باسمه الشريف. وكان هذا الاسم غير معتاد عندهم فقيل له لمَ سمّيته بهذا وليس من أسماء آبائك؟ فقال رجاء أن يحمد في السماء والأرض فكان

in the hope that the name's meaning will turn out to be true, and, as peoples' aspirations differ, this depends on what is intended by the name.

"Why do you name your slaves Beneficial and Blessed and your sons War and Bitterness?" an Arab was asked. "We name our sons for our enemies," he responded, "and our slaves for ourselves." There is no difference between the merit of the pleasantness of names and the protection they provide, but protection is the more important aspect. 3.15

Someone once said the following about the Valley of Beasts, which was in the land of the Arabs:[9] 3.16

I came to the Valley of Beasts; I have never seen
 another valley like it.
Countless riders have stopped there.
 Except for those whom God protects, it terrifies the night traveler.

It is said that the reason for its name is that there was an Arab woman living there with a number of children. One day a man found her by herself when the children were nearby and approached her. She began to scream for her children, calling out "O Lion, O Tiger, O Leopard, O Such and Such," these being their names. They came running to her and the man departed, saying, "This is the Valley of Beasts."

There are two benefits in seeking an auspicious sign when meeting or interacting with someone. One benefit lies in perceiving the meeting to be a good omen and delighting in it. The second benefit lies in the hope that it will bring about its corresponding meaning, and that a favorable name indicates the goodness of the thing named. This was the case with the philosophical science of physiognomy, in which a good physical shape is an indication of a good nature. In the Hadith we find, for example: "Seek goodness in pleasant faces," and it is true that God did not send a prophet without his having a pleasant face and an auspicious name. The common folk have a saying: "The name indicates the thing named." 3.17

One confirmed example of someone seeking a good omen is the case of ʿAbd al-Muṭṭalib regarding our Prophet, God bless him and keep him, when ʿAbd al-Muṭṭalib gave him his noble name. This name was not a common one among them, so ʿAbd al-Muṭṭalib was asked, "Why did you give him this name, which is not one of your ancestors' names?" "In the hope that he would be praised in heaven and on earth," he answered.[10] And true enough, this is what 3.18

ذلك. ويحتمل أن يكون كان عنده من ذلك علم ممّن لقي من أهل ذلك العلم كسيف ابن ذي يزن ونحوه.

١٩،٣ وقد يكون سبب تخيّر الاسم مشايعة من تسمّى به تبركًا به أو حبًا[١] لذكره أو رجاء الشبه به أو نحو ذلك. وفي الحديث ولد لي الليلة ولد فسمّيته باسم أبي إبراهيم. وقيل لمّا نزل قوله تعالى ﴿يا أُخْتَ هَـارُونَ﴾ قيل للنبيّ صلّى الله عليه وسلّم كيف تكون أخت هارون وبينهما دهر طويل؟ فقال صلّى الله عليه وسلّم إنّهم كانوا يسمّون بأسماء أنبيائهم. أي فهو هارون آخر سمّي باسم هارون بن عمران عليه السلام.

٢٠،٣ واعلم أنّ التلذّذ المذكور في هذا القسم خلاف المذكور فيما مرّ فإنّ ذلك تلذّذ بالاسم بسبب حضور معناه الأصليّ كسعد وسعيد ووردة وياسمين. وهذا تلذّذ بالاسم لحضور من كان تسمّى به من غير التفات إلى مدلول اللفظ الأصليّ. فكلّ من سمع اسمًا كان وقع على مسمّى آخر فقد يستشعر ذلك المسمّى الآخر في الاسم فيوجب له ذلك الاستشعار أمورًا. إمّا تعظيمًا ومنه بدل أمير المؤمنين عمر رضي الله عنه اسم ولد كان اسمه محمدًا. فسمع رجلًا يومًا يشتمه ويقول فعل الله بك يا محمد وفعل. فقال لا أرى اسم النبيّ صلّى الله عليه وسلّم يُسَبّ بكَ. وكان بعض الرؤساء كلّم خديمًا له اسمه محمّد في أمر وخاطبه باسم آخر وهمّ أنّه غضبان عليه. فدخل على الخديم من ذلك جزع عظيم حتى بيّن له بعد ذلك أنّه إنّما كان على جنابة فلم يستطع أن ينطق بهذا الاسم الشريف وهو جنب رحمه الله تعالى وجزاه خيرًا. وإمّا تلذّذًا أو استئناسًا أو اشتياقًا أو نحو ذلك لكونه أليفًا أو محبوبًا.

٢١،٣ وكان المجنون لمّا اشتدّ به حاله قام أهله فقالوا نذهب به إلى الحجّ وزيارة البيت. ففعلوا فلمّا أقبلوا على مكّة قالوا له يا قيس هذا بلد الله وهذا بيته فادع الله تعالى أن يعافيك من حبّ ليلى. فأنشأ يقول: [وافر]

---

١ م، ق: إحياء.

happened. It is possible that ʿAbd al-Muṭṭalib had learned to see omens from someone who had experience in such matters, such as Sayf ibn Dhī Yazan.

The choice of name might also be intended as a blessing, on account of love for the name itself, out of hope that the person named will resemble it, and so on. In the Hadith we find, "A son was born to me that evening and I named him after my ancestor Abraham."[11] It is said that when the words of Exalted God «O sister of Aaron»[12] were revealed, the Prophet, God bless and keep him, was asked, "How can she be the sister of Aaron, as so much time has elapsed between the two?" He answered, God bless and keep him, "They were named after the names of their prophets." Thus, he was a different Aaron who was named after Hārūn ibn ʿImrān, peace be upon him. 3.19

Know that the delight mentioned above in this section is distinct from the delight previously discussed, for the latter is delight in the name due to the presence of its original meaning, such as with Saʿd, "Joyous," Saʿīd, "Happy," Wardah, "Rose," and Yāsmīn, "Jasmine." This delight in the name is due to its evocation of the one who bears the name, without reference to the word's original signification. Everyone who hears a name that has been given to another may perceive therein the named person. This perception carries certain associations for him, which may be of exaltation, as in the following account, when the Commander of the Faithful ʿUmar changed the name of a boy whose name was Muḥammad. ʿUmar heard a man one day vilify his son, saying, "May God do such and such with you, Muḥammad," and ʿUmar said, "I cannot have the name of the Prophet, God bless and keep him, being insulted by you." A certain chieftain spoke to a servant of his by the name of Muḥammad concerning a matter, and addressed him by a different name, leading the servant to worry that his master was angry with him. Due to this, a profound distress came over the servant until later it was made clear to him that his master was in a state of ritual impurity. While in such a state he was not able to speak this noble name, God show him mercy and reward him richly. The associations evoked by a name may also be of delight or of desiring familiarity and the like, due to the name being familiar or beloved. 3.20

When Majnūn's condition became grave, his family said, "Let's take him on a pilgrimage to God's House." They did so, and when they approached Mecca, they said to him, "Qays, this is the country of God and this is His House, so pray to Exalted God that He cure you of your love for Laylā." In response, he recited: 3.21

ذَكَرْتُكِ وَالْحَجِيجُ لَهُ ضَجِيجٌ   بِمَكَّةَ وَالْقُلُوبُ لَهَا وَجِيبُ

فَقُلْتُ وَنَحْنُ فِي بَلَدٍ حَرَامٍ   بِهِ لِلَّهِ أَخْلَصَتِ الْقُلُوبُ

أَتُوبُ إِلَيْكَ يَا رَحْمَانُ مِمَّا   جَنَيْتُ فَقَدْ تَكَاءَرَتِ الذُّنُوبُ

فَأَمَّا مِنْ هَوَى لَيْلَى وَحُبِّي   زِيَارَتَهَا فَإِنِّي لَا أَتُوبُ

فَكَيْفَ وَعِنْدَهَا قَلْبِي رَهِينًا   أَتُوبُ إِلَيْكَ مِنْهَا أَوْ أُنِيبُ

فَأَيِسُوا مِنْهُ. ثُمَّ سَكَنَ شَيْئًا مَا فَلَمَّا بَلَغُوا نَاحِيَةً مِنَّى سَمِعَ إِنْسَانًا يَقُولُ يَا لَيْلَى يُنَادِي **٢٢،٣**
امْرَأَةً. فَطَارَ الْمَجْنُونُ وَاسْتَقْبَلَ الْبَرِّيَّةَ[١] وَهُوَ يَقُولُ: [طويل]

وَدَاعٍ دَعَا إِذْ نَحْنُ بِالْخَيْفِ مِنْ مِنَّى   فَهَيَّجَ أَحْزَانَ الْفُؤَادِ وَمَا يَدْرِي

دَعَا بِاسْمِ لَيْلَى غَيْرَهَا فَكَأَنَّمَا   أَطَارَ بِلَيْلَى طَائِرًا كَانَ فِي صَدْرِي

وَقَالَ الْآخَرُ: [طويل]   **٢٣،٣**

وَمَنْ كَبِدِي يَهْفُو إِذَا ذُكِرَ اسْمُهُ   كَهَفْوِ جَنَاحٍ يَنْفُضُ الطَّلَّ طَائِرُهُ

وَبَلَغَ بِأَوْلِيَاءِ اللَّهِ تَعَالَى نَحْوُ هَذَا الْمَعْنَى وَهُمْ أَحَقُّ بِهِ. يُحْكَى عَنْ بَعْضِهِمْ أَنَّهُ لَقِيَ وَاحِدًا **٢٤،٣**
مِنْهُمْ فِي الْبَرِّيَّةِ فَقَالَ لَهُ مِنْ أَيْنَ أَتَيْتَ؟ فَقَالَ هُوَ. فَقَالَ أَيْنَ تُرِيدُ؟ فَقَالَ هُوَ. فَقَالَ
مَا تَعْنِي بِقَوْلِكَ هُوَ؟ فَقَالَ هُوَ. فَقَالَ اللَّهَ تَعْنِي؟ فَصَاحَ وَسَقَطَ مَيْتًا وَإِمَّا نَفْرَةً وَكَرَاهِيَةً
لِكَوْنِهِ بَغِيضًا مَقِيتًا وَإِمَّا غَيْرَ ذَلِكَ.

تَتِمَّةٌ. وَاعْلَمْ أَنَّ الِاسْمَ الَّذِي يُوضَعُ عَلَى الْإِنْسَانِ عَلَمًا عِنْدَ الْوِلَادَةِ أَوْ عِنْدَ تَبْدِيلِ اسْمِهِ **٢٥،٣**
بِاسْمٍ آخَرَ إِمَّا أَنْ يَكُونَ بِصُورَةِ الْكِنْيَةِ كَأَبِي بَكْرٍ وَأَبِي الْقَاسِمِ لِمَنْ سُمِّيَ بِهِ فَيَكُونُ اسْمُهُ
كِنْيَتَهُ. وَإِمَّا أَنْ يَكُونَ بِغَيْرِهَا كَزَيْدٍ وَعَمْرٍو وَهُوَ الْأَغْلَبُ. وَحِينَئِذٍ إِمَّا أَنْ تُقْرَنَ بِهِ الْكِنْيَةُ

---

١ ق: القبلة.

I remembered you at Mecca amid the clamor of the pilgrims,
 when hearts were beating fast.
While we were in the sanctuary,
 where hearts turn sincerely to God, I said,
"I repent to you, God,
 for the sins I've committed, and they are many.
But my infatuation with Laylā
 and my desire to see her—this I do not repent.
When my heart is held hostage by her,
 how could I repent or turn to You?"

So they despaired of him. He proceeded to grow somewhat calmer. When they reached Minā, he heard someone calling out to a woman, "Laylā!" Majnūn was stirred by this, turned toward the desert, and recited the following: 3.22

When we were at al-Khayf at Minā, someone called out
 unknowingly, awakening the sorrows of my heart.
He was calling another Laylā—with Laylā's name
 it was as if he caused a bird to flutter in my chest.

Another poet wrote: 3.23

When his name was mentioned, my heart fluttered
 like a bird's wing shaking off the dew.

A similar thing happened to some Friends of God, as befits them. It is said that one of them met another in the desert and asked, "Where did you come from?" "Him," he replied. The first one asked, "What do you want?" "Him," replied the second. "What do you mean by saying 'Him'?" the first asked. "Him," the second replied. "You mean God?" the first one said, and the other Friend screamed and dropped dead. This happened either due to his having been startled, or due to his having found the mention of God distasteful due to the speaker's base nature. Or it was for some other reason. 3.24

In conclusion, a person's proper name, whether given at birth or when one name is replaced by another, is either a teknonym, as with Abū Bakr or Abū l-Qāsim, so that his teknonym is his name, or, as is more often the case, he has a different name, such as Zayd or ʿAmr. In the first case, one possibility is that the teknonym is associated with him from the start, it being said, for example: 3.25

من أوّل وهلة فيقال مثلاً سمّيت ابني كذا وكنيته كذا. وقد يقرن به اللقب أيضاً فيقال مثلاً سمّيت ابني محمّداً وكنيته أبا عبد الله ولقّبته جمال الدين. وهذا كلّه لا إشكال في عَلَميتّه.

٢٦،٣ وقد لا يكنّى ولا يلقّب أوّلاً فإذا كنّي بعد ذلك أو لقّب كان ذلك عارضاً لا كالاسم اللاّزم أبداً من وجهين. أحدهما أنّه لم يكن شيء منهما ثمّ كان الثاني أنّهما يكونان ثمّ لا يكونان فإنّه قد يكنّى ثمّ لا يكنّى وقد يكنّيه هذا ولا يكنّيه الآخر وكذا اللقب. فصار كلّ منهما بمنزلة الوصف يعرض الاتّصاف به.

٢٧،٣ فقد يقال كيف يحسبان مع هذا في الأعلام؟ والجواب أنّهما متى أطلقا على المسمّى عيناه عند من عرفهما من غير معنى زائد على الذات. وهذا هو[١] حاصل العلميّة أمّا طروءهما فلا يضير فإنّ الاسم أيضاً كثيراً ما يطرأ. والمعتبر ما بعد الطروء كما هو الأمر في التسمية الأولى. وأمّا كونهما يتركان أحياناً فللاستغناء عنهما بالاسم كما يكون في الشيء يسمّى بأسماء مترادفة. فإذا عبّر عنه بواحد منها كفى.

٢٨،٣ وفيه بحث وهو أنّ الأسماء المترادفة فوضى على مدلولها ولا كذلك ما نحن فيه. فإنّ كلاًّ من الكنية واللقب إنّما يجلب لغرض من تعظيم أو تحقير أو غير ذلك ممّا مرّ. فيكون الوصف محطّ التسمية وحينئذ هو كليّ فيكون الاسم اسم جنس أو علم جنس وذلك خلاف ما يقال من أنّه علم شخص. وهذا بحث قويّ لم نبسطه لأنّا لسنا بصدده. ويجاب بمنع ذلك وأنّ محطّ التسمية الذات مع ملاحظة الغرض وكونه يؤتى به عند وجود الملاحظة ويترك عند عدمها. وأنّ ذلك غير معهود في الاسم لا امتناع فيه فافهم.

١ سقط من م.

"I named my son so-and-so and his teknonym is such and such." Perhaps the moniker is also associated with him. One can say, for example, "I named my son Muḥammad; his teknonym is Abū ʿAbd Allāh and his moniker is Jamāl al-Dīn." In all cases, there is no doubt that these are proper names.

A person may be given neither a teknonym nor a moniker at first, and when he later receives it, it is then contingent. In this case, it is nothing like the permanent name in two ways: The first is that neither the teknonym nor the moniker first existed, and then it did. The second difference is that the two of them existed and then did not, in that perhaps someone will address him with a teknonym and then not do so, or one person will do so and another will not. The same is the case with the moniker. Both of them are like descriptions whose application is contingent. 3.26

It may be asked, "Given this, how are they both considered distinguishing markers?" The answer is that when they are bestowed on the one named, they distinguish him for those who know them without any meaning beyond this. This is the essence of signification. When they are bestowed adventitiously, it does no harm, as a given name is also often bestowed in this fashion. What is under consideration here is what takes place after they are given in this fashion, similar to when the name was first given. As for the teknonym and the moniker sometimes being abandoned, this is due to their being superfluous to the proper name, as is the case with something that is named with synonymous names. When one mentions one of them it is enough. 3.27

There is some debate regarding this—namely, whether synonymous names have different connotations—but we are not talking about this here. Both teknonym and moniker are employed for the purpose of praise, scorn, or another reason that I have already mentioned. The significance of naming lies in description, and when a name is given in this fashion it is general in scope. A name is a name or mark of a category, which is different from saying that it is the proper name of a person. This is a matter of profound study that we shall not go into here, as it is not our subject. One might respond by rejecting this line of thought and arguing that the goal of naming is to identify an essence and to take the intended meaning into account: The name is used when the characteristic is observed and is abandoned when it is not—and this is not known to be the case with the given name, although it is not impossible. This should make things clear![13] 3.28

١،٤ فـأقول أنا الحسن بن المسعود بن محمّد بن عليّ بن يوسف بن أحمد بن إبراهيم بن محمّد ابن أحمد بن عليّ بن عمرو بن يحيى بن يوسف وهو أبو القبيلة ابن داوود بن يدراسن ابن ينتو.[١] فهذا ما بعد من النسب إلى أن دخل بلد فركلة في قرية منه تسمّى حارة أقلال وهي معروفة الآن. والكنية أبو عليّ وأبو المواهب وأبو السعود وأبو محمّد. أمّا ذكري للاسم فلمّا مرّ من فوائد التسمّي وأحمد الله تعالى وأشكره إذ جعله حسناً وأسأله سبحانه أن يجعل كذلك فعلي وخلقي وحظي في الدارين منه حسناً. كما أحمده تعالى إذ حسن اسم والدي أيضاً فجعله مسعوداً. واسأله تعالى أن يجعلني كذلك في الدارين ويجعله مسعوداً.

٢،٤ و ممّا اتّفق لي في اسمي هذا واسم والدي أنّي كنت ذات مرّة سافرت إلى زيارة الأستاذ الإمام ابن ناصر رحمه الله. فمررت ببلادنا وكان أخونا في الله البارع الفاضل الخير أبو سالم عبد الله بن محمّد العياشي يشتهي أن أمرّ به في زاويته. فلم يتّفق لي ذلك فكتبت إليه اعتذاراً: [طويل]

أَبَا سَالِمٍ مَا أَنْتَ إِلَّا كَسَالِمٍ ... لَدَيْنَا وَلَمْ يَقْضِ اللِّقَاءُ فَسَالِمِ
وَزَوِّدْ غَرِيبًا طَالَمَا قَذَفَتْ بِهِ ... ضُرُوبُ النَّوَى مِنْ كُلِّ أَفْيَحَ قَاتِمِ
مَرَامًا لِشُرْبِ ٱلْكَأْسِ وَهْيَ مَنُوطَةٌ ... بِكَفِّ الثُّرَيَّا أَوْ بِكَفِّ النَّعَائِمِ
بِوُدٍّ وَإِنَّ ٱلْوِدَّ مِنْ أَطْيَبِ ٱلْقِرَى ... وَدَعْوَةُ صِدْقٍ عِنْدَ عَقْدِ ٱلْعَزَائِمِ
وَسَلِّمْ عَلَى مَنْ ثَمَّ مِنْ جُمْلَةِ ٱلْمَلَا ... تَحِيَّةَ ذِي وِدٍّ إِلَى ٱلْكُلِّ دَائِمِ

٣،٤ وقولي كسالم تلميح إلى قول الشاعر: [طويل]

يُدِيرُونَنِي عَنْ سَالِمٍ وَأُدِيرُهُمْ ... وَجِلْدَةُ بَيْنَ ٱلْعَيْنِ وَٱلْأَنْفِ سَالِمُ

١ ط: ينتن؛ بياض في ق.

I thus declare: I am al-Ḥasan ibn Masʿūd ibn Muḥammad ibn ʿAlī ibn Yūsuf ibn Aḥmad ibn Ibrāhīm ibn Muḥammad ibn Aḥmad ibn ʿAlī ibn ʿAmr ibn Yaḥyā ibn Yūsuf—the last of whom is the progenitor of the tribe—ibn Dāwūd ibn Yadrāsan ibn Yanantū. The first part of the genealogy goes down to when Yūsuf entered a village in the region of Farkalah by the name of Ḥārat Aqlāl, which is well known today. My teknonyms are Abū ʿAlī, Abū l-Mawāhib, Abū l-Suʿūd, and Abū Muḥammad. I mention my name because of what I said above about the merits of naming oneself, and I thank Exalted God and am grateful to Him for making it Ḥasan, "Good." Likewise, I ask Him, may He be praised, to make good my actions, my character, and my fate both in this world and the next. I also thank the Exalted for having given my father a good name—He made it Masʿūd, "Fortunate"—and ask the Exalted to make my father fortunate and to make me so as well in this world and the next. 4.1

Speaking of my name and my father's, I was traveling once to visit the teacher and exemplar Ibn Nāṣir, God show him mercy. I was passing through our region when our excellent, distinguished, and admirable brother in God, Abū Sālim ʿAbd Allāh ibn Muḥammad al-ʿAyyāshī, asked me to visit him in his lodge.[14] This was not possible, so I wrote to him, apologizing: 4.2

Abū Sālim, one without flaws, you are nothing if not like Sālim;
  though we have not met, let our relationship be flawless.
Provision a stranger who has been cast about by
  many journeys in every broad and dark land
Out of desire to drink of a cup suspended
  from the hand of the Pleiades or Sagitta.
Provision him with love: Love is the best hospitality
  and a most sincere invocation when making a resolution.
Greet the entire group for me
  as one who is constantly full of love for all of them.

When I said "like Sālim" it was in reference to the line:[15] 4.3

They drive me away from Sālim, as do I them.
  Sālim is as delicate as the skin between the eye and the nose.[16]

وكتب عبد الملك بن مروان إلى الحجّاج أنت عندي كسالم. فلم يفهم مراده حتّى أنشد البيت المذكور ومراد الشاعر أنّ سالمًا المذكور الذي يدافع الناس عنه ويحامي عنه في محبّته له وعزّته عليه بمنزلة الجلدة التي بين الأنف والعين لأنّ تلك الجلدة هي سالم فهو تشبيه.

٤،٤ ثمّ لمّا قفلنا من زيارتنا كتب إليّ كتابًا يهنّيني بالزيارة ويهنّي من معي بصحبتي. وفي آخره: [بسيط]

مَنْ فَاتَهُ ٱلْحَسَنُ ٱلْبَصْرِيُّ يَصْحَبُهُ   فَلْيَصْحَبِ ٱلْحَسَنَ ٱلْيُوسِيَّ يَكْفِيهِ

٥،٤ ومن غريب الاتّفاق مع ذلك أن كنت في تلك المدّة إمّا قبل هذا الكتاب أو بعده بقريب حدّثني بعض الإخوان أنّه رأى فيما يرى النائم جماعة من الصالحين والكاتب معهم وفيهم الشيخ محمّد بن مبارك التستاوتي وغيره من أمثاله. فتكلّم بعضهم وأظنّه قال ابن المبارك المذكور إلى أن قال إن كان الحسن البصريّ في زمانه فهذا الحسن البصريّ في زماننا يشير إلى الكاتب. وإنّما ذكرت هذا رجاء وطماعيّة في اللحاق بالصالحين أو بمحبّيهم أو بمحبّي محبّيهم وتبرّكًا بذكرهم. وإلّا فليس بعشّك فادرجي: [كامل]

لَمَّا ٱنْتَسَبْتُ إِلَى عُلَاكِ[1] تَشَرَّفَتْ   ذَاتِي فَصِرْتُ أَنَا وَإِلَّا مَنْ أَنَا

٦،٤ وكتب إليّ العلّامة أبو عبد الله محمّد بن سعيد السوسي بأبيات يذكر فيها أنّه على عقد المحبّة وفي آخرها: [بسيط]

لَقَدْ تَحَبَّبْتَ لِي فَضْلاً[2] خُصِصْتَ بِهِ   بَيْنَ ٱلْوَرَى حَبَّذَا حُبُّ ابْنِ مَسْعُودِ

فعلمت أنّه يروي عن ابن مسعود الحبر الصحابيّ رضي الله عنه وألحقنا وآباءنا بزمرته إنّه ذو الجود والإحسان. فقلت إنّ هذا كله من نعم الله التي يسر بها الإنسان.

١ ط: حماك. ٢ ط: حبا.

ʿAbd al-Malik ibn Marwān wrote to al-Ḥajjāj: You are to me like Sālim. The latter didn't understand what he meant until he cited the line of poetry quoted above. The poet means that this Sālim, whom the people defend, and whom the poet protects in his love and care for him, is like the skin between the nose and the eye, as that skin is flawless. In other words, it is a simile.

When we departed, al-ʿAyyāshī wrote a letter congratulating me on my visit 4.4
and congratulating those with me on being my companions. The last line was:

> He who missed the chance to meet al-Ḥasan al-Baṣrī,
> let him be satisfied with the companionship of al-Ḥasan al-Yūsī.

It is a strange coincidence that at that time, either before or shortly after 4.5
writing the letter, one of my brothers told me that he had seen a group of the devout in a dream, with this author among them, along with the teacher Muḥammad ibn Mubārak al-Tastāwatī and others like him. One of them was speaking—I think he said it was the aforementioned Ibn Mubārak—and he happened to say, "What al-Ḥasan al-Baṣrī was in his time, this fellow"—indicating the author—"is in ours." I mention this only out of hope and desire to join the devout, or those who love them or those who love those who love them, and to seek blessings by mentioning them. If this is not to happen, "This is not your nest, go your own way":[17]

> When I became associated with your nobility I was honored
> to my core and became who I am. If not for this, who would I be?

The illustrious Abū ʿAbd Allāh Muḥammad ibn Saʿīd al-Sūsī wrote lines to 4.6
me in which he mentioned that he felt deep affection toward me. The last of these was:

> I have come to adore you for the special qualities you have among mortals.
> How perfect is the affection for Ibn Masʿūd!

I knew that the allusion was to Ibn Masʿūd, the learned Companion, God be content with him and may we and our ancestors be part of his cohort, a devout and beneficent man. I said, "All of this is a blessing of God, with which He has made life easy for men: This blessing entails the correspondence of a person's name or the name of his ancestor with the names of the elect." It is a strange coincidence that when I was writing the preceding passage on genealogy, a

وهو موافقة اسمه أو اسم أبيه لأسماء الخيار.[١] ومن غريب الاتفاق أني كنت أكتب ما تقدم من النسب فجاء أعرابي بقصيدة من الملحون يمدحني بها وفي أثنائها يقول ما معناه إن اسمه أي الممدوح على اسم الحسن بن علي رضي الله عنهما. فقلت في نفسي سبحان الله في هذا كان عملي.

١،٥ تتمّة أخرى في أحكام التسمية. اعلم أنّه وإن كان المطلوب تخيّر الاسم كما مرّ لا بدّ من التوسّط بين طرفي الإفراط والتفريط. فكما أنّه لا ينبغي له أن يتسفّل إلى الأسامي الدنيّة كذلك[٢] لا ينبغي له أن يتعلّى إلى الأسامي العليّة التي لا تنبغي له كأسماء الله تعالى. وللفقهاء كلام في أسماء الملائكة. فعن إمامنا مالك رضي الله عنه أنّه يكره أن يتسمّى الرجل بجبريل وعلّل ذلك بأنّه سبب لأن يقول قائل جاءني البارحة جبريل وكلّمني جبريل وهو بشيع موهم. وروي عنه أيضاً لا ينبغي بياسين.

٢،٥ وتقدّم إلى الحارث بن مسكين القاضي خصمان فنادى أحدهما صاحبه باسمه إسرافيل. فقال القاضي لمَ تسمّيت بهذا الاسم؟ وقد قال صلّى الله عليه وسلّم لا تسمّوا بأسماء الملائكة. فقال له الرجل ولمَ تسمّى مالك بن أنس بمالك؟ وقد قال تعالى ﴿وَنَادَوْا يَا مَالِكُ لِيَقْضِ عَلَيْنَا رَبُّكَ﴾؟ ثمّ قال لقد تسمّى الناس بأسماء الشياطين فما عيب عليهم يعني القاضي فإنّ اسمه الحارث وهو اسم الشيطان إبليس. قال ابن عرفة ويرحم الله الحارث في سكوته والصواب معه لأنّ[٣] محل النهي في الاسم الخاصّ بالوضع أو الغلبة كإسرافيل وجبريل وإبليس والشيطان وأمّا مالك والحارث فليسا منه لصحّة كونهما من نقل النكرات للأشخاص المعيّنة أعلاماً من اسم فاعل مالك وحارث كقاسم. انتهى.

٣،٥ وأمّا أسماء الأنبياء عليهم السلام فيجوز التسمّي بها. وفي الحديث تسمّوا باسمي ولا تكنّوا بكنيتي. وقيل إنّ هذا النهي منسوخ فيجوز التسمّي أيضاً والتكنّي بكنيته صلّى الله

١ ط: الأخيار. ٢ ق: الأسافل لدنيّة ذلك. ٣ م: لأنه. قارن مع النصّ في إبن عرفة، المختصر الفقهي (دبي: مؤسسة خلف أحمد الحبتور، ٢٠١٤)، ٣٦٧.

Bedouin brought me a poem in colloquial Arabic in which he praised me.[18] In the course of it, he said something to the effect that "He," that is, the object of praise, is named after al-Ḥasan ibn ʿAlī, God be pleased with them both. I said to myself, "God be praised! This is just the subject I was working on."

Here is an additional aspect of the rules of naming. When one picks a name, as I have written about here, one needs to find the middle ground between excess and neglect. Just as one should not stoop to using base names, so too there is no call for elevating oneself with lofty names that are inappropriate, such as the names of Exalted God. The jurists provide us with a discussion of the names of angels, and it is related from our own exemplar Mālik, God be pleased with him, that he loathed that a man be named Gabriel. He justified this with the possibility that someone could say, "Yesterday Gabriel came to me and spoke to me in an offensive and deluded manner." It is also related from him that one should not use the name Yāsīn.[19] 5.1

Two adversaries approached the judge al-Ḥārith ibn Miskīn, and one of them called his companion by the name Israfel. The judge asked, "Why were you given this name, when the Prophet said, God bless and keep him, 'Do not give people the names of angels'?" The man said to him, "And why was Mālik ibn Anas named Mālik when God had said: «They will cry: O Mālik! Would that thy Lord put an end to us!»"[20] The man continued, saying, "People have been given the names of devils, with no shame involved"—meaning the judge, whose name was al-Ḥārith, which is a name for the devil, Iblīs. Ibn ʿArafah said, "May God have mercy on al-Ḥārith in his silence, for he was right: The determining factor in forbidding a name lies in its being conventionally appointed as a proper name or generally being so understood, as with Israfel, Gabriel, Iblīs, and Satan. Mālik and al-Ḥārith are not in that category since they are rightly considered to be the kind of nouns that convert into names for specific people, such as the active participles 'possessor,' which gives Mālik; 'tiller,' which gives Ḥārith; and 'divider,' which gives Qāsim." 5.2

As for the names of prophets, peace be upon them, it is permitted for people to be named after them. In the Hadith we find: "Name people after me, but do not call them by my teknonym." It is said that this prohibition has been 5.3

عليه وسلّم. ودخل القاضي أبو القاسم بن زيتون على أمير بلده المنتصر بالله فقال له لم تسمّيت بأبي القاسم؟ وقد صحّ عنه صلّى الله عليه وسلّم أنّه قال تسمّوا باسمي ولا تكنّوا بكنيتي. فقال القاضي إنّما تسمّيت بكنيته صلّى الله عليه وسلّم ولم أتكنَّ بها. وفي المسألة كلام باعتبار علّة النهي وكون ذلك مع وجوده صلّى الله عليه وسلّم مشهور لا حاجة إلى بسطه. ومن المنهيّ عنه في الحديث أن يسمّي الرجل غلامه رباحاً أو أفلح أو يساراً[١] إذ قال أثمّ هو؟ فيقال لا. ولا بأس بتكنية الصبيّ كما مرّ وأصله يا أبا عمير ما فعل النّغير. تنبيه: في الحديث إنّ أخنع الأسماء رجل تسمّى عند الله بمالك الأملاك. ووقع فيه عضد الدولة حيث قال: [رمل]

مَا يَطِيبُ ٱلْعَيْشُ إِلّا بِالسَّمَرْ[٢] وَغِنَاءٍ مِنْ جَوَارٍ فِي سَحَرْ
غَانِيَاتٌ سَالِبَاتٌ لِلنُّهَى سَاقِيَاتُ الرَّاحِ مَنْ فَاقَ ٱلْبَشَرْ
عَضُدُ الدَّوْلَةِ وَٱبْنُ رُكْنِهَا مَلِكُ ٱلْأَمْلَاكِ غَلَّابُ ٱلْقَدَرْ

فهذا من التغالي المنكر وإنّما ذلك لأنّ ملك الأملاك هو الله تعالى وإطلاقه على غيره وإن كان يتأوّل بمن دونه أي ملك أملاك البشر لكنّه في غاية من الإيهام والبشاعة فلا ينبغي. وقد تردّد العلماء في أنّه هل يلتحق به قاضي القضاة ونحوه.

ومن البشيع الواقع في زماننا في الأوصاف أنْ بَنَى السلطانُ رشيد ابن الشريف جسرَ سبو فصنع له بعضهم أبياتاً كتبت فيه برسم الإعلام. أوّلها: [مجزوء الرمل] ٤،٥

صَاغَ[٣] ٱلْخَلِيفَةُ ذَا ٱلْمَجَازِ مَلِكُ ٱلْحَقِيقَةِ[٤] لَا ٱلْمَجَازِ

١ ق: جبارا. ٢ ق: بالسهر. ٣ ق: بني. ٤ ق: الخليفة.

abrogated, and that both naming people after him, God bless and keep him, and giving them his teknonym is permitted. The judge Abū l-Qāsim ibn Zaytūn came to the ruler of his country, al-Muntaṣir billāh, who addressed him, saying, "Why were you named Abū l-Qāsim, when it has been reliably related from the Prophet, God bless and keep him, 'Name people after me, but do not call others by my teknonym.'" The judge said, "I was given his teknonym, God bless and keep him, as my given name, not as my teknonym." The matter involves considering the cause of the prohibition, and it is well known and needs no elaboration that the name was used during the Prophet's time, God bless and keep him. There is a hadith that prohibits a man from naming his slave Profit, Fortune, or Prosperity, since one might ask, "Present?" and one might then reply, "No." As discussed above, there is no harm in giving a young boy a teknonym. The origin of this dispensation is the saying, "Father of ʿUmayr, what happened to *nughayr*, the young sparrow?" Note that there is a hadith that goes, "In God's view, the most perfidious name is that of a man called king of kings." This is what happened with ʿAḍud al-Dawlah, when he said:

Life is not sweet without nightly conversation
and the song of slave women at daybreak.
Singing girls who rob you of your mind
and pour wine for the most excellent men:
"Power of the State," son of "Pillar of the State"—[21]
the king of kings, the conqueror of fate.

This is an example of illicit exaggeration, because the king of kings is Exalted God. Giving the title to any besides Him, even if it can be understood to mean one below Him—the people's king of kings—is supremely delusional and offensive, and should not be done. Scholars have already hesitated regarding whether a judge should be given the title Judge of Judges, and the like.

An offensive matter regarding attributes in our day was the composition of verses as an informative inscription for Sultan Rashīd ibn al-Sharīf when he built the bridge over the Subū. The first line of it was: 5.4

The caliph constructed this bridge, I figure.
He is a true king, not just a figure.[22]

فحمله اقتناص هذه السجعة والتغالي في المدح والاهتبال بالاسترضاء على أن جعل ممدوحه ملكاً حقيقياً لا مجازياً وإنّما ذلك هو الله تعالى. وكلّ ملك دونه مجاز الممدوح وغيره ونسبة الألوهيّة إلى غيره تعالى كفر صراح. وهذا مقتضى اللفظ وقائله يتأوّله بحقيقة دون حقيقة لأنّه موحّد ولكنّه في غاية الإيهام وغاية البشاعة والقبح. وقد أنكر الإشبيليّ وغيره ممّن ألّف في لحن العامّة ما هو أخفّ من هذا بكثير. لله الأمر من قبل ومن بعد.[1]

وأمّا اليوسي فأصله اليوسفيّ كما مرّ من أنّ يوسف هو أبو القبيلة ويسقطون الفاء في لغتهم. وأمّا ذكري لما مرّ من النسب فلفوائد منها أن يعرفه من يقف عليه من ذوي القرابة للتوصّل إلى صلة الرحم والموارثة والمعاقلة وغير ذلك من الأحكام وهذا ممّا لا بدّ منه. وقد قال سيّدنا أمير المؤمنين عمر بن الخطّاب رضي الله عنه تعلّموا من الأنساب ما تصلون به أرحامكم. وقد حمل الأمر في كلامه على الوجوب وذلك أصله. الثانية أن يعلم انقطاع النسب عند انتهائه إلى القرى. فيظهر معنى قول مولانا عمر أيضاً رضي الله عنه فيما يؤثر عنه أنّه قال تعلّموا أنسابكم ولا تكونوا كالقبط ينتسبون إلى القرى. وليس هذا مخصوصاً بالقبط بل المدن كلّها تتلف الأنساب كما قال العراقيّ رحمه الله: [رجز] ١،٦

وَضَاعَتِ ٱلْأَنْسَابُ بِٱلْبُلْدَانِ   فَنُسِبَ ٱلْأَكْثَرُ لِلْأَوْطَانِ

وسبب ذلك أنّ الإنسان إنّما احتاج إلى التمدّن للقيام بالمتاجر والحرف وسائر الأسباب التي ينتظم بها أمر المعاش والتعاون على المنافع الدينيّة والدنيويّة. ولا يتأتّى ذلك عادة إلّا بكثرة الناس لتحصل عمارة الأسواق. ويحصل من كلّ حرفة وصناعة وسبب وعمل عارف أو أكثر يقوم بها. ولا يكون ذلك عادة من عشيرة واحدة بل ولا من قبيلة وعمارة بل من أخلاط شتّى وأفواج جمّة. و ذلك لسببين. أحدهما أنّ ٢،٦

١ سقطت الجملة من م.

The poet's seeking out the rhyming couplet, exaggerating in his praise, and seeking to please the ruler led him to make the object of praise a true and not metaphorical king, when the only true king is Exalted God. Every king, praiseworthy and not, other than God, is a figurative one: Attributing divinity to any other than Him is arrant unbelief. This is the significance of the line, and any monotheist who recites it understands that it is not literally true, although by saying it he has entered a state of extreme delusion, offensiveness, and shame. Al-Ishbīlī, as well as others who have written on solecisms of the common folk, have condemned far less than this. Everything is God's to command.

Regarding the name "al-Yūsī," its orgin is "al-Yūsufī." As mentioned previously, Yūsuf was the father of the tribe who drop the letter "f" in their dialect. As for the abovementioned remarks about my genealogy, I made them because of genealogy's virtues. Among these is that one who has knowledge of genealogy understands who is related to whom in order to be apprised of their ancestry, inheritance, responsibility for blood money, and other such indispensable judgments. Our leader, the Commander of the Faithful, ʿUmar ibn al-Khaṭṭāb, God be pleased with him, said, "Learn genealogy that relates to your own blood." This imperative was understood as one of obligation: It is the origin of the studying of genealogy. Furthermore, we should know that genealogy is interrupted when it ends in a settlement. This is also clarified by the saying of our leader ʿUmar, God be pleased with him: He is reported to have said, "Know your genealogy, and do not be like the Copts who trace their genealogies to settlements." Doing this is not something that is specific to Copts; rather, all cities ruin genealogies. As al-ʿIrāqī, God show him mercy, said: 6.1

> Genealogies are lost in cities,
> since most trace themselves back to tribal areas.

This loss of genealogical knowledge is due to mankind's need to build cities in order to trade, pursue professions, and carry out other matters that involve earning a living and helping each other achieve religious and material benefits.[23] This generally does not come about unless there are a sufficiently large number of people to establish markets. In every profession, craft, and calling, or in the case of specialized tradespeople and so forth, members are usually not from one clan, nor are they from one tribe or tribal division. Rather, they 6.2

هذا هو مظنّة الكثرة الكافية فيما ذكر. الثاني أنّ عادة الله تعالى لم تجرِ باختصاص رهط أو حيّ واحد من الناس بالتفرّد بالمعارف والاستقلال بالمصالح الدينيّة والدنيويّة من دون سائر أصناف الخلق حتّى ينتظم بهم الأمر وحدهم وتحصل لهم المزيّة بذلك والذكر فيه دون من سواهم. بل بثّ الله تعالى بلطيف حكمته الخصائص والمزايا في الناس فيوجد في هذا الرهط عالم وفي آخر شاعر وفي آخر صانع أو تاجر. وهكذا ليتمّ التعاون ويحظى الخلق كلّهم من مائدة الله تعالى في باب الخصوصيّات بنصيب.

٣،٦ ولمّا كانت المدينة تجمع أخلاط الناس صار ساكنها في الغالب غريباً عن نسبه. فقد لا يكون بينه وبين جار بيته نسب ولا معرفة. فإذا نشأ نسله انتسبوا غالباً إلى البلد لا إلى قومهم من وجهين أحدهما أنّه كثيرًا ما ينقطع ما بينهم وبين قومهم فلا يعرفونهم. الثاني أنّ الإنسان يجب ببلده ويتبجّح به لثلاثة أوجه. أحدها أنّه لا يعرف غالباً غيره. الثاني أنّ الله تعالى حبّب إلى الناس منازلهم ليلازموها فتنتظم عمارة الأرض على ما قدّر الله تعالى. كما قال صلّى الله عليه وسلّم اللهم حبّب إلينا المدينة كحبّنا مكّة أو أشدّ. الثالث الإلف الطبعي فإنّ كلّ واحد يألف تربته كإلفه لأمّه وأبيه. ولذا لا يزال يحنّ إلى مسقط رأسه ومحطّ لهوه وأنسه. وقالوا الكريم يحنّ إلى وطنه كما يحنّ النجيب إلى عَطَنِهِ.

٤،٦ وقال الأعرابيّ: [طويل]

أَحَبُّ بِلَادِ اللهِ مَا بَيْنَ مَـنْعِجٍ إِلَيَّ وَسَلْمَى أَنْ يَصُوبَ سَحَابُهَا
بِلَادٌ بِهَا حَلَّ الشَّبَابُ تَمَائِمِي وَأَوَّلُ أَرْضٍ مَسَّ جِلْدِي تُرَابُهَا

are from many tribes and groups. There are two reasons for this. The first, as already mentioned, is that cities are the most likely place to find a sufficiently numerous group of people. The second is that it is God's habit not to single out one group or tribe of people to know something and to be the only ones that possess religious or profane expertise to the point where, achieving superiority and renown, they alone are distinguished in the matter. Instead, Exalted God, in the subtlety of His wisdom, scattered distinctive characteristics and privileges among people, so that in one group there resides a scholar, in another a poet, and in yet another an artisan or a merchant, and so forth. He did this so that people should help each other, and that all of creation obtain its share of talents from the table of Exalted God.

When cities begin to gather together different groups, any given individual living there generally becomes estranged from his genealogy, and he and his neighbor might not be related or even know each other. When his children grow up, they usually trace themselves back to a city, and not to their tribal group. They do so for two reasons: The first is that there is a rupture between them and their people of whose identity they were ignorant, and the second is that a person likes to identify with his city and boast about it. There are three reasons for this: (1) Generally, a person knows no other place. (2) Exalted God has caused people to love their homes so that they remain in them and the earth to be cultivated in accordance with Exalted God's decree. It is as the Prophet said, God bless and keep him: "God made Medina beloved to us to the same extent as Mecca, if not more." (3) Natural inclination, for everyone feels affection for his land, just as he does for his mother or father. Thus, people continue to long for their home, or any place where they have experienced happiness and intimacy. There is a saying: "A noble person longs after his country, just as the camel rider longs for the watering hole." 6.3

Al-Aʿrābī said:[24] 6.4

The part of God's earth I most love
  is between Manʿij and Salmā, may it be watered by clouds.
This land in which I came of age
  was the first earth to touch my skin.

٦،٥ وقال الآخر: [كامل]

بَلَدِي أَلِفتُ بِهِ الشَّبِيبَةَ وَالصِّبَا   وَلَبِسْتُ ثَوْبَ ٱلْعَيْشِ وَهْوَ جَدِيدُ
فَإِذَا تَمَثَّلَ فِي الضَّمِيرِ رَأَيْتُهُ   وَعَلَيْهِ أَثْوَابُ الشَّبَابِ تَمِيدُ

٦،٦ وقال الآخر: [طويل]

وَحَبَّبَ أَوْطَانَ الرِّجَالِ إِلَيْهِمُ   مَآرِبُ قَضَاهَا الشَّبَابُ هُنَالِكَا
إِذَا ذَكَرُوا أَوْطَانَهُمْ ذَكَّرَتْهُمُ   عُهُودَ الصِّبَا فِيهَا فَحَنُّوا لِذٰلِكَا

٦،٧ وهذا المعنى كثير شهير. ومن الأسباب في ذلك أنها أوّل بقعة ذاق فيها النعمة وأوّل جهة ألف منها الرفق وآنس الإحسان. وفي الحديث جبلت القلوب على حبّ من أحسن إليها. ولك في الحديث وجهان أحدهما لطيف وهو أنّ القلوب الطاهرة عن الهوى الصافية من رعونات النفس الزاهرة بأنوار المعرفة جبلت على حبّ الله تعالى لأنّه هو المحسن إليها لا غير. والثاني ظاهري وهو أنّ القلوب من حيث هي جبلت على الميل إلى المحسن من حيث هو. ولا شكّ أنّ كلّ محسن دون الله تعالى لا أثر له وإنّما هو جهة يرد منها إحسان الله تعالى. ومع ذلك يحبّ فكذا تربة الإنسان أوّل جهة ورد منها عليه الإحسان الإلهيّ. فيحبّها قبل غيرها من الترب حبّاً متمكّناً. كما قيل: [طويل]

أَتَانِي هَوَاهَا قَبْلَ أَنْ أَعْرِفَ ٱلْهَوَى   فَصَادَفَ قَلْباً خَالِياً فَتَمَكَّنَا

٦،٨ وقال الآخر: [كامل]

كَمْ مَنْزِلٍ فِي ٱلْأَرْضِ يَأْلَفُهُ ٱلْفَتَى   وَحَنِينُهُ أَبَداً لِأَوَّلِ مَنْزِلِ

Another poet said:[25] 6.5

This is my country: where I spent my youth and childhood
and wore the robe of life when it was new.
When I see it now in my mind's eye
it is draped in those clothes of youth.

Another said:[26] 6.6

The wishes that youths fulfilled in their homelands
cement their attachment to them as men.
When men recall their homelands, they are reminded
of their childhood, and feel a longing to return.

There are many famous poems that convey this meaning. One of the reasons a person longs for the homeland is that it is the first place he tasted happiness, and where he experienced kindness, intimacy, and generosity. There is a hadith: "Hearts are created with a disposition to love those who treat them well." There are two facets to this. One is subtle: Hearts that are free of desire, purified of the soul's frivolities, and bright with the lights of knowledge are drawn to the love of Exalted God because He alone is their benefactor. The second is obvious: By their nature, hearts incline toward any benefactor. Now, it is undoubtedly true that no benefactor has any influence but God, and that any apparent benefactors are a medium through which the beneficence of Exalted God is channeled. Despite this, they are loved. Similarly, the homeland is the first place people experience divine beneficence, so they love it deeply and above all else. As has famously been said:[27] 6.7

I desired her before I ever knew desire;
she struck an empty heart and possessed it.

As has also been said:[28] 6.8

A young man can know many homes in this world
yet his longing is always for the first of them.

٩،٦ ومن أسباب المحبّة والحنين حبّ من كان فيها من ذوي القرابة والأحباب وتذكارهم عند تذكارها. وقد قيل إنّ قوله صلّى الله عليه وسلّم في أُحد: جبل يحبّنا ونحبّه إنّ المراد من كان فيه من الأصحاب لحمزة ومن معه رضي الله عنهم.

١٠،٦ وقال المجنون: [وافر]

أَمُـرُّ عَلَى الدِّيَارِ دِيَارِ لَيْلَى   أُقَبِّلُ ذَا ٱلْجِدَارَ وَذَا ٱلْجِدَارَا
وَمَا حُبُّ الدِّيَارِ شَغَفْنَ قَلْبِي   وَلٰكِنْ حُبُّ مَنْ سَكَنَ الدِّيَارَا

١١،٦ وقال الآخر يخاطب وطنه: [طويل]

تَقَسَّـمَ فِيكَ التُّرْبَ أَهْلِي وَجِيرَتِي   فَفِي الظَّهْرِ أَحْيَائِي وَفِي ٱلْبَطْنِ أَمْوَاتِي

١٢،٦ وهذا سبب ذكر الديار والمنازل والأوطان. ولا ينحصر ما قيل في ذلك وسنلمّ بشيء منه إن شاء الله في هذا الكتاب.

١٣،٦ ثمّ إذا انتسب إلى البلد ذهب قومه وتُنوسيت أسلافه. فصار النسب مجهولاً لا باعث على حفظه ولا حامل على تعرّفه. وهذا بخلاف أهل البادية فإنّهم يحفظون أنسابهم إذ لا ملجأ لهم في الانتساب غير قومهم. فيبقى الأبّ الأوّل محفوظاً وبحفظه وذكره يتذكّر ما بينه وبينهم من سلسلة النسب. وإنّما كان ذلك فيهم لوجهين أحدهما أنّه لا قرار لهم في باديتهم فينتسبوا إليه بل منازلها عندهم سواء. الثاني أنّهم خالصون غالباً من كثير الشوب فكلّ واحد غالباً ينازل قومه إذ لا حاجة بهم إلى التمدّن في باديتهم اكتفاء بالحاضرة فكلّ حيّ فيها يعيشون وحدهم. ومتى خالطهم غيرهم لم يزل معروفاً بكونه ملصقاً. وقد يكون من القرى ما يكون كذلك لانقطاعه عن الاختلاط وعدم التمدّن فيمكنهم حفظ أنسابهم أيضاً.

Another reason for affection and longing for a place is a person's love for his relatives and loved ones there whom he remembers when recalling it. It has been noted about the Prophet's saying, God bless and keep him, regarding Uḥud—namely, "It is a mountain that loves us as we love it"—that he refers to the Companions who lie buried there, such as Ḥamzah and others, God be content with them. 6.9

Majnūn said: 6.10

When I pass the abodes of Laylā
I kiss each of their walls, one at a time.
It is not for love of houses that my heart fills with passion
but love for the one who lived there.

Another has said, addressing his homeland:[29] 6.11

My family and neighbors are divided by the earth—
on the outside are my living relatives, on the inside my dead.

This is why one remembers houses, places one has lived, and one's homeland. Too much has been said about this to treat the subject comprehensively: God willing, we will gather just some of it in this book. 6.12

When a person is associated with a country whose people have disappeared, and whose ancestors are forgotten, his genealogy becomes unknown: No cause remains to remember it, no incentive to know it. The case is different with desert folk: They remember their genealogy and have nothing but their people to associate themselves with. Thus, they continue to remember their first progenitor, and by remembering and recollecting him, they remember all those who lie between him and them in their genealogical chain. There are two reasons for this. The first is that they had never settled in a desert dwelling they would consider their place of origin. Instead, all their residences are the same to them. The second is that they generally do not mix with others; each individual among them generally camps with his people. In the desert they have no need for urban settlements and content themselves with temporary encampments near water. In this way, every clan in the desert lives by itself. When anyone from another tribe associates himself with them they know he is an outsider. Some settlements function like this. Cut off from mingling with others and by virtue of the absence of larger settled communities near them, they too can remember their genealogy. 6.13

١٤،٦ ومن هذا حفظت قريش أنسابها مع كونها في قرية. وكذا الخزرج في طيبة على ساكنها أفضل الصلاة والسلام وكذا نحوها. وقد يكون في المدائن من يحفظ نسبه أيضاً. ولا سيّما من له نسب مخصوص كالعلويّة[١] أو من يكون في محلّة منعزلة في المصر فيكون كالقرية السابقة.

١٥،٦ الثالثة أن يعلم أنّ حفظ الأنساب ليس خصوصيّة للعرب وإن كان لهم مزيد اهتمام بها ومزيد ارتفاع الهمّة. وكنت أنا قبل أن أخالط قومي أظنّ ذلك وأقول إنّ العجم إنّما هم كالمعزى ليس بين الأم وبين ولدها عهد إلّا أن يرعى[٢] فيذهب حيث شاء. وأمّا الأب فلا سؤال عنه. فلما باحثت قومي في هذا ألفيت الأمر على خلاف ما كنت أظن ووجدتهم يحفظون أنسابهم كما مر وإذا فيهم نسّابون يحقّقون الفصائل والشعوب على نحو ما كانت العرب تفعل في أنسابها. والوهن وإن كان يمكن أن يداخل شيئاً من ذلك فليس بعجب فإنّ غيرهم أيضاً ما كان يسلم من ذلك.

١٦،٦ وقد قال صلّى الله عليه وسلّم: كذب النسّابون. قال تعالى ﴿وَقُرُونًا بَيْنَ ذَٰلِكَ كَثِيرًا﴾ وكون هؤلاء أيضاً يكتفون بالقرى ويضيعون أنسابهم فذلك غير مختصّ بهم. فقد وقع أيضاً للعرب حين دخلت قرى الشام والعراق ومصر والمغرب وغيرها. فلا تزال تلقى حلبيّاً أو حمصيّاً أو كوفيّاً أو بصريّاً أو قرطبيّاً أو باجيّاً وهو تميميّ أو قيسيّ أو أزديّ أو غيره. وكثير منهم لا يرفع نسبه. وإنّما قال سيّدنا عمر رضي الله عنه ما قال قبل أن يقع هذا الواقع أو قاله خوفاً منه ثمّ وقع كما ظنّ.

١٧،٦ ويتعلّق بأمر النسب أبحاث. الأوّل اعلم أنّ نسب الإنسان الأصليّ هو الطين. قال تعالى ﴿وَبَدَأَ خَلْقَ ٱلْإِنسَانِ مِن طِينٍ﴾ وقال صلّى الله عليه وسلّم أنتم بنو آدم وآدم من تراب. ويقال لآدم عليه السلام عرق الثرى وأعراق الثرى. قال امرؤ القيس: [وافر]

١ ط: كالغالوية؛ ق: كالعارية. ٢ ق: يسن بها.

It is in this way that the Quraysh remembered their genealogy, despite living in a town. Thus, also the Khazraj in Medina, the greatest blessing and peace be upon its residents, and others as well. Those living in cities may also remember their genealogy, especially those whose lineage is distinguished, such as the descendants of ʿAlī.[30] This is true also of those who live in an isolated part of a garrison town: Their situation is like that of the previously mentioned settlements. 6.14

The third reason for preserving a genealogy is this. Evidently, remembering one's genealogy is not restricted to the Arabs, though they may have greater interest in doing so and lend it greater importance. Before I mingled among my countryfolk, I used to think that the Arabs were the only ones who cared for it. I would say, "The Amazigh are like goats: There is no bond between mother and son other than his being looked after, and then going his own way. As for the father, no one even asks after him." When I asked my countryfolk about this, I found the matter to be different from what I understood. I discovered that they remembered their lineage as I have described previously, with genealogists ascertaining the branches and groups in the fashion of the Arabs. As for their being fallible, such occurrences are not surprising as others are susceptible to error as well. 6.15

The Prophet, God bless and keep him, said, "The genealogists lie." And the Exalted has said: «And many generations between them.»[31] The fact that these tribes are content with living in urbanized areas, thereby losing sight of their genealogies, is not exclusive to them. This happened when they entered the cities of Syria, Iraq, Egypt, the Maghrib, and elsewhere. They still refer to themselves as being from Aleppo, Homs, Kufa, Basra, Cordoba, or Baja, when they are in fact Tamīmī, Qaysī, Azdī, and the like. Many of them cannot trace their genealogies back. Indeed, our leader ʿUmar, God be pleased with him, said so before this ever came to pass: He was fearful it would occur, and it subsequently transpired just as he suspected. 6.16

The following are matters related to the issue of genealogy.[32] First, you should know that man's original genealogy is clay. The Exalted has said: «He began the creation of man through clay.»[33] The Prophet, God bless and keep him, said: "You are the sons of Adam, and Adam came from dust." Adam, peace be upon him, is called both "Root of the earth" and "Roots of the earth." And Imru' al-Qays said: 6.17

إِلَى عِرْقِ الثَّرَى وَشَجَتْ عُرُوقِي   وَهٰـذَا ٱلْمَوْتُ يَسْلُبُنِي شَبَابِي[١]

١٨،٦ وهذا هو الأصل لجملته ثمّ لكلّ فرد منه بعد آدم أصل آخر وهو النطفة. قال تعالى ﴿ثُمَّ جَعَلَ نَسْلَهُ مِن سُلَالَةٍ مِّن مَّآءٍ مَّهِينٍ﴾. فإذا استوى الإنسان كلّه في أنّه من طين وأنّه في الجملة من ماء مهين لم يمكن أن يكون له فضل في نفسه باعتبار أصله. ولا أن يكون لبعضه فضل على بعض بذلك لاستواء الجميع. ولهذا نبّه صلّى الله عليه وسلّم على هذا فقال إنّ الله أذهب عنكم غبيّة الجاهليّة وفخرها بالآباء أنتم بنو آدم وآدم من تراب. ونبّه الله تعالى الإنسان على أصله في آيات كثيرة ليتنبّه فيعرف نفسه ويعرف اقتدار مولاه. وقال مولانا علي كرّم الله وجهه ما لابن آدم والفخر وأوّله[٢] نطفة وآخره جيفة. وقد يقال أوّله نطفة مذرة وآخره جيفة قذرة وهو فيما بين ذلك يحمل العذرة. وعقد الشاعر الكلام الأوّل فقال: [سريع]

مَا بَالُ مَنْ أَوَّلُهُ نُطْفَةٌ   وَجِيفَـةٌ آخِـرُهُ يَفْخَرُ

١٩،٦ وقال آخر: [منسرح]

عَجِبْتُ مِنْ مُعْجَبٍ بِصُورَتِهِ   وَكَانَ مِنْ قَبْلُ[٣] نُطْفَـةً مَذِرَه
وَفِي غَـدٍ بَعْدَ حُسْنِ صُورَتِهِ   يَصِيرُ فِي التُّرْبِ جِيفَةً قَذِرَه
وَهْوَ عَـلَى عُجْـبِهِ وَنَخْوَتِـهِ   مَا بَيْنَ رِجْلَيْهِ تَخْرُجُ ٱلْعَذِرَه

٢٠،٦ نعم يشرّف الإنسان بخصوصيّة تزاد على جسمه الطينيّ كالعقل والعلم والدين مثلاً. فيثبت له الفضل ويثبت لبعضه على بعض ولمّا عمي إبليس اللعين على الخصوصيّة ولم يرَ إلّا الطينيّة السابقة لم يرضَ بآدم ولا بالسجود له. ولم يسلّم الأمر لمولاه فأبى وصرّح بأنّه خير منه وعلّل ذلك بالمنشأ المذكور. فأخطأ من جهات منها أنّه إمّا أن

١ ق: ثيابي. ٢ ق: و إنما أصله. ٣ كذلك في ق؛ م: وأوله.

My veins are closely linked to the root of mankind
while this death strips me of my youth.

Imru' al-Qays's sentiment is a reference to this. Every person after Adam has a different origin than this—namely, a drop of sperm. The Exalted has said: «Then He fashioned his progeny from an extract of base fluid.»[34] If all mankind is equal in originating from clay, and subsequently from base fluid, it is not possible for them to possess merit on the basis of their genealogy. If all are equal, then none are superior to any other. The Prophet, God bless and keep him, drew attention to this fact, saying, "God preserved you from the foibles of the Time of Ignorance and the vaunting of ancestors that took place then. You are the sons of Adam and Adam came from dust." Exalted God drew man's attention to his origins in many verses of the Qur'an, so that he might take note and know himself and his Lord's power. Our leader 'Alī, God honor his countenance, said, "What justification has the son of Adam for boasting, for he begins as sperm and ends as a corpse." 'Alī may have worded it as follows: "His beginning is in a worthless drop of sperm, his end in a dirty corpse, and he carries excrement between the two." A poet has versified the first part as follows:[35] 6.18

How can he boast, when he begins as a drop and ends as a corpse?

Another said:[36] 6.19

Amazing, one who admires his own form
when he began as a worthless drop of sperm.
His beauty tomorrow
will be dirt—a corpse in the earth.
His arrogance and pride
merely excrement emerging between his legs.

People are in fact distinguished by what is singular to them beyond their clay-formed body, such as, for example, possessing reason, knowledge, and religion. These attributes speak to their merit and the merit of some over others. When accursed Iblīs—a malcontent—was blind to Adam's unique nature he saw only Adam's origin in clay. He was not pleased with Adam, nor with bowing down to him. He failed to comply with his Master's order, and refused to bow down, justifying this with his own superior origins. In this, Iblīs erred in several ways. One was that he was unaware of created characteristics, 6.20

يكون لا شعور له بالخصوصيّات أصلاً وإنّما منظره ذوات الأجرام. وهذا جهل عظيم وإمّا أن يشعر بها ولا يعرف أنّها بها يقع التفاضل وهذا أيضاً جهل. وإمّا أن يعرف ذلك ولكن لا يسلّم وجودها في آدم. فيكون قد بادر إلى إنكار الشيء قبل تحقّق انتفائه بل قبل التأمّل وهو أيضاً جهل وطيش وغفلة عن الإمكانات العقليّة وتصرّف الفاعل المختار تعالى.

٢١،٦ وإمّا أن يكون ذلك محتملاً عنده فحمل على الانتفاء لا على الثبوت. وهو أيضاً جهل وزلل في الرأي وتضييع للاحتياط وإهمال لدلالة القرائن المفيدة للعلم. فإنّه لو تأمّل أدنى تأمّل لاستفاد الحقّ من ترشيحه للخلافة. فإنّه لا يخفى عليه قول الله تعالى ﴿إِنِّي جَاعِلٌ فِي ٱلْأَرْضِ خَلِيفَةً﴾ ومن سجود الجمهور ويد الله مع الجماعة. وإمّا أن يكون قد علم ذلك ولكن غلبه ما يجد من الحسد والكبر فاشتغل بالمكابرة والمغالطة وهذا أيضاً جهل. فإنّ العلم إذا لم ينفع كالعدم ومن لا يجري على علمه في حكم الجاهل هذا مع غاية النقصان بعد التزكية وعدم ملك زمام النفس نسأل الله تعالى العصمة. قال الله تعالى ﴿قَدْ أَفْلَحَ مَنْ زَكَّاهَا وَقَدْ خَابَ مَنْ دَسَّاهَا﴾.

٢٢،٦ ومنها أنّه لم يخلص إلى صحيح العلم وصريح التوحيد فيعلم حقّ يقين أو عين يقين أو علم يقين أنّ للفاعل سبحانه أن يتصرّف في مملكته كيف شاء فيرفع من شاء ويضع من شاء ويقدّم من شاء ويؤخّر من شاء. ولا سَبب غير العناية الأزليّة وكلّ شيء بقضاء وقدر ﴿لَا يُسْأَلُ عَمَّا يَفْعَلُ وَهُمْ يُسْأَلُونَ﴾.

٢٣،٦ ومنها أنّ ما اعتمده من فضل جرم النار على جرم الطين ضعيف لا يسلّم له. فإنّ فضل النار إن كان بمجرد حسنها الصوريّ فهذه المزيّة لا تكفي. فإنّ الأشياء خلقت للانتفاع بها فما ينبغي أن يكون تفاوتها إلّا بالمنافع أكثريّة وأهميّة. والحسن الصوريّ من المنافع النظريّة وغيره أهمّ منه. ففي النار منافع كالإحراق والإيقاد والإنضاج والتسخين والتحليل والتعقيد والتعذيب لمن أريد والتذكّر ونحو ذلك. وفيها مفاسد كثيرة ومضار هائلة كالإحراق والإتلاف للنفوس والأموال والزرع والتنشيف والتيبيس والإيلام

looking instead at the attributes of the substances: This was great ignorance on his part. Or else he was aware of them but did not know the merit acquired through them. This was also ignorance on his part. Or he knew their merit, but did not accept their existence in Adam, having already rushed to deny something before verifying his view or before considering that these characteristics were present. This too is ignorance, rashness, and the willful denial of what is rationally possible and of what the freely acting Agent, the Exalted, can do.

Perhaps Iblīs considered it possible for Adam to have these qualities but acted as if they were absent. This position also manifests ignorance, false opinion, a lack of caution, and a disregard of the indicators that lead to knowledge. If Iblīs had contemplated these at all, he would have realized the truth that Adam had been designated as a worthy vice-regent. The words of Exalted God were not kept from him: «I will create a vice-regent on earth»,[37] nor the fact that, with God's support, all bowed down to Adam. Perhaps Iblīs did know this, but was so overcome by envy and arrogance that he hewed to obstinacy and deception—this too is ignorance. Useless knowledge is tantamount to not knowing, and whoever does not act according to what he knows should be counted as ignorant. Such obstinacy is the greatest flaw after self-advancement and the loss of self-control—we ask immunity from it from Exalted God, who has said: «Prosperous is he who purifies his ego, and he who lets himself be seduced by it has failed.»[38] 6.21

Among the reasons a person errs is that he does not attain correct knowledge and pure faith in God's unity until he knows with certainty, conviction, and confidence that the Agent, praise Him, proceeds in His kingdom as He wishes. He raises up and casts down whom He wishes, and promotes and holds back whom He wishes. There is no cause but eternal providence, and everything is subject to the divine decree and predestination: «He cannot be questioned for His acts, but they will be questioned.»[39] 6.22

Among Iblīs's errors is that he relied upon weak argumentation concerning the superiority of fire over clay—this is an unacceptable line of thought. If the superiority of fire subsisted in its beautiful appearance only, that would not be enough of an advantage. Things were created for their benefits; differentiating between them should be only on the basis of the level and importance thereof. A beautiful appearance is among the visual benefits, but others are more important. The benefits of fire include burning, igniting, cooking, warming, disintegrating, thickening, tormenting others, and serving as a reminder. 6.23

والعذاب الأكبر. وحسبك منها أنّها ضرّة الجنة وضدّها حتّى حصل بينهما من التقابل شبه ما بين النفع والضرّ. والعذاب وإن اشتمل على غير النار لكنّ النار أعظمه ولذا صحّ إطلاقها عليه.

٢٤،٦ وأمّا التراب فهو مهاد الإنسان وفراشه حيّاً وكِفاتُهُ مَيتاً. ثمّ هو منبع الماء الذي به الحياة ومنبت الزرع وجميع الأقوات للإنسان وغيره من الحيوانات. ومنبت العقاقير التي بها الاستشفاء والمعادن التي بها قوام العيش والتي بها التعامل. فمنافعه لا تحصى وليس فيه من المفاسد والمضار إلّا ما هو تافه يضمحل في جنب المصالح والمنافع. فهذا هو الشرف والفضل وقد ظهر ما في كلّ منهما في فرعه. فانظر إلى فرع التراب الذي هو الرحمة والمنفعة وهو الإنسان كيف ظهر فيه العلم والدين والرحمة. قال تعالى في نبيّه صلّى الله عليه وسلّم ﴿وَكَانَ بِٱلْمُؤْمِنِينَ رَحِيمًا﴾. وانظر إلى فرع النار التي هي النقمة والمضرّة وهو إبليس كيف ظهر فيه الإفساد والإغواء والاستفزاز.

٢٥،٦ والأمر بيد الله على أنّ الإنسان مخلوق من الاسطقسات الأربعة التراب والماء والنار والهواء. قال تعالى ﴿مِن تُرَابٍ﴾. وقال أيضاً ﴿مِن طِينٍ﴾ كما مرّ وهو التراب والماء. وقال تعالى أيضاً ﴿مِن صَلْصَالٍ﴾ وهو الطين اليابس لما فيه من ناريّة. وقال أيضاً ﴿مِنْ حَمَإٍ مَسْنُونٍ﴾ وهو المتغيّر الرائحة بما تخلّله من الهواء. فقد استولى الإنسان في تركيبه ما في النار وزاد ما في غيره. فافتخار صاحب النار على صاحب النار والماء والتراب والريح حمق عظيم.

٢٦،٦ وهذا المحلّ يسع من الكلام أكثر من هذا بكثير ولكنّه ليس من غرضنا. فلنرجع إلى ما نحن فيه فنقول إنّ ابن آدم متى افتخر قيل له إن كان افتخارك بأصلك فلا فخر لك بل كما يقال ضعيف عاذ بقرملة. ثمّ لا فخر لك به على غيرك لأنّكما سيّان وإن كان بمزيّة فهاتها فمن ثبت له أو لأبيه مزيّة[١] ثبت فخره بنفسه أو بنسبه وإلّا فلا. الثاني اعلم أنّ ما أشرنا إليه من المزايا التي يتشرّف بها الإنسان حتّى يشرّف بشرفه من

١ سقط من م.

It has many negative and extremely dangerous qualities as well, such as burning; destroying people, property, and crops; drying; desiccating; causing pain; and the punishment of hell. It suffices to say that it is a harm, the contrary of paradise, as distinct as the opposition between benefit and harm. There are other types of suffering, but fire is the worst kind, and therefore it is fitting that it be designated a harm.

Earth is man's abode, his berth while he is alive and his resting place when 6.24
dead.[40] It is also the provenance of water, from which issues life, the source of crops, and all nourishment for mankind and other living beings. It is the source of all medicines that heal, and of the metals fundamental to life and with which one does business. Its benefits are innumerable, and it has no negative or harmful qualities except some so insignificant that they fade next to the advantages and benefits. The nobility and distinction of each substance is apparent in what issues from it. Consider what issues from earth—namely, mercy and benefit. In this way, knowledge, religion, and mercy manifest themselves in man. Exalted God said regarding His Prophet, may He bless and keep him: «He is full of mercy for the believers.»[41] Then consider what issues from fire—vengeance and harm. This is the way that corruption, temptation, and provocation are manifested in Iblīs.

Everything is in God's power, for man is created from all four elements: 6.25
earth, water, fire, and air. The Exalted has said: «from earth»,[42] «from clay»,[43] which is earth and water, the Exalted also said: «from dry clay»,[44] which is dry clay that has been cooked. He also said: «from mud molded into shape».[45] This clay has various odors, according to how the air has affected it. Thus, in his composition man has received his full share of fire and more. For the one of fire to vaunt himself over the one of fire, water, earth, and air is arrant stupidity.

Much more could be said about this issue, but that is not our aim. Let us 6.26
return to what we were discussing: that when the son of Adam vaunts, he should be told, "If you vaunt your origin, you have nothing to vaunt." Rather, as the saying goes, "A weak man seeks help from a worthless one." You cannot vaunt superiority over another when the two of you are equal. If one has an advantage, he should produce it, for proof of oneself or one's father having it shows that he has reasonable cause to vaunt about himself or his ancestors. If not, then desist. Second: Know that the qualities we have referred to through which man is honored are many—and it follows that one descended from a person inherits his nobility. There are religious merits, such as prophecy,

انتسب إليه كثيرة منها دينيّة كالنبوءة وهي أجلّها وكالعلم والصلاح ومكارم الأخلاق وغير ذلك. ودنيويّة كالملك وهو أعظمها وكالنجدة والكرم والقوّة وكثرة العدد وكثرة المال والجمال ونحو ذلك. وكثير منها يصلح أن يكون دينياً ودنيوياً كالقوّة والعزّ والكرم وسائر مكارم الأخلاق وبعضها دينيّ ودنيويّ معاً كالنبوءة والخلافة والعلم. وبعض ذلك حسيّ وبعضه معنويّ وبعضه وجوديّ وبعضه عدميّ وشرح ذلك يطول فلنقتصر القول مع تمثيل وتمهيد.

٢٧،٦ أمّا التمثيل فهو أنّه لو اعتبر رجلان متساويان في الخَلق والخُلق والنسب وسائر الأحوال فلا مزيّة لأحدهما على الآخر. وفي مثلهما قال علقمة بن علاثة للمتنافرين صرتما كركبتي البعير الآدم. ولو اختصّ أحدهما بالفقه فهذه مزيّة وجوديّة يفضل بها الآخر. ولو اختصّ أحدهما بكونه ظلوماً فهذه مزيّة مذمومة عند أهل الشرع وقد سلم منها الآخر فله الفضل بمزيّة هي عدميّة. وعند الجاهليّة بعكس هذا ولذا تأتى لشاعرهم أن يهجو بقوله: [طويل]

قُـبَـيِّـلَـةٌ لا يَخْفِـرُونَ بِـذِمَّـةٍ   وَلَا يَظْلِمُونَ النَّاسَ حَبَّةَ خَرْدَلِ

فقد فهمت المزيّة في الجملة.

٢٨،٦ وأمّا التمهيد فاعلم أنّ الأجرام الترابيّة وما توالد منها متشابهة في الأصل. وكانت المزيّة للناميات الثلاثة وهي المعدن والنبات والحيوان. أمّا المعدن فله الفضل على سائر الأجرام الترابيّة بالنموّ والنفاسة والانتفاع. وأمّا النبات فله الفضل على ما قبله بالنموّ والإثمار والانتفاع الخاصّ ووجود النفس النباتيّة حتّى أنّ المعدن جزؤه ككلّه فينتفع بما يقطع منه فهو في ذلك كغير النامي بخلاف الشجرة لو اقتطعت منها قطعة لم ينتفع بها الانتفاع المراد منها كالإثمار فأشبهت الحيوان وربما تموت بقطع رأسها كالنخلة كما يموت الحيوان. وقد ادّعى بعض المتكلّمين أنّ للنبات حياة وزعموا أنّ النخلة يتعشّق بعضها ببعض فيميل إليه. وأمّا ميل عروقها إلى الماء فمشاهد. وزعموا أنّه إلى

which is the most glorious, and others such as knowledge, righteousness, noble morals, and so on. There are also worldly advantages, the greatest of which are rulership, courage, generosity, power, number, wealth, beauty, and the like. Many of these, such as power, glory, generosity, and noble morals, can be either religious or worldly merits. Some of them, such as prophecy, caliphal authority, and knowledge, are both religious and worldly. Some of these merits are tangible and some abstract; some are based in presence, some in absence. To explain this would take too long, so let us summarize it with an example and some preliminary remarks.

The example: Consider two men of equal physical constitution, disposition, genealogy, and other attributes, so that neither has an advantage over the other. Referring to such a pair, ʿAlqamah ibn ʿAlāthah said to a group of disputants, "You have become like two knees of a toothless camel." Were one distinguished in jurisprudence, he would possess an absolute virtue placing him ahead of the other. Were one to distinguish himself through oppression, according to the jurists this would be reprehensible. If the former is preserved from the latter's negative quality, then he has the advantage of its being absent. During the Jāhiliyyah, the situation was quite the reverse. It is related of one of its poets that he mocked others by saying:[46] 6.27

You are a tribe that does not break a contract
nor oppresses others so much as a mustard seed.

Now you have a general comprehension of the privilege some men have over others.

To the preliminary remarks. Different types of earth, and their products, are effectively similar. There is advantage in three things that grow or are extractable: metal, plants, and animals. Metal is superior to other types of earth in the gain it brings, in its preciousness, and in its benefits. Plants are superior to metal in terms of growth, of fruit-bearing, of the particular benefits they possess, and of the presence of a vegetal essence. A piece of metal is like the block it is hewn from, so one benefits from its forging. In this it resembles things that do not grow. This is different from a tree: If one cuts off a part it does not have the desired benefit. This is not like fruit from a tree. Trees resemble animals and may die as animals do when the head is cut off, as is the case with the palm tree. Some theologians have claimed that plants possess life, maintaining that palm trees fall in love and lean toward each other. 6.28

هذا المعنى الإشارة بالحديث أكرموا عمّتكم النّخلة وهو حديث غريب. والذي في الصحيح أنّها مثل المسلم. واختلف المحدّثون في وجه الشبه على أقوال معروفة. وأمّا الحيوان فله الفضل بما ذكر مع زيادة الحياة والإحساس والإلهام. ويختصّ الإنسان عن جملته بزيادة العقل الذي هو محطّ إدراك الكليّات والرأي والتصرّف فللإنسان الفضل على الجميع.

٢٩،٦ والإنسان لفظ واقع على آدم وعلى ذريّته أبدًا اسمًا للقدر المشترك فيه. وهو الحيوان الناطق أي المتفكّر بالقوّة[١] والآدميّ كلّه مشترك في هذه الفضيلة ولذا سخّر له غيره وابتلي هو بالتكليف بمعرفة الخالق تعالى وبعبادته. وهذه مزيّة أخرى لجميعه ولقد خصّه الله تعالى في أرزاقه وفي خَلْقه وفي خُلُقه وفي لباسه وركوبه وغير ذلك بكثير. قال تعالى ﴿وَلَقَدْ كَرَّمْنَا بَنِي آدَمَ وَحَمَلْنَاهُمْ فِي ٱلْبَرِّ وَٱلْبَحْرِ وَرَزَقْنَاهُمْ مِنَ ٱلطَّيِّبَاتِ وَفَضَّلْنَاهُمْ عَلَى كَثِيرٍ مِمَّنْ خَلَقْنَا تَفْضِيلاً﴾. وإنّما قال تعالى عَلَى كَثِيرٍ لبقاء الملائكة على ما في ذلك من النزاع المشهور بين الجمهور.

٣٠،٦ لطيفة: كان بعض المخارفين يقول نحن معشر المحرومين لسنا من ولد آدم لأنّ الله تعالى قد قال فيهم ما تقدّم يعني الآية وليس عندنا شيء من ذلك. ويقول كان لآدم عبد فنحن جميعًا من ولده وليس بيننا وبين آدم نسب أصلاً. قلت وهذا دخل في أحاديث الخرافات والمضحكات الباطلة. والإنسان كلّه ابن آدم كما قال صلّى الله عليه وسلّم أنتم بنو آدم. والآية صحيحة على الجملة وصحيحة أيضًا على التفصيل لأنّ كلّ آدمي ولو بلغ في حرمان الرزق والفقر المدقع ما عسى أن يبلغ هو أفضل من سائر الحيوان ومن الجنّ بعقله وصورته الحسنة وانتصاب قامته وأكله بيديه معًا وسائر تصرّفاته وتناوله من الطيّبات التي لا تصل إليها الحيوانات وتمكّن من الركوب في البرّ والبحر إلى غير ذلك. فهو مكرّم أيّ تكريم ومفضّل أيّ تفضيل.

١ ق: تنقص بعد هذه الكلمة حوالي ٧ فقرات مع أنّ أرقام أوراق المخطوط متواصلة.

For that matter, the attraction of their roots to water is attested. They have claimed that the wording of the following hadith conveys this: "Honor your aunt, the palm tree." But this hadith is poorly attested. Sound hadiths convey that the tree is like a Muslim. Scholars of Hadith have differed on the matter of such similarities in well-known sayings. As for animals, they are superior to both metals and plants since they are animate and have both sensory perception and instinct. Man is distinguished from all the above through his possession of superior intellect, by which he perceives universals; reasoned opinion; and independent action. In this fashion, man is superior to them all.

Humankind is the term applied to Adam and his descendants until the end 6.29
of time and is a name referring to a shared ability. He is a speaking animal, that is, with the potential to think—all humans share in this virtue. Because of this characteristic, the other beings were made subject to him and he was burdened with the responsibility of knowing his Creator, the Exalted, and of worshipping Him. This is another quality all men have, and God distinguished them in their sustenance, creation, disposition, garments, ability to ride animals, and in sundry other ways. The Exalted has said: «We have honored the sons of Adam; provided them with transport on land and sea; given them for sustenance things good and pure; and conferred on them special favors, above a great part of our creation.»[47] Indeed, the Exalted said: «above a great part» to include the angels, as referred to in the famous widely debated argument.[48]

An amusing anecdote: A fool once said, "We are a company of deprived 6.30
souls, not the offspring of Adam, for God has said regarding them"—what has just been recited, referencing the verse—"we don't possess any of these virtues." The fool continued, "Adam had a slave: We are his offspring; we do not share a genealogy with Adam at all." I responded as follows: "This is a fanciful tale, just an amusing fiction. All humankind is descended from Adam. As the Prophet, God bless and keep him, said, 'You are the sons of Adam . . . '." The hadith is correct both in its generality and in its specifics, for every human, even if he suffers exceeding deprivation, poverty, and misery to the greatest extent imaginable, is superior to all living beings and jinn by virtue of his reason, his beautiful form, his upright stance, the fact that he eats with his hands, and other behaviors, including his consumption of refined things unattainable by animals, his ability to ride on land and sea, and so forth. He has been thus honored and privileged in every way.

ثمّ إنّ أفراد الإنسان متفاوتون فيما ذكر من مزيّة العقل كثرة وقلّة تفاوتاً عظيماً. وأعلاهم في ذلك الأنبياء ثمّ الصدّيقون ثمّ سائر الزاهدين في العرض الفاني. وأمّا أقلّهم عقلاً فلا ينضبط وإن وقع التعبير عنه في كثير من كلام الأنبياء والحكماء. فقد انتهى بعض الأفراد إلى مزاحمة البهائم وما يقع من التعبير عنه يرجع إلى الإضافة. ٦،٣١

ثمّ إنّ الله تعالى خصّ آدم وبنيه بمزايا أخرى دينيّة ودنيويّة يمتاز بها البعض عن البعض لا مشتركة كالأولى. أعلاها في الدينيّة النبوّة ثمّ الخلافة عنها في الظاهر أو في الباطن أو فيهما أو في السياسة. وفي الدنيويّة الملك ثمّ النيابة عنه ومنها القوّة وكثرة المال وكثرة الإنفاق واصطناع الصنائع وابتناء المآثر وكثرة العدد والفصاحة والصباحة ونحو ذلك من كلّ وصف محمود في الدين أو في الدنيا. فمن حصل له شيء من ذلك حصل له شرف على قدره وثبت لولده عدّ ذلك في مفاخر أبيهم. وهو المراد بالحسب في لسان العرب فكلّ واحد عندهم حسبه هو ما يعدّ من مفاخر آبائه فهو من الحساب ومن ليس له ما يعدّ فلا حسب له. فالخصلة الحميدة تكون مفخرة لمن اتّصف بها ولمن انتسب إلى من اتّصف بها فيشرف نسبه بذلك. ٦،٣٢

إذا علم هذا فنقول إنّ آدم أبا البشر على نبيّنا وعليه السلام قد حصل له الشرف بالنبوءة وسائر الخصال الحميدة وبسجود الملائكة له وولادته للأنبياء والصدّيقين والشهداء والصالحين. وهذا كلّه من المزايا فجميع بنيه شريفهم ومشروفهم ورشيدهم وغويهم يحصل لهم بالانتساب إليه شرف من هذا الوجه يفضلون به غيرهم ممّن ينتسب إلى جنيّ أو بهيمة. فلا تظنّ أنّ دابّة لكونها لم تعص الله تعالى تكون أشرف من إنسان كافر أو فاسق إلّا من هذا الوجه. وأمّا في النسب والحسب والصورة ٦،٣٣

Individual men and women differ widely in how much they possess of this quality of reason. The prophets possess the most, followed by the devout, followed by those who abstain from transitory vanities.[49] As for who possesses the least amount of reason, it is hard to determine, though both prophets and philosophers have discussed this matter at length. Some individuals have even reached the low point of competing with beasts—this is not the place to go into what has been said about this. 6.31

Exalted God singled out Adam and his offspring with distinct religious qualities, and also worldly qualities, in which some have excelled over others, and which are not shared equally among mankind as are the first. The highest of these qualities in religion is prophethood, followed by its representatives either of an external or internal kind, those who unite both or those who represent it in political matters. Of the worldly qualities, the highest is kingship, followed by being the king's minister. These advantages include worldly power, wealth, the capability to spend generously, the knowledge of producing handicrafts, the ability to construct glorious buildings, being numerous, eloquence, grace, and so forth with regard to every praiseworthy characteristic related to religion and this world. Those who attain some of these qualities also attain honor in the same measure. There is consensus that the children of those with these qualities count them among the glorious deeds of their fathers, and this is what is meant by "pedigree" in the language of the Arabs. The pedigree of a person consists of the glorious deeds of his ancestors. This is a type of reckoning, and he who has nothing to count has no pedigree to reckon. Praiseworthy traits and glorious deeds create distinction, which honors both the ancestry and progeny of those distinguished by them. 6.32

Having established this, we can assert that Adam, the father of mankind, peace be upon him, is our prophet and attained honor through his prophethood, and his other praiseworthy attributes, including the angels prostrating to him, and his role as forefather of the prophets, the devout, the martyrs, and the pious. All of these are virtues, and in this respect all his descendants—the illustrious, the lowly, those rightly guided, and those led astray—attain honor by their descent from him; through it they are superior to others who are descended from jinn or beasts. Thus, do not think that a beast of burden, because it does not disobey Exalted God, is more noble than an unbelieving or sinning human except in obedience. Man is more noble than them with respect to genealogy, esteem, form, and so on. Because of this, when he dies 6.33

وغيرها فهو أشرف منها. ولذا يوارى إن مات ولا توارى هي غير أنّ الافتخار بنسبة آدم قد تُنوسِي لطول العهد كما تُنوسِيت رَحِمه.

٣٤،٦ ومن أطرف ما وقع لسيّدنا معاوية رضي الله عنه أن جاءه إنسان فقال له أسألك بالرحم التي بيني وبينك إلّا ما رفدتني. فقال أنت من عبد مناف؟ قال لا. قال أنت من قريش؟ قال لا. قال أنت من العرب؟ قال لا. قال أيّ رحم بيني وبينك؟ قال رحم آدم. فقال رَحِمٌ مَجفُوَةٌ لأكوننّ أول من وصلها. فأعطاه.

٣٥،٦ ثمّ يتمايزون بعد ذلك فمن كان من ولد نوح عليه السلام فهو أفضل نسباً من بقيّة ولد آدم لأنّ أولئك يعدّون آدم وهؤلاء يعدّون آدم ونوحاً. فإنّ كلّ ما يعدّه الأعلى يعدّه الأسفل ويزيد فإنّ الأخصّ فيه ما في الأعمّ وزيادة. وهذا كما يقال في الحكمة في الأجناس المتوسّطة والسافلة والأنواع الحقيقيّة والفصول إنّ كل ما يتقدّم به الأعلى يتقدّم به الأسفل ويزيد. فالله تعالى قد قال ﴿ إِنَّ ٱللَّهَ ٱصۡطَفَىٰٓ ءَادَمَ وَنُوحٗا وَءَالَ إِبۡرَٰهِيمَ وَءَالَ عِمۡرَٰنَ عَلَى ٱلۡعَٰلَمِينَ﴾. فمن انتسب إلى آدم ونوح فقد انتسب إلى مصطفين ثمّ من كان من ولد إبراهيم بعد ذلك فهو أفضل من بقيّة ولد نوح لأنّه يعدّ آدم ونوحاً وإبراهيم عليهم السلام.

٣٦،٦ وإلى هذا أشار صلّى الله عليه وسلّم بقوله حين قيل له من أكرم الناس؟ الكريم ابن الكريم ابن الكريم ابن الكريم يوسف بن يعقوب بن إسحاق بن إبراهيم نبيّ ابن نبيّ ابن نبيّ ابن نبيّ. وكلامه صلّى الله عليه وسلّم موافق لقوله تعالى ﴿ إِنَّ أَكۡرَمَكُمۡ عِندَ ٱللَّهِ أَتۡقَىٰكُمۡ﴾. فإنّ الأنبياء هم أتقى الناس لأنّهم أعلم وإنّما يَخۡشَى ٱللَّهَ مِنۡ عِبَادِهِ ٱلۡعُلَمَٰٓؤُاْ فهم أكرمُ الناس. فمن انتسب إليهم كرم بنسبه إليهم وإن لم يكن نبيّاً فكيف إذا كان هو أيضاً نبيّاً؟ فله الشرف الطارف والتليد كيوسف عليه السلام فصدق نبيّنا صلّى الله عليه وسلّم. ثمّ أولاد إبراهيم عليه السلام يتفاوتون في الشرف أيضاً بقدر

he is buried and they are not. Yet, people's pride in their descent from Adam has been obscured by the length of time that has passed, just as their kinship has been obscured.

One of the most curious incidents in the life of our leader Muʿāwiyah, God be pleased with him, occurred when a man came to him and said, "I ask you for help on the basis of our kinship, without which you need not help me." "Are you of the ʿAbd Manāf?" Muʿāwiyah asked. "No," he replied. "Are you of the Quraysh?" he asked. "No," he replied. "Are you of the Arabs?" he asked. "No," he replied. "What then is the kinship between us?" asked Muʿāwiyah. "The kinship of Adam," he replied, and Muʿāwiyah said, "A vexing kinship, for me to be the first to be made aware of it," and gave him a token something. 6.34

Some make further distinctions, such that a descendant of Noah, peace be upon him, is held to be superior in terms of genealogy than Adam's other descendants because the latter count Adam as an ancestor, whereas the former count both Adam and Noah. Indeed, everything attributed to one high up on the genealogical tree is also attributed to everyone lower down. The specific encompasses the general, and more besides. This is as described in philosophy regarding the middle and lower categories and the ideal types and categories: Everything that is contained by the higher is contained by the lower and augmented. Exalted God has said: «God chose Adam and Noah and the House of Abraham and the House of ʿImrān above all beings.»[50] Therefore, anyone descended from Adam and Noah is descended from two chosen ones, and anyone subsequently descended from Abraham is superior to the remaining descendants of Noah, as he can count among his ancestors Adam, Noah, and Abraham, peace be upon them. 6.35

This is what the Prophet, God bless and keep him, referred to when he was asked, "Who is the most noble of people?" and he answered, "The one who is noble is the son of someone who is noble, going back three generations: Joseph, son of Jacob, son of Isaac, son of Abraham, thus a prophet who was the son of a prophet, son of a prophet, son of a prophet." His words, God bless and keep him, correspond with the words of the Exalted: «Surely the noblest among you in the sight of God is the most God-fearing.»[51] Prophets are the most God-fearing people as they are the most knowledgeable. Among God's ordinary worshippers, scholars fear Him, so they are the noblest people. Whoever is descended from them is noble through that descent, even if he is not a prophet. How then if he were also a prophet? In this case his nobility is both 6.36

أنسابهم فمن ازداد بنبيّ أو نبيّين أو أكثر ازداد درجة في الشرف. فأمّا أولاد إسحاق بن إبراهيم عليهما السلام فلهم الشرف في الجملة غير أنّ الأسباط أولاد يعقوب بن إسحاق لهم الشرف الشامخ والمجد الباذخ. فإنّهم فازوا بثلاثة أنبياء على نسق ثمّ جلّ الأنبياء بعد ذلك فيهم.

٦،٣٧ وقد قال الله تعالى لبني إسرائيل ﴿ٱذۡكُرُوا نِعۡمَةَ ٱللَّهِ عَلَيۡكُمۡ إِذۡ جَعَلَ فِيكُمۡ أَنۢبِيَآءَ وَجَعَلَكُم مُّلُوكٗا وَآتَاكُم مَّا لَمۡ يُؤۡتِ أَحَدٗا مِّنَ ٱلۡعَٰلَمِينَ﴾. وقال تعالى ﴿يَا بَنِي إِسۡرَٰٓءِيلَ ٱذۡكُرُوا نِعۡمَتِيَ ٱلَّتِيٓ أَنۡعَمۡتُ عَلَيۡكُمۡ وَأَنِّي فَضَّلۡتُكُمۡ عَلَى ٱلۡعَٰلَمِينَ﴾ إلى غير ذلك. وأولاد العِيص بن إسحاق لهم شرف دونهم ولم يكن فيهم نبيّ فيما يقال غير أيّوب[١] عليه السلام. وأمّا أولاد إسماعيل بن إبراهيم فلهم الشرف بإبراهيم وإسماعيل أوّلاً ثمّ استكملوا الشرف آخر بسيّد الوجود وسرّ الكائنات سيّدنا ومولانا محمّد صلّى الله عليه وسلّم. فإنّه صلّى الله عليه وسلّم إليه يساق حديث الشرف العِدّ وباسمه يرسم عنوان صحيفة المجد فيه شرف من قبله كما به شرف من بعده. وقد كان آدم يكنّى به تشريفاً له بأشرف أولاده فيقال أبو محمّد. وكما يشرّف الولد بشرف الوالد قد يشرّف الوالد بشرف الولد. ولله دَر ابن الرومي في قوله: [بسيط]

وَكَمْ أَبٍ قَدْ عَلا بِٱبْنٍ ذُرَى حَسَبٍ كَمَا عَلَتْ بِرَسُولِ اللهِ عَدْنَانُ

٦،٣٨ وسنزيد هذا بسطاً إن شاء الله تعالى. فمن اتصل بالنبيّ صلّى الله عليه وسلّم بعده وهم الفاطميّون أشرف الناس نسباً لأنّ غيره كبني إسرائيل وإن عدّ بكثرة الأنبياء فهو يعدّ بأشرف الأنبياء والمنتسب إلى الأشرف يجب أن يكون أشرف. وهذا باعتبار النسب فقط. أمّا من حصلت له النبوّة من بني إسرائيل فهو أشرف بذاته ممّن ليس

---

١ يبدأ ق من جديد بعد هذه الكلمة.

acquired and inherited, as with Joseph, peace be upon him. The Prophet, God bless and keep him, spoke truly in saying so. In this fashion, the sons of Abraham, peace be upon him, also vied with each other for nobility in the extent of their ancestry, thus, adding a prophet or two, or more, added a degree of nobility. As for the sons of Isaac son of Abraham, peace be upon them, they all possessed nobility; however, the twelve tribes of the sons of Jacob son of Isaac enjoy a towering nobility and great glory, for they possessed three consecutive prophets, and the greatest prophet after them was from their lineage.

Exalted God said, regarding the sons of Israel: «Remember God's blessing upon you, when He appointed among you prophets, and appointed you kings, and gave you such as He had not given to any being.»[52] The Exalted has also said: «Children of Israel, remember My blessing wherewith I blessed you, and that I have preferred you above all beings», and other like things.[53] The sons of Esau son of Isaac possessed a nobility the others did not, and tradition has it the only prophet among them was Job, peace be upon him. As for the sons of Ishmael son of Abraham, their nobility comes first through Abraham and Ishmael, and is perfected in the end with the Lord of Existence, the Secret of Created Things, our Lord and Leader Muḥammad, God bless and keep him. Indeed, when one speaks of unceasing nobility one refers to him, God bless and keep him. His name is written on the very title of the page of glory. He is distinguished by what went before him as well as by what came after. Adam was given a teknonym to honor him as the most distinguished of his sons and was called "Father of Muḥammad." As the son is distinguished by the honor of the father, so the father is distinguished by the honor of the son. How excellent is Ibn al-Rūmī's sentiment: 6.37

How many fathers have been elevated by their sons to the peaks of esteem
as ʿAdnān was elevated by the Prophet of God?

We will elaborate, God willing. Those who trace themselves back to the Prophet, God bless and keep him, are the descendants of Fāṭimah and enjoy the most distinguished ancestry. This is because, regarding the others, such as the sons of Israel, even if they ennumerated a multitude of prophets in their lineage, Muḥammad is reckoned to be the most distinguished of them, and the one who is descended from the most distinguished person is necessarily the most distinguished. This is solely in relation to genealogy. Concerning a son of 6.38

بنبيّ إذ لا يعدل النبوءة إلّا نبوءة أخرى. كما أنّ من كفر منهم فقد اختلّ نسبه واضمحلّ حسبه بالإضافة إلى من لم يكفر منهم.

٦، ٣٩ أمّا لو قيس هذا الكافر إلى كافر آخر قبطيّ أو نوبيّ أو نحوهما فالواجب أن يكون هذا أشرف نسباً ولو قيس إلى مؤمن من هؤلاء لتعارض الوجهان ولكنّ الإسلام يعلو ولا يعلى عليه. وفي السيرة قال المسلمون هذا أبو سفيان وسهيل وكان أبو سفيان لمّا يُسلِم وقدّموه لشرفه. فقال النبيّ صلّى الله عليه وسلّم هذا سهيل وأبو سفيان الإسلام يعلو ولا يعلى عليه. فانتبه لهذا الفصل فإنّي رمزته ولم أبسطه لأنّ بعضه موحش لمن لا فهم له.

٦، ٤٠ وإذا عُلم تفضيل النسب والحسب في باب النبوءة فهم في غيرها كذلك كالعلم والصلاح والهداية والزهد والورع والملك والنجدة والجود وغير ذلك من كلّ ما يُحتسب به. ويصير به من عرف به عيناً من أعيان عشيرته أو قبيلته أو عمارته أو بلده أو جيله ويشرّف به من انتسب إليه. ولم يخل الله تعالى قوماً من سيّد كما لم يخل هجمة من فحل. وبسادة الناس تنتظم أمورهم فهم خلفاء الله في عباده بالحكم التصريفيّ. ولذلك إذا فقدوا أو فقدت الأهليّة منهم اختلّ الأمر كما قال الشاعر: [بسيط]

لَا يُصْلِحُ النَّاسُ فَوْضَى لَا سَرَاةَ لَهُمْ   وَلَا سَـرَاةَ إِذَا جُهَّـالُهُمْ سَـادُوا

٦، ٤١ الثالث الإنسان قد يفتخر بنسبه على ما مرّ وقد يفتخر بنفسه أي بالخصال التي اتّصف بها والدرجات التي نالها من الدين والدنيا. والأوّل هو الفخر العظامي لأنّه افتخار بالعظام والرُفات. والثاني هو الفخر العصاميّ وهو مأخوذ من عصام صاحب النعمان. وكان يقول: [رجز]

Israel who attains prophecy, in his essence he is more distinguished than one who is not a prophet, for prophecy is only equaled by prophecy. Similarly, for one who renounces Islam, his genealogy is corrupted and the nobility of his descent fades in comparison with one who does not renounce Islam.

Now, if this unbeliever who had once been Muslim is compared to another unbeliever who is Coptic or Nubian or the like, it follows that he is nobler in terms of genealogy. If he is compared to a believer of these groups, then the two aspects would conflict, but Islam elevates and is not surpassed by other factors. We find in the Prophet's biography Muslims saying, "Abū Sufyān and Suhayl"—Abū Sufyān had converted to Islam, so they elevated him because of his nobility. The Prophet, God bless and keep him, had actually said, "Suhayl and Abū Sufyān. Islam elevates and is not surpassed." Pay close attention to this section, as I wrote it allusively and have not elucidated fully in order not to trouble those without understanding. 6.39

Given that prophecy grants preference in genealogy and descent, then those being compared are like this in other matters as well, such as knowledge, righteousness, guidance, asceticism, piety, power, bravery, generosity, and so on. Indeed, this is the case in all matters considered here. One who uses these criteria to know a notable in one's clan, tribe, subtribe, village, or generation honors him according to his ancestry. Exalted God does not fail to grant a people a leader, just as He does not fail to grant a herd a stallion. The affairs of a people are arranged according to their nobles, for they are the representatives of God among his worshippers, with authority to rule. This is why, if they are absent or if they lose their competence, the situation becomes dire. As a poet has said:[54] 6.40

People suffer from the chaos of having no rulers:
If the ignorant among them rule, they are still leaderless.

The third point: As has been discussed, a person may vaunt his ancestry, and he may vaunt himself, either the qualities by which he is distinguished or his achievements in religious and worldly matters. The first is the vaunting of bones,[55] because it is pride in bones and mortal remains, while the second is the vaunting of ʿIṣām, which is of one's own achievements, derived from ʿIṣām, who was a companion of al-Nuʿmān. It's been said: 6.41

نَفْسُ عِصَامٍ سَوَّدَتْ عِصَاماً وَعَلَّمَتْهُ ٱلْكَرَّ وَٱلْإِقْدَامَا

٦،٤٢ فكلّ ما جاءه السؤدد من تلقاء نفسه فهو مثل عصام هذا فخره عصاميّ. والناس لم يزالوا مختلفين في هذا المنحى فقوم يعتنون[١] في افتخارهم أو ثنائهم بذكر الآباء كقوله: [وافر]

أَنَا ٱبْنُ مُزَيْقِيَا عَمْرٍو وَجَدِّي أَبُوهُ مُنْذِرٌ مَاءُ السَّمَاءِ

٦،٤٣ وقول النابغة: [طويل]

لَئِنْ كَانَ لِلْقَبْرَيْنِ قَبْرٌ بِجِلَّقٍ وَقَبْرٌ بِصَيْدَاءَ ٱلَّذِي عِنْدَ حَارِبِ
وَلِلْحَارِثِ ٱلْجَفْنِيِّ سَيِّدِ قَوْمِهِ لَيَبْتَغِيَنْ[٢] بِٱلْجَيْشِ دَارَ ٱلْمُحَارِبِ

٦،٤٤ وقول حسّان رضي الله عنه: [كامل]

أَوْلَادُ جَفْنَةَ حَوْلَ قَبْرِ أَبِيهِمُ قَبْرِ ٱبْنِ مَارِيَةَ ٱلْكَرِيمِ ٱلْمُفْضِلِ

٦،٤٥ وقول العرجي العثمانيّ: [وافر]

أَضَاعُونِي وَأَيَّ فَتًى أَضَاعُوا[٣] لِيَوْمِ كَرِيهَةٍ وَسِدَادِ ثَغْرِ
كَأَنِّي لَمْ أَكُنْ فِيهِمْ وَسِيطًا وَلَمْ تَكُ نِسْبَتِي فِي آلِ عَمْرِو

٦،٤٦ وقال الفرزدق: [طويل]

أُولَئِكَ آبَائِي فَجِئْنِي بِمِثْلِهِمْ إِذَا جَمَعَتْنَا يَا جَرِيرُ ٱلْمَجَامِعُ

١ ط، ق: يعيشون. ٢ ط: يلتمس. ٣ في الهامش في ق: وقول العرجي العثماني ليس هو بأول شطر البيت وإن أول شطر البيت: أضاعوني وأي فتىً أضاعوا.

The soul of ʿIṣām ennobled ʿIṣām
and taught him how to attack and advance.

Since what he achieved as a ruler was due to his own effort, he was like this ʿIṣām, and his boasting was ʿIṣām-like (*ʿiṣāmī*). People continue to disagree on this question, one group taking care to mention ancestors in their vaunting, as in the verses: 6.42

I am ʿAmr son of Muzayqiyāʾ and my grandfather
is his father, Mundhir, "the water of the heavens."

There is also this by al-Nābighah:[56] 6.43

If his ancestry had been from two graves, one in Damascus
and one in Ṣīdāʾ in a military graveyard,
As well as from al-Ḥārith al-Jafnī, leader of his people,
he should seek out the warrior's abode in the army!

And the verse of Ḥassān ibn Thābit, God be pleased with him: 6.44

The sons of Jafna surround the grave of their father,
the grave of the noble and favored son of Māriyah.

And the verses of al-ʿArjī al-ʿUthmānī: 6.45

They ignored me, and any young man ignored by them
feels the calamity of his tongue being silenced.
As if I were not a mediator among them
nor descended from the family of ʿAmr.

And Farazdaq said: 6.46

Those are my ancestors, Jarīr, so bring me one like them
when our assemblies come together.

٤٧،٦ وقال النابغة لحسّان رضي الله عنه حين أنشد: [طويل]

لَنَا ٱلْجَفَنَاتُ ٱلْغُرُّ يَلْمَعْنَ بِالضُّحَى وَأَسْيَافُنَا يَقْطُرْنَ مِنْ نَجْدَةٍ دَمَا
وَلَدْنَا بَنِي ٱلْعَنْقَاءِ وَٱبْنَ مُحَرِّقٍ فَأَكْرِمْ بِنَا خَالاً وَأَكْرِمْ بِنَا ٱبْنَمَا

٤٨،٦ إنّك شاعر لولا أنّك قلت الجفنات فقلّلت العدد. ولو قلت الجفان كان أبلغ. وقلت يلمعن بالضحى ولو قلت يشرقن بالدجى كان أبلغ. وقلت يقطرن من نجدة ولو قلت يجرين كان أبلغ. ثمّ افتخرت بمن ولدت ولم تفخر بمن ولدك فهذا مذهب العرب وهو الافتخار بالآباء. ولذا نبّه عليه النبيّ صلّى الله عليه وسلّم وكرهه كما مرّ. وقوم يفتخرون بأنفسهم وهذا الوجه كثير أيضاً جداً لأنّه طبع الآدميّ لا يكاد يسلم منه ولا يحصى ما فيه من كلام الناس نظماً ونثراً ولا حاجة إلى التطويل.

٤٩،٦ ومن أفصح ما ورد في هذا النحو قول السموأل في لاميّته المشهورة منها: [طويل]

إِذَا ٱلْمَرْءُ لَمْ يُدْنَسْ مِنَ اللُّؤْمِ عِرْضُهُ فَكُلُّ رِدَاءٍ يَرْتَدِيهِ جَمِيلُ
وَإِنْ هُوَ لَمْ يَحْمِلْ عَلَى النَّفْسِ ضَيْمَهَا فَلَيْسَ إِلَى حُسْنِ الثَّنَاءِ سَبِيلُ
تُعَيِّرُنَا أَنَّا قَلِيلٌ عَدِيدُنَا فَقُلْتُ لَهَا إِنَّ ٱلْكِرَامَ قَلِيلُ[1]
وَمَا ضَرَّ مَنْ كَانَتْ بَقَايَاهُ مِثْلُنَا شَبَابٌ تَسَامَى لِلْعُلَا وَكُهُولُ
تَسِيلُ عَلَى حَدِّ الظِّبَاتِ نُفُوسُنَا وَلَيْسَتْ عَلَى غَيْرِ السُّيُوفِ تَسِيلُ
وَإِنَّا لَقَوْمٌ مَا نَرَى ٱلْقَتْلَ سُبَّةً إِذَا مَا رَأَتْهُ عَامِرٌ وَسَلُولُ[2]

٥٠،٦ إلى أن قال: [مخلع البسيط]

١ ط يزيد في الهامش: وَما ضَرَّنا أَنَّا قَليلٌ وَجارُنا عَزيزٌ وَجارُ الأَكْثَرينَ ذَليلُ. ٢ ط: سليل.

And al-Nābighah addressed Ḥassān, may God be pleased with him, as follows: 6.47

We have beautiful scabbards that shine in the morning light
and our swords drip blood from our courageous acts.
The sons of the long-necked and the burning belong to us;[57]
how blessed we are in our uncles and our children!

You would have been a true poet had you not said "scabbards"—the plural spoils the effect. It would have been more eloquent to have said "scabbard." You said "shine in the morning light," when it would have been more eloquent had you said "shine at dusk." You said "drip from our courageous acts" when it would have been more eloquent had you said "run with." You also prided yourself on your descendants but not on your ancestors, when it is the way of the Arabs to take pride in one's ancestors. This is the type of act the Prophet, God bless and keep him, referred to, as mentioned above, and that he despised. There is also a kind of people who take pride in themselves; they too are prevalent, for it is human nature and almost unavoidable. Poetry and prose on this subject are plentiful—there is no need to dwell on it here. 6.48

One of the most eloquent examples of this theme is the following lines by al-Samaw'al, from the opening to his famous poem rhyming in *l*: 6.49

If blame does not stain a man's honor
every robe he wears will be beautiful.
If he cannot inflict harm on anyone
he will have no path to praise and glory.
Time has reproached us because we are few in number.
I told her that the noble are few.
Anyone whose deeds resemble ours cannot be harmed—
young and old men competing for nobility.
Our blood streams on the edges of swords;
it flows on nothing but them.[58]
We stem from a tribe that sees no shame in killing.
I see none of this characteristic among ʿĀmir and Salūl.

The lines continue up to where he says: 6.50

وَنُنْكِرُ إِنْ شِئْنَا عَلَى النَّاسِ قَوْلَهُمْ   وَلَا يُنْكِرُونَ ٱلْقَوْلَ حِينَ نَقُولُ
سَلِي إِنْ جَهِلْتِ النَّاسَ عَنَّا وَعَنْهُمْ   وَلَيْسَ سَوَاءً عَالِمٌ وَجَهُولُ
فَإِنَّ بَنِي الدَّيَّانِ قُطْبٌ لِقَوْمِهِمْ   تَدُورُ رَحَاهُمْ حَوْلَهُمْ وَتَجُولُ

٦،٥١ ومثل هذا النمط من الكلام فيه افتخار بالنفس وبالآباء أيضاً لأنّ المقصود أنّهم على هذا الوصف كابراً عن كابر. وقول الفرزدق: [طويل]

أَنَا الذَّائِدُ ٱلْحَامِي الذِّمَارَ وَإِنَّمَا   يُدَافِعُ عَنْ أَحْسَابِهِمْ أَنَا أَوْ مِثْلِي

٦،٥٢ وغير ذلك. ثمّ كثير من الناس لا يلتفتون إلى النسب ولا يقيمون للمفتخر به وزناً. كما قال الحريريّ: [طويل]

لَعَمْرُكَ مَا ٱلْإِنْسَانُ إِلَّا ٱبْنُ يَوْمِهِ   عَلَى مَا بَدَا مِنْ حَالِهِ لَا ٱبْنُ أَمْسِهِ
وَمَا ٱلْفَخْرُ بِٱلْعَظْمِ الرَّمِيمِ وَإِنَّمَا   فَخَارُ الَّذِي يَبْغِي ٱلْفَخَارَ بِنَفْسِهِ

٦،٥٣ وقال الآخر: [منسرح]

كُنِ ٱبْنَ مَنْ شِئْتَ وَاتَّخِذْ[١] أَدَباً   يُغْنِيكَ مَحْمَدَةً عَنِ النَّسَبِ
إِنَّ ٱلْفَتَى مَنْ يَقُولُ هَا أَنَذَا   لَيْسَ ٱلْفَتَى مَنْ يَقُولُ كَانَ أَبِي

إلى غير ذلك ممّا لا ينحصر.

٦،٥٤ والحقّ أنّ كرم النسب فضيلة. قال تعالى ﴿وَكَانَ أَبُوهُمَا صَالِحًا﴾ وقال صلّى الله عليه وسلّم في بنت حاتم إنّ أباها كان يحب مكارم الأخلاق. ووصفُ الإنسان وسعيُه هو الشأن والنسب زيادة. فإلغاء النسب رأساً جور والاقتصار عليه عجز والصواب ما قال عامر بن الطفيل: [طويل]

---

١ ط: اكتسب.

We refute what the people say when we so desire,
and no one can gainsay our words when we speak.
If the people are ignorant about us and them, then ask:
for the knowing and the ignorant are no longer equals.
The Banū Dayyān are the mainstay of their people;
their millstone turns and spins around them.

This type of speech involves pride in oneself and one's ancestors: It connotes that such people have inherited their nobility. Farazdaq said: 6.51

I defend and protect my honor.
The truth is that those like me protect their noble ancestors.

There are other examples. There are also many people who pay no attention to genealogy and place no stock in anyone who takes pride in it. As al-Ḥarīrī said:[59] 6.52

By your life! Man is nothing but the son of today.
This is apparent from his state—he is not the son of yesterday.
What pride is there in rotting bones?
The truth is that one who merits pride takes pride in himself.

Another said:[60] 6.53

If you focus on your behavior, it does not matter whose son you are—
you will not need to vaunt your genealogy.
Upstanding is the young man who says, "I am here,"
not the one who says, "My father was."

There are countless verses like these.

The truth is that noble ancestry is a virtue. Exalted God said: «Their father was a devout man.»[61] The Prophet, God bless and keep him, said regarding the daughter of Ḥātim:[62] "Truly, her father loved generous deeds." At issue here is a person's character and efforts. Ancestry is an additional advantage. To disregard it completely would be wrong and clinging to it exclusively would be misguided. The correct approach accords with ʿĀmir ibn al-Ṭufayl's verse: 6.54

وَإِنِّي وَإِنْ كُنْتَ ابْنَ سَيِّدِ عَامِرٍ ... وَفِي السِّرِّ مِنْهَا وَالصَّرِيحِ ٱلْمُهَذَّبِ
فَمَا سَوَّدَتْنِي عَامِرٌ مِنْ وِرَاثَةٍ ... أَبَى اللهُ أَنْ أَسْمُو بِأُمٍّ وَلَا أَبِ
وَلٰكِنَّنِي أَحْمِي حِمَاهَا وَأَتَّقِي ... أَذَاهَا وَأَرْمِي مَنْ رَمَاهَا بِمَنْكِبِي

فقوله وإن كنت ابن سيّد عامر تعريض بالنسب وإعلام بمكانته منه. وقوله أبى الله أن أسمو بأم ولا أب أي فقط دون شيء يكون منّي ليوافق ما قبله. فمراده أنّي لا أكتفي بالنسب وأخلو عن استحصال الحمد وابتناء المجد.

٦،٥٥ ومثله: [كامل]

لَسْنَا وَإِنْ أَحْسَابُنَا كَرُمَتْ ... يَوْماً عَلَى ٱلْأَحْسَابِ نَتَّكِلُ
نَبْنِي كَمَا كَانَتْ أَوَائِلُنَا ... تَبْنِي وَنَفْعَلُ مِثْلَ مَا فَعَلُوا

٦،٥٦ وقال الآخر: [طويل]

أَنَا ٱلْفَارِسُ ٱلْحَامِي حَقِيقَةَ وَائِلٍ ... كَمَا كَانَ يَحْمِي عَنْ حَقَائِقِهَا أَبِي

٦،٥٧ وقال زهير: [طويل]

وَمَا يَكُ مِنْ خَيْرٍ أَتَوْهُ فَإِنَّمَا ... تَوَارَثَهُ آبَاءُ آبَائِهِمْ قَبْلُ
وَهَلْ يُنْبِتُ ٱلْخَطِّيَّ إِلَّا وَشِيجُهُ ... وَتُغْرَسُ إِلَّا فِي مَنَابِتِهَا ٱلنَّخْلُ

٦،٥٨ وقال الملك الراضي من ملوك بني العبّاس: [كامل]

لَا تَعْذِلِي كَرَمِي عَلَى ٱلْإِسْرَافِ ... رِبْحُ ٱلْمَحَامِدِ مَتْجَرُ ٱلْأَشْرَافِ
أُجْرِي كَآبَائِي ٱلْخَلَائِفِ سَابِقاً ... وَأُشَيِّدُ مَا قَدْ أَسَّسَتْ أَسْلَافِي
إِنِّي مِنَ ٱلْقَوْمِ ٱلَّذِينَ أَكُفُّهُمْ ... مُعْتَادَةُ ٱلْإِخْلَافِ وَٱلْإِتْلَافِ

Truly, even if my father was a leader, I am ʿĀmir,
    whether in secretive or refined and open talk.
It was not my inheritance that made me ʿĀmir.
    God prevent me from being named for my mother or father!
Yet I protect what has been left to me, and fearing damage
    I shoulder away violently anyone who slanders it.

When he says, "Truly, even if my father was a leader, I am ʿĀmir," he is alluding to his genealogy and his place in it. When he says, "God prevent me being named for my mother or father," it implies "without anything stemming from myself," an attitude in common with preceding examples. The meaning of the verse is that I am not constituted solely by my genealogy, and I have no need of praise or vainglory through it.

Similar are the following lines:[63] 6.55

Though it may be honored,
    we do not rely on our ancestry.
We build like the first of us built;
    we do as they did.

Another poet said:[64] 6.56

I am a knight who protects the afflicted in times of hardship
    as my father did before me.

And Zuhayr said: 6.57

All the good he achieved,
    he inherited from his ancestors.
What grows from spears but their like?
    Are palms ever grown from other than their seeds?

The Abbasid caliph al-Rāḍī said: 6.58

Do not reproach my generosity as excessive!
    To profit from laudable deeds is a noble man's business.
I behave like my caliphal forefathers before me
    and cleave to my ancestors' foundations.
For I hew from a people, every one of whom has
    habitually rewarded others and incurred ruin through generosity.

فهذا وأبيك الفخر العليّ البنيان المتأسّس الأركان.

واعلم أنّ الناس في هذا الباب ثلاثة رجل كان أصيلاً ثمّ قام هو أيضاً يشيّد بنيانه ويحوط بستانه كالذي قبله. فهذا أكرم الناس وأولاهم بكلّ مفخر. وفيه كان قوله صلّى الله عليه وسلّم الكريم ابن الكريم كما مرّ. والذروة العليا في هذا الصنف هو نبيّنا صلّى الله عليه وسلّم. فإنّه كان أصيلاً بحسب النبوءة من عهد إبراهيم وإسماعيل. ثمّ لم تزل أسلافه في شرف وسؤدد ومجد مخلّد معروفاً ذلك لهم عند الناس. وأنّهم أهل الحرم وجيران الله وسَدَنَةُ بيته مع إكرام الضيف وإعمال السيف وغير ذلك من المفاخر العظام والمآثر الجسام. وقد اختصّهم الله بين العرب بالاحترام والتوقير وجعل لهم رحلة الشتاء والصيف آمنين لا يعرض لهم لصّ ولا مغير فأطعمهم من جوع وآمنهم من خوف كما أخبر به تعالى في كتابه. وذكر ذلك بعض بني أسد فقال: [وافر] ٦،٥٩

زَعَمْتُمْ أَنَّ إِخْوَتَكُمْ قُرَيْشٌ لَهُمْ إِلْفٌ وَلَيْسَ لَكُمْ إِلَافُ
أُولَئِكَ أُومِنُوا جُوعاً وَخَوْفاً وَقَدْ جَاعَتْ بَنُو أَسَدٍ وَخَافُوا

أي أخطأتم في هذا الزعم لأنّكم لستم مثلهم. وقوله إلاف مصدر على[١] فعال يقال آلفته مؤالفة وإلافاً وتآلفاً وليس من آلفته الشيء إيلافاً كالذي في القرآن.

ثمّ لما جاء المصطفى صلّى الله عليه وسلّم ردّ بدر شرفهم فجراً وجدول كرمهم بحراً. بل جعلهم قرار كلّ مجد ومركز كلّ حمد. وقد أكمل به الله تعالى الدين فكذلك أكمل به سائر المحامد والمحاسن. قال صلّى الله عليه وسلّم بعثت لأتمّم مكارم الأخلاق وهو صلّى الله عليه وسلّم لبنة التمام فشُرّفت به قريش خصوصاً والأمّة كلّها عموماً صلّى الله عليه وسلّم ومجّد وعظّم. وقد بيّن صلّى الله عليه وسلّم هذا كلّه مع الإشارة إلى التدريج السابق بقوله إنّ الله اصطفى من ولد إبراهيم إسماعيل واصطفى من ٦،٦٠

١ ق يزيد كلمة وزن.

This—by your father!—is glory built on firm foundations!

In the matter of ancestry, there are three types of people. The first is a man of noble origin, who constructs his home and protects his garden in the way his predecessor did. He is the most noble of people, and the most deserving of all manner of pride. Regarding this, we have encountered before the Prophet's saying, God bless and keep him: "The noble is the son of the noble." The best example of this type is our Prophet, God bless and keep him, for he had noble prophetic origin going back to Abraham and Ishmael. His ancestors invariably had distinction, honor, power; they had unforgettable glory, and were known to all for these attributes. They are the guardians of the sanctuary, the neighbors of God thereby, the keepers of His house. They distinguish themselves by honoring their guests, by their feats with the sword, and other laudable and momentous deeds and exploits. God had distinguished them among the Arabs as worthy of respect and honor, and He made it safe for them to travel in both winter and summer, protecting them from every thief and raider. As the Exalted informs us in His book, He provisioned them against hunger and protected them from fear.[65] This was mentioned to a member of the Banū Asad, who responded as follows:[66] 6.59

> You have claimed that your Qurayshī brethren
> have security, yet you have no security.
> They are protected from hunger and fear,
> while the Banū Asad hunger and fear.

That is, you err in your claim, for you are not like them. However, the poet uses "have security" as if it is a third-form verbal noun, whereby one can speak of "security," "secureness," and "securedness." But the form used in the Qur'an is different from this.

When the Chosen One, God bless and keep him, was among us, the Battle of Badr occurred and restored Quraysh's honor from the outset and gave them nobility as expansive as an ocean. Indeed, it made them the locus of glory and the focus of gratitude. Through it and other praiseworthy and positive acts, Exalted God perfected the religion. The Prophet, God bless and keep him, said, "I was sent to exemplify noble qualities." He was, God bless and keep him, the cornerstone of perfection, and the Quraysh were ennobled by him, both individually and communally, with glory and greatness. The Prophet, God bless 6.60

ولد إسماعيل بني كنانة واصطفى من بني كنانة قريشاً واصطفى من قريشٍ بني هاشمٍ واصطفاني من بني هاشم.

٦١،٦ ورجل لا أصل له ينتمي إليه ولا حسب يُعَرِّجُ عليه ولكن انتهض في اقتناء المآثر واقتناص المفاخر حتى اشتهر بمحاسن الخلال وصار في عداد أهل الكمال وأنشد لسان حاله. فقال: [خفيف]

وَبِنَفْسِي شَرُفْتُ[١] لَا بِجُدُودِي

فهذا أحرى أن يشرّف بوصفه وحاله وأن يشرف به من بعده وأن يكون هو أساس بيته وعرق شجرته.

٦٢،٦ وكان بعض الملوك استدعى رجلاً ليستوزره. فقال له الرجل أيّها الملك إنّه ليس لي في هذا سلف. فقال له الملك إنّي أريد أن أجعلك سلفاً لغيرك. وأصاب هذا الملك فإنّه لو توقّف كلّ بيت على بيت قبله لكان من التسلسل الباطل. فالله تعالى يخرج الحيّ من الميت ويحيي الأرض بعد موتها. ذلك تقدير العزيز العليم فلم يزل الشرف يتجدّد ويحدّث بالعلم والولاية والجود وسائر الأوصاف. وقد ارتفع الوضعاء بالشعر كما اتّضع الرفعاء به. ولذا قال صلّى الله عليه وسلّم إنّ من الشعر لحكمة. وفي رواية لحكماً.

٦٣،٦ فمن الأوّل المُحَلَّقُ وهو عبد العزيز بن حنتم الكلابي وكان رجلاً خاملاً مقلاً من المال. فلمّا مرّ به الأعشى ذاهباً إلى سوق عُكاظ قالت له أمّه إنّ أبا بصير رجل مجدود في شعره وأنت رجل خامل مقلّ ولك بنات فلو سبقت إليه وأكرمته رجونا أن يكون لك منه خير. فبادر إليه وأنزله ونحر له وسقاه الخمر. فلمّا أخذت منه الخمر اشتكى له حاله وحال بناته. فقال له ستكفى أمرهنّ. فلمّا أصبح قصد إلى السوق فأنشد قصيدته التي أوّلها: [طويل]

---

١ ط: افتخرت.

and keep him, made this clear by referring to the echelons mentioned previously in his words: "Truly, God chose Ishmael from Abraham's sons, and chose the Banū Kanāna from Ishmael's sons, the Quraysh from the Banū Kanāna, the Banū Hāshim from the Quraysh, and me from the Banū Hāshim."

A man who had no origin upon which to rely and no noble descent to elevate him—but rather who drew himself up through glorious deeds and laudable exploits, famous for his qualities and natural disposition, a man who achieved perfection—recited as follows regarding his position and status:[67] **6.61**

> I achieved honor, not through my ancestors but by myself.

It is entirely appropriate for such a person to be honored through his qualities and nature, and for those after him to be honored through him, and for him to be the foundation of his house and the root of his family tree.

A king summoned a man in order to appoint him minister, and the man said, "Your Majesty, none of my ancestors have occupied such a position." The king responded, "I will make you an ancestor for others." This king was right, for if all members of a house depended on their predecessors, this would be a flawed sequence. Indeed, Exalted God brings forth the dead from the living, and He revives the earth after it is dead.[68] This is the opinion of the Powerful, the Knowing. Nobility can be created and renewed through knowledge, closeness to God, excellence, and other qualities. Power has elevated the humble and by the same token brought down those of high rank. Therefore, the Prophet, God bless and keep him, said, "Truly, in poetry there is wisdom"—or in a variant reading, "there is a judgment." **6.62**

An example of someone elevating their descendants is al-Muḥallaq, whose full name was ʿAbd al-ʿAzīz ibn Ḥantam al-Kalābī, a poor man of no distinction. When al-Aʿshā passed by him going to the market of ʿUkāẓ, his mother said to him, "Abū Baṣīr is a man who takes poetry seriously and you are an obscure man of little means who only has daughters. If you were to go up to him and praise him, we might hope for some good." Al-Muḥallaq rushed to al-Aʿshā and asked him to dismount, slaughtered an animal for him, and gave him wine to drink. Once the wine was consumed, al-Muḥallaq bemoaned his state and that of his daughters. "They will be cared for," al-Aʿshā said. The next morning al-Aʿshā set out for the market and recited his poem that begins: **6.63**

أَرِقْتُ وَمَا هٰذَا السُّهَادُ ٱلْمُؤَرِّقُ   وَمَا بِيَ مِنْ سُقْمٍ وَمَا بِي مَعْشَقُ

إلى أن انتهى فيها إلى قوله في المُحلَّق:

نَفَى الذَّمَّ عَنْ آلِ ٱلْمُحَلَّقِ جَفْنَةٌ   كَجَابِيَةِ السَّيْحِ ٱلْعِرَاقِيِّ تَفْهَقُ
تَرَى ٱلْقَوْمَ فِيهَا شَارِعِيْنَ وَبَيْنَهُمْ   مَعَ ٱلْقَوْمِ وَلْدَانٌ مَعَ النَّاسِ دَرْدَقُ
لَعَمْرِي لَقَدْ لَاحَتْ عُيُونٌ كَثِيرَةٌ   إِلَى ضَوْءِ نَارٍ فِي يَفَاعٍ تُحَرَّقُ
تُشَبُّ لِمَقْرُورَيْنِ يَصْطَلِيَانِهَا   وَبَاتَ عَلَى النَّارِ النَّدَى وَٱلْمُحَلَّقُ
رَضِيعَيْ لِبَانٍ ثَدْيِ أُمٍّ تَحَالَفَا   بِأَسْحَمَ دَاجٍ عَوْضُ لَا نَتَفَرَّقُ
تَرَى ٱلْجُودَ يَجْرِي سَائِرًا فَوْقَ جَمْرِهِ   كَمَا زَانَ مَتْنَ ٱلْهُنْدُوَانِيِّ رَوْنَقُ

فما أتمّ القصيدة إلّا والناس يسعون إلى المحلّق يهنّونه والأشراف يتسابقون إلى بناته. فما باتت واحدة منهن إلّا في عصمة رجل أفضل من أبيها بكثير.

ومن ذلك بنو أنف الناقة كانوا يتأذّون بهذا الاسم ويكرهون ذكره حتّى تعرّض بعضهم للحطيئة فأكرمه. فمدحهم وقلب الاسم مدحاً. وفي ذلك يقول: [بسيط] ٦،٦٤

سِيرِي أَمَامَ فَإِنَّ ٱلْأَكْثَرِينَ حَصًا   وَٱلْأَكْرَمِينَ إِذَا مَا يُنْسَبُونَ أَبَا
قَوْمٌ إِذَا عَقَدُوا عَقْدًا لِجَارِهِمُ   شَدُّوا ٱلْعِنَاجَ وَشَدُّوا فَوْقَهُ ٱلْكَرَبَا
أُولٰئِكَ ٱلْأَنْفُ وَٱلْأَذْنَابُ غَيْرُهُمُ   وَمَنْ يُسَوِّي بِأَنْفِ النَّاقَةِ الذَّنَبَا

فصاروا يفتخرون به ويتبجّحون بذكره. فهذا كلّه شرف متجدّد بسبب من الأسباب. وقد يزداد الشريف شرفاً بذلك كما وقع لهرم بن سنان المريّ فإنّه كان من سادات قومه ولكنّ أخوه خارجة بن سنان أسود منه وأشهر. فلمّا وقع لزهير من المدائح ما وقع

I could not sleep, was tormented by sleeplessness
and suffered from sickness and frustrated desire.

and which ends with him saying of al-Muḥallaq:

May Jafnah stave off all censure from the family of al-Muḥallaq,
for it is as a rippling pond of clear Iraqi water
To which you see a people come to drink, among them
those with children, and young animals.
By my life, many eyes have gazed
toward the light of a burning fire atop a hill
It blazed bright for two cold people who warmed themselves by it.
During the night, dew settled on the fire and on al-Muḥallaq.
Two milk brothers by the teat of one mother swore
on hands smeared with dark blood: We will not separate.[69]
You see generosity pouring over its embers, gleaming
just as luster decorates the blades of Indian swords.

The poem had not yet ended when people rushed to al-Muḥallaq to congratulate him, and noble men vied for his daughters. Not a night had passed before each daughter was married to a man better than her father by far.

Another example of elevation is the case of the Banū Anf al-Nāqah. They suffered having the name "Sons of the she-camel's nose," and hated it being mentioned, until the time one of them honored al-Ḥuṭay'ah. He subsequently changed the name's significance with a praise poem in which he said: 6.64

Any leader will see that what they attribute to their ancestor
comes from sound understanding and integrity.
A people who, whenever they conclude an agreement with their neighbor,
tie the knot and then tie it again to be sure.[70]
They are the nose, the rest of us are tails,
and who equates the nose of the camel with the tail?

They prided themselves on this poem and vaunted themselves by reciting it. In such cases, nobility is acquired on a specific occasion. One who is noble may have his nobility increased through such acts, as happened to Harim ibn Sinān al-Murrī, a noble man among his people. His brother Khārijah ibn Sinān

في هرم ازداد شرفاً وشهرة حتّى فاق أخاه في ذلك بل لا يكاد اليوم أخوه يذكر إلى غير هذا ممّا يكثر.

٦،٦٥ ومن الثاني بنو نمير كانوا من جمرات العرب المستغنين بقوّتهم وعددهم عن طلب حلف. وكانوا يفتخرون بهذا الاسم ويمدّون به أصواتهم إذا سُئلوا إلى أن هجا جرير عبيد بن حصين الراعي[١] منهم بقصيدته التي يقول فيها مخاطباً له: [وافر]

فَـغُضَّ الطَّرْفَ إِنَّكَ مِنْ نُمَيْرٍ   فَلَا كَعْباً بَلَغْتَ[٢] وَلَا كِلَابَا
وَلَوْ وُضِعَتْ شُيُوخُ بَنِي نُمَيْرٍ   عَلَى ٱلْمِيـزَانِ مَا عَـدَلَتْ ذُبَابَا

فسقطوا ولم يرفعوا بعد ذلك رأساً حتّى كانوا لا يتّسمون بهذا الاسم. فإذا قيل للواحد منهم من أنت؟ قال عامريّ.

٦،٦٦ ومن أظرف ما وقع في ذلك أنّ امرأة مرّت بقوم منهم فجعلوا ينظرون إليها ويتواصفونها. فالتفتت إليهم. وقالت قبّحكم الله بني نمير ما امتثلتم أمر الله إذ يقول ﴿قُلْ لِلْمُؤْمِنِينَ يَغُضُّوا مِنْ أَبْصَارِهِمْ﴾. ولا قول جرير إذ يقول:

فَـغُضَّ الطَّرْفَ إِنَّكَ مِنْ نُمَيْـرٍ

٦،٦٧ ومن ذلك بنو العجلان كانوا يفتخرون بهذا الاسم لأنّ جدّهم إنّما قيل له العجلان لتعجيله القِرى للضيفان. حتّى هجاهم النجاشيّ فقلب الاسم ذمّاً. وفي ذلك يقول: [طويل]

قُبَـيِّلَةٌ لَا يَخْفِـرُونَ بِـذِمَّـةٍ   وَلَا يَظْلِمُونَ النَّاسَ حَبَّةَ خَرْدَلِ
وَلَا يَـرِدُونَ ٱلْمَـاءَ إِلَّا عَشِـيَّةً   إِذَا صَدَرَ ٱلْوُرَّادُ عَنْ كُلِّ مَنْهَلِ

١ ط: بن عبيد حصين المراعي. ٢ ق: باقت.

was nobler and more famous than him, yet when Zuhayr included Harim in one of his panegyrics, Harim's nobility increased and his renown surpassed his brother's. Today his brother is hardly mentioned, and when he is, it's mainly in relation to this.

Examples of the second type, being brought down, include the Banū Numayr, who were one of the most powerful Arab tribes, not needing to seek alliances on account of their strength and number. They boasted of their name, "Sons of the young panther," and uttered it deliberately when asked about it, until the time Jarīr satirized one of them—'Ubayd ibn Ḥaṣīn the shepherd—in a poem addressing him: 6.65

> Cast your eyes down, you are of the Numayr:
> You have traveled to neither Kulāb nor the Kaaba.
> If you placed all the leaders of the Banū Numayr
> on a scale, they would not weigh so much as a fly.

After this, they hung their heads and no longer called themselves by the name. If one of them was asked, "Who are you?" he would say, "An 'Āmirī."

One of the most enjoyable accounts in connection with this case relates to a woman who passed by a group of them. They began to stare at her and to describe her to one another. So she turned to them and said, "May God make you infamous, Banū Numayr. You have not followed the example ordered by God when he said: «Say to the believers, that they cast down their eyes,»[71] nor the words of Jarīr when he recited the verse beginning 'Cast down your eyes, you are of the Numayr.'" 6.66

Another example is the Banū al-'Ajlān. They boasted of "Sons of the Swift" because of their ancestor al-'Ajlān, who would hasten to bring meals to his guests. But then al-Najāshī mocked them, reversing the name's meaning so it became one of reproach, as follows: 6.67

> It is a puny tribe that reneges on its promises of protection:
> They cannot hold sway over a people even to the extent of a mustard seed.
> They come to water only at nightfall
> when all the rest return from the pools.

تَعَافُ ٱلْكِلَابُ الضَّارِيَاتُ لُحُومَهُمْ   وَتَأْكُلُ مِنْ كَعْبِ بْنِ عَوْفٍ وَنَهْشَلِ
وَمَا سُمِّيَ ٱلْعَجْلَانُ إِلَّا لِقَوْلِهِمْ   خُذِ ٱلْقَعْبَ وَٱحْلُبْ أَيُّهَا ٱلْعَبْدُ وَٱعْجَلِ

فتنكّروا من هذا الاسم وجعل الواحد منهم إذا سئل يقول كعبيّ مخافة أن يسخر منه. ولهم معه في ذلك قصّة مشهورة بين يدي أمير المؤمنين عمر بن الخطّاب رضي الله عنه.

٦،٦٨ ثمّ قد يفيض شرف الإنسان حتّى يستطيل على من قبله من سلفه فتحيا رسومهم بعدما كانت دائرة وتعمر ربوعهم بعدما كانت غامرة. والذروة العليا أيضاً فيمن عاد شرفه على من قبله هو نبيّنا محمّد صلّى الله عليه وسلّم كما مرّ شرحه. وقد أشار إليه ابن الرومي بقوله: [بسيط]

قَالُوا أَبُو الصَّقْرِ مِنْ شَيْبَانٍ قُلْتُ لَهُمْ   كَلَّا لَعَمْرِي وَلٰكِنْ مِنْهُ شَيْبَانُ
تَسْمُو الرِّجَالُ بِآبَاءٍ وَآوِنَةٍ   تَسْمُو الرِّجَالُ بِأَبْنَاءٍ وَتَزْدَانُ
وَكَمْ أَبٍ قَدْ عَلَا بِٱبْنٍ ذُرَى حَسَبٍ   كَمَا عَلَتْ بِرَسُولِ اللهِ عَدْنَانُ

٦،٦٩ وادّعى هذا الوصف أبو الطيّب فقال: [خفيف]

مَا بِقَوْمِي شَرُفْتُ بَلْ شَرُفُوا بِي   وَبِنَفْسِي ٱفْتَخَرْتُ لَا بِجُدُودِي

٦،٧٠ أمّا شرفه هو في بابه فلا ينكر وأمّا شرف قومه به فالشعر أعذبه أكذبه وإلّا فالحكم على الشيء فرع تصوّره نعم كان من عادة العرب أنّه إذا نبغ شاعر في قوم اعتزّوا به. واحتموا عن الشعراء فلو تحقّق لأبي الطيّب قوم لكانوا كذلك.

٦،٧١ ورجل له أصل وقديم شرفٍ ثمّ لم يبنه ولم يجدّده وهو إمّا أن تخفى عوامله فلم يبن ولم يهدم مع أنّه بالحقيقة من لم يكن في زيادة فهو في نقصان. والمراد أن يرجع إلى عمار الناس فلا يحدّد المآثر ولا يخرج إلى المعايب. فهذا لا فضيلة له إلّا مجرّد النسب

Hungry dogs loathe their meat
and eat rather from that of Kaʿb ibn ʿAwf and Nahshal.
They were called al-ʿAjlān not by others but by themselves.
Hurry, slave, to take the drinking cup, and milk!

After this rebuke, they abandoned the name and, if any was asked, he would say his name was Kaʿbī for fear of being mocked. There is a famous story about this concerning them and al-Najāshī before the Commander of the Faithful, ʿUmar ibn al-Khaṭṭāb, God be pleased with him.

The nobility of a person can be so abundant that it is extended to his forebears. Their traces come alive after having been peripheral, their quarters are built up after having been desolate. The greatest example of someone who gave such nobility to his predecessors was our Prophet, God bless and keep him, as previously explained. Ibn al-Rūmī described this when he said: 6.68

They said that Abū Ṣaqr is of the Shaybān. I said,
"Not so, by my life, though the Shaybān are from him.
Men rise to heights by their ancestry and their era,
just as they rise and are adorned by their sons.
How many fathers have been elevated by a son to the peaks of glory
as ʿAdnān was by the Prophet of God?"

Al-Mutanabbī challenged this way of putting it, saying: 6.69

I was not honored by my people; rather, they were honored by me.
I boasted of myself, not my ancestors.

The Prophet's glory is in a class of its own and is unassailable. As for poetry that celebrates the honor of one's people, the sweetest is the falsest; otherwise, one is judging the matter according to only a part of the whole picture. Yes, it was the custom of the Arabs that if a poet of theirs excelled, they would be proud of him. They protected poets. If al-Mutanabbī had truly belonged to a tribe, his people would have responded in the same way.[72] 6.70

If a man has longstanding nobility, but does not build upon it or renew it, his affairs will be concealed, neither growing nor diminishing. Although, in truth, one who does not gain in nobility loses it.[73] That is to say that he will return to being a member of the masses, neither leaving noteworthy traces behind nor being implicated in disgraceful affairs. This person has no virtue 6.71

والفخر العظاميّ كما مرّ. وإمّا أن يهدمه بملابسة ضدّ ما كان أولاً. فهذا بمنزلة من هدم الدار ثمّ حفر البقعة أيضاً فأفسدها فهذا مذموم بما جنى على نفسه وبما جنى على حسبه ونسبه والذروة العليا. في هذا الصنف اليهود والنصارى ونحوهم فقد هدموا أنسابهم وأحسابه بِشَرِّ الخصال وهو الكفر نسأل الله العافية.

٦،٧٢ ومن هذا النمط من يخلف آباءه الصالحين بالفسق وكثرة الرغبة في الدنيا والكبر والدعوى وغير ذلك من القبائح كما هو شأن كثير من أولاد الصالحين في زماننا نسأل الله العافية. وفي هذا الصنف قيل: [بسيط]

لَئِنْ فَخَرْتَ بِآبَاءٍ لَهُمْ شَرَفٌ   لَقَدْ فَخَرْتَ وَلٰكِنْ بِئْسَ مَا وَلَدُوا

٦،٧٣ وقال لبيد: [كامل]

ذَهَبَ ٱلَّذِينَ يُعَاشُ فِي أَكْنَافِهِمْ   وَبَقِيتَ فِي خَلْفٍ كَجِلْدِ ٱلْأَجْرَبِ

٦،٧٤ وقال الآخر: [كامل]

ذَهَبَ ٱلرِّجَالُ ٱلْمُقْتَدَى بِفِعَالِهِمْ   وَٱلْمُنْكِرُونَ لِكُلِّ أَمْرٍ مُنْكَرِ
وَبَقِيتَ فِي خَلْفٍ يُزَيِّنُ بَعْضُهُمْ   بَعْضاً لِيَسْكُتَ مُعْوِرٌ عَنْ مُعْوِرِ

٦،٧٥ الرابع قد يقال فيما ذكرناه من النسب إنّه من النسب الطويل وهو عيب ويذمّ بضدّه وهو النسب القصير. قال الشاعر: [كامل]

أَنْتُمْ بَنُو ٱلْقَصِيرِ وَطُولُكُمْ   بَادٍ عَلَى ٱلْكُبَرَاءِ وَٱلْأَشْرَافِ

والنسب القصير هو أن يقول أنا فلان ابن فلان فيعرف لكون أبيه أو جدّه الأدنى من الأعيان. والطويل هو ألّا يعرف إلى رأس القبيلة.

other than his lineage and vaunting his ancestry, as has been discussed above. Or he destroys his nobility by carrying out acts contrary to his inherited status. This is like someone who destroys a house, then plows up the land and ruins it. Such an action is reprehensible and reaps nothing for the reputation, lineage, and ancestry of its actor. Such are the Christians, Jews, and their like, who destroyed their lineages and the memory of their deeds through that most nefarious quality, unbelief. We ask God to preserve us from this.

Of this kind also are those who disappoint their devout parents with wickedness, excessive worldly desire, arrogance, and their advocacy of all things evil and vile, as is the case with many of the children of the devout in our times. We ask God to preserve us from this. The following verse describes this issue:[74] 6.72

> Though I boasted of the nobility of my ancestors,
> what they gave birth to was wretched.

And Labīd said: 6.73

> Those under whose protection I lived are long gone:
> Here I remain, like the sloughed skin of a mangy camel.

Another poet said:[75] 6.74

> Gone are those who were worthy of imitation
> and who forbade every reprehensible act.
> I remained among stragglers who flatter each other
> and keep quiet about each other's faults.

The fourth relation to ancestors: One may regard the kind of ancestry we have been discussing as distant ancestry, which is weak and can be undermined by its opposite, recent ancestry. As the poet has said:[76] 6.75

> You are people of a recent lineage—
> your ancient lineage passed away with its elders and nobles.

The meaning of a recent lineage is to say, I am so-and-so, son of so-and-so, such that a person is known by the nobility of his father or his immediate ancestor. The meaning of an ancient lineage is that one is known only by the originary ancestor.

٦،٧٦ والجواب أوّلاً أنّنا لم نذكر النسب افتخاراً حتى يعرض على هذا المقياس وإنما ذكرناه لاحتياج إليه في المصالح الدينيّة والدنيويّة عند أهله وثانياً أن كون الإنسان من الأعيان أمر إضافيّ. كما مرّ أنّه قد يكون من أعيان عشيرته أو قومه وهو الأغلب. وقد يكون من أعيان عمارته أو إقليمه أو جيله وهو عزيز الوجود. ولا شكّ أنّ شرف الإنسان واشتهاره باعتبار عشيرته أو قومه إنّما يعرف فيهم ولا يضيره أن لا[1] يعرفه غيرهم لأنّ سادات العرب لا يعرفهم العجم ولا العكس. وكذا فيما بين العرب غالباً.

٦،٧٧ وقال الشاعر: [متقارب]

طَوِيلُ ٱلنِّجَادِ رَفِيعُ ٱلْعِمَا   دِ سَادَ عَشِيرَتَهُ أَمْرَدَا

٦،٧٨ وقال الآخر: [كامل]

لَيْسَ ٱلْغَبِيُّ بِسَيِّدٍ فِي قَوْمِهِ   لٰكِنَّ سَيِّدَ قَوْمِهِ ٱلْمُتَغَابِي

٦،٧٩ ولم يخرج عن هذه الإضافة الملوك كما قال النابغة: [طويل]

وَلِلْحَارِثِ ٱلْجَفْنِيِّ سَيِّدِ قَوْمِهِ   لَيَبْتَغِيَنْ بِٱلْجَيْشِ دَارَ ٱلْمُحَارِبِ

٦،٨٠ وقالت هند بنت عتبة رضي الله عنها لمن قال لها في ابنها معاوية رضي الله عنه أرجو أن يسود قومه ثكلته إن كان لا يسود إلّا قومه. وذلك أنّها سمعت قبل ذلك من الكهّان أنّها تلد ملكاً اسمه معاوية في قصّة مشهورة.

٦،٨١ إذا تقرّر هذا فالمنتسب معروف النسب قصيره بحمد الله في قومه. وهو من صميمهم وإنّما رفعه ليعرف على ما تشعّب عنه من الفصائل والبطون وليعرف انقطاعه

[1] كذا في ط، ق؛ م: ألا.

First and foremost, our aim has not been to introduce the subject of genealogy in order to boast. Rather, we brought it up primarily because it is necessary when people attend to their religious and worldly affairs, and secondarily because being noble is a relative matter. As already discussed, an individual may be a noble in his clan or tribe, as is most frequently the case. Or he may a noble in his city, region, or generation, which is a high honor. Without doubt, man's nobility and fame is reckoned in relation to the group or people he belongs to: They know him and he suffers no harm if outsiders do not know him, insofar as Arab notables are not known to non-Arabs, and vice versa. For the most part, this is the way things stand among the Arabs. 6.76

As the poet said:[77] 6.77

He was of tall stature and exalted nobility
but he ruled over his people as a beardless youth.

Another poet said:[78] 6.78

The lord of a people is not an idiot,
though he seem to be so.

Nor are kings exempt from this relative aspect, for as al-Nābighah has said:[79] 6.79

As well as from al-Ḥārith al-Jafnī, leader of his people,
then let him be a military man!

Hind bint ʿUtbah, God be pleased with her, said to someone who broached the subject of her son Muʿāwiyah, God be pleased with him, "I hope that he will rule his people. If he fails to do this, I will mourn him as if he were dead." The reason for this lies in a well-known story she had once heard from soothsayers that she would give birth to a king whose name would be Muʿāwiyah. 6.80

It is by repeated usage that, by the grace of God, a man becomes known by his short lineage among his people. He is from their inner circles and has abbreviated his lineage so that he might be known among those clans and tribes that are related to him and that his distinction among them be known when he enters settled areas, and as a result obtains other benefits such as have been mentioned above. As for the benefits of teknonyms already discussed, 6.81

عند دخول القرى وغير ذلك من الفوائد التي مرّت.[١] وأمّا ذكري لما مرّ من الكنى فلجريانها على ألسنة فضلاء مع التفاؤل ورجاء تحقّق ما له معنى منها.

٨٢،٦ أمّا أبو علي وهو كنية الحسن المشهورة فكنّاني بها شيخ الإسلام الإمام الهمام أستاذنا وقدوتنا أبو عبد الله سيّدي محمّد بن ناصر الدرعيّ رضي الله عنه وعنّا به. وكنت وردت عليه في أعوام الستّين والألف بقصد أخذ العلم فامتدحته بقصيدة قدّمتها بين يدي نجواي فانبسط إليّ بحمد الله وافتتحنا بكتاب التسهيل فلمّا قرأنا الخطبة دخل مسروراً فكتب إليّ: [بسيط]

أَبَا عَلِيٍّ جُزِيتَ ٱلْخَيْرَ وَٱلنِّعَمَا وَنِلْتَ كُلَّ ٱلْمُنَى مِنْ رَبِّنَا قَسَمَا
يَا مَرْحَباً بِكَ كُلَّ ٱلرَّحْبِ لَا بَرِحَتْ قَرَائِحُ ٱلْفِكْرِ مِنْكَ تَجْنِي حِكَمَا

ولم أزل بحمد الله أتعرّف بركة دعائه وإقبال قلبه إلى الآن. نسأل الله تعالى أن لا يزايلنا فضله ورحمته حتّى نلقاه آمين.

٨٣،٦ وقال ابن عمّنا الفاضل البارع أبو سعيد عثمان بن عليّ اليوسيّ رحمه الله من أبيات: [كامل]

نَفْسِي عَشِيَّةَ قِيلَ مَرَّ أَبُو عَلِيٍّ مِثْلُ ٱلرِّيَاحِ إِذَا تَمُرُّ بِأَثْأَبِ

ولم يزل الشيخ رضي الله عنه يكنّيني بذلك إلى أن توفّاه الله في رسائله[٢] ومخاطبته وعند ذكري. وأمّا البواقي فكنّاني بها فضلاء من الإخوان في رسائلهم. ونحوت في ذلك منحى السيّد خير النسّاج وكان اسمه محمّد بن إسماعيل. فلمّا وقعت عليه المحنة وألقي عليه شُبه خير مملوك لرجل نسّاج فقبض عليه وأدخله ينسج ويخاطبه بهذا الاسم. فلمّا كشفت عنه المحنة وخرج ترك هذا الاسم على نفسه. فقيل له ألا ترجع إلى اسمك؟ فقال ما كنت لأغيّر أو لأترك اسماً سمّاني به رجل مسلم.

١ ط، ق يزيد لله الأمر من قبل ومن بعد. ٢ ط، ق يزيد إليَّ.

truly these are often on the tongues of distinguished men who seek to display their auspicious meanings.

Abū ʿAlī is a teknonym well known to accompany the name al-Ḥasan. It was given to me by the guide to the faith, the magnanimous exemplar, our teacher and our leader, Abū ʿAbd Allāh Sīdī Maḥammad ibn Nāṣir al-Daraʿī, may God be pleased with him and us. I came to him in the 1060s [1650s] with the aim of acquiring knowledge from him. I praised him in a poem that I presented to him privately, and, God be praised, he was pleased with me. We began my studies with *The Facilitation.*[80] Once we had read the introduction, he was happy and wrote to me as follows: 6.82

> Abū ʿAlī, may you be rewarded with goodness and blessings,
> may your destiny be to obtain everything you wish from our Lord.
> We welcome you in all ways possible,
> for your gifted mind continuously brings forth wisdom.

By the grace of God, I continue to experience the blessing of his prayer and his sincerity. We ask Exalted God not to deprive us of His favor and His mercy until we meet Him. Amen.

The following is a verse by our gifted and brilliant cousin Abū Saʿīd ʿUthmān ibn ʿAlī al-Yūsī, may God show him mercy: 6.83

> One evening my soul said to me, there goes Abū ʿAlī!
> like the winds blowing through the tamarisk tree.

As I recall, the shaykh, God be pleased with him, continued to address me with the teknonym Abū ʿAlī in his letters and conversations until God took him. As for my other names, I was given them as teknonyms in letters from distinguished brethren: In this matter, I have acted in the manner of Master Khayr the Weaver, whose name was Muḥammad ibn Ismāʿīl. When tribulation befell him, he was given the appearance of Khayr, the slave of a weaver. He was captured, made to work as a weaver, and addressed by this name.[81] When he was released from this tribulation, he continued calling himself Khayr. When he was asked, "Are you not going to go back to your old name?" he answered, "I am not going to change or desist from using the name that I was given by a fellow Muslim."

واعلم أنّ لهذا السيّد في التزام الاسم المذكور أوجهاً. منها أنّه تسليم لأنّه شاهد فعل الله تعالى فلمّا ألقى الله تعالى عليه الاسم لم يبق له اختيار في التعرّض له. ومنها أنّه يستشعر من مولاه تعالى أنّه أدّبه بجعله عبداً مملوكاً وتسميته باسمه وضربة المحبوب تستلذّ. ومنها أنّه يتذكّر العبوديّة وذلّتها وهذه الطائفة قد صارت الذلّة شرابهم ونعيمهم. ومنها أنّه يذكر به العقوبة فيذكر الهفوة ليتحرّر منها. ومنها أنّه يبقى عليه الاسم ليبقى عليه ذكر الهفوة والعقوبة هضماً لنفسه وإرغاماً لها. ومنها التفاؤل بهذا اللفظ فإنّه على أصله وهو ضدّ الشرّ وعلى أنّه مخفّف من التشديد فهو ذو الخير. وكيف أترك أنا كنية كنّاني به رجل من أفاضل المسلمين ولا سيّما إن تضمّنت معنى حسناً. لله الأمر من قبل ومن بعد. ٨٤،٦

ولمّا كان القصد في هذا الموضوع إلى ذكر المحاضرات بنوادر الفوائد ممّا اتّفق لي خصوصاً أو لغيري عموماً وجب أن ينخرط في سلك ذلك ما وقع في شأني حال الولادة لأنّه أوّل الرحلة إلى هذه الدار مع ما انضاف إليه ممّا يكون له مصداقاً أو يرجى خيره ويذكر على وجه التبرّك والتفاؤل أو التحدّث بالنعم. وفيه مسرّة المحبّ ومساءة البغيض. فأقول إنّي أرجو أن أكون إن شاء الله تعالى رؤيا والدي ودعوة أستاذي. أمّا رؤيا الوالد فاعلم أنّ أبي مع كونه رجلاً أمّياً كان رجلاً متديّناً مخالطاً لأهل الخير محبّاً للصالحين زَوّارًا لهم. وكان أُعطِيَ الرؤيا الصادقة وأعطي عبارتها فيرى الرؤيا ويعبّرها لنفسه فتجيء كَفَلَقِ الصبح. وكان ممّا رأى وتواتر الحديث به عنه في العشيرة رحمه الله أن قال رأيت عينَيْ ماء إحداهما لي والآخر لعليّ بن عثمان وهو والد ابن عمّنا الأديب البارع أبي سعيد عثمان بن عليّ رحمه الله غير أنّ عين عليّ كنّا نسقي بها في بلدنا وعيني خرجت إلى ناحية أخرى. ١،٧

Know that several aspects are reflected in this good man preserving the name. Among them are the following: (1) It is an act of submission, as he had witnessed the providential act of Exalted God, and when Exalted God had bestowed this name on him, he had no choice but to apply it. (2) He realized that his Lord, the Exalted, had admonished him by making him a slave and giving him the name. One takes pleasure in a blow from one's beloved. (3) He retains a memory of slavery and submissiveness, and submissiveness is the drink and happiness of this kind of person. (4) He remembers slavery because of the moniker, and remembers the error in order to be preserved from its reoccurrence. (5) He keeps the name to preserve the memory of the error and its punishment—he submits to it and suffers it. (6) He considered this term to be an auspicious omen in that its meaning is the antithesis of evil—it was not as harsh as it could have been, and it encapsulated goodness. How could I then abandon the use of a teknonym that had been given to me by a most excellent Muslim, especially given its positive signification? Everything is God's to command. 6.84

When I decided to relate discourses with beneficial anecdotes that involved me personally or had occurred to others, I felt it necessary to include the case of my birth, for this was my first journey into this world. I chose to include in this narrative evidence for its truthfulness as well as those matters that promise benefit and that one mentions to attract blessings and for good fortune, or to proclaim God's blessings.[82] It contains the joy of the beloved and the pain of the hated. Because of this, I say, "I wish to fulfill, God willing, the vision of my father and the prayer of my teacher." Concerning the vision of my father: Despite being illiterate, he was a religious man who associated with pious men and loved the devout, whom he visited often. He had been granted the gift of true visions and of discerning their meaning: He would see and interpret them for himself and his understanding would come upon him like the break of dawn. Among the things he saw and described, as related by many of the tribe on his authority: "I saw two springs; one of them belonged to me and the other to ʿAlī ibn ʿUthmān (he was the father of our cousin, the outstanding writer Abū Saʿīd ʿUthmān ibn ʿAlī, God show him mercy). We drank from the spring of ʿAlī in our area, while my own spring surfaced in a different place." 7.1

٢،٧ وزعموا أنّه قال وكانت العين التي هي لي أقوى ماء وأكثر فيضاً ثمّ فسّر ذلك بمولودين ينتفع بهما. فولد أبو سعيد المذكور فانتفع ونفع حتّى مات رحمه الله وظهر أنّه العين المذكورة لأبيه. وولدت أنا أيضاً وقد كان لي أخوان أسن منّي فماتا أميّين رحمهما الله فأرجو أن أكون تلك العين. وقد اتّفق خروجي عن البلد كما قال رحمه الله وكنت بعد ذلك حين ارتحلت في طلب العلم إلى ناحية السوس الأقصى غيّبت عن الوالد رحمه الله أعواماً لا يدري أين أنا.

٣،٧ فلمّا قفلت حدّثني رحمه الله فقال لمّا ضقنا من غيبتك رأيت كأنّ الناس يتجارون خلف فرس أشقر[١] ليقبضوه. فجئت إليه أنا فأمسكته بلجامه فلمّا استيقظت قلت للناس إنّ الحسن ابني سيأتي وأجتمع به فكان ذلك. والفرس الأشهب عند المعبّرين اشتهار بشرف وذكر. وقد حصل لي ذلك بحمد الله. نسأل الله سبحانه أن يكمل ذلك لنا وله ولسائر الأحباب بالفوز يوم الحشر والرضوان الأكبر بجاه نبيّه المصطفى المبعوث إلى الأسود والأحمر صلّى الله عليه وسلّم وعلى آله وصحبه المجلّين في كل مفخر.

٤،٧ وأمّا دعوة أستاذي وهو شيخ الإسلام وعلم الأعلام أبو عبد الله سيّدي محمّد بن ناصر رحمه الله تعالى ورضي عنه فهي تلك بعينها وكان من حديثي معه في ذلك. أنه لمّا تهيّأ للتشريق في حجّته الثانية أرسل إليّ في حاجة أقضيها له ممّا يتعلّق بسفره ذلك. وأنا إذ ذاك بالزاوية البكريّة فقضيت ذلك بحمد الله وسافرت به إليه حتّى بلغته. فلقيني بترحيب ورأيت منه بحمد الله إقبالاً خارجاً عن المعتاد حتّى إنّه متى ذكرت ذلك إلى اليوم يغشاني خجل وإشفاق على نفسي. وأقمت معه حتّى شيعته لوجهته إلى أن جاوزنا سجلماسة بمرحلة فرجعت إلى داري.

٥،٧ ولمّا كنت ببعض الطريق ألهمت الدعاء له فاتخذت الدعاء له بعد أوراد الصبح وردا. فلمّا قفل من الحجّ ذهبنا إليه لنسلّم عليه فخلوت به يوماً وجعلت أطلب منه وأطلب. فقال لي رحمه الله أمّا الدعاء فإنّي في سفرتي هذه ما دخلت مقاماً ولا مزارة

---

١ ط و ق: أشهب.

They claim that he said, "The spring that was mine had more water and was more abundant." He then explained this through the two births from which he had benefited. The aforementioned Abū Saʿīd was born, was successful, and provided benefit to others until he died, God show him mercy. It was clear that he was the spring of his father. I too was born, having had two older brothers who had died, may God show them mercy. I hope to be that spring, which corresponds with my leaving the area as he had interpreted it, God show him mercy. After my birth, when I traveled in search of knowledge to distant Sūs, I was absent for years from my father, God show him mercy, during which he didn't know where I was. 7.2

When I returned, he, God show him mercy, spoke to me, saying, "When we were troubled by your absence I had a vision in which people ran after a light-colored horse, trying to catch it. I ran to it and seized it by the reins. When I woke I told the people, 'My son al-Ḥasan will come and I will be reunited with him.' And, thanks be to God, we were." Among interpreters of dreams, a gray horse represents repute, nobility, and renown, and this has come to pass for me, God be praised. We ask Exalted God to bring this about for us, for him, and for our loved ones, in a victorious fashion on the day we are gathered to witness our greatest delight. We ask this on the honor of our Chosen Prophet, who was sent to all mankind, God bless and keep him, his family, and his Companions distinguished with every glory. 7.3

As for the prayer of my teacher, the guide to the faith, the most distinguished of men, Abū ʿAbd Allāh Sīdī Maḥammad ibn Nāṣir, may Exalted God show him mercy and be pleased with him, it resulted from my talking with him about this. When he was preparing himself to go east for his second pilgrimage, he sent a letter asking me to do something for him in connection with his trip. I was at that time at the Bakriyyah lodge. God be praised, I took care of the matter, then set out to meet him. He welcomed me, and, God be praised, I received from him greater affection than usual, to the point that until today when I remember this, I am overcome and overwhelmed. I stayed with him, and accompanied him till we were a day's journey beyond Sijilmāsah. I then headed for home. 7.4

On the road, I was inspired with a prayer for him. I uttered it after reciting a passage of the Qur'an in the morning. When he had returned from the pilgrimage we went to greet him. I took him aside, asking for guidance. He said, may God show him mercy, "On this journey, I did not enter a house or shrine, nor 7.5

ولا توجّهت إلى الدعاء لأحد إلّا جاء بك الله تعالى في لساني أوّلاً. ثمّ لا أدعو لك إلّا بهذا الدعاء اللّهم اجعله عيناً يستقي منها أهل المشرق وأهل المغرب. قال حتّى كنت أتعجّب في نفسي وأقول سبحان الله بماذا استحقّ هذا الرجل هذا؟

٦،٧ ولمّا صنّفت القصيدة الداليّة في مدحه وتهنئته بالحجّ أدخلها إليه ولده الفقيه الناسك الفاضل أبو محمّد عبد الله بن محمّد. فخرج إليّ وقال يقول لك الشيخ جعلك الله عيناً يستقي منها أهل المشرق وأهل المغرب وشمساً يستضيء بها أهل المشرق وأهل المغرب. وهذا اللفظ يحتمل الدعاء والخبر نسأل الله تعالى أن يحقّق لنا نحن وللمسلمين ذلك. آمين.

٧،٧ ومن هذا ما كلّمه جماعة من فقراء الغرب وأنا حاضر معهم فقال لهم يشير إليّ هذا شمسكم هذا ضوءكم. وهذا كلّه أصرح ممّا حكى تاج الدين بن عطاء الله عن شيخه القطب العارف أبي العبّاس المرسيّ رضي الله عنهما. قال جاء الشيخ مرّة من سفر فلقيناه فدعا لي وقال فعل الله لك وفعل وبهاك بين خلقه. قال ففهمت يعني من قوله وبهاك بين خلقه أنّي مراد بالظهور إلى الخلق. واعلم أنّ مواطأة دعوة الشيخ رضي الله عنه لرؤيا الوالد[1] مع كونه لم يحضر لذلك ولم ينقل إليه من عجيب الاتّفاق. قد ذكرت هنا ما وقع في الحديث عن أصحاب النبيّ صلّى الله عليه وسلّم أنّهم قالوا له يا رسول الله[2] أخبرنا عنك. فقال لهم أنا دعوة أبي إبراهيم عليه السلام ورؤيا أمي.

١،٨ تنبّـه أيّها الناظر. فإيّاك أن يختلج بفهمك أو يخطر بوهمك أنّي أنزع بهذه الحكاية قصداً إلى المحاكاة معاذ الله فإنّ درجات الأنبياء لا تنبغي لغيرهم. ولا يصل أحد إلى مزاحمتها فكيف بسيّد الأنبياء؟ صلوات الله وسلامه عليه وعليهم أجمعين

١ ق: رحمه الله. ٢ م يزيد عليه.

did I pronounce a prayer for anyone without Exalted God placing you on my tongue first. I always prayed for you as follows: 'Make him, God, a spring from which the people of the East and the West can drink.'" He said, "I was amazed by this and asked myself, God be glorified, why does al-Yūsī deserve this?"

When I composed the poem ending in *d* in praise of him, and gave it to him on the occasion of the pilgrimage, his son, the fine and pious Abū Muḥammad ʿAbd Allāh ibn Maḥammad brought it in to him, then returned to me, saying, "My shaykh says to you, 'May God make you a well from which the people of the East and West will drink, a sun from which the people of the East and the West will seek light.'" This phrase contained both a prayer and a blessing. We ask Exalted God that this be accomplished for us and for all Muslims. Amen. 7.6

This was the gist of what he told a group of devotees from the West when I was present. Pointing to me, he said to them, "This is your sun. This is your light." This is clearer than what Tāj al-Dīn ibn ʿAṭāʾ Allāh said of his shaykh, the knowledgeable authority Abū l-ʿAbbās al-Mursī, God be pleased with them both: "The shaykh returned once from a trip. We met him and he prayed for me, saying, 'May God accomplish and carry this out for you, and make you shine among His creation.' Tāj al-Dīn said, 'I understood by his saying, "Make you shine among His creation," that I was marked out to become prominent among mankind.'" Know that the correspondence between the prayer of my shaykh, God be pleased with him, and my father's dream, at which my shaykh had not been present and of which he had not been told, was a wondrous coincidence. I have already mentioned above what took place in the account regarding the Prophet's Companions, God bless and keep them, when they said, "Tell us about yourself, Prophet of God," and he said to them, "I am the prayer of my father Abraham, eternal peace be his, and the dream of my mother." 7.7

Reader, take heed! You should tremble if your fancy leads you to think that I desire to establish an equivalence—God is my refuge. The rank of prophets cannot appropriately be compared to those of ordinary men. No one can compete with them, so how then with the lord of the prophets, God bless and keep him and his family as well as all of them and their families? Convince yourself that there is no shared kinship or lineage involved here, nor any shadow 8.1

وعلى آله وعلى آل كلّ ثمّ إياك أيضاً أن تتوهّم أن لا نسبة ولا نسب ولا شبهة ولا شبه فتقع في الغلوّ من الطرف الآخر. وقد قال صلّى الله عليه وسلّم خير الأمور أوسطها ولا بدّ لهذا من تقرير. فنقول إنّ الله جلّ اسمه وهو الذي لا مثل له ولا نظير ولا شبه ولا وزير قد شرّع لعباده التعلّق بأسمائه الحسنى. ثم شرّع لهم أيضاً التخلّق بها في الجملة حتّى إذا علمنا مثلاً أنّ الله تعالى حليم انتهض العبد في التخلّق بالحلم فيكون حليماً.

٢،٨ كذا إذا علمنا أنّه تعالى عليم أو وهّاب أو صبور أو شكور انتهض العبد في الاتّصاف بالعلم وبالجود وهكذا حتّى يكون عليماً وهّاباً. ومعلوم أنّ حلم العبد ليس كحلم الله وهكذا ولكن له به نسبة هي توجب قرب العبد من الله تعالى في المعنى ومن هذا حديث خلق الله آدم على صورته أي خلقه حيّاً عالماً قديراً وليس كالجمادات والحيوانات العجماوات. وبهذا تأهّل لأن يكون عبد الحضرة دونها.

٣،٨ ثمّ إنّ العباد المختارين يرضون لرضى الله ويغضبون لغضبه ويشتدّون لأجله ويلينون لأجله وهكذا في سائر الأحوال والأفعال. قال تعالى في أصحابه صلّى الله عليه وسلّم ورضي عنهم ﴿أَشِدَّاءُ عَلَى ٱلْكُفَّارِ رُحَمَاءُ بَيْنَهُمْ﴾. وقال أيضاً ﴿أَذِلَّةٍ عَلَى ٱلْمُؤْمِنِينَ أَعِزَّةٍ عَلَى ٱلْكَافِرِينَ﴾ وهو مسايرة ومشايعة في الأفعال والأحوال. وذلك شأن عبيد الملك وإذا كان هذا في حقّ الله تعالى ففي حقّ الأنبياء أقرب وأيسر فلا إشكال في صحّة تعاطي أوصافهم وأخلاقهم وأفعالهم وسائر أحوالهم وإن لم تكن في ذلك مشابهة ولا مزاحمة للنبوءة بل اتّباع واقتباس و نسبة[١] توجب لصاحبها أيضاً القرب منهم.

٤،٨ ولهذا قيل في الوارث إنّه من كان على قدم النبيّ صلّى الله عليه وسلّم أي متحقّقاً في الاقتداء به قولاً وفعلاً وحالاً. وقال صلّى الله عليه وسلّم الرُّؤْيَا الصالِحَةُ مِنَ الرَّجُلِ الصَّالِحِ جُزْءٌ مِنْ سِتَّةٍ وأَرْبَعِينَ جُزْءاً مِنَ النُّبُوءةِ. فقد علم من لفظ الحديث أنّ الرؤيا

---

١ م: شبه.

of resemblance, and do not fall into exaggeration from another angle. He said, God bless and keep him, "Matters are best at their mean." This warrants clarification, so we declare that God—His name be glorified, there is none like Him nor any equal, no one similar, nor any minister to Him—has decreed for His worshippers that they should take His blessed names. He then decreed for His worshippers that they be shaped by these names in their entirety, to the extent that if we know, for example, that Exalted God is gentle, the worshipper devotes himself solely to cultivating gentleness and in so doing becomes gentle.

In the same fashion, if we know that the Exalted is Knowing, Granting, 8.2
Enduring, and Bounteous, the worshipper rises to the occasion with knowledge, excellence, and so on, so as to become distinguished and generous. It is well known that the worshipper's patience is not like God's, and so on. Yet in the worshipper's patience, he shares a portion that brings him closer in essence to Exalted God. From this comes the hadith, "God created Adam in his image." That is to say, He created him alive, knowing, and powerful, not like minerals and dumb beasts. In this fashion, the worshipper is cheered, as he, unlike the rest of God's creations, worships His exalted presence.

Then there are the select worshippers who are pleased when God is 8.3
pleased, angry when He is angry, and grow either violent or gentle for His sake. The same is the case with regard to other states and acts. The Exalted has said regarding the Prophet's Companions, God bless and keep him and be content with them: «They are hard against the unbelievers, merciful to one another.»[83] He also said that they were «humble toward the believers, disdainful toward the unbelievers.»[84] This is consistent, and is coherent with regard to both acts and states. This is also the case with a king's slaves. If this is true with respect to Exalted God, then how much more so with regard to the prophets? Undoubtedly, it is appropriate to ascribe their attributes, characteristics, acts, and other states to the worshipper, so long as in doing so there is no assertion of resemblance or claim of prophecy, but rather emulation, adaptation, and adherence; as a result, the one who possesses these attributes becomes closer to the prophets.

It is said, therefore, that the true inheritor is the one who was at the feet of 8.4
the Prophet, God bless and keep him; that is, in terms of achieving emulation of his speech, acts, and station. He said, God bless and keep him, "The sincere vision of a devout man is one forty-sixth of the measure of prophecy." From the wording of this hadith we know that a vision that comes to someone who is not

الواقعة من غير النبيّ لعموم لفظ الصالح قد أخذت بنسبة من النبوءة فهي منها غير أنّه لقلّة النسبة لا تقع بها مزاحمة.

٨،٥ وقال الشيخ أبو يزيد رضي الله عنه مثل ما أعطي الأنبياء مثل زقّ مملوء ماء أو عسلاً. ومثال ما أعطي الأولياء كلّهم مثال قطرات تقطر من ذلك الزقّ. فانظر في هذا المثال فإنّ القطرات هي من ماهيّة ما في الزقّ قطعاً ولكنّها لقلّتها جدّاً لا تقع بها مزاحمة. ولم يزل أهل الدين من العلماء العاملين والمجاهدين السالكين والواصلين العارفين يأخذون أقوالهم وأفعالهم وأحوالهم من أحوال الأنبياء عموماً وحال نبيّنا صلّى الله عليه وسلّم خصوصاً. وهذا هو الشأن كلّه.

٨،٦ وقد يقع لهم ممّا هو في معنى الاقتباس والإشارة والتمثيل ما يزيد على هذا كما قال الشيخ أبو مدين رضي الله عنه لأبي عمران موسى ابن يدراسن الحلاّج حين توجّه إليه فإن أمن الغرب فأنت موسى وأنا شعيب وإنّ موسى لمّا بلغ شعيباً أمن. ومن هذا ما وقع له رضي الله عنه في القرآن وقد دخل عليه رجل من أهل الإنكار والمصحف بين يديه. فقال للرجل ارفع المصحف وافتحه وانظر إلى أوّل ورقة منه فإذا فيها ﴿ٱلَّذِينَ كَذَّبُوا شُعَيْبًا كَانُوا هُمُ ٱلْخَاسِرِينَ﴾. ومن هذا النمط كان رضي الله عنه يقول لا يكون المريد مريداً حتّى يجد في القرآن كلّ ما يريد.

٨،٧ وقال الشيخ أبو العبّاس المرسيّ رضي الله عنه في شأن ابن عطاء الله الفقيه جدّ الشيخ تاج الدين إنّ النبيّ صلّى الله عليه وسلّم يوم ثقيف جاءه ملك الجبال. فقال له ما شئت إن شئت أن أطبق عليهم الأخشبين؟ فقال صلّى الله عليه وسلّم بل أرجو أن يخرج الله من أصلابهم من يعبد الله ولا يشرك به شيئاً. قال فكذلك صبرنا لجدّ هذا الفقيه لأجل هذا الفقيه يعني تاج الدين. إلى غير هذا ممّا يكثر.

٨،٨ فما وقع من الحكاية بعد أن يكون قصد به اقتباس وضرب من المناسبة يكون كلّ شيء ممّا مرّ وإلّا فهو استطراد للعلم وتذكير بفائدة. وقد يقال على أنّه ممّا مرّ فأين منزلتك؟ أي هذا المتشبّع بما لم يعط من درجات الشيخين المذكورين ونحوهما حتّى

a prophet does so as a measure of his righteousness, and that he has acquired a portion of prophecy. The vision thus partakes of prophecy, yet because it is such a small part of it, there is no resemblance between the two.

The shaykh Abū Yazīd, God be pleased with him, said, "What the prophets were given is like a skin filled with water or honey. What all of the saints were given together is like drops dripping from this skin." Consider this simile: The drops are part of the essence that is in the skin, yet they represent only a very small amount and therefore bear no resemblance to it. The people of religion—the scholars who work, exert themselves, engage in spiritual practices, and have attained spiritual insights and knowledge—base their words, acts, and states on those of the prophets in general and the state of our Prophet in particular, God bless him and keep him. This is the entirety of the matter. 8.5

People may experience more than this in the way of acquisition, instruction, and assimilation of the attributes of prophets. As the shaykh Abū Madyan, God be pleased with him, said to Abū ʿImrān Mūsā ibn Idrāsan al-Ḥallāj when he came to him, "The West is safe, for you are Moses and I am Shuʿayb, and when Moses reached Shuʿayb he was safe."[85] This is also reflected in what happened to Shuʿayb, God be content with him, in the Qurʾan, and when one of those who denied Abū Madyan's message entered unto him when the text of the Qurʾan was in front of him, he said to the man, "Pick up the book, open it, and look at the first page," and in it was: «Those who cried lies to Shuʿayb, they were the losers.»[86] This is similar to Abū Madyan, God be pleased with him, saying, "The disciple will never become a disciple until he finds all that he desires in the Qurʾan." 8.6

Abū l-ʿAbbās al-Mursī, God be pleased with him, said regarding the jurist Ibn ʿAṭāʾ Allāh, ancestor of Tāj al-Dīn, "The angel of the mountains came to the Prophet, God bless and keep him, on the day of Thaqīf, and said to him, 'What do you wish? Shall I cast the two peaks of al-Akhshabayn upon them?' He, God bless and keep him, said, 'I implore you rather that God bring from their loins worshippers of God who associate none with Him.'"[87] Abū ʿAbbās said, "Thus we have put up with this jurist because of his descendant," that is, Tāj al-Dīn. There are many more examples of this. 8.7

All of the above has been told as instruction or analogy. When not the case, it was a digression to edify and to serve as a beneficial reminder. It may be asked regarding what has preceded: How does your ranking compare in this? That is, as one who is satisifsied with less than the gifts of these two 8.8

يصحّ منك ما صحّ منهم؟ فنقول إذا انفصلنا من جانب النبوءة بخير فقد خرجنا عن مضيق الممتنع إلى فضاء الجائز وهو رحب ومن تشبّه بقوم فهو منهم. كما قيل: [خفيف]

لَمْ أَكُنْ لِلْوِصَالِ أَهْلاً وَلٰكِنْ   أَنْتُمُ بِٱلْوِصَالِ أَطْعَمْتُمُونِي

لله الأمر من قبل ومن بعد.

١،٩ كان الشيخ الصالح أبو محمّد الحسين بن أبي بكر رحمه الله ينشدنا كثيرًا تحريضاً على جميل الصبر وتعريفاً بتقلّبات الدهر ونحن إذ ذاك صبيان. قول الشاعر: [طويل]

ثَمَانِيَةٌ تَجْرِي عَلَى ٱلنَّاسِ كُلِّهِمْ   وَلَا بُدَّ لِلْإِنْسَانِ يَلْقَى ٱلثَّمَانِيَةْ
سُرُورٌ وَحُزْنٌ وَاجْتِمَاعٌ وَفُرْقَةٌ   وَيُسْرٌ وَعُسْرٌ ثُمَّ سُقْمٌ وَعَافِيَةْ

٢،٩ ونحو قول أبي الطيب: [طويل]

عَلَى ذَا مَضَى ٱلنَّاسُ اجْتِمَاعٍ وَفُرْقَةٍ   وَمَيْتٍ وَمَوْلُودٍ وَقَالٍ وَوَامِقِ[1]

٣،٩ فهذه أحوال تعرض لابن آدم على التوارد لا يسلم منها في الجملة ولا تنحصر لبقاء العزّ والذلّ والقوّة والضعف والحركة والسكون وغير ذلك ممّا لا يُحصَى. وكثير منها يصلح ردّه إلى ما ذُكِرَ بضرب من التأويل. ولو اشتغلنا بتفصيل ذلك وشرحه لغةً واصطلاحاً لطال واحتاج إلى ديوان وحده أو أكثر فلنقتصر على الإجمال مع الإلمام.

٤،٩ فالأوّل وهو السرور والحزن فنقول هما مترتّبان على المحابّ والمكاره ومن المحبوب فوات المكروه ومن المكروه فوات المحبوب والإنسان لا يخلو من أن يظفر بمحبوب

١ ق: وافق.

aforementioned shaykhs and their like, how can what is true for them be true for you? To this we say, "If we leave aside the rank of prophecy, as we should, then we can escape the straits of what is inaccessible and attain the space of the permissible, which is wide open." "Whoever resembles a people is one of them."[88] As has been said:

I did not merit being reunited
but you sustained me by reuniting with me.

Everything is God's to command.

The devout shaykh Abū Muḥammad al-Ḥusayn ibn Abī Bakr, God show him mercy, often used to recite poetry to us when we were boys, stressing to us the beauty of fortitude, and teaching us about the vicissitudes of time. Regarding this, a poet has said:[89] 9.1

All mankind experiences eight things
with which every person inevitably must meet.
Happiness and sadness, union and separation,
hardship and ease, and finally, sickness and health.

Al-Mutanabbī expressed a similar sentiment: 9.2

This is the way people experience union and separation:
death and birth, hatred and love.

These are the states the sons of Adam continually experience and from which they are never completely safe. They are not confined to the states of either glory or baseness, strength or weakness, movement or stillness—and innumerable other pairings. Many of these should be explained further in some fashion in light of what has been related. Yet, if we concerned ourselves with presenting the matter in detail and with explaining it all in discursive language and expression, it would take too long and require at least a volume to itself. With this understanding, let us restrict ourselves to a general discusson of the matter. 9.3

Regarding the first pair, happiness and sadness, we say that they stem from love and hate. From what we love comes our ability to transcend what we hate, and from what we hate comes our ability to transcend what we love. No one 9.4

فيسرّ به أو يفوت فيحزن. وفي الحديث عن عائشة رضي الله عنها قالت كان صلّى الله عليه وسلّم يوماً في البيت يعمل عملاً فنظرت إلى وجهه صلّى الله عليه وسلّم وهو يتهلّل. أو كما قالت فقلت يا رسول الله أنت والله أحقّ بقول أبي كبير. تعني الهذليّ:

[كامل]

وَمُبَرَّأً مِنْ كُلِّ غُبَّرِ حَيْضَةٍ وَفَسَادِ مُرْضِعَةٍ وَدَاءٍ مُغِيلِ
وَإِذَا نَظَرْتَ إِلَى أَسِرَّةِ وَجْهِهِ بَرَقَتْ كَبَرْقِ ٱلْعَارِضِ ٱلْمُتَهَلِّلِ

قالت فطرح ما في يده وأخذني وقبّل ما بين عينيّ وقال صلّى الله عليه وسلّم يا عائشة ما سررت بشيء كسروري بك. وقد ذكر القصّة في الإحياء. وقال صلّى الله عليه وسلّم يوم فتح خيبر وقد قدم عليه جعفر ابن أبي طالب رضي الله عنه فعانقه لا أدري بمَ أُسَرّ أبفتح خيبر أم بقدوم جعفر. وقال صلّى الله عليه وسلّم يوم مات ابنه إبراهيم: العين تدمع والقلب يحزن ولا نقول إلّا ما يرضي ربّنا. وإنّا بفراقك يا إبراهيم لمحزونون.

ثمّ الإنسان في أيّام دهره لا يكاد يخلو من سوء فإنّ الدنيا دار بلاء ومحنة. ولا سيّما في حقّ المؤمن الذي هي في حقّه سجن. فقد قال الله تعالى ﴿وَلَنَبْلُوَنَّكُمْ حَتَّىٰ نَعْلَمَ ٱلْمُجَاهِدِينَ مِنكُمْ وَٱلصَّابِرِينَ﴾. وقال الله تعالى ﴿الٓمٓ أَحَسِبَ ٱلنَّاسُ أَن يُتْرَكُوٓا أَن يَقُولُوٓا آمَنَّا وَهُمْ لَا يُفْتَنُونَ وَلَقَدْ فَتَنَّا ٱلَّذِينَ مِن قَبْلِهِمْ فَلَيَعْلَمَنَّ ٱللَّهُ ٱلَّذِينَ صَدَقُوا وَلَيَعْلَمَنَّ ٱلْكَاذِبِينَ﴾. وقال تعالى ﴿وَلَنَبْلُوَنَّكُم بِشَيْءٍ مِّنَ ٱلْخَوْفِ وَٱلْجُوعِ وَنَقْصٍ مِّنَ ٱلْأَمْوَالِ وَٱلْأَنفُسِ وَٱلثَّمَرَاتِ﴾. وقال تعالى ﴿لَتُبْلَوُنَّ فِيٓ أَمْوَالِكُمْ وَأَنفُسِكُمْ وَلَتَسْمَعُنَّ مِنَ ٱلَّذِينَ أُوتُوا ٱلْكِتَابَ مِن قَبْلِكُمْ وَمِنَ ٱلَّذِينَ أَشْرَكُوٓا أَذًى كَثِيرًا﴾ إلى غير ذلك. ٩،٥

وقال صلّى الله عليه وسلّم أشدّكم بلاء الأنبياء ثمّ الأمثل فالأمثل. وقال الشيخ أبو القاسم الجُنَيد رضي الله عنه أصلت لنفسي أصلاً فلا أبالي بعده وهو أنّي قدّرت ٩،٦

attains what he desires and remains unhappy, or fails to do so and is not saddened. ʿĀʾishah, God be pleased with her, related a hadith: "The Prophet, God bless and keep him, was working one day in the house, and I glanced at his face, God bless and keep him, and he was visibly happy." In another version, she recounted: "I said, 'Prophet of God, by God, you are the most deserving of the words of Abū Kabīr,'" referring to al-Hudhalī's lines:[90]

He is free of traces of menstrual blood, the filth of the wet nurse,
or the sickness of the nursing pregnant mother.
And when you look at the features of his face,
they light up like the lightening of a passing cloud.

She said, "He set down what was in his hands and took me in his arms, kissing me on the forehead, and said, God bless and keep him, "ʿĀʾishah, I have never been happy with anyone the way I am with you.'" This story is found in *The Revival*.[91] He also said, God bless and keep him, on the day of the victory at Khaybar when Jaʿfar ibn Abī Ṭālib, God be pleased with him, approached him and embraced him: "I don't know what makes me happier, the victory at Khaybar, or the arrival of Jaʿfar." And he said, God bless and keep him, on the day that his son Abraham died, "The eye weeps, the heart grieves, and we say only what pleases our Lord. O Abraham, I grieve at your departure."

It is almost impossible for a person not to encounter difficulty during his 9.5
life, for this world is a place of trials and tribulations. This is especially so for the believer, for whom it is a veritable prison. Regarding this, Exalted God has said in the Qurʾan: «And We shall assuredly try you until We know those of you who struggle and are steadfast.»[92] «Alif. Lām. Mīm. Do the people reckon that they will be left to say, "We believe," and will not be tested? We certainly tried those who came before them, and assuredly God knows those who speak truly, just as He knows the liars.»[93] «Surely We will try you with something of fear and hunger, and diminution of goods and lives and fruits.»[94] «You shall surely be tried in your possessions and your selves, and you shall hear much that is hurtful from those who were given the Book before you, and from those who are idolaters.»[95]

The Prophet, God bless and keep him, said, "Prophets will face the greatest 9.6
trials, and yet be the most exemplary." Shaykh Abū Qāsim al-Junayd, God be pleased with him, said, "I determined to live in such a way that nothing could bother me, having determined that this world was evil in its entirety; I had

أنّ هذا العالم كلّه شرّ ولا يلقاني منه إلّا الشرّ فإن لقيني الخير فنعمة مستفادة وإلّا فالأصل هو الأوّل.

٩،٧ ومن غريب ما اتّفق في هذا المعنى أنّ بعض الملوك نظر في كتاب الحكمة فإذا فيه إنّ الدهر لا يخلو من المصائب وإنّه لا يصفو فيه يوم من كدر. فقال لأكذّبنّ هذا. وأعدّ ليلة لسروره وأحضر فيها كلّ ما يحتاج. وكانت عنده جارية حظيّة هي مجمع لذّته ومنتهى أنسه. فأحضرها لذلك وأمر أن تُصرَف عنه الصوارف وتُقطع عنه الأشغال ليتفرّغ لمتعته وأنسه ويقضي الأرب كلّه من هوى نفسه. فحين أمسى كان أوّل ما قرّب للجارية العنب فأخذت حبّة وجعلتها في فيها فغصّت بها. وكان ذلك آخر العهد بها. فلم يرَ الملك أمرّ من تلك الليلة ولا مصيبة ولا همًّا ولا حزنًا أفظع ممّا فيها فسبحان القاهر فوق عباده الغالب على أمره ﴿وَلَٰكِنَّ أَكْثَرَ ٱلنَّاسِ لَا يَعْلَمُونَ﴾.

٨،٩ هذا ومتى تأمّل العبد أحواله واستقرأ عوارضه وجد لطف الله تعالى أغلب ونعمته عليه أوسع. قال تعالى ﴿ٱللَّهُ لَطِيفٌۢ بِعِبَادِهِۦ﴾. وقال تعالى ﴿وَإِن تَعُدُّوا۟ نِعْمَتَ ٱللَّهِ لَا تُحْصُوهَآ﴾. وفي الخبر يقول الله تعالى إنّ رحمتي سبقت غضبي. ولا يشكّ العاقل أنّ أيّام البلاء أقلّ من أيّام العافية وأوقات العسر أقلّ من أوقات اليسر وهكذا. وقد قال الله تعالى في قصّة آل فرعون ﴿فَإِذَا جَآءَتْهُمُ ٱلْحَسَنَةُ قَالُوا۟ لَنَا هَٰذِهِۦ﴾ الآية.

٩،٩ ثمّ لا يخلو وقت من لطف. ولذا قال أئمّة التصوّف رضوان الله عليهم العارف من عرف شدائد الزمان في الألطاف الجارية.[١] ثمّ المؤمن كما في الحديث كلّه بخير إن أصابه الخير شكر الله تعالى فكان له خيرًا. وإن أصابه شرّ صبر فكان خيرًا له. وقال بعض العارفين الناس كلّهم في مقام الشكر وهم يحسبون أنّهم في مقام الصبر. وبيان هذا من أوجه.

١٠،٩ الأوّل أنّ موجب الشكر وهو النعمة أغلب والحكم للأغلب. الثاني أنّه ما من شرّ وبلاء يصيب العبد إلّا وفي مقدور الله تعالى من البلاء ما هو أفظع منه قد صرفه

١ ق: الخارجية.

never experienced anything in it but evil. When I am met with good it is a beneficial blessing, but the norm is evil."

Among the wondrous things related to this was the king who looked into a book of wise sayings and found written there: "Time is never free from disasters, nor is there ever a day without trouble." "I will prove this wrong," he said. He prepared himself for a night of happiness and had everything that he needed brought to him. He had a slave—a concubine who was the source of all his pleasure and desires—and had her brought and ordered that all distractions be kept from him: to be rid of worry and to be free to enjoy his delights and relaxation, to achieve every desire. That evening, before anything else happened, the slave was given some grapes. She took one, placed it in her mouth, and choked on it. And that was the end of her. The king never experienced a night more bitter than that one, nor a calamity, trouble, or sorrow more terrible than what that night brought. Praise be to the One who is victorious over his worshippers, and who controls every matter. «But most men have no understanding.»[96] 9.7

When the worshipper contemplates his affairs, and ponders all the difficulties he faces, he finds that the kindness of Exalted God and His blessing upon him is greater than these trials. Exalted God said: «God is Gentle with His servants,»[97] and «If you count God's blessings, you will never number them.»[98] There is also the following hadith: "Exalted God said: 'Truly, my mercy has precedence over my anger.'" A reasonable person never doubts that days of tribulation are fewer than those of good health, and that hard times are fewer than easy ones, and so on. Exalted God has said regarding the family of Pharaoh: «So, when good came to them, they said, "This belongs to us"»[99] . . . to the end of the verse. 9.8

What is more, no moment exists without kindness; because of this the foremost Sufis, God be pleased with them, have said, "The one who possesses mystical knowledge keeps in mind the vicissitudes of time when circumstances are good."[100] For the believer, as it is related in the Hadith, all is good. If he encounters goodness, he thanks God and it is good for him. If he encounters evil, he endures it and it is good for him. One of those who had attained mystical knowledge said, "All people stand at the station of thanks while believing that they are at the station of fortitude." There is several ways to interpret this. 9.9

The first is that the obligation to give thanks, which is God's grace, is stronger and one should judge according to what is preferable. The second is that no 9.10

الله تعالى. فيجب الشكر على الاقتصار على ما وقع. الثالث ما يفيده البلاء من رياضة النفس وتشجيعها للنوائب وإخماد سَوْرَتِها والنجاة من طغيانها وما يجرّ إليه من البلاء دينًا ودنيا وتربية العقل بتعريفه تقلّبات الدهر وفتح البصيرة في الأمور. وهذه الأوجه عامّة في المؤمن وغيره. الرابع ما يحصل بالبلاء في الدنيا من مزيد المعرفة بالله تعالى وقهره وقوّته وبطشه وفي الآخرة من الأجر العظيم. الخامس ما يحصل للنفس من الخشوع لخالقها والانفكاك عن المعصية. السادس سلامة ثوابه من شوب الرياء وما يفسده إذ لاحظ للنفس فيه فهو خير قد دخل عليها بلا تعمُّل فالشكر عليه أحقّ. إلى غير ذلك من الفوائد التي يطول تعدادها فمن علم ذلك كان البلاء عنده محلّ الشكر فصار في مقام الشكر على كلّ حال. لله الأمر من قبل ومن بعد.

١،١٠ كان بسجلماسة أيّام ارتحلنا إليها للقراءة زمان الصبا شجرة يقال لها الشجرة الخضراء مشهورة في تلك البلاد وفي سائر بلاد القبلة. وهي قدر الزيتونة أو السدرة الكبيرة وورقها يقرب من ورق السدر. وسبب شهرتها أنّها غريبة الشكل دائمة الخضرة وغريبة في محلّها لأنّها في البلد وليست من شجر البلد. وهي منفردة ليس معها شجر أصلًا. وكانت نابتة خارج سور المدينة الخالية بينه وبين النهر قبالة الرصيف الذي يعبر عليه لناحية الزلاميط. ويقال إنّ ذلك باب من أبواب تلك المدينة والله أعلم.

٢،١٠ ثمّ إنّ الأستاذ الفاضل أبا يزيد عبد الرحمن بن يوسف الشريف بعث إليها جماعة من الطلبة فقطعوها. وكان ذلك يوم الخميس وكنت جئت من ناحية المراكنة ذلك اليوم قصدًا إلى سوق الخميس. فلمّا بلغت إلى الشجرة وجدت الطلبة حين بلغوا إليها بقصد قطعها فقعدت حولها أنظر. فلمّا انفصل أهل السافلة من السوق

trial or evil befalls the worshipper but that it lies in God's power to makes things worse and yet He prevents this. Therefore, gratitude is the requisite response to everything that happens. The third interpretation is that what tries and tests us is beneficial, as it trains and encourages the spirit to cope with calamities, to cushion their force, and provides comfort against their onslaught, and against the religious and worldly trials that occur. Trials educate the mind by familiarizing it with the vicissitudes of time and granting insight into the way of things. These, in general, are ways for the believer and others to understand the issue. The fourth is that trials of this world provide more knowledge of Exalted God, of His force, power, and strength, and this leads to a great reward in the next world. The fifth is the fear and awe the spirit feels before its Creator, which cause it to refrain from sinning. The sixth is the preservation of the believer's reward in the next world from being tarnished by hypocrisy and other corrupting factors that are observed in the soul. It is a good that benefits the spirit without exertion, and is therefore most deserving of thanks. There are other benefits that would take too long to enumerate. The one who knows all this will be grateful for trials and will remain in the station of thanks through all the other states that he reaches. Everything is God's to command.

In the days of our youth, we used to travel to Sijilmāsah to study. There was a tree there known as the green tree. It was famous in the area as well as the surrounding regions in the south. It was the size of a lemon tree or a large lotus tree, with leaves like those of the lotus tree. It was famous on account of its strange appearance: It always remained green. And its presence was peculiar as it was not indigenous to the region. It was alone, with no other tree near it. It grew outside the outermost wall, between it and the river, across from the wooden bridge that you cross to go to al-Zalāmīṭ (it is said that this is one of the gates of this city; God knows best). 10.1

One day, the distinguished teacher Abū Yazīd ʿAbd al-Raḥmān ibn Yūsuf al-Sharīf sent a group of students to cut it down. This was on a Thursday. That day I had come from the area of al-Marākanah in order to attend the Thursday market. When I reached the tree, I saw that the students had gotten there before me, and were intent on cutting it down. I sat nearby to watch. When the common folk had left the market to head home, everyone who passed by and saw that tree had been cut down cried out in lamentation, "What did the 10.2

وكانت طريقتهم كان كلّ من يمرّ فيراها تقطع يصيح ويتأسّف ويقول ما فعلت لكم المسكينة؟ وكان أهل سجلماسة لمّا استغربوا أمرها يزورونها ولا سيّما النساء فيكثرون عليها من تعليق الخيوط ويطرحون الفلوس أسفلها. وربّما تغالت النساء في تعظيمها والتنويه بشأنها حتّى يسمّينها باسم امرأة صالحة كالسيّدة فاطمة ونحو ذلك. فلهذا أمر الأستاذ المذكور بقطعها وكأنّه يرى أنّها صارت ذات أنواط كما قال الشيخ أبو العبّاس المرسيّ رضي الله عنه.

٣،١٠ فذكرناها نحن للتنبيه على ذلك. فإنّ عوام الناس أكثروا عليها منذ عقلنا حتّى كانوا ينسبون إليها من ترّهات الأراجف نحو قولهم قالت الشجرة الخضراء هذا زمان السكوت من قال الحقّ يموت. فليعلم الناظر أنّها إنّما هي شجرة لا تضرّ ولا تنفع ولا تبصر ولا تسمع ومثلها أحقّ أن يقطع. ومن هذا نسيت شجرة بيعة[1] الرضوان حتّى لم يثبت عليها الصحابة الذين كانوا تحتها فضلاً عن غيرهم وذلك مخافة أن تعبد.

٤،١٠ وسمعت الفاضل الناسك البكري بن أحمد بن أبي القاسم بن مولود الجاوزيّ رحمه الله يحدّث عن أسلافه أنّ شيخ المشايخ أبا القاسم الغازيّ رضي الله عنه ونفعنا به كان يقول لهم إنّه نزلت عليه القطبانية تحت شجرة ببلد أجاوز. فيقولون له يا سيّدنا لِمَ لَمْ ترنا تلك الشجرة؟ فيقول خفت أن تتركوا السبع وتعبدوا النغورة أي مغارته أي يتركونه فلا ينتفعون به ويشتغلون بالشجرة. وكانت بقرب تاغية مقام الشيخ أبي يعزّى شجرة أخرى من هذا المعنى وكدس من أحجار يقال له البقرة. وكلّ ذلك حقيق بالإزالة غير أنّ العالِم سيفُه لسانه وما وراء ذلك إنّما هو لأهل الأمر ومن له قدرة على الأمر.

٥،١٠ نعم التبرّك بآثار الصالحين مع صحّة العقيدة لا بأس به وله أصل في فعل الصحابة رضوان الله عليهم فقد كان ابن عمر رضي الله عنهما يدير راحلته حيث رأى النبيّ

١ سقط من ط، ق.

poor thing ever do to you?" The people of Sijilmāsah, especially the women, had previously visited the tree on occasions when the city was in trouble. The women often tied strings to it or threw copper coins at its foot. It may be that they were excessive in praising the tree and commending it to the point of calling it Lady Fāṭimah, or another name of some devout woman. This is why the teacher mentioned above ordered that it be cut down—it was as if he thought it had become like the *dhāt al-anwāṭ* tree,[101] as surmised Shaykh Abū l-ʿAbbās al-Mursī, God be pleased with him.

We draw attention to it here, since from as far back as we can remember commoners attributed much to that tree, even falsehoods and lies, such as the claim that it had said, "This is the time of silence; whoever speaks the truth will die." Whoever looks into this should know that it was just a tree—it neither caused harm nor granted benefit, it could neither see nor hear—but the likes of it have to be cut down. The tree where the oath of assent was given was cut down and forgotten, to the point where it could no longer be established which of the Companions had stood beneath it and which had not.[102] This was done for fear that it would be worshipped. 10.3

I heard the distinguished ascetic al-Bakrī ibn Aḥmad ibn Abī l-Qāsim ibn Mawlūd al-Jāwzī, God show him mercy, talking about his ancestors, and how the great shaykh Abū l-Qāsim al-Ghāzī, God be pleased with him, used to say to them that his status as Axis of the age was bestowed upon him while sitting under a tree in the region of Ajāwaz. He was asked, "Lord, why do you not show us this tree?" and answered, "For fear that you neglect the seven verses of the opening chapter of the Qur'an and worship the *naghūrah*," referring to his cave. By this he meant that he feared they would abandon him and the benefit of his presence, and devote themselves to the tree instead. At Tāghiyā there was a similar tree like this near the tomb of the shaykh Abū Yiʿzzā, and heaped stones, which people called The Cow.[103] Such practices should be done away with. The scholar's sword is his tongue: It is, rather, for those in power, or who have authority, to deal with what lies beyond the reach of words alone.[104] 10.4

It is true that there is no harm in finding blessings in the relics of figures, as long as one does so with proper faith. This practice has a basis in the acts of the Companions, God be pleased with them. Ibn ʿUmar, God be pleased with him, used to guide his female camel to the same place as did the Prophet, God bless and keep him, and inquired about the places where the Prophet, God bless and 10.5

صلّى الله عليه وسلّم أدارها ويتحرّى الأماكن التي صلّى فيها صلّى الله عليه وسلّم. وذلك مذكور في الصحيح. وفيه قيل: [طويل]

خَلِيلَيَّ هٰذَا رَبْعُ عَزَّةَ فَاعْقِلَا   قَلُوصَيْكُمَا ثُمَّ ٱبْكِيَا حَيْثُ حَلَّتْ
وَلَا تَيْأَسَا أَنْ يَمْحُوَ اللهُ عَنْكُمَا   ذُنُوبًا إِذَا صَلَّيْتُمَا حَيْثُ صَلَّتْ

٦،١٠ ورأيت في بلاد المصامدة وخصوصاً بلاد رجراجة من هذا كثيراً بقي عندهم موروثاً خلفاً عن سلف. عندما يدورون على صلحائهم زائرين ولمّا حضرت معهم في الدور في هذه السفرة التي بدأت فيها هذه الأوراق وذلك سنة خمس وتسعين وألف لم أوافقهم في فعل كثير ممّا يفعلون من ذلك مخافة أن يتّخذني العوام حجّة فيتغالون في ذلك. ومع ذلك لم أخل نفسي من التبرّك بأمور قريبة لا بأس فيها.

٧،١٠ وفي بلاد المغرب مواضع اشتهرت بآثار الصالحين ووقع التغالي فيها. منها شالة في رباط سلا فلا يعرف لها إلّا أنّها مزارة يزورها الناس ويتبرّكون بمن فيها. ولم يظهر فيها بهذا العهد إلّا يحيى بن يونس وهو مشهور عند الناس ولا تعرف له ترجمة وملوك بني عبد الحقّ وهم معروفون ولا بأس بهم. وكلّ ما يذكر فيها ممّا سوى ذلك ويوجد في بعض الأوراق المجعولة من الأخبار فلا يعرف له أصل ولا يعوّل عليه. ومنها ميسرة في بلاد ملوية حيث مدفن الشيخ أبي الطيّب بن يحيى الميسوريّ ويقال لها تامغروات قد اشتهرت عند الناس. وتوجد فيها أخبار وأحاديث في الأوراق وألسنة الناس.

٨،١٠ وسألت عن ذلك بعض أولاد الشيخ المذكور وهو الفاضل أبو عبد الله محمّد بن أبي طاهر عند نزولنا عليه. فقال ما ثبت عندنا في هذا الموضع إلّا أنّه كان رابطة لأسلافنا يتعبّدون فيه. فقلت له نعم الوصف هذا فإنّ متعبّد الصالحين حقيق أن يتبرك به فهذا أيضاً غاية ما يثبت في هذا الموضع وما وراء ذلك لا يلتفت إليه.

٩،١٠ ومنها رباط شاكر وهو مشهور وكان مجمعاً للصالحين من قديم ولا سيّما في رمضان يفدون إليه من كلّ أوب. حتّى حكى صاحب التشوّف عن منية الدكاليّة

keep him, prayed. This is mentioned in the *Sound Collection*.[105] On this topic it has also been said:[106]

> My two friends, this is the land of ʿAzzah,
> so hobble your young female camels and weep where they settle.
> Do not despair that God will wipe
> away your sins if you pray where she prayed.

In the lands of the Maṣmūdah, specifically of the Rijrājah, I saw a great deal of this sort of inherited practice. Aping their ancestors, when they visited the graves of their holy figures, they circumambulated them. When I stayed among them on the trip during which I began to write these pages—in the year 1095 [1683–84]—I disagreed with much of what they were doing in this regard, but I kept quiet, lest the common folk follow my example and then commit excesses. Because of this, I have abstained from seeking blessings from harmless things that are readily at hand. 10.6

In Morocco, there are places that have become famous on account of stories about holy men and their excessive practices in those places. One such place is the Chellah in Rabat-Salé, known for the vistors who seek the blessings of those buried there. In our day, it is known only for Yaḥyā ibn Yūnus, famous among the people though his biography is unknown, and for the kings of the Banū ʿAbd al-Ḥaqq, who are well-known and unobjectionable. Everything else said about the Chellah, as reported in written anecdotes, has no basis in fact and is not reliable. Another such place is Maysarah in the area of the Moulouyah River, where the shaykh Abū l-Ṭayyib ibn Yaḥyā al-Maysūrī is buried. The place is known as Tāmaghrawāt and is famous. People tell anecdotes and stories about it and have written about it too. 10.7

I asked a son of the abovementioned teacher—namely, the distinguished Abū ʿAbd Allāh Muḥammad ibn Abī Ṭāhir—about this when we stayed with him, and he said, "As far as we're concerned, the only thing we can say for sure about this place is that our ancestors used it as a spiritual retreat and worshipped there." "An elegant characterization," I responded. A place where devout worship is worthy of having blessings sought from it. This is the extent of what has been proven regarding this place. One should not be concerned with anything beyond that. 10.8

Ribāṭ Shākir is also famous: It has been a gathering place of the devout for years, especially during Ramadan, when they congregate there.[107] The author 10.9

رضي الله عنها أنها حضرت ذات مرة في رباط شاكر فقالت لبعض من معها إنه حضر هذا العام في هذا الرباط ألف امرأة من الأولياء. فانظر إلى عدد النساء فكيف بالرجال! فلا شكّ أنّ هذا الموضع موضع بركة ومجمع خير. ولكن لم نقف من أمره إلّا على ما وقع في التشوّف من أنّ شاكرًا ذكر أنه من أصحاب عقبة بن نافع الفهريّ وأنّه هنالك. وأنّ يعلى بن مصلين الرجراجيّ بناه. وكان يقاتل كفّار برغواطة وغزاهم مرّات وأنّ طبله هو الباقي هنالك إلى الآن والله أعلم. ولم يظهر فيه في العهد من مشاهد الصالحين إلّا أبو زكرياء المليجيّ والله أعلم. لله الأمر من قبل ومن بعد.

١٠١١ ممّا وقع بسجلماسة قريبًا من هذه القصّة أنّه شاع في البلد ذات ليلة أنّه قد ظهر رجل في المدينة الخالية. فأصبح الناس يهرولون إليه أفواجًا. وخرجنا مع الناس فقائل يقول وليّ من أولياء الله. وآخر يقول صاحب الوقت. فلمّا بلغنا المدينة وجدنا الخلق قد اجتمعوا من كلّ ناحية على ذلك الرجل حتّى أنّ أمير البلد وهو محمّد بن الشريف خرج في موكب حتّى رآه. فلمّا كثر الناس اشتدّ الزحام عليه وتعذّرت رؤيته دخل في قبّة هناك في المقابر فأخرج كفّه من طاق في القبّة فجعل الناس يقبّلون الكفّ وينصرفون. وكان كلّ من قبّل الكفّ اكتفى ورأى أنه قضى الحاجة فقبّلناه وانصرفنا. ثمّ بعد أيّام سمعنا أنه ذهب إلى ناحية الغرفة وأنّه سقط في بئر هنالك ومات. فظهر أنّه رجل مصاب وكأنّه يشتغل باستخدام الجانّ ونحو ذلك فهلك. وإنّما ذكرنا هذا ليعلم وينتبه لمن هذا حاله فكم تظاهر بالخير من لا خير فيه من مجنون أو معتوه أو موسوس أو ملبس. فيقع به الاغترار للجهلة الأغمار. [بسيط]

مَا أَنْتَ سَارٍ غَرَّهُ قَمَرٌ وَرَائِدٍ أَعْجَبَهُ[١] خُضْرَةُ ٱلدِّمَنِ

١ ق: خدعته.

of *Contemplating the Sufis* has even recounted that Munyat al-Dukkāliyyah, God be pleased with her, was once in Ribāṭ Shākir and said to her companion, "This year a thousand female saints are present at this *ribāṭ*." If there were this many women, how many men must there have been! There is no doubt that this a site of grace and a place of goodness. Yet all we know about it is from *Contemplating the Sufis*—namely, that Shākir stated he was one of the companions of ʿUqbah ibn Nāfiʿ al-Fihrī, the location of the *ribāṭ*, and that it was built by Yaʿlā ibn Mṣlīn al-Rijrājī. We have also learned that he fought the unbelievers of the Barghawāṭah, raided them many times, and that his drum remains there until now. God knows best. In our age, none of the devout have been seen there except Abū Zakariyyāʾ al-Malījī, but God knows best. Everything is God's to command.

A similar story is told about Sijilmāsah, that one night word spread around town that a man had appeared on the outskirts of the city. People rushed to him in large numbers, myself included. One person said, "He is one of the saints of God!" Another said, "He is the savior!"[108] When I reached the city I found this man surrounded by a crowd of people from all parts. Even Maḥammad ibn al-Sharīf, the ruler of the region, came out with a retinue. As the crowd grew, the throng pressed in, and it became impossible to see him. He entered one of the domed shrines in the graveyard and stretched his hand out of one of the windows of the dome. The people kissed the hand and left. Everyone who kissed the man was content and believed he had achieved his goal. I too kissed it and then left. A few days later, we heard that he had gone to the region of al-Ghurfah, and that he had fallen into a well and died. It emerged that he was insane and that he may have colluded with jinn and other beings and perished as a result. We relate this so that people might know and take heed of such people. Many appear to be good, yet have no good in them, and are either possessed, crackbrained, delusional, or confused. In cases like these, gullible and ignorant people are deceived. 11.1

You are not the first night traveler deceived by the moon,
nor the first visitor who has found pleasure in the green of manure.[109]

وقد يشايعه من هو على شاكلته من الحمق ومن الفجّار وشبه الشيء منجذب إليه. إنّ الطيور على أجناسها تقع. فيغترّ الأغبياء بذلك إلّا من عصمه الله.

٢،١١ وقد صعدت في أعوام الستين وألف إلى جبل من جبال هسكورة فإذا برجل نزل عليهم من ناحية الغرب واشتهر بالفقر. وبنى خباء له وأقبل الناس عليه بالهدايا والضيافات. وكان من أهل البلد فتى يختلف إليه ويبيت عنده. فاستراب من أمره بعض الطلبة فتلطّف مساء ليلة حتّى ولج الخباء فكمن في زاوية منه فلمّا عسعس الليل قام المرابط إلى الفتى فاشتغل معه بالفاحشة نسأل الله العافية. ثمّ علم أن قد علموا به فهرب وبلغ الخبر إلى أخوة الفتى فتبعوه. ولم أدر ما كان من أمره ومثله كثير.

٣،١١ ومن أغرب ما وقع من هذا أيضاً بسجلماسة ما حدث به أخونا في الله الولي الصالح أبو عبد الله محمّد بن عبد الله بن علي بن طاهر الشريف المعروف بابن علي رضي الله عنه. قال ما لعب بإخواننا يعني أشراف سجلماسة إلّا رجل جاءهم في البلد واتّسم باسم الصلاح ووقع الإقبال عليه. فكان يأتيه الرجل فيعده بأن يبلغه إلى مكة ويحجّ به طرفة عين واستمرّ على ذلك مدّة. ثمّ قام نفر من الأشراف اتّفقوا على اختباره فكمنوا قريباً منه. وتقدّم إليه أحدهم وعنده نحو خمسين مثقالاً فقال له يا سيّدي إنّ هذه الصلاة تثقل عليّ فعسى أن ترفعها عنّي؟ وأفرغ تلك الدراهم بين يديه وكأنّه هشّ لذلك. فبادره الآخرون قبل أن يستوفي كلامه وأوجعوه ضرباً وطردوه. ثمّ بعد مدّة سافر بعضهم إلى الغرب فمرّ بعين ماء هنالك. فإذا الرجل عندها يستقي قربة له منها وإذا هو يهودي من يهود معروفين هنالك نسأل الله العافية.

٤،١١ فالحذر مطلوب ولا سيّما فيما نحن فيه من آخر الزمان الذي استولى فيه الفساد على الصلاح والهوى على الحقّ والبدعة على السنّة إلّ من خصّه الله وقليل ما هم. وفيه قيل: [بسيط]

Such people are likely to be followed by others, insane or profligate like him, because like attracts like, and birds of a feather flock together. The ignorant are deluded by them, except those protected by God.

In the 1060s [1650s] I climbed one of the mountains in the Haskūrah region, and encountered a man famed for his poverty who had come to the area from the west. He had set up a tent and people came to him with gifts and provisions. Among the locals was a young man who visited him frequently and would spend the night with him. One evening, a student who was suspicious of the situation secretly followed the young man right up until he had entered the man's tent, and concealed himself in a corner of the tent. When night fell, the stranger went to the young man and performed an abomination with him—God preserve us! He then realized he had been found out and fled. News reached the young man's brothers, so they followed the stranger: I don't know what happened to him. There are many like him. 11.2

One of the strangest such cases also took place in Sijilmāsah, and was recounted by our brother in God, the devout saint Abū ʿAbd Allāh Muḥammad ibn ʿAbd Allāh ibn ʿAlī ibn Ṭāhir al-Sharīf, better known as Ibn ʿAlī, God be pleased with him. He related as follows: "No one ever deceived our brethren, the Prophet's descendants of Sijilmāsah, except for one man who came to the region. He distinguished himself through a reputation for righteousness, and became renowned. A man came to the pretender, who promised that very moment to convey him to Mecca to carry out the pilgrimage. He carried on with these promises for some time. Then a group of the Prophet's descendants decided to investigate. They concealed themselves nearby, and then one of them approached, carrying close to fifty dirhams, saying, 'My lord, this prayer is hard for me. Perhaps you could remove it from me?' He placed the dirhams before him, and the man seemed to smile at this. The others fell upon him before he was finished speaking, beat him up, and drove him away. After some time, one of them traveled to the west and passed by a well. There the man was, at the well filling his waterskin. It was obvious he was a Jew, one known to people there." God preserve us from the like. 11.3

Caution is therefore essential, especially as we are currently in the end times when corruption dominates over righteousness, vanity over truth, and heretical innovation over proper custom. Only the few God has singled out are exempt from this. It has been said regarding this: 11.4

هٰذَا ٱلزَّمَانُ ٱلَّذِي كُنَّا نُحَاذِرُهُ   قَوْلَ كَعْبٍ وَفِي قَوْلِ ٱبْنِ مَسْعُودِ
إِنْ دَامَ هٰذَا وَلَمْ يَحْدُثْ لَهُ غِيَرٌ   لَمْ يُبْكَ مَيْتٌ وَلَمْ يُفْرَحْ بِمَوْلُودِ

بل نقول ليته يدوم فإنّه لا يأتي زمان إلّا والذي بعده شرّ منه كما في الحديث الكريم. ٥،١١
نعم لا بدّ للناس من تنفيس فنسأل الله تعالى أن يرزقنا تنفيساً نقضي فيه ما بقي من أعمارنا في خير ونستعتب ممّا مضى إنّه الكريم المنّان. هذا ولا بدّ مع الحذر من حسن الظنّ بعباد الله ولا سيّما من ظهر عليه الخير والتغافل عن عيوب الناس.

٦،١١ وفي الخبر خصلتان ليس فوقهما شيء من الخير حسن الظنّ بالله وحسن الظنّ بالناس. وخصلتان ليس فوقهما شيء من الشرّ سوء الظنّ بالله وسوء الظنّ بالناس ومن تتبّع عيوب الناس تتبّع الله عيوبه حتّى يفضحه في قعر بيته. فالاعتراض بلا موجب جناية واتّباع كلّ ناعق غواية.

٧،١١ وفي كلام مولانا عليّ كرّم الله وجهه الناس ثلاثة عالم ربّاني ومتعلّم على سبيل النجاة وهَمَجٌ رَعاعٌ أتباع كلّ ناعق. فمن ثبتت استقامته وصحّ علمه وورعه وجب اتّباعه ومن اتّسم بالخير وجب احترامه على قدره والتسليم له في حاله. ومن ألقى جلباب الحياء عن وجهه وجب لومه. وإذا ظهرت البدعة وسكت العالم فعليه لعنة الله. ولا بدّ من مراعاة السلامة. وهذا باب واسع لا يكفيه إلّا ديوان وحده وإنّما ذكرنا هذه الإشارة استطراداً. لله الأمر من قبل ومن بعد.

١،١٢ من الشعر المستملح في باب التكرّم قول المقنّع الكِنديّ أنشده القالي في النوادر:

[طويل]

This is the age about which we were warned
in the words of Kaʿb and Ibn Masʿūd.
If it continues and is not replaced with another
we will no longer mourn death, nor rejoice in birth.

Yet I hope it continues, as every era is succeeded by a worse one, as stated in a noble hadith of the Prophet. Truly, people require comfort and we ask Exalted God to grant us comfort that we may enjoy for the remainder of our lives. We ask God to look favorably on the past, for He is the Generous Benefactor. On account of all the above we must be careful to think well of the worshippers of God, especially of those in whom good appears, and we must not pay too much attention to people's failings. 11.5

As the account goes: "There are two characteristics better than any other: thinking well of God and thinking well of people. And there are two characteristics that are worse than any other: thinking poorly of God and thinking poorly of people." He who keeps an account of the failings of other people, God will keep an account of his failings, to the point of uncovering the sins he commits in the privacy of his house. It is a sin to raise objections without cause, and it is an error to follow everyone who raises a hue and cry. 11.6

In the words attributed to our leader ʿAlī, God honor his countenance: "There are three kinds of people: mystics, the learned on the path to salvation, and the rabble and the riffraff, who follow anyone who raises a hue and cry."[110] Now, whoever's uprightness is verified—whose knowledge and piety are sound—must be followed. Whoever is characterized by goodness should be respected to the same extent, and one should submit to him because of his qualities. Whoever behaves shamelessly is worthy of shame, and a scholar who remains silent in the face of heresy shall be cursed by God. It is obligatory to foster communal peace. This is a broad subject that could fill a volume of its own—we have only alluded to it in passing. Everything is God's to command. 11.7

Of the poetry considered beautiful on the subject of giving generously are the lines by al-Muqannaʿ al-Kindī, included by al-Qālī in his *Anecdotes*: 12.1

يُعَاتِبُنِي فِي ٱلدَّيْنِ قَوْمِي وَإِنَّمَا   دُيُونِيَ فِي أَشْيَاءَ تُكْسِبُهُمْ حَمْدَا
أَسُدُّ بِهِ مَا قَدْ أَخَلُّوا وَضَيَّعُوا   ثُغُورَ حُقُوقٍ مَا أَطَاقُوا لَهَا سَدَّا
وَفِي جَفْنَةٍ مَا يُغْلَقُ ٱلْبَابُ دُونَهَا   مُكَلَّلَةٍ لَحْمًا مُدَفَّقَةٍ ثَرْدَا
وَفِي فَرَسٍ نَهْدٍ عَتِيقٍ جَعَلْتُهُ   حِجَابًا لِبَيْتِي ثُمَّ أَخْدَمْتُهُ عَبْدَا
وَإِنَّ ٱلَّذِي بَيْنِي وَبَيْنَ أَبِي   وَبَيْنَ بَنِي عَمِّي لَمُخْتَلِفٌ جِدًّا
فَإِنْ يَأْكُلُوا لَحْمِي وَفَرْتُ لُحُومَهُمْ   وَإِنْ يَهْدِمُوا مَجْدِي بَنَيْتُ لَهُمْ مَجْدَا
وَإِنْ ضَيَّعُوا غَيْبِي حَفِظْتُ غُيُوبَهُمْ   وَإِنْ هُمْ هَوَوْا غَيِّي هَوَيْتُ لَهُمْ رُشْدَا
وَلَا أَحْمِلُ ٱلْحِقْدَ ٱلْقَدِيمَ عَلَيْهِمْ   وَلَيْسَ رَئِيسُ ٱلْقَوْمِ مَنْ يَحْمِلُ ٱلْحِقْدَا
لَهُمْ جُلُّ مَالِي إِنْ تَتَابَعَ لِي غِنًى   وَإِنْ قَلَّ مَالِي لَمْ أُكَلِّفْهُمْ رِفْدَا
وَإِنِّي لَعَبْدُ ٱلضَّيْفِ مَا دَامَ نَازِلًا   وَمَا شِيمَةٌ لِي غَيْرُهَا تُشْبِهُ ٱلْعَبْدَا

ونحوه قول عروة بن الورد: [طويل] ٢،١٢

أَيَا بِنْتَ عَبْدِ اللهِ وَٱبْنَةَ مَالِكٍ   وَيَا بِنْتَ ذِي ٱلْبُرْدَيْنِ وَٱلْفَرَسِ ٱلْوَرْدِ
إِذَا مَا صَنَعْتِ ٱلزَّادَ فَٱلْتَمِسِي لَهُ   أَكِيلًا فَإِنِّي لَسْتُ آكِلَهُ وَحْدِي
أَخًا طَارِقًا أَوْ جَارَ بَيْتٍ فَإِنَّنِي   أَخَافُ مَذَمَّاتِ ٱلْأَحَادِيثِ مِنْ بَعْدِي
وَكَيْفَ يَسِيغُ ٱلْمَرْءُ زَادًا وَجَارُهُ   خَفِيفُ ٱلْمِعَى بَادِي ٱلْخَصَاصَةِ وَٱلْجَهْدِ
وَلَلْمَوْتُ خَيْرٌ مِنْ زِيَارَةِ بَاخِلٍ   يُلَاحِظُ أَطْرَافَ ٱلْأَكِيلِ عَلَى عَمْدِ
وَإِنِّي لَعَبْدُ ٱلضَّيْفِ مَا دَامَ ثَاوِيًا   وَمَا فِيَّ إِلَّا تِلْكَ مِنْ شِيمَةِ ٱلْعَبْدِ

My people censure me for my debts,
yet what I owe earns their thanks.
I cover what they've lost, and cannot repay
the gaps in the obligations they cannot meet.
My door is always open, a bowl set out
crowned with meat floating in broth.
With a noble, spirited horse I made a curtain for my house,
and I ordered a slave to serve my guest.
What is between my father and me
and my cousins is very different.
While they eat my meat, I provide them with theirs.
While they destroy my reputation, I shore up theirs.
While they fritter away the fat of my kitchen, I preserve theirs.
While they wish for me to sin, I wish only to guide them.
I bear them no grudge—
one who does so is no leader of his people.
When I am rich, most of my money is theirs.
When I am poor, I do not ask them for support.
I am a servant to my guest as long as he abides with me,
but it is only in this that I am a servant.

Similar are the lines of ʿUrwah ibn al-Ward:[111] **12.2**

Daughter of ʿAbd Allāh,[112] daughter of Mālik,
daughter of the man with two robes and a red horse.
When you prepare, note well that I always share my food—
I do not eat alone—
Destined for a brother on the road, a neighboring house.
I fear what people say about me when I am gone.
How can a man eat when his neighbor
goes hungry, when there is arrant poverty and hardship?
Better to die than to visit a miser
who aims to take from the hands of one who is eating.
I am the servant of the guest as long as he stays,
but I have nothing else in common with a servant.

وقول الآخر: [طويل]

لَعَمْرُ أَبِيكِ ٱلْخَيْرِ إِنِّي لَخَادِمٌ   لِضَيْفِي وَإِنِّي إِنْ رَكِبْتُ لَفَارِسُ

لله الأمـر من قبـل ومن بعـد.

١٫١٣ قـال معاوية رضي الله عنه يوماً لصعصعة بن صوحان وكان من البلغاء صف لي الناس. فقال خلق الناس أخيافاً فطائفة للعبادة وطائفة للتجارة وطائفة خطباء وطائفة للبأس والنجدة ورجرجة فيما بين ذلك يكدرون الماء ويُغلُون السّعر ويضيّقون الطريق.

٢٫١٣ وقال الآخر في نحو هذا: [مجزوء الرمل]

ٱلنَّاسُ هُمْ ثَلَاثَةٌ   فَوَاحِدٌ ذُو دَرَقَه
وَذُو عُلُومٍ دَارِسٌ   كُتُبَهُ وَوَرَقَه
وَمُنْفِقٌ فِي وَاجِبٍ   ذَهَبَه وَوَرِقَه
وَمَنْ سِوَاهُمْ هَمَجٌ   لَا وَدَكٌ لَا مَرَقَه

٣٫١٣ وفي كلام مولانا عليّ كرّم الله وجهه لكميل بن زياد الناس ثلاثة عالم ربّاني ومتعلّم على سبيل النجاة وهمج رعاع أتباع كلّ ناعق.

٤٫١٣ وقال الآخر: [كامل]

مَا ٱلنَّاسُ إِلَّا ٱلْعَارِفُونَ بِرَبِّهِمْ   وَسِوَاهُمُ مُتَطَفِّلٌ فِي ٱلنَّاسِ

٥٫١٣ وهذا المعنى له تفصيل وتحقيق والاشتغال به يطيل ويكفي اللبيب فيه ما مرّ عند ذكر الحسب وتفصيل المزايا في الناس. لله الأمـر من قبـل ومن بعـد.

Another said:[113]

By the life of your father, I am a servant
to my guest, yet when I ride I am a knight.

Everything is God's to command.

One day Muʿāwiyah, God be pleased with him, said to the eloquent Ṣaʿṣaʿh ibn Ṣuḥān, "Describe people for me." "God created humankind in groups," he answered, "one for servitude, one for trade, one to be preachers, one for fighting and valor, and then a motley crowd that fouls the water, raises prices, and makes the roads unsafe." 13.1

Someone else said on this: 13.2

There are three kinds of people:
One possesses a shield.
Another knows the sciences and
studies his books and papers.
A third spends his gold and notes
on what is necessary.
Other than these are foolish men
with no substance to them.

In the speech of our leader ʿAlī, God honor his countenance, to Kumayl ibn Ziyād, we find the following: "There are three kinds of people: mystics, the learned on the path to salvation, and the rabble and the riffraff, followers of braying donkeys." 13.3

And another: 13.4

Concerning men, there are those who know their Lord,
and then there are the party crashers.

More detail and discussion can be brought to bear on this matter, but to do so would be to draw the matter out. For the thinking person, what we discussed of nobility and what we detailed about how people are distinguished by their virtues will suffice. Everything is God's to command. 13.5

١،١٤ كان شيخنا الأستاذ المشارك الفاضل الناسك أبو بكر بن الحسن التطافيّ ينشدنا كثيرًا في التنويه بالعلم قول القائل: [طويل]

وَمَا عَرَّفَ ٱلْأَرْجَاءَ إِلَّا رِجَالُهَا   وَإِلَّا فَلَا فَضْلُ لِتُرْبٍ عَلَى تُرْبِ

٢،١٤ والمعنى أنّ القطر من الأرض وكذا المدينة والقرية تعرف وتشرّف بنسبة المعروف إليها كأبي عثمان المغربيّ وابن عامر الشاميّ والحسن البصريّ وأبي الحسن الحراليّ وغيرهم. واعلم أنّ بقاع الأرض كأفراد الإنسان هي كلّها مشتركة في كونها أرضاً وتربة ثمّ تتفاوت في المزايا الاختصاصيّة إمّا من ذاتها بأن يجعلها الله منبتاً للعشب وهي أفضل من السبخة أو مزرعة وهي أفضل من الكنود أو سهلة وهي أفضل من الحزن وقد ينعكس الأمر أو معدناً وتتفاوت بحسب الجواهر المودعة فيها أو منبعاً للماء. وتتفاوت بحسب المياه إلى غير ذلك من مختلفات الفواكه والأشجار والأزهار وسائر المنافع. وإمّا من عارض كأن يختصّها الله تعالى بكونها محلاً لخير إمّا نبوءة بيته كمكّة. فهي أشرف البقاع ما خلا المدينة من ثلاثة أوجه الأوّل كونها محلاً لبيته وقبلة لعباده. والثاني كونها عمارة خليله إبراهيم عليه السلام. الثالث كونها مولد ومبعث أشرف الأنبياء عليه وعليهم الصلاة والسلام.

٣،١٤ إلى وجوه أخرى ككونها وسط الأرض أو أرفع الأرض أو من تحتها دحيت الأرض وكونها حراماً وغير ذلك. ولبيت المقدس قسط من هذا الفضل لأنّها مأوى الأنبياء وكانت قبلة. واختصّت المدينة طيبة بكونها مهاجر أشرف الخلق ومدفنه مع أكابر أصحابه رضي الله عنهم فصارت خير البقاع حتّى مكّة عند علمائنا. أمّا التربة التي تضمّنت شخصه الكريم صلّى الله عليه وسلّم فلا مثل لها في الأرض ولا في السماء قطعاً.

Our shaykh and teacher, Abū Bakr ibn al-Ḥasan al-Taṭāfī, a distinguished ascetic, knowledgeable in many fields, often recited the following line in praise of knowledge to us: 14.1

The regions of the world are known only by their inhabitants.
But for this, no region has precedence over another.

The meaning of this is that regions, as well as cities and villages, are known and given honor through their attributive nouns, as with Maghrib in Abū ʿUthmān al-Maghribī, Shām in Ibn ʿĀmir al-Shāmī, Baṣra in al-Ḥasan al-Baṣrī, Ḥarāllah in Abū l-Ḥasan al-Ḥarāllī, and so on.[114] The regions of the earth are like human individuals. In their essence they are all composed of earth and soil; beyond this they differ only in their specific characteristics. One essential attribute could be that God makes them fertile for plants to grow, which makes them superior to salt marshes. Or that He makes them agricultural fields, which are superior to infertile lands. Or that He makes them sandy earth, which is superior to rough ground. Or the matter may be the opposite, and relate to minerals. Areas may differ according to the gems placed there, or whether they have a spring. They may differ, among other benefits, according to the quality of the water and other attributes related to fruits, trees, flowers, and other plants. Or it could be an accidental attribute, as when Exalted God selects a place to be characterized by goodness, or to be the abode of prophecy, as with Mecca. This is the noblest place, surpassing Medina in three ways: by being the site of His house and the direction of prayer for His worshippers; by having been built by His True Friend, Abraham, peace be upon him; and by being both the birthplace of the noblest prophet, God bless and keep him, and the place he was sent. 14.2

There are also other ways of being differentiated, such as it being the center of the world, or the highest place in the area, or having land stretch out below it into the lowlands, or that it is sacred, and so on. Jerusalem has a share of this virtue, for it is the sanctuary of the prophets, and was the direction of prayer. Medina was distinguished with virtue by being made the place of exile of the noblest of all people, as well as his burial place alongside the greatest of his Companions, God be pleased with them.[115] Because of this it became more propitious even than Mecca for our scholars. As for the land that contains his noble person, God bless him and keep him, there is absolutely none like it on earth or in heaven. 14.3

وأمّا نبوءة فتشرّف كلّ بلدة ولد فيها نبيّ أو بعث أو أقام أو دفن وتشتهر بذلك وتتعرّف كما قال صلّى الله عليه وسلّم يوم الطائف للغلام وقد قال له إنّه من نينَوى قرية أخي يونس عليه السّلام. وأمّا علم فكلّ قرية أيضاً أو بلدة كان فيها عالم أو كان منها فهي تشرّف بذلك وتتعرّف كما في البيت المذكور وإمّا زهدٌ أو عبادة أو نحو ذلك أو ملك أو جود أو نجدة أو جمال أو خلق حسن أو غير ذلك حتّى رخاء العيش وصحّة الهواء. فكلّ ذلك ونحوه يكون به الشرف والاشتهار كما يكون الاشتهار في النقصان[١] والمذمّة بأضداد ذلك. ٤،١٤

واعلم أنّ المولى تبارك وتعالى من لطيف حكمته وسابغ منّته كما لم يُخْلِ عبدًا من عباده من فضل عاجل أو آجل ظاهر أو باطن كثير أو قليل كذلك لم يُخلِ بقعة من بقاع الأرض من فضل. ولم يُعْرِ بلدة من مزيّة يتعلّل بها عُمّارُها حتّى لا يتركوها وقد جعل الله تعالى الأهواء مختلفة والطباع متفاوتة وحبّب لكلّ أحد ما اختصّه به ذلك تقدير العزيز العليم الحكيم. فتجد هذا يمدح أرضه بكثرة المياه للاتّساع في الشرب والطهارة والنقاوة ونحو ذلك. وهذا يمدح أرضه بالبعد عن كثرة المياه لجودة منابتها وصحّة هوائها وذهاب الوخم عنها. وهذا يمدح أرضه بالسهولة لوجود المزارع فيها وكثرة ريفها واتّساع خيرها. وهذا يمدح أرضه بكونها جبالاً لتمنعها وعزّة أهلها وحسن مائها وهوائها وقناعتها وغير ذلك. ٥،١٤

وللشعراء قديماً وحديثاً في هذا ما يحسن ترداده ويطول إيراده. فمن ذلك لأبي بكر ابن حجّة الحمويّ يتشوّق إلى بلده قوله: [طويل] ٦،١٤

١ ق: العصيان.

Prophecy grants honor to any town in which a prophet is born or dies, to which he is sent, or where he announces his message. Through such an association it becomes esteemed and renowned, as when on the day he went to Ṭā'ifah the Prophet, God bless and keep him, said to a boy who had told him that he was from Nineveh, "That is the city of my brother Jonah, peace be upon him." This applies to knowledge too, so that any village or town with a scholar or from which a scholar hails is honored by the association and gains renown, as in the verse quoted earlier. Either by virtue of asceticism, worship and the like, kingship, excellence, courage, beauty, good character, or even easy living and healthy air, through all of this and the like, honor and fame can be attained, just as, through the opposite, infamy and deficiency accrue. 14.4

From the subtleties of the wisdom of the Lord, Blessed and Exalted, and from the abundance of His favor proceeds the fact that just as He did not deprive any of His servants in this life or the next of virtue, apparent or concealed, great or small, in the same fashion He did not leave any piece of earth without some virtue. He gave to each town a merit that its inhabitants could invoke to justify not leaving it. Exalted God made climates and natural qualities differ and inspired a love for each one according to its divinely gifted distinction. Such is the determination of One who is Powerful, Knowing, Wise. You will find that one person praises his land for its plentiful waters, sufficient for drinking, ritual purity, purification, and the like, while another praises his land for its distance from waters, for the excellence of its springs, the purity of its air, and the absence of squalor. Similarly, someone else praises his land for the ease with which one sows crops in it, the plenitude of its fertile areas, and the expanse of its goodness, while another praises his land for its mountainous nature and isolation, its fierce inhabitants, sweet water, pure air, temperate climate, and so on. 14.5

Poets ancient and modern have composed verses worth repeating, though to present them all would take too long. They include lines by Abū Bakr ibn Ḥijjah al-Ḥamawī, in which he longs for his country: 14.6

بِوَادِي حَمَاةِ ٱلشَّامِ عَنْ أَيْمَنِ ٱلشَّطِّ ... وَحَقِّكَ تُطْوَى شُقَّةُ ٱلْهَمِّ بِٱلْبَسْطِ
بِلَادٌ إِذَا مَا ذُقْتُ كَوْثَرَ مَائِهَا ... أَهِيمُ كَأَنِّي قَدْ ثَمِلْتُ بِإِسْفِنْطِ
فَمَنْ يَجْتَهِدْ فِي أَنَّ فِي ٱلْأَرْضِ بُقْعَةً ... تُمَاثِلُهَا قُلْ أَنْتَ مُجْتَهِدٌ مُخْطِ
وَصَوِّبْ حَدِيثَيْ مَائِهَا وَهَوَائِهَا ... فَإِنَّ أَحَادِيثَ ٱلصَّحِيحَيْنِ مَا تُخْطِي

٧،١٤ وللآخر في تلمسان مثل هذا: [كامل]

بَلَدُ ٱلْجِدَارِ مَا أَمَرَّ نَوَاهَا ... كَلِفَ ٱلْفُؤَادُ بِحُبِّهَا وَهَوَاهَا
يَا عَاذِلِي فِي حُبِّهَا كُنْ عَاذِرِي ... يَكْفِيكَ مِنْهَا مَاؤُهَا وَهَوَاهَا

٨،١٤ ولابن حمديس الصقليّ في بلده: [متقارب]

ذَكَرْتُ صِقِلِّيَةَ وَٱلْأَسَى ... يُهَيِّجُ لِلنَّفْسِ تِذْكَارَهَا
فَإِنْ كُنْتُ أُخْرِجْتُ مِنْ جَنَّةٍ ... فَإِنِّي أُحَدِّثُ أَخْبَارَهَا
وَلَوْلَا مُلُوحَةُ مَاءِ ٱلْبُكَا ... حَسِبْتُ دُمُوعِي أَنْهَارَهَا

٩،١٤ وللأعرابيّ: [وافر]

أَقُولُ لِصَاحِبِي وَٱلْعِيسُ تَخْدِي ... بِنَا بَيْنَ ٱلْمُنِيفَةِ فَٱلضِّمَارِ
تَمَتَّعْ مِنْ شَمِيمِ عَرَارِ نَجْدٍ ... فَمَا بَعْدَ ٱلْعَشِيَّةِ مِنْ عَرَارِ
أَلَا يَا حَبَّذَا نَفَحَاتُ نَجْدٍ ... وَرَيَّا رَوْضِهِ بَعْدَ ٱلْقِطَارِ
وَأَهْلُكَ إِذْ يَحُلُّ ٱلْحَيُّ نَجْدًا ... وَأَنْتَ عَلَى زَمَانِكَ غَيْرُ زَارِ
شُهُورٌ يَنْقَضِينَ وَمَا شَعَرْنَا ... بِأَنْصَافٍ لَهُنَّ وَلَا سِرَارِ

The plains of Ḥamāh in Syria on the right bank—
the gardens' expanse banishes hardship brought by worry.
When I taste the Kawthar-like water of this land
I am in rapture, as if drunk on aromatic wine.
Say to the one who argues that there is in the world
another place like it: Your reasoning is flawed!
Consider the two hadiths on its air and water sound,
for the hadiths of the *Sound Collections* do not lie![116]

Another said something like this regarding Tilimsān:[117] **14.7**

How bitter is this distance from the walled city[118]
that has afflicted my heart with love and desire.
You who rebuke my love for her—forgive me!
May her sweat and fragrance be enough to convince you.

And Ibn Ḥamdīs al-Ṣaqallī has these verses about his country: **14.8**

I remembered Sicily, and the grief of reminiscence
troubled my soul.
If you were cast out from paradise—
that is of what I speak.
And were it not for the saltiness of my sobs,
you would think my tears her rivers.

One Bedouin poet says:[119] **14.9**

I said to my companion, when our reddish-white camel
carried us between al-Munīfah and al-Ḍimār:
Enjoy the smell of the wild narcissus of Najd;
after nightfall they are no longer fragrant.
How lovely the scents of Najd,
the lushness of its gardens after rain.
If your tribe visits Najd I will welcome you—
you will have no cause for complaint.
Long months pass there without us having felt even
the half of them, much less their last night.

١٠،١٤ وللآخر في تونس: [متقارب]

لَتُونِسُ تُونِسُ مَنْ جَاءَهَا وَتُودِعُهُ لَوْعَةً حَيْثُ سَارَ
فَيَغْدُو وَلَوْ حَلَّ أَرْضَ ٱلْعِرَاقِ يَحِنُّ إِلَيْهَا حَنِينَ ٱلْحُوَارِ
وَيَأْمَلُ عَوْدًا وَيَشْتَاقُهُ ٱشْ تِيَاقَ ٱلْفَرَزْدَقِ عَوْدَ ٱلنَّوَارِ

١١،١٤ وللآخر في مدينة فاس: [كامل]

يَا فَاسُ حَيَّا ٱللّٰهُ أَرْضَكِ مِنْ ثَرًى وَسَقَاكِ مِنْ صَوْبِ ٱلْغَمَامِ ٱلْمُسْبِلِ
يَا جَنَّةَ ٱلدُّنْيَا ٱلَّتِي أَرْبَتْ عَلَى عَدْنٍ بِمَنْظَرِهَا ٱلْبَهِيِّ ٱلْأَجْمَلِ
غُرَفٌ عَلَى غُرَفٍ وَيَجْرِي تَحْتَهَا مَاءٌ أَلَذُّ مِنَ ٱلرَّحِيقِ ٱلسَّلْسَلِ

١٢،١٤ وكثيرًا ما يقع الحنين إلى المنازل والبلدان من أجل من فيها من الإخوان والأخدان كما قال القائل: [طويل]

أُحِبُّ ٱلْحِمَى مِنْ أَجْلِ مَنْ سَكَنَ ٱلْحِمَى وَمِنْ أَجْلِ مَنْ فِيهَا تُحَبُّ ٱلْمَنَازِلُ

١٣،١٤ وقال المجنون: [وافر]

وَمَا حُبُّ ٱلدِّيَارِ شَغَفْنَ قَلْبِي وَلٰكِنْ حُبُّ مَنْ سَكَنَ ٱلدِّيَارَا

١٤،١٤ وهي خصوصيّة في البقعة عارضة من سكّانها كالذي في البيت. فإنّ الميل إليها يقتضي فضلها على غيرها بالنسبة إليه ومن هذا المعنى أكثر العرب ذكر الحِمى كقوله: [طويل]

Another poet has said regarding Tunis: 14.10

Whoever comes to Tunis
will bid farewell to suffering, no matter where he wanders.
Having been there, even if he is in Iraq
he will long for it as a young camel does for its mother.
Missing it, he will want to return,
just as Farazdaq longed for the return of al-Nawār.

Another poet said of Fez:[120] 14.11

Fez! May God make your moist earth fertile
and water you with the rain of low-lying clouds.
Paradise on earth, more beautiful
and resplendent than Eden.
Lofty chambers heaped on each other, below which water runs
sweeter than the sweetest wine.

Longing for home and country is often because of the relatives and loved ones left behind, as when the poet said: 14.12

I love the sanctuary because of the one who lives there.
Homes are cherished on account of their inhabitants.

Majnūn said:[121] 14.13

It is not homes that have afflicted my heart with love
but those who dwelled in them.

This is a characteristic a place acquires on account of its inhabitants, such as is the case with a house. One's fondness for a given place renders it superior to comparable places. On this matter, the Arabs spoke often of sanctuaries, as in the following example:[122] 14.14

فَإِنْ كَانَ لَمْ يُغْرِضْ فَإِنِّي وَنَاقَتِي بِحَجْرٍ إِلَى أَهْلِ ٱلْحِمَى غَرِضَانِ
تَحِنُّ فَتُبْدِي مَا بِهَا مِنْ صَبَابَةٍ وَأُخْفِي ٱلَّذِي لَوْلَا ٱلْأَسَى لَقَضَانِي

الغرض المشتاق.

وكقول الآخر: [طويل] ١٥،١٤

وَإِنَّ ٱلْكَثِيبَ ٱلْفَرْدَ مِنْ جَانِبِ ٱلْحِمَى إِلَيَّ وَإِنْ لَمْ آتِهِ لَحَبِيبُ

وكقول الآخر: [طويل] ١٦،١٤

وَكُنْتُ أَذُودُ ٱلْعَيْنَ أَنْ تَرِدَ ٱلْبُكَا فَقَدْ وَرَدَتْ مَا كُنْتُ أَذُودُهَا
خَلِيلَيَّ مَا بِٱلْعَيْشِ عَتْبٌ لَوَ أَنَّنَا وَجَدْنَا لِأَيَّامِ ٱلْحِمَى مَنْ يُعِيدُهَا

وكقول الآخر: [طويل] ١٧،١٤

أَلَا أَيُّهَا ٱلرَّكْبُ ٱلْمُجِدُّونَ هَلْ لَكُمْ بِسَاكِنِ أَجْزَاعِ ٱلْحِمَى بَعْدَنَا خُبْرُ؟
فَقَالُوا قَطَعْنَا ذَاكَ لَيْلًا وَإِنْ يَكُنْ بِهِ بَعْضُ مَنْ تَهْوَى فَمَا شَعَرَ ٱلسَّفْرُ

وكقول الآخر: [طويل] ١٨،١٤

بَكَتْ عَيْنِي ٱلْيُسْرَى فَلَمَّا زَجَرْتُهَا عَنِ ٱلْغَيِّ بَعْدَ ٱلشَّيْبِ أُسْبِلَتَا مَعًا
فَلَيْسَتْ عَشِيَّاتُ ٱلْحِمَى بِرَوَاجِعٍ إِلَيْكَ وَلَكِنْ خَلِّ عَيْنَيْكَ تَدْمَعَا

إلى غير ذلك.

ويكثرون أيضاً ذكر اللوى كقوله: [طويل] ١٩،١٤

Even if it was not intended, my camel and I in Ḥijr
pine for the people in the sanctuary.
It yearns, and openly displays its deep longing,
while I conceal what—if I could not comfort myself—would kill me.

(To "pine" is to yearn.)

And as another poet has said:[123] **14.15**

A solitary sand dune next to the sanctuary,
dear to me even when I am not there.

This is also like what another poet said:[124] **14.16**

I tried to keep my eye from tearing up again,
but what I wished to hold back flowed.
My friends, there would be nothing in life to reproach if we
could find someone to bring back our days in the sanctuary.

And similar to what another poet said:[125] **14.17**

Swift riders, have you any news
of those who lived in the high hills of the sanctuary after us?
We passed there at night, they said.
If someone there was in love, they did not pay us heed.

This is akin to what another poet said:[126] **14.18**

My left eye teared up, and when I scolded it for being inappropriate
for an old man, both eyes began to cry.
The evenings in the sanctuary will never come to you again;
you may as well let your eyes weep.

And so on.

The poets also often mention curving sand dunes in lines such as the following:[127] **14.19**

شَيَّبَ أَيَّامُ ٱلْفُرَاقِ مَفَارِقِي وَأَنْشَزْنَ نَفْسِي فَوْقَ حَيْثُ تَكُونُ
وَقَدْ لَانَ أَيَّامُ ٱللِّوَى ثُمَّ لَمْ يَكَدْ مِنَ ٱلْعَيْشِ شَيْءٌ بَعْدَهُنَّ يَلِينُ

وكقول جرير: [كامل] ٢٠،١٤

أَوَلَا مُرَاقَبَةُ ٱلْعُيُونِ أَرَيْنَنَا مُقَلَ ٱلْمَهَا وَسَوَالِفَ ٱلْآرَامِ
هَلْ يَنْهَيَنْكَ أَنْ قَتَلْنَ مُرَقِّشاً أَوْ مَا فَعَلْنَ بِعُرْوَةَ بْنِ حِزَامِ
ذُمَّ ٱلْمَنَازِلَ بَعْدَ مَنْزِلَةِ ٱللِّوَى وَٱلْعَيْشَ بَعْدَ أُولَئِكَ ٱلْأَيَّامِ

إلى غير ذلك.

وأمّا نجد وهو ما ارتفع من الأرض من بلادهم فأكثر من ذلك كلّه كقوله: [طويل] ٢١،١٤

سَقَى اللهُ نَجْداً وَٱلسَّلَامُ عَلَى نَجْدِ وَيَا حَبَّذَا نَجْدٌ عَلَى ٱلنَّأْيِ وَٱلْبُعْدِ

وقول الآخر: [وافر] ٢٢،١٤

أَشَاقَتْكَ ٱلْبَوَارِقُ وَٱلْجَنُوبُ وَمِنْ عَلْوِيِّ ٱلرِّيَاحِ لَهَا هُبُوبُ
أَتَتْكَ بِنَفْحَةٍ مِنْ شِيحِ نَجْدٍ تَصُوبُ وَٱلْعَرَارُ بِهَا مَشُوبُ
وَشِمْتَ ٱلْبَارِقَاتِ فَقُلْتُ جِيدَتْ جِبَالُ ٱلْبَتْرِ أَوْ مَطَرُ ٱلْقَلِيبِ
وَمِنْ بُسْتَانِ إِبْرَاهِيمَ غَنَّتْ حَمَائِمُ بَيْنَهَا فَنَنٌ رَطِيبُ
فَقُلْتُ لَهَا وُقِيتِ سِهَامَ رَامٍ وَرُقْطَ ٱلرِّيشِ مَطْعَمُهَا ٱلْجَنُوبُ
كَمَا هَيَّجْتِ ذَا حُزْنٍ غَرِيباً عَلَى أَشْجَانِهِ فَبَكَى ٱلْغَرِيبُ

The parting of my locks turned white in the days of separation
and roused my soul from its state.
The days of curving sand dunes were pleasant in a way
that nothing since has equalled.

This is similar to Jarīr's words: 14.20

Has observing their eyes not shown us
the eyes of wild cows and the locks of white gazelles?
Did they warn you they had killed al-Muraqqish
or say what they did to ʿUrwah ibn Ḥizām?
After that curving dune, curse all abodes
and curse my life after those days.

And so on.

Najd is the elevated part of Arabia, and there is a great deal of poetry about it, such as:[128] 14.21

May God grant Najd rain and peace—
I love Najd beyond measure when I am far removed from it.

And such as these lines by another poet:[129] 14.22

The south wind and the glow of lightning, the gusts of the celestial winds,
have made you the object of my desires.
When I came to you the scent of Najd wormwood struck me,
mixed with wild narcissus.
I smelled the lightning and said: The mountains of Bitr and al-Qalīb
have been given generous amounts of rain.
On a young branch, the doves were calling
from the Garden of Abraham.[130]
May you be protected from the arrows of the archer, I said,
and from speckle-feathered birds come from the south.
They stirred up the sorrows of a mournful stranger,
bringing him to tears.

وقول الآخر: [طويل] ٢٣،١٤

وَمَا وَجْدُ أَعْرَابِيَّةٍ قَذَفَتْ بِهَا صُرُوفُ ٱلنَّوَى مِنْ حَيْثُ لَمْ تَكُ ظَنَّتِ
تَمَنَّتْ أَحَالِيبَ ٱلرُّعَاءِ وَخَيْمَةً بِنَجْدٍ فَلَمْ يُقْدَرْ لَهَا مَا تَمَنَّتِ
إِذَا ذَكَرَتْ مَاءَ ٱلْغَضَاءِ وَطِيبَهُ وَرِيحَ ٱلصَّبَا مِنْ نَحْوِ نَجْدٍ أَرَنَّتِ
بِأَعْظَمَ مِنْ وَجْدٍ بِلَيْلَى وَجَدتُهُ غَدَاةَ غَدَوْنَا بُكْرَةً وَٱطْمَأَنَّتِ
وَكَانَتْ رِيَاحُ تَحْمَلُ ٱلْحَاجَ بَيْنَنَا فَقَدْ بَخِلَتْ تِلْكَ ٱلرِّيَاحُ وَضَنَّتِ][1]

٢٤،١٤ وتقدّم شيء من ذلك وهو كثير وذلك في الغالب لحسنه في نفسه هواء وماء ومنابت ومسارح. والناس كلّهم مجمعون على ذكر ديار الأحباب ومعاهد الشباب ولا خصوصيّة للعرب وإن كان لهم مزيد رقّة. لله الأمر من قبل ومن بعد.

٢٥،١٤ أنشد في النوادر لمحرز العكليّ: [طويل]

يَظَلُّ فُؤَادِي شَاخِصاً مِنْ مَكَانِهِ لِذِكْرِ ٱلْغَوَانِي مُسْتَهَاماً مُتَيَّمَا
إِذَا قُلْتُ مَاتَ ٱلشَّوْقُ مِنِّي تَنَسَّمَتْ بِهِ أَرْيَحِيَّاتُ ٱلْهَوَى فَتَنَسَّمَا

وفي البيت فائدة وهي أنّ لفظ الأَرْيَحيّة هو بسكون الراء وفتح الياء.

٢٦،١٤ ووقع في شعر المولدين أيضاً ما يوافق ذلك.[2] ممّا علق بحفظي من أشعار المعاني عند العرب قول الشاعر: [وافر]

فَجُنِّبْتَ ٱلْجُيُوشَ أَبَا زُنَيْبٍ وَجَادَ عَلَى مَسَارِحِكَ ٱلسَّحَابُ

يحتمل أن يكون دعاء له بالعافية والخصب. ويحتمل أن يكون دعاء عليه بالإفلاس حتّى لا تقصده الجيوش ثمّ بالخصب مع ذلك لأنّه أوجع لقلبه حيث يرى الرّعيَ ولا راعية.

١ سقط من م. ٢ يزيد ق، ط: لله الأمر من قبل ومن بعد.

Another said:[131] 14.23

Consider the passion of a Bedouin woman whom the misfortunes of
separation
have unexpectedly afflicted.
She desired the milk the camel herders sent from the pastures
and a tent in Najd, yet what she desired could not be given.
She recalled the purity of the water of al-Ghaḍā',
and the east wind of Najd delighted her
More than the one who had found his love in Layla
on the morning when we departed early—so she grew calm.
The winds carry the smell of bitter desert trees between us:
winds stingy and tightfisted.

We have presented only a little of this type of poetry. There is quite a lot of 14.24
it, on account of the intrinsic beauty of Najd's air, water, plants, and vistas. It is a common attribute of mankind to remember the houses of loved ones, and the places of their youth. In this, the Arabs are not exceptional, even though they do it with greater delicacy than others. Everything is God's to command.

In *Anecdotes*, al-Qālī included the lines of Muḥriz al-ʿUklī: 14.25

My heart remains fixed to the spot,
enthralled and captivated by the memory of beautiful women.
If I say that my passion died, the munificence
of passion would breathe upon it, and it would return to life.

There is a particular benefit to this line—the use of the word *aryaḥiyyah*, vocalized *arya*, meaning "munificence."[132]

There are similar examples in the postclassical poets. One of the lines, 14.26
which I recall can be read as containing opposing meanings,[133] is the following:

May the armies avoid Abū Zaynab
and the clouds rain on your pastures.

It is possible that this is a prayer for his good health and his fertility, and it is also possible that it is a curse against him for him to become insolvent so that armies would not seek him out. Fertility, along with such insolvency, would cause his heart greater pain as he would see the pasture but would have no herds to graze on it.

كما قال الراجز: [رجز] ٢٧،١٤

أَمْرَعَتِ ٱلْأَرْضُ لَوَ أَنَّ مَالَا
لَوْ أَنَّ نُوقًا لَكَ أَوْ جِمَالَا
أَوْ ثُلَّةً مِنْ غَنَمٍ إِمَّا[١] لَا

أي إن كنت لا تجد غيرها.

وقال الآخر: [طويل] ٢٨،١٤

سَتَبْكِي ٱلْمَخَاضُ ٱلْجُرْبُ أَنْ مَاتَ هَيْثَمٌ ... وَكُلُّ ٱلْبَوَاكِي غَيْرُهُنَّ جُمُودُ

أي إنّه كان يستحييها بخلاً ولا ينحرها للضيفان. فهي تبكي عليه ولا يبكي عليه أحد من الناس إذ لا خير فيه. وهذا هجو وقد استعمل الجمود في مجرّد عدم البكاء. وكأنّه لاحظ فيه المبالغة فإنّ الناس لعدم اكتراثهم بالهالك أصبحوا في حقّه لا يتصوّر منهم البكاء ولا انحدار دمع كمثل الأحجار ونحوها. ويستعمل الجمود حيث يراد البكاء ولا تسمح العين بالدموع كقوله: [طويل]

أَلَا إِنَّ عَيْنًا لَمْ تَجِدْ يَوْمَ وَاسِطٍ ... عَلَيْكَ بِجَارِي دَمْعِهَا لَجَمُودُ

ولذا عيب قول القائل: [طويل] ٢٩،١٤

سَأَطْلُبُ بُعْدَ ٱلدَّارِ عَنْكُمْ لِتَقْرَبُوا ... وَتَسْكُبُ عَيْنَايَ ٱلدُّمُوعَ لِتَجْمُدَا

ومتى اعتبر[٢] بالمعنى الأوّل فلا عيب. وقول الآخر: [طويل] ٣٠،١٤

قَتِيلَانِ لَا تَبْكِي ٱلْمَخَاضُ عَلَيْهِمَا ... إِذَا شَبِعَتْ مِنْ قَرْمَلٍ وَأَفَانِ

١ كذا قرأت. و في م، ق، ط: أما. ٢ م: اعتبرنا.

This has been described by a poet of the *rajaz* meter as follows:[134] **14.27**

If you find livestock in the fields—
Female and male camels, a flock of sheep—
They must be full of pasture. If not, then there are none.

The last line means: if you don't find other than them.

Another poet said: **14.28**

Mangy, pregnant camels will weep at the death of Haytham
while all others remain unmoved.

This means that Haytham was ashamed of his stinginess: that he had not slaughtered the camels for his guests. Therefore, the camels cried for him, but none of the people wept, as there was no good in him. This is mockery, with the poet having used the word "unmoved" to denote the absence of crying. It is as if he noted hyperbole in the term, with no one crying for the deceased due to their indifference to him; they were like stones, not shedding a tear. The word "unmoved" is used when one wants to cry but the eye won't tear up. This is like the saying:[135]

You did not find on the day of Wāsiṭ an eye
shedding a tear for you, but rather they remain unmoved.

For this very reason, people have found fault with the line:[136] **14.29**

I will look beyond the campsite for your return,
my eyes shedding tears yet remaining unmoved.

Consider the use in the first example—no fault there. Another similar line goes:[137] **14.30**

Two killings for whom the pregnant camels do not cry,
satiated as they were with *qarmal* and *afānī* shrubs.

وهذا مدح ضدّ الأوّل أي إنهما كانا يهلكانها بالنحر. فإذا ماتا استراحت وشبعت فلم تبك عليهما. والقرمل واحده قرملة وهي شجرة ضعيفة تنفضخ إذا وطئت. ومنه قولهم في المثل إذا التجأ الضعيف إلى مثله ضعيف عاذ بقرملة.

والأفاني واحده فانية وهي شجرة أخرى وقول الآخر وهو حميد بن ثور: [كامل] ٣١،١٤

وَلَقَدْ نَظَرْتُ إِلَى أَغَرَّ مُشَهَّرٍ بِكْرٍ تَوَسَّنَ بِٱلْخَمِيلَةِ عُونَا
مُتَسَنِّمٍ سَنَمَاتِهَا مُتَبَجِّسٍ بِٱلْهَدْرِ يَمْلَأُ أَنْفُسًا وَعُيُونَا
لَقِحَ ٱلْعِجَافُ لَهُ لِسَابِعِ سَبْعَةٍ وَشَرِبْنَ بَعْدَ تَحَلُّؤٍ فَرُوِينَا

يصف السحاب وفعله وانتفاع الأرض به على طريق التمثيل فقوله أغرّ أي سحاب فيه برق أو أبيض. وقوله بكر أي لم يمطر قبل ذلك. وقوله توسّن بالخميلة عونًا أي طرقها ليلاً وقت الوسن أي النعاس. والخميلة رملة ليّنة ذات شجر. والعون جمع عوان وهي في النساء التي كان لها زوج وهنا هي الأرض التي أصابها المطر قبل على التشبيه. وقولهم تسنّم سنماتها أي طالع على الأكام والتلال وأصله في الجمل يتسنّم الناقة أي يعلو عليها وهي سَنِمة أي عظيمة السنام مرتفعته. قوله متبجّس أي متكبّر بالهدر أي رعده يملأ أنفسًا وعيونًا عجبًا به أو رعبًا منه. قوله لقح العجاف أي الأرضون المجدبة حملت به الماء فأنبتت العشب. وذلك بعد تحلّؤٍ أي امتناع من السقي لعدم المطر فهذا كلّه تمثيل.

وقول الآخر: [بسيط] ٣٢،١٤

حِلُّوا عَنِ ٱلنَّاقَةِ ٱلْحَمْرَاءِ أَرْحُلَكُمْ وَٱلْبَازِلَ ٱلْأَصْهَبَ ٱلْمَعْقُولَ فَٱصْطَنِعُوا
إِنَّ ٱلذِّئَابَ قَدِ ٱخْضَرَّتْ بَرَاثِنُهَا وَٱلنَّاسُ كُلُّهُمُ بَكْرٌ إِذَا شَبِعُوا

In contrast to the first verse, this is one of praise, and signifies that the two were slaughtered, and that when they died, the camels were relieved and satisfied and did not cry for them. The singular of *qarmal* is *qarmalah*, a small shrub whose frailty is evident when it is trampled underfoot. There is a saying that is used when a weak man seeks help from someone like himself: "A weak person seeks refuge under the *qarmalah*."

The singular of *afānī* is *fāniyyah*, another type of shrub, regarding which there is another line, by Ḥumayd ibn Thawr: **14.31**

I looked at the virgin cloud, with a white blaze
approaching the moist ground covered by a shrub at night.
Looking up at the clouds' heights, eyes and souls are filled
with thunderous awe.
It fertilizes the earth on the seventh day
giving drink, quenching thirst after drought.

The poet uses a metaphor to describe clouds, their behavior, and how they benefit the earth. His saying "with a white blaze" signifies that there is lightning in the cloud. His saying "virgin" means that the cloud has not rained before this. His words "Approaching the moist ground covered by a shrub at night" means that it left it at night at the time when one goes to sleep, that is, when one seeks rest. "A shrub" is a plant like the slender branch of a tree. The word for moist ground, *ʿawn*, plural *ʿawān*, signifies women who have been married. Here it refers metaphorically to the earth that has previously experienced rain. His words "Looking up at the clouds' heights" means ascending above the mounds and hills. The origin is in the male ascending, that is mounting, the female camel. The latter is the height, as it possesses tall humps. His saying "are filled" means overwhelming with roaring, that is, its thunder fills eyes and souls with wonder or fear. His words "fertilizes the earth" refer to a piece of ground that soaks up water and produces grass after drought, which is an inability to drink due to an absence of rain. All of this is metaphorical.

There is another saying:[138] **14.32**

Remove your saddles from the red camel
and the hobbled ruddy camel, and bind them.
Truly, the wolf's claws have become green from hunger—
people, when satiated, are like the Bakr.

أراد بالناقة الحمراء الدهناء وبالجمل الأصهب الصمّان كأنّه يقول ارتحلوا عن السهل وألجئوا إلى الجبال مخافة الغارات. والقائل كان أسيرًا فكتب إلى قومه ينذرهم وكانت بكر لهم عدوًا فهو يقول الناس كلّهم إذا شبعوا أعداء لكم كبكر احذروهم. وهذا المعنى مذكور في قصة أخرى يحكى أنّ رجلًا من بني العنبر كان أسيرًا في بكر بن وائل فسألهم رسولًا إلى قومه. فقالوا له لا ترسل إلّا بحضرتنا وكانوا أزمعوا غزو قومه فتخوّفوا أن ينذرهم وذلك هو ما أراد هو أيضًا فأتوه بعبد أسود. فقال له أبلغ قومي التحيّة وقل لهم ليكرموا فلان يعني أسيرًا من بكر كان عندهم فإنّ قومه لي مكرمون. وقل لهم إنّ العرفج قد أدبني وقد شكت النساء. وأمرهم أن يعرّوا ناقتي الحمراء فقد أطالوا ركوبها وأن يركبوا جملي الأصهب بآية ما أكلت معهم حيسًا. واسألوا الحارث عن خبري. فلمّا أبلغهم العبد الرسالة قالوا جُنّ الأعورُ والله ما نعرف له ناقة حمراء ولا جملًا أصهب. ثمّ سرّحوا العبد ودعوا الحارث فحدّثوه بالحديث. فقال قد أنذركم أمّا قوله العرفج قد أدبني فكناية عن الرجال وأنّهم استلأموا أي لبسوا الدروع للغزو. وقوله شكت النساء أي اتّخذن الشكاء للسفر وهي جمع شكوة معروفة. والحيس أراد به الأخلاط من الناس المجتمعون للغزو لأنّ الحَيْسَ يجمع الأقِط والسمن والتمر. لله الأمر من قبل ومن بعد.

كنت في أعوام الستّين وألف مرتحلًا في طلب العلم فدخلت قرية في أرض دكالة. ١٫١٥
فرأيت فيها رجلًا مسنًا قد لازم المسجد منقطعًا عن الناس فجلست إليه مستحسنًا لحاله. وفي الحديث: إذا رأيتم الرجل قد أعطي زهدًا في الدّنيا وقلّة منطق فادنوا منه فإنّه يلقّن الحكمة. فلما دنوت منه إذا هو يعظم العلم وأهله تعظيمًا بالغًا فازددت به عجبًا.

By red camel, the poet meant the desert, and by ruddy camel the hard, rugged ground, as if he had been saying: They left the easy places and sought refuge in the mountains out of fear of raids. Now the speaker was a prisoner writing his people to warn them. The Bakr were their enemy, and he said: When people are full, all of them are your enemies, like the Bakr. This was a warning for them.[139] This interpretation is mentioned in another story as well: It is said that a man of the Banū al-ʿAnbar was a prisoner of the Bakr ibn Wāʾil and that he asked them for a messenger to be sent to his people. They responded: "We will not let you send anyone without us accompanying you." They were planning to raid his tribe, and were wary that he would warn them, which was in fact what he intended to do. They brought him a black slave, and he said to the slave, "Convey my greetings to my tribe and tell them to honor so-and-so"—a prisoner of the Bakr who was with them—"for his tribe has honored me. And tell them that the *ʿarfaj* plant has chastised me, and the women have taken the skin of a young goat to churn milk. Order them to catch my red female camel, for they have ridden her too long, and tell them to ride my reddish male camel, since I have not eaten *al-ḥays* with them. And have them ask al-Ḥārith about news of me." When the slave conveyed the message, they said, "The one-eyed one has gone crazy! By God, we don't know of any red female camel or reddish male camel of his." They then dismissed the slave and called al-Ḥārith and recounted to him what they had been told. He said, "He has warned you. When he said 'the *ʿarfaj* plant has chastised me' it was a metaphor for men who have girded themselves, that is, who are wearing armor for raiding. When he said 'and the women have taken the skin of a kid to churn milk,' it meant that they have taken skins in preparation for travel (it is well known that the word *al-shikāʾ* is the plural of *shakwah*, 'skin'). By *ḥays* he meant a mixture of people preparing for a raid, since *al-ḥays* is a blend of curd, butter, and dates." Everything is God's to command.

In the 1060s [1650s] I was traveling for my studies. I entered a village in the region of Dukkālah and saw an old man who kept to the mosque, and away from other people. I approved of his lifestyle and sat with him. There is a hadith: "If you see a man who has been granted renunciation of the world and is of few words, draw close to him—he imparts wisdom." When I drew close, he began to praise knowledge and the people of knowledge in the grandest 15.1

فكنت أجلس بين يديه ويحدّثني ويصبّرني على الغربة ويحضّني على العلم رحمة الله عليه. وأنشدني في شأن الغربة ملحونًا:

أَنَا ٱلْغَـرِيبُ ٱلْمُتَوِّحُ   صَابِرٌ عَلَى كُلِّ هَانَا
إِلَى نَتْجَرَّحُ مَا نَقَلَ احَ   فِي قَلْبِ مَنْ قَطَعْتُ أَنَا

٢،١٥ وفي نحو هذا يقول الشاعر: [طويل]

إِذَا كُنْتَ فِي قَوْمٍ عِدًا لَسْتَ مِنْهُمُ   فَكُلْ مَا عُلِفْتَ مِنْ خَبِيثٍ وَطَيِّبِ
وَإِنْ حَدَّثَتْكَ ٱلنَّفْسُ أَنَّكَ قَادِرٌ   عَلَى مَا حَوَتْ أَيْدِي ٱلرِّجَالِ فَكَذِّبِ

٣،١٥ وقال الآخر: [بسيط]

لَا يُعْدَمُ ٱلْمَرْءُ كِنًّا يَسْتَقِرُّ بِهِ   وَبُلْغَةً بَيْنَ أَهْلِيهِ وَأَحْبَابِهْ
وَمَنْ نَأَى عَنْهُمُ قَلَّتْ مَهَابَتُهُ   كَٱللَّيْثِ يُحْقَرُ لَمَّا غَابَ عَنْ غَابِهْ

٤،١٥ وقال الحريري: [بسيط]

إِنَّ ٱلْغَرِيبَ ٱلطَّوِيلَ ٱلذَّيْلِ مُمْتَهَنٌ   فَكَيْفَ حَالُ غَرِيبٍ مَا لَهُ قُوتُ

٥،١٥ وأنشدني في مدح العلم ملحونًا:

أَلْعِلْمُ شَمْعًا مُنِيرًا   يَتَنَاوَلُهُ ٱلْأَكْيَاسُ
مَا فَوْقَ مِنُّو ذَخِيرًا   يَزُولُ عَنِ ٱلْقَلْبِ ٱلْإِحْسَاسُ[1]

وفضل العلم وشرفه أبهر وأشهر من أن يذكر وأوضح من أن ينكر ويكفي في ذلك النظر.

---

١ ق: الادناس.

fashion. My wonder increased, so I sat in front of him as he spoke with me, urging me to endure being far from home, and inciting me to acquire knowledge, may God have mercy upon him. He recited a poem in colloquial Arabic to me on the subject of being far from one's home:

I am far from home, wandering,
Enduring every calamity.
One who does not even say "ah!"
When pierced in the heart. That's me.

On this subject, a poet has said:[140] 15.2

If you are with a foreign tribe,
then eat what you are fed, exquisite or vile.
If your desires tell you that you can take
what their men possess, they lie!

Another poet said:[141] 15.3

A man does not lack a place in which to seek shelter,
nor the means to reach his loved ones and family.
Whoever is far from these has lost dignity,
like a lion who is despised when he is far from his hollow.

Al-Ḥarīrī said:[142] 15.4

A rich man is humbled when he is far from home.
What then the state of the stranger without food?

He recited another colloquial poem to me in praise of knowledge: 15.5

Knowledge is a shining candle
Acquired by the prudent.
There is no treasure greater than it;
It removes all pain from the heart.

One only has to look at it to see that the virtue and nobility of knowledge are greater than can be expressed and too clear to be denied.

ومن غريب ما حكي أنّه اتّفق للفقيه الخليل الإمام ابن عرفة رضي الله عنه وكان قد مرض فأصابه غشي. قال فجاءتني طائفتان إحداهما عن يميني وجعلوا يرجون الإسلام والأخرى عن يساري وجعلوا يرجون الكفر عياذاً بالله تعالى. قال فأخذ هؤلاء يلقون شبه الكفّار ويلهمني الله تعالى الجواب عنها بما كنت عرفت من قواعد العقائد. فعلمت أنّ العلم ينفع صاحبه في الدنيا والآخرة. لله الأمر من قبل ومن بعد. ٦،١٥

خرجت في أعوام التسعين وألف من حضرة مراكش حرسها الله وكنت إذ ذاك منزعجًا عن الوطن مبايًا للقطين والسكن. فلقيت أعرابياً من هوارة وهم حيّ من شبانة فإذا هو قد انزعج عن وطنه في السوس الأقصى. فحدّثني عن أحمد بن عبد الله بن مبارك الوقاوي أنّه كان هبّت له ريح فحسده قومه. وقالوا عنه وهو في غربته حتّى خرج عن وطنه إلى وداي السوس. قال فجئته ذات مرّة وهو في غربته فقال لي أين العرب وأين القوالون؟ قال فقلت هم بحالهم لم يزالوا يقولون. قال ثمّ أنشد هو ملحونًا: ٧،١٥

إِلَى بَـرَكَ لِي ٱلزَّمَانُ أَرْكَبْتُ عَلَيْهِ   وَلَّى دَارَ ٱلْمَوْلَى نَلْقَاهُ عِـرَاضَـا
بَـرَكَ لِي مَرْكُوبٌ فَإِنِّي ضَارِي بِهِ   مَا نَحْسَبْشِ أَيَّامِي عَلَيَّ مُغْتَاضَـا
نَصْبِرُ لِأَحْكَامِ ٱلْمَوْلَى حَتَّى تَتَقَاضَـا

في قوله مغتاضاً من الغيظ وأبدل من الظاء هنا ضاداً.

وكان هذا من عجيب الاتّفاق فإنّ هذا القول مناسب لأحوالنا معشر الثلاثة أعني القائل والراوي والسامع. وقوله نصبر لأحكام المولى حتّى تتقاضا هذا هو أدب العبد. وهو الصبر لأحكام الله تعالى والسكون تحت مجاري الأقدار. قال تعالى ﴿وَٱصْبِرْ لِحُكْمِ رَبِّكَ﴾ ونحوه من نصوص الكتاب والسنّة وأقوال أئمّة الدين لا يحصى. لله الأمر من قبل ومن بعد.[١] ٨،١٥

١ سقطت الجملة من ق، ط.

One of the strange things that people recount regards the great jurist and exemplar Ibn ʿArafah, God be pleased with him, when he fell ill and fainted. Ibn ʿArafah related: "Two groups came to me. The one on my right began to argue in favor of Islam, the one on my left in favor of unbelief, Exalted God preserve us! The latter began to put themselves forward in the manner of unbelievers, and Exalted God inspired me with a rebuttal of their positions based on what I knew of the tenets of their creeds. Thus, I know that knowledge benefits the one who possesses it both in this world and the next." Everything is God's to command. 15.6

In the 1090s [1680s] I left the city of Marrakesh, may God protect it. At that time, I was restless in my own homeland, not disposed to staying in one place or settling down. I met a Bedouin from the Hawārah, a tribe of the Shabānah. He had been restless in his homeland in distant Sūs and spoke to me of Aḥmad ibn ʿAbd Allāh ibn Mubārak al-Waqāwī, who had been blessed by fortune, and whose people envied him. They had spread gossip against him while he had been abroad, so he left his homeland for the Sūs Valley. The Bedouin continued, "I came to him once when he was far from his homeland, and he asked, 'How are the gossiping Arabs?' and I replied, 'Status quo, still gossiping.' He then recited a poem in colloquial Arabic:[143] 15.7

> I ride upon my blessings,
> And accept what the Lord has granted us.
> He blessed me with a painful mount,
> Yet I don't think time is angry with me.
> We endure the decrees of the Lord until they are fulfilled."

(In his use of the word *mughtāḍ*, derived from anger, *al-ghayẓ*, he replaced the *ẓāʾ* with a *ḍād*.)

This is a wonderful account—the poem applies to the conditions of all three who are implicated: I mean the speaker, the transmitter, and the listener. Saying "We endure the decrees of the Lord until they are fulfilled" decribes the proper comportment of the worshipper, which consists in enduring the rulings of Exalted God, and quiet acceptance of what has been decreed. The Exalted has said: «And be thou patient under the judgment of thy Lord.»[144] There are innumerable passages like this in the Qur'an, in Prophetic Practice, and in the sayings of the religious scholars. Everything is God's to command. 15.8

١،١٦ واعلم أنّ الحكم حكمان حكم تكليفيّ وحكم تصريفيّ وكلاهما يجب الإذعان له والتسليم. أمّا التكليفيّ فهو الوجوب والندب والتحريم والكراهة والإباحة التي وردت بها الشريعة المطهّرة. وأمّا التصريفيّ فهو ما قدّر على العبد من غير ذلك ممّا يردّ عليه كالغنى والفقر والعزّ والذلّ والصحّة والمرض والسرور والحزن وغير ذلك. ومورد الأوّل كلام الله تعالى أمرًا ونهيًا. ومورد الثاني قدرته تعالى إيجادًا وإعدامًا على وفق مشيئته وعلمه. وكما لا بدّ من قبول الأوّل وامتثاله فعلًا وتركًا وتلقّيه بالصبر على ما فيه من المشقّة على النفس وقد تضمحلّ أيضًا دواعي النفس فيرتقي العبد إلى الرضى والاستلذاذ.

٢،١٦ كذلك لا بدّ في الثاني من تلقّي محبوبه بالشكر ومكروهه بالصبر وقد تضمحلّ أيضًا دواعي النفس فيرتقي العبد إلى الرضى. ثمّ إنّ كلّ شيء قدّر على العبد فلا محالة يقدّر له وقت يقع فيه لا يتقدّمه ولا يتأخّر عنه. فمتى حان وقت شيء فهو بارز لا محالة خيرًا كان أو شرًّا لا يمكن أن لا يبرز ولا أن يبرز غيره في موضعه. فالبصير يستكنّ حتّى ينقضي بانقضاء وقته فيجمع بين راحة قلبه والأدب مع ربّه. والجاهل يقلق منه أو يروم ظهور غيره دونه فيصير أحمق الحمقاء ولا يحصل إلّا على الشقاء.

٣،١٦ وقال صاحب الحكم العطائيّة ما ترك من الجهل شيئًا من أراد أن يظهر في الوقت غير ما أظهر الله فيه. وقالوا الوقت سيف وأنشدوا: [طويل]

وَكَالسَّيْفِ إِنْ لَايَنْتَهُ لَانَ مَسُّهُ   وَحَدَّاهُ إِنْ خَاشَنْتَهُ خَشِنَانِ

ولله الأمر من قبل وبعد.[١]

٤،١٦ وأنشدني أبو القاسم بن بوعتل الشبانيّ ثمّ الزراريّ لبعض الأعراب ملحونًا:

١ سقطت الجملة من ق، ط.

Divine decree consists of two judgments, one a legal obligation, and one allotted to you. Both require compliance and submission. Legal obligation entails the categories required, recommended, forbidden, discouraged, and permitted, all present in the pristine, divine law. The allotted deals with what has been determined for the worshipper beyond these categories, such as wealth, poverty, glory, humiliation, health, sickness, happiness, grief, and so forth. The source for the first is the speech of Exalted God, which contains both obligation and prohibition. The source for the second is the power of Exalted God to create and undo in accordance with His will and knowledge. It is necessary to accept the first and comply with it, either by performing or refraining from action, and to accept with forbearance the difficulties for the ego that it brings with it, so that the impulses of the ego might fade and the worshipper rise to the stage of contentment and pleasure. 16.1

In the same way, it is also necessary to accept the second and receive what one loves with gratitude and what one dislikes with forbearance. Here too, the demands of the ego may fade away and the worshipper can rise to the stage of contentment. As everything is decreed for the worshipper, it is inevitable that a time is decreed for everything that cannot be advanced or postponed. When something's time comes, it inevitably takes place, whether good or bad. It is impossible for it not to take place or for something else to take place instead. The clear-sighted person has faith that what has been decreed takes place at its appointed time; his heart is thus at peace, and he displays the proper comportment to his Lord. The ignorant person, anxious about what is going to happen or desirous that something else happen, becomes the greatest fool, and experiences nothing but hardship. 16.2

The author of *The Wise Sayings of Ibn ʿAṭāʾ Allāh* writes: "One cannot demonstrate ignorance any better than by desiring something else to occur than what God has decreed for that moment." People say, "Each moment is a sword," and quote the following: 16.3

> It is like a sword, soft when touched gently,
> but with sharp edges if treated roughly.

Everything is God's to command.

Abū l-Qāsim ibn Būʿtal al-Shabbānī, later known as al-Zarrārī, recited to me a poem in colloquial Arabic that he had heard from a certain Bedouin: 16.4

يَا رَأْسِي عَيْبُكْ بَانْ | وَالِى عَيْبُو فِي وَجْهُو مَا يَصِيبُ اِيدْسُو
قَالُوا عِلَّةْ ٱبْنِ آدَمِ شَيْطَانْ | وَإِنَّا نَقُولُ عِلَّةُ ٱبْنِ آدَمِ نَفْسُو
قَبْلَ لَا يَزِيغْ إِبْلِيسْ | اِشْ يَكُونْ اِبْلِيسُو

٥،١٦ فانظر إلى هذا الأعرابيّ كيف غاص على معنى كبير وهو أنّ نفس الإنسان سبب هلاكه بإذن الله تعالى إلّا من عصمه الله. وكيف وقع على حجّة برهانيّة وقياس منظوم في النفس وتقريره أن يقول لو كان كلّ زائغ إنّما يزيغ بشيطان لكان إبليس حين زاغ بإبليس آخر. والتالي باطل للزوم التسلسل فالمقدّم مثله. ونحو هذا في الاستدلال ما وقع للنبيّ صلّى الله عليه وسلّم حيث أبطل العدوى بمعنى أنّه لا تأثير فيها لغير الله تعالى. فقال له الأعرابيّ ما بالنا نرى الإبل تكون في الرمل كأنّها الظباء فيدخلها جمل أجرب فتجرب كلّها؟ فقال له صلّى الله عليه وسلّم فمن أعدى الأوّل؟ أي لو كان جمل إنّما يأتيه هذا البلاء من آخر قبله لزم التسلسل وهو باطل. فلا بدّ أن ينتهي الأمر إلى بعير يصيبه البلاء من عند الله بلا سبب هذه العدوى. فيعلم عند ذلك أنّ الله تعالى هو الفاعل المختار يفعل الشيء عند الشيء وهو قادر أن يفعله بلا شيء ولا عند شيء. سبحانه عمّا يشركون.

٦،١٦ واعلم أنّ ما ذكره هذا الأعرابيّ في ملحونه من أنّ علّة الإنسان نفسه صحيح وعزله الشيطان عن ذلك غير صحيح. إن أراد أنّه لا مدخل له وإن أراد أنّه غير مستقلّ بالإضرار لمشاركة النفس له أو أنّ ضرر النفس هو الأعظم لأنّها المباشرة والشيطان متسبّب فصحيح. وتقرير هذه الجملة باختصار إنّ كلاً من النفس والشيطان مضرّ بالعبد فهما متظاهران على العبد كما قال بعضهم وقد ضمّ إليهما الدنيا والهوى:

[كامل]

My goodness, your fault has become apparent:
Those who fault you to your face have it wrong.[145]
They said mankind is afflicted by the devil.
We say the sons of Adam are afflicted by the ego.
Before Satan went astray
Who was his Satan?

Consider how this Bedouin has immersed himself in the greater meaning—namely, that by the leave of Exalted God, and leaving aside those God protects, man's ego is the reason for his destruction. How did he stumble upon the logical proof and reasoned analogy regarding the self? His statement is equal to your saying, "If everyone who deviates does so because of the devil, then when he deviates, Satan does so because of another Satan." The latter example is invalid as it forces an infinite regression, and the first example is exactly like it. This type of inference took place when the Prophet, God bless and keep him, denied contagion in the sense that nothing but Exalted God has influence on anything. A Bedouin said to him, "What are we to think when we see camels like gazelles upon the sand, and then a mangy camel joins them and all become mangy?" The Prophet, God bless and keep him, said, "Who infected the first one?" That is to say, if the camel has received this affliction from another before him it would necessarily imply an infinite regression, which is invalid. The matter has to have its origins in a camel that had been afflicted by God, not from contagion.[146] This is how it is known that Exalted God is the freely acting Agent, who creates something in association with something else, but is able to create it from nothing or in association with nothing. «High be He exalted above that they associate with Him.»[147] 16.5

What the Bedouin said in his poem is true—namely, that mankind's disease is his ego. But his separating the devil from this is false if he meant that he has nothing to do with the matter. If he meant that the devil cannot harm independently as the ego must be complicit with him, or that the damage done by the ego is greater, as it carries it out while the devil provides the impulse, then he is correct. In brief, the explanation of this sentence is the following: Both the devil and the ego are harmful to the worshipper. As someone has said, the worshipper faces both of these along with this temporal world and vain desire: 16.6

إِنِّي بُلِيتُ بِأَرْبَعٍ يَرْمِينَنِي ... بِٱلنَّبْلِ عَنْ قَوْسٍ لَهَا تَوْتِيرُ
إِبْلِيسُ وَٱلدُّنْيَا وَنَفْسِي وَٱلْهَوَى ... يَا رَبِّ أَنْتَ عَلَى ٱلْخَلَاصِ قَدِيرُ

وسبب ذلك أنّ الآدميّ لمّا أبدعه الله تعالى بقدرته مؤتلفاً من الأخلاط ذا مزاج جعله سبحانه بباهر حكمته وسابق مشيئته مفتقرًا عادة في بقاء وجوده الشخصيّ إلى القوام. وهو الغذاء بالطعام والشراب وفي بقاء وجوده النوعيّ إلى التوالد بواسطة النكاح. فطبع فيه عند ذلك شهوة الأكل وشهوة النكاح. و لولم يكن ذلك طبعاً لافتقر إلى داع آخر فيتسلسل أو يبقى فاترًا عن ذلك فيهلك شخصاً أو نوعاً فسبحان المدبّر الحكيم.

٧،١٦ ثمّ لمّا كانت الشهوتان أعني الأكل والنكاح لا تحصلان إلّا من مادّة وهي المال وبه يحصل المأكول والنساء وبهنّ يحصل النكاح المؤدّي إلى التناسل المذكور والنساء لا يحصلن إلّا بالمال أيضاً. طبع الله فيه حبّ المال وحبّ النساء وكلّ ما يستعان به في ذلك الباب من صحّة وقدرة وجاه. وذلك هو مجموع الدنيا فكانت الدنيا محبوبة طبعاً للحكمة المذكورة. وكان ميل النفس إلى شيء من هذه المحبوبات بمقتضى الشهوتين المذكورتين وهو المعبّر عنه بالهوى طبعاً في الإنسان. وكلّ ذلك في أصله رحمة من الله تعالى للإنسان كما ترى إذ لولا ذلك لم يستمرّ له وجود.

٨،١٦ ثمّ جعل الله تعالى العبد متأثرًا بالعوارض في بدنه وفي ماله وفي حريمه ونحو ذلك. فافتقر إلى احتماء عن ذلك ودفاع فطبع فيه الغضب. وهو أيضاً رحمة منه تعالى إذ لولا هو لم ينتهض للدفع عن نفسه ولا حريمه ولا ماله ولا جاره ولا غير ذلك ولا لتغيير منكر ولا نحو ذلك. ثمّ إنّ النفس لمّا كان فيها ذلك طبعاً استعدّت لأن تتقاضاه من كلّ وجه طلباً لحصول المرام على التمام. فتأكل مثلاً وتبالغ ولا تقتصر على القدر المحتاج

I am afflicted by four things
launched against me, arrows from a taut bow:
Satan, this world, my ego, and vain desire.
Lord, salvation is through Your power.

The reason is that when Exalted God created man through His power, composing his temperament out of the humors, the Almighty used His splendid wisdom and express will to make him habitually require sustenance for the continuation of his personal existence. This sustenance consisted of nourishment through food and drink, and the continuing of his existence as a species required reproduction through sex. For this reason, God placed in man a desire to eat and a desire for sex. If this desire had not been imprinted in him, he would have lacked an impetus to do so and he would become or remain listless and would die as an individual and as a species. Glory be to the Wise Arranger of events.

These two desires—I mean food and sex—cannot be fulfilled except through means, that is, through assets. With assets one acquires food and women.[148] One can have licit sex with women, which leads to procreation as I've mentioned. Women can only be acquired with assets—God placed in man a love for assets, for women, and for everything required to ensure health, power, and rank. These things all belong to the temporal world. By his nature man desires the temporal world in accordance with the wisdom mentioned above. The ego's inclination to any of the things that are beloved by the temporal world is in accordance with these two desires—this inclination is referred to as man's natural desire. As you can see, all of this is in its very origin a mercy of Exalted God for mankind, since without it he would not continue to exist. 16.7

Then Exalted God contrived that the worshipper be influenced by the changing circumstances of his body, his possessions, his women, and so forth. Since man needs to protect and defend all of these, He placed anger in his nature. This too is a mercy from the Exalted, since in its absence, man would not rise up to defend himself, nor his women, his possessions, his neighbor, or anything else. Neither would he rise up to change what is wrong, and such. When these were instilled in the nature of the ego, it became prepared to seek to fulfill its desire in any way possible. For example, it eats and does so excessively, not keeping itself to the necessary amount, nor holding back from harmful excess. It drinks and has sex in a similar fashion and does not then 16.8

ولا تتنزّه عن الزائد المضرّ. وتشرب كذلك وتنكح ثمّ لا تبالي من أيّ وجه حصل ذلك أمن مأذون فيه أم محرّم لأنّ سعيها طبعيّ لا شرعيّ.

٩،١٦ وكذا في غضبها ودفاعها. فمتى تركت وذلك أضرّت بالعبد عاجلاً بحصول الأمراض وإتلاف الأموال في الشهوات وانتهاك الأعراض والمروءات وكثرة اللجاج والعدوان والهلاك والبوار. وآجلاً بالتعريض لطول الحساب وأليم العقاب عند وجوب التكليف. وهذه هي المضرّة المنسوبة للنفس فخلق الله تعالى العقل ليكون محتسباً عليها حتّى تكون فيما ذكر من الشهوة والغضب تابعة لإشارة العقل أخذاً وتركاً. وأودع الله تعالى في العقل إدراك المصالح والمفاسد والمنافع والمضارّ حتّى يعلم ما يشير به أمراً ونهياً ليجري الأمر على السداد فلا يقع قصور عن المراد ولا التعدّي إلى ما يوجب الفساد.

١٠،١٦ ثمّ لمّا كان العقل أيضاً معرّضاً للخطأ وللقصور عن كثير من المصالح وللجهل بكثير من المدارك ولا سيّما المغيبات لأنّ النقصان شأن المخلوق افتقر هو أيضاً إلى مؤيّد إمّا إلهام من الله تعالى وإمّا عقل آخر أكمل كما في حال التربية وتلقين الحكمة. وإمّا وحي سماوي وهو أكمل فأنزلت الأحكام وشرّعت الشرائع وانتسبت الأحكام إليها عند أهل الحقّ لا إلى العقل فصار العقل مؤيّداً للشرع ومتأيّداً به.

١١،١٦ ثمّ إنّ إبليس اللعين عندما وقع له من الخزي والطرد مع صفيّ الله آدم عليه السلام ما وقع صار عدوّاً له حسوداً حقوداً وكذا لذرّيّته إلى يوم القيامة. قال تعالى ﴿يَٰٓـَٔادَمُ إِنَّ هَٰذَا عَدُوٌّ لَّكَ وَلِزَوْجِكَ﴾. وقال تعالى ﴿إِنَّ ٱلشَّيْطَٰنَ لَكُمْ عَدُوٌّ﴾. وقال تعالى ﴿إِنَّهُۥ لَكُمْ عَدُوٌّ مُّبِينٌ﴾. وقال تعالى ﴿إِنَّ ٱلشَّيْطَٰنَ لَكُمَا عَدُوٌّ مُّبِينٌ﴾ إلى غير ذلك. فكان دأبه السعي في مضرّة الآدميّ كما يسعى كلّ عدوّ في مضرّة عدوّه. ولم يجد إلى مضرّته سبيلاً أيسر ولا سبباً أنجح من أن يأتيه من قبل النفس وطريق الطبع فيزيّن له ما طبع من الشهوات ويسوّل له كلّ قبيح. قال تعالى ﴿ٱلشَّيْطَٰنُ يَعِدُكُمُ ٱلْفَقْرَ وَيَأْمُرُكُم بِٱلْفَحْشَآءِ﴾.

consider why it does this or whether it was permitted or forbidden, since its drive derives from its nature and not revelation.

The same is the case with its anger and self-defense. For when the ego is left alone, this harms the worshipper in the short run through his becoming sick, losing his possessions to base desires, violating reputations and honor, and through excessive obstinacy, enmity, destruction, and ruin. In the long run, in light of man's legal obligation before God, it exposes the believer to the full extent of the Divine reckoning and the torment of the punishment. This is the harm that proceeds from the ego, and Exalted God created reason to watch over it, so that when it came to desire and anger, it would guide it when choosing what to do and what not to. Exalted God granted reason the ability to perceive beneficial and harmful matters so that the worshipper should know which actions God signaled him to perform, and from which to refrain, so as to carry out his affairs in the appropriate manner. In this way, he does not fall short of the desired goal, nor does he venture into something that would entail corruption. 16.9

Now, reason is also susceptible to error, to falling short in achieving many beneficial matters, and to ignorance in many matters of sensory perception, especially regarding the unseen world. This is because every created being is deficient and requires some type of help, either in the form of inspiration from Exalted God or from the more developed reason that comes from instruction and the imparting of wisdom. In the case of heavenly revelation—the most perfect form of instruction—through it, rulings were revealed and divine laws were legislated. Those with proper understanding attribute divine rulings to it and not to reason—reason supports revelation and is dependent on it. 16.10

When God chose Adam, peace be upon him, accursed Satan experienced shame and expulsion, and became his enemy out of jealousy and hatred, and will remain so to all Adam's offspring until the day of resurrection. The Almighty said: «Adam, surely this is an enemy to thee and thy wife.» «Surely the devil is a foe to you.» «Surely, he is a manifest foe to you.» «Verily the devil is for you a manifest foe,»[149] among other examples. He has persevered in attempting to harm mankind, as every enemy attempts to harm his foe, and he has found no easier fashion nor better way to do this than to come at him through the ego and his nature. He cultivated in him the desires he had been given and enticed him to every vile act. The Exalted said: «Satan promises you poverty, and bids you unto indecency.»[150] 16.11

١٢،١٦ فحصل اتّفاق بين النفس والشيطان على مضرّة الآدميّ غير أنّ المقصد مختلف فإنّ النفس لم تكن منها المضرّة عن قصد وعداوة. كيف ولا أحبّ إلى كل أحد من نفسه بل جهلاً وغلطاً وذلك أنّها أدركت ما في طبعها من الشهوات الحاضرة فاستحسنته وظنّت أنّ ذلك هو كمال صاحبها إذا ناله. فجاء الشيطان فأغراها ممّا استحسنت وزيّن لها ما ظنّت فاعتقدته نصيحاً واتّخذته خليلاً تلبّي دعوته وتجيب رغبته فأُتيَ الإنسان منها وتمكّن منه عدوُّه من طريقها فصارت من هذه الوجه عدّوة بل أكبر الأعداء.

١٣،١٦ وأمّا الشيطان لعنه الله فهو يفعل ما يفعل عن عداوة وقصد إضرار. فإنّه لمّا خاب من رحمة الله وطرد عن بابه نسأل الله العافية أراد أن يسعى في خيبة الآدميّ وبعده عن الله وحرمانه من نعيم الجنّة باتّباع الدنيا وغرورها والإكباب على شهواتها. واعلم أنّ الشيطان لشدّة عداوته للإنسان ليس له غرض في اتبّاع الإنسان للشهوات وتمتّعه باللذات.

١٤،١٦ بل لو أمكنه أن يسعى في حرمانه دائماً فلا ينال لذّة عاجلة ولا آجلة. ولا يحصل على منفعة في الدنيا ولا في الآخرة لكان ذلك هو منيته ورغبته. وهو مقتضى العداوة وثمرة الحسد إلّا أنّه لمّا لم يمكنه ذلك لفيضان رحمة الله على عباده وسبوغ نعمه عليهم رأى أن يرتكب به أعظم الضررين فيستزلّه عن أعظم الحظّين بل الحظّ الذي هو الحظّ وهو الأخرويّ. ويستهويه إلى الحظّ الدنيويّ ورأى أنّه إذا خاب عن النفيس الباقي واستبدله بالخسيس الفاني فقد خاب والأمر كذلك. فإنّ ما في الدنيا لو كان نفيساً وهو بصدد الانقطاع لم يلتفت إليه فكيف وهو مع ذلك خسيس مشوب متكدّر؟

١٥،١٦ بل لو كان نعيم الآخرة النفيس ينقطع لوجب أن يلتفت إليه إذ النفس إنّما تجد النعمة ما دامت متناولة لها فإذا انقطعت عنها تكدّرت كالصبيّ الراضع متى صرف الثدي عن فيه صاح.

There was then an agreement between the ego and the devil to harm mankind, despite their differing goals. The harm done by the ego is not caused intentionally or due to enmity. How could this be the case when no one loves another more than himself? Instead, the harm is done out of ignorance and inadvertence. It happens because the ego perceives the desires that are within its nature and considers them to be positive, and to lead to perfection if obtained. At that moment, the devil approaches and seduces the ego away from what it considered to be good, and embellishes what it had been thinking about so that it will take its advice. The ego takes the devil to be its friend, answering his appeal and responding to his wishes. The devil approaches mankind through the ego and by means of it overpowers his enemy. In this sense, the ego is the greatest of mankind's enemies. 16.12

As for the devil, God curse him, he does what he does out of enmity and out of a desire to cause harm. When his hopes for the mercy of God were dashed and he was expelled from His door—we ask God to preserve us from this—he strove to defeat mankind, and to distance it from God and from the divine sanctity that comes from the grace of heaven by having mankind pursue the temporal world, its deception and its desires. By dint of the intensity of the devil's enmity toward mankind, his goal is not to pursue man out of pleasure or for his enjoyment. 16.13

On the contrary, even if he assailed God's sanctity for all eternity he would not attain pleasure, in either the short or long run. Nor would he achieve any benefit in this world or the next had this been his goal or desire. He is bound to enmity and the fruit of envy, except when this is not possible for him because God has granted His mercy to His worshippers and bestowed His grace upon them. The devil turns then to committing the greatest of harm through the ego: He seeks to have man slip from the greater of the two fates—man's fate in the hereafter. The devil tempts him to the fate of the temporal world, believing that if mankind is prevented from the eternal goal and replaces it with the contemptible temporal one, mankind will go astray. And this is indeed the case. For if the temporal world were precious and about to cease, man would not turn toward it; how then when the world is vile, adulterated, and impure? 16.14

However, if the grace of the pure world to come were cut off from him, mankind would have to turn toward it: The ego finds grace as long as it is available, and if it is withdrawn, it is annoyed, like a nursing child who cries when the breast is taken from it. 16.15

١٦،١٦ وما مثال النفس في ذلك إلّا مثال المرأة في قوله صلّى الله عليه وسلّم إنّهنّ يكفرن العشير وإنّك لو أحسنت إلى إحداهنّ الدّهر كلّه ثمّ رأت منك شيئاً قالت ما رأيت منك خيراً قطّ. فقد تحصل من هذا أنّ النفس مضرّة بالإنسان من وجهين. أحدهما أنّها تميل طبعاً إلى الشهوات وتخلد إلى الرعونات. الثاني أنّها مسلك الشيطان إلى الإنسان كما مرّ وإنّ الشيطان مضرّ للإنسان أبداً بوسوسته وتزيينه للنفس.

١٧،١٦ وهذه كلّها أسباب جعليّة اقتضتها الحكمة والنافع والضارّ بالحقيقة هو الله تعالى وتبيّن أنّ النفس تابعة للشيطان في مضرّة الإنسان سفهاً منها وغلطاً لا عداوة. ولسان حالها ينشد قول القائل: [وافر]

وَخِلْتُهُمُ سِهَاماً صَائِبَاتٍ   فَكَانُوهَا وَلٰكِنْ فِي فُؤَادِي

١٨،١٦ ومن أجل ما ذكرنا بين النفس والشيطان من اختلاف الوجه وتباين المقصد فرّق أئمّة التصوّف رضوان الله عليهم بين الخاطر النفسانيّ والخاطر الشيطانيّ بعد اشتراكهما في الحضّ على السوء في الجملة. وهو أنّ الخاطر إذا تقاضى معصية مثلاً بعينها فإن أصرّ على ذلك فهو نفسانيّ. وإن جعل يتحوّل من معصية إلى أخرى فهو شيطانيّ. ووجه ذلك أنّ النفس إنّما تطلب المعصية بمقتضى طبعها فيها من حيث أنّها شهوة لا غير فلا تريد أن تنفكّ عنها حتّى تنالها بعينها.

١٩،١٦ وأمّا الشيطان فليس طلبه من الإنسان أن ينال شهوة ومتعة من حيث التنعّم بها فإنّه عدوّ بل من حيث إنّها معصية موجبة للعقاب. فمتى دعاه إلى واحدة وتعسّرت أو تلكّأ عليه فيها دعاه إلى أخرى لقيامها مقامها في المقصود. وهو حصول الإثم واستحقاق النار نعوذ بالله تعالى من شرّه. لله الأمر من قبل ومن بعد.

There is no better metaphor for the ego in this matter than that of the woman in the saying of the Prophet, God bless and keep him: "Truly, these women are ungrateful to their closest family. If you were kind to one of them for time eternal and she then took offense at something you did, she would say, 'I have never seen you do anything good.'" From this we can understand that the ego harms mankind in two ways: The first is that it inclines by nature to vain desires and is disposed to frivolity. The second is that it is the devil's path to mankind, as we have discussed, and Satan is an eternal harm to man through his temptations and the fantasies he creates for the ego. 16.16

All of these are efficient causes in accordance with God's wisdom—the true one who grants benefits and causes harm is Exalted God. Wisdom clarifies that the ego is subservient to the devil in harming mankind out of foolishness and by mistake, not out of enmity. This is expressed in the following line: 16.17

I considered them to be arrows that strike their mark.
They were—but it was my heart they struck.

As in our discussion of the distinct natures of the ego and the devil and our clarification of their goals, the foremost Sufi authorities, God be pleased with them, differentiated between the suggestions of the ego and those of the devil, while also grouping them together as incitements to evil. This differentiation consisted in the suggestion that if, for example, a specific sin was called for and insisted upon, then it was attributed to the ego. And if the suggestion called for the person to change from one sin to another, then they attributed it to the devil. The reasoning for this was that the ego seeks after sin in accordance with its nature due to its specific desire, and does not wish to leave off from doing so until it attains that precise sin. 16.18

As for the devil, he does not ask mankind to fulfill desire or pleasure for the sake of enjoying them—he is surely mankind's enemy; instead, he seeks to have man commit sin that leads to punishment. When he calls man to a sin, which is difficult to carry out or from which he hesitates, the devil calls him to commit another in its place. The goal is to have man commit a sin and become deserving of the fire, from the evil of which we seek refuge with Exalted God. Everything is God's to command. 16.19

خطر لي ذات ليلة بيت للملك الضلّيل امرئ القيس بن حجر. فوجدته قد احتوى على مقتضى الشريعة الظاهرة والباطنة وتضمّن كلّ ما تحصل عن دواوين أئمّة الدين وأقاويل الصوفيّة فقضيت العجب من ذلك وعلمت أنّ الله تعالى من باهر قدرته وعجيب حكمته يبرز الحكمة على لسان من شاء وإن لم يكن من أهلها. كما قال بعض السلف حين سمع بعض الولاة نطق بحكمة خذوها من قلب خَرِبٍ. وتبيّنت إشارة قوله صلّى الله عليه وسلّم: الحكمة ضالّة المؤمن. أي[١] فحقّه أن يتلقّفها ممّن وجدها عنده وإن لم يكن مُرضياً كما يأخذ ضالّته من الدنيا كذلك وتبيّنت صدق قوله صلّى الله عليه وسلّم إنّ من الشّعر لحكمةً. وقول الحكماء[٢] الأوّلين: أنزلت الحكمة على ثلاثة أعضاء في الجسد على قلوب اليونان وأيدي أهل الصين وألسنة العرب. ١٧،١

والبيت المذكور هو قوله: [كامل] ١٧،٢

ٱللهُ أَنْجَحُ مَا طَلَبْتَ بِهِ وَٱلْبِرُّ خَيْرُ حَقِيبَةِ ٱلرَّحْلِ

فالشطر الأوّل قد احتوى على الحقيقة كلّها وهي باطن الشريعة. فإنّ معناه أنّ ما طلبته بالله فأنت منجح فيه.

وهو كما قال في الحكم العطائيّة ما تعسّر مطلب أنت طالبه بربّك وما تيسّر مطلب أنت طالبه بنفسك. ومعلوم أنّك لست تروم ذلك إلّا وأنت تعرف الله تعالى وأنّه حقّ لا شريك له وأنّه هو الفاعل المدبّر النافع الضارّ. ثمّ تنفي عن نفسك وعن حولها وقوّتها وتدبيرها واختيارها وتبغي بربّك. وهذا هو سرّ العبوديّة وهو الكنز الذي يحوم حوله المريدون ويعنو إليه السالكون. وهو المشار إليه في قوله صلّى الله عليه وسلّم: لا حول ولا قوّة إلّا بالله كنز من كنوز الجنّة. ١٧،٣

١ سقط من ط. ٢ ط: الشعراء.

One evening a line by the errant king Imru' al-Qays ibn Ḥujr came to my mind and I realized that it encompassed both the internal and external intent of the revealed law, and contained everything you can obtain from the tomes written by religious authorities and from the sayings of the Sufis. I was struck with wonder at this, and knew that it was a reflection of the scintillating power of Exalted God and the marvel of His wisdom that He places it on the tongue of whomever He wishes, even if that person is not one of the wise. As one of the pious predecessors said, upon hearing a worldly ruler say something wise: "Take it from a destructive heart." The whole matter is explained by a saying of the Prophet, God bless and keep him: "The wise saying is the lost camel of the believer."[151] That is to say, it is the believer's right to seize lost property from whoever possesses it. If he is not content with having obtained his goal from the temporal world in this fashion, let the matter be clarified by the truth of the Prophet's saying, God bless and keep him, "There is wisdom in poetry." There is also the saying of the first philosophers: "Wisdom has been placed in three organs: the hearts of the Greeks, the hands of the Chinese, and the tongues of the Arabs." 17.1

The line of poetry by Imru' al-Qays to which I referred earlier is: 17.2

> God grants success to whatever you seek through Him.
> The best provision to take when traveling is piety.

The first line contains the entire truth, which is the core meaning of the revealed law. Its meaning is that you will be successful in what you seek if it is through God.

This is as the author of *The Wise Sayings of Ibn ʿAṭāʾ Allāh* has said: "The goal you seek through your Lord will not be hard for you; that which you seek through yourself will not be easy." It is well known that you should not seek something unless you know Exalted God to truly have no partner, and to be the determining Agent who grants benefit and inflicts harm. Banish everything but this from your ego, from what surrounds it, from its management, and from what it chooses, and seek your Lord. This is the secret of worship, the treasure around which the disciples circle and before which the seekers humble themselves. This is what the Prophet, bless and keep him, was referring to when he said, "Saying that there is no might or power except in God is one of the treasures of heaven." 17.3

وهذا هو كليّة الأمر ولا حاجة إلى التطويل. والشطر الثاني قد تضمّن الشريعة كلّها وهي أنّ البرّ خير ما تحمّله العبد وادّخره أي والفجور شر ما تحمّله. ويدخل في البرّ برُّ العبد مع ربّه بطاعته له قولاً وفعلاً واعتقاداً. وكذا مع من أوجب الله تعالى طاعته من نبيّ وأمير ومالك ووالد ونحوهم. وبرّه مع الناس بالإحسان فعلاً وقولاً وخلقاً وهو مجموع ما يطلب شرعاً ولا حاجة إلى التطويل. لله الأمر من قبل ومن بعد.[1] ٤،١٧

واعلم أنّ البيت قد اشتمل على مثلثين مستقلّين كما رأيت فرأيت أن أستطرد هنا من أبيات الحكمة والتمثيل نبذة صالحة يقع بها الإمتاع ويحصل الانتفاع. فمن ذلك قول لبيد: [طويل] ٥،١٧

أَلَا كُلُّ شَيْءٍ مَا خَلَا اللهَ بَاطِلُ   وَكُلُّ نَعِيمٍ لَا مَحَالَةَ زَائِلُ

واعلم أنّ هذا البيت مع كونه في غاية الحكمة وكونه قد شهد له الرسول صلّى الله عليه وسلّم بذلك كما ورد في الحديث أصدق كلمةٍ قالها الشّاعر قول لبيدٍ ألا كلّ شيء ما خلا البيت يسأل عنه.

فيقال مثلاً في المصراع الأوّل إنّ معرفة الله تعالى وشرعه ودينه وأنبياءه ونحو ذلك داخل فيما جعله باطلاً وليس بباطل. وفي الثاني إنّ نعيم الآخرة غير زائل فيلزم انتقاض الكلّيتين. والجواب عن الأوّل من وجهين أحدهما أنّ المراد ما سوى الله تعالى وما انضاف إليه كما وقع في الحديث الدّنيا ملعونة ملعون ما فيها إلّا ذكر الله وما والاه وعالم أو متعلّم وهذا واضح. فإنّ صفات الله تعالى لا تدخل في الباطل لانضيافها إلى الذات وشمول الاسم لها فكذلك كلّ مُنضاف. ٦،١٧

الثاني أنّ هذا كلام في الحقائق ولا شكّ أنّ الله تعالى هو قديم واجب الوجود فهو حقّ ثابت والعالم كلّه محدث فهو باطل لا ثبوت له من ذاته لكن بإثبات الله تعالى. ٧،١٧

[1] سقطت الجملة من ق، ط.

This is all there is to it; there is no need to elaborate on it. The second line encompasses all of the revealed law—namely, that piety is the best the worshipper can pursue and amass, immorality the worst. Piety consists of the God-fearing nature of the worshipper before his Lord in the form of obedience to Him in word, deed, and belief. This is in addition to those to whom Exalted God has declared obligatory obedience, such as prophets, rulers, kings, parents, and so forth. The worshipper's piety in interactions with people consists of demonstrating what is beautiful in act, word, and character. This is all that revelation demands and there is no need to elaborate further. Everything is God's to command. 17.4

Consider that this line contains two independent lessons, as you have seen, and observe how I adduce here apposite lines containing both wisdom and example—ones that bring pleasure and provide benefit. One such line is Labīd's: 17.5

> Everything except God is vain.
> Without doubt, every delight is transient.

This line, despite its display of the great wisdom, attested to by the Prophet, God bless and keep him, and its being found in the hadith: "The truest saying spoken by a poet was that of the poet Labīd: Everything except . . ." until the end of the line, was open to question.

It could be said, for example, regarding the first hemistich: "Exalted God's knowledge, His revelation, His religion, His prophets, and the like are among what the poet calls vain, yet they are not vain." And regarding the second hemistich: "The delight of the hereafter is not transient. So, both of these must be rejected." The answer to the first of these criticisms consists of two aspects. One of them is that what is intended is nothing other than Exalted God and what is attached to Him, as described in the hadith: "The world and everything in it is damned, except for the remembrance of God and what facilitates it, the scholar, and the seeker of knowledge." This is clear, for none of the attributes of Exalted God can be considered vain due to their association with His being and the fact that they are encompassed in God's name. It is the same with everything that is associated with Him. 17.6

The second aspect is that these words are about theological truths. There is no doubt that Exalted God is eternal and necessarily existent. He is the constant reality. Similarly, there is no doubt that the world is created in its entirety, and that it is vain, with no subsistence through its own being but rather subsistence 17.7

وهذا الوجه أيضاً واضح لا شبهة فيه والموجودات كلّها متى اعتبرت إضافتها وتعلّقها بالله تعالى كانت حقّاً به وهي باطلة بحسب ذاتها ومنها ما هو حقّ باعتبارين أعني بهذا التعلّق وبإثبات الله له شرعاً كما في الوجه الأوّل.

٨،١٧ وهو مع ذلك باعتبار ذاته ولا تنافي في شيء من ذلك فافهم. والجواب عن الثاني ثلاثة أوجه الأوّل أنّ المراد نعيم الدنيا لأنّه هو المعروف المشاهد لا سيّما في حقّ هذا القائل. فإنّه كان حين قوله ذلك جاهليّاً لا ذكر للآخرة عنده. فإن قيل من لك بأنّه إذ ذاك جاهليّ؟ ولعلّه قال هذا بعد الإسلام. قلت قد استفاض في شأنه أنّه لم يقل بعد الإسلام إلّا بيتاً واحداً وهو قوله: [بسيط]

أَلْحَمْدُ لِلّٰهِ إِذْ لَمْ يَأْتِنِي أَجَلِي   حَتَّى لَبِسْتُ مِنَ ٱلْإِسْلَامِ سِرْبَالَا

٩،١٧ على أنّه لو كان بعد الإسلام لكان إرادة الدنيويّ في غاية الوضوح. إذ المراد تهوين أمر الدنيا والتنفير عنها والتزهيد فيها كما وقع ذلك في كلام كثير من أهل الإسلام.

١٠،١٧ الثاني أن يكون أيضاً كلاماً في الحقائق فإنّ النعيم كلّه ممكن حادث فهو بصدد الزوال والفناء فعلاً أو قوّة وما بقي منه إنّما بقي بإبقاء الله تعالى لا بذاته. الثالث أن يراد أنّ كلّ نعيم ناله العبد وتنعّم به فهو زائل عنه قطعاً بالشخص وإنّما تتجدّد أمثاله وهذا قدر مشترك بين الدنيويّ والأخرويّ.

١١،١٧ قال النبيّ صلّى الله عليه وسلّم في متاع الدنيا وإنّما لك من مالك ما أكلت فأفنيت أو لبست فأبليت أو تصدّقت فأمضيت. وقال تعالى في نعيم الآخرة ﴿ كُلَّمَا رُزِقُوا مِنْهَا مِنْ ثَمَرَةٍ رِزْقًا قَالُوا هَٰذَا ٱلَّذِي رُزِقْنَا مِنْ قَبْلُ﴾.

through Exalted God. This matter too is clear, with no doubt regarding it. When one considers creation's association and connection with Exalted God, one must remember that it is only real through Him and possesses no reality on its own. There are things that can be considered real in two ways, and by this I mean, as with the first matter, through connection with God and through having been given subsistence by God's decree.

Despite this, these things can be considered by themselves—this does not contradict any of the above. Understand this correctly! There are three aspects to answering the second objection: The first is that the temporal world is intended by "delight," for that is what is known and what has been experienced. This is especially the case of this speaker—Labīd—as he said what he did during the Jāhiliyya and never mentioned the hereafter. To the question, "Who are you to say that he was ignorant of Islam when he said this? Perhaps he said this after the coming of Islam," I answer, "There is abundant evidence regarding his life that he only recited one line of poetry after his conversion to Islam, that being: 17.8

God be thanked my time did not come
before I had donned the robe of Islam."

If he had written after Islam then worldly desires would be even more clearly discernible. What was intended was to belittle the affairs of the temporal world, and to deter people from it while advocating asceticism. This sentiment is similar to what one can find in many of the sayings of the people of the faith. 17.9

The second aspect is that this is also about theological truths. Every delight is possible and created, and is subject to transience and passing away, in its essence or its potential. What remains of a delight remains through the sustaining power of Exalted God, not through itself. The third aspect is that the line expresses that every delight attained by the worshipper and enjoyed by him is completely transient for him as a person. Similar delights will recur—this is a factor shared by the temporal and the hereafter. 17.10

The Prophet, God bless and keep him, said regarding the enjoyment of the temporal world, "Your only true possessions are the food you have already consumed, the clothes you have already worn out, and the alms you have already given away." Regarding the delight of the hereafter, Exalted God said: «Whenever they are provided with fruits therefrom they shall say, "This is what we were previously granted."»[152] 17.11

وقول الحطيئة: [بسيط] ١٢،١٧

مَنْ يَفْعَلِ ٱلْخَيْرَ لَا يُعْدَمْ جَوَازِيَهُ   لَا يَذْهَبُ ٱلْعُرْفُ بَيْنَ اللهِ وَٱلنَّاسِ

وقول طرفة بن العبد: [طويل] ١٣،١٧

سَتُبْدِي لَكَ ٱلْأَيَّامُ مَا كُنْتَ جَاهِلاً   وَيَأْتِيكَ بِٱلْأَخْبَارِ مَنْ لَمْ تُزَوِّدِ

وكان صلّى الله عليه وسلّم ينشده أحيانًا استحسانًا فيقول: ويأتيك من لم تزوّده بالأخبار ويقول: هُمَا سَوَاءٌ أي التركيبان يعني في المعنى. فيقول أبو بكر رضي الله عنه أشهد أنّك رسول الله قال تعالى ﴿وَمَا عَلَّمْنَاهُ ٱلشِّعْرَ﴾.

وقول النابغة: [طويل] ١٤،١٧

وَلَسْتُ بِمُسْتَبْقٍ أَخًا لَا تَلُمُّهُ   عَلَى شَعَثٍ أَيُّ ٱلرِّجَالِ ٱلْمُهَذَّبُ؟

وقول امرئ القيس: [طويل] ١٥،١٧

وَإِنَّكَ لَمْ يَفْخَرْ عَلَيْكَ كَفَاخِرٍ   ضَعِيفٍ وَلَمْ يَغْلِبْكَ مِثْلُ مُغَلَّبِ

وأخذه أبو تمّام فقال: [كامل] ١٦،١٧

وَضَعِيفَةٍ فَإِذَا أَصَابَتْ قُدْرَةً   قَتَلَتْ كَذٰلِكَ قُدْرَةُ ٱلضُّعَفَاءِ

وقول زهير: [طويل] ١٧،١٧

وَمَنْ يَجْعَلِ ٱلْمَعْرُوفَ مِنْ دُونِ عِرْضِهِ   يَفِرْهُ وَمَنْ لَا يَتَّقِ ٱلشَّتْمَ يُشْتَمِ

وأخوات هذا البيت في ميميّته مثله وهي مشهورة لا نطيل بها.

There is also al-Ḥuṭay'ah's line: 17.12

> One who does good will not lack for people to give him water—
> accepted custom does not come between God and man.

And Ṭarafah ibn al-'Abd's line: 17.13

> The days will reveal what you did not know;
> one you did not task will bring unexpected news.[153]

The Prophet, God bless and keep him, would recite this line sometimes with admiration, but he put it as follows: "Someone will bring you unexpected news whom you did not task." He said, "The two are equal," meaning the constructions are the same in terms of meaning. Abū Bakr, God be content with him, said about the Prophet, "I bear witness that you are the Prophet of God, yet Exalted God said: «We have not taught him poetry.»"[154]

Then there is al-Nābighah's line: 17.14

> You would not ask a brother to stay without putting
> his affairs in order: Which refined man behaves like this?

And the line by Imru' al-Qays: 17.15

> Only the weak would try to boast over you;
> only the defeated would try to vanquish you.

Abū Tammām borrowed this motif, as follows: 17.16

> When a weak person acquires power,
> he lords it over others who are weak.

There is also Zuhayr's line: 17.17

> Whoever does a good deed for a lesser one preserves his honor;
> whoever does not guard himself against insult will be insulted.

In his poem rhyming in *mīm*, this line has too many famous analogues to mention.

١٨،١٧ غيره: [طويل]

لِذِي ٱلْحِلْمِ قَبْلَ ٱلْيَوْمِ مَا تُقْرَعُ ٱلْعَصَا   وَمَا عُلِّمَ ٱلْإِنْسَانُ إِلَّا لِيَعْلَمَا

١٩،١٧ وقوله: [وافر]

قَلِيلُ ٱلْمَالِ تُصْلِحُهُ فَيَبْقَى   وَلَا يَبْقَى ٱلْكَثِيرُ مَعَ ٱلْفَسَادِ

٢٠،١٧ غيره: [مجزوء الكامل]

أَلْعَبْدُ يُقْرَعُ بِٱلْعَصَا   وَٱلْحُرُّ تَكْفِيهِ ٱلْمَلَامَه

٢١،١٧ وقول عبد الله بن معاوية: [طويل]

فَعَيْنُ ٱلرِّضَا عَنْ كُلِّ عَيْبٍ كَلِيلَةٌ   وَلٰكِنَّ عَيْنَ ٱلسَّخْطِ تُبْدِي ٱلْمَسَاوِيَا

٢٢،١٧ وقول القُطامي: [طويل]

قَدْ يُدْرِكُ ٱلْمُتَأَنِّي بَعْضَ حَاجَتِهِ   وَقَدْ يَكُونُ مَعَ ٱلْمُسْتَعْجِلِ ٱلزَّلَلُ

٢٣،١٧ وقوله: [طويل]

وَٱلنَّاسُ مَنْ يَلْقَ خَيْرًا قَائِلُونَ لَهُ   مَا يَشْتَهِي وَلِأُمِّ ٱلْمُخْطِئِ ٱلْهَبَلُ

٢٤،١٧ وسبقه إلى الأوّل عديّ بن زيد في قوله: [سريع]

قَدْ يُدْرِكُ ٱلْمُبْطِئُ مِنْ حَظِّهِ   وَٱلْخَيْرُ قَدْ يَسْبِقُ جُهْدَ ٱلْحَرِيصِ

Another poet said:[155] **17.18**

A forbearing man does not strike before it's time,
as man is taught only in order to know.

The same poet said: **17.19**

Having little money suited him and he flourished.
Most do not flourish when corrupt.

A different poet said:[156] **17.20**

The slave is beaten with a stick;
for the free man, censure is sufficient.

There is also the line by ʿAbd Allāh ibn Muʿāwiyah: **17.21**

The kind eye looks languidly upon faults.
The angry eye reveals all evil things.

And the line by al-Quṭāmī: **17.22**

The patient achieve some of what they need;
those in a hurry make mistakes.

And the same poet also said: **17.23**

People tell those who are successful what they wish to hear,
but the mothers of the errant mourn them.

ʿAdī ibn Zayd anticipated this poet with regard to the first line quoted above: **17.24**

Those who are slow reach their destiny
while good fortune outruns the efforts of the greedy.

٢٥،١٧ وقول عمرو بن براقة: [بسيط]

فَمَا هَدَاكَ إِلَى أَرْضٍ كَعَالِمِهَا وَلَا أَعَانَكَ فِي عَـزْمٍ كَعَزَّامِ

٢٦،١٧ وقول عبد الله بن همّام: [طويل]

وَسَاعٍ مَعَ ٱلسُّلْطَانِ لَيْسَ بِحَارِسٍ وَمُحْـتَرِسٌ مِنْ مِثْلِهِ وَهْوَ حَـارِسُ

٢٧،١٧ وقول عبيد بن الأبرص: [بسيط]

اَلْخَيْرُ يَبْـقَى وَإِنْ طَالَ ٱلزَّمَانُ بِهِ وَٱلشَّـرُ أَخْبَثُ مَا أَوْعَيْتَ فِي زَادِ

٢٨،١٧ وقول حسّان بن ثابت رضي الله عنه: [خفيف]

رُبَّ حِلْمٍ أَضَاعَـهُ عَـدَمُ ٱلْمَا لِ وَجَهْلٍ غَطَّى عَلَيْهِ ٱلنَّعِيمُ

٢٩،١٧ وزعموا أنّ حسّان بينما هو في أُطمِه وذلك في الجاهليّة إذ قام في جوف الليل فصاح يا للخزرج .فجاءوا وقد فزعوا فقالوا ما لك يا ابن الفريعة؟ قال بيت قلته فخفت أن أموت قبل أن أصبح فيذهب ضيعة خذوه عنّي. فقالوا وما قلت؟ فأنشد البيت المذكور.

٣٠،١٧ وقول أبي ذؤيب: [كامل]

وَٱلنَّفْسُ رَاغِبَةٌ إِذَا رَغَّبْتَهَا وَإِذَا تُـرَدُّ إِلَى قَلِيـلٍ تَقْنَعُ

٣١،١٧ وقول زهير: [طويل]

وَهَلْ يُنْبِتُ ٱلْخَطِّيَّ إِلَّا وَشِيجُهُ وَتُغْرَسُ إِلَّا فِي مَنَابِتِهَا ٱلنَّخْلُ

And there is a line by ʿAmr ibn Barrāqah: 17.25

No one can guide you to a place quite like one who knows it;
no one can help you be determined quite like one who is.

And one by ʿAbd Allāh ibn Hammām: 17.26

One who struggles against the sultan is careless
even as he believes he is taking care.

Then there is the line by ʿAbīd ibn al-Abraṣ: 17.27

What is good remains sound, no matter how much times passes,
while evil is the most malignant thing you set aside as provision.

And also one by Ḥassān ibn Thābit, God be content with him: 17.28

How much forbearance has been lost due to indigence!
How often has ignorance been coddled by luxury!

People claim that once during the Jāhiliyya, when Ḥassān was at home, he woke up in the middle of the night and screamed, "To me, Khazraj!" Struck with fear, they all came and asked, "What is it, son of al-Farīʿah?" "A line that came to me, and I was afraid I would die before morning and it would be lost. Take it!" "What was the line?" they asked, and he recited the line cited above. 17.29

Abū Dhuʾayb has a line that goes: 17.30

The soul is greedy if you give it what it wants.
It is satisfied if you only give it a little.

One by Zuhayr goes: 17.31

Do the arrows of Khaṭṭ grow in other trees?
Does the palm take root outside its grove?[157]

غيره: [طويل] ٣٢،١٧

أَرَى كُلَّ عُودٍ نَابِتًا فِي أَرُومَةٍ   أَبَى مَنْبِتُ ٱلْعِيدَانِ أَنْ يَتَغَيَّرَا

وقول بشّار: [كامل] ٣٣،١٧

تَأْتِي ٱلْمُقِيمَ وَمَا سَعَى حَاجَاتُهُ   عَدَدَ ٱلْحَصَا وَيَخِيبُ سَعْيُ ٱلطَّالِبِ

غيره: [طويل] ٣٤،١٧

مَتَى مَا تَقُدْ بِٱلْبَاطِلِ ٱلْحَقَّ يَأْبَهُ   وَإِنْ قُدْتَ بِٱلْحَقِّ ٱلرَّوَاسِي تُنْقَدِ

وقول عبيد: [مخلع البسيط] ٣٥،١٧

مَنْ يَسْأَلِ ٱلنَّاسَ يَحْرِمُوهُ   وَسَائِلُ اللهِ لَا يَخِيبُ

غيره: [طويل] ٣٦،١٧

يَفِرُّ جَبَانُ ٱلْقَوْمِ عَنْ أُمِّ نَفْسِهِ   وَيَحْمِي شُجَاعُ ٱلْقَوْمِ مَنْ لَا يُنَاسِبُهُ
وَيُرْزَقُ مَعْرُوفَ ٱلْجَوَادِ عَدُوُّهُ   وَيُحْرَمُ مَعْرُوفَ ٱلْبَخِيلِ أَقَارِبُهُ

٣٧،١٧ فهذا كلّه ونحوه مشتمل على مثلين كبيت امرئ القيس وقد يكون مثلاً واحداً كقول طرفة: [طويل]

رَأَيْتُ ٱلْقَوَافِي يَتَّلِجْنَ مَوَالِجًا   تَضَايَقُ عَنْهَا أَنْ تَوَالَجَهَا ٱلْإِبَرْ

وهو معنى قول الأخطل والقول ينفذُ ما لا تنفذ الإبر.

Another poet said:[158] 17.32

I see every branch growing from its root.
The source of the branches refuses to change.

And Bashshār said: 17.33

The desires and aspirations of one who waits are fulfilled
A hundredfold, while the labor of one who strives is frustrated.

Another poet said: 17.34

If you cut with what is false, the truth rejects it.
The well-rooted falls when cut with the truth.

And ʿAbīd said:[159] 17.35

Whoever seeks help from people is rejected,
while whoever turns to God will not be disappointed.

Someone else said: 17.36

The coward flees from his own mother,
while the brave one protects those unrelated to him.
The one known for uprightness is generous to his enemy,
while the one famed for stinginess refuses to help relatives.

Such sentiments are encapsulated in two examples, just as with the line by 17.37
Imru' al-Qays. One is similar to Ṭarafah's line:

I have seen rhymes pass through gaps
that needles were unable to penetrate.

This is the meaning of al-Akhṭal's words: Words can do what needles cannot.

وقول علقمة: [طويل] ١٧،٣٨

إِذَا شَابَ رَأْسُ ٱلْمَرْءِ أَوْ قَلَّ مَالُهُ   فَلَيْسَ لَهُ فِي وِدِّهِنَّ نَصِيبُ

وهو لامرئ القيس في قوله: [طويل] ١٧،٣٩

أَرَاهُنَّ لَا يُحْبِبْنَ مَنْ قَلَّ مَالُهُ   وَلَا مَنْ رَأَيْنَ ٱلشَّيْبَ فِيهِ وَقَوَّسَا

ومنه قول الأعشى: [كامل] ١٧،٤٠

وَأَرَى ٱلْغَوَانِيَ لَا يُوَاصِلْنَ ٱمْرَءًا   فَقَدَ ٱلشَّبَابَ وَقَدْ يَصِلْنَ ٱلْأَمْرَدَا

وقول أبي تمّام: [كامل] ١٧،٤١

أَشْهَى ٱلرِّجَالِ مِنَ ٱلنِّسَاءِ مَوَاقِعًا   مَنْ كَانَ أَشْبَهَهُمْ بِهِنَّ خُدُودَا

وقول علقمة بن عبدة: [بسيط] ١٧،٤٢

وَكُلُّ قَوْمٍ وَإِنْ عَزُّوا وَإِنْ كَثُرُوا   عَدِيدُهُمْ بِأَثَافِي ٱلدَّهْرِ مَرْجُومُ
وَكُلُّ حِصْنٍ وَإِنْ طَالَتْ سَلَامَتُهُ   عَلَى دَعَائِمِهِ لَا بُدَّ مَهْدُومُ

وقول الآخر: [طويل] ١٧،٤٣

وَمَا رُزِقَ ٱلْإِنْسَانُ مِثْلَ مَنِيَّةٍ   أَرَاحَتْ مِنَ ٱلدُّنْيَا وَلَمْ تُخْزِ فِي ٱلْقَبْرِ

وقول ابن حازم: [طويل] ١٧،٤٤

لَا تَكْذِبَنَّ فَمَا ٱلدُّنْيَا بِأَجْمَعِهَا   مِنَ ٱلشَّبَابِ بِيَوْمٍ وَاحِدٍ بَدَلُ

Then there is ʿAlqamah's line: 17.38

If a man's hair turns white or he has little money,
he will have no luck in gaining women's affection.

That was in response to Imruʾ al-Qays's line: 17.39

I see they do not love one with little money,
nor one on whom they see spreading white hair.

Similar is al-Aʿshā's line: 17.40

I see that beautiful women do not show a mature man affection.
Young and beardless men are more likely to find success.

Or the line of Abū Tammām: 17.41

The men who are desired by women
are those whose cheeks are most like their own.

There are also these lines by ʿAlqamah ibn ʿAbadah: 17.42

All people, even if powerful and numerous,
will be slain by the cornerstones of time.
And every fortress, even those preserved for ages,
will be destroyed to the very foundations.

Another poet said: 17.43

Nothing that man desired was granted
that did not give pleasure in this world then debase in the grave.

And Ibn Ḥāzim said: 17.44

Do not be deceived! The world in its entirety
cannot replace a lost day of your youth.

٤٥،١٧ ومثله قول منصور النمريّ: [بسيط]

مَا كُنْتُ أُوفِي شَبَابِي حَقَّ غُرَّتِهِ   حَتَّى مَضَى فَإِذَا ٱلدُّنْيَا لَهُ تَبَعُ

٤٦،١٧ وقول امرئ القيس: [طويل]

إِذَا ٱلْمَرْءُ لَمْ يَخْزُنْ عَلَيْهِ لِسَانَهُ   فَلَيْسَ عَلَى شَيْءٍ سِوَاهُ بِخَزَّانِ

٤٧،١٧ ونحوه: [طويل]

إِذَا ضَاقَ صَدْرُ ٱلْمَرْءِ عَنْ كَتْمِ سِرِّهِ   فَصَدْرُ ٱلَّذِي يَسْتَوْدِعُ ٱلسِّرَّ أَضْيَقُ

٤٨،١٧ وقوله: [طويل]

إِذَا جَاوَزَ ٱلْإِثْنَيْنِ سِرٌّ فَإِنَّهُ   يُبَثُّ وَإِفْشَاءُ ٱلْحَدِيثِ قَمِينُ

وقد قيل الاثنان هنا الشفتان.

٤٩،١٧ وقول طرفة: [طويل]

وَإِنَّ لِسَانَ ٱلْمَرْءِ مَا لَمْ يَكُنْ لَهُ   حَصَاةٌ عَلَى عَوْرَاتِهِ لَدَلِيلُ

الحصاة العقل وهو إشارة إلى قول الحكماء لسان العاقل من وراء عقله ولسان الأحمق على العكس.

٥٠،١٧ وقول الخنساء رحمها الله: [وافر]

وَلَوْلَا كَثْرَةُ ٱلْبَاكِينَ حَوْلِي   عَلَى إِخْوَانِهِمْ لَقَتَلْتُ نَفْسِي

This is similar to the line of Manṣūr al-Namarī: 17.45

I was not aware of the illusions of my youth until
it passed and was succeeded by this world.

And also to the saying of Imruʾ al-Qays: 17.46

If a man cannot control his tongue
there is nothing else that he will control!

Similarly:[160] 17.47

If the chest of a man who keeps a secret is constricted,
how much more so the chest of a man who shares one!

And the line:[161] 17.48

If a secret passes beyond two,
it belongs on every tongue.

It has been said that the "two" referred to here are the lips.

There is also Ṭarafah's line: 17.49

The tongue of a person who has no sense
is proof of his shame.

"Sense" means reason. This line is a reference to the saying of the philosophers: The tongue of an intelligent man comes after his reason—he speaks after he thinks—whereas the reverse is the case with the tongue of a fool.

Al-Khansāʾ, God have mercy on her, said: 17.50

If not for the multitude around me
weeping for their brothers, I would kill myself.[162]

٥١،١٧ وقول الآخر: [طويل]

إِذَا ٱنصَرَفَتْ نَفْسِي عَنِ ٱلشَّيْءِ لَمْ تَكَدْ إِلَيْهِ بِوَجْهٍ آخِرَ ٱلدَّهْرِ تُقْبِلُ

٥٢،١٧ وغيره: [طويل]

وَظُلْمُ ذَوِي ٱلْقُرْبَى أَشَدُّ مَضَاضَةً عَلَى ٱلْمَرْءِ مِنْ وَقْعِ ٱلْحُسَامِ ٱلْمُهَنَّدِ

٥٣،١٧ غيره: [طويل]

إِذَا أَنْتَ لَمْ تُعْرِضْ عَنِ ٱلْجَهْلِ وَٱلْخَنَا أَصَبْتَ حَلِيمًا أَوْ أَصَابَكَ جَاهِلُ

٥٤،١٧ غيره: [بسيط]

كُلُّ ٱمْرِئٍ رَاجِعٌ يَوْمًا لِشِيمَتِهِ وَإِنْ تَخَلَّقَ أَخْلَاقًا إِلَى حِينِ

٥٥،١٧ ونحوه: [طويل]

وَمَنْ يَبْتَدِعْ مَا لَيْسَ مِنْ سُوسِ نَفْسِهِ يَدَعْهُ وَيَغْلِبْهُ عَلَى ٱلنَّفْسِ خِيمُهَا

السوس والخيم الطبيعة.

٥٦،١٧ ونحوه: [بسيط]

إِنَّ ٱلتَّخَلُّقَ يَأْتِي دُونَهُ ٱلْخُلُقُ

٥٧،١٧ وقد يكون المثل جزءًا لبيت كهذا. ونحوه للنابغة: [طويل]

حَلَفْتُ فَلَمْ أَتْرُكْ لِنَفْسِكَ رِيبَةً وَلَيْسَ وَرَاءَ ٱللهِ لِلْمَرْءِ مَطْلَبُ

Another poet said:[163] 17.51

> If my soul turns away from something
> it will never revert to it again.

And another said:[164] 17.52

> Suffering oppression at the hands of those close to you
> is a greater agony than being struck with a blade of Indian steel.

Still another said:[165] 17.53

> If you do not turn away from ignorance and obscenity
> you will strike down a forbearing man, and be struck down by a fool.

And another said:[166] 17.54

> Sooner or later everyone reveals their nature.
> Until then, they are shaped by their morals.

Similarly: 17.55

> Whoever undertakes something that is not in his soul's essence,
> his disposition calls to him, overpowering his soul.

Both essence and disposition are equivalent to nature.

And again:[167] 17.56

> Feign the opposite of your character; your true nature will still emerge.

A proverb may be part of a similar line of poetry. Along the same lines is a 17.57
verse by al-Nābighah:

> I swore an oath, not leaving you in any doubt:
> Mankind desires nothing more than God.

وقوله: [طويل] ٥٨،١٧

لَمُبلِغُكَ ٱلْوَاشِي أَغَشُّ وَأَكْذَبُ

وقول دريد: [كامل] ٥٩،١٧

مُتَبَذِّلًا تَبْدُو مَحَاسِنُهُ   يَضَعُ ٱلْهِنَاءَ مَوَاضِعَ ٱلنُّقْبِ

وقول الصَّلَتان العَبْدي: [متقارب] ٦٠،١٧

نَرُوحُ وَنَغْدُو لِحَاجَاتِنَا   وَحَاجَاتُ مَنْ عَاشَ[١] لَا تَنْقَضِي

وقول الآخر: [طويل] ٦١،١٧

تَدُسُّ إِلَى ٱلْعَطَّارِ سِلْعَةَ بَيْتِهَا   وَهَلْ يُصْلِحُ ٱلْعَطَّارُ مَا أَفْسَدَ ٱلدَّهْرُ

وقول زهير: [وافر] ٦٢،١٧

لَهُمْ فِي ٱلذَّاهِبِينَ[٢] أَرُومُ صِدْقٍ   وَكَانَ لِكُلِّ ذِي حَسَبٍ أَرُومُ

وقوله: [وافر] ٦٣،١٧

كَذٰلِكَ خِيمُهُمْ وَلِكُلِّ قَوْمٍ   إِذَا مَسَّتْهُمُ ٱلضَّرَّاءُ خِيمُ

وقول الآخر: [وافر] ٦٤،١٧

تُسَائِلُ عَنْ حُصَيْنٍ كُلَّ رَكْبٍ   وَعِنْدَ جُهَيْنَةَ ٱلْخَبَرُ ٱلْيَقِينُ

١ ط: مات. ٢ ق: السابقين. وط: الصادقين.

He also said: 17.58

The slanderer who told you this is most deceitful and mendacious.

And Durayd said: 17.59

When one's clothes are worn out one's virtues appear.
Place tar on the places where scabs form.[168]

And the line of al-Ṣalatān al-ʿAbdī: 17.60

We go to and fro taking care of our affairs—
the affairs of the living are never completed.

Another poet said: 17.61

She sneaks the wares of the perfumer into her house:
How does the perfumer remedy what time has corrupted?

And Zuhayr said: 17.62

Among their ancestors are those with noble roots;
everyone who has a reputation has roots.

He also said: 17.63

Such is their character, and all people
reveal their character when touched by hardship.

Another poet said:[169] 17.64

Ask every rider regarding Ḥuṣayn.
Among the Juhaynah you will find certain news.

١٧،٦٥ وهذه الأنواع لا يأتي عليها الحصر وإنّما أردنا بعضاً من مختار ذلك ومشهوره وما تركناه أكثر. وقد يشتمل البيت على ثلاثة أمثال أو أربعة وهو قليل بالنسبة إلى غيره فمن ذلك قول زهير: [طويل]

وَفِي ٱلْحِلْمِ إِذْعَانٌ وَفِي ٱلْعَفْوِ دُرْبَةٌ   وَفِي ٱلصِّدْقِ مَنْجَاةٌ مِنَ ٱلشَّرِّ فَٱصْدُقِ

١٧،٦٦ غيره: [بسيط]

اَلْعِلْمُ يَجْلُو ٱلْعَمَى وَٱلْجَهْلُ مَهْلَكَةٌ   وَٱللَّاعِبُ ٱلرَّفْلُ ٱلْأَذْيَالِ مَكْذُوبُ

١٧،٦٧ وقول صالح: [خفيف]

كُلُّ آتٍ لَا بُدَّ آتٍ وَذُو ٱلْجَهْـ   ـلِ مُعَنًّى وَٱلْهَمُّ وَٱلْغَمُّ فَضْلُ

١٧،٦٨ وقولي من قصيدة: [طويل]

فَلَا تَهْتَبِلْ لِلْحَادِثَاتِ وَلَا تَثِقْ   بِمَا وَهَبَتْ يَوْمًا فَمَوْهُوبُهَا مُعْرَى
مُقَرَّبُهَا مُقْصًى وَمَرْفُوعُهَا لُقًى   وَمُنْهَلُهَا مُظْمٍ وَمَكْسُوُّهَا مُعْرَى

١٧،٦٩ وقولي فيها: [طويل]

وَإِنْ أَبْصَرُوا بِٱلْمُمَلَّقِ ٱهْتَزُّوا بِهِ   وَمَدُّوا إِلَيْهِ طَرْفَهُمْ نَظَرًا شَزْرَا
وَقَالُوا بَغِيضٌ إِنْ نَأَى وَمَتَى دَنَا   يَقُولُوا ثَقِيلٌ مُبْرِمٌ أَدْبَرَ ٱلْفَقْرَا
فَإِنْ غَابَ لَمْ يُفْقَدْ وَإِنْ عَلَّ لَمْ يُعَدْ   وَإِنْ مَاتَ لَمْ يُشْهَدْ وَإِنْ ضَافَ لَمْ يُقْرَا

١٧،٧٠ وهذا الباب لا ينحصر وقد أودعنا منه كتاب الأمثال والحكم قدراً صالحاً. ولنقتصر على هذا القدر هنا خوفاً من الملل. لله الأمر من قبل ومن بعد.

Examples abound. We have selected some of the famous ones and omitted the majority. A line of poetry may contain three or four proverbs, though this is rare. One line is by Zuhayr: 17.65

In forbearance there is submission and in forgiveness habituation,
in sincerity there is salvation from evil, so be sincere!

Another poet said: 17.66

Knowledge removes blindness, ignorance is a place of death,
and a flirtatious person with trailing hems is full of deceit.

And Ṣāliḥ ibn ʿAbd al-Quddūs said: 17.67

Future events are unavoidable: Only the ignorant are pained by this,
for worry and anxiety are a blessing.

I myself wrote in a poem: 17.68

Do not take advantage of events or trust
in what you once benefited from them: Their gift is barren.
What they bring close is distant, what they raise up high is within reach.
Their well leaves you thirsty; their garments leave you bare and naked.

I also wrote on this subject: 17.69

When they contemplate a penniless person they mock him,
casting a suspicious glance his way.
Whether far or close, they say he is hateful.
They say he is burdened, bent, with a twisted spine.
Absent, he is not missed; sick, not visited;
dead, not prayed over; and when a guest, given no hospitality.

This section is not exhaustive—we have placed a substantial amount of this type of material in *The Book of Proverbs and Wise Sayings*.[170] Out of fear of inducing boredom I confine myself here to what I have presented. Everything is God's to command. 17.70

١،١٨ حـدّثني الرئيس الأجلّ أبو عبد الله محمد الحاج بن محمد بن أبي بكر الدلائيّ رحمه الله. قال لمّا نزلنا في طلعتنا إلى الحجاز بمصر المحروسة خرج للقائنا الفقيه النبيه أبو العباس أحمد بن محمد المقريّ. قال وكنت أعرفه عند والدي لم يشب فوجدته قد شاب. فقلت له شبت يا سيدي. فاستضحك ثم قال: [خفيف]

شَـيَّبَتْنِي غَـرَنْـدَلُ وَيَحَارُ   وَبِحَارٌ فِيهَا ٱللَّبِيبُ يَحَارُ

٢،١٨ قال وحدث أنّهم كانوا ركبوا بحر سويس فهال بهم مدّة من نحوستة أشهر وهم يدورون دورانًا. وأنّه ألّف في تلك المدّة موضوعًا في علم الهيئة وسارت به الركبان. فلمّا خرج من البحر وتصفّحه وجد فيه الخطأ الفاحش وقد فات تداركه وذلك ممّا وقع له من الهول. قال وإذا هو قد خرج معه برجل ضرير البصر. فقال هذا الضرير من أعاجيب الزمان في بديهة الشعر فألقِ عليه أيّ بيت شئت يأت عليه ارتجالًا بما شئت من الشعر. ثمّ عهّدُه به أن يقوله فلا يبقى شيء منه في حفظه. فأتيتكم به لتشاهدوا من عجائب هذه البلاد ونوادرها وتذهبوا بخبر ذلك إلى بلادكم. قال فاقترحوا مني بيتًا يقول عليه فحضر في لساني بيت ابن الفارض: [رمل]

سَائِقَ ٱلْأَظْعَانِ يَطْوِي ٱلْبِيدَ طَيِّ   مُسْرِعًا عَـرِّجْ عَلَى كُثْبَانِ طَيِّ

٣،١٨ قال فذكرته فاندفع على هذا الرويّ مع صعوبته حتّى أتى بنحو مائة بيت ارتجالًا. قلت وهذا غريب فإنّ هذا القدر كلّه يعزّ وقوعه من العرب المطبوعين فكيف بالمولّدين؟ فكيف بآخر الزمان الذي غلبت فيه العُجمة على الألسن؟ ولكن رب الأولين والآخرين واحد تبارك الله أحسن الخالقين! وحدّثني أنّ الفقيه أبا العباس المذكور كان أيام مقامه بمصر قد اتّخذ رجلًا عنده بنفقته وكسوته وما يحتاج على أن يكون كلّما أصبح ذهب يقتري البلد أسواقًا ومساجد ورحابًا وأزقّة وكلّ ما رأى من أمر

The great leader Abū ʿAbd Allāh Maḥammad al-Ḥājj ibn Maḥammad ibn Abī Bakr al-Dilāʾī, God have mercy on him, related the following to me: "On our way to the Ḥijāz, we stopped in Cairo the Protected, where the renowned jurist Abū ʿAbbās Aḥmad ibn Muḥammad al-Maqqarī came to meet us. I had met him at my father's before he had grown old, and now I found him having turned gray. 'My lord, you have grown gray,' I said, which made him laugh, and he said: 18.1

Gharandal made me gray:
In the seas, the intelligent man loses his way.

"Al-Maqqarī recounted that they had been sailing in the sea of Suez and went in circles for the six months of their trip. During this time, he wrote a work on astronomy, and the travelers sailed according to it. When he was on land and read it over, he found a grievous mistake since his discernment failed him after the terror he had experienced. He had come to meet us with a blind man who, he said, was one of the wonders of the ages due to the splendor of his poetry. Al-Maqqarī said, 'This blind man can extemporize upon any line you recite to him—anything you wish. But nothing of what he says remains in his memory. I brought him so that you would witness one of the wonders and rarities of this place and that you would take news of this to your country.'" Abū ʿAbd Allāh said, "They demanded that I cite a line to him, and a line of Ibn al-Fāriḍ came to me: 18.2

Camel driver, folding up the deserts, traveling swiftly through them,
turn to the dunes of Ṭayy.

"When I related this line to him, he took up what had been recited in spite of its difficulty, and produced close to one hundred lines extemporaneously. This is wondrous! An ability of this kind is rarely found among pure Arabs, so how could it exist among those who have intermarried with them—especially when people have recently lost the ability to speak Arabic properly? Still, the Lord of the First and the Last is One, God bless the best of Creators!" Abū ʿAbd Allāh related that during his stay in Egypt, the aforementioned jurist, Abū ʿAbbās, undertook to pay for the maintenance, clothing, and all the needs of a certain individual, so that every morning he would wander through the markets, mosques, squares, and alleys of the city. He would visit him every 18.3

واقع أو سمع يُريحُه عليه بالليل فيقصّه عليه. قلت وهذا اعتناء الأخبار والنوادر والتواريخ.

٤،١٨ وقد كان نحو هذا لشيخ مشايخنا أبي عبد الله محمد العربيّ ابن أبي المحاسن يوسف الفاسيّ. فكان من دأبه أنّه متى لقي إنسانًا يسأله من أيّ بلد هو. فإذا أخبره قال من عندكم من أهل العلم و[١]من عندكم من أهل الصلاح ومن الأعيان؟ فإذا أخبره بشيء من ذلك كلّه سجله. وهذا الاعتناء بالأخبار والوقائع والمساند ضعيف جدًا في المغاربة فغلب عليهم في باب العلم الاعتناء بالدراية دون الرواية وفيما سوى ذلك لا همّة لهم.

٥،١٨ وكان أبو عبد الله المذكور يذكر في كتابه مرآة المحاسن أنّه كم في المغرب من فاضل ضاع من قلّة اعتنائهم وهو كذلك. وقد سألت شيخنا الأستاذ أبا عبد الله ابن ناصر رحمه الله ورضي عنه يومًا عن السند في بعض ما كنت آخذه عنه. فقال لي إنّا لم تكن لنا رواية في هذا وما كنّا نعتني بذلك. قال وقد قضيت العجب من المشارقة واعتنائهم أمثال هذا حتّى إنّي لمّا دخلت مصر كان كلّ من يأخذ عنّي عهد الشاذليّة يكتب الورد والرواية والزمان والمكان الذي وقع فيه ذلك.

٦،١٨ رجعنا إلى الحديث الأوّل. قال ووجدت الفقيه أبا العباس المذكور قد وقع بينه وبين طلبة العلم من أهل مصر شحناء عظيمة وحدث أنّ سببها اتّفاق غريب وهو أنّه حضر ذات يوم سوق الكتب وهو إذ ذاك لم يعرف. فوقع في يده سِفرٌ من تفسير غريب ففتح على تفسير سورة النور. فإذا هو قد تعرّض لمسألة فقهيّة غريبة وذكر فيها اختلافًا وتفصيلًا وتحقيقًا فحفظ ذلك كلّه على الفور وكان رجلًا حافظًا. ثمّ اتّفق عن قريب أن اجتمع علماء البلد في دعوة وحضر معهم فلمّا استقرّ بهم المجلس إذا سائل في يده بطاقة يسأل عن تلك المسألة نفسها. فدفعت للأوّل من أكابر أهل المجلس فنظر فكأنّه لم يحضره فيها ما يقول. فدفعها لمن يليه ثمّ دفعها الآخر للآخر وهكذا حتّى بلغت أبا العباس المذكور.

---

١ سقط من م، ق.

evening and tell him what he had seen and heard. I said, "This is what it means to take a real interest in events, anecdotes, and accounts."

Something similar had been related about our shaykhs' shaykh, Abū ʿAbd Allāh Muḥammad al-ʿArbī ibn Abī l-Maḥāsin Yūsuf al-Fāsī. It was his habit that whenever he met a person he asked what area they were from. When he was told the place, he would say, "Which men of knowledge do you know? Which people of piety? Which notables?" He would record whatever he was told. This attention to relations, events, and verifiable traditions is quite lacking among the Moroccans—in matters of knowledge they have given preference to intellectual appreciation over the transmission of knowledge, and for them nothing else is important.[171] 18.4

The abovementioned Abū ʿAbd Allāh noted in his *Mirror of Virtues* that many distinguished men in Morocco were forgotten due to their neglect of this transmission. This is indeed the case. I once asked our teacher Abū ʿAbd Allāh ibn Nāṣir, God have mercy on him and be pleased with him, for the line of transmission of something I had learned from him. He told me, "I do not have a verified transmission for this; this was not something to which we paid attention." Abū ʿAbd Allāh said, "I have been overawed by those from the East and their superior attention to such matters, to the degree that when I entered Egypt, everyone who took the pledge of the Shādhiliyya from me wrote down the prayer, its line of transmission, and the time and place at which this occurred." 18.5

Let us return to what we started with. Abū ʿAbd Allāh said, "I found that great rancor had developed between the jurist Abū ʿAbbās and the students of religious knowledge in Egypt. The cause was a curious coincidence—namely, that he had one day gone to the book market at a time when he was still unknown. He came upon a rare volume of a Qurʾanic exegesis and opened it to the exegesis of Sūrat al-Nūr. This passage addressed a curious juridical matter and described a disagreement in precise detail. He memorized all of this immediately, being a man with this ability. Soon after this, it happened that the scholars of the city came together for some occasion and he was present. When the gathering was underway, someone holding a card asked about precisely this issue. The card was given to the first of the great scholars attending the gathering. He looked at it, and it appeared that nothing occurred to him on the subject. He gave it to the person next to him. That person then gave it to the next, and so on, until it reached the aforementioned Abū ʿAbbās. 18.6

٧،١٨ فلمّا تناولها استدعى الدواة فكتب عليها الجواب بنحو ما حفظ فجعلوا ينظرون إليه متعجّبين. فلمّا فرغ تعاطوها فقالوا من ذكر هذا؟ فقال لهم ذكره فلان في تفسير سورة النور فالتمسوا التفسير فإذا الأمر كما ذكر. فدخلهم من ذلك ما هو شأن النفوس. قلت وليس هذا ببدع فما زال هذا الجنس يتحاملون على من توسّموا فيه شفوفًا عليهم أو مزاحمة في رتبة أو حظّ إلّا من عصمه الله وقليل ما هم. [كامل]

كَضَرَائِرِ ٱلْحَسْنَاءِ قُلْنَ لِوَجْهِهَا   حَسَدًا وَبُغْضًا أَنَّهُ لَدَمِيمُ

٨،١٨ وقد أفتى بعض الفقهاء أنّه لا تقبل شهادة بعضهم على بعض لهذا المعنى ولا شكّ أنّه ليس على العموم ولكنّه شائع معلوم. فمن ذلك ما وقع للإمام سيبويه مع أهل الكوفة وقصّته مشهورة. وما وقع لسيف الدين الآمديّ مع أهل مصر فإنّه لمّا برز عليهم في العلوم أنكروه ونسبوه إلى الأهواء وكتبوا عليه رسمًا بذلك. فكانوا يدفعونه بعضهم لبعض ليوقعوا فيه الشهادة على ذلك فكانوا يشهدون حتّى انتهى إلى بعض من وفّقه الله وعصمه فوقع تحت الشهادات. [كامل]

حَسَدُوا ٱلْفَتَى إِذْ لَمْ يَنَالُوا سَعْيَهُ   فَٱلْقَوْمُ أَعْدَاءٌ لَهُ وَخُصُومُ

٩،١٨ وقد تناهى به ذلك حتّى خرج من مصر. وما وقع للفقيه محمّد بن تومرت المعروف بالمهديّ إمام الموّحدين فإنّه دخل مدينة مراكش مَقْفَلَهُ من المشرق فحرّك العلوم العقليّة وكانوا أهل بادية لا يعرفون ذلك فقالوا هذا أدخل علينا علوم الفلاسفة ووَشوا به إلى اللمتونيّ حتّى كان من أمره ما كان.

١٠،١٨ ومثله ما وقع للإمام أبي الفضل بن النحويّ حين دخل سجلماسة فجعل يُدرّس أصول الدين وأصول الفقه فمرّ به عبد الله بن بسّام أحد رؤساء البلد. فقال ما العلم الذي يُدرّسه هذا؟ فأخبروه وكانوا قد اقتصروا على علم الرأي. فقال هذا يريد

"When he had read it, he called for an inkwell and wrote out the answer he had memorized. They looked at him with amazement. When he was finished writing, they asked, 'Who wrote this?' and he said, 'So-and-so wrote it in his exegesis of Sūrat al-Nūr.' They asked for the exegesis and found it to be as he had said. Their egos became troubled on account of this. This was not the first time this has occurred, and, save for the few whom Exalted God has preserved from the vice, they continue to be prejudiced against those whom they perceive to be superior to themselves, or against those who compete with them for rank or distinction. 18.7

Like the fellow wives of a beautiful woman who say of her face
Out of envy and hatred, 'Truly, it is hideous.'"[172]

Because of this type of thing, a certain jurist issued a legal opinion that scholars should not testify against each other. No doubt this is not generally the case, but the prejudice is widespread. Other examples of this are what famously happened to the exemplar Sībawayhi with the people of Kufa. Or to Sayf al-Dīn al-Āmidī with the people of Egypt—when he demonstrated his superiority over them in the sciences, they disavowed him, accused him of heresy, and wrote an official decree to that effect. They passed this decree among themselves, so that each would sign it and bear witness. They did this until it reached one whom God had granted success and preserved from error, and he wrote underneath the testimonies: 18.8

Unable to match him, the people envied the young man;
they were his enemies and adversaries.

Abū ʿAbbās refrained from anything similar while in Egypt. This is also what occurred to Ibn Tūmart, known as "the Savior,"[173] the leader of the Almohads. When he entered the city of Marrakesh he was on his way back from the East and was advocating for the rational sciences. The people of the countryside were ignorant of this and said, "This fellow has introduced the sciences of the philosophers among us." They denounced him to the Almoravid ruler, and matters took their course. 18.9

A similar thing happened to the exemplar Abū l-Faḍl ibn al-Naḥwī when he entered Sijilmāsah and began teaching theology and legal theory. ʿAbd Allāh ibn Bassām, one of the leaders of the city, passed by and said, "What is this science this fellow is teaching?" so they told him. They had previously refrained 18.10

أن يُدخل علينا علوماً لا نعرفها وأمر بإخراجه. فقام أبو الفضل ثمّ قال له أَمَتَّ العلمَ أماتك الله ههنا.

١١،١٨ قالوا وكانت عادة أهل البلد أن يعقدوا الأنكحة في المسجد. فاستحضروا ابن بسّام لعقد نكاح صبيحةَ اليوم الثاني من ذلك اليوم. فخرج سَحرًا وقعد في المكان المذكور فمرّت عليه جماعة من ملوانة إحدى قبائل صنهاجة فقتلوه برماحهم. وارتحل أبو الفضل إلى مدينة فاس فتسلّط عليه القاضي ابن دبوس ولقي منه ما لقي من ابن بسّام فدعا عليه أيضاً فهلك. ولمّا رجع إلى وطنه القلعة واشتغل بالتقشف تسلّط عليه إبن عصمة أيضاً فقيه البلد بالإذاية.

١٢،١٨ وهذا النوع أعني الفقهاء ولا سيّما أرباب المناصب منهم كالقضاة لم يزالوا متسلّطين على أهل الدين كما وقع لهذا وكما وقع للقاضي ابن الأسود مع الإمام العارف أبي العباس بن العريف ولابن أبي البراء مع القطب الجامع أبي الحسن الشاذليّ. وكلّهم قد أخذهم الله بذنوبهم في الدنيا قبل الآخرة نسأل الله تعالى العصمة من اتّباع الهوى ونعوذ بالله أن نَظلم أو نُظلم إنّه الحفيظ الرحيم.

١٣،١٨ وحدّثني الحاج المذكور أيضاً قال دخلنا مكّة شرّفها الله فدخلت ذات يوم المسجد الحرام فإذا هو غاص بأهله والناس مزدحمون فقلت ما هذا؟ فقالوا جنازة ولد توفي للشيخ يوسف الوفائيّ وكان حاضرًا في تلك الجنّة. قال وكنت أعرفه فجئت إليه لأعزّيه في مصيبته فاستأذنت عليه فأذن لي فدخلت عليه وهو مع أصحابه فإذا هو يتحدّث وهو في غاية ما يكون من البسط والسرور. قال فجلست أمامه وقلت أعظم الله أجرك. فأنكر عليّ غاية الإنكار وقال أمثلك يقول هذا؟ وقد طالما كنت أتمنّى أن يجعل الله جسدي في هذه البقاع المشرّفة واليوم قد جعل الله بعضي فيها فله الحمد وله الشكر أو كلاماً هذا معناه رحمة لله ورضي عنه.

from the study of the speculative sciences. Ibn Bassām said, "This fellow wants to introduce sciences to us of which we were ignorant," and ordered that Ibn al-Naḥwī be cast out. Abū l-Faḍl stood up and said to him, "As you put knowledge to death, so God will kill you in this very spot."

Now it was the habit of the people of the town to hold marriage ceremonies in the mosque. They called for Ibn Bassām to perform a wedding on the morning of the following day. He went out in the early morning and sat in the aforementioned place. A group of the Malwānah, one of the branches of the Ṣanhājah, passed by and killed him with their lances. Abū l-Faḍl traveled to the city of Fez, where the judge Ibn Dabbūs opposed him and at whose hands he experienced the same as he had from Ibn Bassām. He prayed for his destruction, and Ibn Dabbūs died. When Abū l-Faḍl returned to his home in al-Qalʿah he lived a rustic life. Ibn ʿAṣmah, a jurist of the area, also opposed him, causing him harm. 18.11

These people, I mean jurists and especially those who hold official positions such as judges, continue to try to exercise control over men of faith, as in Abū l-Faḍl's case. This is what happened in the case of the judge Abū l-Aswad with the exemplar and gnostic Abū l-ʿAbbās ibn al-ʿArīf and Ibn Abī l-Barāʾ and the universal Axis of the age Abū l-Ḥasan al-Shādhilī, all of whom God has purified of their sins in this world before the coming of the next. We ask Exalted God to preserve us from following vain desires, and we seek refuge in God from oppressing or being oppressed. Truly, He is a merciful Protector. 18.12

The aforementioned al-Ḥājj al-Dilāʾī also related the following to me: "We reached Mecca, God honor it. I entered that very day into the mosque of the Sanctuary and found it teeming with the city's people and very busy. When I asked, 'What is going on?' I was told, 'It is the funeral ceremony of the son of Shaykh Yūsuf al-Wafāʾī, who was present for that year's pilgrimage.'" Al-Ḥājj continued, "I knew him, so I went to him to express my condolences for the disaster that had afflicted him. I asked permission to approach, which he granted. I entered and found him holding forth to his companions, happy and in the best of moods. I sat in front of him and said, 'May God increase your reward!' He rejected this strenuously and said, 'How can one such as you say this? How long have I desired for God to inter my body in this blessed piece of earth and today God has placed part of me in it—all thanks and gratitude belong to Him.' He said this or words like it, God have mercy on him and be pleased with him." 18.13

وإنّما أذكر مثل هذه القصّة للاعتبار والائتساء. وحدّثنا أيضاً قال بتنا عند الفقيه الشيخ علي الأجهوريّ برسم زيارة. فبات ليله على النظر في كتب العلم وهو يشرب الدخان فكان له صاحب يعمر له الدواة حتّى إذ فرغت عمر أخرى ويرى حلّيته. قال وكان الشيخ إبراهيم اللقانيّ معاصره وبلديه يفتي بحرْمته. لله الأمر من قبل ومن بعد. ١٤،١٨

وكان يحدّثنا عن أسلافه أنّ ثلاثة من صلحاء الغرب قد جرّب عندهم قضاء الحاجات الشيخ عبد السلام بن مشيش والشيخ أبو يعزى يلنور والشيخ أبو سلهام. غير أنّهم اختلفوا فالأوّل في أمور الآخرة والثالث في أمور الدنيا وأبو يعزى في الكلّ نفعنا الله بهم وبأمثالهم. وقد ذكر غيره كالشيخ زروق أنّ هؤلاء الثلاثة أبا يعزى وأبا العباس السبتيّ وأبا مدين قد وقع الانتفاع بهم بعد الموت. وهذا بحسب ما اشتهر وانتشر وإلّا فالانتفاع واقع بأولياء الله كثيراً في كلّ أرض. ١،١٩

وقد شاهدت المولى أدريس بن إدريس رضي الله عنه أيّام مقامي بمدينة فاس ترياقاً مجرّباً في كلّ ما أنزل به من حاجة. وحدّثونا في درعة عن الشيخ سيدي أحمد بن إبراهيم أنّه كان يقول لهم إنّ سيدي أبا القاسم الشيخ وهو معروف هنالك يقضى عنده ما يقضى عند الشيخ أبي يعزى. ٢،١٩

وحدّثني بمدينة مراكش الفاضل أبو العباس أحمد بن أبي بكر الهشتوكيّ. قال رأيت ذات ليلة فيما يرى النائم أنّي دخلت مقام الشيخ أبي عبد الله محمد بن سليمان الجزوليّ فإذا هو جالس وهو يقول من كانت له إلى الله حاجة فليأتنا. قال فلمّا أصبحت وكان أمير الوقت قد بعث إلى أهل المدينة أن يعطوا الرماة وشقّ عليهم ذلك كثيراً. وكان قوم قد ذهبوا إليه وعزموا أن يسعوا في إذايتي. فجئت إليه فقلت إنّك قلت كذا وها أنا ذا قد جئت في هاتين الحاجتين. قال فقضى الله الحاجتين معاً. ٣،١٩

I mention stories like this for the sake of the morals and examples they contain. Al-Ḥājj al-Dilāʾī also related the following to me, saying, "We spent a night visting the jurist and teacher ʿAlī al-Ujhūrī. He spent the evening smoking and studying scholarly works. He had a companion who would fill the inkwell for him, and when it ran dry, would fill another. He believed smoking was permitted. The teacher Ibrāhīm al-Laqānī, a contemporary and compatriot of his, issued a legal opinion that it was forbidden."[174] Everything is God's to command. 18.14

Al-Ḥājj al-Dilāʾī related to us from his ancestors that three devout men from the West experienced the fulfillment of their desires, albeit in different ways: these were the shaykhs ʿAbd al-Salām ibn Mashīsh, Abū Yiʿzzā Yallanūr, and Abū Salhām. The first experienced this with respect to the afterlife, the third with respect to this world, and Abū Yiʿzzā with respect to both, God grant us blessings through them and their like. Someone else, possibly Shaykh Zarrūq, mentioned that, according to what is widely held, the three we benefited from after their deaths were Abū Yiʿzzā, Abū l-ʿAbbās al-Sabtī, and Abū Madyan. Everywhere in the world the saints of God frequently benefit people. 19.1

During my time in Fez, I witnessed Master Idrīs ibn Idrīs, God be content with him, provide proven antidotes for all the problems brought to him. They told us in Darʿah about Shaykh Sīdī Aḥmad ibn Ibrāhīm, that he would tell them regarding Shaykh Sīdī Abū l-Qāsim,[175] who is well known there, that the same thing would happen with him as happened with Shaykh Abū Yiʿzzā. 19.2

In Marrakesh, the distinguished Abū ʿAbbās Aḥmad ibn Abī Bakr al-Hashtūkī related the following to me: "One night I dreamed that I had entered the tomb of Shaykh Abū ʿAbd Allāh Muḥammad ibn Sulaymān al-Jazūlī. He sat before me and said, 'Let anyone who desires something from God come to us.' When I awoke, I found that the then ruler had sent for the people of the city to provide archers, which caused them great distress. A group of people had already gone to him and had resolved to try to do me harm. I came to him and said, 'You said such and such, and here I am, come regarding both these matters.' He said, 'God has granted both desires at the same time.'"[176] 19.3

٤،١٩ وحدّثني أيضاً الأخ الصالح أبو عبد الله محمّد بن أحمد الهشتوكيّ. قال بلغني عن الفقيه سيدي عبد الواحد الشريف أنّه حدّث أصحابه فقال لهم كنّا خرجنا ونحن نفر ثلاثة لزيارة الشيخ عبد الخالق بن ياسين الدغوغيّ. فلمّا كنّا ببعض الطريق قلنا تعالوا فليذكر كلّ واحد منكم حاجته التي يريدها. قال فأمّا أنا فقلت لهم إنّي أريد كرسي جامع المواسين. وأمّا الثاني فقال أريد أن أتولّى الحكومة في البلد. وأمّا الثالث فقال أريد محبّة الله تعالى. قال فزرنا فأمّا أنا وصاحبي فقد تولّينا ما طلبنا. وأمّا الآخر فبخروجه من مقام الشيخ تحرّك وفغر فاه واستقبل البريّة فكان ذاك آخر العهد به وقد قضى الله الحاجات كلّها.

٥،١٩ وكانت أهلي أيّام كنّا بالزاوية البكريّة قد تراخت عنها الولادة فدخلها من ذلك غمّ عظيم. فأصبحت ذات يوم فأخبرت أنّها رأت أنّها ذهبت إلى مقام سيدي أبي عليّ الغجاتيّ. فقالت فوجدته جالساً وأنا في غاية العطش. فإذا حوله عين يرشح منها ماء قليلٌ لا يغني. فقلت يا سيدي ما هذا؟ جئت إليك عطشى رجاء أن أشرب أفأرجع كما جئت؟ قال لا إنّ الماء ثمّ انبشي يخرج. فقالت فنبشت بيدي فخرج الماء وشربت حتّى رويت. وطلبت منّي أن نزوره وأن نطعم عنده طعاماً. ففعلنا فولد ولدنا محمّد الكبير أصلحه الله وأمتع به.

٦،١٩ ولمّا نزلنا بالزاوية المرّة الثانية مَقْفَلَنَا من حضرة مراكش كانت لنا بُنَيّة عجزت عن النهوض وهي في سنّ من يمشي فظنّناها مقعدة. فذهب بها الخدم إليه وزوروها فقامت بالفور على رجلها تمشي. وأمثال هذه الأمور لو تتبّعنا منها ما رأينا وما سمعنا لملأنا بها الدواوين. نعم رأيت لبعضهم أنّ الولي إذا مات أنقطع تصرّفه من الكون. وما يحصل لزائره مثلاً إنّما يحصل له على يد قطب الوقت بحسب درجة ذلك الولي. والله تعالى أعلم. لله الأمر من قبل ومن بعد.[1]

[1] سقطت الجملة من ق، ط.

The devout brother Abū ʿAbd Allāh Muḥammad ibn Aḥmad al-Hashtūkī also recounted the following to me: "I heard from the noble jurist Sīdī ʿAbd al-Wāḥid that he said to his companions, 'Three of us went to visit the teacher ʿAbd al-Khāliq ibn Yāsīn al-Daghūghī. When we were on the road we resolved, "Let each of us state his desire." "As for me," I said to them, "I want the teaching chair of the al-Mawāsīn mosque." The second said, "I want to be ruler of the country." And the third, "I want the love of Exalted God." We visited the shrine. My companion and I received what we requested. As for the other, when he left the grave of the shaykh, his mouth was agape and moving. Some dust entered it and his life came to an end. Thus, God granted all our desires.'" 19.4

When my wife and I were at the Bakriyyah lodge, she had difficulty bearing children, which greatly distressed her. One day, I woke up and she told me she had had a dream in which she had gone to the tomb of Sīdī Abū ʿAlī al-Ghujātī. "I found him sitting there, and I was very thirsty," she said. "Next to him was a well from which a little water was trickling, which was hardly enough. I said, 'O Sīdī, what is this? I came to you thirsty, desiring to drink. Shall I return the same way I came?' and he said, 'There is water. Dig and it will appear!' Then he left." She said, "So I dug with my hands and water welled up. I drank until I was satisfied." She asked that we visit him and distribute food at his tomb. We did so, and our oldest son Muḥammad was born, may God be pleased with him and make him thrive. 19.5

When we stayed in the lodge the second time, on our way back from Marrakesh, we had a young daughter who couldn't stand up, even though she was of the age to do so—we thought she was lame. The servants took her to visit him and she immediately stood and walked. If we set down all such cases we have seen or heard of, it would fill many volumes. One of the agreeable things I have witnessed is that while a saint's actions cease when he dies, what a visitor to this saint then experiences is at the hands of the Axis of the age and depends on the rank of the saint. God knows best—everything is God's to command. 19.6

وكان أيضاً رحمه الله كثيراً ما ينشدنا لبعضهم: [طويل] ١،٢٠

إِذَا لَمْ يَكُنْ فِي مَنْزِلِ ٱلْمَرْءِ حُرَّةٌ تُدَبِّرُ أَمْرًا نَابَهُ فَهْوَ ضَائِعُ

وقوله في البيت حرّة يحتمل أن يريد بها ضدّ الأمة لأنّ الحرائر مظنّة العقل والتجربة والغناء والكفاية. والظاهر أنّ المراد أخصّ من ذلك وهي الكاملة الحرّية كما يقال لكامل الرجوليّة فلان رجل وذلك أنّ ليس كلّ حرّة تكفي وتغني بل ربّ أمة لبيبة أقوم من حرّة. فالمرأة الصالحة الكيّسة الصيّنة هي التي تراد.

٢،٢٠ وفي الحديث تنكح المرأة لدينها وجمالها ومالها فاظفر بذات الدّين. وفي الحديث أيضاً الدّنيا كلّها متاع وخير متاع الدّنيا المرأة الصّالحة. وفي الحديث إنّ المرأة الصّالحة بين النساء كالغراب الأعصم بين الغربان. وذلك لعزّة من تستكمل المعتبر من الأوصاف أو لعزّة الدين فيهنّ فإنّهنّ ناقصات عقل ودين. وروي عن نبيّ الله داود أنّه قال لابنه سليمان عليهما السلام يا بنيّ إنّ المرأة الصالحة كمثل التاج على رأس الملك وإنّ المرأة السوء كالحمل الثقيل على الشيخ الكبير.

٣،٢٠ وعن أمير المؤمنين عمر رضي الله عنه النساء ثلاث. امرأة عاقلة مسلمة عفيفة هيّنة ليّنة ودود ولود تعين أهلها على الدهر ولا تعين الدهر على أهلها. وقليلاً ما تجدها. وأخرى وعاء للولد لا تزيد على ذلك. وأخرى غُلّ قمل يجعله الله في عنق من يشاء. ثمّ إذ شاء أن ينزعه نزعه. وقوله غلّ قمل تمثيل وأصله أنّ الأسير مثلاً يجعل عليه الغلّ فيبقى حتّى إذا طال قَمِلَ أي دخله القمل فيأكله القمل في عنقه. ولا يمكنه أن يزيل القمل منه ولا أن يزحزح الغُلّ من محله ما لم يحلّ من أصله فيلقى من ذلك عذاباً لازماً.

٤،٢٠ وكذلك المرأة إذا كانت سيّئة الأخلاق أو ذميمة الخلقة أو جمعتها فالرجل يتأذّى منها أذًى عظيماً لازماً ما لم يطلّقها. فالمرأة إذا كانت جميلة حسنة الشباب مليحة ألفها الطبع وشربتها النفس فكان سيّئها حسناً وذنبها مغفوراً. كما قال أبو فراس: [طويل]

Abū ʿAbd Allāh al-Hashtūkī, God have mercy on him, would also often recite this to us by one of the saints: 20.1

> If a man's house has no free woman
> looking after entrusted matters, then he is lost.

When he says "free woman," it is possible that he intended the opposite of a slave girl, as free women typically exhibit intelligence, experience, ability, and competence. But it is clear that he intended something more specific, to wit, absolute freedom, just as one says of absolute manliness: Such and such a person is a man. For not every free woman is capable and competent: On the contrary, a particular slave girl may be more intelligent than a free woman. The woman meant here is pure, astute, and devout.

In the Hadith we find: "Marry a woman for her piety, her beauty, and her possessions, but most of all for her piety." In the Hadith we find also: "The whole world is pleasure, but the greatest pleasure is a devout woman." And also: "A devout woman is like a white-feathered crow among crows." This is due to the scarcity of the one who possesses such characteristics, or the rarity of her piety, for women are deficient in reason and piety. It is related that God's prophet David said to his son Solomon, peace upon them both: "My son, a pure woman is like the crown on a king's head, whereas a bad woman is like a heavy load on an old man." 20.2

It is reported that ʿUmar, the Commander of the Faithful, God be pleased with him, said, "There are three kinds of women. An intelligent Muslim woman, chaste, tender, devoted, and fertile, who helps her people against the depredations of time—never the reverse. Such a woman is rarely to be found. Second, women who are just vessels for children; and finally, those who are a collar of lice placed by God on the neck of whomever He wills, which He then removes as He wishes." "Collar of lice" is a metaphor, the origin of which is that a prisoner, for example, would have an iron collar placed on him that would remain even if lice climbed under it and relentlessly bit his neck. Nor would he be able to move the collar about, so suffering from it would be uninterrupted torture. 20.3

This is the way with a woman of poor morals, of unpleasant character, or both. A man will necessarily experience great harm, until he divorces her. If a woman is beautiful, in the prime of youth, comely, of a friendly nature, and with a sweet soul, then her evil deeds are considered good and her sins are forgiven. As Abū Firās[177] has said: 20.4

يَعُدُّ عَلَيَّ ٱلْوَاشِيَاتُ ذُنُوبَهُ   وَمِنْ أَيْنَ لِلْوَجْهِ ٱلْمَلِيحِ ذُنُوبُ

ولا بدّ مع ذلك من كفاية بيتها. فإذا جمعت الحسن والدين والكفاية فهي الحرّة المعدودة والضالّة المنشودة. وفي أمر النساء كلام يكثر لا يفي به إلّا تصنيف مستقلّ وهذا القدر يكفي في هذا المحل.

٥،٢٠ وكان يقول كثيرًا لا تواكل من لا يواكل ولا تجالس من لا يجانس. وكان يقول في حديثه بما سمع ممّن لقي إنّ الوليّ الصالح سيدي عبد العزيز بن عبد الحقّ الحرار المعروف بالتبّاع كان يقول لأصحابه وهم سيدي سعيد بن عبد المنعم المنانيّ الحاحيّ وسيدي علي بن إبراهيم البوزيديّ تادلاويّ وسيدي رحّال المعروف بالكوش سعيد فقيهكم وعلي عابدكم ورحّال مجذوبكم والغزوانيّ سلطانكم نفعنا الله بجميعهم آمين.

٦،٢٠ وسمعته يحدّث عن والده سيدي محمّد بن أبي بكر أنّ شيخه سيدي محمّد ابن أبي القاسم المعروف بالشرقيّ التادلاويّ كان وقع بينه وبين ولده سيدي الغزوانيّ كلام وعتاب إلى أن قال الولد أنت ترزقني؟ فقال الشيخ نعم أنا أرزقك فأعظم الناس هذا الكلام. قال فقال الوالد لا شيء في هذا فإنّ الشيخ هو القطب في الوقت والقطب تجري الأرزاق على يده فصحّ بهذه الإضافة أن يكون رازقًا. لله الأمر من قبل ومن بعد.[1]

١،٢١ وحدّث عنه أيضاً قال قدمت على الوالي الصالح سيدي عبد الله بن حسوّن دفين سلا. فقعدت إلى جنبه وقد مدّ رجليه والأعراب يتساقطون عليه يقبّلون يديه ورجليه. قال فخطر ببالي أنّه كيف أطلق هذا الرجل نفسه للناس هكذا؟ فلم يتمّ الخاطر إلّا وقد قال أيّها الناس رجل قيل له من مسّ لحمك لم تمسّه النار أو لم تأكله النار أو نحو هذا فيبخل بلحمه على المسلمين؟

١ سقطت الجملة من ق، ط.

The slanderers count the faults of ʿAlī;
how can one with a pleasant face have faults?

The line will have to suffice. Beauty, piety, and efficiency combined give you the rare free woman, the long-sought-after goal. In the matter of women, there is much to be said that would only be adequately addressed in a separate book. The foregoing suffices.

Al-Hashtūkī often said, "Do not trust someone who cannot be trusted, and **20.5**
do not sit with someone who is not sociable." He also said, having heard this from someone he met, "The devout saint, Sīdī ʿAbd al-ʿAzīz ibn ʿAbd al-Ḥaqq al-Ḥarrār, known as al-Tabbāʿ, used to say to his companions—Sīdī Saʿīd ibn ʿAbd al-Munʿim al-Mannānī al-Ḥāḥī and Sīdī ʿAlī ibn Ibrāḥīm al-Būzīdī al-Tādlāwī and Sīdī Raḥḥāl, known as al-Kūsh—'May your jurist be felicitous, your follower be noble, your saint be a wanderer, and your ruler be a raider. God grant us benefit through them all. Amen.'

"I also heard him relate from his father, Sīdī Muḥammad ibn Abī Bakr, **20.6**
that an admonishing conversation took place between the latter's teacher, Sīdī Muḥammad ibn Abī l-Qāsim, known as al-Sharqī al-Tādlawī, and his son, Sīdī al-Ghazwānī. It reached the point where the son said, 'Do you grant me blessings?' and the shaykh said, 'Yes, I do give you blessings.' People made a great deal of this exchange. The father said, 'This is a matter of no consequence, for Shaykh al-Sharqī al-Tādlawī is the Axis of the age, and blessings occur at the hand of the Axis. He was correct in ascribing the granting of blessings to himself.'" Everything is God's to command.

It is also related that Abū ʿAbd Allāh al-Hashtūkī said, "I went to the devout **21.1**
saint Sīdī ʿAbd Allāh ibn Ḥassūn, who is now buried in Salé. He had stretched out his legs and I sat next to him. Some Bedouin came to him one after another, kissing his hands and feet. I wondered how this man came to offer himself up to people like this. Just as that thought occurred to me, he said, 'People! If it is said of a man that if someone touched his flesh, fire would not burn that person, nor consume him, or the like, should such a man refuse the touch of Muslims?'"

٢،٢١ قال فلمّا سمعت كلامه وعلمت أنّه على خاطري تكلّم تبت إلى الله تعالى في نفسي. فجعلت إذا مدّ إليه أحد كاغد وكان يكتب الحروز تلقّفته من يده وناولته الشيخ وقبّلت يده فإذا كتبته أخذته منه وقبّلت يده فيحصل لي في كل حرز تقبيلتان. قال ورأيت عنده أمورًا أشكلت عليّ منها أنّه يؤتى بالثياب هديّة وصدقة فيأمر بها فترمى في بيت وتبقى كذلك يأكلها السوس. ومنها أنّه كلّ يوم يصبح عليه أهل الآلات فيضربون عليه.

٣،٢١ قلت أمّا الثياب فالذي يظهر في أمرها أنّه إمّا غيبة حصلت للشيخ عنها وليس ذلك بمستنكر في أمثاله من المستهترين في ذكره. وإمّا خارج مخرج القلنسوة التي رمى بها الإمام الشبليّ في النار ومائة الدينار التي رمى بها في دجلة.

٤،٢١ وتأويل ذلك معروف عند أهل الطريق لا نطيل به. وأمّا أمر الآلات فإمّا أنّه كان يستفيد من تلك الأصوات أسرارًا ومعاني.

٥،٢١ ونظيره ما حكى الإمام أبو بكر بن العربيّ في سراج المريدين عن الشيخ أبي الفضل الجوهريّ أنّه بات بجواره ذات ليلة أصحاب الآلات. فشغلوه عن ورده بما هم عليه من لهوهم وباطلهم فلمّا أصبح وجلس في مجلسه قال إنّه بات بجوارنا البارحة قوم ملئوا مسامعنا علمًا وحكمة. قال أوّلهم لي لي لي. فقال الآخر لي ولك لي ولك. فقال الآخر كذا. ومثل ذلك بمتناظرين وجعل يقرّر ذلك حتّى قضى المجلس كلّه بأنواع من الحكم واللطائف والأسرار.

٦،٢١ وهذا من أعجب ما يتحف الله به أولياءه فقد غيّبَهُ الله عن صورتها الباطلة وأشهده سرّه الباطن فيها. [متقارب]

وَفِي كُلِّ شَيْءٍ لَهُ آيَةٌ   تَدُلُّ عَلَى أَنَّهُ وَاحِدُ

Al-Hashtūkī said, "When I heard what he said, I knew he was talking about the thought that had crossed my mind, and I repented in my soul to Exalted God. When someone held out a piece of paper to him—he used to write amulets—I would seize it from him and pass it to the shaykh and kiss his hand. When he was done writing, I would take it from him and kiss his hand. For each amulet I was thus able to kiss him twice." He said, "When I was with him I saw things that troubled me. One of these was that when clothing was brought to him as gift and alms, he ordered that it be thrown into a house, where it would remain until it was moth-eaten. Another was that every day musicians would come to him and play their instruments for him." **21.2**

Regarding the clothing, it is clear that it either took place when the shaykh was in an ecstatic state—no one will deny such recounted events occurring among those who are devoted to the remembrance of God—or that it took place in the same way with the hat the exemplar al-Shiblī threw into the fire, or the hundred dinars he cast into the Tigris.[178] **21.3**

The correct interpretation of this is well known among people on the Sufi path, so there is no need to expand upon it here. Regarding the musical instruments, one possible explanation is that he found a way to benefit from their sounds by receiving secrets or insights through them. **21.4**

The exemplar Abū Bakr ibn al-ʿArabī recounts in *The Lamp of the Disciples* that Shaykh Abū Faḍl al-Jawharī spent a night in the vicinity of some musicians. They distracted him from his personal devotions as they engaged in their idle amusement and vanity. When morning came and he had taken his seat in his circle, he said, "A group of people spent last night nearby and filled our ears with knowledge and wisdom. The first of them said, 'Mine, mine, mine.' The next said, 'Mine and yours, mine and yours.' The other said, 'Thus.' They were like disputants." He proceeded to affirm this until the circle had determined that all of these sounds were types of wise sayings, subtleties, and hidden meanings. **21.5**

This is among the most wondrous things that God has bestowed upon his saints, for God has hidden their vain natures from them, and has made His secret essence manifest in them. **21.6**

Everything is a sign of Him,
pointing to His Oneness.[179]

٧،٢١ وإمّا أنّ ذلك يوافق حالة له جماليّة تحضر في الوقت. ومن هذا المنبع يقع الطرب وما يشهد من حالات أهل الوجد. وإمّا أنّه يكون قطباً فتناسبه النوبة الملوكيّة. [طويل]

وَقُـلْ لِمُـلُوكِ ٱلْأَرْضِ تَجْهَـدُ جُهْـدَهَا فَذَا ٱلْمُلْكُ مَلْكٌ لَا يُبَاعُ وَلَا يُهْدَى

لله الأمـر من قبـل ومن بعـد[1]

٨،٢١ ونحو هذا ما يحكى عن سيدي محمّد الشرقيّ التادلاويّ. وأنّه لمّا وقع له الظهور بعث إليه السلطان أحمد المنصور نفرًا من خواصّه يختبرون أمره. فأضمر كلّ واحد منهم حاجة. فأحدهم قال تركت جارية لي مريضة وأريد أن يخبرني بأمرها. وقال الآخر أشتهي خبزًا خالصاً ودلاّعة وذلك في غير مكان وغير إبان. فلما انتهوا إليه خرج إليهم في لباس رفيع. فقال بعضهم هذا لباس الملوك فكيف يكون هذا وليّاً؟ فلما استقرّ المجلس بهم قال للمتكلم أنا قطب وقتي وهذا هو اللباس اللائق بي أو نحو هذا. وأخبر الآخر عن جاريته وأنّها عوفيت. وكان رجل قد خبأ له دلاّعة من الصيف فأتاه بها ذلك اليوم واستحضر خبزًا على الوصف. فقال للمشتهي تطلّبت ما لا يكون فها هو ذا قد جاء الله به.

٩،٢١ وحدّث أيضاً أن بعض الناس ممّن كان مملّقاً دوام حياته ذهب إلى سيدي محمّد الشرقيّ المذكور فاشتكى إليه الفقر. فقال له اذهب فقد رفع الله عنك الفقر. قال فذكر ذلك للوالد رحمه الله يعني سيدي محمّد ابن أبي بكر. فقال كلام الشيخ لا مطعن فيه ولكن يا عجباً أين يذهب الفقر عن فلان؟ فهذا لا بدّ له من مخرج. قال فلم يلبث ذلك الرجل أن مات عاجلاً فكان ذلك هو ارتفاع الفقر عنه واستراحته منه.

١٠،٢١ قلت: ومن معنى هذه ما حدّثوا عن بعض الصلحاء مراكش القرباء العهد أنّه جاءه إنسان فقال له يا سيدي إنّ الصلاة تثقل عليّ فعسى أن ترفعها عنّي. فقال له على الفور قم قد رفعها الله عنك فلم يقم إلّا مجنونًا خارجاً عن التكليف والله على كلّ شيء قدير.

[1] سقطت الجملة من ق، ط.

Another possibility is that the playing of music corresponded with a beatific state that he experienced at this particular time; that this was a source of musical rapture, known to correspond to the states of the people of ecstasy. Yet another possibility is that he was a spiritual Axis, and therefore deserving of a regal musical performance. 21.7

Say to the kings of the earth: Strive to make it better—
this realm that can neither be sold nor given away.

Everything is God's to command.

Something similar has been recounted regarding Sīdī Muḥammad al-Sharqī al-Tādlāwī. When his status became known, Sultan Aḥmad al-Manṣūr sent some of his close advisors to look into his case. Each had a secret desire. One said, "I have left behind a sick slave—I'd like him to tell me how she is doing." Another said, "I crave purest bread and watermelon"—these were not available anywhere at the time. When they arrived, he emerged, wearing elegant clothing, and one of them said, "This is the clothing of a king. How can he be a saint?" When they had joined the gathering and seated themselves, he responded to the man who had spoken last, saying "I am the Axis of this age; this clothing is appropriate to me." Or words to that effect. He informed the other that his slave had recovered. And a man who had hidden a watermelon from the summer heat brought it to him that very day. He had bread brought that fit the man's description, and said to the one who wished for it, "You asked for what wasn't available, and here it is—God has brought it to you." 21.8

Someone who had been destitute his whole life went to this Sīdī Muḥammad al-Sharqī and complained to him of poverty. "Go," he responded, "for God has removed poverty from you." Al-Hashtūkī said, "This was mentioned to Sīdī Maḥammad ibn Abī Bakr, the father, God have mercy on him. He was asked, 'The shaykh's speech is without fault, no, it is wondrous! What happened to this man's poverty? The matter must have been resolved.' Ibn Abī Bakr replied, 'This man did not have to wait long before he died suddenly—that resulted in the removal of and recovery from poverty.'" 21.9

I added: Similar accounts have in recent years been recounted about a saint of Marrakesh. A man came to him and said, "O Sīdī, prayer is difficult for me. Is it possible to exempt me from the obligation?" He replied straightaway, "Stand up. God has already removed it from you." When he stood, he had become insane, and was no longer obligated to pray.[180] God is capable of anything. 21.10

١١،٢١ وقد شهدت أنا بعض الناس ممّن كان ذا رياسة ودنيا فنكب وذهب ماله كتب معي كتاباً إلى أستاذنا الإمام ابن ناصر رضي الله عنه يشكو عليه بما نابه وما تخوّف من العيلة والضيعة. فأجابه الأستاذ بكتاب وفيه فلا تخشى الفقر فاتّفق أن مات ذلك الرجل عن قريب فكان ذلك راحته ممّا خاف. لله الأمر من قبل ومن بعد.

١،٢٢ حدّثني الأديب الفاضل أبو عبد الله محمّد بن المرابط الدلائيّ. قال كنت مع والدي رحمه الله وأظنّه قال في درب الحجاز نزولاً فإذا بعجوز أعرابيّة مرّت بنا وقد رفعت عقيرتها وهي تقول: [كامل]

حَجَّ ٱلْحَجِيجُ وَنَاقَتِي مَعْكُولَةٌ[١] يَا رَبِّ يَا مَوْلَايَ حُلَّ عِكَالَهَا[٢]

بقاف معقودة على ما هو لغة العرب اليوم. قال فقام أبي يهرول وراءها عجباً بما سمع من كلام العرب في غير زمانه. والظاهر أنّها أرادت بالناقة نفسها وأنّها لم تنشرح لهذا الأمر. أو أرادت تمثيل حالها في عدم التحرّك بحال الناقة المعقولة أو حال من ناقة معقولة.

٢،٢٢ ومثل هذه اللغة ما حدّثني الفاضل أبو عبد الله محمّد بن عبد الكريم الجزائريّ. قال حجّ بعض الأشراف فلمّا وقف على الروضة المشرفة على ساكنها الصلاة والسلام قال: [مخلع البسيط]

إِنْ كِيلَ زُرْتُمْ بِمَا رَجَعْتُمْ بِهِ يَا أَكْرَمَ ٱلرُّسْلِ مَا نَكُولُ[٣]؟

بالقاف المعقودة. فسمع من الروضة بتلك اللغة:

كُولُوا[٤] رَجَعْنَا بِكُلِّ خَيْرٍ وَٱجْتَمَعَ ٱلْفَرْعُ وَٱلْأُصُولُ

لله الأمر من قبل ومن بعد.

١ ط: معقولة. ٢ ط: عقالها. ٣ ط: نقول. ٤ ط: قولوا.

I witnessed someone of high position and stature experience a change in fortune and lose all his possessions. He sent a letter through me to our Teacher, the Exemplar Ibn Nāṣir, God be content with him, complaining of his affliction, and his fear of poverty and want. Our Teacher wrote in answer: "Do not fear poverty." And it happened that this man died soon after, and that this was the respite from what he feared. Everything is God's to command. 21.11

The distinguished scholar Abū ʿAbd Allāh Muḥammad ibn al-Murābiṭ al-Dilāʾī recounted the following to me: "Once, when I was with my father, God have mercy on him, I believe he said, 'Descending the Ḥijāz road, an old Bedouin woman passed by us, reciting with raised voice: 22.1

> The pilgrims have performed the pilgrimage and yet my camel is hobbled.
> Lord and Master, loosen her ties.'[181]

"—she pronounced the letter *qāf* differently from the way the Arabs do today. My father jumped up and rushed after her, surprised to hear the Arabic of another time." It is clear that by camel she was referring to herself, and that she was not happy. Or that she meant metaphorically to compare her state and the absence of movement with that of a hobbled camel, or some such thing.

The distinguished Abū ʿAbd Allāh Muḥammad ibn ʿAbd al-Karīm al-Jazāʾirī recounted something similar to me: "A noble performed the pilgrimage. When he stood in the *rawḍah*, adjacent to the grave of the one buried there, prayers and peace upon him, he said: 22.2

> If asked, 'You visited, what did you return with?'
> Noblest of prophets, what should we say?

"pronouncing the *qāf* as a 'g.' He then heard the following from the *rawḍah*:

> Say, 'We have returned with all that is good:
> The branch has been reunited with the root.'"[182]

Everything is God's to command.

١،٢٣ وجدت في بعض التقاييد لبعضهم ما معناه لو رأى أرسطوقدر البرنس في اللباس والكسكسون في الطعام والحلق بالموسى لاعترف للبربر بحكمة التدبير الدنيويّ وأنّ لهم قصب السبق في ذلك. انتهى. وقدكتبت الكسكسون بالنون على ما وجدته مكتوبًا خلاف ما ينطق به الناس. وبالنون حدّثنا الرئيس الأجلّ أبو عبد الله محمّد الحاج المتقدّم الذكر. قال ذهب رجلان فاضلان من بلاد المغرب وأظنّه قال أخوان. فدخلا بلاد الشام فمرض أحدهما وطال به المرض حتّى يئسوا منه فرأى الآخر النبيّ صلّى الله عليه وسلّم. فقال له أطعموه الكسكسون بهذه العبارة. قال فاستصنعوه له فأكله فبرئ وهذا إمّا خصوصيّة لهذا الطعام أو بذكره صلّى الله عليه وسلّم فيثبت له الشرف. ويستدرك بذلك ما فاته من كونه لم يأكله صلّى الله عليه وسلّم في حياته وإمّا من باب ما تقرّر من أنّ دواء الجسم عادته.

٢،٢٣ وقد دخلنا مدينة فاس حرسها الله عام تسع وسبعين وألف فأصابني إسهال مفرط وطال بي. وكان الطبيب بعثني بأمري فلم يترك دواء يستحسنه إلّا صنعه لي فلمّا لم يفد ذلك أرسل في غيبة منّي إلى عمّالي يقول لهم انظروا إن كان ثَمّ من الطعام ما يعتاده في بلده فأطعموه. فذكروا الأَقِط واصطنعوا عليه طعامًا فأكلته فعافاني الله تعالى. وقد أصابني مرّة أخرى ذلك فدخلت على السلطان رشيد ابن الشريف وكان يكرّمني ويجلّني. فرأى تغيّرًا في وجهي فسألني فأخبرته. فقال وماذا صنعت من علاج؟ فقلت له إنّ الطبيب يصنع لي شراب الريحان. فتضاحك ثم قال سبحان الله! ما لنا ولشرب الريحان؟ وأين عهدناه؟ خذ سويق الشعير واخلطه بالماء فذلك دواؤه. ثمّ ضحك. فقال هذه مثل قصّة العمرانيّ الشريف بات في ملويّة عند بني فلان فجعل يقول أعندكم شيء من شراب رمانتين؟ وهذا أعني التداوي بالشيء المعتاد ولو في الأعراق أمر شهير واضح.

I found the following proposition in someone's book: "Had Aristotle acknowledged the value of the burnoose as a piece of clothing, couscousūn as a food, and razors for shaving, he would have recognized the wisdom of the Berbers and their preeminence in worldly matters." I have spelled couscousūn with an "n," just as I found it, which is different from the way people pronounce it. The greatest ruler, the aforementioned Abū ʿAbd Allāh Maḥammad al-Ḥājj, pronounced it with an "n." He said, "Two devout men from Morocco went abroad," and I believe he said that they were brothers. "They arrived in the Levant, and one took ill. His illness lasted so long, they despaired for him. Then the other one dreamed of the Prophet, God bless and keep him, who said, 'Give him couscousūn to eat!' using this very pronunciation. They prepared it, he ate it, and he recovered." He recovered either because of a property of this food or because the Prophet, God bless and keep him, mentioned it, thereby endowing it with blessing. Thus the Prophet, God bless and keep him, anticipated something he had never known, as he had not once in his life eaten couscous. Or this is an example of the best medicine being what the body is used to. 23.1

We entered Fez, may God protect it, in the year 1079 [1668], and I was struck with an extreme case of diarrhea. It persisted, so the doctor applied himself to my case. He only gave me medicine he himself prepared and that he believed beneficial. When this did not help, he sent a note to my servants without my knowledge: "See if you can find some of the food he usually eats back home, and feed it to him." They thought of cheese curd and made some for me to eat. I ate it and Exalted God cured me. I was suffering the same affliction on another occasion when I entered before the Sultan Rashīd ibn al-Sharīf, who honored and esteemed me highly. He saw a change in my face and asked me about it. I told him about my affliction, and he asked, "What treatment have you undergone?" "The doctor has made a draft of basil for me," I replied. We shared a good laugh, and he said, "Good God! What good is a draft of basil? Have we ever encountered this? Take barley mush and mix it with water. That's the medicine indicated for your condition." Then he laughed, and said, "This is like the story of the Prophet's descendant from the city who spent the night in the desert with such and such a tribe. He asked, 'Do you have any pomegranate juice?'" This shows that taking as medicine something that one habitually consumes, even a homegrown remedy, is well-attested and clearly valid. 23.2

٣،٢٣ وقد ذكره ابن الحاجّ رضي الله عنه في المدخل وذكر قصّة الملك النصرانيّ الذي مرض فأعيا الأطباء علاجه حتّى جاء بعض أهل الخبرة. فسأل أمه وقال إن أردت أن يعافى ابنك فاصدقيني عنه. فقالت نعم كان أبوه عقيماً فلمّا خفت ذهاب ملكهم مكنّت أعرابياً كان عندنا من نفسي فهو أبو الملك. فقال الرجل على الفور عليّ بحوار فجيء به وذبح وشوي قدّامه وهو يشمّ رائحته. فكان ذلك بإذن الله تعالى سبب برئه. وهذا من العجب فإنّ هذا الملك الظاهر أنّه ما أكل قطّ لحم الجمل وإنّما العروق نزعته. فكيف بمن اعتاد أكل الطعام وربا عليه جسمه.

٤،٢٣ ومن أظرف ما وقع في هذا ما حدّثني به الطبيب المذكور وهو الفاضل أبو عبد الله محمّد الدراق الفاسيّ. قال كنت دخلت طنجة بقصد ملاقاة الأطبّاء ورؤية الشخص الذي صوّروه تعلّم التشريح معاينةً. قال فكان بعض أطبّاء الروم هنالك يعجب من أكلنا الكسكسون المذكور ويضحك منّا ويقول إنّما تأكلون العجين في بطونكم. قال فبينما نحن كذلك إذ دخلت عليه يوماً فوجدته عند رأس مريض محموم شديد الحمّى وهو يسقيه الخمر. قال فقلت له ما هذا الذي تصنع أنت؟ وأي مناسبة بين الخمر والحمّى والكلّ في غاية الحرارة؟ فقال إنّها لن تضرّه لاعتياده لها فإنّه كان يرضعها من ثدي أمّه وهو طفل صغير. قال فقلت له سبحان الله! ونحن هكذا كنّا نرضع ما تتكرّمن الكسكسون من ثدي أمّهاتنا ونحن صغار فأي شيء يضرّنا؟ فقال صدقت ولم يجد ما يقول. ومن هذا المعنى اختلفت طباع الناس في الطعام باختلاف الإلف والعادة فكلٌّ يستمرئ ما يألفه من الطعام ويشتهيه ويعاف الآخر. قال صلّى الله عليه وسلّم في الضبّ إنّه ليس بأرض قومي فتجدني أعافه. فعلّل ذلك بكونه ليس في أرضه.

٥،٢٣ ودخلت في أعوام الستّين وألف مدينة مراكش عند رحلتي في طلب العلم وأنا إذ ذاك صغير السنّ. فخرجت يوماً إلى الرحبة أنظر إلى المدّاحين. فوقفت على رجل مسنّ عليه حلقة عظيمة وإذا هو مشتغل بحكاية الأمور المضحكة للناس. فكان أوّل ما قرع سمعي منه أن قال اجتمع الفاسيّ والمراكشيّ والعربيّ والبربريّ والدراويّ. فقالوا

Doing so was mentioned by Ibn al-Ḥājj, God be content with him, in his book *The Introduction*, in which he recounted the story of a Christian king who fell sick. The doctors were unable to treat him until an experienced scholar came and questioned the king's mother. "If you want your son to be cured," he said, "then tell me the truth about him." "I will," she said. "His father was impotent, and as I was afraid of not being able to provide an heir, I gave myself to a Bedouin who was staying with him. He is the father of the king." The man immediately responded, "Bring me a young camel!" One was brought, slaughtered, and roasted in front of the king, who inhaled its scent. By Exalted God's leave, this cured him. This is truly amazing, since it is clear that while the king had never eaten camel meat, his preferences were those of his ancestors. Imagine the effect on someone whose body is accustomed to eating this food and who was raised on it. 23.3

I heard one of the best stories on this subject from this same doctor, the learned Abū ʿAbd Allāh Muḥammad al-Darrāq al-Fāsī. "I went to Tangier," he said, "hoping to meet doctors—in particular, one who was teaching anatomy. One Christian doctor was surprised that we ate the aforementioned couscousūn, and laughed at us, saying, 'You're just filling your stomachs with dough!' Then one day, on this particular visit, I found him standing over a sick man with a severe fever. He was making him drink wine, so I said, 'What are you doing? What's the value of wine when treating fever? Both are "hot" in nature!' 'It won't hurt him,' he said, 'since he is used to it—he used to get it as an infant when he nursed at his mother's breast.' 'Good God!' I said. 'We used to get couscousūn, the benefit of which you denied, in the same way, at our mothers' breasts when we were babes. How can it harm us now?' 'Too true,' he said, and was then at a loss for words. Peoples' natures differ according to habit and custom. Everyone enjoys eating food they are familiar with and everyone is averse to everything else. The Prophet, God bless and keep him, said about lizards: 'There are none in the land of my people, so you will find that I have an aversion to them.' He justified this opinion by their not being found where he lived." 23.4

In the 1060s [1650s] I arrived in Marrakesh during my travels for my studies. I was young at the time. One day I went to the square to see the storytellers.[183] I stopped by an old man surrounded by a large group who was telling the people funny stories. The first thing I heard was, "A man from Fez, a man from Marrakesh, an Arab, a Berber, and a man from the Darʿah Valley met and 23.5

تعالوا فليذكر كلّ منّا ما يشتهي من الطعام ثمّ ذكر ما تمنّاه كلّ واحد بلغة بلده وما يناسب بلده ولا أدري أكان ذلك في الوجود أم شيء قدره وهو كذلك يكون.

٦،٢٣ وحاصله أنّ الفاسيّ تمنّى مرق الحمام ولا يبغي الزحام والمراكشيّ تمنّى الخالص واللحم الغنميّ والعربيّ تمنّى البركوكش بالحليب والزبد والبربريّ تمنّى عصيدة انلي وهو صنف من الذرة بالزيت والدراويّ تمنّى تمر الفقوس في تجمدرت وهو موضع بدرعة يكون فيه تمر فاخر مع حريرة أمّه زهراء. وحاصله تمر جيّد وحريرة. ولو عرضت هذه الحريرة على العربيّ لم يشر بها إلّا من فاقة إذ لا يعتادها مع الاختيار ولو عرضت العصيدة على الفاسيّ لارتعدت فرائصه من رؤيتها وهكذا.

٧،٢٣ وأغرب شيء وقع في أمر الاعتياد ما حكي في جارية الملك الهنديّ مع الاسكندر. فإنّ الاسكندر لمّا دوّخ الملوك واستولى على الأقاليم احتال بعض ملوك الهند في هلاكه وكانت عنده جارية بديعة الحسن كاملة الأوصاف فجعل يغذّيها بالسموم ويتلطّف لها حتّى اعتادت ذلك ثمّ تناهت إلى أن تطبّعت بذلك وصارت مسمومة. فأهداها للإسكندر وقصد بذلك أن يمسّها فيهلك وهذا غريب. وقد ذكر الأطبّاء هذه الحكاية فاستغربوا شأنها. وقد ذكرنا في اختلاف البلدان مع اختلاف طبائع الناس بها فيما مرّ ما يقرب من هذا المعنى ويرشّحه. لله الأمر من قبل ومن بعد.

١،٢٤ من كلامهم ما أدري أسلم أو ودّع. وهو مذكور في قِصَرِ الزيارة. ونحوه قولهم ما سلم حتى ودّع. وقال فيه الشاعر: [رمل]

بِأَبِي مَنْ زَارَنِي مُكْتَتِمًا خَائِفًا مِنْ كُلِّ حِسٍّ جَزِعَا
حَذِرًا نَمَّ عَلَيْهِ نُورُهُ كَيْفَ يُخْفِي ٱللَّيْلُ بَدْرًا طَلَعَا

said, let's each mention what food we crave." He then recounted what each wished for in the local dialect corresponding to each one's place of origin. I do not know if this was how they said it, or if they merely supposed it to have transpired this way.

The upshot was that the man from Fez wanted clear pigeon soup, the man from Marrakesh clarified butter and goat meat, the Arab desired large-grained couscous with milk and butter, the Berber *anlī* paste, which is a kind of millet with oil, and the man from the Darʿah Valley, besides his mother's *ḥarīrah*, wanted Faqūsh dates from Tajamdart, a place in Darʿah with excellent red-flowering date palms. Essentially, he wanted good-quality dates and *ḥarīrah*. Now, if the *ḥarīrah* had been offered to the Arab who had never eaten it before, other than out of necessity, that is to say if he did not habitually choose it, his whole body would have shivered with shock at its sight, or the same would have happened if the paste had been offered to the man from Fez, and so on. 23.6

The most curious thing that ever took place in connection with becoming habituated to something is related about an Indian king's slave and Alexander. When Alexander had subjugated the rulers of India and subjected the various regions to his control, one of the kings plotted to have him killed. This king had an extraordinarily beautiful slave, perfect in every way, to whom he began to feed poison, little by little, till she was accustomed to it. She consumed the poison till it became second nature to her and she herself became poisonous. The king then gave her to Alexander, hoping he would caress her and die. Truly curious! Doctors have reported this story and have wondered at it.[184] We already mentioned above something similar when talking about the differences between countries and between the natures of their inhabitants. Everything is God's to command. 23.7

One thing people say is: "I don't know whether he was saying hello or goodbye." This is mentioned in connection with short visits. Similarly, people say: "Hardly had he said hello than he said goodbye." Regarding this, a poet said:[185] 24.1

I swear, someone visited me secretly,
  fearful and anxious that someone would see him,
Wary his light would give him away.
  But can the night conceal the full moon rising?

رَصَدَ ٱلْخَلْوَةَ حَتَّى أَمْكَنَتْ وَرَعَى ٱلسَّامِرَ حَتَّى هَجَعَا
كَابَدَ ٱلْأَهْوَالَ فِي زَوْرَتِهِ ثُمَّ مَا سَلَّمَ حَتَّى وَدَّعَا

٢،٢٤ وقال العباس بن الأحنف: [خفيف]

سَأَلُونَا عَنْ حَالِنَا كَيْفَ أَنْتُمْ؟ فَقَرَنَّا وَدَاعَهُمْ بِٱلسُّؤَالِ
مَا أَنَاخُوا حَتَّى ٱرْتَحَلْنَا فَمَا نَفْـ ـرِقُ بَيْنَ ٱلنُّزُولِ وَٱلتَّرْحَالِ

٣،٢٤ وقال محمّد بن أميّة الكاتب: [خفيف]

يَا فِرَاقًا أَتَى بِعُقْبِ فِرَاقِ وَٱتِّفَاقًا جَرَى بِغَيْرِ ٱتِّفَاقِ
حِينَ حَطَّتْ رِكَابُهُمْ لِتَلَاقِ زَفَّتِ ٱلْعِيسُ مِنْهُمْ لِلانْطِلَاقِ
إِنَّ نَفْسِي بِٱلشَّامِ إِذْ أَنْتَ فِيهَا لَيْسَ نَفْسِي ٱلَّتِي بِٱلْعِرَاقِ
أَشْتَهِي أَنْ تَرَى فُؤَادِيَ فَتَدْرِي كَيْفَ وَجْدِي بِكُمْ وَكَيْفَ ٱحْتِرَاقِي

٤،٢٤ وقال الحسين بن الضحّاك: [رمل]

بِأَبِي زَوْرٌ تَلَفَّتُّ لَهُ فَتَنَفَّسْتُ عَلَيْهِ ٱلصُّعَدَا
بَيْنَمَا أَضْحَكُ مَسْرُورًا بِهِ إِذْ تَقَطَّعْتُ عَلَيْهِ كَمَدَا

٥،٢٤ وكنت خرجت ذات مرّة لزيارة أقاربي فلقيت أختًا لي. فبنفس ما سلّمت عليّ جعلت تبكي. فقلت لها ما يبكيك؟ أليس هذا وصقت سرور وفرح؟ فقالت ذكرت يوم فراقك. فقلت في ذلك: [طويل]

وَمَحْزُونَةٍ بِٱلْبَيْنِ طَالَ بِهَا ٱلْجَوَى عَلَيْنَا وَشَوْقٌ بِٱلْجَوَانِحِ لَدَّاغُ
تَبِيتُ وَجَفْنَاهَا يُبَارِيهِمَا ٱلْحَيَا وَمَا تَحْتَ جَنْبَيْهَا مِنَ ٱلْفَرْشِ لَدَّاغُ

He lay in wait in a private moment,
watching the night owls till they fell asleep.
He braved terrors during his visit, and, in the end,
no sooner had he said hello than he said goodbye.

Al-ʿAbbās ibn al-Aḥnaf said: 24.2

They asked after us, How are you doing?
We chose to bid farewell with a question.
They had not made their camels kneel before we left;
We did not distinguish between making and striking camp.

The scribe Muḥammad ibn Umayyah said: 24.3

Separation upon separation—
each meeting without reunion!
When their riders dismount to meet,
already the camels groan to leave.
My soul is in Syria, where you are—
not in Iraq!
If you could see my heart, you'd know
how much I love you and burn for you.

Al-Ḥusayn ibn al-Ḍaḥḥāk said: 24.4

I swear, a beautiful breast caused my demise
and forced a deep sigh from me.
Though I laughed from the pleasure it gave me,
it made me fall apart with grief.

Once, on a visit to my relatives, I saw one of my sisters. At the very moment she greeted me, she began to cry. "What's making you cry?" I asked. "Isn't this a moment of happiness and joy?" "I was thinking of the day you'll leave," she said. About this I wrote: 24.5

Saddened by separation, she is affected by love for me,
passion aching in her ribs.
To the point that her eyes vie with the rain,
and the bed on which she reclines burns her sides.

إِلَى أَنْ تَسَخَّى ٱلدَّهْرُ بِٱلْوَصْلِ بَيْنَنَا وَلَاحَ ضِيَاءٌ لِلْمَسَرَّاتِ بَزَّاغُ
فَلَمَّا ٱنْقَضَى ٱلتَّسْلِيمُ مَا بَيْنَنَا بَكَتْ وَفَاضَ لَهَا دَمْعٌ مِنَ ٱلْعَيْنِ نَشَّاغُ
فَقُلْتُ أَلَمْ يَأْنِ ٱلسُّرُورُ وَلَمْ يَدُرْ شَرَابٌ لِلُقْيَانِ ٱلْأَحِبَّاءِ سَوَّاغُ
فَقَالَتْ تَذَكَّرْتُ ٱلْفِرَاقَ غَدًا فَذَا لِقَلْبِي عَنْ تِلْكَ ٱلْمَسَرَّاتِ صَدَّاغُ
فَيَا لَكَ مِنْ حُزْنٍ يُبَارِي مَسَرَّةً بِسَهْمَيْنِ كُلٌّ فِي ٱلْمُنَاضِلِ بَلَّاغُ
وَيَا لَكِ مِنْ نُعْمَى بِبُؤْسِي مَشُوبَةٍ كَمَا مَحْضًا شَابَ بِٱلدَّمِ ٱلْمَوْرُ نَسَّاغُ
بَلِ ٱلشَّرُّ فِي ٱلدُّنْيَا عَلَى ٱلْمَرْءِ صَائِلٌ تَجُوجُ عَلَيْهِ ٱلدَّهْرُ وَٱلْخَيْرُ رَوَّاغُ
عَلَى أَنَّ لُطْفَ اللهِ لِلْعُسْرِ دَامِغٌ كَمَا ٱلْحَقُّ مِنْهُ لِلْأَبَاطِيلِ دَمَّاغُ

٦،٢٤ واعلم أنّ أمور الدنيا مشوبة خيرها بشرّها وحلوها بمرّها ثمّ هي متبدّلة متغيّرة لا تكاد تثبت في حدّ ولا تقف على مركز. وحكمة ذلك شيئان أحدهما أنّ الدنيا لمّا جعلت مقدّمة للآخرة يقع فيها الاستعداد لدخول الجنّة والنجاة من النار. جعلت مظهرًا لما هنالك من نعيم وعذاب ودالّة عليه ومذكّرة له وقاضية بالترغيب والتنفير. فلم تجعل خيرًا محضًا وإلّا نسي العذاب ولا شرًّا محضًا وإلّا نسي النعيم. وأيضًا جعلت دالّة على أوصاف الربّ المنشئ لها سبحانه من جمال وجلال لتحصل المعرفة لعباده.

٧،٢٤ وهذا كلّه كلام واسع الذيل لو بسطناه والإشارة تكفي. الثاني أنّها حادثة حادث ما فيها. وشأن الحادث أن يتبدّل من عدم إلى وجود ومن وجود إلى عدم ذاتًا وصفة وحالًا ومكانًا وزمانًا فلزم من ذلك التحوّل من عزّ إلى ذلّ ومن غنى إلى فقر ومن اجتماع إلى افتراق ومن ارتفاع إلى اتّضاع ومن سرور إلى حزن ومن صحّة إلى سقم. وبالعكس في الجميع إلى غير ذلك.

Until time unites us again
  and shines a bright light on our happiness.
When our greetings ended she cried;
  tears welled up and flowed.
"Isn't this a time of joy?" I asked.
  "The draft of loved ones meeting should be easy."
"I am reminded of tomorrow's separation," she said,
  "which keeps my heart from happiness."
How often sadness contends with joy,
  two arrows that both hit the mark.
You mixed my misery with good fortune,
  like pierced, immaculate skin tainted by flowing blood.
Evil assails us in this world,
  Time is a relentless adversary, and good remains elusive.
God's grace triumphs over hardship,
  As His Truth triumphs over false belief!

In worldly matters, good and evil are mixed, as are sweet and bitter. What is more, they alternate, one swapping roles with the other, scarcely ever fixed in their borders or their center. The wisdom in this is twofold: The first is that when this world was created as a prelude to the hereafter, the potential to enter heaven and be saved from the fire was made possible. This world was created to embody both the blessings and punishment of the next, evoking it to engender both desire and aversion. It was not made completely good, so that punishment would not be forgotten, nor completely evil, so that blessings would not be forgotten. It was also created as a sign of the attributes of the Lord who produced it out of beauty and splendor, praise Him, to convey knowledge to His worshippers. 24.6

All this would be a vast subject if we expanded on it here—it suffices to allude to it. The second piece of wisdom is that the world and everything in it were created. Everything created has the characteristic, with regard to its essence, attributes, state, location, and time, of proceeding from nonbeing to being, and from being to nonbeing. The shift from glory to humiliation follows necessarily from this, as does wealth to poverty, being together to being separate, being elevated to being humbled, happiness to sadness, and health to illness. The reverse is also true of all of these, as well as of other similar pairs. 24.7

وفي الحديث كانت العضباء وهي ناقة للنبي صلّى الله عليه وسلّم معروفة لا تسبق. ٨،٢٤
فجاء أعرابيّ على قعودٍ فسبقها فقالوا سبقت العضباء. وشقّ ذلك على المسلمين فقال النبي صلّى الله عليه وسلّم إنّ الله لن يرفع شيئاً من الدّنيا إلّا وضعه. وقد جاء رجل إلى بعض الوزراء فقال له إنّي رأيتك فيما يرى النائم طالعاً على رأس نخلة أو شجرة. ورأيت فلاناً يعني وزيراً آخر كان يساميه في المرتبة أنّه شرع في الطلوع ولم يصل بعد إلى أعلاها وأراد بذلك أن يبشّر الوزير ليستجديه. فقال له الوزير وكان ذا فطنة يا أخي اذهب إلى فلان ليعطيك فإنّه في الزيادة وأمّا أنا فقد انتهيت وليس بعده إلّا الانحطاط.

وقد أذكرتني هذه الحكاية حكاية أبي عبد الله وزير المهديّ وكان متمكّناً في منزلته ٩،٢٤
عنده. ثمّ إنّ الخليفة زاره في داره ذات مرّة وكانت زيارة الخليفة لخواصّه في عرفهم ليس فوقها درجة تطلب. فلمّا همّ بالانصراف أخذ الوزير يدفع له من نفائس الذخائر ما يليق بتجهيزه ثمّ جعل يبكي. فقال الخليفة ما يبكيك؟ لقد علمت أنّ فيك بخلاً تسمّيه حزماً. فإن كان بك ما أعطيت أعفيناك منه. فقال أبو عبد الله والله ما بكيت للمال وللدنيا كلّها أحقر شيء في حقّك ولكن علمت أنّ زيارتك لي درجة ليس فوقها درجة ترام فأخاف الآن من السقوط. فلمّا رأى ذلك أشفق وأعطاه من العهود والمواثيق أن لا يغدر به ولا يسمع فيه قول قائل ما اطمأنّ به. فلم يلبث إلّا أيّاماً يسيرة حتّى سعوا فيه فنكب وقصته مشهورة. والعامّة يقولون: [رجز]

ثَلاثَـةٌ لَيسَ لَهـا أَمـانُ   ٱلبَحرُ وَٱلسُّلطَانُ وَٱلزَّمانُ

وفي هذا المعنى الذي نحن فيه قيل: [طويل] ١٠،٢٤

تُوَقَّى ٱلبُدُورُ ٱلنَّقصَ وَهيَ أَهِلَّةٌ   وَيُدرِكُها ٱلنُّقصانُ وَهِيَ كَوامِلُ

From the Hadith we learn the following: Al-ʿAḍbāʾ was the she-camel of the Prophet, God bless and keep him, and was known for being unbeatable in a race. Then a Bedouin came on a young camel and bested her, and people said, Al-ʿAḍbāʾ has been beaten. This distressed the Muslims. The Prophet, God bless and keep him, said, "God will never elevate anything in this world without humbling it." A man came to a minister and said, "I saw you in a dream, ascending to the top of a palm tree or some other tree. And I saw someone—referring to another minister who was seeking to surpass him in rank—ascend without reaching the top." He wanted to give the minister this news so that he would give him alms. Being astute, the minister said, "My brother, go to so-and-so that he may give you some charity—he has more than he needs. As for me, my ascent is done; now there is nothing but decline." 24.8

The story reminds me of the story about Abū ʿAbd Allah, al-Mahdī's influential minister. Once, the caliph visited him in his house. It was the habit of caliphs to visit their close advisers and it represented the highest sign of favor. When the caliph wanted to leave, his minister began to give him gems from his storerooms, suitable to his outfit, and then began to cry. "What is making you cry?" the caliph asked, "I know you consider your miserliness a form of self-restraint. If what you have given is dear to you, we forgive you for it." Abū ʿAbdāllah replied, "By God, it's not wealth that makes me cry. Owning the whole world is more loathsome still. It's this: I know that your visit is the greatest distinction I could wish for; now I fear the inevitable fall." When the caliph heard this, he felt pity and granted him promises and assurances that he would not suffer from any treachery or gossip directed against him and could feel at ease. And yet, it was only a few days before he was pursued and he fell out of favor. His story is famous.[186] People say: 24.9

There are three things you can't rely on:
The ocean, power, and time.

Someone has said, on this very issue: 24.10

The moons are protected from loss when they are crescents;
depletion reaches them once they are full.[187]

وإذا كانت الدنيا وما فيها عرضاً زائلاً لا ثبات له فلا ينبغي لعاقل أن يتبجّح بخيرها ولا أن يجزع من شرّها. بل إذا كان حلوها تتوقّع بعد المرارة ومرّها ترجى بعده الحلاوة فقد صار حلوها مرّاً ومرّها حلواً. وإذا كان المفروح به لا يبقى فهو بصدد أن يكون محزوناً عليه قلّ أو كثر فكثرة الفرح بها إذن مقدّمة كثرة الحزن فلا ينبغي أن يلتفت إليه.

١١،٢٤ وقال الشاعر: [طويل]

عَلَى قَدْرِ مَا أُولِعْتَ بِٱلشَّيْءِ حُزْنُهُ   وَيَصْعُبُ نَزْعُ ٱلسَّهْمِ مَهْمَا تَمَكَّنَا

١٢،٢٤ وقال الآخر: [طويل]

وَمَنْ سَرَّهُ أَنْ لَا يَرَى مَا يَسُوءُهُ   فَلَا يَتَّخِذْ شَيْئًا يَخَافُ لَهُ فَقْدَا
فَإِنَّ صَلَاحَ ٱلْمَرْءِ يَرْجِعُ كُلُّهُ   فَسَادًا إِذِ ٱلْإِنْسَانُ جَازَ بِهِ ٱلْحَدَا

١٣،٢٤ وفي الحكم العطائية ليقلّ ما تفرح به يقلّ ما تحزن عليه وذكر شارحها ابن عبّاد رضي الله عنه أنّه حمل لبعض الملوك قدح من فيروزج مرصّع بالجواهر لم يُرَ له نظير ففرح الملك به فرحاً شديداً. فقال لبعض الحكماء عنده كيف ترى هذا؟ فقال أراه مصيبة وفقراً. قال وكيف ذلك؟ قال إن انكسر مصيبة لا جبر لها وإن سرق صرت فقيراً إليه ولم تجد مثله وقد كنت قبل أن يحمل إليك في أمن من المصيبة والفقر. فاتّفق أن انكسر القدح يوماً فعظمت مصيبة الملك فيه. وقال صدق الحكيم ليته لم يحمل إلينا.

١٤،٢٤ وقال الشاعر: [طويل]

وَمَنْ يَحْمَدِ ٱلدُّنْيَا لِشَيْءٍ يَسُرُّهُ   فَسَوْفَ لَعَمْرِي عَنْ قَرِيبٍ يَلُومُهَا
إِذَا أَدْبَرَتْ كَانَتْ عَلَى ٱلْمَرْءِ حَسْرَةً   وَإِنْ أَقْبَلَتْ كَانَتْ كَثِيرًا هُمُومُهَا

If the world and everything in it is just a passing manifestation without constancy, there is no need for any reasoning person to boast of its good or to bemoan its evil. Instead, if one anticipates bitterness after sweetness, and hopes for sweetness after bitterness, then its sweetness becomes bitter, and its bitterness sweet. If what is joyful in the world is not permanent, but will be mourned to a greater or lesser extent, then finding great pleasure in the world is prelude to great sorrow, and one should not seek it out.

As a poet has said: 24.11

Your grief for something is equal to your passion for it—
try as we may, the arrow is hard to remove.

Another poet has said: 24.12

Whoever is happy not to heed what harms him
will not acquire anything he is afraid to lose.
One's prosperity is corrupted utterly
when crossing the border into death.

In the *Wise Sayings of Ibn ʿAṭāʾ Allāh* we find: "May the amount you rejoice 24.13
in something be small so that the amount you grieve for it is similar." The commentator of the work, Ibn ʿAbbād, God be content with him, recounted that a king had a goblet of turquoise brought to him, studded with jewels, the like of which had never been seen. The king took great pleasure in it, and said to one of the wise men in his entourage, "What is your opinion of this?" "I deem it a loss calamitous," he replied. "How so?" asked the king. "If it breaks," he said, "it will be an irreversible disaster, and if it is stolen then you will have lost it and you will never find its like. Before it was brought to you, you were safe from both disaster and loss." It happened one day that the goblet broke and the king experienced it as a great disaster. "The wise man was right," he said. "I wish it had never been brought to me."

As the poet said: 24.14

Whoever praises the world for something that gladdens him,
by my life, he will soon come to blame it.
If it is removed, it is a source of sorrow;
if it remains, countless worries attend it.

١٥،٢٤ وفي الحكم أيضاً إن أردت أن لا تعزل فلا تتولّ ولاية لا تدوم لك. وهذا صادق في الولاية نفسها ولذا قال صلّى الله عليه وسلّم فيها نعمت المرضعة وبئست الفاطمة. وفي غيرها من كلّ ما يتناول الإنسان من الدنيا زائداً على قدر الضرورة أو يصحبه من أهلها فكلّ ذلك لا يخلو من علاقة بالنفس ثمّ هو لا يدوم إمّا أن تفارقه أو يفارقك فمآله إلى الحسرة والأسف.

١٦،٢٤ وكنت في سفرتي إلى السوس الأقصى لقيني فقير من شبانة فصحبني أيّاماً قلائل وأنس بي. فلمّا بلغنا المحلّ ودّعته فرأيته يبكي على فراقي وسمعته يقول لا تعرف أحداً. ويكرّر هذا الكلام أي إذا كنت أيّها العاقل تعلم أنّ الذي دخل في قلبك سوف تفارقه فيتألّم قلبك عليه فلا تسع في دخول أحد فيه بمعرفتك له ولا تعرف أحداً واترك قلبك خاليًا مستريحًا. [متقارب]

رَأَى ٱلْأَمْرَ يُفضِي إِلَى آخِرٍ فَصَيَّرَ آخِرَهُ أَوَّلَا

١٧،٢٤ وهذا كلّه من واد واحد والكلام فيه يتّسع. نعم إن أمكنك أن تدخل في قلبك من لا يخشى عليه الزوال والهلاك والفناء فافعل وليس ذلك إلّا الحقّ تعالى. فمن أحبّه فهو جدير أن يدوم محبوبه ومن أنس به فهو جدير أن يدوم أنسه ومن استعزّ به دام عزّه ومن استغنى به دام غناه. كما قيل: [مجزوء الكامل]

لِيَكُنْ بِرَبِّكَ عِزُّ نَفْـ سِكَ يَسْتَقِرُّ وَيَثْبُتُ
وَإِنْ ٱعْتَزَزْتَ بِمَنْ يَمُو تُ فَإِنَّ عِزَّكَ مَيِّتُ

لله الأمر من قبل ومن بعد.

١،٢٥ دخلت مدينة فاس حرسها الله تعالى سنة تسع وسبعين وألف إذ خربت الزاوية البكريّة. فأقبلت طلبة العلم للأخذ عنّي وتخلّفت جماعة من المشاهير وهم أو جلّهم

We also find in the *Wise Sayings*: If you do not want to be deposed, do not agree to govern what you know won't last for you. This is true for the essence of government itself, and for this reason the Prophet, God bless him and keep him, said in this context: "The nursing woman is fortunate, the weaning woman unfortunate." In all matters in which you take of this world something more than you need or that you acquire from its people, until you relinquish it or it is taken from you, your ego is excessively attached to it. Possessions bring nothing but sorrow and regret. 24.15

When I was traveling to the southernmost part of the Sūs, I met a devotee of the Shabānah, who accompanied me for several days and whom I got to know well. When we reached our destination, I bade him farewell. He wept when we parted and I heard him say, "Do not make anyone's acquaintance." He repeated these words, by which he meant: You who are intelligent, since you know that you will be separated from anyone you admit into your heart, and since your heart will suffer in the process, admit no one. Do not make anyone's acquaintance. Let your heart be empty and at peace.[188] 24.16

He saw how it would end,
So he made the end the beginning.

This is related to the same subject, about which a great deal has been said. Truly, if you are able to admit into your heart someone whom you need not fear will fade, disappear, or die, then do so: This will be none other than God, the Exalted Truth. Whoever loves Him merits lasting love; whoever is intimate with Him deserves to remain intimate with Him; whoever holds Him in high esteem, his glory continues forever. He who finds sufficiency in God alone will find this to be an eternal state. As has been said: 24.17

Through your Lord, your own power
is established and maintained.
If you seek power through one who dies
your power is as good as dead.

Everything is God's to command.

I arrived in the city of Fez, Exalted God protect it, in 1079 [1667] after the Bakriyyah lodge had been destroyed. Some students thirsting for knowledge 25.1

محتاجون إلى المجلس وكأنّهم غلبهم ما هو المألوف من الطبع الآدميّ في أمثالهم. وكنت آنست ذلك فيهم.

٢،٢٥ فاتّفق أن خرجنا لزيارة صلحاء الساحل فلمّا انتهينا إلى مقام الشيخ أبي سلهام جلسنا على شاطئ البحر: [خفيف]

فِي عَشِيٍّ كَأَنَّمَا ٱخْتَلَسَتْهُ   مِنْ نَعِيمِ ٱلْفِرْدَوْسِ نَفْحَةُ لُطْفِ
قَدْ قَطَفْنَا بِهِ جِنَى جَنَّتَيْ أُنْـ   ـسٍ وَعِلْمٍ أَشْهَى ٱجْتِذَابٍ وَقَطْفِ
وَٱرْتَضَعْنَا أَلَذَّ مِنْ كَأْسِ وَصْلٍ   بَعْدَ هَجْرٍ مِنْ ذِي وِدَادٍ وَعَطْفِ
وَلَقَدْ كَانَ فِي ٱلْحَشَا جِذْوَةُ ٱلْوَجْـ   ـدِ فَكَانَ مِنْهُ لِذٰلِكَ مُطْفِ

٣،٢٥ فحصل للنفس ارتياح وانبساط وتجدّد لها عزم ونشاط فكتبت ارتجالاً ما صوّرته حافظته لمّا انقدح في الفكرة من الشعر. أذكره بحسب ما اتّفق غثّاً وسميناً ورخيصاً وثميناً وجدّاً وهزلاً وصدقاً وإزلاً حتّى إذا آن لمضروبه الترويج وبلغت بناته أوان التزويج. دفع الخالص الإبريز وأحظيت الحسان بالتبريز. وكان الردي أولى أن يكسر أو يعطّل والدميمة منه أحقّ أن تُوأَدَ أو تعضل. هذا وليت شعري ماذا أكتب اليوم؟ وقد ضاع أكثر شعري: [طويل]

لَيَالِي كَانَ ٱلْقَلْبُ فِي مَوْكِبِ ٱلْهَوَى   عَلَى مَتْنِ يَعْبُوبٍ مِنَ ٱللَّهْوِ سَابِقِ
وَكَانَ ٱلشَّبَابُ ٱلْغَضُّ فَيْنَانَ مُورِقًا   فَكَانَتْ رِيَاضُ ٱلْغَيِّ أَزْهَى ٱلْحَدَائِقِ

٤،٢٥ وللنَفسُ إذ ذاك أقدر على القيل والقال وأعرف بالسحر الحلال. فكنت إذ ذاك أقول الفذّ والنتفة والقصيدة عن نشاط إلى القول وارتياح. ثمّ ادع ذلك يذهب مدرج الرياح ولم أستفق لتقييد إلّا وقد كدت أراهق التفنيد. ويقصر من وسواس النفس باطله ويعرّى أفراس الصبا ورواحله. [كامل]

came to study with me, while a group of well-known scholars kept their distance. Most of these scholars were in need of instruction, and it seemed they had been overwhelmed by what is well-known about human nature in similar cases. I found this amusing.

Now, it happened that we visited the graves of the holy men on the coast. 25.2
When we came to the tomb of Shaykh Abū Salhām, we sat on the beach:

> In the evening, it was as if a pleasant breeze
> had escaped from the grace of paradise.
> From it we gathered the harvest of two gardens—
> intimacy and knowledge are the sweetest crops.
> We drank sweetness from the cup of union
> after being separated from our intimate loved ones.
> We felt the firebrand of passion burning our insides,
> which the drink put out.

In this way, my soul relaxed and experienced peace, and my resolve and 25.3
activity were renewed. I then wrote spontaneously what I had preserved of the poetry that inspired me. What I remembered was by turns lean and fat, worthless and valuable, serious and frivolous, sincere and deceitful. Soon it was time to write it down and circulate what had been composed, and for its daughters to marry. The most beautiful were given for a dowry of gold. The basest lines were prone to break or fall apart and the worst ones deserved to be buried alive or prevented from marriage altogether. This is how I applied myself to poetry. If only I knew what to write today! Most of my poetry has been lost.

> On such nights, my heart joined a procession of desire
> racing on the swift horse of pleasure.
> The young were vibrant, their hair loose, aglow,
> the most brilliant gardens in an orchard of temptation.

At such times, the ego becomes adept at prattle and skilled in a kind of licit 25.4
magic. I would recite with briskness a single line, a fragment, or a poem until I was delighted with it. I then bid it farewell, and it would be carried away by the winds. I was not bothered to write any of it down until I was almost senile. Its vanity is no longer capable of tempting my ego; its riding beasts—my muse—are now saddleless and unridden.

وَٱلْقَلْبُ يَرْجُو أَنْ تَرِقَّ شِفَارُهُ   وَتَطُولَ فِي سُبُلِ ٱلْهُدَى أَسْفَارُهُ
وَيَبِينُ عَنْ شَرَكِ ٱلْغُرُورِ نَوَّارُهُ   وَتَلُوحُ فِي رُتَبِ ٱلْعَلَى أَنْوَارُهُ
فَيَقِلُّ فِي سُوقِ ٱلصِّبَا أَوْطَارُهُ   وَيَشِطُّ عَنْ وَطَنِ ٱلْهَوَى أَقْطَارُهُ

٥،٢٥ ولعمري إنّ النفس عند هذا أحقّ أن يجدّ في طلب الجدّ جدُّها. ويقف عند الأهمّ حدّها فتبعد عن قول الشعر بمراحل وعن سبل اللهو التي هي له أفراس ورواحل. ولكن للنفس فرطات ولا بدّ لها أحيانًا من سقطات. فمن ذلك قولي: [كامل]

مَا أَنْصَفَتْ فَاسُ وَلَا أَعْلَامُهَا   عِلْمِي وَلَا عَرَفُوا جَلَالَةَ مَنْصِبِي
لَوْ أَنْصَفُوا لَصَبُوا إِلَيَّ كَمَا صَبَا   رَاعِي سِنِينَ إِلَى ٱلْغَمَامِ ٱلصَّيِّبِ

٦،٢٥ ثمّ أثبتُّ في هذه الحافظة ما وقع لي من الشعر في ذلك العهد وهو مجموع في الديوان فلا حاجة إلى الإطالة به هنا. وإنّما الغرض من ذكر هذين البيتين الواقعين على السبب الذي ذكرناه قبل. وأظنّ أنّ البحتري وقع له شبه هذا الشعر في ذمّ بغداد ولكنّي لم أقف عليه بعد ولم يطرق سمعي حين قلت ذلك. وإنّما رأيت بعد ذلك أبا العلاء المعرّي أشار إلى ذلك منتقدًا عليه حيث قال: [بسيط]

ذَمَّ ٱلْوَلِيدُ وَلَمْ أَذْمُمْ جِوَارَكُمُ   وَقَالَ مَا أَنْصَفَتْ بَغْدَادُ حُوشِيتَا
فَإِنْ لَقِيتُ ٱلْوَلِيدَ وَٱلنَّوَى قَذَفُ   يَوْمَ ٱلْقِيَامَةِ لَمْ أُعْدِمْهُ تَبْكِيتَا

٧،٢٥ فلمّا رأيت هذا نبّهت بهذا الكلام لئلّا أنسب إلى الأخذ فإن وقع شيء فمن توافق الخواطر. و في البيت الثاني تلميح إلى قول الأعرابيّ في حسن الحديث: [كامل]

The heart wishes to be merciful
  and to continue on the path of righteousness.
Its blossoms discern the snares of deception
  and its lights illuminate the highest ranks.
Its desires in the marketplace of youthful impulse are few
  and its expanses exceed the terrain of vanity.

By my life, the ego is clearly worthy of more serious things, and should contemplate more important matters. Thus, it should distance itself from the recitation of poetry, and the paths that, like horses and riding camels, carry you to indulgence. Yet the ego can exceed its limits and is bound to make mistakes. Regarding this, I composed: 25.5

Neither Fez nor its scholars did justice to my knowledge,
  Nor did they acknowledge the greatness of my stature.
If they had behaved righteously, they would have yearned for me
  As a farmer of barren land yearns for clouds heavy with rain.

In recollecting, I have set down the poetry that occurred to me at that time; it is gathered in the collection of my poetry so there is no need to include more here.[189] My intention in mentioning these two lines was for the reason I stated. I believe it was al-Buḥturī to whom similar poetry occurred when he censured Baghdad. But I had not yet stumbled upon his verses, nor had they been brought to my attention, when I composed my lines. I later saw that Abū l-ʿAlāʾ al-Maʿarrī censured al-Buḥturī's lines as follows: 25.6

Al-Walīd censured your neighborhood, not I.
  Baghdad, he said, was unjust at its core.
If I meet al-Buḥturī on Judgment Day, when the stones are cast about,
  I will not hold back from rebuking him.

I drew attention to his lines when I came upon them so as not to be accused of plagiarism. If my lines happen to be similar, that is the result of a coincidence of ideas. The second line has an allusion to what the Bedouin say about beautiful speech: 25.7

وَحَدِيثًا كَٱلْقَطْرِ يَسْمَعُهُ   رَاعِي سِنِينَ تَتَابَعَتْ جَدْبَا
فَأَصَاخَ يَرْجُو أَنْ يَكُونَ حَيًا   وَيَقُولُ مِنْ فَرَحٍ هَيًّا رَبَّا

وإنّما استسهلت وأستغفر الله التمدّح والافتخار لأنّ ذلك مباح في الشعر مسلوك في سائر الأعصار والأمصار. لله الأمر من قبل ومن بعد.[1]

٨،٢٥ وما ذكر من عدم الإنصاف سببه الكبر والحسد وهما الداء العضال الذي هلك به إبليس نسأل الله العافية. وذلك معجون في طينة الآدميّ ومبتلى به إلّا من طهّره الله من أصفيائه وقليل ما هم. ولم يزل ذو الفضل محسوداً وكلّما كثر الفضل كثر الحسّاد فوجود الحسّاد دليل على وجود الفضل وعدمهم على عدمه فإذا قيل للشخص كثّر الله حسّادك كان دعاء له وإذا قيل قلّل الله حسّادك كان دعاء عليه. وقد أكثر الشعراء من هذا المعنى قال الكميت الأسديّ: [بسيط]

إِنْ يَحْسُدُونِي فَإِنِّي غَيْرُ لَائِمِهِمْ   قَبْلِي مِنَ ٱلنَّاسِ أَهْلُ ٱلْفَضْلِ قَدْ حُسِدُوا
فَدَامَ لِي وَلَهُمْ مَا بِي وَمَا بِهِمْ   وَمَاتَ أَكْثَرُنَا غَيْظًا بِمَا يَجِدُ
أَنَا ٱلَّذِي يَجِدُونِي فِي صُدُورِهِمْ   لَا أَرْتَقِي صَدَرًا مِنْهَا وَلَا أَرِدُ

٩،٢٥ وأنشد أبو علي الحاتميّ في حلية المحاضرة بدل البيت الأخير:

لَا يُبْعِدُ اللهُ حُسَّادِي فَإِنَّهُمْ   أَشَرُّ عِنْدِي مِنَ ٱللَّائِي لَهَا ٱلْوِدَدُ

والظاهر أنّ قوله أشرّ تصحيف من الكاتب وإنّما هو أحبّ.

[1] سقطت الجملة من ق، ط.

Her speech is like a raindrop heard by a shepherd
following years of drought.
He listened, hoping it was rain,
saying out of joy, Lord, let it come!

I used to find it easy to write eulogies and boasts, and I seek God's forgiveness for doing so, since it is permitted, and has been undertaken in every time and place. Everything is God's to command.

The cause for the lack of justice I mentioned is arrogance and envy. These constitute the inveterate evil that destroyed Satan, God preserve us! This evil is mixed into the very clay of humanity, and afflicts all humans, except those close friends of God whom He has purified—but these are few in number. A virtuous person will be envied: The more virtue he has, the greater the envy. Thus, the presence of envy is an indication of the presence of virtue and the absence of one represents the absence of the other. If a person is told, "May God increase the number of those who envy you," it is a prayer for him. If he is told, "May God lessen the number of those who envy you," it is an invocation against him. The poets have said a great deal on this subject. Al-Kumayt al-Asadī said: 25.8

I do not blame them for their envy—
before they envied me they envied people of virtue.
As long as we remain like this,
most of us will die of chagrin at this state of affairs.
I am the one they find at their vanguard;
I did not seek this elevation, nor did I refuse it.[190]

In *Discourse's Adornment*, Abū ʿAlī al-Ḥātimī includes a different last line: 25.9

May God not remove those who envy me—
they are more hateful to me than those who bear me affection.

It is clear that his saying "more hateful" is an error of transcription on the part of the scribe and that it should instead be "more beloved."

١٠،٢٥ وقال عروة بن أذينة: [بسيط]

لَا يُبْعِدُ اللهُ حُسَّادِي وَزَادَهُمْ حَتَّى يَمُوتُوا بِدَاءٍ غَيْرِ مَكْنُونِ
إِنِّي رَأَيْتُهُمْ فِي كُلِّ مَنْزِلَةٍ أَجَلَّ فَقْدًا مِنَ ٱللَّائِي أَحَبُّونِي

١١،٢٥ وقال نصر بن سيّار: [بسيط]

إِنِّي نَشَأْتُ وَحُسَّادِي ذَوُو عَدَدٍ يَا ذَا ٱلْمَعَارِجِ لَا تُنْقِصْ لَهُمْ عَدَدَا
إِنْ يَحْسُدُونِي عَلَى مَا بِي وَمَا بِهِمْ فَمِثْلُ مَا بِي لَعَمْرِي جَرَّ لِي ٱلْحَسَدَا

١٢،٢٥ وقال معن بن زائدة: [بسيط]

إِنِّي حَسَدْتُ فَزَادَ اللهُ فِي حَسَدِي لَا عَاشَ مَنْ عَاشَ يَوْمًا غَيْرَ مَحْسُودِ
مَا يُحْسَدُ ٱلْمَرْءُ إِلَّا مِنْ فَضَائِلِهِ بِٱلْعِلْمِ وَٱلظَّرْفِ أَوْ بِٱلْبَأْسِ وَٱلْجُودِ

١٣،٢٥ وقال أبو نواس: [طويل]

دَعِينِي أُكَثِّرْ حَاسِدِيكِ بِرِحْلَةٍ إِلَى بَلَدٍ فِيهِ ٱلْخَصِيبُ أَمِيرُ

١٤،٢٥ وقال الأوّل: [بسيط]

لَوْ كَانَ يَقْعُدُ فَوْقَ ٱلشَّمْسِ مِنْ كَرَمٍ قَوْمٌ بِأَوَّلِهِمْ أَوْ مَجْدِهِمْ قَعَدُوا
مُحَسَّدُونَ عَلَى مَا كَانَ مِنْ كَرَمٍ لَا يُنْقِصُ اللهُ عَنْهُمْ مَا لَهُ حُسِدُوا

١٥،٢٥ وقال أبو تمّام: [كامل]

وَإِذَا أَرَادَ اللهُ نَشْرَ فَضِيلَةٍ طُوِيَتْ أَتَاحَ لَهَا لِسَانَ حَسُودِ
لَوْلَا ٱشْتِعَالُ ٱلنَّارِ فِيمَا جَاوَرَتْ مَا كَانَ يُعْرَفُ طِيبُ عَرْفِ ٱلْعُودِ

ʿUrwah ibn Udhaynah said: 25.10

May God not remove those who envy me, and instead increase them
that they may die for all to see.
I have seen them in every dwelling.
I value them more than those who love me.

And Naṣr ibn Sayyār said: 25.11

When I was growing up, enviers were numerous.
Night journeyer, do not decrease their number!
They envy me for what I have and they do not.
By my life, the place I've reached courts envy!

Maʿn ibn Zāʾidah said: 25.12

I was envied and God increased it.
Whoever lives a day unenvied has not lived!
A person is only envied for his achievements
in knowledge, elegance, courage, and excellence.

Abū Nuwās said: 25.13

Let me, who envies you most, travel
to the land al-Khaṣīb rules.[191]

The first to address this said:[192] 25.14

If he exceeded the sun in generosity,
they would do the same, according to their station and glory.
They envy the nobility he enjoyed—
may God not decrease how much they envy him.

Abū Tammām said: 25.15

If God wished to unveil a once-secret virtue,
He would put it on the tongue of an envier.
If not for fire's irradiant brightness,
the sweetness of aloe wood would remain unknown.

١٦،٢٥ واعلم أنّ هذا الشعر ونحوه يخيّل استحسان الحاسد واستحباب وجوده بل كثرته. ولم يزل الناس يكرهونه ويتخوّفون منه ويستعيذون من شرّه. وقال تعالى ﴿وَمِن شَرِّ حَاسِدٍ إِذَا حَسَدَ﴾ فقد يقف القاصر على هذا فيحار ولا يدري ما يختار. وفصل القضيّة في ذلك أنّ وجود الحاسد كما مرّ دليل على وجود الفضل. وذلك لما عرف أنّ الحسد هو حبّ زوال ما ظهر على الغير من خير إمّا دينيّ أو دنيويّ حسيّ أو معنويّ عاجل أو آجل حقيّ أو ادّعائيّ. فلزم من وجود الحسد وجود الخير.

١٧،٢٥ ثمّ إنّ الحاسد إذا أحبّ زوال الخير فهو لا محالة يسعى في زواله أو في إلحاق مضرّة تذهب بها طلاوة ذلك الخير ما لم يحجزه حاجز. وهذه مضرّة تتوقّع من الحاسد فالحاسد خبيث شرّير مضرّ. إذا علم هذا فمن استحبّ وجود الحاسد فلم يحبّه لذاته بل أحبّ ما يقارنه من الخير لا من حيث إنّه محسود عليه به من حيث كونه خيراً. وإلّا فيودّ الإنسان أن لو أعطي الخير وأعفي من الحسّاد فإنّ ذلك أهنأ لعيشه وأروح لقلبه وأبعد له عن الأذاية والهول.

١٨،٢٥ ولم تجرِ حكمة الله تعالى غالباً بذلك إذ نعم الدنيا مشوبة بالنقم وصفوها مشوب بكدر. فأمام كلّ عين قذى وعلى كل خير أذى. فلمّا لم يكن بدّ من وجود الحاسد غالباً كان وجوده مبشّراً بالخير معلّماً بالنعمة فيفرح بوجوده لذلك لا لذاته. ومثاله في ذلك الذباب الواقع على الطعام والفأر الناقب على المخزن فإنّهما دليلان على الخير من حيث ذلك حتّى إنّه يكنّى عن البيت الخالي عن الخير بأنّه لا تطور فيه فارة فمن أحبّ وجود الذباب ووجود الفار فلم يحبّهما لذاتهما فإنّهما مؤذيان مكروهان بل لما يقارنهما من الخير. ولو وجد الإنسان الخير مع السلامة عنهما كان هو الغنم البارد[1] ولم تجر بذلك الحكمة.

١٩،٢٥ وبلغني أنّ ناساً من الجند قدموا من بلاد السودان أيّام السلطان أحمد المنصور وقاسوا في تلك الفيافي ما هو المعهود فيها من العناء وشظف العيش. فلمّا لحقوا

١ يكرر م كلمة بارد مرتين.

Such poetry is intended to make one think well of enviers, and to seek their presence, one or a great number of them. Yet, people continue to dislike them, to be afraid of them, and to seek refuge from their evil—the Exalted said: «And from the evil of an envier when he envies».[193] A person of limited understanding might encounter this verse and be confused, and not know what to choose. The final judgment in this matter is that the presence of the envier, as related, indicates the presence of virtue. This is because envy is the desire for the good in another to cease, whether spiritual or worldly, tangible or intangible, sooner or later, manifest or hidden. The presence of envy necessitates the presence of good. 25.16

When an envious person desires to put an end to goodness, he will necessarily try to bring this about, or, insofar as he is not impeded from doing so, to do something to bring an end to its beauty. This is the harm that is to be expected from an envious person, for an envious person is malicious, evil, and hurtful. When one knows this, then whoever desires the presence of an envious person does not love him for himself. Instead, he loves the good associated with him, which has nothing to do with the envied person being envied per se, but is because of his good nature. A person might desire to receive goodness while being protected from having enviers; this means a more pleasant life, a more peaceful heart, and greater distance from harm and fright. 25.17

The wisdom of Exalted God generally does not manifest in this manner, for the blessings of this world are mixed with trials, and its purity is mixed with turbidity. There is a speck in every eye, and harm in every good. So, while there is no avoiding the presence of the envious, his presence generally promises goodness and is a sign of blessing. For this reason, one should rejoice at his presence, though not because of the person himself. A metaphor for this is the vermin that appear in food, and the rats that steal from storerooms. The vermin and the rats are indicators of the good inhering in the food, to the point that it is said of a house entirely empty of good that no rat will approach it. Whoever welcomes the presence of vermin and rats does not do so out of love for them—they are harmful and hateful—but because he associates them with the presence of good things. If mankind were indeed able to locate good and be preserved from vermin and rats, that would be a rare thing indeed, but this is not how God's wisdom works. 25.18

I was told that members of the army approached from West Africa during 25.19
the time Aḥmad al-Manṣūr was ruler and that in the trackless desert they

بقرية من قرى السوس الأقصى خرج منها نفر من اليهود. فحين بصر بهم الجنديّ قال مرحباً بوجوه الخير. فاليهود بغضاء عند كلّ مسلم ومع ذلك استبشر بهم الجنديّ التفاتاً منه إلى النعمة التي تقارنهم إذ لا يزايلون غالباً الحاضرة ومحلّ الخصب والرفاهية.

٢٠،٢٥ وهكذا الحاسد. وقد يكون في وجود الحاسد نعمة ولذّة أخرى للمحسود إذا وقي شرّه. فإنّه ينعم هو والحاسد يحترق على عينيه وهو يزداد ظهوراً وشفوفاً فيلتذّ باحتراقه وإقصاره عنه وشفوفه عليه. ومن كره الحاسد فإنّما كرهه لِذاته إذ هو مُنغِّص بما يبدو من أقواله وأفعاله ولما يُتوقَّع من شرّه وضرره. ولا شكّ أنّه محذور ولذا أمر بالتعوّذ منه بالله تعالى ولا دواء له إلّا هي مع الصبر أعلى ما يرى ويسمع. وبذلك ينعكس على الحاسد البلاء فيموت غمّاً.

٢١،٢٥ قال تعالى ﴿قُلۡ مُوتُوا۟ بِغَيۡظِكُمۡ﴾ وقال الشاعر: [مجزوء الكامل]

اِصْبِرْ عَلَى مَضَضِ ٱلْحَسُو　　دِ فَإِنَّ صَبْرَكَ قَاتِلُهُ
فَٱلنَّارُ تَأْكُلُ نَفْسَهَا　　إِنْ لَمْ تَجِدْ مَا تَأْكُلُهُ[١]

٢٢،٢٥ فائدة من ابتلي بالحسد لشخص فعلاجه بإذن الله أن يكلّف نفسه السعي في زيادة الخير على المحسود ولو بالدعاء له بذلك. فإنّه إذ لازم ذلك ولو تكلّفا سيثيبه الله تعالى من فضله انسلال السخيمة من قبله وسلامة الصدر. فإن بقي شيء فليغمّه في صدره مع كراهته ولا يظهره ولا يسع في مقتضاه بقول ولا فعل فذلك غاية ما يطلب منه والله الموفّق. لله الأمر من قبل ومن بعد.

١،٢٦ كنت في أعوام السبعين وألف قصدت إلى زيارة شيخنا البركة وقدوتنا في السكون والحركة أبي عبد الله محمّد بن ناصر سقى الله ثراه. فمررت ببلد سجلماسة فوجدت فتنة ثارت

١ يزيد ق: وكتبت من خطه اكرمه الله و رأيت إلحاقها هنا: إذا ما شئت إرغام الأعادي/بلا سيف يسل ولا سنان//فزد من مكرماتاك فهي أعدى/على الأعداء من نوب الزمان.

endured the toil and hardship for which it is well-known.[194] When they reached a village in the farthest Sūs, some of the Jews there came forward.[195] When the soldier saw them, he said, "Hello! What a sight for sore eyes!" Now, Jews are hateful to every Muslim, and despite this the soldier rejoiced in them. In doing so he took into consideration the blessing that he associated with them, since they generally reside in areas that are settled, fertile, and comfortable.

It is the same with the envious person. The presence of the envious person may be another blessing and sweetness for the envied if he guards against his evil. While the envied person is blessed, the envious burns in front of him and the envied can take pleasure in his burning and wasting away. Whoever hates the envious hates him for himself, being troubled by his words and deeds, and the associated evil and harm. There is no doubt that one needs to be wary of him and this is why we are commanded to take refuge from him with Exalted God. There is no remedy for him, other than the greatest forbearance ever seen or heard. Through this, the calamity is turned back upon the one who is envious and he dies of grief. **25.20**

The Exalted said: «Say: Die in your rage.»[196] And a poet said:[197] **25.21**

Forbearance when afflicted by the envious!
Your forbearance resists him.
The fire consumes itself
when it finds nothing to consume.

The moral: Whosoever is afflicted with envy for a person, his response—by God's leave—should be to try to increase the good of the one he envies, even if only by praying for him. If he does this constantly, even if reluctantly, Exalted God will reward him through His virtue by withdrawing the hatred from his heart and purifying his breast. If anything remains, let him conceal it along with his hatred, and never display it, nor pursue this desire in word or deed. This is the full extent of what is asked of him. God grant success! Everything is God's to command. **25.22**

In the 1070s [1660s] I decided to visit our Blessed Shaykh, our Guide in times of calm and times of trouble, Abū ʿAbd Allāh Maḥammad ibn Nāṣir, may God reward him. I passed through the town of Sijilmāsah, where conflict had broken out between the students regarding the meaning of the expression "There is no **26.1**

بين الطلبة فيها في معنى كلمة الإخلاص. فكان بعض الطلبة قرّر فيها ما وقع في كلام الشيخ السنوسي من أنّ المنفي هو المَثَل المُقدَّر. فأنكر عليه بعض من لهم الرياسة في النوازل الفقهيّة وفصل الأحكام الشرعيّة وليس لهم نفاذ في العلوم النظريّة. وأخذوا بنحو ما أخذوا به الشيخ الهبطيّ في مشاجرته المشهورة مع أهل عصره حتّى امتحنوه بالسياط. فجعلت أقرّر لأولئك المنكرين الكلمة بوجه يقرّب بين المأخذين ويصلح بين الخصمين. فلم يفهموا ذلك وصمّموا على ما طرق أسماعهم من أن الهبطيّ أخطأ في هذه المسألة وضلّ ضلالاً مبيناً. ثمّ وقعت هذه الفتنة أيضاً[1] بمدينة مراكش عن قريب من هذه بين طلبتها حتّى ضلّل بعضهم بعضاً. فمن أجل ذلك ألّفت كتاب مناهج الخلاص من كلمة الإخلاص كما نبّهت على ذلك في خطبته فجاء بحمد الله كافياً في الغرض شافياً للمرض.

٢،٢٦ ثمّ رجعت في زورة أخرى بعد هذه فمررت أيضاً بسجلماسة فوجدت فتنة أبشع من هذه وأشنع وقعت لهؤلاء مع عوامّ المسلمين ثمّ مع المسلمين كافّة عامّة وخاصّة. وذلك أنّهم نظروا في كلام من حرّض من الأئمّة على النظر في علم التوحيد وحذّر من الجهل فيه ومن التقليد. فجعلوا يسألون الناس عمّا يعتقدون ويكلّفونهم الجواب والإبانة عن الصواب فربّما عثروا على قاصر العبارة عمّا في قلبه أو متلجلج اللسان لدهش ناله أو جاهل بشيء ممّا يقدح في العقيدة أو يظنّونه قادحاً. وإن لم يقدح فيشنّعون عليه الجهل والكفر ثمّ أشاعوا أنّ الفساد قد ظهر في عقائد الناس وجعلوا يقرّرون العقائد للعوامّ.

٣،٢٦ فشاع عند الناس أن من لم يشتغل بالتوحيد على النمط الذي يقرّرون فهو كافر. وشاع عندهم أن من لم يعرف معنى لا إله إلّا الله أي النفي والإثبات على التقرير الذي يقرّره العلماء فهو كافر فدخل من ذلك على عوامّ المسلمين أمر عظيم وهول كبير. فلمّا دخلت البلد جاءني الناس أفواجاً يشتكون من هذا الأمر وأن ليس كلّ أحد يبلغ إلى فهم تقارير العلماء. فأقول لهم إنّ الله تعالى إنّما تعبّدكم باعتقاد الحقّ في

---

١ سقط من ق.

god but God." One student was relying on what the shaykh al-Sanūsī had said—namely, that what was denied was an implicit equal. This view was rejected by several who were knowledgeable in jurisprudence, but who were not competent in the discursive sciences. They tackled the matter in the same way others had dealt with the shaykh al-Habṭī in his famous argument with his contemporaries, to the point that they had had him whipped.[198] I began to explain the expression to the deniers, in a way that might bring the participants closer, and bring peace between the opposing parties. They did not understand, and decided, based on what they heard, that al-Habṭī had made a mistake in this matter and clearly erred. Soon after, this argument also broke out among the students in Marrakesh, to the point that they led each other astray. For this reason, I wrote a book, *Methods of Deliverance Regarding Declaring One's Faith in the Unity of God*, and drew attention to this question in the introduction.[199] It was, God be thanked, equal to its task and healed the sickness.

I returned for another visit after this, and again passed through Sijilmāsah. 26.2
I discovered that a more bitter, nastier discord had erupted between this same group and the common folk, and then the whole Muslim community, the common folk and elites alike. They looked into what the religious leaders who had encouraged scrutiny of the belief in God's oneness said, into their warnings of ignorance of its proper understanding and of blindly following received opinion. These leaders began to ask people what they believed, requiring proper answers, stating clearly what was correct. Now it would happen that they stumbled upon someone who could not express himself well regarding what was in his heart, or who stammered out of anxiety, or someone ignorant of an aspect of the creed or of some other aspect they deemed significant. When that person did not state it properly, they denounced his ignorance and unbelief. They spread the view that people's knowledge of creedal matters had been corrupted and began lecturing the masses on these issues.

Soon after, the belief spread among people that whoever did not profess 26.3
God's oneness in the way the leaders explained was an unbeliever. The view also spread that whoever did not know the meaning of "There is no god but God"—that is, the meaning of denial and affirmation in the way the scholars professed it—was an unbeliever. Among the Muslim commoners a massive commotion and great fear occurred. When I came to town, people came to me in large numbers, complaining of this, saying not everyone could grasp the scholars' pronouncements. "God is Exalted," I told them. "You worship

أنفسكم أفلا تشهدون أنّ الله تعالى حقّ موجود؟ فيقولون بلى. أفلا تعلمون أنّه واحد في ملكه لا شريك له ولا إله معه وكلّ معبود سواه باطل. فيقولون بلى هذا كلّه يقين عندنا لا نشكّ فيه ولا نرتاب. فأقول لهم هذا هو معنى كلمة الإخلاص المطلوب منكم اعتقاده سواء عرفتموه من لفظها أو لا فإنّ الكلمة عربيّة والأعجميّ لا حظّ له في دلالتها وإنّما حسبه أن يترجم له مضمونها فيعتقده. وكذا العقائد كلّها المطلوب منكم اعتقادها بالمعنى ولا يشترط فهم ألفاظها التي يعبّر بها عنها في كتب العلماء ولا إدراك حدودها ورسومها التي تعرف بها. فإنّ فهم هذه العبارات والإحاطة بهذه الحقائق والتقريرات علم آخر لم يكلّف به العوامّ. فإذا أجبتهم بذلك انطلقوا مسرورين حامدين شاكرين.

٤،٢٦ ثمّ جاءني رئيس هذه الفتنة وسألني عن مسائل في هذا المنحى فأجبته ثمّ تقدّمت إليه بالنصيحة. وقلت له أكثر النحل وجلّ الطوائف الضالّة إنّما خرجت في هذا العلم. فإن أردت نفع الناس فقرّر لهم العقائد بالقدر الذي يبلغون وحدّث الناس بما يفهمون كما في الحديث الكريم. ودع عنك هذه الامتحانات والتدقيقات والتشنيعات التي لم تجرِ بها سنّة أهل الدين في عصر من الأعصار. فإذا هو قد أشرب ذلك وتمكّن فيه التظاهر به وإذا تمييزه قد نقص عمّا كنت أعرف منه قبل ذلك. نسأل الله العافية.

٥،٢٦ فتمادى على ذلك وأصفقت عليه العوامّ حتّى سمعوا مقالته فيهم. وجعل يتغالى في تقرير العقائد وبيان وجوه المخالفة ونحوها على التفصيل بما لا حاجة إليه حتّى يقع في ذكر ما هو سوء الأدب في حقّه تعالى وما لا يستطيع كلّ من في قلبه رائحة من عظمة الله تعالى أن يفوه به.

٦،٢٦ ويحضر مجلسه أوباش الأعراب من جراوة ونحوها. فإذا رجعوا إلى قومهم ذهبوا بتلك المقالات وجعلوا يلقون على أمثالهم من الرعاع الأسئلة من هذا

with the proper faith within yourselves. Don't you bear witness to the truth and existence of Exalted God?" "Yes," they said, "we do." "And don't you know that He is one in His dominion, that He has no partner, that no other god exists alongside Him, and that anything worshipped beside Him is false?" "Yes," they said, "we do. We are certain about all of this and do not doubt it." So, I said to them, "This is what you are required to believe regarding the meaning of declaring one's belief in the unity of God, whether you know it from this phrase or not. For the words are in Arabic, and an Amazigh need not understand it; he should have it translated for him so that he can profess it. It is the same with all creedal matters one must profess, according to their significance. It is not stipulated that one understand the phrases as expressed in the books of scholars, nor that one grasp the definitions and designations by which they are known. Understanding these terms and having a full understanding of the facts and the pronouncements belongs to another domain altogether, something commoners are not obligated to know." When I answered them in this fashion, they left happy, grateful, and appreciative.

Then the leader in this conflict came to ask me about aspects of this dispute and I responded.[200] I offered him advice as follows: "Most of the heretical sects and the majority of the errant groups have transgressed in this matter. If you wish to benefit people, present creedal matters to them at a level they can access and speak to them in a way they can understand, as the noble hadith says.[201] Stop these interrogations, investigations, and condemnations, which have never been the behavior of the pious in any time." Now, either he was dominated by his opinion and remained steadfastly determined, or his powers of discernment had diminished from what I remember of him. God preserve us from such things. 26.4

He persevered, so I brought the common folk to him so they could hear what he said about them. He became excessive in his discussion of creedal issues and in his explanation of the many ways one can err and such, launching into an unnecessary degree of detail. He persisted and ended up displaying poor manners when discussing the Truth Divine, and got to the point that he uttered things that no one with even a whiff of Exalted God in his heart ever would. 26.5

Common Jarāwah Bedouin and others like them were present. When they returned to their people they carried his pronouncements with them and began to ask the same questions of other riffraff like themselves, saying, "Where does God spend the night? Where does God wake up? Where does He stay? 26.6

المنحى. فيقولون لهم أين بات الله؟ وأين يُصبح؟ وأين يظلّ؟ وأين هو؟ وكيف هو؟ إلى ما هو أبشع من ذلك ممّا لا أذكره. وقد نبّهت على طرف من هذا المعنى في كتابي المذكور. ثمّ أشاعوا أنّ عوامّ المسلمين لا تؤكل ذبائحهم ولا يناكحون مخافة أن يكونوا لم يعرفوا التوحيد.

٧،٢٦ فحدّثني الفقيه المشارك الصالح أبو عبد الله مبارك بن محمّد العنبريّ الغرفيّ رحمه الله أن أعرابياً من هؤلاء الشيعة جاء مع قوم من بلد توات. فكانوا إذا طبخوا زادهم وفيه الخليع يمتنع من الأكل معهم ويقول إنّ الجزّار الذي ذبح هذه البهيمة لا ندري أيعرف التوحيد أم لا. ولمّا دخل البلد جيء بطعام عليه لحم وجماعة من الأشراف حضور فدعوه للأكل فأمتنع وقال إنّ العبد الذي ذبح تلك الذبيحة لا ندري أيعرف التوحيد أو لا. فقالوا له ما ذبحها عبد وإنّما ذبحها المولى فلان الشريف منهم. فامتنع أيضاً وبات طاوياً.

٨،٢٦ ثمّ لم يقفوا في هذا بل لمّا انتهكوا حرمة عوامّ المسلمين ابتلاهم الله بانتهاك حرمة خاصّتهم أيضاً. فتناولوا فقهاء وقتهم ووقعوا في أهل العلم والدين ومن هم على سنن المهتدين وضلّلوهم إذا لم يضلّلوا العامّة. فوقع لهم قريب ممّا وقع للكميليّة من الروافض فإنّهم كفّروا الصحابة حيث لم يقدّموا عليّاً كرّم الله وجهه ثمّ كفّروا عليّاً حيث لم ينازعهم في حقّه.

٩،٢٦ وكان أهل البلد أتبعوني وأنا في الطريق سؤالاً فيما هو من حكم الذبائح ونحوها في بطاقة. فأجبتهم بما علم من دين الإسلام أنّ كلّ من تشهّد شهادة الحقّ فإنّه تؤكل ذبيحته وتحلّ مناكحته ويدفن في مقابر المسلمين ما لم يظهر منه ما يخالف ظاهره ونحو هذا الكلام. فلمّا بلغ إلى أولئك قالوا سبحان الله! كنّا نعرف فلاناً من العلماء ثمّ هو يقتصر على مثل هذا الكلام ويكتفي به. فلم يقع كلامي منهم موقعاً حيث اقتصرت على الحاجة وما هو الحقّ ولم أتعدّ إلى ما يشتغلون به من الفضول والضلال.

Where is He? What is His state?" They continued with such questions and even more offensive ones that I won't mention. I have already drawn attention to some of this matter in my abovementioned book. They then spread the view that one cannot marry Muslim commoners, or eat what Muslim commoners have slaughtered, out of fear that they do not know the nature of God's oneness.

The erudite and devout jurist Abū ʿAbd Allāh Mubārak ibn Muḥammad al-ʿAnbarī al-Ghurfī, God have mercy on him, recounted to me that a Bedouin of this party arrived with a group of people from Tuwāt. When they cooked their supplies while this profligate was present, he would refrain from eating with them, saying, "The butcher who slaughtered this beast—do we know if he grasped monotheism or not?" When he entered the town, food was prepared that contained meat. A group of the Prophet's descendants who were present invited him to eat with them. He refused, saying, "We don't know if the slave who slaughtered this animal has grasped monotheism or not." They said to him, "It was not a slave who slaughtered it." In fact, it was a prominent descendant of the Prophet, one of their group. He refused again and went hungry. 26.7

They persisted in this way, and when they failed to respect the Muslim masses, God afflicted them by causing them to disrespect the elites too. In this way, they took on the jurists of their time and slandered the people of knowledge and religion, and those who followed the habits of the rightly guided. When they did not lead the elites astray, they did so with the masses. What happened to them is similar to what happened to the heretical Kamīliyyah, who declared to be unbelievers the Prophet's Companions who did not advance the cause of ʿAlī—God honor his countenance—and then declared ʿAlī to be an unbeliever because he did not fight for his due.[202] 26.8

While I was traveling, the townspeople sent me a letter, asking about the ruling concerning slaughtered animals and similar matters. I answered them according to attested Islamic practice—that for anyone who testifies to the Truth, what he slaughters can be eaten, that it is licit to marry him, and that he should be buried in Muslim graveyards, all as long as he does nothing at odds with his outward belief—adding other things to this effect. When my letter reached them, they said, "Good God! We considered this fellow a scholar; then he goes and says only this, thinking it suffices." For them, my words had missed the mark, as I had limited myself to the matter at hand, and to the truth, without addressing the superfluous and false matters they busied themselves with. 26.9

١٠،٢٦ وكانوا قبل هذه الفتنة تلمذوا لشيخنا الإمام ابن ناصر رضي الله عنه وأخذوا عهده. فلمّا لم يشتغل بما اشتغلوا به أنكروا عليه حتّى وقعوا فيما يؤتى به إليه من الهدايا والصدقات وفيما يذكره للفقراء من كلام الإمام الثعالبي. فإنّه كان يحكي بسنده إلى الثعالبي أنّه قال من رأى من رآني إلى سبعة ضمنت له الجنّة بشرط أن يقول كلّ لمن رأى أشهد أنّي رأيتك فيشهد له. فكان الشيخ رضي الله عنه يذكر ذلك على طريق الترجية ولئلاّ يفوت المسلمين ذلك الخير إن حقّقه الله تعالى. فقالوا هذا يوقع الناس في الأمن وفي الإعراض عن تعلّم التوحيد مع أنه لا وثوق به فإنّ أمور المنامات لا تنضبط ولا يعوّل عليها. ثم برئوا من صحبته وكتبوا في ذلك كرّاسة.

١١،٢٦ فقيّض الله لها الشاب اللبيب الفاضل أبا العبّاس أحمد بن محمّد بن السيّد الشريف الحسنيّ رحمه الله ورحم سلفه. فتكلّم عليها بما نقض أباطيلها عروة عروة. فلمّا انتهى إلى براءتهم من الشيخ كتب عليها ما معناه إنّ هذه السلسلة المباركة الفاضلة يعني سلسلة الشيخ رضي الله عنه هي أمنع جناباً وأطهر ساحة من أن يبقى فيها أمثالكم فطهّرها الله منكم. وقد اشتعلت فتنتهم حتّى كادت تخرج إلى الآفاق كلّها ثمّ أطفأها الله تعالى بفضله. فجاء الطاعون عام تسعين وألف فأجتثّ شجرتهم من فوق الأرض فلم يبق لها قرار.

١،٢٧ فـائدة. أمّا السلسلة التي أشرنا إليها عن الإمام الثعالبي فإنّ شيخنا الإمام ابن ناصر رضي الله عنه يحدّث بها عن شيخه الفقيه الصالح سيدي عليّ ابن يوسف الدرعيّ عن شيخه سيدي عبد الرحمن بن محمّد من بني مهرة عن سيدي محمّد بن محمّد بن ناصر من أهل الرقبة عن سيدي عبد الكبير وهو جدّ سيدي عبد الرحمن

Before this conflict, they had studied with our shaykh Ibn Nāṣir, God be content with him, and had pledged loyalty to him. When he did not adopt the views they adopted, they criticized him to the point that they took issue with what he was given as gifts and alms, and criticized him for recounting the words of the exemplar al-Thaʿālibī to his followers. He used to relate, based on a chain of authorities going all the way to al-Thaʿālibī, that the latter said, "Whoever sees someone in a dream who has seen me in a dream—to the seventh degree—heaven is promised to him, on the condition that everyone who saw me says in front of witnesses, 'I testify that I saw you.'" Now, the shaykh, God be pleased with him, recounted this out of hopefulness, and so that this good would not be lost to the Muslim community—assuming that Exalted God had established it. They responded, saying, "This just makes people feel secure and makes them resist learning about monotheism, when there is no proof that it is true, since the stuff of dreams cannot truly be determined or relied on." So they ended their companionship with him, and wrote a pamphlet on the matter. 26.10

Now, God ordained that the insightful young man, Abū ʿAbbās Aḥmad ibn Muḥammad ibn al-Sayyid al-Sharīf al-Ḥasanī—God have mercy on him and his ancestors—spoke against this pamphlet and criticized its falsehoods point by point. When he came to their dissociating themselves from the shaykh, he wrote words to the effect of "This blessed, noble chain"—that is, the shaykh's chain of teachers and students, God be content with him—"is both too well established and too pure for the likes of you to remain in it. God has purged you from it." Their dissension flared to the point that it nearly extended to the whole world, but Exalted God extinguished it through His grace. The plague came in 1090 [1679] and tore the trunk of their community from the earth, leaving it without a solid base. 26.11

A beneficial anecdote: According to our shaykh Ibn Nāṣir, God be content with him, the chain of transmitters to the exemplar al-Thaʿālibī, referred to above, went through Ibn Nāṣir's teacher, the devout jurist Sīdī ʿAlī ibn Yūsuf al-Darʿī, through his shaykh Sīdī ʿAbd al-Raḥmān ibn Muḥammad of the Banū Mahra, through Sīdī Muḥammad ibn Muḥammad ibn Nāṣir of the Ruqaybah, through Sīdī ʿAbd al-Kabīr, who was the ancestor of the abovementioned Sīdī ʿAbd al-Raḥmān, through the Great Axis, ʿAbd al-Raḥmān al-Thaʿālibī, God be 27.1

المذكور عن القطب الكبير سيدي عبد الرحمن الثعالبي أنّه قال رضي الله عنه من رآني إلى سبعة ضمنت له الجنة. وفي سلسلة كلّ واحد يقول لصاحبه أشهد أنّي رأيتك و قد رأيت والحمد لله الإمام ابن ناصر وأشهدته على ذلك. حقّقه الله لنا وللإخوان آمين. واعلم أنّ مثل هذا يذكر على طريق الرجاء كما أشرنا إليه. وهو أمر جائز لا يمنعه عقل ولا شرع وذلك أنّ فضل الله عظيم لا يحدّ بمقياس وأولياء الله تعالى أبواب يخرج منها هذا الفضل ولهم مكانة عند ربّهم الكريم المتفضّل. فأيّ شيء يستبعد في أن يعطي[1] بعضهم الشفاعة في قرنه أو أكثر أو أنّ من مسّه لم تمسّه النار كما في قصّة ابن حسّون أو أنّ من رآه دخل الجنة أو أنّ من رأى من رآه إلى سبعة أو أكثر. هذا كلّه قريب.

وقد أخبر النبيّ صلّى الله عليه وسلّم في خبره عن أويس القرنيّ رضي الله عنه أنّه يشفع في مثل أو عدد ربيعة ومضر. وحدّثني الثقة أنّ نفرًا من أصحاب ابن مبارك التستاوتي دخلوا على سيدي محمّد الشرقيّ فقال لهم أيّها الفقراء ما الذي قال ابن مبارك؟ فقالوا له قد قال أهل زماني محسوبون عليّ أو في ذمتي أو نحو ذلك. فقال سيدي محمّد الشرقيّ اشهدوا علينا إنّا من أهل زمان ابن مبارك. فانظر إلى هذا الإنصاف وهذا التسليم. فكذا يجب التسليم لمن وقع منه شيء من هذا من أهل الصلاح والدين. ويظنّ به الخير ويحصل الرجاء. ولا يوجب ذلك أمنًا من مكر الله والاستغناء عمّا يجب تعلّمه أو العمل به. بل التكليف باق بحاله والخوف والرجاء بحالهما. وقد شاع عند هذه الطائفة الغازيّة أنّ الشيخ قد أخذ من الله تعالى عهدًا أن لا يسوق إليه إلّا المقبول. ولم يوجب لهم ذلك أمانًا ولا غرورًا إلّا أن يشذّ جاهل فلا التفات إليه. وأمّا الهديّة من الأخ في الله فهي مباحة في الجملة بل هي محسوبة في الفقه من وجوه الحلال فإن عرض عارض في المعطى أو في وجه الإعطاء فالآخذ أعرف بما يأتي وما يذر. ثمّ أحوال الصوفيّة في قبول الفتوح مختلفة تبعًا ٢،٢٧

[1] ط: يمنع.

content with him, to wit: "Who sees someone in a dream who has seen me in a dream—to the seventh degree—heaven is promised to him." Everyone in this chain said to his companion, I bear witness that I saw you in a dream. As for me, God be thanked, I saw Ibn Nāṣir in a dream, and bore witness to him regarding this. God has established this for us, and for others—amen! These things are mentioned with hope of good fortune, as we have already indicated. Doing so is permissible, forbidden neither by reason nor revelation. This is because God's grace is limitless and the friends of Exalted God are the doors through which this grace passes. They have a standing with their generous and gracious Lord, and it is not farfetched to think that one of them has been granted intercession for a companion or for others, or that whoever touches one of them will not be touched by fire, as in the story of Ibn Ḥassūn, or that someone who saw someone in a dream, or that one who saw one in a dream who had seen him—to the seventh degree—would enter heaven. All this is easily possible.

The Prophet, God bless him and keep him, in his account of Uways al-Qaranī, God be content with him, said that he would intercede for some members of the Rabīʿah and Muḍar tribes. Now, a reliable source has told me that a group of the companions of Ibn Mubārak al-Tastāwatī came to Sīdī Muḥammad al-Sharqī, who said to them, "Devotees, what did Ibn Mubārak say?" "He said, 'The people of my time are accountable to me,' or 'They are under my protection,'" they answered, or words to that effect. Sīdī Muḥammad al-Sharqī responded, "Bear witness that we are of the people of Ibn Mubārak's time!" Consider this kind of just behavior and submission! In this fashion one should submit to the people of virtue and religion who experience something of this sort. One should think well of him and be hopeful. Doing so does not protect one from God's plan, nor does it mean that one can neglect what one is required to know or do.[203] What is obligatory remains obligatory, and the role played by fear and hope remain unchanged. It was common knowledge among this rebellious faction that the shaykh had received from Exalted God a promise that only good would be granted him. He did not enforce this closeness to God on them to dispel fear or deceive them, but when an ignorant person goes astray one should not pay attention to him. As for the gift from a brother in God, it is quite permitted—indeed, in jurisprudence it is condoned and legally permissible. If there is something wrong with what is given or with an aspect of the giving, the one who receives it knows best what he should take or leave. Nonetheless, the spiritual states of the Sufis regarding their ability to receive 27.2

لما اقتضته الواردات والتحفّظ عن الآفات. وهي في كلّ من الأخذ والترك كما قال الأستاذ السريّ للإمام أحمد بن حنبل رضي الله عنهما احذر آفة الردّ كما تحذر آفة الأخذ. وكلّ من عرف بصحّة العلم والعمل ومتانة الديانة كشيخنا المذكور فأمره موكول إلى دينه ولا سبيل إلى الانتقاد عليه والله الموفّق. لله الأمر من قبل ومن بعد.

١،٢٨ كنت ذات مرة اشتريت رمكة من رجل صحراويّ أسود شديد السواد. فظهر فيها عيب وتعذّر إثبات قدمه لتُردّ. فأدّى الأمر إلى موتها منه وتلف الثمن. فأقبل رجل من قومي والمشترى منه[1] عندي ونحن نتكلّم في المسألة. فلمّا بصر بالمشترى منه[2] قال سبحان الله! كنت أعجب من أين جاء هذا الخسران فإذا أنت تعامل الغِرْبان. ألم تعلم أنّا لا نعامل مثل هذا حتّى إنّا لا نزجر الكلب الأسود عنّا إذا مرّ بنا لئلّا يقع خطاب منّا أليه. فكيف بغيره؟ وجعل يتأسّف من خسران الثمن ومن معاملة ذلك الشخص. وجعلت أنا أضحك من عظمة الدنيا في عينيه ومن تحكيمه الأمور العادية.

٢،٢٨ وكان قومنا كما قال يفرون من السواد فلا يلبسون ثوبًا أسود ولا يركبون فرسًا أدهم وهكذا. واعلم أنّ هذه الأمور العاديّة يضلّ فيها العامّة والقاصرون من الخاصّة. أمّا العامّة فإنّهم إذا رأوا شيئًا عند شيء نسبوه إلى ذلك الشي وغفلوا عن الله تعالى ولم يعلموا أنّ الله تعالى هو الفاعل وحده ولا تأثير لشيء من الكائنات بحال. فوقعوا في الشرك وفاتهم التوحيد. وأمّا القاصرون من الخاصّة المعتقدين لانفراد المولى تعالى بالفعل وأنّ لا شريك له فإنّهم يجرون على هذا المعنى وينكرون حكمة الله تعالى في أرضه وسمائه. فإذا قيل لهم إنّ هذا الشيء يكون عند وجود هذا السبب قالوا هذا لا معوّل عليه فإنّ السبب لا تأثير له ووجوده وعدمه سواء. وهذا أيضًا جهل عظيم

١ ق: البائع وط: المشتري. ٢ ق: بالبائع وط: المشتري.

spiritual insights differ according to circumstances and to the precautions taken against evil. These states apply both to accepting and refusing gifts. As the teacher al-Sarī said to the exemplar Aḥmad ibn Ḥanbal, God be content with them both, "Beware the evil of rejecting gifts, just as you are wary of the evil of accepting them." The affairs of those such as our aforementioned teacher, who are renowned for the soundness of their knowledge and action and the strength of their religious conviction, are attested to by their faith, and there is no way to criticize them. Success comes from God. Everything is God's to command.

I once bought a mare from an exceedingly black man from the desert. I then 28.1
found a defect in her and it was impossible to establish how long it had been there such that she could be returned. She eventually died of it, and I lost what she was worth. One of my people came when the seller and I were talking over the matter. When he saw the seller, he said, "Good God! I was wondering how this loss came about—here you are dealing with a crow! Don't you know that we don't get involved with his kind, just as we drive away a black dog if he passes by so that he doesn't overhear our speech? How then do you think we deal with other things that are black?" He began to lament the financial loss and his dealings with this person. I began to laugh at the importance of this world in his eyes and at his assessment of things that happen.

Our people, as he said, would avoid the color black. They would not wear 28.2
black clothes, or ride black horses, or the like. When it comes to ordinary events, both the common folk as well as those among the elect of limited understanding are lost. When common folk see something taking place while something else is happening, they attribute one to the other, ignoring Exalted God. They do not see that Exalted God alone is the active Agent, and nothing created has any causal effect in itself. They fall into polytheism and stop believing in the oneness of God. The elect who are limited in understanding believe that the Lord alone is involved in each act, and that He has no partner. They proceed in this fashion and deny the wisdom of God on His earth and in His heaven. If you say to them that a given thing is a cause for the presence of another, they say that it has not been determined to be the case, that the cause has no effect, and that it is the same if it is present or not. This position is also one of great ignorance, for while God is powerful, willing, and peerless, He is also wise and makes things happen in association with other things.

فإنّ الله تعالى كما أنّه قادر مريد لا شريك له كذلك هو حكيم يفعل أشياء عند أشياء ويرتّب أسباباً ومسبّبات حكمةً منه تعالى ورفقاً بعباده في تأنيس نفوسهم بالأسباب المشهودة.

٣،٢٨ فإنّ الإيمان بالغيب وانتظاره عسير عليها وابتلاء لهم ليتميّز من انخرقت له الحجب فأبصر الحقّ ومن حجب بها فتاه في أودية الضلال. نسأل الله تعالى العافية. ألا ترى إلى ما جعل تعالى لعامة الخلق من الشبع عند الأكل والريّ عند الشرب والتدفّي عند اللبس والراحة عند الركوب واللذة المخصوصة عند الوقاع وهكذا ممّا لا يحصى. وكلّ ذلك يجوز من الله تعالى أن يخلقه بلا شيء.

٤،٢٨ فهل ينكر أحد من العقلاء هذه الحكمة فيقول مثلاً إنّ الطعام لكونه لا تأثير له وجوده وعدمه سواء ويستجهل من يأكل ليشبع وكذا ما جعله الله تعالى من المنفعة في الأدوية والعقاقير وما لها من الخواصّ وألهم ذلك الأطباء وأهل التجاريب. فهل ينكر أحد ذلك؟ وكذا ما نحن فيه من كلّ أمر جرت العادة بوجود شيء عنده فلا ينكر بل يعتقد حكمة من الله تعالى مع صحّة التوحيد وهو أن لا ينسب إليه أثرًا أكثر من أنّ وجوده سبب لبروز القضاء الأزليّ عنده لا به. فمن نسب إلى شيء دون الله تعالى تأثيرًا في وجود شيء أو عدمه فهو مشرك. ومن أنكر الحكمة المودعة في قوالب الكائنات فهو جاهل أعمى البصيرة. ولو لم يكن إلّا جموده عن إدراك ما جرت به العادات وأفصحت به التجريبات لكان أمرًا سهلاً.

٥،٢٨ ولكنّه إنكار لحكمة المولى سبحانه وبديع تصرّفه في الكائنات الدالّ على إحاطة العلم والمشيئة بالمصالح والمنافع والمضارّ وعظمة الملك. فهو ينظر بإحدى العينين دون الأخرى. فمتى حكم التجريب مثلاً بأنّ يوماً من الأيّام لا يسعد بحاجة من سافر فيه أو تزوّج أو أخذ في سبب من الأسباب أو أنّه يسعد فلا نبادر إذا سمعنا ذلك بإنكاره ونقول قد أشرك مع الله تعالى.

He arranges causes and effects in accordance with His wisdom, out of kindness to His worshippers, to put their souls at ease through perceived causes.

Believing in the unseen and living in expectation of it is difficult. It is a burden for them to distinguish between those for whom the veils have been pierced, who have seen Truth, and those who remain veiled and go astray in valleys of error. We ask Exalted God to protect us from this. Don't you see that for the common people God creates satiety through eating, slaking of thirst through drinking, cover through the wearing of clothes, rest through lying down, distinct pleasure through sexual relations, and so on? Such examples are far too numerous to count. It is possible for Exalted God to create all of this from nothing. 28.3

Does any rational person deny the wisdom of this, claiming for instance that "The fact that foods exist has no influence, its presence or absence makes no difference," and considering the person who eats in order to become full ignorant? This is also true of the benefits God created in medicines, remedies, and their properties, knowledge of which He granted to doctors and those with experience. Can anyone deny this? This is true of every matter that habitually occurs in association with something else. This habitual occurrence is not to be denied; rather, it should be considered divine wisdom, in accordance with true faith in God's unity. One should not attribute influence to it beyond its existence as an occasion for the manifestation of the eternal decree—not by its very means but attendant with it. If someone attributes to something other than God influence for the presence or absence of something else, he is a polytheist. And whoever denies the wisdom God placed in the forms of all that exists is ignorant and blind. If such ignorance consisted merely in his refusal to perceive this, and habitual events and experimental knowledge would inform him correctly, then it would be an easy affair to correct. 28.4

But this is a denial of the wisdom of the Lord, praise Him, and of the splendor of His Dispensation, which guides one to knowledge, and provides cognizance of His Will for what is good and harmful. It is looking out of a single eye without using the other. When experience shows, for example, that a person is unhappy on a given day because of someone's departure, or someone's marriage, or because of any other particular circumstance, or conversely that he is happy because of these things, then when we hear this, we do not rush to deny it, saying that that person has associated something with Exalted God. 28.5

٦،٢٨ بل لا بأس بالاعتراف بذلك واعتباره عادة مع سلامة العقيدة من نسبة التأثير لليوم أو غيره من سائر الكائنات. والناس في نحو هذا ثلاثة. شخص يعتبره أخذاً وتركاً مع الغفلة عن الله تعالى إمّا مع نسبة التأثير إلى السبب وهم المشركون وإمّا بلا نسبة ولكن استغراقاً في الركوب إلى الأسباب والالتفات إلى الأغيار وهو من الغافلين. وشخص لا يعتبره أصلاً استغراقاً في التوحيد والتوكّل على الله تعالى والفناء عن الأسباب لا إنكاراً للحكمة وهذا لا بأس به. وإذا صحّ توكّله وتجرّده عن الأسباب فذلك سبب لنجاته بفضل الله تعالى من مقتضيات العادة. حتّى إنّه لو ألقم الحيّة رجله لم تضرّه. فإنّه لمّا خرق العادة على نفسه بحسمها عن المألوفات وتجريدها عن الرعونات خرق الله تعالى له العادة بإعفائه عن جري العادات وما تقتضيه بإذن الله الأسباب الحادثات. وشخص يعتبر ذلك تأدّباً مع الله تعالى في مراعاة الحكمة الجارية مع صحّة العقيدة وصحّة التوكّل على الله تعالى عند الأسباب لا على الأسباب. وهذا هو الكامل.

٧،٢٨ وكان صلّى الله عليه وسلّم يعالج ويستعمل الرُّقى. وقد يكون من ذلك ما هو خفي يكون اعتباره تعمّقاً في الأسباب فيترك وجعل بعض الأئمّة من هذا نهيه صلّى الله عليه وسلّم الأمّة عن الكيّ مع الاعتراف له بأنّه سبب من الأسباب. إذا علم هذا كلّه فكلّ ما ورد من نصوص الشريعة وأقوال أهل الدين وفعلهم يتنزّل على هذا.

٨،٢٨ وبما قرّرنا يعرف عذر من اعتبر شيئاً من ذلك وعذر من لم يعتبر. وفي الحديث لا عدوى ولا طيرة فالحقّ عندنا في تأويله أنّه إثبات لانفراد المولى جلّ وعزّ بكلّ التأثير وأنّ لا تأثير لشيء ممّا يتوهّم العرب أنّه مؤثّر لا في باب العَدْوى ولا في باب الطِّيَرة لا أنّه

On the contrary, there is nothing wrong with acknowledging this with proper faith, and when taking this divine Habit into account, to attribute influence to a day or to anything else. Concerning this, people are of three kinds: (1) A person who considers something a reason to do or not to do something, while ignoring Exalted God. He does so either while attributing influence to the occasion—these are the polytheists—or without doing so, but overly emphasizing the occasions and relying on what he set aside for himself. Such people are heedless. (2) A person who does not consider it at all and immerses himself in believing in the oneness of God, relying upon Exalted God, ignoring the occasions while not denying God's wisdom. There is no harm in this. If his reliance on God and his ridding himself of a belief in causes are sound, then this itself is a cause for his salvation by the grace of Exalted God through the necessary contingency of His Habit. Even if a snake bites his foot, it will not hurt him, for when he breaks the Habit for himself by separating it from customary things and frivolous things, Exalted God breaks the Habit for him by curing him from what habitually takes place and from His Habit's normal effects. (3) The best position to take is that of the person who considers this an education in how to preserve correct belief in light of God's ceaseless wisdom, and how to exercise proper reliance upon God in attendance with the occasions, not relying on them. 28.6

The Prophet, God bless and keep him, used to seek medical treatment and use curative prayers. The workings of some of this may be obscure and entail dwelling on the occasions things happen. In such a case it should be abandoned. One religious authority, having acknowledged that it was a specific occasion, derived this position from the Prophet, God bless and keep him, having forbidden cauterization to the Muslim community. If all of this is known, then all the texts of the revealed law and statements and actions by the people of religious knowledge can be reduced to a proper understanding of causality. 28.7

We have presented enough for the arguments of both those who support and those who oppose this matter to be known. Regarding the interpretation of the hadith "There is no contagion and no evil omen," we believe firmly that it is an affirmation of the Lord, Great and Powerful, being the sole influence, and that nothing of what the Arabs of the pre-Islamic period imagined had influence, neither with regard to contagion nor evil omens. The hadith is not a denial of what God's Habit causes habitually to occur, should God will it so. It is 28.8

نبي لما جرت العادة بوجوده عند ذلك بإذن الله تعالى. وهذا هو الجمع بين التوحيد والحكمة. وهو جمع بين الحقيقة والشريعة في المعنى.

٩،٢٨ وقوله صلّى الله عليه وسلّم وفرّ من المجذوم فرارك من الأسد. وكذلك قوله صلّى الله عليه وسلّم لا يوردنّ ممرض على مصحّ أي ذو الإبل المريضة على ذي الإبل الصحيحة. يحتمل معنيين أحدهما أنّه سدّ للذريعة بمعنى أنه ترك ذلك مخافة أن يقع شيء بإذن الله فيظنّ من وقع له أو غيره أنّه ناشئ عن ذلك السبب فيقع في الشرك. الثاني أنّه إثبات لما جرت به العادة من حكمة الله تعالى كما قرّرنا. فيعتبر ذلك شرعاً ولو لم يكن إلّا تنزّهاً عن تغيير القلوب وآية الناس.

١٠،٢٨ وفي الحديث أيضاً اطلبوا الخير عند حسان الوجوه وهو يحتمل أموراً. الأوّل اطلبوا الخير عند الناس الحسان الوجوه فإنّ الخير مقرون بهم وهذا من نمط ما نحن فيه. الثاني اطلبوا الخير منهم فإنّه يصدر عنهم الخير بإذن الله تعالى. إذ حسن الخَلق عنوان حُسْنِ الخُلق كما تقرّر في الفِراسَة الحكمية وهو قريب ممّا قبله. الثالث اطلبوا الخير عندهم ومنهم فإنّ النفس تنبسط إليهم وتتمتّع برؤيتهم. وفي الحكمة اعتمد بحوائجك إلى الصباح الوجوه فإنّ حُسن الصورة أوّل نعمة تلقاك من الرجل. الرابع اطلبوا الخير أي الرزق عند الوجوه المُستحسنة شرعاً كالبيع والتجارة والقراض والهبة والصدقة وسائر الوجوه الحِلّية دون السرقة والغصْب والخيانة ونحو ذلك.

١١،٢٨ وكان صلّى الله عليه وسلّم يقول إذا أبردتم إليّ بريداً فأبردوه حسن الوجه حسن الاسم. وهو أيضاً يحتمل أنّه لمجرّد النظر أو لزائد على ذلك. ولهذا بعث الله الأنبياء ولا سيّما نبيّنا ومولانا محمّد صلّى الله عليه وسلّم في أحسن صورة.

١٢،٢٨ وفي ترجمة الإمام الشافعيّ رضي الله عنه كان يتجنّب أهل العاهات والناقصين خلقة. وكان يقول احذروا الأعور والأحول والأعرج والأحدب والأشقر والكوسج

a joining of a belief in God's oneness with a belief in God's wisdom, a bringing together and synthesis of the reality of the Truth with the revealed Law.

It is the same with his saying, God bless and keep him, "Flee from the leper as you flee from the lion," as well as his saying, God bless and keep him, "Do not water the sick animals with the healthy." He refers here to the owner of sick camels with the owner of the healthy camels. This hadith can mean two things: One is that the hadith is a case of preventing the means to sin: He should not do this for fear that, with God's leave, something could happen, leading him to believe that it was the cause for what happened to him or another, thus leading him to fall into polytheism.[204] The second possibility is that, as we have previously established, the hadith is a confirmation of how God's Habit proceeds in accordance with His wisdom. This is considered to be in accordance with revealed law, if only in the sense that it is a sign for people and is meant to avoid changing their hearts toward the sick. **28.9**

In the Hadith we find the phrase: "Seek good from those with beautiful faces," which has various possible interpretations. The first is: Seek good from people with beautiful faces, for good resides in them. This is the type of interpretation we support. The second: Seek good from them, as, by Exalted God's leave, good comes from them. A beautiful physical constitution is the sign of a noble character, as has been established in the philosophical science of physiognomy, an interpretation similar to the previous one. The third: Seek good with and from them, for the soul is at ease in their presence and enjoys seeing them. The proverb goes: "Part of wisdom is depending on beautiful faces, for a beautiful image is the first blessing you receive from a man." The fourth: Seek what is good—meaning one's livelihood—with faces people find pleasant in legal matters, such as selling, trade, loans, gifts, and charity and other licit matters, as opposed to theft, extortion, treachery, and the like. **28.10**

The Prophet used to say, God bless and keep him, "If you send me a letter, send it with someone who has a beautiful face and a beautiful name." Though this too suggests appearance is the sole essential element, there is perhaps more to it. This is why God sent prophets, especially our Prophet and master Muḥammad, God bless and keep him, with an excellent appearance. **28.11**

In the biography of the exemplar al-Shāfiʿī, God be content with him, it states that he used to avoid people with deformities or disfigurements. He used to say, "Beware of the one-eyed, the cross-eyed, the lame, the hunchback, the light-skinned, the hairless, and all those with bodily defects: In them **28.12**

وكلّ من به عاهة في بدنه فإنّ فيه التوّى ومعاشرته عسيرة. ومن غريب ما وقع له في ذلك أمران الأوّل أنّه حكى أنّه بعث رجلاً من أصحابه ذات مرّة ليشتري له نوعاً من العنب معروفاً. قال الرجل فذهبت فلم أجده إلّا عند رجل من هذا الجنس إمّا أشقر أو أزرق. قال فأتيته به فلمّا طرحت الطبق بين يديّ الإمام قال أين وجدت هذا؟ قلت عند فلان وكان يعرفه. فقال أردد إليه عنبه. قال فقلت يا أبا عبد الله إن لم ترد أن تأكله أكله غيرك. فقال ما أحبّ أن تتمّ المعاملة بيننا وبينه.

١٣،٢٨ فانظر في هذا ولا تظنّ أنّ الإمام به حبّ الثمن يستردّه ولا يتصدّق بالعنب. كلّا فإنّ جوده قد طبق الآفاق وهو الذي وضع بين يديه عشرة آلاف خارج مكة. فكلّ من سلّم عليه يعطيه حتّى لم يقم إلّا وقد فرغت. وإنّما الحامل له على ما قال ألا تتمّ المعاملة بينه وبينه. والظاهر من القصّة أنّ الرجل المبعوث قد اشترى العنب شراء بتّاً وهو العادة في مثل ذلك. ففسخ العقدة إن لم يكن فضلاً من البائع. إنّما هو أن يدّعي أنّه من مثل ذلك الشخص عَيب وهذا نهاية هذا الأمر وليس بعجب. فقد حكي عن بعض القضاة من السلف أنّه ردّ فرساً على بائعه بشيّة قد عيبت فيه.

١٤،٢٨ الثاني أنّه حكي عنه أنّه كان في بعض أسفاره مرّ برجل من هذا الجنس فقام الرجل إليه ورحّب به ترحيباً بالغاً واستدعاه للنزول والتضييف بغاية الاستحثاث. فنزل رضي الله عنه فبالغ الرجل في ضيافته وإكرامه مع غاية التأديب معه وتبجيله والبرّ به. فلمّا رأى الإمام ذلك قال في نفسه سبحان الله! مثل هذا الخير لا يصدر عن مثل هذا الشخص بما تقرّر الحكمة في أمثاله. وهذا الإنسان ينقض علينا القاعدة.

١٥،٢٨ فاغتمّ لذلك وبات مغموماً متحيّرًا فلمّا أصبح وتهيّأ للرحيل لم يشعر إلّا وقد ناوله الرجل سجِلاً فيه مكتوب كلّ ما أكل وكلّ ما انتفع به عنده مقوّماً بقيمة مضاعفة.

is perdition, and intimate contact with them brings difficulties." Two anecdotes are related to the curious things he experienced in this respect: First, it is said that he once sent one of his students to buy a certain well-known type of grape for him. The man reported, "So I set out but could not find any except from such a man." That is, somone fair-skinned or blue-eyed. "I returned with the grapes, and when I placed the plate in front of the exemplar, he asked, 'Where did you find this?' and I said, 'At so-and-so's,' and he knew the person. 'Return his grapes to him,' he said. And I said, 'Abū 'Abd Allāh, if you do not wish to eat them, give them to someone else.' 'I don't wish there to be any transaction with that man.'"

Ponder this, and do not for a moment believe that the exemplar wanted his money back or that he did not trust the grapes. Far from it. His generosity exceeded every measure—it was he who, outside Mecca, placed ten thousand dinars in front of him and did not leave until he had given a dinar to every person who greeted him, till they were all gone. Rather, according to what is reported, the carrier should not have completed the transaction between himself and the seller. It is clear from the story that the man who was sent had bought the grapes in a binding sale. This was customary in such cases. Al-Shāfiʿī would have annulled the contract, were it not for the seller's rights. Nonetheless, he claimed it was a source of shame for it to be from such a person. So ended the affair, which was not unusual. It has been similarly recounted about a judge from the first generations of Muslims that he returned a horse to its seller due to the latter possessing an ugly face. 28.13

The second curious anecdote told regarding al-Shāfiʿī is that on one of his trips he passed by such a man. The man stood up and welcomed him effusively, calling on him with great urgency to stop and receive hospitality. He stopped, God be content with him, and the man was exceedingly hospitable and honored him greatly, was exceedingly polite, and exhibited great reverence and piety toward him. When the exemplar saw this, he said to himself, "Good God! According to what has been established in received wisdom regarding his like, this kind of good does not come from this kind of person. This person counters the basis of our thinking." He was distressed by this and spent the night unhappy and confused. 28.14

No sooner had he woken and readied himself to leave than the man gave him a bill on which was written everything that he had eaten and enjoyed, which amounted to twice its normal cost. "Pay me for what you ate," he said 28.15

وقال له ادفع لي ما أكلت. وإذا هو رجل صاحب مكر واحتيال على الناس بالضيافة ليتّجر فيهم. فعند ذلك سُرِّيَ عن الإمام رضي الله عنه وعلم أنّ القاعدة لم تنخرم فوزن له ذلك عن طيب نفس وسرور بصحّة القاعدة. انظر الأمثال الحديثة.

١٦،٢٨ ودخل الشعبيّ سوق الرقيق فقالوا له هل من حاجة؟ فقال حاجتي صورة حسنة أتنعّم بها يلتذّ بها قلبي وتعينني على عبادة ربّي. وكأنّه يتذكّر ما عنده والتشويق إليه. وأدام النظر إلى جارية حسنة. فقال مولاها لمَ؟ فقال ما لي لا أتأمّل منها ما أحلّ الله. وفيه دليل على حكمة الله واشتياق إلى ما وعد الله.

١٧،٢٨ وقال الراجز: [رجز]

ثَلَاثَةٌ تَجْلُو عَنِ ٱلْقَلْبِ ٱلْحُزُنْ ٱلْمَاءُ وَٱلْخُضْرَةُ وَٱلْوَجْهُ ٱلْحَسَنْ

١٨،٢٨ وقال إسحاق الموصلي: [بسيط]

لَا أَشْرَبُ ٱلرَّاحَ إِلَّا مِنْ يَدَيْ رَشَأٍ تَقْبِيلُ رَاحَتِهِ أَشْهَى مِنَ ٱلرَّاحِ

١٩،٢٨ ولا بدّ من التنبيه في هذا الباب لأمور منها أنّ هذه الأسباب الحكميّة قسمان. قسم ظاهر وهو ما يرجع إلى قوام الإنسان في معاشه غذاء ودواء مباشرة أو بواسطة قريبة أو بعيدة كما في التمثيل ببعضه. وقسم خفي وهو ما لم يصل إلى تلك المنزلة بذاته وإن كان له بها مساس. فالأوّل لا ينكر على من يتعاطاه لوضوحه. والثاني هو الذي يقع فيه الإنكار كما مرّ كلّ ذلك.

٢٠،٢٨ ومنها أنّ الأمر العاديّ كما أنّه لا تأثير فيه إلّا لله تعالى كذلك لا ارتباط فيه عقلاً. وإنّما هو أمر يجعله الله تعالى وتستمرّ عادته تعالى به اختياراً منه ومتى أراد أن يخرقه خرقه كما شوهد ذلك في معجزات الأنبياء وكرامات الأولياء وسحرة السحرة. فكلّ ذلك خرق من الله تعالى لحكمة كما أجراه أوّلاً لحكمة. وقد أخرج أهل الحيرة السمّ القاتل

to al-Shāfiʿī. It emerged that he was a man who deceived and tricked people with hospitality in order to exploit them. At this the exemplar ceased to worry and he knew, God be content with him, that this did not constitute an exception, and he was very reassured and pleased to have his thinking confirmed. Consider current examples of this!

Once, al-Shaʿbī entered the slave market and was asked, "What do you need?" and he replied, "I need a beautiful face that will bring me pleasure, that will delight my heart, and that will inspire me to worship my Lord." In doing so, he was listing his desires and what he longed to possess. He stared so fixedly at a beautiful slave girl that her owner said to him, "What are you doing?" "I am doing nothing but contemplating in her what God has permitted." In this there is a sign of God's wisdom, and a longing for what God has promised. **28.16**

A *rajaz* poet has said: **28.17**

Three things remove sorrow from the heart:
Water, greenery, and a beautiful face.

Isḥāq al-Mawṣilī said: **28.18**

I only drink wine from the hands of a young gazelle:
Kissing his palm is more appealing than the wine.

In this context, it is necessary to draw attention to some matters, one of which is that there are two kinds of manifestations linked to God's wisdom: an external kind, examples of which we have given, which entails the livelihood of man being directly or indirectly—in one way or another—dependent on food and medicine. There is also a kind that is concealed, which is the sort that does not quite attain this category, even though it comes close to it. The first of these, being obvious, is not denied by the one who receives it. It is with the second that denial occurs, as we have discussed at length. **28.19**

One aspect of this is that, just as nothing but Exalted God has influence in habitual occurrences, in the same fashion there is no rational connection between them. Rather, these are matters created by Exalted God, maintained by His Habit and His choice. When He wishes to break the Habit, He does so, as has been witnessed in the miracles of the prophets, the marvels granted the saints, and the magic of sorcerers. All of this represents Exalted God rupturing the wisdom He initially put in place. The people of al-Ḥīrah brought out lethal poison for Khālid ibn al-Walīd, God be content with him, hoping to kill him. **28.20**

للسيّد خالد بن الوليد رضي الله عنه طمعاً منهم في أن يقتلوه. فلمّا علم به أخذه فسمّى الله تعالى وأكله ولم يضرّه شيئاً. ولا يحصى كم من عابد بقي حيّاً بلا طعام ولا شراب.

٢١،٢٨ ولمّا حاصر المعتصم عمورية نهاه المنجّمون أن يتقدّم لقتالهم في ذلك اليوم. فلمّا بلغ ذلك بعض أهل الدين في عسكره دخل عليه فقال له: [بسيط]

دَعِ ٱلنُّجُومَ لِطُرْقِيٍّ يَعِيشُ بِهَا   وَقُمْ لِوَقْتِكَ وَٱنْهَضْ أَيُّهَا ٱلْمَلِكُ
إِنَّ ٱلنَّبِيَّ وَأَصْحَابَ ٱلنَّبِيِّ نَهَوْا   عَنِ ٱلنُّجُومِ وَقَدْ أَبْصَرْتَ مَا مَلَكُوا

فنهض إليهم لوقته ففتح عليه. وأصل هذا ما في الحديث أنّ النبيّ صلّى الله عليه وسلّم قال لأصحابه إثر سماء وقعت أتدرون ما قال ربّكم؟ قالوا الله ورسوله أعلم. قال يقول الله تعالى أصبح من عبادي مؤمن بي وكافر فأمّا من قال مطرنا بفضل الله وبرحمته فذاك مؤمن بي وكافر بالكواكب. وأمّا من قال مطرنا بنوء كذا فذاك كافر بي مؤمن بالكواكب. وهذا هو الذي قرّرناه قَبْلُ من تحقيق التوحيد وليس فيه إنكار العادة الجارية.

٢٢،٢٨ والنوء عند العرب أن يطلع نجم وقيل أن يغرب وهو الأصحّ فيقع المطر بإذن الله فينسبونه إليه ويقولون أمثال نوء السماك ونوء النعائم وهكذا. وقد أجرى الله تعالى عند طلوع النجوم وعند غروبها وعند اقتران[١] بعضها ببعض أموراً كثيرة في المملكة اختباراً منه تعالى ونبّه إليها من شاء من عباده. فحصل لهم علم الأنواء وعلم الاقترانات وسائر علم التنجيم وهي كلّها عادات جارية بإذن الله تعالى. والمتنبّهون إليها لمعتبرون لها منهم من آمن ومنهم من كفر.

٢٣،٢٨ والمقياسُ الحديثُ السابقُ على ما مرّ من تفصيل أحوال الناس. ومنها أنّه قد يُعدّ من هذا الباب ما ليس منه ممّا يرجع إلى مجرّد تخيّلات ووساويس. ولم يظهر فيه حكمة منوطة ولا عادة صحيحة جارية. وأكثره يكون بتسلّط شياطين يعبثون

١ ق وط: إقتراب.

When he became aware of this, he took it, invoked Exalted God, and consumed it. He was not harmed in the slightest. The number of worshippers who have survived the deprivation of food or drink is uncountable.

When al-Muʿtaṣim had surrounded Amorium, the astrologers forbade him from bringing the fight to them on that day. When this news reached one of the religious scholars among his troops, he came to al-Muʿtaṣim and said: 28.21

> Leave stars to adherents who live by them—
> seize your moment, King, and attack.
> The Prophet and his Companions forbade belief in stars
> and you have seen the extent of their dominion.

That day, he attacked them and conquered the city. The root of this ruling is in the Hadith, for the Prophet, God bless and keep him, said to his Companions after nightfall: "Do you know what your Lord said?" They said, "God and His Prophet know best." He said, "Exalted God says, 'It appears that among those who worship me, some are believers and some unbelievers. The one who says, "It rained on us by the virtue and mercy of God" believes in Me and disbelieves in the stars. The one who says, "It has rained on us because of the rising" disbelieves in Me and believes in the stars.'" This is what we determined previously in establishing belief in the unity of God, and does not involve a denial of God's Habit taking place.

For the Arabs, the rising refers to a rising star or, it is also said, to a setting star, which is more accurate. When rain falls by God's leave, they attribute it to this star and speak similarly of the rising of Arcturus or the rising of Sagittarius, and so on. Exalted God has chosen to make many things happen in Creation simultaneous with the rising and setting of stars and with their being in conjunction with each other. He has drawn them to the attention of those of His worshippers He wishes to, and they learned the science of the setting of stars, conjunctions, and the rest of astrology. These are all habitual occurrences, by Exalted God's leave. Those who pay attention to the conjunctions hold them in high regard: Some are believers, some unbelievers. 28.22

The distinguishing factor between the two groups is detailed in our previous discussion of peoples' conditions. One aspect sometimes added to this subject but that does not belong is based in mere speculation and rumor. Such things are not linked to God's wisdom, nor are they truly the result of God's Habit. Most often they occur because devils seize power and manipulate 28.23

بمن يتوهّم ذلك فلا يلتفت إلى هذا النوع بوجه من الوجوه. ولا سيّما إن أبطل سنّة وعارض حكماً شرعياً.

٢٨،٢٤ كالذي يقول إنّي جرّبت أنّي متّى أعرت أو سلفت أو تصدّقت أو أضفت ضيفاً تصيبني مضرّة. فهذه شيطانيّة. وقد حكي عن بعض الناس أنّهم ما يذبحون الضحيّة. وأنّهم متى ذبحوها أصابتهم مصيبة. فلمّا اعتادوا ذلك تركوها فتمادوا على هذا الضلال حتّى انتهى الأمر إلى رجل منهم موفّق. فقال والله لا أترك السنّة ولأضحينّ. فلمّا ضحّى يبِسَتْ يده اليمنى فقالوا هذا الذي حذرناك. فقال لا أبالي. فلمّا أتت الضحيّة من قابل ضحّى أيضاً فيبست يده الأخرى. فلمّا ضحّى الثالثة يبست رجله ولمّا ضحّى الرابعة يبست رجله الأخرى ولمّا ضحّى الخامسة انطلق ولم يبق به بأس. وانقطعت تلك العادة الباطلة وتبيّن أنّه شيطان يعبث بهم ويفسد عليهم دينهم. لله الأمر من قبل ومن بعد.

٢٨،٢٥ كنت في هذه السفرة التي كتبت فيها هذه الأوراق سافرت زمن البرد. فلمّا انفصلت من البلد قلت: [وافر]

أَيَا رَبُّ ٱلْبَـرَايَا يَا رَحِيـمُ وَيَا مَوْلَى ٱلْعَـطَايَا يَا حَفِيظُ
أَجِـرْنَا مِنْ عَذَابِكَ وَٱمْتِحَانٍ تَجِيشُ ٱلنَّفْسُ مِنْهُ أَوْ تَفِيظُ
وَمِنْ وَعْثَاءَ فِي سَفَـرٍ وَسُوءٍ وَمِنْ صُرَدٍ وَسَائِرِ مَا يَغِيظُ

يقال فاظت نفسه إذا مات والوعثاء بعين مهملة وثاء مثلّثة المشقّة.

٢٨،٢٦ فلمّا أمسينا وضعت بين أيدينا فاكهة الشتاء فنعمنا بها. فلمّا رأيت ذلك قلت سبحان من جعل رحمته في عذابه أي النار وجعل عذابه في رحمته أي المطر ثمّ نظمت هذا المعنى فقلت: [سريع]

those who imagine such things. One should not be sympathetic to this in any way, especially not when it falsifies Prophetic precedent and opposes revealed wisdom.

Such is the case of someone who says, "In my experience, when I gave a loan, advanced money, gave charity, or invited a guest, I was afflicted with harm." This is the devil's work. It has been reported about one group that they did not give offerings as sacrifices. And when they did, they were struck with an affliction. They became accustomed to this and stopped making offerings. They continued in this error until a prosperous man among them got wind of it. "By God," he said, "I will not renounce Prophetic precedent and I will make sacrifices." When he made a sacrifice, his right hand shriveled up, and they said, "We warned you about this!" and he said, "I do not care!" When the next time for sacrifice came, he did so again and his other hand shriveled up. When he sacrificed a third time, his foot shriveled up, and when he sacrificed a fourth time his other foot shriveled up. When he sacrificed a fifth time, he was relieved of all affliction. The false habit ended among them, and it became clear that it had been Satan manipulating them and corrupting their faith. Everything is God's to command. **28.24**

On the trip during which I wrote these pages, I was traveling at a cold time of year. When I left this area, I composed: **28.25**

Lord of Creation, Merciful One,
Lord of Bestowals, Preserver,
Save us from Your punishment,
prepare the soul for the Trial or have it depart.
Preserve us from tribulation and evil on the road,
from birds of omen and all things that vex.

(People say "his soul departed" when a person dies. *Waʿthāʾ*, "tribulation," means difficulty, and is written is with an *ʿayn*, and a *thāʾ*.)[205]

When we stopped for the night, a fire was kindled in front of us, which delighted us. When I saw it, I said, "Praise the One who placed His mercy in His punishment"—meaning the fire—"and who placed His punishment in His mercy"—meaning the rain. I then set it to verse as follows: **28.26**

سُبْحَانَ مَنْ يَقْدِرُ أَنْ يَرْحَمَا بِمَا بِهِ يُعَذِّبُ ٱلْمُجْرِمَا
وَأَنْ يُعَذِّبَ بِمَا يَرْحَمُ ٱلْعَبْدَ بِهِ يَوْمًا إِذَا أَنْعَمَا
فَظَهَرَ ٱقْتِدَارُهُ وَٱعْتَلَى فِي كُلِّ أَمْرٍ شَأْنُهُ وَٱسْتَمَى
وَظَهَرَتْ حِكْمَتُهُ فِي ٱلَّذِي رَكَّبَ فِي ٱلدُّنْيَا وَمَا أَحْكَمَا
فَمُرُّهَا لَمْ يَخْلُ مِنْ حُلْوِهَا وَحُلْوُهَا قَدْ أَشْرَكَ ٱلْعَلْقَمَا

في أبيات أخرى أنسيتها الآن.

٢٧،٢٨ وتقرير هذا المعنى من وجهين أحدهما أنّ هذه الأمور التي يباشرها الإنسان ذات وجهين نافع وضارّ. ألا ترى أنّ النار مثلاً تدفئ من البرد وتحرق والمطر مثلاً ينبت الزرع والنوار ويخلف المياه الغزار ولكن يخرب الديار ويقطع المسافر عن التسيار. وهكذا والحكمة في ذلك التركيب المشار إليه في الدنيا لما مرّ من الدلالة على ما في الآخرة من النعيم والعذاب والترغيب والترهيب وغير ذلك ممّا يطول تتبّعه. ثانيهما أنّ كلّ ما هو نافع فالله تعالى قادر أن يجعله ضارًّا وبالعكس.

٢٨،٢٨ وذلك لمّا تقرّر في العقيدة من أنّ ما يوجد في هذه الحوادث من الفوائد والخواصّ ليس ناشئًا عنها لا باختيار ولا علّة ولا طبع بل عن الفاعل المختار تعالى بقدرته ومشيئته. وليس ثمّ ارتباط عقليّ فيجوز وجود ذلك وعدمه فللّه تعالى أن يجعل النار مثلاً مُحرقة مرّة ثم يجعلها غير مُحرقة وأن يجعل الخبز مثلاً مقتاتًا ثمّ يجعله غير مقتات كالحجر وهكذا. ولكن أجرى الله تعالى عادته بما وقع لما مرّ من الحكمة وكثيرًا ما يخرق ذلك وقد مرّ كلّ ذلك. لله الأمر من قبل ومن بعد.

١،٢٩ كان الرئيس أبو عبد الله محمّد الحاج بن محمد بن أبي بكر قد ملك المغرب سنين عديدة واتّسع هو وأولاده واخوته وبنو عمّه في الدنيا. فلمّا قام الشريف السلطان رشيد بن الشريف ولقي جيوشهم ببطن الرمّان فهزمهم. وذلك أوائل المحرّم فاتح سنة تسع

Praise the One who can show mercy
  through that with which He punishes the criminal.
He punishes worshippers through that with which He shows mercy
  when He blesses.
His Wisdom is made manifest
  in what He fashions and decrees in this world.
Its bitterness is not empty of sweetness;
  its sweetness is mixed with vexation.

And there are other lines I've now forgotten.

There are two aspects to the significance of these words. The first is that the matters that attend mankind have two facets, one beneficial and one harmful. Don't you see, for example, that fire warms when it is cold out, but fire also burns? And rain, for example, causes crops to grow and blossom and brings copious rainfall, but also destroys houses and prevents the traveler from beginning his journey. And so forth. The wisdom of having this design in the world has been discussed above. It is an indication of blessing and punishment, attraction and horror, and so on in the world to come—the examples are too numerous to list. The second aspect is that Exalted God is capable of making something beneficial harmful, and vice versa. 28.27

It has been established in doctrine that the benefits and attributes of these created things do not proceed from them, neither by choice, nor as a cause, nor by nature, but from the power and volition of the Exalted Chosen Agent. There is then no rational connection between events: It is possible for an association to be present or absent. Exalted God can, for example, make fire burn at one point, and not burn at another. He can make bread, for example, satiate at one time, and, like stone, not satiate at another. And so forth. Yet Exalted God has arranged His Habit according to established wisdom, though He often breaks it. All this has already been discussed. Everything is God's to command. 28.28

The leader Abū ʿAbd Allāh Maḥammad al-Ḥājj ibn Maḥammad ibn Abī Bakr had ruled over Morocco for many years, and he and his sons, brothers, and nephews grew powerful in this world. When the descendant of the Prophet, the sultan Rashīd ibn al-Sharīf, rose up, he met their army at Baṭn al-Rummān and defeated them. This was in the first days of Muḥarram, at the beginning 29.1

وسبعين وألف. فدخلنا عليه وكان لم يحضر في المعركة لعجزه من كبر سنّه. فإذا بالفَلّ يدخلون فدخل عليه أولاده واخوته وأظهروا جزعاً شديداً وضيقاً عظيماً. فلمّا رأى منهم ذلك قال لهم ما هذا؟ إن قال لكم حسبكم فحسبكم يريد الله تعالى. وهذا كلام عجيب وإليه يساق الحديث. والمعنى إن قال الله تعالى لكم حسبكم من الدنيا فكفّوا راضين مسلمين.

٢،٢٩ والإشارة بهذه إلى أنّ الله تعالى وضع في الدنيا مائدة لعباده وجعلها دُوَلاً كما قال تعالى ﴿وَتِلْكَ ٱلْأَيَّامُ نُدَاوِلُهَا بَيْنَ ٱلنَّاسِ﴾. فكلّ من جلس على هذه المائدة وتناول منها ما قسم له فلا بدّ أن يقام عنها بالموت أو العزل ليجلس غيره. ولا تدوم لأحد بل لا يقام عنها من أقيم غالباً إلّا بمرارة وعنف. ولذا قال صلّى الله عليه وسلّم في الولاية نعمت المرضعة وبئست الفاطمة.

٣،٢٩ ثمّ من الناس من لم يشعر بهذا المعنى ولم يتنبّه له فهو يسعى إليها عجباً بأوائل زِبْرِجها وانخداعاً بظاهر زينتها. كما قيل: [كامل]

ٱلْحَرْبُ أَوَّلُ مَا تَكُونُ فَتِيَّةٌ   تَسْعَى بِزِينَتِهَا لِكُلِّ جَهُولِ
حَتَّىٰ إِذَا ٱشْتَعَلَتْ وَشَبَّ ضِرَامُهَا   عَادَتْ عَجُوزًا غَيْرَ ذَاتِ حَلِيلِ
شَمْطَا تَنَكَّرَ لَوْنُهَا وَتَغَيَّرَتْ   مَكْرُوهَةٌ لِلشَّمِّ وَٱلتَّقْبِيلِ

٤،٢٩ ومن الناس من علم ذلك وتنبّه له. ثمّ من هؤلاء من نفعه الله بعمله فأوجب له أحوالاً محمودة إمّا قبل ولوجها بالزهد فيها والفرار عنها علماً بغايتها ديناً وتقوى أو حزماً في الدنيا. وأمّا بعد الولوج بالتعفّف والعدل والإحسان والرفق ومجانبة البغي والجور إمّا ديناً أيضاً وحذاراً من المطالبة في الآخرة وإمّا حزماً دنيوياً وحذار من اختلالها واضمحلالها. لله الأمر من قبل ومن بعد.

of 1079 [June 1668]. I went to Abū ʿAbd Allāh—he had not attended the battle, his advanced age having prevented him from doing so—and at that time, the remnants of his army were gathering to him, and his sons and brothers came to him, showing great sorrow and deep pain. When he noticed this, he asked them, "What is this? If you were told this was your measure, then He has measured it out for you," referring to Exalted God. This was a wondrous thing to say and merits further discussion. His meaning was: If Exalted God said, "This is your measure in this world," then be content and submit.

There was an indication in this to Exalted God having placed a table for his worshippers in this world, and having made its fortunes alternate, as when the Exalted said: «We alternate these days between the people.»[206] Everyone who sits at this table and eats what has been allotted to him will have to give up his spot, by dying or by leaving it to someone else. It lasts for no one, and generally anyone who sits there leaves bitter, and against his will. Because of this, the Prophet, God bless and keep him, said, "In governance, the nursing woman is fortunate, the weaning woman unfortunate." 29.2

Then there are people who do not feel this way and do not pay attention to the table. Such individuals may approach the table wondering at its exquisite decoration, and deceived by its superficial finery. As has been said:[207] 29.3

At first, War is a young woman in finery
   commanding every ignorant person
Until her fire begins to burn.
   It ages and she turns into an old spinster,
Gray-haired, her color changed for the worse,
   foul-smelling and vile to kiss.

There are people who know this and take heed. Among them are some whom God has aided in their actions, guaranteeing them blessed states, either before war, because of which they renounce it, or, conversely, as they flee from it, knowing the outcome by virtue of their piety, fear of God, or prudence in this world. Or it happens that after engaging in war, God aids them by granting them the ability to show restraint, justice, benevolence, and compassion, and to avoid what is hateful and unjust. They do this either out of faith and with an eye to accountability in the hereafter, or out of worldly prudence and fear of this world's imperfection and evanescence. Everything is God's to command. 29.4

١،٣٠ وقد حكي عن فرعون لعنه الله أنّه دخل عليه بعض أشياعه بمال عظيم فوضعه بين يديه. فقال له من أين هذا؟ فأخبره أنّ بعض القرى من أعمالهم كان لهم ماء فتبطّل وأنّه قد أذن لهم في إحيائه وإجرائه على هذا المال. فقال له فرعون الماء ماؤهم وقد أجروه ففيم يدفعون المال؟ هذا ظلم وجور والملك لا يستقرّ على الجور فاردد إلى الناس أموالهم. قال بعض أئمّتنا فانظروا يا معشر المسلمين هذا كافر لا يلتفت إلى الدار الآخرة ثمّ حافظ بالعدل على دنياه فقط. فكيف بمن يدّعي الدين ثمّ لا يلتفت إلى العدل ولا يحافظ على الدين ولا دنيا.

٢،٣٠ قلت وقد قال الحكماء إنّ الملك يستقرّ ويستقيم مع الكفر ولا يستقيم مع الجور[١] والعلّة فيه أنّ الملوك هم خلفاء الله تعالى على عباده مؤمنهم وكافرهم. غير أنّ المؤمن خليفة في الطرفين والكافر في الدنيا فقط والملك هو نظام العالم والعدل هو روحه. فمتى ذهب العدل اختلّ النظام ووقع الفساد في العالم. ولذلك قال أرسطوطاليس في ضوابطه العالم بستان سياجه أي حائطه الدولة. الدولة سلطان تحيا به السنّة. السنّة سياسة يسوسها الملك. الملك راع يعضده الجيش. الجيش أعوان يكفلهم المال. المال رزق تجمعه الرعيّة. الرعية عبيد تعبّدهم العدل. العدل مألوف وهو حياة العالم.

٣،٣٠ ومن كلام الفرس لا ملك إلّا برجال ولا رجال إلّا بمال ولا مال إلّا بعمارة ولا عمارة إلّا بعدل. وقال الإمام عليّ كرّم الله وجهه الدين أس والملك حارس وما لا أسّ له مهدوم. وفي الحديث صنفان من أمّتي إذا صلحا صلح الناس الأمراء والعلماء. وقال أبو بكر رضي الله عنه لا يصلح هذا الأمر إلّا شدّة في غير عنف ولين في غير ضعف. وقال عمر رضي الله عنه لا يقيم هذا الأمر إلّا رجل يخاف الله في الناس ولا يخاف الناس في الله. وقال عمرو بن العاص رضي الله عنه إمام عادل خير من مطر وابل وأسد حَطوم خير من إمام ظلوم وإمام ظلوم خير من فتنة تدوم.

١ يزيد ق وط: وهو صحيح.

There is a story about one of Pharaoh's men who came to Pharaoh, God curse him, and placed a large amount of money in front of him. "Where does this come from?" Pharaoh asked. The man informed him that the water in the village of one of the workers had dried up and that he had permitted them to restore it and to make it flow in exchange for money. Pharaoh said, "If the water is theirs and they caused it to flow, why are they paying? This is tyranny and injustice. Rule is not based on tyranny," and he returned the people's money to them. One of our exemplary leaders said to us, "Consider, community of Muslims: This unbeliever pays no attention to the hereafter, and yet maintains justice on earth. What to make then of someone who calls to the true religion but does not incline to justice, nor preserves the faith or this earth?" 30.1

The philosophers have said, "Rule can exist and be sound in the face of unbelief, but not in the face of tyranny." The reason for this is that the kings are representatives of Exalted God to His worshippers, believers and unbelievers alike, although the believer is a representative in this world and the next, and the unbeliever is solely a representative in this world. Rule is order in the world, and its essence is justice. When justice is absent, order is upset and corruption spreads in the world. For this reason, among Aristotle's principles is: "The world is a garden, the fence of which—that is, its wall—is the dynasty. The dynasty is power whose life blood is the example provided by the king's political conduct. The king is the guardian who is supported by the army. The army is composed of armed guards who are retained with finances. Finances are the sustenance gathered by the subjects. The subjects are the servants who venerate justice. The meaning of justice is well known and represents the life of the world."[208] 30.2

The Persians have a saying: "There can be no rule without men. There can be no men without money. There can be no money without cities. There can be no cities without justice." The exemplar ʿAlī, God honor his countenance, said, "Religion is the foundation and rule is the guardian. What has no foundation is as good as destroyed." In the Hadith we find: "There are two types of people in my community who, when they are devout, the people are well: rulers and scholars." Abū Bakr, God be content with him, said, "The matter can only be fixed through strength without violence and flexibility without weakness." ʿUmar, God be content with him, said, "No man can rule unless he fears God more than the people, and not the reverse." ʿAmr ibn al-ʿĀṣ, God be content with him, said, "A just leader is better than heavy rain, an enraged lion 30.3

وفي أمثالهم إذا رغب السلطان عن العدل رغبت الرعيّة عن الطاعة ولم يزل الحازمون من أهل الدين يهربون منها.

٤،٣٠ ولذا قال صلّى الله عليه وسلّم إنّا لا نولّي أمرنا هذا من سأله أو من أراده. إمّا رعياً للغالب من أنّه لا يطلبه إلّا شهوانيّ أو مضيّع للحزم وإمّا استنانًا ليتّبع عند غلبة الشهوة وضعف الديانة كأزمنتنا هذه.

٥،٣٠ وقال أبو عمر بن عبد البرّ تكلّم يوماً معاوية رضي الله عنه فقال أمّا أبو بكر فهرب عنها وهربت عنه. وأمّا عمر فأقبلت إليه فهرب عنها وأمّا عثمان فأصاب منها وأصابت منه وأمّا أنا فداستني ودُستها. قال أبو عمر أمّا عليّ فأصابت منه ولم يصب منها. قلت إنّ أبا بكر هرب عنها من أوّل مرّة. وقد قال يوم السقيفة ووضع يديه على عمر وأبي عبيدة بايعوا أحد هذين الرجلين. قال عمر فلم أكره ممّا قال غيرها. فهما هاربان منها.

٦،٣٠ وقال عمر رضي الله عنه بعد ذلك في قصّته مع أويس القرنيّ من يأخذها بما فيها؟ يا ليت عمر لم تلده أمه. وقال في آخر رمق يا ليتني تخلّصت منها كفافًا لا لي ولا عليّ. هذا مع استقامته وعدله الشهير حتّى صار يضرب به المثل في متابعة الحقّ. وقد شهد له صلّى الله عليه وسلّم بذلك الحديث المشهور وقال له أيضاً ما سلكت فجًّا إلّا سلك الشيطان فجًّا غير فجّك. فكيف يكون حال من لم يبلغ أدنى من هذه المرتبة ولا قارب وهو يتبجّح بالولاية ويستبشر بنيل الدرجة بها عند الله تعالى. وقال عليّ كرّم الله وجهه يا بيضاء ويا صفراء غرّي غيري ولا تغريني.

٧،٣٠ وكلّ من تعرّض لها من السلف فإمّا انتهاضاً لنصح المسلمين من نفسه بإقامة الحقّ لئلّا يضيع وإمّا نزعة بشريّة حرّكها سبب من الأسباب. أمّا على الثاني فلا يقتدي به وأمّا على الأوّل فيقتدي من بلغ مقامه في التمكين والقوّة والنزاهة. وفي مثل زمانه الصالح الذي لم يزل فيه الدين طريًّا والحقّ جليًّا والأعوان عليه قائمين. وهيهات ذلك في آخر الزمان الذي غلب فيه حبّ الدنيا واستولى سلطان الهوى على الناس

is preferable to a tyrannical ruler, and a tyrannical ruler is better than unremitting conflict."[209] Their proverbs also include the saying: "If a ruler disdains justice, his subjects will disdain obedience, and those devoted to their faith will flee from it."

Because of this, the Prophet, God bless and keep him, said, "We do not entrust our affairs to one who desires this or requests it." He said this either to make the point that political authority is usually only sought by the dissolute or those lacking in prudence, or to provide a model for times such as these, when greed has become overpowering and faith is weak. 30.4

Abū ʿUmar ibn ʿAbd al-Barr said, "Muʿāwiyah, God be content with him, said, 'In Abū Bakr's case, he fled from power and it fled from him. In ʿUmar's, power came to him, but he fled from it. In ʿUthmān's, he got it and it got him. As for me, it trampled me, so I trampled it.'" Abū ʿUmar added, "As for ʿAlī, power took from him but he got nothing of it." Truly, Abū Bakr fled from power from the beginning. On the Day of the Portico, he placed his hands on ʿUmar and Abū ʿUbaydah, and said, "Give your allegiance to one of these two men." ʿUmar said, "This is the only thing he ever said that I disliked." The two of them fled rule. 30.5

ʿUmar, God be content with him, said, regarding the matter between him and Uways al-Qaranī, "Who seizes power by means of power? Would that ʿUmar's mother had never given birth to him."[210] With his last breath, he said, "If only I had avoided it by refusing it for myself and rejecting its imposition on me." He said this despite being upright and being known for justice to the point that his pursuit of the truth became proverbial. The Prophet, God bless and keep him, had attested to this in a famous hadith and had also said to him, "Never do you go down a road without the devil choosing another." How then one far lower than this, who boasts of his rule and welcomes it as a sign of God's favor? As ʿAlī, God honor his countenance, said, "Silver, gold, do not tempt me: Cleave to others, not me." 30.6

Each of the early Muslims who achieved power did so either by deciding of his own accord to advise the Muslims in establishing what is right so that it would not be lost, or from a natural human motivation. This second situation should not be emulated. But the first should be by those who have the ability, the power, and the rectitude to do so, who live in a moral age like the Prophet's in which faith is still fresh and truth resplendent, and whose supporters are ready to help protect it. How preposterous it is to do so in these end times 30.7

فلا ترى إلّا حرصاً على الجمع والمنع. ولا ترى إلّا نفاقاً ومداهنة وملقاً. فالمرء فيه لا يعدل بالسلامة شيئاً ومن له بوجودها إن لم يكن له من المولى تعالى لطف ظاهر. وقد أنذر نبيّنا محمّد صلّى الله عليه وسلّم بهذا الزمان وحضّ فيه على تجنّب أمور العامّة وإيثار السلامة فقال صلّى الله عليه وسلّم إذا رأيت شحّاً مطاعاً وهوى متّبعاً وإعجاب كلّ ذي رأي برأيه فعليك بخويصّة نفسك. ولله الأمر من قبل ومن بعد.[1]

١،٣١ فمن انتهض اليوم للانتصاب رَوْماً منه لإقامة الحقّ وإنصاف المظلوم من الظالم فهو مغرور. ولعلّ ذلك لا يتأتّى له كما ينبغي في بيته فضلاً عن قريته فضلاً عن البلد فضلاً عن الإقليم. وقد يسمع فضائل الأمر بالمعروف والنهي عن المنكر والقيام بمصالح المسلمين ودرجة الإمام العادل. وذلك كلّه حقّ ولكن أين يتأتّى؟ فيتحرّك المسكين لانتقاص الأجر والظفر بعلي الدرجات. فلا يفطن إلّا وقد وقع به العشاء على سرحان وربّما حان فيمن حان. وقد يكون ذلك وهو الأغلب دسيسة دنيويّة ونزعة شيطانيّة. وقد يقع في بعض هذه المهاوي بعض أبناء الطريق يحسدهم الشيطان على باب الله والتفرّغ للحضور بين يديه وتجنّب المعاصي التي هي أقرب شيء إلى الغفران برحمة الله. فلا يزال بهم حتّى يضمّهم إليه ويجاوز بهم مزالق من كانوا يتّبعونه إلى هاوية من يتبعهم. كما قال الشاعر: [طويل]

وَكُنْتُ ٱمْرَءًا مِنْ جُنْدِ إِبْلِيسَ فَٱنْتَهَى   بِيَ ٱلْأَمْرُ حَتَّى صَارَ إِبْلِيسُ مِنْ جُنْدِي

نسأل الله العافية.

٢،٣١ فيجد الواحد قوّة إيمانيّة في قلبه أو حالة جماليّة واردة فيوهمه ذلك أنّه قويّ على أن يصدع بالحقّ. وربّما أوهمه ذلك أنّه هو الحقيق بذلك دون غيره. أو أنّه هو المهدي

١ سقطت الجملة من ق، ط.

when love for this world has become dominant and when the sway of vain desire has taken power over the people! One sees nothing but hypocrisy, flattery, and adulation! An individual in such a time could not set anything right—safely or otherwise—if he were not granted explicit grace by the Exalted Lord. Our Prophet Muḥammad, God bless and keep him, warned of this time, and called for avoiding public affairs and for promoting peace. He said, God bless and keep him, "If you see miserliness take hold and vain desires being followed, and everyone adoring their own opinion, then draw away." Everything is God's to command.

Anyone rising up today wishing to establish what is right, and to see that the 31.1
oppressed receive justice from the oppressor, is deluded. It may not be feasible for him to do so in his home, let alone in his village, or the area or the region he comes from. He may hear about the virtue of commanding right and forbidding wrong, about establishing the public good of the Muslims, and about the rank of a just leader. This is all true, but where will it lead? This poor man is motivated by fear of losing the divine reward and the hope for a victory of the highest kind. He does not understand that pursuing his desire will lead him to be a wolf's meal and that he may perish. Such a delusion may indeed be, as is most often the case, a worldly scheme motivated by the devil. One of the travelers on the spiritual path, against whom the devil holds a grudge, might fall prey to such a desire at God's door, when applying himself to avoid sin—which is the closest thing to being forgiven through the mercy of God. The devil will stick to these travelers until he attracts them to himself, carrying them past the perils of those that follow him in order to deliver them to the abyss of him who makes them follow. As the poet says:

> I was a soldier in the army of Satan—the affair
> turned in my favor and Satan became one of my soldiers.

We ask God to preserve us!

Someone might find his heart full of strong faith or might enjoy a pass- 31.2
ing state of grace, and Satan could then make this person believe that he is strong enough to speak the truth openly and perhaps even make that person believe he and no one else is the right one to do so. Or he might make a person believe he is the awaited savior: This person might then become motivated by

المنتظر فيتحرّك على طمع أن ينقاد له الأمر وينقاد له أبناء الزمان. ويحفر فيُكدي ولا يعيد ولا يبدي. ثمّ يصير أشقر إن تقدّم نُحِر وإن تأخّر عُقِر. فلا يسعه على زعمه إلّا فتح أبواب التأويلات والترخصات وإسعاف الناس بعد أن قام ليتبعوه. ومن هنالك يهدم الدين عوض ما قام ليبنيه ويخفض الحقّ مكان ما انتهض ليعليّه فإيّاك وإيّاك. [وافر]

إِذَا أَرْخَى ٱلْخُمُولُ عَلَيْكَ ذَيْلًا   فَنَمْ فِي ظِلِّهِ لَيْلًا طَوِيلًا[١]

٣،٣١ وقد رأينا في وقتنا هذا من استولت عليه هذه الوساوس حتّى وقع في شبه صاحب المالنخويا بحيث لو اطّلع الناس على ما هو فيه رموه في المارستان. ولكن ستر الله تعالى يغطّي على عبيده.

٤،٣١ وممّن ابتلي بهذا قريباً أحمد بن عبد الله بن أبي محلّي. وكان صاحب ابن مبارك التستاوتي في الطريق حتّى حصل له نصيب من الذوق وألّف فيها كتباً تدلّ على ذلك. ثمّ نزعت به هذه النزعة فحدّثونا أنّه في أوّل أمره كان معاشرًا لابن أبي بكر الدلائي المتقدّم الذكر. وكان البلد إذ ذاك قد كثرت فيه المناكر وشاعت. فقال لابن أبي بكر ذات ليلة هل لك أن تخرج غداً إلى الناس فتأمر بالمعروف وتنهى عن المنكر؟ فلم يساعفه لما رأى من تعذّر ذلك لفساد الوقت وتفاقم الشرّ.

٥،٣١ فلمّا أصبحا خرجا فأمّا ابن أبي بكر فانطلق إلى ناحية النهر فغسل ثيابه وأزال شَعَثَهُ بالحلق وأقام صلاته وأوراده في أوقاتها. وأمّا ابن أبي محلّي فتقدّم لما همّ به من الحسبة فوقع في شرّ وخصام أدّاه إلى فوات الصلاة عن الوقت ولم يحصل على طائل. فلمّا اجتمعا بالليل قال له ابن أبي بكر أمّا أنا فقد قضيت مآربي وحفظت ديني وانقلبت في سلامة وصفاء ومن أتى منكرًا فالله هو حسيبُهُ أو نحو هذا. وأمّا أنت

١ ق: فنم في ظله نلت الفلاحا. و يزيد البيت: فمن لم يسأل اجيران عنه ولا عن حاله فقد استراحا.

the desire for power and the desire to make the people of that time submit to him.[211] He becomes lean and achieves little, and neither begins things nor takes them up again. He becomes red, and if he rushes ahead he will be slaughtered; if he holds back he will be wounded.[212] In his claim to power, there is nothing for him to do but open the doors of esoteric interpretation and opportunism, and, after rising up, to ask people for help in order for them to follow him. In this fashion, the faith is torn down when he had set out to shore it up, and justice is decreased when he had set out to increase it. Beware! Beware!

> If obscurity drapes the train of its cloak over you,
> sleep then in its shade the night long.

In our days, we have seen someone overpowered by these whisperings to the point that he fell into a state similar to melancholy: When people find melancholics, they throw them into a hospital. May God the Almighty guard and protect his worshippers! 31.3

One who was recently afflicted in this fashion was Aḥmad ibn Abī Maḥallī, a companion of Ibn Mubārak al-Tastāwatī on the Sufi path, who was fortunate to have tasted mystical knowledge and who has written books attesting to this experience. Then ambition overcame him. We learned that at the beginning of his career he was associated with the aforementioned Ibn Abī Bakr al-Dilāʾī.[213] At that time, many sinful acts were being committed throughout the land. One night he said to Ibn Abī Bakr, "Will you go tomorrow to the people and command them to do right and forbid them from doing wrong?" The latter did not support him, thinking the task impossible because of the corruption at that time and the alarming amount of evil then present. 31.4

When the two awoke, they set out. Ibn Abī Bakr headed toward the area by the river, washed his robe, shaved off his unkempt hair, and performed his prayer and devotions at the prescribed time. Ibn Abī Maḥallī set out to give moral instruction, as he had decided, but fell into mischief and quarreling that led him to miss the prayer at its proper time, and to be unsuccessful. When they met that evening, Ibn Abī Bakr said, "I attained my goal, safeguarded my faith, and sought peace and pureness of heart. Whoever came, attempting to do anything reprehensible, God held him to account." He said this or words to this effect. "As for you, look at the state you're in." Ibn Abī Maḥallī resumed his career when he went to the south of Morocco and called people to him, 31.5

فانظر ما الذي وقعت فيه. ثمّ لم ينته إلى أن ذهب إلى بلاد القبلة ودعا لنفسه وادّعى أنّه المهدي المنتظر وأنّه بصدد الجهاد فاستخفّ قلوب العوامّ واتّبعوه.

٦،٣١ فدخل بلد سجلماسة وهزم عنه والي الملوك السعديّة واستولى عليه ثمّ أخرجهم من درعة ثمّ تبعهم إلى حضرة مراكش وفيها زيدان بن أحمد المنصور فهزمه وأخرجه منها. وذهب فاستغاث بأهل السوس الأقصى فخرجوا إلى ابن أبي محلّي فقتلوه وهزموا عسكره شذر مذر. فكان آخر العهد به ورجع زيدان إلى ملكه.

٧،٣١ وحدّثونا أنّه كان ذات يوم عند أستاذه ابن مبارك قبل ذلك فورد عليه وارد حال فتحرك وجعل يقول أنا سلطان أنا سلطان. فقال له الأستاذ يا أحمد هب أنّك تكون سلطانًا ﴿إِنَّكَ لَن تَخْرِقَ ٱلْأَرْضَ وَلَن تَبْلُغَ ٱلْجِبَالَ طُولًا﴾.

٨،٣١ وفي يوم آخر وقع للفقراء سماع. فتحرّك فقير[١] وجعل يقول أنا سلطان أنا سلطان فتحرّك فقير آخر في ناحية وجعل يقول ثلاث سنين غير ربع ثلاث سنين غير ربع. وهذه هي مدّة ملكه. وقد رمزوا له ذلك فقالوا قام طيشاً ومات كبشاً. أي قام في تسعة عشر بعد ألف ومات في اثنين وعشرين بعدها.

٩،٣١ وزعموا أنّ إخوانه من الفقراء ذهبوا إليه حين دخل مراكش برسم زيارته وتهنئته. فلمّا كانوا بين يديه أخذوا يهنّئونه ويفرحون له بما حاز من الملك. وفيهم رجل ساكت لا يتكلّم. فقال ما شأنك لا تتكلّم؟ وألحّ عليه في الكلام. فقال له الرجل أنت اليوم سلطان فإن أمّنتني على أن أقول الحقّ قلته. فقال له أنت آمن فقل. فقال إنّ الكرة التي يلعب بها يتبعها المائتان وأكثر من خلفها وينكسر الناس وينجرحون وقد يموتون ويكثر الصياح والهول. فإذا فتّشت لم توجد بداخلها إلّا شراويط أي خرقاً بالية ملفوفة. فلمّا سمع ابن أبي محلّي هذا المثال وفهمه بكى وقال رمنا أن نحيي الدين فأتلفناه.

---

١ سقط من المخطوطات.

claiming he was the awaited savior, and that he was going to undertake jihad. He incited the hearts of the people and they followed him.

He entered Sijilmāsah, chased out the governor appointed by the Saʿdi kings, and took over the city. He then drove the Saʿdis out of the Darʿah Valley, pursuing them to Marrakesh. Ibn Abī Maḥallī defeated Zaydān ibn Aḥmad al-Manṣūr and drove him from the city. Zaydān sought help from the people deep in the south, who came out in force against Ibn Abī Maḥallī, killed him, and defeated his army, scattering it in all directions. This was the end of his affair, and Zaydān returned to power. 31.6

We have been told that one day before this happened, Ibn Abī Maḥallī was with his teacher Ibn Mubārak. He entered into a spiritual state, became agitated, and said, "I am the sultan, I am the sultan!" and his teacher said, "Aḥmad, suppose you were the sultan, «certainly thou wilt never tear the earth open, nor attain the mountains in height.»"[214] 31.7

On another occasion, some devotees experienced a state of spiritual exaltation. One became agitated and began saying, "I am the sultan! I am the sultan!" Another devotee who was nearby also became agitated, calling out, "Three years without a fourth, three years without a fourth!" This was the length of Ibn Abī Maḥallī's rule. They made a riddle out of his affair, saying, "He rose up rashly and died as a three-year-old ram." That is, he rose up in 1019 [1610] and died after that in 1022 [1613]. 31.8

They claim that his brethren from among the devotees went to him when he entered Marrakesh in order to visit and congratulate him. When they stood before him, they began to congratulate him and celebrate him for the power he had seized. Among them was a man who remained silent, not uttering a word. Ibn Abī Maḥallī said to him, urging him to speak, "Why won't you speak?" "Today you are the sultan," the man replied, "and if you guarantee my safety if I speak the truth, I will do so." "Granted—speak!" "This ball you are playing with will result in great slaughter and more. People will be broken and wounded; some may even die. Screaming and terror will prevail. If you examine the ball, you will find nothing but tatters—that is, wet, rolled-up rags." When Ibn Abī Maḥallī understood the imagery, he wept and said, "I wanted to revivify the faith; instead, I destroyed it." 31.9

١٠،٣١ واعلم أن هذه الدعوى أعني دعوى الفاطميّة بلوى قديمة كما أشار إلى ذلك بعض الأئمّة. وكان الشيعة ادّعوا ذلك لزيد بن عليّ. فلمّا قام على هشام ظفر به يوسف بن عمر فصلبه. فقال بعض شعراء بني مروان يخاطب الشيعة: [طويل]

صَلَبْنَا لَكُمْ زَيْداً عَلَى جِذْعِ نَخْلَةٍ وَلَمْ نَرَ مَهْدِيّاً عَلَى ٱلْجِذْعِ يُصْلَبُ

لله الأمر من قبل ومن بعد.[1]

١١،٣١ وأوّل من تظاهر بهذا جدّاً ببلاد المغرب فيما علمنا يهدي الموحّدين وهو أبو عبد الله محمّد بن تومرت السوسي. وكان رجلاً فقيهاً له رحلة إلى المشرق ولقي فيها المشايخ كالإمام الغزالي رضي الله عنه. فلمّا قفل إلى المغرب لقي في طريقه عبد المؤمن بن عليّ قد ارتحل في طلب العلم وهو شاب صغير. وكان عنده فيما يقال علم من علم الحدثان. فلمّا بصر به توسّم فيه أنّه صاحب الأمر فقال له اذهب معي وأنا أعلّمك ما تشاء من العلوم. فصحبه عبد المؤمن في دخوله إلى المغرب. فلمّا وصلوا إلى حضرة مراكش حرسها الله وجدوا فيها آخر المرابطين ووجدوا أموراً مختلفة كما هو المعهود في أذناب الدول. فدخل ابن تومرت وأظهر شيئاً ممّا حمل من العلوم العقليّة.

١٢،٣١ فأنكر أهل البلد ذلك وكانوا إذ ذاك أهل بادية. فوشوا به إلى صاحب الوقت فاستدعى وناظر حتّى ظهر عليهم فخلّى السلطان سبيله وبقي في البلد. ثمّ جعل يأمر بالمعروف وينهى عن المنكر. وشاع ذلك فأنهوا أمره ثانية إلى السلطان وأغروه به فأمر بإخراجه. فخرج إلى تلك الجبال وجعل يدعو إلى الدين وأقبل عليه الناس ثمّ تظاهر بأنّه هو المهدي. فلمّا اجتمع إليه الناس حضّهم على إعلاء الدين وجهاد المفسدين. فتقدّم بهم إلى مراكش وجرت بينهم وبين المرابطين حروب شديدة مات في خلالها بعد أن أوصى بعبد المؤمن وهيّأ الأمر له.

١ سقطت الجملة من ق، ط.

This claim—I mean the claim to be the savior descended from Fāṭimah—is, as has been described by one of the great religious scholars, an old calamity. The Shiʿah claimed this status for Zayd ibn ʿAlī. When he rose up against Hishām, Yusūf ibn ʿUmar defeated him and crucified him. One of the poets of the Banū Marwān recited as follows, addressing the Shiʿah on this occasion: 31.10

We crucified Zayd for you on the trunk of a palm tree:
We have never seen a savior crucified as he was.

Everything is God's to command.

The first person in Morocco to seriously profess to be a savior, as far as we know, was the leader of the Almohads, Abū ʿAbd Allāh Muḥammad ibn Tūmart al-Sūsī. He was a jurist who traveled to the East, where he met many scholars, including the exemplar al-Ghazālī, God be content with him.[215] On his return to Morocco he met ʿAbd al-Muʾmin ibn ʿAlī, who as a young man had traveled for his studies. According to popular account, Ibn Tūmart knew how to foretell thc future.[216] When Ibn Tūmart saw the signs that this man would be a ruler, he said to him, "Come with me, and I will teach you everything you want to know." So ʿAbd al-Muʾmin accompanied him to Morocco. When they reached Marrakesh, God protect it, they found the last Almoravids and saw that everything was in confusion, as is the case in the final days of any dynasty. Ibn Tūmart entered the city and exhibited some of what he knew of the rational sciences. 31.11

The local people, who at the time came from the countryside, criticized him for this and denounced him to the ruler. He invoked God and continued to argue until he defeated them. The sultan let him go his own way, and he remained in the region. He then began to command the right and forbid the wrong far and wide. They condemned his actions again to the sultan and urged him to do something. So, the sultan ordered that Ibn Tūmart be driven out. He retreated to the mountains and began summoning people to the faith from there. People came to him, and he said he was the savior. When people gathered around him, he urged them to elevate the faith and to struggle against the corrupt. He led them to Marrakesh and fierce battles took place between them and the Almoravids. He died in one of these battles after giving his testament to ʿAbd al-Muʾmin and entrusting rule to him. 31.12

فولي عبد المؤمن واستوسق الأمر له ولولده من بعده وهم أتباع المهدي مع كلّ من يشايعهم في أنّه هو المهدي من الطائفة التومرتيّة. وقد أنكر الفقهاء عليهم ذلك وضلّلوهم. ولا شكّ في ضلالهم في ذلك عند كلّ من يعترف بوجود المهدي في آخر الزمان. ١٣،٣١

وقد ألف بعد ذلك الجلال السيوطي كتابه العرف الوردي في أخبار المهدي والكشف في مجاوزة هذه الأمّة الألف. وبسط القول في ذلك بما فيه غنية من أن المهدي متأخّر حتّى يكون في آخر الزمان لوقت خروج الدجّال ونزول عيسى ابن مريم عليه السلام. وأنّه ليس هو ابن تومرت ولا أمثاله من كلّ من يدّعي ذلك إلى زماننا. وكنت لا أحسب أنّ للطائفة التومرتيّة في دعواهم أزيد من مجرد الدعوى وتقليد شيخهم المذكور. ١٤،٣١

فكان من غريب الاتّفاق أنّي منذ نظرت في كتب التصوّف وقع في يدي كتابان في هذا العلم ينسبان لأبي زيد عبد الرحمن اللجائي. أحدهما قطب العارفين والآخر شمائل الخصوص. ١٥،٣١

فكنت أستحسنهما مع العلم من نفسهما أنّ مؤلّفهما ليس من فحول العلماء. ولكن ما فيهما حسن المسلك وسهل المدرك. فكنت أتمنّى زيارة المؤلّف لاعتقادي أنّه من أهل الطريق. وكنت إذا ارتحلت لزيارة الشيخ عبد السلام بن مشيش رضي الله عنه أسأل عنه فأجده بعيداً عنّي حتّى إذا كان الحصار على مدينة فاس حرسها الله حين قتلوا القائد زيدان خرجت منها وأخذت على جبل بني زروال فإذا بجبل لجاية قريباً منّي. فأجمعت زيارته وتركت الركب وانخزلت إليه في نفر من أصحابي. ١٦،٣١

فصعدنا الجبل إليه وإذا هم يسمّونه سيدي عبد الرحمن التراري[1] فلمّا وصلنا إلى مقامه خرج إلينا أولاده فأنزلونا وأكرموا مثوانا. فلمّا اطمأنّ بنا المنزل وزرنا قالوا هل لك في أن نخرج إليك كتب الشيخ لتراها. فقلت نعم فأخرجوا الكتابين المذكورين ١٧،٣١

١ ط: التزاري.

ʿAbd al-Muʾmin, thus invested with power, consolidated his rule and the rule of his son after him. These were the followers of the savior along with all the like-minded members of the Tūmart faction. The jurists denounced this belief and declared they were in error. For all who acknowledge the coming of the savior at the end of time, there can be no doubt, of course, about the error of Ibn Tūmart's followers on this score. 31.13

The great al-Suyūṭī later wrote his book *Rose-Scented Perfume: Accounts of the Savior*, revealing the transgressions of the millennial community. In this work, he explained clearly how the savior will come later, at the end of time, when the al-Dajjāl appears and Jesus son of Mary, peace be upon him, descends. Neither Ibn Tūmart, nor others like him who up to today have claimed this status, are the savior. I had never believed that in making these claims the Tūmart faction was doing anything other than proselytizing and unthinkingly following their teacher. 31.14

Now, it was a strange coincidence that when I was studying works on Sufism, two books on this subject attributed to Abū Zayd ʿAbd al-Raḥmān al-Lajāʾī came into my hands. One was called *The Axis of the Spiritually Elect*, and the other *The Excellent Qualities of the Essence*. I had a good opinion of these works, in spite of realizing that their author was not the best scholar. And yet, the material was well put and easy to understand. 31.15

I hoped to visit the author's grave, believing him to be one of the people of the path. When I visited the tomb of Shaykh ʿAbd al-Salām ibn Mashīsh, God be content with him, I asked about it, and learned that he was a long way away. Later, when Fez, God protect it, was besieged and the leader Zaydān ibn ʿUbayd killed, I left, heading for the Banū Zirwāl mountains, and found that I was near Mount Lajāiyyah, so I tagged a visit onto my trip. I got off my steed and clambered up with one of my companions. 31.16

We climbed the mountain to his grave—there they call him ʿAbd al-Raḥmān al-Tarārī. When we arrived at his resting place, his descendants came to greet us, and honored us by hosting us in their home. Once we were settled in and had spent some time together, they said, "Would you like us to bring out the teacher's books for you to peruse?" "Yes," I said, and they brought out the two books I mentioned above. They pleased me, and I inferred that he was indeed the author. Then they brought out a thick third volume. I opened it and saw he had named it *The Most Brilliant Meaning Regarding the Most Honorable Savior*. When I saw this I thought that he was speaking of the awaited savior, 31.17

فلمّا رأيتهما سررت بهما واستدللت بذلك على أنّه هو ذاك وأنّه هو المؤلّف لهما. وأخرجوا كتابًا ثالثًا مجلّدًا ضخمًا ففتحته فإذا هو يسمّيه المقصد الأسنى في المهدي الأقنى. فلمّا رأيت ذلك ظننت أنّه يتكلّم في المهدي المنتظر على نحو ما تكلّم عليه الأئمّة. وإذا هو يخرج أحاديث لعبد الرزاق ويذكر حسابًا يتضمّن ظهوره إثر المائة الخامسة. وإذا هو يصفه ويذكر أحواله وإذا كلامه في ابن تومرت المذكور وإذا هو من الطائفة التومرتيّة. وذكر في أثناء الكتاب المذكور أنّه امتحن على يد قضاة الوقت في ذلك حتّى دعي إلى فاس ثمّ إلى مراكش وأنّه أنقذه الله من المحنة ورجع إلى بلده سالمًا.

١٨،٣١ فلمّا رأيت ذلك استضحكت في نفسي وقلت كما قال أبو علي الفاسي[١] حين وجد الياء منقوطة. ضاعت خطواتنا واستعجلت القيام والخروج عن ذلك المقام ولم أنتظر ما يضعون من طعام وتخلّصت بالاعتذار بأصحابي الذين خلفت بعدي في الدار. ولمّا فصلنا عنهم تأمّلت فقلت حصل العلم بأنّ هذا الرجل من تلك الطائفة والعلم بأنّ تلك الطائفة قد كان فيها من يحتجّ لدعواهم الباطلة من أهل العلم. وهاتان فائدتان غريبتان فلم تضع الخطوات مع أنّ الخَطْب سهل والمجتهد مصيب مأجور أو مخطئ معذور. [لله الأمر من قبل ومن بعد.][٢]

١،٣٢ وإذ قد ألممنا بذكر الرياسة والشهرة وضدّيهما وذلك ممّا يبتلى به العامّ والخاصّ مع إشكاله والتباسه إلّا على البصير. فلنشر إلى شرح ذلك باختصار حتّى يكون الإنسان منه على محجّة واضحة في رشده وغيّه واستقامته وانحرافه في سعيه. فاعلم أنّ في كلّ من الرياسة والشهرة وعدم ذلك شهوة للنفس ونفرة ومصلحة في الدين والدنيا أو مفسدة.

٢،٣٢ فمن أُلهِم المصلحة في الرياسة أو في الشهرة وسلم من المفسدة ومن الشهوة وأصاب الإمكان فقد حصل على الشرف في الدارين. وفي مثله يقال المؤمنون أو

١ ط: الفارسي. ٢ سقطت الجملة من ق، ط.

the way prominent religious scholars do. But he included narratives from ʿAbd al-Razzāq[217] and gave accounts of the savior's appearance in the fifth [eleventh] century, describing him and his circumstances. It was clear that this was about Ibn Tūmart and that he was part of the Tūmart faction. In the book, he mentioned that he was tried for this by the judges of the day, including being summoned to Fez and then to Marrakesh, and that God saved him from persecution and returned him safely to his region.

Seeing this, I laughed to myself and said the same thing Abū ʿAlī al-Fāsī said when he found the letter *yāʾ* with diacritical marks: We have gone astray.[218] I hastened to leave the place without waiting for the food. I made my apologies to the companions I was leaving behind in the house, and left. Once gone, I reflected and said to myself: I have learned from these writings that this man belonged to a faction among whom were scholars who had been won over by its false propaganda. These are two curious lessons here: (1) Despite the matter being easy, you misstepped, and (2) the qualified jurist is rewarded when correct and is forgiven when he errs. Everything is God's to command. **31.18**

Since we have already broached the subject of leadership and fame and their opposites—matters that affect both the common folk and the elite by causing confusion and doubt in all but those with deep insight—let us expound briefly on the subject so that people can acquire a clear method to distinquish both their moral actions and their errors, their good behavior and their going astray. Know that the ego can either desire the presence or absence of leadership and fame, or be averse to either, and that in this regard, both in this world and the next, are matters that benefit and corrupt. **32.1**

Those inspired to work for the common interest through leadership or fame, and able to achieve this while being preserved from desire and corrupting influence, have achieved honor in both worlds. It has been said of such people: "The state of the believers—or the pious—is strong; how do you think their leader will be?" If such a person does not possess this implied quality **32.2**

المتّقون بخير فكيف بإمامهم. وإن لم يتوفر له ذلك فإن أنفقت له المصلحة والإمكان أصبح كالسراج يضيء للناس وهو يحترق. وفيه يقال إنّ الله يؤيّد هذا الدين بالرجل الفاجر وإن اتّفقت له المفسدة والإمكان أصبح من الذين يفسدون في الأرض ولا يصلحون. وفي أمره ورد أنَّ هَذَا الأمْرَ يَكُونُ نُبُوءَةً ثُمَّ خِلافَةً ثُمَّ مُلكًا ثُمَّ عُتُوًّا وَفَسَاداً في الأرْضِ.

٣،٣٢ وهو الموجود اليوم. وكثير من الحمقى في زماننا يشتكون الجور ويطلبون العدل ولم يدروا أنّ الجور قد مضى مع الملوك بعدما مضى العدل مع الخلفاء ولم يبق إلّا الفساد. فيا ليت الناس وقف لهم الأمر في الجور فيعيشوا. وإن لم ينفق له الإمكان فهو الفضيحة إن أبدى صفحة عنقه والغمّ والوسواس إن شرق بريقه. أمّا إن لم يلهم المصلحة وإنّما جمحت به الشهوة أو قصد المفسدة فلا سؤال عليه.

٤،٣٢ أمّا شهوة الناس في الرياسة مثلاً فواضحة لما مرّ غير مرّة من تعشّقها لصفات الألوهيّة. ولذا يقال دعوى فرعون الألوهيّة في ضمير كلّ أحد مع تعشّق ما يتوهّم من ثمرات ذلك من التنعّم والترفّه والاحتواء على الدنيا وأهلها. ونفرتها عن ذلك بتوقّع ما فيه عادة من المتاعب والمعاطب وإيثار راحة القلب والبدن. وتشتعل الشهوة وتتقوّى بعلوّ الهمّة في الدنيا وقوّة الحرص وشهامة النفس وتضعف بضعف ذلك. ومصلحة ذلك في الدنيا إطفاء الفتن وإخماد الإحن وقمع البغاة وإغاثة ملهوف وإنصاف مظلوم وتهدين السبل. كما قال عبد الله بن مبارك رضي الله عنه:

[بسيط]

لَوْلَا ٱلْخِلَافَةُ لَمْ تَأْمَنْ لَنَا سُبُلٌ   وَكَانَ أَضْعَفُنَا نَهْبًا لِأَقْوَانَا

٥،٣٢ وجباية الأموال وتحصينها وقسم الأرزاق على أهلها إلى غير ذلك. وفي الدين إقامة الصلاة والزكاة والجهاد ونشر العلم وكفاية أهله ونحو ذلك. وفي مطلق الشهرة في

to a sufficient extent, then both the common good and his power have been squandered, and he becomes like a lantern that guides people while he himself burns up. It has been said of such men, “God may indeed strengthen this faith through a profligate, but if power and corruption come together in him, then he will become someone who wreaks corruption in the land, and who turns away from right action.” It has also been said of such a person’s case, “Leadership was first with the prophets, then the caliphs, then the kings, and then it devolved to arrogance and corruption throughout the land!”

This is the situation today. Many imbeciles in our time complain of tyranny and seek justice while ignoring the fact that tyranny has already disappeared with kings and justice with caliphs. Nothing is left but corruption. Would that people still lived under tyranny—they then would prosper! When such a person has not been given the ability to lead, it leads to tragedy if he shows himself vulnerable, or, if his star rises, to sorrow and idle talk. When such a person is not motivated by the common good, but the desire or intention to corrupt has overtaken him, then there is no need to discuss him. 32.3

Now, it is clear that people desire leadership due to it being linked to their love for God’s attributes. It is said, accordingly, that Pharaoh’s assertion of divinity resides in the conscience of all of us, along with an infatuation with what we imagine to be the fruits of a blessed and easy life, as well as possession of this world and those living in it. Conversely, people’s aversion to leadership lies in their anticipation of the hardships and calamities it entails, and in their preference for emotional and physical comfort. This desire is kindled and nurtured when they place importance in this world and by the power of their greed and the boldness of the ego, and it is weakened when these lessen. The common good produced by this in this world lies in eliminating social strife, ending feuds, suppressing hatred, saving the anxious, treating the oppressed justly, and ensuring calm on the roads. As ʿAbd Allāh ibn Mubārak said, God be content with him: 32.4

If not for the caliphate, our roads would not be safe
and the weak among us would be spoils for the powerful.

Leadership consists also in the levying of taxes on commodities and storing them, in distributing provisions to those in need, and the like. In matters of religion it consists of establishing communal prayer and collecting alms, carrying out jihad, disseminating knowledge, and supporting believers in such 32.5

الدنيا السعي في مصالح الناس والمسادّة بينهم وغير ذلك. وفي الدين نصح المستنصحين وتعليم المتعلّمين وهداية الضالّين وتربية المريدين وغير ذلك. وفي حديث الهداية[١] يقول صلّى الله عليه وسلّم لعليّ كرّم الله وجهه لأنْ يهدي الله بك رجلاً واحداً خير لك من حمر النّعم. والمفسدة في ذلك في الجملة ظلم العباد والسعي في الأرض بالفساد وتضييع الحقوق وإظهار العقوق وإضلال الناس والتحريف والإلباس وشهوة النفس في الخمول والضعة إيثار الراحة والسلامة.

٦،٣٢ كما مرّ في مقابله: [طويل]

وَقَائِلَةٍ مَا لِي أَرَاكَ مُجَانِبًا أُمُورًا وَفِيهَا لِلتِّجَارَةِ مَرْبَحُ؟
فَقُلْتُ لَهَا مَا لِي بِرِبْحِكِ حَاجَةٌ فَنَحْنُ أُنَاسٌ بِٱلسَّلَامَةِ نَفْرَحُ

٧،٣٢ ونفرتها عنها لعدم الحظّ السابق والمصلحة في ذلك بانتفاء المفسدة التي في المقابل. وذلك كلّه واضح فقد تبيّن ما هو حظّ النفس في البابين. فقد تدعو إلى جانبٍ موهِمةً أنّها تريد استحصال مصلحته والتخلّص من المفسدة في مقابله. وهي إنّما تريد حظّها الطبيعي منه والشيطان يحثّها إلى ذلك طلباً لحصول المفسدة التي فيه وفوات المصلحة التي في المقابل. وعلى البصير الحازم أن يزُمَّ نفسه بزمام التقوى ويزنها بميزان العدل وينتقدها بسراج الهدى ويصفّيها من بهرج الهوى.

٨،٣٢ فإذا دعته مثلاً إلى طلب الرياسة والقيام بالأمر موهمة أنّها تريد جمع الكلمة وإقامة الشريعة وبسط العدل وكفّ الظلم ونحو ذلك فلا ثق بها في هذه الدعوى حتّى يمتحنها. فإنّها تدّعي أنّها لم ترد متعة الدنيا وإنّما طلبت استحصال الأجر والدرجة عند الله تعالى. فيكفيك في امتحانها شيئان أحدهما أن تعاقدها فيما تدعو إليه بأن تقوم فيه أشعث أغبر لا تنال ممّا يناله من دخل ذلك من أهل الدنيا عادة من مطعوم

١ ق، ط: الراية.

acts. The height of fame in this world results from addressing the needs of the people, providing leadership to them and such. In matters of religion it results from giving advice to those who need it, teaching those who require instruction, guiding those who have strayed, mentoring spiritual disciples, and so forth. In the "guidance hadith," the Prophet, God bless and keep him, said to ʿAlī, God honor his countenance, "It is better for you for God to guide one man through you than for you to possess a red prize camel." The things that lead to the corruption of leadership can be summarized as follows: oppressing worshippers, spreading corruption on the earth, usurping rights, promoting disobedience, leading people astray, spreading perversion and confusion, and the desire of the ego for the indolence and humility that comes with being peacefully at ease.

Regarding this, it has been said: 32.6

A woman said to me, Why is it I see you avoid
business matters that would make you a profit?
I have no need for your profit, I replied.
We are people who delight in being at ease.

The ego's aversion to leadership comes from not possessing the allotment 32.7
mentioned above, which has the advantage of no associated corruption. This is clear: We have in two preceding chapters clarified the nature of the fulfillment of the ego. Now, you might hypothetically claim that the ego desires to achieve the benefit of this fufillment and, correspondingly, to rid itself of corrupting influence. On the contrary, it desires its natural allotment, and in so doing Satan prompts it to seek the corruption that it contains along with the corresponding absence of benefit. The determined and clear-sighted should restrain the ego with the reins of piety, weigh it with the scales of justice, scrutinize it with the lamp of guidance, and cleanse it of the dregs of vain desire.

If, for example, the ego urges a person to seek leadership and rule, and gives 32.8
the impression that it wishes for harmony and the establishment of the revealed law, to extend justice and constrain oppression and the like, then it should not be trusted until it is tested. If the ego claims that it does not desire worldly pleasures and is instead after reward and acknowledgment from Exalted God, then it suffices for you to test it in two matters: First, you should make an agreement with the ego regarding what it calls you to do: You will undertake to do this, disheveled and covered in dust; you will abstain from what is normally

ولا ملبوس ولا مركوب ولا منكوح ولا مسكون ولا عظمة. وأنّك تكون كواحد من الناس لا تميّز عنهم إلّا بما تحمّلت من المشاقّ والمتاعب والهموم في مصالحهم كما كان حال الخلفاء رضي الله عنهم. حتّى إنّك لو كنت في رفاهية قبل ذلك تركتها شغلاً عنها.

٩،٣٢ كما كان فعل عمر بن عبد العزيز رضي الله عنه. فقد حكي أنّه قبل الخلافة اشتريت له حلّة بنحو أربعين أو سبعين ألفًا. فجسّها فقال ما أحسنها لولا خشونة فيها! ولمّا ولي الأمر اشتريت له حلّة بنحو أربعة دوانق فجسّها فقال ما أحسنها لولا لينها! فقيل له ما هذا يا أمير المؤمنين؟ فقال إنّ نفسي ذوّاقة توّاقة كلّما ذاقت مكانة تشوّقت إلى غيرها فلمّا حصلت الخلافة تاقت إلى ما عند الله تعالى. وسمع البكاء بداره حين ولي. فدخل مسلمة بن عبد الملك إلى أخته فاطمة[١] زوجة أمير المؤمنين فسألها عن ذلك. فأخبرته أنّ أمير المؤمنين دخل عليهن فقال إنّي قد شغلني عنكنّ ما نزل بي يعني من الخلافة فمن أحبّت منكنّ أن تصبر على ذلك فلتصبر رضي الله عنه وجُعلنا في حماه.

١٠،٣٢ ولمّا انعقد له الأمر وكان قد تعب فيه هم بأن يَقِيلَ فذهب ليدخل الدار. فقال له ابنه عبد الملك بن عمر رضي الله عنهما ما تريد أن تفعل يا أبت؟ فقال له يا بنيّ إنّي قد سهرت من هذا الهمّ فأردت أن أصيب راحة. فقال له وأين حقوق الناس؟ فقال يا بنيّ إلى الظهر. فقال يا أبت ومن لك بأن تعيش إلى الظهر؟ فأخذه وقبّل ما بين عينيه وقال الحمد لله الذي خلق منّي من يعينني على ديني فترك القيلولة وخرج إلى الناس. وقال من كانت له مظلمة فليأتنا. وجعل يردّ على الناس ضياعهم وأموالهم وينصفهم ممّا وقع عليهم من الظلم قبله. [خفيف]

هٰكَذَا هٰكَذَا وَإِلّا فَلَا لَا طُرُقُ ٱلْجِدِّ غَيْرُ طُرُقِ ٱلْمُزَاحِ

---

١ يزيد ق "بنت عبد الملك".

attained in the way of food, clothing, steed, spouse, home, or the greatness that accrues to such people of this world who embark upon such matters; you will be like those lacking in distinction, save for the trials, hardships, and worries they endured in their affairs, as was the case with the caliphs, God be pleased with them, to the extent that if you had previously enjoyed refinement you will renounce it due to your preoccupation with other matters.

This was the case of ʿUmar ibn ʿAbd al-ʿAzīz, God be pleased with him. It is said that before he became caliph he was brought a robe worth forty thousand or seventy thousand. He felt it and said, "If it were not rough, there would be no better!" When he came to power, a robe was bought for him for four *dāniq*s. He felt it and said, "If it were not soft, nothing would be better than this!" "What do you mean, Commander of the Faithful?" he was asked. "My ego has refined tastes and is desirous," he answered. "Whenever it attains one place it longs after another, and when I attained the caliphate it desired to be with Exalted God." Lamentation was heard in his house when he assumed power, so Maslamah ibn ʿAbd al-Malik went to his sister Fāṭimah, a wife of the Commander of the Faithful, to ask about this. She told him that the Commander of the Faithful, God be content with him, had come to them and said, "What has beset me"—that is, the caliphate—"has distracted me from you, so let anyone who wishes to endure this, do so. We are in His protection." 32.9

Once his rulership was established and he had grown weary, he wished to rest. He went to his house, and his son ʿAbd al-Malik ibn ʿUmar, God be content with them both, asked, "What do you intend to do, Father?" "My son," he replied, "I was awake all night with this responsibility, and I want to rest." His son asked, "And what about the rights of the people?" and he replied, "My son, let me sleep until noon." "Father, can you trust that you will live until noon?" responded the son, and ʿUmar took ʿAbd al-Malik's face, kissed him on the forehead, and said, "God be thanked for giving me a son who reminds me of my faith." He abandoned his nap and went out to the people, saying, "Anyone who has been wronged, let him come forward." He began to return possessions and other losses to their rightful owners, and to treat them with justice after the oppression they had experienced before him. 32.10

In this fashion, and not in another,
the ways of the earnest are not those of the frivolous.

١١،٣٢ ومن هذا سئل إمامنا مالك رضي الله عنه أيقاتل عن الإمام؟ قال إن كان كعمر ابن عبد العزيز فنعم. وإلّا فدعه ينتقم الله من الظالم بالظالم حتّى ينتقم من الجميع. فإذا عرضت على نفسك هذا الشرط فتنبّه إليها فإن انشرحت له بأوّل عارض فعسى أن تصدّق. وإن رأيت في أديمها انكماشاً ما فهي كذّابة تريد أن تتذرّع بتسويلتها الباطلة إلى اقتناص اللذّات والانهماك في الشهوات. ولا تغترّ بانشراح يظهر منها ثانيَ حالٍ لأنّه يكون متكلّفاً احتيالاً.

١٢،٣٢ الثاني أن تقدّر أن لو ظهر غيرك في الوجود ممّن يقوم بهذا الأمر مثل ما ترجو أو أفضل. هب تكتفي بذلك وتحمد الله تعالى على ما كفاك مئونة ما تريد أم لا. فإن اكتفيت بذلك وعلمت أنّ المراد انتفاع المسلمين وصلاحهم وقد حصل بلا مشقّة منك فقد تصدّق وإن وجدت نفسك مع ذلك مضرّة على طلب ذلك متنكّدة من فواته فاعلم أنّها كاذبة إنّما تطلب حقّها. فإن زعمت أنّها إنّما طلبت الفوز بدرجة ذلك عند الله تعالى وإنّما تنكّدت من فواتها فاعرض عليها أنّه لو حصل ذلك أو أرفع منه وهي بين يدي الله تعالى في خلوتها مراقبة له لهجة بذكره سارحة في رياض المعارف ليلاً ونهاراً هل تطلب هذه الخطّة؟ فإن قالت إذن لا حاجة لي بها إذ أصبت الغنيمة الباردة ووقعت على الدرّ النفيس فعسى أن تكون صادقة وإن أصرّت على الطلب فهي كاذبة هذا على أنّ دسائس النفس أدقّ شيء وأغمضه. فقد تسخو بالحظوظ الحسيّة كلّها حتّى تتوهّم أنها صادقة. وإنّما تريد حظوظاً معنويّة مثل الصيت والذكر في الدنيا على ما وقع للرهبان نسأل الله السلامة من شرّها.

١٣،٣٢ ثمّ إن ألفيتها صادقة مع الامتحانات وما أغرب وجود ذلك فانظر حينئذ في الإمكان. فإنّ القيام بذلك متوقّف عادة على أمور كالعقل والقوّة والعدد والعدّة والمال والإخوان والأعوان فإن تيسّر ذلك فمن علامة الإذن التيسير. ولا يكاد يتّفق ذلك ولا سيما فيما نحن فيه من آخر الزمان الذي قلّ خيره وكثر شرّه. وإن اتفق فلا يكاد

Our exemplar Mālik, God be content with him, was asked whether one should fight for the caliph. "If the caliph is like ʿUmar ibn ʿAbd al-ʿAzīz," he replied, "then one should fight for him. If not, then let God exercise vengeance on the unjust through the unjust, until he does so on all." When you present this condition to your ego, pay close attention to it, for if the ego is relieved when first exposed to it, then it is likely it is being truthful. If you see on its surface any wrinkle, know that it is deceptive, seeking an excuse with its empty enticements to take advantage of the self, to dedicate itself to its desires. Do not be deceived by the ego being relieved at a later stage, for this is contrivance and trickery. **32.11**

The second way you can test it is if someone else undertakes this matter in the fashion that your ego desires or in a better fashion: Does it rush to be content with this, thanking Exalted God for what He has provided? Does it desire this or not? If it is content with someone else undertaking the matter, knowing that the true goal is the benefit and well-being of Muslims, and that attitude comes about without any qualms on your part, then it may be truthful. If, despite this, you find your ego compelling you to seek after power, and are miserable at the chance of it passing by, then know that it is dishonest and that it is indeed aspiring to power for itself. If it claims that it actually sought victory in order to achieve a degree of regard from Exalted God and that it was miserable at losing this possibility, present it with the argument that if it achieved this or more while it was in a spiritual retreat before Exalted God, contemplating Him, constantly mentioning His name, roaming freely day and night in the garden of spiritual knowledge—would it still be content with this plan? If it then says, "I have no need of it if I have already won the ready spoils and acquired the most precious pearl," then it may be sincere. If it persists in seeking after power, then it is deceitful. This is because the machinations of the ego are most subtle and obscure. The ego may confer such tangible fortunes as to convince you to believe it is sincere. Instead, as happened with the monks, it actually desires intangible fortunes such as fame and renown in this world. God preserve us from its evil! **32.12**

If, after testing it, you find the ego to be sincere—and there is nothing more wondrous than this—then look into the feasibility of seeking to rule. For doing so is generally dependent on factors such as reason, power, troops, goods, money, brethren, and supporters. If all this can be easily arranged, the ease is a sign of permission to do so. But these conditions hardly ever obtain, **32.13**

يتّفق إلّا بعد فتن ومفاسد لا يقوم بها ما يرجى من مصلحة. فلا يصل إلى الطاعة على زعمه إلّا بعد اقتحام معاص عظام.

١٤،٣٢ وما أشبهه حينئذ بما شاع في ألسنة المتطبّبين من أنّه لا يكون الرجل طبيباً حتّى يعمل مقبرة أي ممّن يقتله بعلاجه الفاسد. فلا كانت هذه الصنعة ولا كان صاحبها ولكنّ الناس مبتلون مقوّدون بسلاسل القدر لينتظم أمر الدنيا على حسب ما شاء الحكيم العليم. نسأله سبحانه أن يصرفنا فيما فيه رضاه. وكذا ما نحن فيه. وإن لم تر إمكاناً أصلاً أو لم تره على مقتضى المصلحة الشرعيّة فخلّ عنها واعلم أنّك لست من أهلها. [بسيط]

دَعِ ٱلْمَكَارِمَ لَا تَرْحَلْ لِبُغْيَتِهَا وَٱقْعُدْ فَإِنَّكَ أَنْتَ ٱلطَّاعِمُ ٱلْكَاسِي

١٥،٣٢ غيره: [بسيط]

وَدَعْ غِمَارَ ٱلْعُلَى لِلْمُقْدِمِينَ عَلَى رُكُوبِهَا وَٱقْتَنِعْ مِنْهُنَّ بِٱلْبَلَلِ[١]

١٦،٣٢ ولا تغترّ بصلاح نيّتك وتمنيك الخير وتظنّ أنك تُعطى لا محالة ما تمنى فهيهات! [بيسط]

مَا كُلُّ مَا يَتَمَنَّى ٱلْمَرْءُ يُدْرِكُهُ تَجْرِي ٱلرِّيَاحُ بِمَا لَا تَشْتَهِي ٱلسُّفُنُ

١٧،٣٢ واعلم أنّك متى رمت النهوض إلى هذا الأمر بلا عُدّته تكون كالمجبوب يروم أن يتزوّج ليولد له ولد صالح يدعو له أو ليكثر الأمّة المحمّديّة بنسله. فهذا أحمق مبين وحسبه أن يحتسب على الله تعالى نيّته الصالحة فعسى أن يعطى بها خيراً. وفي الحديث نيّة المؤمن أبلغ من عمله. وفي الحديث من همّ بحسنة فلم يعملها كتبت له حسنة. وكذا أنت في هذا كلّه. وانظر إلى الملك الذي أشرف على تلّ ونظر إلى

١ ط: اليأس.

especially in the end of days we now live through, in which there is little good and much evil. If they do obtain, then rulership can only be acquired after strife and heinous acts that no one who desires the public good would undertake. For, according to what is claimed, no one achieves obedience without committing many sins.

Nothing encapsulates this better than a saying that is widespread among aspiring physicians—namely, that a man cannot be a physician until he has produced a cemetery, that is, of people he killed through his flawed practice. This is not an example of the art, nor of its practitioner, yet people are afflicted and bound by the chains of fate. Let the affairs of this world be arranged according to the wish of the One Who is Knowing and Wise. We ask that He, praise Him, direct us according to His pleasure. This is our state of affairs. If power is not attainable, or you cannot acquire it in accord with what is good for the community according to revelation, then know that you are not one who would attain it. 32.14

Abandon virtue, do not hasten to achieve it;
stay seated, you are both well-fed and clothed.[219]

Another poet has said:[220] 32.15

Abandon the depths to those who ride into them
and be content with the shallows.

Do not be deceived by the soundness of your intention or by your desire for good, and believe that you will inevitably be given what you desire! How impossible and preposterous that would be! 32.16

A man does not achieve everything he wishes for,
Nor do the winds blow according to the ships' desires.[221]

When you set out to advocate for justice without the necessary preparation, you are like a castrated man setting out to get married in order to have an upright, praiseworthy son or to increase the community of Muḥammad through his offspring. This is clear stupidity. His actions will be judged by Exalted God according to the purity of his intention and may well bring him reward. In the Hadith, we find: "A believer's intention is more eloquent than his acts," and "Whoever intends to do a good deed but does not act on it, a good deed is nevertheless recorded for him." Precisely the same applies 32.17

جنوده تحته فأعجبوه. فتمنّى أن لو كان حاضراً مع النبيّ صلّى الله عليه وسلّم لينصره. فرحمه الله تعالى بفضله على هذه النيّة.

١٨،٣٢ فانوِ أنت أيضاً أن لو كانت لك قوّة على إظهار الشريعة وإحياء السنّة وإخماد البدعة وحسم الباطل وإغاثة الملهوف ونصرة المظلوم وإقامة ميزان العدل وإصلاح العباد والبلاد فعسى أن تنال بهذه النيّة خيراً. وقف هاهنا وطبّ نفساً عمّا وراءه. فلا تلج تلك المضايق ولا تتبّع تلك الطرائق. وإذا فهمت الدسيسة في هذا القسم فافهمها في غيره والله الموفّق. لله الأمر من قبل ومن بعد.

١،٣٣ حدّثنا شيخنا العلاّمة أبو بكر بن الحسن التطافي رحمه الله قال دخلت على شيخنا العلاّمة أبي بكر بن الحسين التطافي رحمه الله. قال دخلت على شيخنا العلاّمة الزاهد أبي محمّد عبد الله بن عليّ بن طاهر الحسنيّ رضي الله عنه يوماً وهو إذ ذاك بقرية أولاد الحاج من بلد مضغرة. فقال لي إنّ بني يفوس وهم قرية من الخنق وقع بينهم قتال. قال فقلت يا سيّدي أجاء أحد من هنالك؟ قال لا ولكن أخبرني بذلك قلبي وقلبي لا يكذب عليّ فقد جرّبته. وكان بينه وبين هؤلاء مرحلة. قال فجاء الخبر بعد ذلك بوقوع الأمر كما أخبر به.

٢،٣٣ وقد رأيت أن أثبت في هذا المعنى كلاماً تتميماً للفائدة كما هو سبيل هذا الكتاب كلّه. وأنا أبرأ إلى السامع من نفسي فلا يتوهّم أنّي من أهل هذا المضمار وأنّي خبرت عن وجدان وتكلّمت عن ذوق وبيّنت عن مشاهدة. كلا. وإنّما أقرّر شيئاً أتعقّله فهماً أو شيئاً وجدته في كتبهم مشروحاً. ولا أدّعي أنّه ليس في حكمة الله البالغة وموهبته السابغة أزيد من ذلك. بل أذكر ما انتهى إليه فهمي فأقول إنّ الغيب المدّعى الاطّلاع عليه.

to you. Consider the king who climbed a hill and looked out over his troops below him and was pleased by them. He wished he could have been present at the Prophet's side, God bless and keep him, in order to be of help. For this intention, Exalted God had mercy on him through His grace.

You too ought to resolve that should you have the power to establish the revealed faith, to revive Prophetic example, to eradicate innovation and put an end to all that is vain, to aid the sorrowful and help the oppressed, to establish the scales of justice and the well-being of both Muslims and their territories, you should do so—you could attain good with this intention. Stop at that point, and treat your ego according to its underlying desire. Do not persist in taking up these difficulties, and do not follow where they lead. If you understand the deception involved, God help you to understand it in other matters too. Everything is God's to command. 32.18

Our illustrious shaykh Abū Bakr ibn al-Ḥasan al-Taṭāfī, God have mercy on him, related the following to us: I entered the presence of our illustrious shaykh Abū Bakr ibn al-Ḥusayn al-Taṭāfī, God have mercy on him, who said: One day I entered the presence of our illustrious shaykh, the ascetic Abū Muḥammad ibn ʿAbd Allāh ibn ʿAlī ibn Ṭāhir al-Ḥasanī, God be content with him, when he was in the village of Awlād al-Ḥājj in the land of the Maḍgharah. "Fighting has broken out among the Banū Yafūs, who constitute a village in al-Khanq," he said, and I said, "My Lord, did someone come with news?" "No," he said, "but my heart informed me of this and my heart does not lie to me—I have tested it." There was a day's travel between him and them. Soon after, news reached us that matters transpired as he had related. 33.1

I have seen fit to corroborate reports that deal with this issue and that are beneficial, which is the goal of this book as a whole. I am not claiming to the listener that I am among those who have this experience or that I have reported my own passion, or my mystical rapture and vision. Not at all. Rather, I am reporting on what I have understood through reason, or on what I have found described in books. I do not claim that this is not part of God's great wisdom, and His abundant generosity encompasses even more. I mention only what I have been able to understand and maintain that what is unseen requires examination. 33.2

٣،٣٣ وهو ما لا يعلمه عامّة الناس قسمان. قسم متقرّر في نفسه وللعقول وصول إليه وقد يدركه بعض العقول دون بعض. وذلك كصفات الله تعالى وأسمائه وحكمته في أرضه وسمائه وأحكام المعاد وغير ذلك. وكذا كلّ علم مستنبط في الأصول والفروع وغير ذلك فهذا اطّلاع صحيح. ولكن لا يسمّى في الاصطلاح كشفاً نعم هو الكشف الصحيح النافع وسنشير إليه آخر الترجمة إن شاء الله. وقسم مرجعه الموهبة ولكن لا مجال فيه للعقول. ويكون إمّا بلا تقدّم سبب يناسبه كحال مجذوب لم يجر له سلوك وحال نائم كذلك. وإمّا مع تقدّم سبب من رياضة وتصفية أو طلب مثلاً. ثمّ هذا القسم إمّا أن يكن مناماً أو شبه منام بوجود غيبة أو يقظة.

٤،٣٣ أمّا المنام فيكون إمّا بمشاهدة الأمر على ما هو عليه وهي الرؤيا المستغنية عن التعبير وإمّا بمشاهدة مثاله وهي الرؤيا التي تعبر. وإمّا بسماع خطاب أو آية أو قراءتها ونحو ذلك. ولا حاجة إلى بيان حقيقة الرؤيا لأنّ ذلك مستوفى في علم التعبير. وأمّا الغيبة فأن يشاهد فيها شيء أيضاً أو مثاله أو يسمع الخطاب أو نحو ذلك. وكون المشاهدة حينئذ بالعين الباصرة أو بعين القلب أمر محتمل. ولا حاجة إلى التعرّض لتحقيقه فإنّه لا يتعلّق به غرض.

٥،٣٣ وأمّا اليقظة فبأن يرى الشيء بعينه إن كان ممّا يرى أو مثاله. أو يراه بقلبه إمّا بأن يتجلّى له كرؤية البصر أو يخطر فيه أنّه كذا. أو يحدث به وقد يرى الشيء مكتوباً في اللوح المحفوظ أو في الصحف المستنسخة يقظة أو غيبة أو مناماً أو مكتوباً على صفحة جدار أو على جبين السائل أو غير ذلك. وقد يفهم ذلك من صوت يسمعه أو فعل أو حال يراه لغيره أو لنفسه أو نحو ذلك. فهذا النوع كلّه هو الذي يراد بالكشف والمكاشفة في عرف الناس. وقد يختصّ ذلك بالقسم الثاني والثالث أو بالثالث فقط. ولمّا كان أمراً معشوقاً للإنسان وذلك من وجهين أحدهما من حيث كونه علماً والعلم هو غذاء الروح وكلّما كان أغرب كان أشهى وأعجب.

What the common people do not know of this matter is in two parts. The first part is self-evident and rational minds can grasp it, some perceiving it, others not. This includes the attributes and names of Exalted God, as well as His wisdom on His earth and in His heaven, the rulings of the world to come, and so on. In this way, every type of knowledge can be traced to its roots and branches and so forth—this is proper examination. What is given the label "unveiling" is not the type of unveiling that we will refer to at the end of the section, God willing, and that is true and most beneficial. The basis of the second part is a bestowed ability in which rationality has no place. It occurs without any prior cause accompanying it, such as the state of a holy madman, which cannot be brought about by doing anything specific. The state of a sleeping person is the same. Or it comes about due to the prior cause of spiritual practice and purification or, for example, from seeking it. This occurs either in a dream or during the kind of dream that takes place in an ecstatic or waking state. 33.3

The dream involves either witnessing matters the way they are in a vision that cannot be expressed in words, or observing their representation in a vision that can be described. Or it involves the hearing of speech, or hearing or reading a sign and the like. There is no need to define the true meaning of the term "vision" here, as this has been done extensively in the science of dream interpretation. As for ecstasy, in that state one can perceive something or its representation, or one can hear speech, and so forth. The nature of perception at such a time is possibly with the physical eye or with the eye of the heart. There is no need to verify such a vision, as it does not have an ulterior motive. 33.4

As for the waking vision, it consists of seeing something, or seeing its representation, if it is of the type of things that can be seen. Or one sees with one's heart: The vision appears to the heart as if seen with one's eyes, or the heart apprehends it to be so. Or it may happen that one sees something written on the Preserved Tablet or in pages that have been transcribed, while awake, in an ecstatic state; while asleep, written on a wall or the forehead of a questioner, or elsewhere. One may also realize this vision through a voice that is heard, or through an act or state of one's own or of someone seen, and the like. These are what people customarily refer to as unveiling and disclosure. A particular case could involve the second and the third parts, or solely the third. People are fascinated by such matters: First, because it is a branch of knowledge and knowledge is the food of the spirit, and the stranger the type of knowledge, the more wondrous and appetizing it is. 33.5

٦،٣٣ ثانيهما من حيث كونه غيباً والعلم به من أوصاف الربوبيّة والعبد مرتاح إلى ذلك كارتياحه إلى القدرة والعلوّ. فكان للناس ولوع بذلك وتشوّف إليه لما ذكرنا وتشوّف إلى من يظهر عليه شيء منه لاستلذاذ الغرائب واستعظام العجائب واستنجاح المآرب. حتّى إنّ العامة مُطبِقون على جعل ذلك آية لثبوت ولاية الوليّ من غير تعريج على المستقيم منه والسقيم. وكذا صاحبه في نفسه. فنشأ من ذلك كلّه لعوام المتوجّهين شغف به وحرص عليه لأوّل قدَمٍ. فكثرت فيه الدعوى وعمّت به البلوى والتبست السبل بالمنهاج وغطّى على شمس الخصوصيّة دخان الاستدراج. رأينا أن ننبّه على وجوه الغلط في الأوجه السالفة بقدر ما حضر في الفكر ليتأتّى للإنسان التحرّز من مغالطة نفسه ومغالطة غيره له والله أعلم.

٧،٣٣ وسمعت الشيخ أبا عبد الله ابن ناصر رحمه الله يقول قال سيدي أحمد ابن إبراهيم رحمه الله لا تكونوا كذّابين ولا يلعب بكم الكذّابون. فنقول أمّا ما يكون من جهة المنام فيمكن الغلط فيه من جهات منها أن لا يضبط أمور نفسه فإنّ أمور النوم قلّما تنضبط. فيتوهّم أنّه رأى صورة الشيء أو المثال الدالّ عليه أو خوطب به أو نحو ذلك والأمر بخلافه. ومنها أن يرى صورته لكونها حاضرة في خياله. فإنّ من أكثر تصوّر الشيء لشغفه به أو لاستغرابه أو للخوف منه أو عليه ربّما تخيّله بذلك السبب.

٨،٣٣ ولا حاصل لذلك كما في قصّة الذي بشّر الملك بطول العمر. وأنّه بقي في عمره أربعون سنة وأنّ أمارة ذلك أن يرى في الليلة القابلة كذا لصورة غريبة صوّرها له فظل الملك يقلب تلك الصورة في وهمه فلمّا أمسى رآها فأصبح مصدّقاً بكلام ذلك الشخص فنال الحظوة منه وهو كذّاب. وما زال العامّة يقولون إنّ فلاناً يحلم بفلان أي لخوف منه أو لمحبّته فيكثر ذكره نهاراً ويحلم به ليلاً. ومنها أن يرى مثالاً فيعبره بذلك ويخطئ في العبارة ويبني على الخطأ. وقد لا يذكر المنامة بل يقتصر على تفسيرها

The second way unveiling happens is when it occurs to a person in an ecstatic state. Knowledge of this is one of the attributes of divinity and the worshipper is comfortable with this in the same way that he is at ease with God's power and exaltedness. For the reasons we have discussed, people have a desire and a longing for unveiling. And, due to their seeking pleasure in strange occurrences, making much of wondrous affairs, and looking for their desires to be fulfilled, they also have a longing for anyone who exhibits unveiling. The general population even agrees that it is a sign for determining the status of a saint, without pausing to differentiate between the upright who exhibit this ability and those who are deluded. It is similar for the ego of the one who experiences it. For all these reasons, an infatuation developed among commoners who were so inclined: an infatuation for unveiling and a desire to be the first to experience it. Many prayed for it and affliction spread through this desire, the paths were confused, and a fog gradually covered the sun of distinction. I wish here to point out aspects of this error from past examples that come to mind, so that people can be wary of committing the same error, or of others committing it, and God knows best. 33.6

I heard the shaykh Abū ʿAbd Allāh ibn Nāṣir, God have mercy on him, say, "My lord Aḥmad ibn Ibrāhīm, God have mercy on him, said, 'Do not lie and liars will not toy with you.'" We say therefore: Concerning what takes place in dreams, there are several reasons why this can be false. One is that matters are not what they seem, for the affairs of sleep can rarely be verified. A person can imagine that he saw something, or an image representing that thing, or that he heard something, and such, when the matter is actually quite different. Another possibility is that he sees its image because he had already imagined it. One most often imagines something out of a longing for it, or because one finds it strange, or because one is afraid—perhaps this is the reason one imagined it. 33.7

And then what one imagines does not take place, as with the story of the person who foretold a long life for the king. He told him that he would live for forty more years, and that the sign for this was that the next night he would see in a dream a strange image that he then described to him. The king contemplated this image in his imagination for a long time, and when night fell, he saw it and came to believe the man. He thereby obtained the king's grace, even though he was a liar. The common people often say that so-and-so dreams of so-and-so—out of fear of him or love for him—and this is because that person is frequently spoken of during the day, and is then the subject of dreams at 33.8

على زعمه إمّا حُسْنَ ظنّ بنفسه أنّ الأمر هو ذلك وإمّا إيهاماً للناس أنّه إنّما أخبر عن مشاهدة لا عن منام ليعدّ من الأولياء أهل الكشف. فإنّ المنامات لا تختصّ بهؤلاء بل تقع لسائر الناس حتّى الكفرة.

٩،٣٣ ولذا وقع الحديث الرّؤيا الصّالحة من الرّجل الصّالح وفي الحديث أيضاً إذا تقارب الزّمان لم تكد رؤيا المؤمن تكذب.

١٠،٣٣ ومنها أن يسمع خطاباً في منامه ولا يدري ممّن سمعه فيبني عليه ظنّاً منه أنّه من الله تعالى أو من ثقة من عباده وإنّما هو شيطان يلعب به وكذا قد يكون كلّ ما ذكر شيطانيّاً. فقد صحّ أنّ الرّؤيا من الله والحلم من الشّيطان. وقد يرى الشّخص المخاطب فيظنّه من أولياء الله أو فلاناً بعينه منهم وإنّما هو شيطان تراءى به. وقد يسمعه من وليّ من الأولياء ويبني عليه فيخرج خطأً فإنّ الوليّ غير معصوم من مثل هذا وإذا جاز على الوليّ الوقوع في هفوة من كبار الذنوب عمداً بلا اضطرار[١] فكيف بالخطأ؟

١١،٣٣ وسنذكر بعد وجوهاً من الخطأ في الكشف وقد يكون ذلك من الوليّ تصرّفاً في المملكة بتولية أو عزل أو نحو ذلك فينقض عليه ذلك غيره من أهل الحلّ والعقد بعدما حمله السامع وتحدّث به. وقد يحضر أوّل كلام من مجلس الصالحين في أمر ثمّ يفوته آخره وهو بخلاف ما سمع إلى غير ذلك. واعلم أنّ مواقع صدق الرؤيا وشروط اعتبارها مشروحة في فنّها. وإنّما قصدنا الإشارة إلى بعض ما يقع للناس ممّا ينبغي التحرّز منه. وأمّا ما يرجع إلى حال الغيبة فيمكن أيضاً أن يقع فيها الخطأ بتلاعب الخيال أو تلاعب الشيطان تَرائِياً وإلقاءً. وقد تكون غيبته بوارد ربانيّ أو شيطانيّ وذلك مشروح في محلّه عند أهله.

١٢،٣٣ واعلم أنّه في كلّ من المنام والغيبة يمكن أن يرى النبيّ صلّى الله عليه وسلّم ثمّ يسمع في تلك الحالة كلاماً يظنّه من النبيّ صلّى الله عليه وسلّم سمعه. وهو إنّما سمعه من

١ ق، ط: إصرار.

night. Another possibility is also that one sees an image and interprets it, but errs in the interpretation and then builds on this error. Perhaps the dreamer does not recount the dream but, because he wishes to do so, summarizes its interpretation. He does this either because according to the best of his ability he believes it to be so; or in order to make people believe that he is telling them something he witnessed in person, not in a dream, so that they may count him among the saints, the people of unveiling. Saints are not the only ones who dream—everyone does, even unbelievers.

Regarding this, there is the hadith that begins "The sound vision of an upstanding man . . .".[222] There is also the hadith: "During the last days hardly any believer's dream will be false." 33.9

One type of false dream consists of a person hearing speech in a dream and not knowing the speaker. He acts on it, believing that it is from Exalted God or from one of His trustworthy servants. Instead, it is the devil playing with him, and everything he has heard may well be satanic in origin. It is true that "The vision is from God, the dream from the devil."[223] One may see the one who speaks, and believe him to be a saint, or even a specific saint, when in reality it is the devil who has taken a saint's appearance. The dreamer may hear what he does from one of the saints, trust that, and, as saints are not protected from error, make a mistake. If a saint can slip and commit one of the gravest sins without being compelled to do so, is it not possible for a saint to err? 33.10

Below, we will mention types of errors that can occur in unveiling. This can happen through the saint acting in worldly matters by putting someone in power or by removing them or a similar action, only to have another religious authority contradict him after the dreamer passed on what he heard. Or maybe the dreamer is present for the beginning of the discussion at a gathering of saintly men but misses the end, which differed from what he had heard. And so on. The requirements for a vision to be true and the conditions for interpreting it are explained in the respective art. We simply want to draw attention to those things that befall people about which one needs to be careful. As for a vision that occurs in an ecstatic state through the cunning of one's own imagination or the devil's, an error may also occur in it in terms of what one sees or encounters. This ecstatic state can come either from God or the devil. This is explained in its proper place by the authorities on the subject. 33.11

In both dreams and ecstatic states, it is possible for a person to see the Prophet, God bless and keep him, and in that state to hear speech he believes 33.12

ناحية أخرى فيبني على ذلك ويغترّ به ويغرّ من سمعه. وكون الشيطان لا يتمثّل به صلّى الله عليه وسلّم لا يوجب امتناع أن يحضر الشيطان في ناحية ولا أن يتكلّم هو أو إنسيّ آخر فيطرق ذلك أذن السامع وهو في حالته يعسر عليه الضبط فيظنّه ما ذكرنا. إذا فهمت هذا فمن حدّثك بأمر سماعاً من النبيّ صلّى الله عليه وسلّم في النوم ونحوه فلا تعوّل عليه. ولا بدّ ولو كان المحدّث صدوقاً بل حتّى يبرز ثمّ إذا أخلف ذلك فلا تحكم ولا بدّ بأنّ المحدّث متحمّل كاذب. بل قد يكون صادقاً في وقوع الرؤيا وإنّما غلط فيما سمع.

١٣،٣٣ فافهم. وما اشتهر في كلام الناس من أنّ الرؤيا التي يحضر فيها النبيّ صلّى الله عليه وسلّم رؤيا حقّ لا حلم يسلم في الرؤيا نفسها لا فيما وراء ذلك من كلام وخطاب مثلاً. وإذا أمكن هذا في جانب النبوءة ففي الأولياء أقرب وأولى. وأمّا ما يكون في اليقظة فيمكن فيه أيضاً الغلط في رؤية البصر بأن يكون المرئيّ خيالاً لا حاصل له كما يقع ذلك للمحموم وصاحب المَيَدِ وراكب البحر ونحوهم. وفي رؤية القلب كذلك وفي الخاطر بأن يكون شيطانياً أو مجرّد حديث نفس أو قوة رجاء وظنّ أو نحو ذلك. إذا علمت هذا فأعلم أنّ الواجب على الإنسان في حقّ نفسه أن لا يغترّ وأن يتّهم رأيه. وفي حقّ غيره أن لا ينخدع لكلّ مبطل ولا يسيء الظن بكلّ مسلم. وفي هذا غموض لا يقوم به إلّا اللبيب الموفّق ولا بدّ من شرح هذا كلّه بعون الله وتوفيقه.

١٤،٣٣ فأمّا الإنسان في خاصّة نفسه ففي باب الرؤيا إن رأى ما يكره فليتعوّذ بالله كما جاء في السنّة المطهّرة. وليقل اللّهم إنّي أعوذ بك من شرّ ما رأيت أن يضرّني في ديني ودنياي فإنّها لن تضرّه. وإن رأى ما يحبّ فهي مبشّرة وفي الحديث ذهبت

to be the Prophet's, God bless and keep him. And yet, in actuality he has heard it from a different source, and because he trusts it, he is deceived by what he heard. The devil's nature does not allow him to take the form of the Prophet, God bless and keep him. This inability does not prevent the devil from appearing in a particular place or for him or another person to speak, which makes it difficult for the listener, when he is in this state, to verify the origin of what he hears. Thus, he believes it to be as we have outlined. If you have understood this, then when someone tells you that while asleep he heard the Prophet speak, God bless and keep him, do not rely on him. Even if the speaker is trustworthy, he can make his claim and then go back on it—do not follow his judgment, for it is certain he is lying and has falsely claimed to have had a vision. Or it can also be the case that he is honest with regard to having seen a vision but has erred in what he heard.

Understand this well! The widely held opinion that the vision in which the 33.13
Prophet appears, God bless and keep him, is a true vision and not a dream, should be accepted regarding the vision itself but not, for example, regarding the words or speech that accompany it. If such mistakes can happen in the context of seeing prophets, they are much more likely and probable to occur with saints. Concerning waking visions, errors may also occur in them with regard to seeing, because what is seen can be imaginary and baseless, as with someone afflicted with fever, or someone who is violently nauseous when on a ship at sea, and so on. As for the vision of the heart, it is the same as with the passing thought, which can be from the devil, merely the speech of the ego-self, or due to the power of hope, suspicion, and the like. If you know all this, then know that it is obligatory for people not to lie to themselves and to test their own opinions. When it comes to others, let them not be deluded by every prattler, nor think poorly of every Muslim. Such recondite matters can only be grasped by the intelligent and those blessed with guidance, and it all must be explained with the assistance and guidance of Exalted God.

It has been related in the noble Hadith that if a person who is alone sees 33.14
something he dislikes in a vision, he should seek refuge with God by reciting, "O God, I seek refuge with you from the evil that I have seen that could harm my faith and my worldly life." The vision will then not harm him. If he sees something he likes, it is a portent of good things to come—in the Hadith we find "Prophecy has ended, but there remain portents of good things to come"—and despite this the recipient of the vision is not deceived by what

النبوءة وبقيت المبشّرات ومع ذلك لا يغترّ لما ذكرنا قبل. ولهذا يقال الرؤيا تسرّ ولا تغرّ.

١٥،٣٣ وأمّا تحدّثه بذلك فإن كان يتّقي فيه فتنة أو غرورًا أو عجبًا لنفسه أو نحو ذلك فليكتم ذلك ولا يلتفت إليه. وإن لم يكن به بأس لنفسه ولا لغيره فليذكرها إن شاء الله بصورتها لا استغناء بمضمونها على زعمه. فإن خرجت على المراد فذاك وإلّا بقي بريء الساحة. وقد يعرض ما يقتضي ذكرها كاستدعاء أستاذه ذلك منه. وقد كان صلّى الله عليه وسلّم إذا أصبح يقول من رأى رؤيا فليقصّها. أو أن يكون في ذلك للإخوان سرور ومزيد. وكان الشيخ أبو مهدي الدغدوغي رحمه الله يقول لا تكتموا عن إخوانكم ما تشهدونه من الكرامات فإنّ ذلك يحبّب إليهم طاعة الله تعالى. غير أنّ هذا مزلقة للنفس فالحذر الحذر. والعاقل لا يعدل بالسلامة لنفسه شيئًا.

١٦،٣٣ وأمّا في باب الغيبة فلا اختيار له في حالتها كما لا اختيار له في حالة النوم. ولكن بعد السكون يجب عليه أن يتحرّز في حقّ نفسه وفي الإفشاء للغير كما في النوم وأكثر لأنّها ملعَبَة للشيطان إلّا من عُصم. وليتحرّز قبل ذلك من الوقوع في ذلك بتصحيح التقوى وترك الدعوى ومجانبة المخلطين والشاطحين المدّعين. وقد نقل الأخ أبو العباس زروق رضي الله عنه أنّ من اعتاد من نفسه الغيبة عند السماع أنّه لا يحلّ له تعاطيه لأنّ حفظ العقل واجب. وبهذا تعلم حال متفقرة الوقت في طلبهم الخمرة. وما مثالهم إلّا مثال سفيه مسافر وبين يديه قُطّاعٌ ومعه خفير يحميه منهم. فَدسّوا إليه من أغراه بقتل ذلك الخفير أو طرده عن نفسه وذلك ليستمكنوا منه بلا مدافع. ففعل ذلك أو سعى في فعله سَفَهًا منه لقلّة معرفته بمصالح نفسه ومكايد عدوّه. وهكذا المريدُ خفيرهُ من تلبيس الشياطين عقله مع توفيق الله تعالى. فإذا ذهب عنه استمكن منه وهو يطلب ذلك ويحرص عليه لأنّه رأى أو سمع أهل الشراب الصافي من أولياء الله

we have previously mentioned. Accordingly, the saying goes: Visions delight; they do not deceive.

As for his talking openly about such a vision, if the recipient fears that this will cause discord, deception, and the like, he should keep the matter quiet and pay no attention to it. If there is no harm in it for himself or others, then he should recount it in detail without omitting any of its content in his description. If the vision results in what was sought after, it is so, and if not, he is not disgraced. Something may occur that makes it necessary to mention the dream, such as when his teacher calls upon him to do so. The Prophet, God bless and keep him, used to say when he awoke: "Whoever has had a vision, let him recount it." Another reason to do so is that it can bring happiness and other benefits to one's brethren. The shaykh Abū l-Mahdī al-Daghdūghī, God have mercy on him, used to say, "Do not hide from your brethren the miracles that you witness, for recounting these leads them to love obeying Exalted God." Not doing so is also perilous for the ego—one must be careful and take precautions. The intelligent man does not hold anything to be equal to the well-being of his soul. 33.15

In the case of ecstatic states, one has no power to choose, much as one has no power to choose in the case of sleep. Yet, after it is over, one must be wary for one's own sake and, even more than is the case with sleep, wary of divulging to others, because, except for those who are protected, the ecstatic state is the devil's playground. One should take precautions against it by strengthening one's piety, abandoning pretension, and avoiding those who sow confusion and claim ecstatic utterances. Brother Abū ʿAbbās Zarrūq, God be content with him, has related how it is not permissible for one who expects to enter into an ecstatic state during a listening session to do so, for one is obligated to preserve one's reason. This explains the state of those who waste time searching for wine. There is none like them save for the traveling fool who has a guard to protect him from the brigands who lie ahead. These brigands ingratiate someone to the fool, who tempts him to kill the guard or to drive the guard away from him so they can overpower him when he is defenseless. He does this, or tries to do this, because he is foolish or ignorant of his own best interests and of his enemy's trickery. In the same fashion, the disciple's guard against the devils' deception is his reason, as well as the success granted by Exalted God. If reason abandons him, he will be overpowered. He is seeking out an ecstatic state and is desirous of it, for he has seen it or heard about 33.16

تعالى. ورأى ما يطّلعون عليه من المغيبات وما يدركون من الحقائق وما يتصرّفون في المملكة من التصرّف وما يقع للخلق من الإقبال عليهم والتنويه بهم فيشتهي المسكين تلك الحالة لذلك. ولا يدري أنّ أولئك لم يكونوا أهل شهادات[1] مثله ولا نالوا ذلك بحولهم واحتيالهم ولا قوّتهم ولا بالترّهات التي يشتغل بها هو. وإنّما اختصّهم الله بموهبته وأهّلهم لحضرته من غير تدبيرٍ منهم ولا اختيار.

١٧،٣٣ ولو كان لهم اختيار لاختاروا البقاء في خدمته وأن لا يغيبوا عنها لحظة. فإنّ أدب العبد وشرفه إنّما هو في خدمة مولاه لقيامه فيها بحقّ سيّده لا بحظّ نفسه. وما مثال من يطلب الخروج عن ذلك بالولهِ والسكر إلّا مثال عبد نصّبه سيّده لخدمته وهو يريد الإباق عنها أو يريد أن يتركها اختياراً منه ليدخل إلى مجلس سيّده؟

١٨،٣٣ فما أحقّه في الحالتين بالعصا تأديباً أو طرداً! نسأل الله تعالى العافية. نعم ما مرّ من أنّه لا ينبغي له تعاطي السماع مثلاً إنّما هو ما دام اختياره معه. وأمّا المغلوب فلا حكم عليه. وبهذا يجمع بين ما نذكر وبين ما يقع للصوفيّة في باب السماع وباب الوجد.

١٩،٣٣ وبلغنا أنّ جماعة قدموا على سيدي محمّد الشرقيّ التادلاويّ المتقدّم الذكر فخرج إليهم وتحرّك سماع. فلم يشعروا به إلّا وهو في وسطه يتواجد وليس عليه إلّا القميص. قال بعض الجالسين لآخر سرّاً هذا رجل خفيف. فإذا هو على الفور تكلّم على خواطرهم. فقال:

اللهُ اللهُ يا اللهُ اللهُ اللهُ يا لَطِيفُ
اَلْحُبُّ يَهِزُّ ٱلرِّجَالَ لَا وَاللهِ مَانِي خَفِيفُ

٢٠،٣٣ ومن هذا قول القطب العارف الشيخ أبي مدين رضي الله عنه حيث قال: [طويل]

---

١ ط: شهوات.

it among the people of pure intoxication who are the Friends of God. He has seen the ecstatic states they attain, the mystical insights they come to, what they command in the temporal realm, and how the masses are drawn to them and praise them. The poor fellow desires this state for these reasons, not comprehending that those are not people gifted with visions like him, nor have they obtained this state through their power, effort, or strength, or through the trifles that he is engaged in. Instead, God has selected them for His gift and has enabled them to come into His presence without their deliberation or choice.

If they had a choice, they would choose to remain constantly in His ser- 33.17
vice, not leaving it for a moment. This is because the proper comportment and honor of a slave is established in service to and for the sake of his lord and master, not for his own fortune. Anyone who seeks to end this service, through witlessness or intoxication, is like a slave whose master assigned him service, and who then wishes to escape it, or like one who leaves it voluntarily in order to enter the audience of his master.

Which of the two is more deserving of being beaten with the rod and ban- 33.18
ished? We ask Exalted God to preserve us from this. What was written above, for example, regarding the fact that he should not participate in a listening session, is valid as long as he remains able to exercise his ability to choose. As for the one who is overcome with ecstasy, there are no rules governing him. In this fashion, what we mentioned is reconciled with what Sufis experience in the matters of listening sessions and ecstatic love.

We have been told that a group came to Sīdī Muḥammad al-Sharqī 33.19
al-Tādlāwī, mentioned above. He went to them and was transported by a listening session. None of them was moved by it; only he in the midst of it, wearing nothing but a shirt, was transported by passion. One attendee said to another privately, "This man is a lightweight." At once he addressed their passing thoughts, saying:

God, God, O God,
  God, God, Most Gentle,
Love makes men tremble;
  by God, nothing about me is lightweight!

On the same subject there is what the spiritual Axis and gnostic, the shaykh 33.20
Abū Madyan, God be content with him, recited, from:

فَقُلْ لِلَّذِي يَنْهَى عَنِ ٱلْوَجْدِ أَهْلَهُ إِذَا لَمْ تَذُقْ مَعَنَا شَرَابَ ٱلْهَوَى دَعْنَا

إلى أن قال:

فَإِنَّا إِذَا طِبْنَا وَطَابَتْ عُقُولُنَا[1] وَخَامَرَنَا خَمْرُ ٱلْعَشِيقِ تَهَتَّكْنَا
فَلَا تَلُمِ ٱلسَّكْرَانَ فِي حَالِ سُكْرِهِ فَقَدْ رَفَعَ ٱلتَّكْلِيفَ فِي سُكْرِنَا عَنَّا

٢١،٣٣ والأبيات مشهورة غير أنّ هذه الغلبة لا يتحققها الجهال ولا ينتظرونها. نعم استدعاء حال يرجى عنه رقّة القلب وانشراح الصدر وذهاب جساوة النفس ورعونتها بلا زائد مع صحّة القصد. لا ينبغي أن ينكر بل يلتحق بما أذن فيه شرعاً بل حضّ عليه ممّا يفيد رقّة القلب وخشوعاً وتذكير الآخرة. كحضور مجالس الذكر وقراءة القرآن بالتدبّر وزيارة القبور والمسح على رؤوس اليتامى ونحو ذلك.

٢٢،٣٣ وقد انجرّ بنا الكلام إلى ما لا حاجة بنا إليه في هذا المحلّ لكثرة أبوابه واتّساع شعابه. فلنرجع إلى ما نحن فيه فنقول وأمّا في حال اليقظة فليحذر أيضاً من الغلط في رؤيته كما مرّ وفي خاطره. فلا يثق بكلّ ما يرد عليه في قلبه في نفسه فضلاً عن أن يخبر به الناس. وليفرض ذلك الوارد كأنّه شخص مجهول ورد عليه من سفر فأخبره بأمر وقع في بلد آخر. فلا يثق به وهو لا يعرف صدقه من كذبه ولا يخبر أحداً بخبره حتّى ينظر. ولو وثق به وحدّث الناس بكلامه دخل في مضمون كَفَى بِالْمَرْءِ كَذِبًا أَنْ يُحَدِّثَ بِكُلِّ مَا سَمِعَ. بل حتّى ينظر هل صدّق ما أخبر به ثمّ إن صدق فأخبره كرّة[2] أخرى فلا يثق به أيضاً لأنّه قد يتّفق للكاذب الصدق مرّة أو أكثر.

٢٣،٣٣ ثمّ إنّ صدّق فأخبره أيضاً فكذلك حتّى يحصل له اليقين بالتكرار والقرائن أنّه صدوق. فعند ذلك يثق به فيقول حدّثني الثقة. وهكذا خاطر القلب وهيهات تحقق

---

١ ق، ط: نفوسنا. ٢ ق: مرة.

Say to one who denies love to its adepts:
If you have not tasted the draft of passion with us, leave us be.

up to:

When our bodies and our minds are in a state of delight
and the wine of the lover has filled our veins, we are exposed.
Do not blame the drunkard for his drunkenness;
in our intoxication, we are no longer responsible.

The lines are famous, but the ignorant do not attain such overwhelming states, nor can they expect to. It is a wonderful thing to pray sincerely for a state that produces a gentle heart, an open breast, the shedding of the ego's roughness and thoughtlessness, and nothing more. Such an act should not be condemned, but be considered part of what has been legally permitted if not signaled as an act that results in a heart's tenderness and produces humility and remembrance of the afterlife. So too attending gatherings for the remembrance of God, reciting the Qur'an in contemplation, visiting graves, stroking the heads of orphans, and so forth. 33.21

All this leads us to a subject we need not go into as it has many subsections and branches out widely. Let us return to what we had been discussing and say: Regarding the state of wakefulness, let a person be wary here too of error in his visions and passing thoughts. A person should not trust everything that comes to him in his heart, much less tell others of it. Let a person who experiences such a state treat it as if it were someone unknown that he happened upon while traveling. This person talks about something that happened in another country, and not knowing whether he is telling the truth or lying, he does not trust it, and tells no one until he has looked into it. If he trusts what he had been told and has told others, it falls under "Spare us the liar who relates everything he hears." Even if he looks into it and it is true, and the traveler repeats the same account, he still does not believe it, for a liar can be right once or twice. 33.22

Then there is the case of the one who speaks and relates the truth, and this happens until through repetition and the accumulation of evidence, he becomes certain that this person is trustworthy. At that point, he comes to trust the traveler, and says, "A trustworthy source has spoken to me." It is the same with the passing desire of the heart, but what a mistake if it only establishes itself in him in this way! For the person in the metaphor is a particular 33.23

ذلك فيه بمجرد هذا. فإنّ الشخص في المثال يكون معروفاً بعينه فإذا ثبت له وصف من الصدق عرف به.

٣٣،٢٤ أمّا الخاطر القلبيّ فمتى يعرف أنّ هذا الذي أخبره الآن هو الذي صدّق قبله وهو يعلم أنّ القلب ميدان للربّانيّ والملكيّ والشيطانيّ والنفسانيّ فلعلّ هذا شيطانيّ أو نفسانيّ. نعم إن كان من جنس من قال كنت بوّاباً على قلبي ثلاثين أو أربعين سنة فمتى تحرّك خاطر سوء صرفته عنه فعسى أن يثق بما حصل في قلبه. وكذا إن علم من ربّه أنّه أعطى الخاطر أو تجريب صادق من أهله في قلبه كما مرّ أو مع ربّه أنّه يعلمه بما يحدث في المملكة.

٣٣،٢٥ وقد روي أنّ امرأة من تلامذة الشيخ السريّ رضي الله عنه أرسلت ابناً لها في حاجة فوقع في النهر وغرق. فبلغ الخبر إلى الشيخ قبلها فقال للجنيد قم بنا إليها فأتياها. فجعل الشيخ يكلّمها في مقام الصبر. فقالت ما أردت بهذا يا أستاذ؟ فقال إنّ ابنك من أمره كذا أي مات. فقالت ابني؟ ما كان الله ليفعل ذلك. ثمّ ذهبت تهرول إلى الماء فنادت يا فلان. فقال لبّيك وخرج إليها يسعى. فنظر السريّ إلى الجنيد وقال ما هذا؟ فقال إن أذن الشيخ تكلّمت. قال تكلّم. فقال هذه امرأة محافظة على ما لله عليها ومن شأن من كان كذلك أن لا يُحدِثَ الله أمرًا حتّى يعلمه. فلمّا لم يعلمها الله علمت أنّه لم يكن. ولذا قال بعض المشايخ للتلامذة أيّكم إذا أراد الله أن يحدث شيئاً في المملكة أعلمه إيّاه؟ قالوا لا أحدَ مِنّا. فقال ابكوا على قلوب لا تجد من الله شيئاً أو نحو ذلك.

٣٣،٢٦ وقد شهد الذوق أنّه ما يتّفق ذلك عادة على استقامة إلّا بعد صفاء المداخل كلّها. فيعمّ ما يتّصل بمعدته من مطعوم وبأُذنه من مسموع وبعينه من مَرئيٍّ وبلسانه من مقُولٍ و بعقله من معقول. وهكذا في سائر الجوارح. أمّا المخلّط فلا يشرب إلّا كدراً. ولا يثق أيضاً بما يقع له من التجلّي في باطنه فإنّ كلّ ما سوى الأنبياء عليهم السلام معرّض للخطأ والغلط. وقد يتجلّى الشيء بتمامه وقد ينتقص.

one, so when it becomes accepted that he is sincere, he becomes known for this quality.

As for the fleeting desire of the heart, when he ascertains that the one now 33.24
relating to him is the same whom his heart trusted—knowing that the heart is a field for influences that are divine, angelic, satanic, and egoistic—then this desire could be satanic or egoistic. How wonderful if he is of those who say: "I have been a doorkeeper of the heart for some thirty or forty years. Whenever a bad passing desire of the heart stirs, I drive it away." It is hard to trust what happens in one's heart. In the same fashion, as discussed above, we know that it is his Lord who gives a passing desire or true experience to the heart He has prepared for it, or who teaches him about what is happening in the temporal realm.

It has been related that a woman among the students of the shaykh al-Sarī, 33.25
God be content with him, sent her son on an errand and he fell into a river and drowned. News of this event reached the shaykh before it did her, and he said to Junayd, "Up, let's go to her." They did, and the teacher began speaking to her about the station of forbearance. "Teacher, what do you mean by this?" she asked, and he said, "Your son is dead." "My son?" she said. "God would not do this!" And she rushed to the water and called out his name. "Here I am!" he replied, and came running to her out of the water. Al-Sarī looked at Junayd and said, "What's this?" "With the shaykh's permission, I will speak," Junayd said. "Go on," said al-Sarī, and Junayd explained, "This woman embraces what God determines for her, and for such as these, God allows nothing to happen until He has informed them of it. Since God had not informed her, she knew that it had not happened." Because of this, one shaykh said to his students, "Listen. If God wishes to make something happen in the temporal realm, does he inform someone of it?" "Not any one of us," they said. And the shaykh said the following, or words to this effect: "Weep for the hearts in which you find nothing from God."

Mystical experience generally does not occur in a reliable fashion until 33.26
the sensory and bodily orifices have been purified. All the food that reaches the stomach, everything heard by the ear, seen by the eye, and spoken by the tongue, spreads throughout the body. It is similar with the other organs. What is mixed turns cloudy when consumed. Nor can one trust appearances since everyone is prone to error and mistakes, except for prophets, peace be upon them all. Something may manifest in a complete or incomplete fashion.

٢٧،٣٣ وضرب الإمام حجّة الإسلام في الإحياء لذلك مثلاً وهو أنّ القلب في مطالعته اللوح المحفوظ بواسطة التجلّي يكون كما لو كان بينك وبين جدار أو إنسان أو متاع ستر مرخىً. فإذا انسدل لم تر شيئاً من ذلك الجدار ونحوه وقد تهب ريح فتحرّكه وترفعه حتّى ترى الجدار بتمامه. وقد ترفعه حتّى ترى بعض الجدار فترسله ولا ترى الباقي. أو ترسله قبل أن تبيّن ما رأيت. وهكذا قلت ومن ثمّ يقع لأهل الفراسة من الصالحين اختلال أو نقصان. فيظنّ بهم الكذب وإنّما يؤتون من عدم التجلّي كما ذكرنا أو من غلط في فهم خطاب أو نحو ذلك وذلك مشهور.

٢٨،٣٣ وقد حدّثونا عن صلحاء تادلا أنّه لمّا قام على السلطان أحمد المنصور ابن أخيه أو ابن عمّه الناصر قال سيدي أحمد بن أبي القاسم الصومعيّ إنّ الناصر يدخل تادلا بمعنى دخول الملك. فلمّا بلغ الخبر إلى سيدي محمّد الشرقيّ قال مسكين بابا أحمد رأى الناصر قد دخل تادلا فظنّها الناصر يدخل. فكان الأمر كذلك أنّه هزم في نواحي تازا ثمّ قطع رأسه وجلب إلى مراكش فدخل تادلا في طريقه.

٢٩،٣٣ وعن صلحاء سلا أنّ رجلاً من رؤساء البحر جاء إلى سيدي عليّ أبي الشكاوي فشاوره على السفر في البحر. فقال له لا تفعل وإن فعلت فلا تربح مالك ولا نفسك. وخرج من عنده فأتى سيدي عبد الله بن حسّون فشاوره. فقال له سافر تسلم وتغنم. فسافر فاتّفق عند دخولهم البحر أن أسرهم الروم. فذهبوا بهم إلى أن لقوا بعض سفن المسلمين فوقع بينهم قتال. فظهر المسلمون فاستمكن هؤلاء من سفينتهم التي أسرتهم فقبضوا عليها وغنموها ورجعوا سالمين غانمين.

٣٠،٣٣ ومثل هذا من أحوالهم كثير. وقد ذكر الشيخ عبد الوهاب الشعرانيّ أنّه لا ينبغي لمن يطالع ألواح المحو والإثبات أن يتكلّم وإنّما يتكلّم من يطالع اللوح بنفسه. وذلك لأنّ ما في اللوح لا يتبدّل بخلاف الصحف فإنّه يقع فيها التبديل. كما قال تعالى

For this reason, the exemplar al-Ghazālī, the Proof of Islam, used a simile in his *Revival of the Islamic Sciences*—namely, that when the heart contemplates the Preserved Tablet by means of a vision it is as if there were a lowered veil between you and a wall, person, or object. When the veil descends, you see nothing of this wall, and then a gust of wind may come and move it, lifting it so that you see the entire wall. Or it may lift in such a way that you see some of the wall, and then it falls so that you do not see the rest. Or it may fall before you get a clear sense of what you see. This is why I say an error or lapse can befall devout believers who practice divination. They are then considered to have lied, when, as mentioned above, they did not experience a vision, or erred in their understanding of what was said, and so on. This is well-known. 33.27

We have been told by devout men in Tādlā that when al-Nāṣir, who was the cousin or nephew of Sultan Aḥmad al-Manṣūr, rose up against him, Sīdī Aḥmad ibn Abī l-Qāsim al-Ṣūmaʿī said, "Al-Nāṣir is entering Tādlā," in the sense of taking sovereign possession of it. When this news reached Sīdī Muḥammad al-Sharqī, he said, "Poor Bābā Aḥmad saw that al-Nāṣir entered Tādlā and thought that was a vision of al-Nāṣir conquering it. In reality, he had been defeated near Tāzā and his head had been cut off and taken to Marrakesh, passing through Tādlā on the way." 33.28

We have been told by devout men in Salé that a sea captain came to Sīdī ʿAlī Abū l-Shakāwī to seek his advice regarding a journey by sea and he responded, "Do not set off, for if you do you will not profit materially or spiritually." The captain then went to Sīdī ʿAbd Allāh ibn Ḥassūn for advice, and he said, "Travel—you will be safe and you will find riches." They set out, but a Christian ship took them prisoner, and so they remained until they crossed a Muslim ship and clashed with it. The Muslims were victorious, and those who had been captured by the Christian ship took over that vessel, pillaged it, and returned unscathed and wealthy. 33.29

Many have had experiences like this. The shaykh ʿAbd al-Wahhāb al-Shaʿrānī related that the one who views the pages of erasing and affirmation should not speak, and the one who views the Tablet should only relate this to himself.[224] This is because what is on the Tablet does not change, in contrast to the pages in which alterations can take place. As the Exalted said: «God erases, and affirms whatever He wills.»[225] Someone may be told of something in the pages only for it to be erased by Exalted God so that it differs from what he was told. 33.30

﴿يَمْحُوا ٱللَّهُ مَا يَشَآءُ وَيُثْبِتُ﴾ . فقد يخبر بما فيها ثمّ يمحوه الله تعالى فيختلف خبره ويدخل وهناً على الخرقة وتهمة بالكذب والدعوى.

٣١،٣٣ وذكر في صلحاء مصر في وقته أنّ فلاناً منهم كان يتكلّم عن اللوح فكان كلّ ما يكون يحتفظ به. وفلاناً كان يتكلّم عن الألواح فكان ربّما يخبر بالشيء ولا يقع. والظاهر أنّ حكاية الشيخ عبد القادر رضي الله عنه من هذا المعنى. وذلك أنّ رجلاً من التجّار شاور بعض المشايخ وأظنّه الشيخ الدبّاس على السفر. فقال له لا تفعل فإنّك إن سافرت تقتل وينهب مالك. فلقي الرجل الشيخ عبد القادر فكلّمه. فقال له سافر ولا بأس عليك. فسافر الرجل فلمّا كان ببعض الطريق طرح بضاعته ثمّ قام فنسيها. وتنحّى إلى مكان آخر فنام. فرأى في منامه أن قد خرج عليهم اللصوص فقتلوه ونهبوا أموالهم. فاستيقظ مذعوراً وإذا به أثر الدم كأنّه أثر الطعنة التي رآها في منامه. ثمّ ذكر بضاعته فهرول إلى الموضع الذي نسيها فيه فإذا هي سالمة. فأخذها ورجع إلى أهله سالماً بماله. فلمّا دخلَ لقي الشيخ الأوّل فقال له ذلك الشيخ يا ولدي الشيخ عبد القادر محبوب طلب من الله تعالى كذا وكذا مدّة أن يرد القتل مناماً والنهب نسياناً ففعل.

٣٢،٣٣ فهذه الحكاية مع عبارة هذا الشيخ إذا سمعها الجاهل يتوهّم أنّ الله تعالى قضى في أزَلِهِ على هذا الشخص أن يقتل في هذه السفرة ويذهب ماله وأنّه أطلع الشيخ على ذلك فأخبر به ثمّ تبدّل ذلك بدعاء الشيخ عبد القادر. وذلك باطل لا يكون فإن علم الله تعالى لا يتبدّل وما قضي في أزله وهو المعبّر عنه باللوح المحفوظ لا يتحوّل. وإنّما ذلك يخرج على ما ذكرنا من المحو والإثبات. وهو أن يظهر الله تعالى القتل والنهب ويطلع عليه الشيخ المذكور ويكون قد قضى في علمه أنّ ذلك منام لا حقيقة. وأنّ دعاء عبد القادر منوط به فلمّا دعا برز ما علّمه الله تعالى أن يكون وقضاه. وهو الصحيح. وإظهار المعنى الآخر يكون لحكمة يعلمها الله تعالى كصدور الدعاء والتضرّع

Because of the errors in such claims, people associate those in Sufi garb with fallibility and accuse them of lying and baseless claims.

Al-Shaʿrānī related that among the devout men of his time in Egypt was one who used to speak about the Tablet on which everything in existence is preserved. This person used to speak about the pages and might report something that would not happen. It is evident that the story of the shaykh ʿAbd al-Qādir, God be content with him, was an example of this. That account involved a merchant seeking advice from one of the masters—I think it was Shaykh al-Dabbās—regarding travel, who said to him, "Do not do it! If you travel you will be killed and robbed of your possessions." The merchant went to speak about the matter with Shaykh ʿAbd al-Qādir, who said, "Travel! No harm will come to you." The man set out, and when he had gone some way, he set down his goods. When he got up and left, he forgot his goods. He retired to another place and went to sleep. In a dream he saw that thieves had set out after him, killed him, and robbed him of all his possessions. He awoke, terrified. There were traces of blood on him, like the traces from the cuts he had seen in his dream. It was then that he remembered his goods, hurried to where he had left them, and found them untouched. He gathered them up and returned safely to his family with all his possessions. When he arrived, he met the first shaykh, who said to him, "My son, the shaykh ʿAbd al-Qādir is beloved by God—he asked Exalted God at a certain time for the killing to be reduced to a dream and the theft to forgetfulness, and God did so." 33.31

Now, if an ignorant person were to hear this story and this teacher's words, he would imagine that Exalted God had made an eternal decree for this person to be killed on this trip and for his possessions to be taken, and that He had made the teacher fully aware of this. Yet he had then altered the decree due to the prayers of Shaykh ʿAbd al-Qādir. This is false and erroneous, for the knowledge of Exalted God does not change, and what He has decreed in eternity—consisting of what He has set down on the Preserved Tablet—does not change. Instead, this affair took place in the fashion that we have mentioned in terms of erasing and affirming. That is, Exalted God made the killing and robbery known, and the aforementioned teacher perceived this, with God having decreed that these things take place in a dream instead of reality. The prayers of ʿAbd al-Qādir are linked to this, and when he prayed to Exalted God, what God had decreed became evident to him. This is the correct interpretation. The other meaning imparted by Exalted God consists of His teaching 33.32

من الشيخ عبد القادر في هذه الصورة وظهور شفوف منزلته وحظوته عند ربّه. وهكذا يفهم كلّ ما يشبه هذا ممّا يقع من الكرامات أو المعجزات.

٣٣،٣٣ واعلم أنّ كلّ ما أشرنا إليه من التحذيرات وقرّرنا من التحرّزات إنّما هو في حال المريدين وعوام المتوجّهين المعرّضين للغلط والزّلق. وأمّا العارفون الكاملون وإن كانوا أيضاً غير معصومين ولا مستغنين عن التحفّظ فلا حديث لنا عنهم لأنّهم أعرف بأحوالهم فيما يأتون[1] ويذرون وما يبدون وما يكتمون. وتوصية أمثالنا لهم حماقة وسوء أدب.

١،٣٤ وأمّا الإنسان في حقّ غيره فهو بين إحدى ثلاث. إمّا شيء يصدّق به لمعرفته له بالبصيرة أو تقليد من يثق به من أستاذ أو نحوه فيقبله. وإمّا شيء تنكره الشريعة أو الحقيقة أو العقل فينكر بالشروط المقرّرة في إنكار المنكر في الفقه وفي التصوّف مع حسن الظنّ في الباطن. وإمّا شيء محتمل فيسلم لا ينكر ولا يتّبع. ولا تتمّ هذه الجملة إلّا بسلامة الصدر للمسلمين وحُسن الظنّ بهم وتغافل عن مساويهم مع فطنة ويقظة ومعرفة بالزمان وأهله. والمؤمن كيّس فطن ثلثاه تغافل. ويقال اللبيب العاقل هو الفطن المتغافل.

٢،٣٤ أمّا الزمان فلا تسأل عنه. وقد مرّ في الحديث صنفان إذا صلحا صلح النّاس وإذا فسدا فسد النّاس الأمراء والعلماء. وقد فسدا معاً وإلى الله المشتكى.

٣،٣٤ وكان الأمر يصلح بأئمّة العدل وفقه الفقهاء وأدب الصوفيّة. وقد فسد هؤلاء الثلاثة بالجور والمداهنة والبدعة. ففسد الدين بهم أوّلاً والدنيا ثانياً كما قيل:

[متقارب]

١ ط: يوتون.

His wisdom, as with the prayers and supplications made by the shaykh ʿAbd al-Qādir in this manner, manifesting the refined nature of his own station and standing with his Lord. This is the manner in which one should understand all other saintly and prophetic miracles.[226]

Everything we have warned about and cautioned against applies to disciples and commoners on the path vulnerable to errors and lapses. About accomplished gnostics, even if they are not protected from error and not exempt from caution, we have nothing to say, as they know best their spiritual states, what they have been granted and can communicate, what they can express openly, and what they must conceal. It would be ludicrous as well as bad form for one such as me to counsel them. 33.33

A person has three options when it comes to something beyond himself: (1) He believes in it because of having seen it, or he accepts what one receives through following a trusted teacher and the like; or (2) it is something denied by either the revealed law, truth, or reason, so he rejects it according to established norms for rejecting what is wrong in jurisprudence and in Sufism, and feels at ease doing so; or (3) it is something that is possible and he accepts it, neither denying nor following it. It would be insufficient to discuss this issue without mentioning the importance of keeping an open heart toward all Muslims, thinking well of them, and ignoring their flaws, while remaining cognizant and wary of the nature of the times and people. Two-thirds of the insight and understanding of a believer lies in disregarding what is nonessential. There is a saying: "The smart and intelligent person is the one who is wise and disregards what is irrelevant." 34.1

As for when this applies, do not ask about it. In the Hadith we find: "There are two kinds of people, rulers and scholars: When they are upright, the people are secure, and when they are corrupt so are the people." They have both become corrupted—let any who complain about this do so to God! 34.2

The situation could be rectified through the justice of rulers, the understanding of jurists, and the comportment of Sufis. All three groups have been corrupted through tyranny, deception, and innovation. First they corrupted the faith and then this world. As has been said:[227] 34.3

وَهَلْ أَفْسَدَ ٱلدِّينَ إِلَّا ٱلْمُلُوكُ   وَأَحْبَارُ سُوءٍ وَرُهْبَانُهَا
وَبَاعُوا ٱلنُّفُوسَ وَلَمْ يَرْبَحُوا   وَلَمْ تَغْلُ فِي ٱلْبَيْعِ أَثْمَانُهَا
لَقَدْ وَقَعَ ٱلْقَوْمُ فِي جِيفَةٍ   يَبِينُ لِذِي عَقْلٍ إِنْتَانُهَا

٤،٣٤ وقيل: [رجز]

يَا مَعْشَرَ ٱلْقُرَّاءِ يَا مِلْحُ ٱلْبَلَدْ   مَا يُصْلِحُ ٱلْمِلْحَ إِذَا ٱلْمِلْحُ فَسَدْ؟

والمراد بالقرّاء الفقهاء وبهم يصلح ما فسد كما يصلح الطعام بالملح. فإذا فسدوا تعذّر الصلاح.

٥،٣٤ أمّا التصوّف فقد كان شيخ الطائفة أبو القاسم الجنيد في زمانه يقول رضي الله عنه: [مجزوء الكامل]

أَهْلُ ٱلتَّصَوُّفِ قَدْ مَضَوْا   صَارَ ٱلتَّصَوُّفُ مَخْرَقَةْ[١]

الأبيات المعروفة. فما بالك بزماننا؟ فقد صارت هذه المخرقة مخرقة ولم يزل الخلق ينقص إلى الآن. وقد قيل قبل هذا بزمان دعوى عريضة وضعف ظاهر. أمّا اليوم فالدعوى من وراء حجاب.

٦،٣٤ وقد طرق أسماع العوامّ من قبل اليوم كلام أهل الصولة كفحول القادريّة والشاذليّة رضي الله عنهم وكلام أرباب الأحوال في كلّ زمان. فتعشّقت النفوس ذلك وأذعن له الجمهور وفاضوا بالتشبّه بهم. فلمّا شئت أن تلقى جاهلاً مسرفاً على نفسه لم يعرف بعد ظاهر الشريعة فضلاً عن أن يعمل به فضلاً عن أن يخلص إلى الباطن فضلاً عن

١ يزيد ق: كان التصوف ركوة/ و سجادة و ملزقة // صار التصوف صيحة / و تواجدًا و مطبقة // كذبتك نفسك ليس ذي / سنن الطريق الملحقة.

Has faith been corrupted and not the kings?
Have the bishops become evil and not the monks?
They sold their souls and made no profit in the selling
as these did not bring in their price.
The community has become like a putrid corpse;
its rot clear to anyone with sense.

And as has also been said:[228] 34.4

Congregation of reciters, salt of the earth!
What restores the salt if the salt has been corrupted?

By "reciters," the line refers to the jurists, who can restore what has been corrupted, just as salt preserves food: When they are corrupted, well-being becomes an impossibility.

With regard to Sufism, the shaykh of the community, Junayd, God be con- 34.5
tent with him, said of his time:

The people of Sufism have all passed away—
Sufism has become a shadow of itself.

These lines are very well known. What then of our own time? This shadow has itself become a shadow, and people's morals continue to decline. As was observed long before this: Pretense is widespread, weakness is everywhere. Today, prayers are veiled from God.

The words of the people of great authority, such as the luminaries of the 34.6
Qādiriyyah and the Shādhiliyyah, God be pleased with them, have reached the ears of the commoners, as has the speech of those who have mastered spiritual states from every period. The commoners' egos have been infatuated with them. The masses have been drawn to them, and have dived headlong into imitating them. When you wish to meet someone who is ignorant and exceedingly focused on his ego without knowing the external aspects of the revealed law—much less acting according to it, reaching its internal aspects, experiencing a spiritual state, or having attained a station on the path—you will find

أن يكون صاحب حال فضلاً عن أن يكون صاحب مقام إلّا وجدته يصول ويقول وينابذ المنقول والمعقول.

٧،٣٤ وأكثر ذلك في أبناء الفقراء يريد الواحد منهم أن يتحلّى بحلية أبيه ويستتبع أتباعه بغير حقّ ولا حقيقة بل لمجرّد حطام الدنيا. فيقول خدّام أبي وزربة أبي ويضرب عليهم كمغرم السلطان. ولا يقبل أن يحبوا أحداً في الله أو يعرفوه أو يقتدوا به غيره. وإذا رأى من خرج يطلب دينه أو من يدلّه على الله تعالى يغضب عليه ويتوعّده بالهلاك في نفسه وماله.

٨،٣٤ وقد يقع له عليه شيء من المصائب بحكم القضاء والابتلاء فيضيفه إلى نفسه. فيزداد بذلك هو وأتباعه ضلالاً. يخترق لهم من الخرافات والأمور المعتادات ما يدّعيه سيرة وديناً يستهويهم به. ثمّ يضمن لهم الجنّة على مساوئ أعمالهم والشفاعة يوم الحشر فيقبض على لحة ذراعه فيقول للجاهل مثله أنت من هذه اللحة. فيكتفي ابتهال العوامّ بذلك ويبقون في خدمته ولداً عن والدٍ قائلين نحن خدّام الدار الفلانيّة وفي زربة فلان. لا نخرج عنها وكذا وجدنا آبائنا.

٩،٣٤ وهذا هو الضلال المبين وهؤلاء قطّاع العِباد عن الله وعن دينه داخلون في شبه ما قال النبيّ صلّى الله عليه وسلّم في ملوك السوء وخصوصاً في بني أميّة. في الحديث إذا بلغ بنو أبي العاصي ثلاثين رجلاً اتّخذوا عباد الله خولاً ومال الله دولاً الحديث.

١٠،٣٤ ولم يعلم الجهّال أنّهم كيف يكونون من لحة ذراعه بمجرّد دعواه إذا لم يجعلهم الله تعالى منها؟ وبعد أن يجعلهم كيف يغترّون بذلك قبل أن يعلموا أين مصير تلك اللحة؟ ولعلّه النار وماذا ينفعهم اجتماعهم في النار؟ نعوذ بالله من البوار.

١١،٣٤ قال تعالى ﴿وَلَن يَنفَعَكُمُ ٱلْيَوْمَ إِذ ظَّلَمْتُمْ أَنَّكُمْ فِي ٱلْعَذَابِ مُشْتَرِكُونَ﴾. فالناس عند الله ثلاثة مقبول مقبول له ومقبول غير مقبول له ومردود. فالمردود لم ينج

him belligerent, gossipy, and opposed to both the traditional and intellectual sciences.

This happens a great deal among the scions of spiritual ascetics, when one of them wishes to adorn himself with the jewelry of his father, without right or truth urging his father's followers to follow him for the sake of nothing more than the detritus of this world. He then addresses them: "Servants of my father and my father's lodge!" Infatuated with power, he imposes himself on them. He does not accept that they love anyone for the sake of God; he rejects the time they spend imitating anyone but him. If he sees anyone setting out in search of faith, or someone guiding him to Exalted God, he grows angry and threatens him with the destruction of both his soul and possessions. 34.7

Such a person may experience hardship because of the tribulation God has decreed, and the scion attributes this punishment to himself, thus increasing his and his followers' error. He invents fanciful stories and mundane matters for them, from which he claims a hagiography and religious practice to seduce them. He then promises them heaven as well as intercession on the day of resurrection in return for their misguided practice. He grabs the flesh of his arm and says to one who is just as ignorant, "You are of this flesh!" It suffices him to address the masses in this fashion for them to remain in his service, generation after generation, saying, "We are the servants of the house and lodge of this person! We will not leave it since this is where our fathers were!" 34.8

This is manifest error. Such people separate worshippers from God and His faith, and approximate what the Prophet, God bless and keep him, said regarding evil kings, applicable especially to the Umayyads. The hadith begins: "If the Banū Abū l-ʿĀṣī reach thirty men in strength, they will take the servants of God as chattel and the property of God as an empire . . . ." 34.9

Do the ignorant not realize—how could they be part of the flesh of his arm solely based on his supplication, without Exalted God having made them so? And after having made them so, why should they desire to remain so before having learned the fate of this arm? Perhaps its fate is in the fire of hell: What benefit to them, then, to be united in the fire? We seek refuge in God from perdition. 34.10

The Exalted has said: «Since you did evil, it shall not profit you today that you are partners in the chastisement.»[229] In God's eyes there are three types of people: One who is accepted and who can intercede; one who is accepted and who cannot intercede; and one who is rejected. The one who was rejected 34.11

بنفسه فكيف ينجو الناس على يده؟ والمقبول لنفسه غايته نفسه والمقبول المقبول له التكلّم في الغير هو الذي يرجى الانتفاع به بإذن الله تعالى إمّا في العموم أو في الخصوص كثيراً أو قليلاً. فهذا المدّعي الذي يتألّى على الله تعالى ويغرّ عباده ما يُدريه أيّ الثلاث هو؟ فإن كان مردوداً فيا ويله. وإن كان مقبولاً في خاصّة نفسه فما له وللناس؟ وإن كان مقبولاً له الشفاعة فلا يدري أفي كلّ هؤلاء أم في بعضهم أم في غيرهم؟ فحقّه أن يدع الناس ويبكي على نفسه حتّى يرى أين هي. وإن قوي رجاؤه حيناً في الله لنفسه أو لغيره فليقل إن قبلني الله وقبل لي نسأل الله التوفيق.

١،٣٥ وأمّا ما نحن فيه من ادّعاء الاطّلاع على الغيب والتظاهر بالكشف والتصرّف في الوجود فهو الكثير في زماننا في المنتسبين دعوى منهم وتشبّعاً بما لم يعطوا إلّا من عصمه الله وقليل ما هم. فمنهم من يستند إلى مجرّد خيالات مناميّة ويتأوّلها لنفسه ويحكم بها كما مرّ. ومنهم من يحكم ظنّاً وخرصاً وثمّ لا يبالي بالفضيحة ولا ينتهي عن غيّه. فإذا اتّفق صدقه مرّة اتّخذ ذلك حجّة واتّخذه له جهّال العوامّ. فيقولون والله لقد سمعنا منه كلاماً حقّاً فصاروا في ذلك كأصحاب الكهّان من جاهليّة العرب.

٢،٣٥ فقد أخبر صلّى الله عليه وسلّم عنهم بأنّ الرَّئِيّ من الجنّ يخطف الكلمة من الملك فيقرّها في أُذن وليّه من الإنس ثمّ يخلط معها مائة كذبة. فيقول الناس ألم يخبرنا يوم كذا بكذا؟ فكان حقّاً للكلمة التي تلقّفها من الجنيّ. وهكذا المذكورون. وترى الواحد منهم يخبر بأمر أو بعد قضاء حاجة لوقت. فإن اتّفق صدق ذلك بمصادفة قوله للقضاء

was not himself saved, so how can he save people by his hand? The one who is accepted for his own sake is limited to himself. The one who is permitted to speak regarding others is the one through whom, with the permission of Exalted God—in general or specific cases, however often or seldom—one can expect benefit. So, this pretender who carries out religious observances for God and deceives His servants, how can it be known which of the three he is? If he is rejected by God, woe to him! If he is accepted for his own sake, then what about him and the people? If his intercession is accepted, then it is not known if that is for all of them, for some of them, or for others altogether. The right thing for him to do is to abandon the people and to plead for his own soul until he knows where its fate lies. If at that point his hope grows strong for his own soul and those of others, then let him say, "May God accept me and accept others through me." We ask God for success.

As for those we now face who claim to perceive the unseen and to have been given concealed knowledge, and who pretend to alter reality, there are many in our time. They claim to belong to and cleave to a practice that has not been given to them, but to those protected by God, of whom there are very few. There are those who rely merely on illusions they saw in dreams and interpret them for their own purposes and act on their basis, as discussed above. There are those who make such judgments based on opinion and conjecture, without caring about the resulting disaster, and without ceasing their transgressions. If such a person happens to be right once, he takes this as proof of his status and the ignorant masses do the same. They then say, "By God, we have heard him utter the truth," thereby becoming like the followers of the Arab soothsayers before Islam. 35.1

The Prophet, God bless and keep him, related about them that one of the jinn who instructed men in magic would capture a word from an angel and report it in the ear of his human master, mixing it with a hundred lies. The people would say, "Did he not inform us that day of such a thing?" And it was true, in accordance with the word that he had snatched from the jinn. So it is with those mentioned above. You see one of them foretelling a matter, or something decreed after the passage of time. If it corresponds with the truth—a coincidence between his words and the eternal decree—he boasts of this and 35.2

الأزليّ تبجّح بذلك ورعَد على الناس وبَرَق. وإن كذب اكفهرّ في وجوه الناس وتنكّر أو تغيّب أيّاماً حتّى ينسى ذلك فيعود إلى ترّهاته.

٣،٣٥ وما مثاله في ذلك إلّا مثال امرأة أيّم عندها عدّة بنات مشهورات بالملاحة ولكنّهن بغايا فاسدات. كما قال ذو الرمة: [طويل]

عَلَى وَجْهِ مَيٍّ مَسْحَةٌ مِنْ مَلَاحَةٍ وَتَحْتَ ٱلثِّيَابِ ٱلْعَارُ لَوْ كَانَ بَادِيَا

٤،٣٥ فجعلت تنوّه بذكرهنّ وتستميل إليهنّ قلوب السفهاء أمثالهنّ حتّى اشتهر أنّ عند فلانة البنات الحسان. فجاء مغرور فخطب إليها فأنكحته واحدة منهنّ فانقلب جذلان لا يبالي ما أنفق ولا ما أهدى منشداً بلسان حاله: [طويل]

وَمَنْ طَلَبَ ٱلْحَسْنَاءَ لَمْ يُغْلِهِ ٱلْمَهْرُ

٥،٣٥ وجعلت للدخول موعداً فلمّا دخل أخفق فأصبح بئساً خاسر الصفقة. وحين أحسّت العجوز بذلك تنكّرت وتعيّبت حتّى نُسِيَ ذلك. فرجعت تذكر بناتها أيضاً. فيجيء أحمق آخر خاطباً فإذا قال له النصحاء ويحك أليس لك فيما وقع لفلان مع هذه الفاجرة عبرة؟ يقول من فرط شغفه بما سمع من الحسن ذلك أمر قد يتّفق ولعلّه في تلك البنت فقط لا في غيرها. فيتقدّم ويقع له كما وقع للآخر. ثمّ يجيء مغرور آخر لا علم له بما كان وهكذا إلى أن يتّفق لواحد أن يجد الأمر كما يجب. فتخرج وتطيل لسانها وتقول من عنده في الوجود مثل بناتي؟

٦،٣٥ ويقول الناس والله إنّ فلاناً تزوّج منها بنتاً فوجدها كما يحبّ وتذهب تلك المساوي كلّها في هذه الحسنة الواحدة. فما أظرف هؤلاء الحمقى إذ يحكمون بأنّ الحسنات وإن قلّت يذهبن السيئات وإن كثرت. وهكذا الفقير المدّعي يتظاهر بإخبارات وتصرّفات هي حسنة لذيذة عند العوامّ لموافقتها لشهواتهم وحاجاتهم. وهي فاسدة

instills terror in people. If it fails to come true, he frowns and denies it, or disappears for days until it is forgotten and then returns to his fakery.

This can best be likened to a widow with several daughters well known for their sweetness, who are in fact corrupt and promiscuous women. As Dhū l-Rummah said: 35.3

Upon Mayya's face is the appearance of sweetness
but under her dress is her shame, were it only visible.

The widow would praise her daughters, and sought to make the hearts of the foolish incline toward others like them. It soon became known that this woman had beautiful daughters. A man who was duped asked for one in marriage, and she agreed to marry him to one of them. He was overwhelmed with happiness and gave no thought to what he spent or the presents he bestowed. While in in this state, he recited: 35.4

No dowry too high for one who seeks beautiful women.

The mother set a date, and on the wedding night, when he went in to his wife he was disappointed and distressed because he had made a bad bargain. When the old woman became aware of this, she denied it and made excuses until the matter was forgotten, and resumed praising her daughters. Then another fool arrived asking for one of them in marriage, and well-meaning observers advised him, saying, "Be careful! Isn't what happened to so-and-so with this debauched woman a lesson for you?" Out of the excessive infatuation resulting from what he had heard of their beauty, he responded with, "That may be the case, but perhaps it is only true of that daughter, and not the others." He then proceeds to experience the same thing as the first. Then another deluded man comes along without any knowledge of what has proceeded, and so it continues until one of them happens upon the truth of the matter. The woman then presents herself and says insolently, "Who in the world has daughters like mine?" 35.5

Regarding this, the people say, "By God, one fellow married one of her daughters and found her to be as he liked and this one good woman compensates for the rest!" How charming are these fools in their judgment that even if there are only a few good women, they compensate for the bad ones, however many they be![230] This is the way it is with the alleged dervish, who fabricates stories and striking behaviors, an attractive prospect that appeals to their 35.6

لبطلانها وانبنائها على غير أساس. فإذا ظهر كذبه في الواحدة قالوا سبحان الفاعل لما يشاء والقادر يحنث عبد القادر. وبهذا أيضاً يعتذر هو.

٧،٣٥ وكنت تحدّثت مع بعض الأصحاب في هذا المنزع فقلت لهم إنّ المدّعين لا يدخلون في الإسلام حتّى يفتضحوا. فاستعجبوا من ذلك وسألوا عن تأويله. فقلت لهم إنّ المدّعي حين تهيج له الظنون الكاذبة والوساوس الباطلة يحكم بوقوع أمور ولا يذكر الله تعالى ولا يعرّج على مشيئته وسعة علمه وعظيم قهره. حتّى إذا افتضح ببطلان ما قال رجع إلى الحقّ وجعل يقول الأمر أمر الله والحكم حكمه وما شاء كان وما لم يشأ لم يكن. [طويل]

فَـهلّاَ تَلاَ حَامِيمَ قَبْلَ ٱلتَّقَدُّمِ[1]

٨،٣٥ ومنهم من يتظاهر بالوجد والسكر ويقول ما يقول في ذلك. فإذا كذّب ولِيمَ يقول والله ما أدري حين تكلّمت ما أقول وما لي اختيار. ويظنّ أنّه يتخلّص بهذا من الملامة وهيهات ذلك! فإنّه إن كان نطقهُ عن عمْد فهو افتراء للكذب وإلّا فالشيطان يلعب به ترقيصاً وضرباً واستنطاقاً وناهيك بها نقيصة.

٩،٣٥ ودخل ذات مرّة عليّ الأديب الفاضل أبو عبد الله محمّد الصالح بن المعطي وأنا إذ ذاك بمدينة مراكش حرسها الله ومعه رجل أسود من ناحية المشرق. فتحدّث الأسود وقال إنّه من وادي العبّاس وزعم أنّه كان ذهب إلى بغداد زائرًا للشيخ عبد القادر رضي الله عنه. وأنّه بقي في مقامه أيّاماً وأنّه رآه فاستتابه ثمّ أمره بالتوجّه إلى شيخ من أهل الوقت في نهر تِيرا يقال له أبو عبد الله. وأنّ بين بغداد وبين ذلك البلد نحو عشرين مرحلة كلّها قفار معاطش لا يعمرها إلّا الحيات والثعابين. وأنّه قال له إنّك ستبلغ في ثلاث ولا ترى بأساً. فبلغ في ذلك سالماً وأنّه بقي عند الشيخ الآخر أيّاماً فردّه إلى بغداد وبلغها في ذلك أيضاً. وأنّه أمره الشيخ عبد القادر بالتوجّه إلى

[1] يزيد ق، ط: وهلا دخل بالله وخرج بالله اوكان من الصديق.

desires and needs. But these actions are false and baseless. If his deception regarding a specific matter becomes evident, they say, "Praise the Agent who does whatever He wishes, and the Almighty who forces His worshipper to lie." And the man in question here excuses himself in like fashion.

I was talking with some of my companions about this issue and told them 35.7
that these pretenders do not enter Islam until they disgrace themselves publically. They were amazed by this and asked how it should be interpreted. "When the false opinions and vain whisperings stir in the pretender," I said, "he makes statements about the things that will happen and fails to recall Exalted God, or to pay heed to His will, the breadth of His knowledge, and the might of His power. Until, when the falsity of what he has said becomes exposed, he returns to the truth, saying, 'This is God's affair and the judgment is His alone: What He wills takes place, what He does not does not.'"

Why not recite the Ḥā Mīm surahs before advancing?[231]

Some of these pretenders feign ecstasy and spiritual intoxication and say 35.8
what they say in such transportations. If someone is accused of lying and is blamed for doing so, he says, "By God, when I spoke I did not know what I was saying. I had no choice." He thinks that by doing so he can rid himself of blame—how wrong he is! If what he said was deliberate, then it was a lie; if not, it was the devil playing with him, knocking him about and causing him to speak—what a terrible thing to befall him.

On one occasion I was in Marrakesh, God protect it, when the distin- 35.9
guished scholar Abū ʿAbd Allāh Muḥammad al-Ṣāliḥ ibn al-Muʿṭī came to see me, accompanied by a black man from the East. The black man said he was from the valley of ʿAbbās. He claimed he had gone to Baghdad to visit the grave of ʿAbd al-Qādir, God be pleased with him, and that he had stayed at the shrine several days. He claimed he had seen ʿAbd al-Qādir, who called on him to repent and ordered him to go to Abū ʿAbd Allāh, a teacher of people in our time, by the River Tīrā. It was twenty days' travel between Baghdad and that place, the entire journey one of desolation and thirst, populated only by serpents and snakes. He told me that ʿAbd al-Qādir had said to him, "You will reach it on the third day and will experience no harm." He reached it safely in that time, and stayed for several days with the other teacher, who sent him back to Baghdad, where he arrived after three days. He told me that the teacher ʿAbd al-Qādir ordered him to travel to Morocco to visit the saints' shrines. When I

بلاد المغرب لزيارة الصالحين. فلمّا رأيت ذلك طمعت أن تكون له رائحة. وكانت لي حاجة فأردت استنجاده فيها.

١٠،٣٥ فحرّكت الصالح وكانت تعتريه هزّة فتحرّك وصاح. فلمّا تحرّك تحرّك ذلك الرجل وكثر اضطرابه وزعيقه. ثمّ وعد بالحاجة لأمد قريب وزعم أنّ الشيخ عبد القادر هو الحاكم بذلك. فلم يلبث أن حلّ الأجل ولم يقع ذلك وروجع فلم يوجد عنده حاصل فعلّم أنّ الشيطان استفزّه. فقلت للصالح ارتجالاً مطايبة ونصحاً: [سريع]

أَيْنَ ٱلَّذِي قَدْ قَالَ يَا صَالِحُ مَنْ هُوَ عِنْدَ زَعْمِهِ صَالِحُ
وَإِذْ بَدَا مَا قَالَهُ زَائِفاً فَهْوَ لَعَمْرِي ٱلْكَاذِبُ ٱلطَّالِحُ
يَلْعَبُ شَيْطَانٌ بِهِ جَهْرَةً فَهْوَ إِلَى وَسْوَاسِهِ جَانِحُ
يَحْسَبُهُ ٱلْقُطْبَ ٱلَّذِي يَدَّعِي وَٱلْقُطْبُ لَا يَكْذِبُ يَا صَالِحُ
فَأَنْصَحُهُ كَيْ يُقْلِعَ عَنْ غَيِّهِ فَحَسْبُهُ ٱلْمُنْتَهَجُ ٱلْوَاضِحُ
تَقْوَى ٱلْإِلٰهِ وَٱعْتِصَامٌ بِهِ فِي سُنَّةٍ وَٱلْعَمَلُ ٱلصَّالِحُ
هٰذَا لَعَمْرِي غَنِيَّةُ ٱلْمُغْتَنِي وَذَا لَعَمْرِي ٱلْمَتْجَرُ ٱلرَّابِحُ
يَا أَيُّهَا ٱلنَّاسُ ٱعْلَمُوا إِنَّمَا عَبْدُ ٱلْإِلٰهِ ٱلظَّافِرُ ٱلنَّاجِحُ
مَنْ يَعْبُدُ ٱلْمَوْلَى وَيُعْنَى بِمَا يَعْنِيهِ لَا وَانٍ وَلَا مَازِحُ
وَلَا أَخُو دَعْوَى وَلَا مُفْتَرٍ وَلَا بِمَرْتَعِ ٱلْهَوَى سَارِحُ
وَلَا عَنُودٌ عَنْ سَبِيلِ ٱلتُّقَى يَوْماً وَلَا عَنِ ٱلْهُدَى جَانِحُ
وَٱلْمَرْءُ لَا يَجْنِي سِوَى غَرْسِهِ غَادٍ إِلَيْهِ كَسْبُهُ رَائِحُ
وَهْوَ لِمَا يَعْتَصُّ فِي نَفْسِهِ مِنْ مَأْرَبٍ يَقْتَادُهُ كَادِحُ

learned this, I hoped that he possessed the scent of heaven. There was a matter for which I wanted to ask his help.

I roused al-Ṣāliḥ, who was trembling, and he stirred and shouted. When he moved, this man moved as well, and his distress and cries only increased. He then foretold that something would occur after a short interval and claimed that the teacher ʿAbd al-Qādir would be the one to make it happen. It did not take long for the time to arrive and for it not to take place. He returned to himself, having achieved nothing and knowing that the devil had provoked him. I then extemporized to al-Ṣāliḥ, in both jest and counsel: 35.10

Where is the one who said, O Ṣāliḥ, pure one?
Who is he to claim he is pure—
When it is clear what he said was false?
By my life, a wicked liar is he.
The devil plays with him openly
as he inclines to his whispering.
The Axis he calls upon holds him to account
and the Axis does not lie, Ṣāliḥ.
I counsel him to give up his transgressions,
for the conduct he pursued is clear.
Fear God and hold fast to piety.
Follow the Prophet's conduct, do good works.
By my life! This is all you need.
By my life! This is a profitable business!
People, know that the true servant of God,
successful and victorious,
Worships Him, concerned only
with what God assigns, unflagging, without jest.
He neither complains nor is idle;
does not graze in vanity's pastures
Or stray from the pious path
for even a day, adhering to the true faith.
He harvests no more than he grows,
achieving his yield before the sun is high.
When commited to something in his soul,
he works tirelessly toward that end.

وَٱلطَّبْعُ مَلَاكُ زِمَامِ ٱلْفَتَى وَسَيْرُهُ بِسِرِّهِ بَائِحُ
وَٱلصِّدْقُ سَيْفٌ صَارِمٌ حَدُّهُ كَشَّافُ كُلِّ مَعُوصٍ فَائِحُ
وَكُلُّ مَنْ أَسَرَّ مَكْتُومَةً فَوَجْهُهَا فِي وَجْهِهِ لَائِحُ
إِنْ تَكُ نُورًا فَهْوَ مِنْهَا مُضِي أَوْ ظُلْمَةً فَهْوَ بِهَا كَالِحُ
وَمَنْ يُرُمْ نَيْلَ ٱلْمُنَى بِٱلْمُنَى فَهْوَ عَنِ ٱلْفَوْزِ بِهَا نَازِحُ
وَمَنْ يَخِمْ عَنْهَا وَلَا يَقْتَحِمْ أَبْوَابَهَا فَهْوَ ٱمْرُؤٌ دَالِحُ
وَمَا عَلَى ٱلْمَرْءِ سِوَى جِدِّهِ وَجُهْدِهِ وَرَبُّهُ ٱلْمَانِحُ

وقد انحصرت دعاويهم في الحدثان الكوائن ومآرب الناس. ولم يرتقوا إلى ما فوق ذلك لجهلهم. فاشتغلوا بما يطلبه العوامّ من الأمور المذكورة. وذلك لو فتح لهم دون ما فوقه لكان أمرًا تافهًا لا يلتفت إليه ذو همّة. فإنّ أولياء الله تعالى يكشف لهم عن الذاتّ والصفات والأسماء كشفًا لا تبلغه العقول وعن ملكوت السماوات والأرض وعن العرش والكرسيّ والجنّة والنار والملك والروح وغير ذلك. ١١،٣٥

فمن لم يبلغ ذلك واطّلع على كون المسافر يقدّم غدًا وفلان يتولّى وفلان ينعزل وفلان يتزوّج ونحو ذلك وفرح به. كان بمنزلة من دخل سوقًا فيها صيارفة الذهب والفضّة والجوهر والياقوت وباعة الحرير وسائر البزّ والعبيد والخيل والإبل والبرّ والأرز. فوقع على بائع نبق فاشترى منه النبق وذهب به فرحًا وقال إنّه قد تسوّق كما تسوّق الناس. ولا ريب أنّ ما ذهب به يفرح الصبيان به ومن لا عقل له من النسوان. وكذلك الكوائن يفرح بها صبيان العقول وكلّ من لم يبلغ مبلغ الرجال من عوامّ الناس. ١٢،٣٥

Character is what guides a young man.
His conduct reveals what's hidden within.
Sincerity is a sharp sword,
the edge illuminating every obscurity.
All who keep a secret hidden,
it shows clearly on their face.
If you are light it will illuminate you.
If you are darkness you will stay in its shadow.
Whoever seeks to achieve his desires through false hopes
will not achieve success.
Whoever denies his desires and does not storm their gates
carries a heavy burden.
Diligence is man's only possession,
along with his efforts and God's generosity.

The claims of these frauds can be reduced to foreknowledge of future occurrences and peoples' desires. Their ignorance has prevented them from knowing anything more than this. Thus, they have exerted themselves in the matters sought after by the masses. If anything less were revealed to them, it would be insignificant and unworthy of attention. The divine essence, characteristics, and names are revealed to the Friends of Exalted God in a manner that is beyond rational comprehension, as is the case regarding the realms of heaven and earth, the throne and the footstool, heaven and hell, dominion and the spirit, and so on. 35.11

One who has not reached this level and then perceives the world of the spiritual traveler will the following day utter things such as "So-and-so will become ruler," and "so-and-so will be deposed," and "so-and-so will get married," and will take joy in doing so. He is like someone who enters a market in which there are dealers in gold, silver, jewels, gems, silk and other fabrics, slaves, horses, camels, wheat, and rice. He happens upon a seller of lotus blossoms, buys some from him and happily leaves. He says that he has traded in the market as people do. Such acts would doubtless bring joy to young boys and simple-minded women. In the same fashion, those with juvenile minds take pleasure in foretelling future events, as do the common people who have not reached maturity. 35.12

ومنهم من يستخدم جنيّاً فيأتيه بخبر الناس وخبر من يَرِد عليه مثلاً وما أتى به من الهدية وما وقع له في الطريق. فيخبر بذلك قبل مجيئه ويخبره إذا ورد. فلا يشكّ العوامّ أنّه كشف ربّانيّ وأنّه من أولياء الله وقد يكون من أعداء الله كما أخبرونا عن رجل ممّن تصدّر للمشيخة والناس مقبلون عليه. فأتى رجل إلى مسجده فجلس في زاوية منه. فإذا بالمرابط قد دخل فنظر يميناً وشمالاً فلمّا لم يرَ أحداً رفع ثوبه وجعل يبول في المسجد يميناً وشمالاً حتّى نجّسه. فحينئذ خرجت جنيّة فمثلت بين يديه. فقال لها أيّ شيء جئتني به؟ فقالت ذهبت إلى قبيلة بني فلان فلم أزل أحرّضهم على الزيارة حتّى اتّفقوا وجمعوا من الهديّة كذا وكذا وهم خارجون يوم كذا. فخرج المرابط إلى مجلسه فقال تهيّئوا لبني فلان فإنّهم قادمون عليكم بهديّة كذا. فلمّا قدموا قالوا قد أخبرنا الشيخ بكم وبما جئتم به منذ يوم كذا. فهذا والعياذ بالله كافر والكرامات تحسب له. ١٣،٣٥

ومنهم من يستند إلى التنجيم وعلم الاقترانات وإلى خط الرمل أو نيروجات أخرى تشبهه. ومنهم من يحتال احتيالاً فإذا قدم الوفود مثلاً دسّ إليهم من يسألهم عن سفرهم وما وقع لهم فيخبره ذلك. فإذا خرج جعل يشير إلى تلك الأمور فيقولون قد اطّلع الشيخ على أحوالنا. وقد يحتال في ساعته فينظر مثلاً إلى من بين يديه ثمّ يبتسم أو يحرّك رأسه أو يقول سبحان الله أو لا إله إلّا الله ويكون ذلك الشخص قد خطر له شيء. فيقول ما فعل الشيخ هذا إلّا على ما في قلبي. ويفهم من ذلك إمّا تعجّباً وإمّا إنكاراً و إمّا استحساناً. ويعده مطّلعاً على ذلك وهو لم يطّلع وقد يتكلّم على ما في خاطر السامع صريحاً فلا يشكّ السامع في أنّه كشف ويكون إنّما خطر له ذلك اتّفاقاً حين خطر للآخر كما يقع الحافر على الحافر. فتكلّم عليه ولا اطّلاع له. ١٤،٣٥

There are also those who employ a jinn to acquire information about a person: Who is coming to him, for example, and what presents he brings with him, and what happened to him on the way. The jinn informs them of this before he comes and tells them when he arrives. The common people do not doubt that this is a divine unveiling and that such people are Friends of God. Yet they may in fact be one of the enemies of God, as we were told regarding a man who claimed the rank of a shaykh and had people attending to him. A man came to his mosque and sat in a corner. The ascetic entered and looked around. Seeing no one, he raised his robe and began to urinate in the mosque to the right and the left to render it impure. At that point, a female jinn appeared and stood before him. "What have you brought me?" he asked. "I went to the tribe of the sons of so-and-so," she replied, "and I urged them to visit you until they decided to do so, and they gathered such and such presents together. They will set out on such and such a day." The ascetic then went to his circle and said, "Send greetings to the tribe of the sons of so-and-so, for they are coming to you with such and such a gift." When they arrived, his followers said, "On such and such a day the shaykh told us about you and what you were bringing." This person—God is our refuge—is an unbeliever, and yet these miraculous events are attributed to him. 35.13

There are those who rely on astrology and the science of planetary conjunctions, on geomancy or on other similar divinatory practices. And there are also those who employ stratagems, so that if, for example, delegations approach, such a person may send someone of this kind to infiltrate the delegation and ask them questions about their trip and what had happened to them. This person then reports back to him, so that when he emerges and begins referring to these matters those around him say, "The shaykh has insight into our affairs." He may employ a stratagem extemporaneously and gaze, for example, at the person in front of him, and then smile, shake his head, or say, "God be praised!" or "There is no god but God!" as if something had occurred to him because of this person. The person in question then says, "The shaykh would not have done this if not for what is in my heart," and understands the teacher's action to represent either wonder, rebuke, or approval. He attributes it to the shaykh having spiritual insight into the matter when he does not. He may also speak directly to what is on this listener's mind and his listener will consider this an unveiling when it was mere coincidence. In this case, the shaykh spoke without any spiritual insight. 35.14

١٥،٣٥ وقد يتكلّم بكلام في غرض فيحمله السامع على أنّه إشارة إلى ما في قلبه أو حاجته وإنّه كوشف بذلك. وأكثر ما يحكى من هذا النوع في أهل الزمان إنّما هو من أحد هذه المداخل احتيال من المتبوع أو جهل من التابع. والعوامّ يستنطقون من لا ينطق ويفسدون من لم يفسد. فهم الشياطين في زيّ المؤمنين وما بالك بشيطان في زيّ محبّ؟ وإن استعذت منه عاداك ووقّع فيك في الغيب بالإذاية زيادة على ما فعل في الحضور. فهو شرّ من الشيطان الآخر بكثير. فكن منهم على حذر كما قيل: [وافر]

فَخَفْ أَبْنَاءَ جِنْسِكَ وَٱخْشَ مِنْهُمْ كَمَا تَخْشَى ٱلضَّرَاغِمَ وَٱلسَّبَنْتَى
وَخَالِطْهُمْ وَزَايِلْهُمْ حِذَارًا وَكُنْ كَٱلسَّامِرِيِّ إِذَا لَمَسْتَا

١،٣٦ واعلم أنّ أشرف ما يكاشف به العبد ما يرجع إلى معبوده تعالى من معرفته وما له من الجلال والجمال ومن أسماء عليّة وصفات سنيّة كما مرّ. ثمّ ما يرجع إلى حكمته في مملكته ثمّ ما يرجع إلى أحكامه من معرفة ما تعبّد به عباده أصلاً وفرعاً وكلّ علم يعين على ذلك. وقد وقع في كلام الشيخ الصالح أبي عبد الله السنوسيّ رضي الله عنه حين تكلّم عن مذهب أهل السنّة في أفعال الحيوان وأنّهم أطلعهم الله على المعنى الجامع بين الحقيقة والشريعة وجنّبهم جانبي القدر والجبر ذلك. فقال هذا هو الكشف الذي ينبغي أن يسمّى كشفاً لا ما يبتلى به الجاهلون من أحلام شيطانيّة يتوهّمونها كرامات وهي استدراجات أو نحو هذا من الكلام.

٢،٣٦ فهذه الجملة كلّها كلّما يزداد فيها العبد ازداد كمالاً لأنّه أمر مطلوب منه الاطّلاع عليه. فطلبه قُربة وحصوله درجة ووجوده منفعة. وأمّا ما خرج عن هذا من جزئيات الكون التي هي متعلّقات القضاء والقدر ولا يتعلّق بها حكم فليست مطلوبة من

He may also speak regarding an issue and the listener can interpret it to be a reference to what is in his heart or to what he is preoccupied with, and believes it was revealed to the shaykh. Most such things recounted about the people of our time consist of this type of behavior: a stratagem of the one being followed, or the ignorance of the follower. The common folk seek words from those who do not speak and they corrupt the uncorrupted. They are devils dressed up as believers—what do you make of a devil dressed as a dear friend? When you seek refuge with him, he treats you as an enemy and causes far more harm when absent than when present. He is worse than any other devil by far. So be on your guard! As the poet has said:[232] 35.15

Fear your brethren and be wary of them
as you are wary of lions and wolves.
Mingle and interact with them with care;
be like the Samaritan when they touch you.[233]

The noblest things revealed to the worshipper through unveiling relate to knowledge of Exalted God—His power, beauty, exalted names, and majestic characteristics, as already discussed. This includes what relates to God's wisdom in His Kingdom, to the root and branches of His ordinances regarding what His worshippers worship, and cognizance of the sciences that deal with the subject. There was something regarding this in the speech of the devout shaykh Abū ʿAbd Allāh al-Sanūsī, God be pleased with him, when he spoke about the Sunni position on the actions of living things. To wit, that Exalted God had granted them knowledge of how to reconcile truth and revelation, and had spared them knowledge of His decree and their fate. On this he said, "This is the nature of unveiling deserving of the name, not the satanic dreams that afflict the ignorant and that they believe to be miracles. Those are all temptations." Or words to that effect. 36.1

The more the worshipper understands this sentence, the more perfect he becomes, for this is a matter he is required to look into. He therefore seeks it out through investigation, acquires it in stages, and then benefits from possessing it. The particulars of creation that emerge from this study, connected with divine Decree and Decision unrelated to God's prescriptions, are not required of the worshipper. Since they are concealed from him, he should not occupy himself with them or concern himself with the plan of Exalted God. 36.2

العبد. إذا أخفيت عنه فأدبه أن لا يشتغل بها شغلاً بالله تعالى وبما لله تعالى عليه. فإن رزقه الله معرفته وشغله بما له عليه وغطّى عنه مملكته وتركه كذلك حتّى يلقاه موفوراً. فقد أسبغ عليه النعمة وحماه من جميع موارد النقمة. وإن أطلعه على شيء من ذلك فليعلم أنّ ذلك لا جدوى له في باب العبوديّة. وإنّما فيه أمر واحد وهو أنّ الكرامة كلّها في الجملة إن صحّت دليل على صدق من ظهرت عليه وعلامة على الخصوصيّة وتثبيت لقدم من أريد تثبيته في الطريق مع ما ينضاف إلى ذلك من الشكر ومن الرجاء والخوف.

٣،٣٦ وفيها مع ذلك من المخاطرة خوف الركون والمساكنة لها والمكر. كما قيل إنّها خدع من الحقّ للمتوجّهين ليقفوا على الحدّ الذي أريد بهم ولا يجاوزوا إلى مقام لم يكن لهم. وذلك فيمن أريد بذلك نسأل الله العافية. فحقّ العبد التسليم والاعتناء بحقوق الله والإعراض عن حظوظه. وإن طلب شيئاً من ذلك طلبه بإذن ليصير من الحقوق كما أنّه أيضاً لا يهرب منها إلّا بأدب لئلّا يصير الهرب من الحظوظ.

٤،٣٦ وهذا الكلام ربما يحتاج إلى تفسير غير أنّا نقتصر. فقد خرجنا أو كدنا نخرج عمّا نحن فيه. وِمنْ حُسْنِ إسْلامِ المَرْءِ تَرْكُهُ مَا لا يَعْنِيهِ. واعلم أنّ ما ذكر من أحوال المدّعين على وجه النصح لهم ولمن يغترّ بهم. إنّما أردنا تخليده في بطون الأوراق ليقع عليه الخواصّ أهل الأدب والفقه الذين يضعون الهناء موضع النقب فيعطون كلّ ذي حقّ حقّه مع حفظ الحُرْمَة وإقامة حقّ النسبة كما أشرنا إليه في صدر هذا الكلام.

٥،٣٦ ولم نرد أن نفتح الباب لكلّ جامد على الظاهر أو خبيث جريء على أهل النسبة مسقط للحرمة فيتّخذ مثالب المنتسبين إلى الله تعالى فاكهةً ويمزّق أديمهم في مجالس السفهاء حتّى يدخل الوهن على النسبة والطعن في الخرقة. فيُزْري العُرْيانُ باللابس

For God granted him what he knows, occupied him with what is encumbent on him, and concealed His kingdom from him—leaving him until he becomes immersed in what he was given. God bestowed blessings on him liberally, and protected him from all sources of affliction. If He granted him knowledge of some of His kingdom, it was to emphasize the fact that it was empty of value for worship. Indeed, there is just one issue here, which is that if the miracle is authentic, its overarching significance lies in the sincerity of the one with whom it appeared. It is a sign of his having been signaled out, and is proof of God having previously established him on the spiritual path with all the thanksgiving, supplication, and piety that involves.

Despite this, in the matter of miracles there are dangers, including the fear 36.3
of trusting in them, of being associated with them, and of their being a trick. It has been said that a miracle is a perversion of the truth for those inclined to accept it; that they should hold to the limits set for them, not exceed it in striving toward a station that is not theirs to attain. This is the case for those I am considering. We ask God to protect us from this. It is the duty of the worshipper to submit and attend to what God has established, and not be preoccupied with his allotted fortune. If he seeks some element of this fortune, he should do so in order that, with God's permission, it may become part of his God-given rights. Similarly, he should not flee what God has established save with the proper comportment, so that he does not seem to be fleeing from his fortune.

What has been said here may require explanation beyond the summary 36.4
I have given. We have deviated, or have come close to deviating, from what we were discussing: "It is a positive aspect of a person's submission to God to eschew what does not concern him." Mentioning the antics of imposters is meant as advice for them and for those deluded by them. I wanted to place it for eternity in the midst of these pages so that the elect may come upon it—the jurists and the people of proper comportment—those who hide blemishes and who give each person his due, preserving that which is holy and establishing the truth of a miracle's attribution, as we indicated at the beginning of this section.

We did not wish to open the door for all those who are fixed on what is obvi- 36.5
ous, or those who are unseemly toward the saints, toppling their sanctity—as such a person mocks the faults of those associated with Exalted God and rips their reputation in gatherings of fools to the point that their association with God becomes weak and the adept's cloak is rent. The naked will then revile clothing and burn the wet with the dry. Let the obstinate and ignorant

ويحترق الرطب باليابس. وليعلم الجاهل الجمود أنّ هذه الأمّة المطهّرة المشرّفة كالمطر لا يدرى أوّلها خير أم آخرها. ولا تزال طائفة منها ظاهرين على الحقّ لا يضرّهم من خالفهم كما أخبر به الصادق المصدوق صلّى الله عليه وسلّم.

٦،٣٦ في كلّ زمان سادة وفي كلّ قُطر قادة فكم من طالع في الدين كالشمس وإن لم يبصره العُميُ والعُمشُ؟ وكم من محبوب يرفل في حلل الأنس والإدلال ويرتضع كؤوس الجمال والإجلال؟ لو تحمّل الشفاعة في قرنين قبيلاً فقبيلاً لكان ذلك في جنب حظوته من مولاه قليلاً. وكم من وليّ أرخى عليه الخمول ذيلاً وصار نهاره في أعين أبناء الدهر ليلاً. فأصبح من ضنائن الله بين أوليائه يلعب بالدهر كما لعب الدهر بأبنائه.

٧،٣٦ وقال أبو نواس: [طويل]

تَسَتَّرْتُ مِنْ دَهْرِي بِظِلِّ جَنَاحِهِ فَعَيْنِي تَرَى دَهْرِي وَلَيْسَ يَرَانِي
فَلَوْ تَسْأَلِ ٱلْأَيَّامَ عَنِّي مَا دَرَتْ وَأَيْنَ مَكَانِي مَا عَرَفْنَ مَكَانِي

٨،٣٦ وقال الآخر فيهم: [بسيط]

لِلّٰهِ تَحْتَ قِبَابِ ٱلعِزِّ طَائِفَةٌ أَخْفَاهُمُ فِي رِدَاءِ ٱلْفَقْرِ إِجْلَالَا
هُمُ ٱلسَّلَاطِينُ فِي أَطْمَارِ مَسْكَنَةٍ جَرُّوا عَلَى فَلَكِ ٱلْخَضْرَاءِ أَذْيَالَا
غُبْرٌ مَلَابِسُهُمْ شُمٌّ مَعَاطِسُهُمْ ٱسْتَعْبَدُوا مِنْ مُلُوكِ ٱلْأَرْضِ أَقْيَالَا
هٰذِي ٱلْمَكَارِمُ لَا قَعْبَانِ مِنْ لَبَنٍ شِيبَا بِمَاءٍ فَعَادَا بَعْدُ أَبْوَالَا
هٰذِي ٱلْمَنَاقِبُ لَا ثَوْبَانِ مِنْ عَدَنٍ خِيطَا قَمِيصاً فَعَادَا بَعْدُ أَسْمَالَا

والبيت الرابع لأميّة بن أبي الصلت في سيف بن ذي يزن وهو مشهور.

know that "This honorable, sincere community is like the rain—one does not know whether it is better at the beginning or the end."[234] And as was related by one who is both truthful and trustworthy, God bless and keep him: "A group of this community continues to render the truth manifest and is immune from those who would harm them."

In every age there are the Prophet's descendants and in every region leaders and vicegerents. How many have in the faith soared like the sun, unseen by the blind and the weak of sight? How many of the beloved have paraded in the apparel of joy and pride and have drunk from the cups of grandeur and delight? If such a person, for two generations, one after another, were granted intercession, this would be but a paltry part of what his Lord has granted as his portion. How many of those given power have been brought low and abased by idleness, their days, in the eyes of their contemporaries, turned to darkness? They join the saints and God's friends, playing with Time the same way Time plays with its denizens. 36.6

Abū Nuwās said: 36.7

I was concealed from Time by the shadow of its wing:
  I saw it—it did not see me.
If you ask the days about me, they know nothing.
  If you inquire where I am, they cannot answer.

Another has said regarding these people: 36.8

Under the canopies of glory is a group;
  the least of them, cloaked in poverty, is exalted.
Sultans decked in torn rags,
  dragging their hems in this worldly sphere,
Their clothes dusty, their breaths fragrant,
  bringing the princes of the earth to heel.
These virtues are not like two bowls of milk,
  cut with water, that become urine.
These qualities are not like two robes from ʿAdan,
  revealed later to be sewn shirts become ragged.

The fourth line is by Umayyah ibn Abī l-Ṣalt regarding Sayf ibn Dhī Yazan, and is famous.

٩،٣٦ وكم من راكع ساجد أو متورّع زاهدٍ لا يدنيه الجاهل من ساحة المتقرّبين؟ لكونه لم يرَ عليه سِيما العارفين ولا بهجة المحبّين. ولم يدر أنّ الزهر ألوان والتمر صنوانٌ وغيرُ صِنْوانٍ والعبيد كلّهم عبيد الحضرة من ممسك الكأس إلى مشتري الخضرة. غير أنّه لكلّ حدّ مرسوم ﴿وَمَا مِنَّآ إِلَّا لَهُۥ مَقَامٌ مَّعْلُومٌ﴾ . فعليك بحسن الظنّ وسلامة الصدر للمسلمين وحفظ الحرمة لأهل الدين والتغافل في عين الحذر والتبصّر فيما تأتي وما تذر والله الموفّق. لله الأمر من قبل ومن بعد.

١،٣٧ حدّثني الأخ الصالح الفاضل أبو عبد الله محمّد الصغير بن أبي عمرو المراكشيّ رحمه الله ورحم سلفه. قال أخبرني الوليّ الصالح أبو عبد الله محمّد بن أبي بكر الدلائيّ أنّ شيخ المشايخ سيدي أحمد بن يوسف الراشديّ الملياني لم يكن في وقته يطعم في زاويته. فقالوا له في ذلك فقال نحن أردنا انتفاع المسلمين فإذا قمت أنا وبناتي وتعبنا واحترقنا في طعام المريد الزائر فأيّ نفع يحصل له؟ وفي المعنى أيضاً كلام يتشعّب ونحن نختصر منه قدراً صالحاً إن شاء الله.

٢،٣٧ فنقول إنّ الزاوية المشتهر اسمها اليوم عند أهل الطريق من إطعام الطعام للوافدين والمساكين والملازمين على الدوام حتّى صارت عند العوام كأنّها من الفروض أو الشروط. لا يعلم لها من حيث خصوصها أصل ولا يجري لها ذكر في الكتاب ولا السنّة. وإنّما مرجعها إلى القرى وإكرام الضيف. ولا شكّ أنّه مأمورٌ به. ففي الحديث من كان يؤمن بالله واليوم الآخر فليكرم ضيفه. ولكنّه أمر مشترك بين جميع المؤمنين لا يختصّ بالصوفيّ ولا القدوة وإن كان هؤلاء أحقّ بمنازلة كلّ خلق محمود.

٣،٣٧ وكان صلّى الله عليه وسلّم يقري الضيف ويحضّ أصحابه على ذلك. وربّما ورد الضيوف فيذهب ببعضهم ويذهب أصحابه بالباقي. ويقول من كان عنده طعام واحد فليذهب بثان ومن كان عنده طعام اثنين فليذهب بثالث وهكذا. وكان عنده أصحاب الصُفة نحو أربعين رجل وهم أضياف الإسلام. وكان إذا أتته صدقة

Of those who bow in prayer, who are pious in their asceticism, how many does an ignorant man fail to associate with the ranks of those close to God? He does not see in them the attributes of the spiritually enlightened, nor the splendor of those who love God. He does not know there are differently colored flowers, that no two dates are alike. All slaves are slaves of God, from the cupbearer to the market-goer. Everything has been defined: «Every one of us has a prescribed station.»[235] You should think well of Muslims and approach them with a pure heart, preserve respect for people of faith, avoid casting suspicion, and look into everything that occurs. Success comes from God. Everything is God's to command. 36.9

My devout and distinguished brother Abū ʿAbd Allāh Muḥammad al-Ṣaghīr ibn Abī ʿAmr al-Murrākushī, God have mercy on him and his ancestors, related the following to me: "The devout Friend Abū ʿAbd Allāh Maḥammad ibn Abī Bakr al-Dilāʾī told me that the Shaykh of Shaykhs, Sīdī Aḥmad ibn Yūsuf al-Rāshidī al-Malyānī, was not given to distribute food in his lodge. When asked about this, he said, 'We wanted to benefit Muslims, so my daughters and I did so, exerting and exhausting ourselves by providing food to every visiting disciple, but how does he benefit?'" On this subject, many different things have been said. We will try to summarize this in profitable measure, God willing.[236] 37.1

To that purpose, we can say that today the lodge is renowned among the people of the path for assiduously distributing food to visitors and to the poor, to the point that among the common folk it has come to be seen as one of the lodge's duties or obligations. The origin of this practice is not known, nor is it mentioned in the Qur'an or Hadith. Its origin is rather in the villages and where guests are hosted. There is no doubt that it is something we were directed to do, for in the words of the Prophet we find: "Whoever believes in God and the Last Day should honor his guest." Yet this is shared by all believers and is not specific to Sufis nor to those worthy of emulation, even though they are the most appropriate hosts for all of blessed creation. 37.2

The Prophet, God bless and keep him, used to entertain guests, and would urge his Companions to do the same. When guests were in attendance, he might take the remains of his food to some of them and give his Companions the rest. He would say, "Whoever has food for one, let him feed two. Whoever has food for two, let him feed three," and so on. In his entourage were 37.3

دفعها إليهم وإذا أتته هديّة أخذ منها معهم. وربّما يدخل إلى داره حتّى إذا لم يجد شيئاً دفع الضيف إلى غيره.

٤،٣٧ ولا شكّ أنّ هذا كلّه يكون أصلاً للإطعام في الجملة من غير اختصاص بكيفيّة ولا بدوام ولا تعميم للناس مع أنّه صلّى الله عليه وسلّم اجتمعت له أحوال الظاهر والباطن والولاية والخلافة. فمن حاله الشريف يستمدّ الموفّق من كلّ صنف. ثمّ كان الخلفاء بعده يطعمون على حسب سيرتهم المعلومة ثمّ الملوك بعد ذلك. لله الأمر من قبل ومن بعد.[1]

٥،٣٧ ولمّا ظهرت الصوفيّة لم يعرف من حالهم وجود هذه الزاوية والقيام بكلّ وارد من الجنس وغير الجنس كما هو اليوم. بل كانوا رضي الله عنهم مَعنيّين بما يعنيهم فمنهم المنقبض عن الناس شغلاً بحاله ومنهم المخالط ينتفع الناس منه بعلومه ومعارفه وآدابه. وقد يكون منهم من يستقرّ بين أظهر الناس ومنهم من يكون سائحاً إنّما يلقى في الخلوات والفلوات. وقد يكون منهم من يكون أصحابه هم الذين يقومون بمئونته أو يسأل قدر قوّته. فكان أبو جعفر الحدّاد وهو من أكابر المشايخ يخرج بين العشائين فيسأل من الديار حتّى يحصل على القدر المحتاج في ليلته فيرجع. قالوا وكان له قدم في التوكّل معروف ولم يُزْرِ به ذلك عند أحد.

٦،٣٧ نعم تكون لهم رباطات فيكون فيها المتجرّدون من أصحابهم للعبادة كشبه حال أهل الصُّفّة. وذكر اليافعيّ رحمه الله في ذلك حكاية عن الإمام أبي بكر الشبليّ رضي الله عنه. قال كان عنده في رباطه نحو أربعين مريداً يعبدون ويعيشون بالفتوح. وأنّه اتّفق له ذات مرّة أن يفتح عليهم بشيء حتّى ضاقوا فخرج الشيخ إليهم فحدّثهم في مقام التوكّل وحضّهم على الصبر. ثمّ ذهب عنهم فبقوا بعده أيّاماً أُخر لم يأتهم شيء فلحقتهم الضرورة. فلمّا كان ذلك خرج إليهم فقال لهم إنّ الله تعالى أمرنا بالتوكّل ورخص لنا في الأسباب فتسبّبوا.

١ سقطت الجملة من ط.

people who slept in the mosque's vestibule, close to forty men, the guests of the Muslim community.[237] When alms were handed to him, he would distribute it among them, and when he was given a gift, he shared it with them. When someone entered his house when he had nothing to offer, he would send them to another house.

Doubtless, in this lies the origin of distributing food generally, without any specification as to how it should be done, nor if it should be done constantly, nor whether it was incumbent on all, despite the fact that he, God bless and keep him, united material and spiritual states with power and vicegerency. All permissible actions derive from his noble example, which, according to their well-known biographies, the caliphs followed by distributing food, and kings followed the practice after them. Everything is God's to command. 37.4

When the Sufis made their first appearance, they were not associated with lodges as they are each linked to one or other of them today. Rather, they were, God be content with them, distinctive in other ways: Some withdrew from society, preoccupied with their condition; others mixed with people, who benefited from them and their knowledge, their spiritual insight, and their morals. Some of them settled down publicly in society; some wandered abroad, only to be found in retreats and remote places. Some were brought provisions by their companions or begged for their sustenance. Abū Jaʿfar al-Ḥaddād, one of the greatest shaykhs, would go from house to house to those taking their evening meal. When he had obtained what he needed for the night, he would return with it. People said, "He had set a famous precedent for relying upon God, so no one rebuked him for begging." 37.5

The Sufis did have retreats, in which their renunciant companions devoted themselves to prayer, just as the "people of the vestibule" did. Al-Yāfiʿī, God have mercy on him, related a story about the exemplar Abū Bakr al-Shiblī, God be content with him, on this subject: "In his retreat, he had about forty devotees who worshipped and lived on alms. On one occasion, it happened that he did something so they might experience distress: The shaykh went to them and spoke to them of the station of reliance upon God and urged forbearance. He then left and they spent many days without any food being brought to them. When their situation became dire, he returned to them and said, 'Truly, Exalted God has commanded us to rely upon Him and has also permitted us to take causes into account—reflect on them!' And they did so. 37.6

٧،٣٧ ففعلوا ذلك وخرج الواحد منهم إلى البلد وجعل يجول في الأسواق والمجامع من غير أن يسأل أحداً. وإنّما يعرض نفسه لما يفتح الله تعالى من رزق. فلم يفتح عليه بشيء حتّى انتهى إلى طبيب نصرانيّ قد حلّق الناس عليه وهو يصف لهم الأدوية. فجلس بين يديه ومدّ إليه يده ليجسّ نبضه بلا كلام. فجسّ الطبيب يده فقال له أنا أعرف مرضك وأعرف دواءه. ثمّ قال لغلام له عليّ برطل من الشواء مع خبز وحلواء. فأحضر الغلام ذلك. فقال الطبيب للفقير أنت جائع وهذا دواؤك. فقال الفقير إن كنت صادقاً فمن ورائي أربعون كلّهم بهذا المرض. فقال الطبيب لأصحابه أحضروا من هذا الطعام ما يكفي أربعين. فأحضروا ذلك فأمر الطبيب من يحمله وأمر الفقير أن يمشي معهم إلى أصحابه. فلمّا خرجوا تبعهم الطبيب مستخفياً ليعلم أَصَدَقَ الفقير أم لا. فأدخلوا ذلك إلى الرباط واستدعوا الشيخ فخرج اليهم فوضعوا الطعام بين يديه فقال ما هذا؟ فقصّ عليه الفقير القصّة على وجهها. فقال لهم أَفَتَرضون أن تأكلوا طعام رجل من غير أن تكافئوه؟ فقالوا فكيف نكافئه يا أستاذ؟ فقال تدعون له. فأخذوا في الدعاء له.

٨،٣٧ والطبيب في كلّ ذلك ينظر إليهم من طاق. فلمّا رأى صدق القول ورأى حالهم من المحافظة على الحقوق وارتفاع هممهم مع غاية الحاجة من غير أن يتناولوا الطعام قبل المكافأة ألقى الله تعالى الأيمان في قلبه. فدخل عليهم وقال للشيخ مدّ يدك وتشهّد شهادة الحقّ ودخل في صحبتهم فصار من الصوفيّة ولله الحمد. فانظر أيّها الناظر في حكمة المولى المتفضّل كيف أمسك عن أوليائه الرزق ليخرجوا إلى الخلق فيصطادوا هذا الوليّ الروميّ حين حان أوان الوصال والخروج من سجن القطيعة إلى حضرة مولاه. فسبحان من يقرّب من يشاء وهو ذو الفضل العظيم. وإنّما هي السابقة وكلّ ميسّر لما خلق له. فكم من وليّ لله تعالى في وسطه زنّار وكم من كافر يؤذن فوق المنار؟ نسأل الله تعالى السلامة والعافية. ويظهر من القصّة أنّ هؤلاء الفقراء يأتيهم

"One of them then went to the city and began to roam through the markets and meeting places without begging from anyone, instead accepting whatever sustenance Exalted God bestowed. He was given nothing until he came to a Christian doctor around whom people were gathered for medical prescriptions. He sat in front of the doctor and without speaking extended his hand to have his pulse taken. The physician examined his hand and said, 'I know what ails you and how to cure it,' and told one of his slaves, 'Bring me a pound of grilled meat with bread and halva.' When the slave brought this to him, the doctor said to the devotee, 'Your sickness is hunger and this is your medicine.' The devotee responded, 'If you are sincere in this, you should know that there are forty others behind me suffering from the same sickness.' The physician said to his companions, 'Bring enough food for forty men.' When they had, the physician ordered them to transport it and instructed the devotee to take them to his companions. The physician followed them surreptitiously to find out whether the devotee had been truthful or not. They brought the food to the retreat and called the shaykh. When he appeared, they placed the food before him, and he said, 'What is this?' The devotee told him what had transpired and the shaykh said, 'Are you content to eat a man's food without compensating him for it?' 'Teacher,' they answered, 'how are we to do this?' 'Pray for him,' he said, so they began to pray for him. 37.7

"The physician had been watching throughout from an archway. When he had gathered that what had been said was true, and saw how they upheld the rights of those involved and the extent of their concern for doing so while nearly starved, not eating the food before offering compensation for it, Exalted God placed true faith in his heart. He revealed himself to them and said to the shaykh, 'Extend your hand and witness my testimony of faith.' He joined them and followed the Sufi path. God be thanked!" Consider, reader, the wisdom of the blessed Lord—how He removed sustenance from his saints so that they would wander among the masses and hunt down this Byzantine saint when the time had come for his reunion with God, that is, of his release from the prison of estrangement into the presence of his Lord. Praise the One who brings close whom He wishes, Possessor of virtue boundless. Truly, the precedent for this is in the hadith: "Everything that comes easily to him was created for him." How many of God's friends wear the *zunnār* around their waist, and how many unbelievers sound the call to prayer from the minaret? We ask Exalted God for safety and preservation. As is clear from the story, these devotees brought 37.8

الفتوح لرباطهم لا أنّ الطعام يخرج لهم من دار الشيخ كما جرى في عرف اليوم. بل قد أشركوا الشيخ في طعامهم في هذه القصّة.

٩،٣٧ وكان بعد ذلك الشيخ يوسف العجميّ فيما حكى من سيرته يخرج الواحد من أصحابه ويذهب بدابّة معه. فيسأل النهار كلّه إلى الليل وما اجتمع يأتي به إلى الفقراء وبذلك يعيشون. وصورة السؤال أن يقف بباب الدار والحانوت فيقول الله ويمدّ بها صوته حتّى يكاد يغشى عليه ويسقط. قالوا وكانوا يتناوبون في الخروج بينهم وبين الشيخ يخرج الخارج يوماً لأنفسهم ويوماً للشيخ. فكان الخارج لهم يأتي بالدابّة مُوقرة لحماً وخبزاً وجبناً وبصلاً وغير ذلك.

١٠،٣٧ وفي يوم الشيخ إنّما يأتي بكسيرات يأكلها فقير واحد. فقالوا له في ذلك فقال أنتم بشريّتكم باقية فبينكم وبين الخلق ارتباط فيعطونكم. وأنا بشريّتي قد فنيت حتّى لا تكاد ترى فليس بيني وبين التجّار والسوقة وأبناء الدنيا كبير مجانسة. قالوا وكان يأمر بإغلاق باب الزاوية طول النهار لا يفتح لأحد إلّا للصلاة. وإذا دقّ أحد يقول للنقيب اذهب وانظر من شقّ الباب. فإن كان معه شيء من الفتوح للفقراء فافتح له وإلّا فهي زيارات فشارات. فقال بعض الناس في ذلك فقال الشيخ أعزّ ما عند الفقير وقته وأعزّ ما عند أبناء الدنيا مالهم إن بذلوه لنا بذلنا لهم وقتنا.

١١،٣٧ وقد شاع اليوم إقامة الصوفيّة الزوايا بإطعام الطعام ولا سيّما في بلادنا المغربيّة وخصوصاً في البوادي. وما يكون من فتوح يأتي إلى يد الشيخ وهو ينفق فيه على المجاورين والواردين. وهذا قد كان فيهم من قديم. ففي ترجمة الشيخ أبي يعزى أنّ الناس كانوا يأتون إليه من كلّ بلد فيطعمهم من عنده ويعلف دوابهم. وأنّ الفتوح كانت تأتيه من إخوانه في الله تعالى فينفقها على زائريه.

١٢،٣٧ وأنّ أهل القرى القريبة منه كانوا يضيفون الواصلين لزيارة أبي يعزى ويتبرّكون بهم. فلمّا مات أبو يعزى رِيءَ في النوم وهو يطير في الهواء. فقيل له بم نلت ما

donations to their retreat, and the food did not come to them from the house of the shaykh, as is the custom today; in this story, the shaykh shares his food with them.

The following is recounted in the biography of the shaykh Yūsuf al-ʿAjamī: 37.9
One of his companions ventured out, leading a donkey. From dawn till dusk he would beg, bringing what he received to the other devotees. This was how they lived. They would beg like this: One would stop at the door of a house or shop and say, "God!" raising his voice so high that he almost swooned and fell to the ground. They would alternate in selecting one of their number and their shaykh: one day one of them, the following day the shaykh. When a devotee went out, the donkey would return weighed down with meat, bread, cheese, onions, and other things.

On the shaykh's day, it would return with only enough pieces of bread for 37.10
one devotee. They spoke to him about this and he explained, "Your human nature remains, sustaining a connection between you and the masses, and they bestow much on you. My human nature has been subsumed to the point where it can't be seen, and there is no great traffic between me and the merchants, the rabble, and the denizens of this world." He used to order the door of the lodge to be locked during the day, not opening for anyone except at prayer-time. When someone knocked, he would tell the gatekeeper, "Go and see who is knocking at the door. If he has any type of donation for the acolytes, open it for him. If not, it is an idle visit." Someone complained about this, and the shaykh responded, "The dearest thing to the devotee is his time and the dearest thing to the inhabitants of this world is their money. If they share it with us, we will share our time with them."

It is a widespread practice today for the Sufis of the lodges to distribute 37.11
food, especially in our lands of North Africa, specifically in the countryside. Whatever donations come into the hands of the lodge are given to those near them and to visitors. This has been the custom for a long time. In the biography of the teacher Abū Yiʿzzā we find that the people used to visit him from everywhere and he would feed them with what he had at hand and would give fodder to their riding beasts. Donations came from his brothers in Exalted God, which he spent on visitors.

The people of the neighboring villages would host those who visited Abū 37.12
Yiʿzzā, obtaining blessing through them. When Abū Yiʿzzā died, someone saw him in a dream, flying through the air. "How did you do that?" he was asked,

نلت؟ فقال بإطعام الطعام. ويحكى عن الشيخ أبي محمد عبد الخالق بن ياسين الدغوغيّ أنّه كان يقول طلبنا التوفيق زماناً فأخطأناه فإذا هو في إطعام الطعام. وقد اشتهر ذلك اليوم حتّى إنّ عوام البادية يرون ذلك كأنّه شرط فيمن انتصب للزيارة أو تصدّى للمشيخة. ويعدّون قوّة ذلك وتيسّره من كراماته ولا يبالون بمن لم يروا ذلك على يده. فوقع في ذلك منافع عظام وآفات جسام.

١٣،٣٧ وأهل الزوايا مختلفون منهم من يطعم الناس من مال أبيه أو من كدّ يمينه من غير أن يدخل عليه فتوح أصلاً فهذا أقرب الناس إلى السلامة وأبعد عن الشبهة. وهو منتفع بحصول الأجر فيما أنفق وفي سدّ خلّة المحتاج وفي ترغيب الناس في الخير بما يحصل لهم من الميل الطبيعي وفي اجتماع أهل الخير عنده وفي تعاونهم على البرّ وتعلّم العلم والأدب والمعرفة وتربية الخير وإحياء مراسم الطريق وتكثير سواد أهله وغير ذلك من الوجوه المستحسنة والمصالح المتبيّنة. وينتفع الناس معه بما ذكر وبحسن الظنّ به وبالطريق وبأهلها وبسلامتهم من كلّ ما يقابل ذلك من الآفات. إن كانت لا تأتيه الفتوح فذاك وإن كانت تأتيه ويردّها فلا شكّ أنّها حالة رفيعة. ولكن لا بدّ أن يحذر آفة الردّ كما يحذر آفة الأخذ ولا سيّما في الردّ على إخوانه وأتباعه.

١٤،٣٧ ومن الآفات المشاهدة اليوم في ذلك أنّ الشحّ عياذاً بالله قد غلب على الناس ولا سيّما فيما هو لله خالصاً إذ لا باعث عليه من النفس. فتجد الفقير يثقل عليه أن يتصدّق بدرهم لمسكين محتاج ويتيم وأرملة. ويخفّ عليه أن يحمل الدينار والدينارين إلى دار شيخه وذلك إما لبواعث شهوانيّة كطلب الأعواض العاجلة أو مساعفة الغير أو المراياة أو نحو ذلك وإمّا تصريف من الله تعالى وتسخير في هذا الوجه. ثمّ إنّ ردّ عليه شيخه ذلك وأغلق عليه بابه انغلقت عليه أبواب الخير والنفقة. فبأيّ وجه يرتاض في صفة البخل حتّى يتخلّى منها أو بمجرّد الموعظة والتذكير من شيخه من غير أن

and he replied, "By distributing food." It is recounted that the master Abū Muḥammad ʿAbd al-Khāliq ibn Yāsīn al-Daghūghī would say, "We have long sought success, but it eluded us, for it consists in distributing food." This saying has become famous today, and is related by common people in rural areas as if it were a precondition for visiting a saint's tomb or aspiring to the rank of shaykh. They count the power of distributing food and of it being easy for him among a saint's miracles and pay no attention to those from whose hand they receive nothing. This issue has resulted in great benefits and prodigious vices.

The people of the lodges differ. There are those who feed the people with 37.13
inherited money or from the fruits of their own labor, without recourse to donations. Such a person is closest to salvation and furthest from suspicion. He will be rewarded for his expenditure; for addressing the difficulty of the one in need; for awakening a desire in people to do the good that comes to them through natural inclination; for gathering good people around them and helping them to piety; for the acquisition of knowledge, proper comportment, and spiritual insight; for developing what is good; and for reviving the principles of the order and increasing its numbers, along with other commendable and clearly virtuous matters. The people benefit along with him in the way mentioned, by holding him in high esteem along with the order and its members, and by being preserved from the respective vices. When he receives no donations, he accepts this. If he does receive them but declines them, doubtless this represents an elevated station. Yet he must beware of the vice of refusal as much as the vice of acceptance, especially when the refusal is to his brethren and followers.

Among the vices we see today is avarice, which has come to predominate, 37.14
God protect us, especially concerning those matters relating solely to God for which people have no internal motivation. You will find that the devotee finds it difficult to give a dirham in alms to a needy poor person, an orphan, or a widow. Yet how quick he is to carry a dirham or two to the house of his shaykh, either because of his personal motivation, such as seeking rapid compensation, or in order to curry favor, or from a desire for public recognition and the like; or it is behavior determined and compelled by Exalted God. If his shaykh then returns this to him and locks him out, the door of goodnesss and spending will be closed to him. For how can he train himself to be freed from the quality of avarice? Can this occur merely through the sermons and admonitions of his master without his implementing them in action? How preposterous this

ينازلها بالفعل؟ وهيهات منه ذلك. وإذا كان كذلك كان شيخه قد غشّه في تربيته له. ولو أنّه قبض منه ذلك وأنفقه له في وجوه الخير كان أعود عليه وأرجى لاعتياده ذلك في جهات أخرى ولحصول نور ينتفع به.

١٥،٣٧ نعم الأمر مخطر والناس فيه ثلاثة. رجل طالب دنيا آكلٌ بدينه يقبض لنفسه شهوة. فهذا فاسد مفسد وربما انتفع معه من أنفق لله تعالى إنّ الله يؤيّد هذا الدين بالرجل الفاجر. ورجل صادق في حاله غير كامل في تصرّفه يخشى العطب في الأخذ ويؤثر جانب السلامة. فهذا سالم في نفسه ولا ربح معه للناس من هذا الوجه. ورجل كامل قد تضلّع من العلم والحال فهذا حقّه الأخذ لحقّ الغير نصحًا له وإعانة له على الخير. اللّهمّ إلّا أن يعرض ما يمنع كاطّلاعه على اختلاف قصد المتصدّق أو فساد في المال أو نحو ذلك.

١٦،٣٧ وكان صلّى الله عليه وسلّم يقبل من أصحابه ما يأتون به من النفقة إعانة لهم على الخير وتزكية لهم عن الأخلاق المذمومة ونفعًا للمسلمين بما أنفقوا. وإلّا فهو صلّى الله عليه وسلّم أغنى الخلق ظاهرًا وباطنًا. وقد عرض عليه أن تجعل له الجبال ذهبًا يتّفق منها فلم يرض وقد لا يقبل لعوارض. وقد قال صلّى الله عليه وسلّم في آخر الأمر هممت ألّا أقبل إلّا من قرشيّ أو ثقفيّ أو دوسي. والكامل من المشايخ له مدخل في ذلك.

١٧،٣٧ ومنهم من يطعم من الفتوح أو من الأمرين فإن استقام أخذه وتصرّفه فهو ينتفع بما مرّ في الأوّل. وإن كان لا يبلغ في أجر النفقة مبلغ من أنفق في كدّ يمينه وعرق جبينه وبمعاونة الناس على الخير وإدخال السرور عليهم في الأخذ وتربية أحوالهم المحمودة وتزكيتهم من المذمومة وبالسلامة من الأنفة والاشتهار بالنزاهة المتوقّع في الأوّل وبتيسّر رزقه في خلال ذلك ليتفرّغ للعبادة إلى غير ذلك من المنافع الدينيّة

would be! If this were the case, then his shaykh would be deceiving him in his education. Even if the shaykh did acquire this sum from him and spent it on good causes, the devotee would backslide and resist doing the same in other circumstances, failing thereby to attain a light that would benefit him.

Truly, the matter is fraught with peril and implicates three types of people: 37.15
(1) A man who seeks the benefits of this world, profiting from his religion, and following his desire to acquire things. This is both corrupt and corrupting, though it may be that the pious will benefit from such a person: "Truly, God supports this faith by means of the man who sins."[238] (2) A man who is sincere in his nature, but imperfect in his actions, fearing ruin from accepting gifts and its negative impact with regard to salvation. Such a man is saved, yet fails to profit people. (3) A complete man, fully versed in knowledge and spiritual insight. It is his right to accept and distribute donations to others, advising them and helping them to do what is good. May he encounter no obstacle, Lord, such as discovering that the almsgiver's motives are flawed, or the involvement of monetary corruption, and the like.

The Prophet, God bless and keep him, used to accept any donations his 37.16
Companions brought him, thus helping them to do good, purifying their morals, and benefiting Muslims from their donations. In addition, he, God bless and keep him, benefited mankind both materially and spiritually. He was once offered to have mountains turned into their weight in gold, and he refused, possibly because of opposing factors.[239] At the end of his life, God bless and keep him, he said, "I took care not to accept anything from anyone who was not of the Quraysh, the Thaqīf, or the Daws."[240] The most perfect shaykhs have insight into this.

There are those who distribute food from donations or from alms and char- 37.17
ity, and if he receives the money properly and with sound behavior, he benefits according to what was previously discussed. Even if the sum of the donated amount falls short of the amount required by one who has labored with his own hands and the sweat of his brow in order to attempt to help people do well and to make them happy to accept donations, to educate their blessed states, to purify them from sins, to protect them from pride and the self-glory proceeding from initial respectability, or to provide sustenance so that one might be free to worship—and to take advantage of other similar spiritual and worldly benefits—then, according to what has been said, the people will still benefit along with him. Those who spend in this way will benefit by receiving

والدنيويّة وينتفع الناس معه بما مرّ والمنفقون بذلك مع حصول أجر ما أنفقوا والتخلّي والتحلّي كما مرّ وغير ذلك.

١٨،٣٧ ومن سوى هذين الشخصين من كلّ من يستظهر بالخرقة ويتّجر باللقمة فلا عبرة به. وقد ينتفع المنفق كما مرّ إن سلم من أتباعه على زيغه والسقوط في مهاوي بدعته. وهذا كلّه في الإطعام والإنفاق جملة.

١٩،٣٧ وأمّا أكل المريد لطعام شيخه والنزول في مثواه وافتراش فراشه وغير ذلك من الانتفاعات فقد يسلم في ذلك وقد يحصل له انتفاع زيادة على السلامة لحصول بركة ونور في قلبه أو رحمة من الله تعالى بذلك. وقد جاءت امرأة من لكاوة إلى دار أشياخنا وأظنّه في حياة سيدي أحمد بن إبراهيم بقصد الزيارة. فأكلت من طعام الزاوية ثمّ رجعت إلى بلدها وبقيت أيّاماً فماتت. فرئيت بعد موتها فقيل له ما فعل الله بك؟ فقالت رحمني بالطعام الذي أكلت من الزاوية.

٢٠،٣٧ وقد يتضرّر المريد بذلك من جهات منها أن يتشوّف إلى ذلك أو إلى المَزِية فيه فيفسد قصده ويختلّ حاله. ومنها أن يستشعر شيخه منه أحياناً ثقلاً في ذلك لما يقتضيه الطبع البشريّ فينفر منه وفي ذلك ضرره. وقد تذهب زيارته وخدمته في بطنه وذلك هو الخسران المبين. ومن ذلك وقع ما ذكر في صدر هذه الترجمة للشيخ أحمد بن يوسف من ترك الإطعام كما قال. وقد يدخل عليه في ذلك من مزاحمة الإخوان والواردين الشغل والفتنة والشحناء والتدابر والتقاطع وغير ذلك. وقد حدّثونا عن شيخ شيوخنا سيدي عبد الله بن حسين الرقي رضي الله عنه أنّه كان إذا ذهب مع الفقراء لزيارة شيخهم سيدي أحمد بن علي يأخذ معه زاداً تحت إبطه.

٢١،٣٧ فإذا وصلوا إلى زاوية الشيخ انفرد عنهم ودخل المسجد واشتغل بحاله واقتات من زاده. فلا جَرَمَ أن كان هو الذي أنجح وأفلح. هذا ولا يخلو شيء من مصالح وآفات والمعصوم من عصمة الله والموفّق من وفقه الله والورع من ورعه الله. فلا يمكن

a reward for what they have spent, and as has been explained, by emptying themselves of all but the worship of God, by adorning themselves with virtues, and so forth.

Aside from these two types of people, pay no attention to those who wear the cloak of the Sufis and barter for a morsel of bread. Perhaps, as has been discussed, the one who spends money will reap benefit, if any of his followers are protected from his deception and from falling into the chasm of his heresy. In sum, this is what there is to say about distributing food and about spending money doing so. 37.18

Concerning the disciple eating his shaykh's food with his assent, dwelling with him, sleeping in his bed, and other such benefits, he may assent to this, and accrue other blessings beyond good health, such as his heart being filled with light and the mercy of God the Exalted. A woman from Laktāwah visited the house of our master, when Aḥmad ibn Ibrāhīm was still alive, I believe. She ate the lodge's food and returned to her village. She remained there some days and then died. She was seen in a dream after her death and was asked, "How have you fared with God?" "He has had mercy on me," she answered, "thanks to the food I ate from the lodge." 37.19

The disciple can be harmed in several ways by eating such food, one of which is that he comes to long for it or to gain some advantage through it, thus corrupting his intention and disturbing his state. Another way he can be harmed is that his shaykh—due to what follows from human nature in matters like this—may at times find the disciple irksome, resulting in the shaykh withdrawing from him, which leads to harm accruing to the follower. He may cease to visit shrines or fail to discipline his appetite—this is real loss. This sort of thing was described at the beginning of this section, regarding how, according to what he said, the shaykh Aḥmad ibn Yūsuf stopped distributing food. He may experience such loss when he encounters a crowd of followers—then toil, discord, grudges, opposing attitudes, broken relations, and so on can ensue. It was related to us regarding our head shaykh, Sīdī ʿAbd Allāh ibn Hussayn al-Raqqī, God be content with him, that when he accompanied his devotees to visit the shaykh Sīdī Aḥmad ibn ʿAlī, he carried provisions under his arm. 37.20

When they arrived at the lodge, he withdrew, entered the mosque, immersed in his own spiritual state, and ate his provisions. It is certain that he alone prospered on this occasion. This discussion has omitted nothing of the respective virtues and vices—sinlessness, success, and piety are all bestowed 37.21

الاعتراض على من أكل ولا من ترك ولا من أطعم ولا من ترك ولا من اشتهر ولا من اختفى اللّٰهمّ إلّا على من كان في تربيته على يده بوجهه. فمن عرف فليتّبع ومن جهل فليسلم والنصح والأمر بالمعروف والنهي عن المنكر باقية في محلّها بشرطها.

٢٢،٣٧ وبلغني أن الفقيه الصالح سيدي الصغير ابن المنيار مرّ ذات مرّة بسيدي محمّد بن أبي بكر الدلائيّ فأخرج إليه الطعام من الزاوية فلم يأكله فبلغ ذلك ابن أبي بكر فذكر ذلك وكأنّه اعتلّ بما يقع من خدمة الناس في الحصاد والدرس. فقال له ابن أبي بكر أيّما أفضل أنت أم جدّك؟ يعني سيدي علي بن إبراهيم وقد جاءه بنو موسى بسبعمائة منجل ليحصدوا. فلمّا رأى عددهم قال لهم بخلتمونا يا بني موسى. فقال له سيدي الصغير جدّي أعرف بحاله وأقدر على ما يفعل وأنا أتصرّف بمقتضى حالي أو نحو هذا من الكلام.

٢٣،٣٧ وقد يكون للوليّ حال مع الله تعالى فيسأل الناس ويأخذ من الله تعالى لا من الناس. ويتصرّف بالله وفي الله ولا يصحّ الاعتراض عليه لاستقامته. وقد قيل للإمام الجنيد إنّ النوريّ يسأل الناس. فقال دعوه في حاله ولكن هاتوا الميزان فوزن قدرًا من الدراهم ثمّ أخذ قبضة من الدراهم بغير وزن فقذفها على الموزون. وقال لصاحبه اذهب بتلك المجموع إليه.

٢٤،٣٧ فلمّا بلغ النوري قال النوريّ هات الميزان فوزن القدر الموزون وردّه وأخذ الباقي. فقال له الحامل كنت عجبت من فعل الجنيد وأنّه كيف خلط الموزون بغير الموزون. فأيّ فائدة للوزن؟ وفعلك هذا أعجب فما هذا؟ فقال له النوريّ إنّ الجنيد رجل حكيم وإنّه أحبّ أن يأخذ الحبل بطرفيه فوزن قدرًا لنفسه وجعل الآخر لله تعالى ونحن قد أخذنا ما لله تعالى. فلمّا رجع الرسول إلى الجنيد بكى وقال أخذ ماله وردّ علينا مالنا. فتبيّن بذلك أنّه يأخذ ما لله من الله عن بصيره صادقة. فلا بأس عليه بذلك والله الموفّق والمعين. لله الأمر من قبل ومن بعد.

by God. One should not object to one who eats or who refuses to do so, to one who distributes food or who refrains from doing so, to one who boasts of doing this or one who does so surreptitiously: Object only to the shaykh who does not provide for his devotees. Follow the one who knows, let the ignorant one submit, and may sound advice and commanding right and forbidding wrong be carried out properly and in the correct circumstances.

It has been related to me that the devout jurist Sīdī al-Ṣaghīr ibn al-Manyār once passed by Sīdī Maḥammad ibn Abī Bakr al-Dilāʾī, who sent food to him from the lodge. He did not eat it. News of this reached Ibn Abī Bakr, and he understood the reaction to his own gift to be similar to when people offer service during harvest time or teaching. Ibn Abī Bakr said to him, "Who is superior, you or your ancestor?" By this he meant Sīdī ʿAlī ibn Ibrāhīm, to whom the Banū Mūsā had come with seven hundred scythes to carry out the harvest; when he saw their number, he said, "You have been stingy with us, O Banū Mūsā!" Sīdī al-Ṣaghīr answered him in something like the following manner: "My ancestor was most knowledgeable concerning his circumstances, and most competent in his actions. I too act according to my circumstances." 37.22

A friend of God can be in a state with God in which he begs from the people and receives from Exalted God, not the people. He carries out his actions through God and in God, and by virtue of his righteousness one should not oppose him. When the exemplar Junayd was told, "Al-Nūrī is begging from people!" he answered, "Leave him be, but bring a scale and weigh a certain number of dirhams. Then take a handful of dirhams without weighing them and throw them on top of what was weighed. Take him this amount." 37.23

When he reached al-Nūrī, al-Nūrī said, "Give me the scale." He weighed the amount that had been weighed, returned it to him, and kept the rest. The one who carried it said, "I was astonished at what Junayd did and the fashion in which he mixed what was weighed and what was not, for what benefit was there in the weighing? What you have done is more astonishing. How?" "Truly," responded al-Nūrī, "Junayd is a wise man and he preferred to take the rope by both ends. So he weighed a portion for himself and left the other for Exalted God. We have taken that which belongs to Exalted God." When the messenger returned to Junayd, he wept and said, "He took his money and returned ours to us." This anecdote demonstrates that al-Nūrī took from God what was God's with true sight. He did nothing wrong by doing so. Both success and succor are from God. Everything is God's to command. 37.24

كان بعض الطلبة من أصحابنا في قرية وكانت القرية قرية سوء وأهلها كذلك. ثمّ إنّ بعض الأصحاب رام لوم ذلك الطالب على الاستقرار فيها فقال له كيف تبقى في تلك القرية وهي كيت وكيت يعدّد عليه مساويها. فقال الطالب أحمد الله وأشكره. فلمّا قال ذلك استحمقه اللائم وازداد في الإنكار عليه وأنّه كيف يحمد على هذا. فقال له الطالب قد رأيت كلّ ما ترون من مساويها وعلمت منها ما تعلمون أو أكثر. ومع ذلك فأجد قلبي غير نفور عنها فأحمد الله تعالى إذ قضى عليّ الاستقرار فيها ولم ينفر قلبي عنها. فلو أنّه تعالى قضى عليّ وكرّهها لي وأنا لا أجد بدّاً منها بحكم القضاء فما ترون يكون عيشي عند ذلك؟ ١،٣٨

فلمّا قرّر هذا المعنى وجدوه معنى لطيفاً تنبّه إليه وسلموا له. وشرح ذلك باختصار أنّ الله تعالى أودع في طبع الآدميّ ميلاً إلى شيء ونفوراً عن شيء ويسمّى الأوّل ملائماً إمّا حسيّاً كالشراب والطعام واللباس والنكاح في الجملة ونحو ذلك وإمّا معنويّاً كالعزّ والجاه والراحة والصحّة والعافية ونحو ذلك. ويسمّى الثاني منافرًا إمّا حسيّاً أيضاً كالعَذِرة والبول والدم والميتة والشوك والجرح والضرب والسجن والقيد ونحو ذلك وإمّا معنويّاً كالذلّ والمهانة والعجز والضيم والغمّ والحزن ونحو ذلك. ٢،٣٨

ثمّ إنّ الأعيان الموجودة في الدنيا كالأموال المكتسبة وغيرها من الحيوانات العجماوات والجمادات مثل الأمكنة والأزمنة والجهات والقرناء والأصحاب ونحو ذلك. منها ما يكون من القسم الأوّل ملائماً لمقارنته للملائم كالأنعام لما فيها من الأكل والشرب والركوب والحمل والزينة والرباع لما فيها من الاشتغال بأنواعه والنساء في الجملة لما فيها من الاستمتاع وسائر الانتفاع. وعلى الخصوص فيمن وجد ذلك فيه حقيقة أو توهّماً وكذا في سائر ما ينفع له. ولذا قال تعالى ﴿زُيِّنَ لِلنَّاسِ حُبُّ ٱلشَّهَوَاتِ مِنَ ٱلنِّسَاءِ﴾ الخ. ومنها ما يكون من القسم الثاني منافرًا لمقارنته للمنافر كالسباع والحيّات والعقارب والأعداء ونحو ذلك. وكذا الأمكنة والأزمنة والجهات تكون ملائمة إذا كانت ظرفاً للملائم ومنافرة إذا صارت ظرفاً للمنافر وهذا هو الأمر المعتاد. ٣،٣٨

A student among our companions was once in a village, a vile place with equally vile inhabitants. Another of our companions took to blaming this student for remaining there. “How is it that you stay in this village when it is like this?” he asked, and enumerated its evils. The student replied, “I thank God and offer him my gratitude.” When he said this, the one who had blamed him took him for a fool and denounced him further, querying how he could give thanks for this. The student said, “I have seen the evils you see in it, and have learned from them all you have learned, if not more. Despite this, I find that my heart is not averse to it, so I thank Exalted God for having decreed that I remain in it and that my heart feel no aversion to it. For if the Exalted had decreed that I remain there and made it hateful to me without any possibility of leaving, how do you think my life there would be?” 38.1

Once he had explained the matter in this fashion, our companions found it to be a subtle understanding to which they should pay heed, and they agreed with it. The explanation for this, in brief, is that Exalted God has placed in the nature of mankind inclinations and aversions to things. These can be attractive, either in a sensory fashion as with, in general, food, drink, clothing, marriage, and so forth, or in an abstract fashion, as with glory, honor, relaxation, health, well-being, and so on. Or they can be repellent, again either in a sensory fashion, as with excrement and urine, blood, corpses, thorns, wounds, blows, prison, binding, and the like, or in an abstract fashion, as with subjugation, humiliation, incapacity, injustice, anxiety, sorrow, and so forth. 38.2

Then there are entities present in this world, such as acquired goods and beasts, inanimate things such as places, times, and directions, as well as spouses and companions and so on. Some are of the first type and are comparatively attractive, such as livestock on account of the food, drink, riding, carrying, and adornment they provide; or homes, on account of all the work that went into them; or women in general, on account of the pleasure they can give, and other benefits besides. This is especially the case for the one who finds this attraction within himself, be it real or imagined. The same is true of everything else that benefits him, and for this reason the Exalted said: «People are drawn to the love of pleasures, of women» until the end of the verse.[241] Some things are of the second type and are comparatively repellent, such as predators, snakes, scorpions, adversaries, and the like. Places, times, and directions are attractive or repellent if they contain attractive or repellent qualities, respectively. This is the customary order of things. 38.3

٤،٣٨ وقد تخرق هذه العادة في شخص فيُجعل في قلبه ميل إلى غير ملائم أو نفرة عن غير المنافر. إمّا بسبب كالسحر ونحوه أو بمحض الحكم الأزليّ. ولا بدّ أن يتوهّمه في نفسه ملائمًا في تلك الحالة أو منافرًا فلا تنتقض العادة الجارية. ثمّ إنّ الله تعالى قدّر على العبد قبل إيجاده كلّ ما يلقاه من هذه الأشياء. فإن قدرّ عليه أن يلقى الملائم فعندما يلقاه ينعم من جهتين. إحداهما وجود الانتفاع الذي فيه كما قرّرنا. والأخرى أنس قلبه به فيكون كما قال عمر بن عبد العزيز رضي الله عنه إذا وافق الحقّ الهوى فهو العسل والزبد. وإن قدّر عليه أن يلقى المنافر فهو عندما يلقاه يعذّب من جهتين وهما التضرّر الظاهر والتألّم الباطن بالكراهة. وهذان القسمان في الملائم والمنافر الحقيقيّين وهما واضحان جاريان على المعتاد ووراءهما أربعة أقسام فيما يرجع إلى القلب من الميل والنفرة.

٥،٣٨ الأوّل أن يقضى عليه بعدم ملاقاة اللائم ولا يخلق في قلبه ميل إليه كحال المجانين أو يخلق له كراهيته. الثاني أن يقضى عليه بملاقاة المنافر ولا تخلق في قلبه نفرة عنه أو يخلق له الميل إليه. وفي كلا القسمين تقع السلامة من العذاب وإن لم يحصل نعيم أو يحصل نعيم موهوم أو خسيس تابع لخسّة عقل صاحبه أو ضعف حسّه كالصبيّ الذي يأكل التراب. ومن القسم الثاني قصّة صاحب القرية المذكور. الثالث أن يبتلى بالميل إلى شيء ومحبّته بحكم القضاء ملائمًا أو غير ملائم ولا يقضى له بملاقاته. الرابع أن يبتلى بالنفرة عن شيء وكراهته بحكم القضاء منافرًا أو غير منافر ويقضى عليه بملاقاته. وفي كلا القسمين يقع العذاب والمحنة بالنظر إلى الباطن. وإلى الأوّل يشير المجنون في قوله: [طويل]

قَضَاهَا لِغَيْرِي وَٱبْتَلَانِي بِحُبِّهَا فَهَلَّا بِشَيْءٍ غَيْرِ لَيْلَى ٱبْتَلَانِيَا

It may happen that this order is breached for a person and that his heart begins to incline toward inauspicious things or be repelled by what is not repellent. This can either happen due to a cause, such as magic and the like, or in accordance with the Eternal Ruling. In this case, he must necessarily imagine it within himself to be attractive or repellent so that it does not conflict with the normal habitual order. Exalted God has decreed everything that the believer will encounter of such matters before He brought him into existence. If He decrees for him to encounter something auspicious, then when he encounters it he may be delighted in two ways: the first on account of it being beneficial, as we have described. The other on account of it being familiar to his heart. It is as ʿUmar ibn ʿAbd al-ʿAzīz, God be content with him, said, "When truth and desire are in accordance with each other, it is like butter and honey." If He has decreed for him to encounter something repellent, then when he does so he suffers in two ways: from external harm and, due to the feeling of disgust, from internal pain. The two categories of being attractive and repellent are real, clear, and occur predictably. They stem from four kinds of inclination and aversion that affect the heart. 38.4

The first is that it be decreed for him not to experience the auspicious as such, and that no inclination toward it be placed in his heart, as is the case with the insane, or that an aversion to it be created in him. The second is that it be decreed for his heart not to feel any aversion to that which is repellent, or for it to be inclined to it. In these two cases, suffering does not take place even if nothing pleasant happens, or something originally imagined to be pleasant takes place, or something vile appears appealing due to the vileness of the person's mind or the weakness of his senses, as with a boy who eats dirt. The abovementioned story of the inhabitant of the village is of this second type. The third type is that due to divine Decree he is afflicted with an inclination toward something and a love for it, be it auspicious or not, but it is not decreed for him to encounter it. The fourth is that due to the Decree he is afflicted with an aversion to something, either repellent or not, and a dislike for it, and it is decreed for him to encounter it. In both categories an ordeal of suffering takes place when internal reactions are considered. Majnūn refers to the first in his line: 38.5

He decreed her for someone else and afflicted me with love for her.
Could He not have afflicted me with someone other than Laylā?

٦،٣٨ وكأنّه يقول لو قضاها لي أي الربّ سبحانه بأن أتزوّجها حين ابتلاني بحبّها لنعمت. ولو لم يبتلني بحبّها حين قضاها لغيري أن يتزوّجها لاسترحت فلا أنا بحصولها في يدي ولا أنا بخروجها من قلبي فهذا هو العذاب المبين.

٧،٣٨ وإلى القسمين معاً يشير الآخر في قوله: [بسيط]

مَنْ لَمْ يَعِشْ بَيْنَ أَقْوَامٍ يَسُرُّ بِهِمْ   فَعَيْشُهُ أَبَدًا هَمٌّ وَأَحْزَانُ
وَأَخْبَثُ ٱلْعَيْشِ مَا لِلنَّفْسِ فِيهِ أَذًى   خُضْرُ ٱلْجِنَانِ مَعَ ٱلْأَعْدَاءِ نِيرَانُ
وَأَطْيَبُ ٱلْعَيْشِ مَا لِلنَّفْسِ فِيهِ هَوًى   سَمُّ ٱلْخِيَاطِ مَعَ ٱلْأَحْبَابِ مَيْدَانُ

٨،٣٨ وحاصله تحكيم القلب وأنّه المرجع في النعيم والعذاب ولا عبرة بالمحسوس إلّا بما فيه من التأدية إلى ما في القلب. وإلى هذا المعنى يشير الصوفيّة في النعيم والعذاب الموعود في الدار الآخرة. كما قال في الحكم النعيم وإن تنوّعت مظاهره إنّما هو لشهوده واقترابه والعذاب وإن تنوّعت مظاهره إنّما بوجود حجابه فسبب العذاب وجود الحجاب وإتمام النعيم بالنظر إلى وجهه الكريم. وإلى هذا المعنى يرجع كلّ ما يذكر من الحنين إلى الأوطان النائية والبكاء على المراسم الخالية وذكر الأحباب النازحة والأيّام الصالحة ومن مرارة الفراق ولوعة الاشتياق. وما قيل في ذلك يملأ الأرض ويفوت الطول والعرض كقول الأوّل: [طويل]

وَكُلُّ مُصِيبَاتِ ٱلزَّمَانِ رَأَيْتُهَا   سِوَى فُرْقَةَ ٱلْأَحْبَابِ هَيِّنَةَ ٱلْخَطْبِ

٩،٣٨ وكتب المهدي وهو بمكّة إلى الخيزران: [خفيف]

It is as if he is saying: "If He decreed her for me—that is, if the Lord, praise Him, decreed—that I might marry her when He afflicted me with love for her, I would have been blessed. And if He had not afflicted me with love for her when He decreed that another marry her, I would live at ease. I cannot hold her in my arms, nor can I remove her from my heart. This is clear torture!" 38.6

Another poet refers to both categories at the same time: 38.7

The one who does not live among people who bring joy
leads a life of constant worry and sorrow.
The worst life is one that harms the ego:
green gardens where enemies are like fire.
The best life is one in which the ego experiences desire.
The eye of the needle is as wide as a playing field when loved ones are present.

To conclude, it is the heart that decides and determines pleasure and suffering. What is perceived by the senses has no bearing except through what they transmit to the heart. This is what the Sufis allude to regarding the pleasure and suffering promised in the life to come. It is as Ibn ʿAṭāʾ Allāh said in his *Wise Sayings*: "Whatever the manifestations of pleasure may be, it comes from witnessing and being close to Him. Whatever the manifestations of suffering may be, it comes from being veiled from Him. The cause of suffering is the presence of the veil, and the utmost pleasure lies in looking at His noble face." Everything that has been mentioned about longing for faraway homelands, crying for empty dwellings, recalling distant loved ones and better days, the bitterness of separation, and the pain of longing is rooted in this concept—what has been said about this would cover the whole earth, far and wide. The following resemble the earlier lines:[242] 38.8

All the disasters I experienced
matter little except my separation from loved ones.

When he was in Mecca, Caliph al-Mahdī wrote to al-Khayzurān: 38.9

نَحْنُ فِي أَفْضَلِ ٱلسُّرُورِ وَلٰكِنْ   لَيْسَ إِلَّا بِكُمْ يَتِمُّ ٱلسُّرُورُ
عَيْبُ مَا نَحْنُ فِيهِ يَا أَهْلَ وِدِّي   أَنَّكُمْ غِبْتُمُ وَنَحْنُ حُضُورُ
فَأَجِدُّوا ٱلْمَسِيرَ بَلْ إِنْ قَدِرْتُمْ   أَنْ تَطِيرُوا مَعَ ٱلرِّيَاحِ فَطِيرُوا

فأجابته: [خفيف] ١٠،٣٨

قَدْ أَتَانَا ٱلَّذِي وَصَفْتَ مِنَ ٱلشَّوْ   قِ فَكِدْنَا وَمَا فَعَلْنَا نَطِيرُ
لَيْتَ أَنَّ ٱلرِّيَاحَ كُنَّ يُؤَدِّيـ   ـنَ إِلَيْكُمْ مَا قَدْ يُجِنُّ ٱلضَّمِيرُ
لَمْ أَزَلْ صَبَّةً فَإِنْ كُنْتَ بَعْدِي   فِي سُرُورٍ فَدَامَ ذَاكَ ٱلسُّرُورُ

وقال أبو تمّام: [كامل] ١١،٣٨

لَوْ حَارَ مُرْتَادُ ٱلْمَنِيَّةِ لَمْ يَجِدْ   إِلَّا ٱلْفِرَاقَ عَلَى ٱلنُّفُوسِ دَلِيلَا

وقال أبو الطيّب: [بسيط] ١٢،٣٨

لَوْلَا مُفَارَقَةُ ٱلْأَحْبَابِ مَا وَجَدَتْ   لَهَا ٱلْمَنَايَا إِلَى أَرْوَاحِنَا سُبُلَا

وقال أحمد بن رجاء الكاتب أخذ منّي تميم بن المعزّ جارية كنت أحبّها وتحبّني. ١٣،٣٨
فأحضرها ليلة في منادمته فنام فأخذت العود وغنّت عليه صوتاً حزيناً من قلب قريح وهو: [مخلع البسيط]

لَا كَانَ يَوْمُ ٱلْفِرَاقِ يَوْمَا   لَمْ يُبْقِ لِلْمُقْلَتَيْنِ نَوْمَا
شَتَّتَ مِنِّي وَمِنْكَ شَمْلًا   فَسَاءَ قَوْمًا وَسَرَّ قَوْمَا
يَا قَوْمُ مَنْ لِي بِوَصْلِ رِيمٍ   يَسُومُنِي فِي ٱلْغَرَامِ سَوْمَا
مَا لَامَنِي ٱلنَّاسُ فِيهِ إِلَّا   بَكَيْتُ كَيْمَا أُزَادَ لَوْمَا

We enjoy the greatest happiness,
which only you render complete.
My beloved folk, we are in a perilous state
because you have left, yet we remain here.
So find your way to us;
fly with the winds if you can.

And she answered: 38.10

Your description of longing has reached us—
we almost flew, but then fell short.
Would that the winds had carried to you
what makes the conscious mind mad.
My love is still deep—if you find happiness after me
may it be long-lasting.

Abū Tammām said the following: 38.11

If one does not know what one wishes, one finds
only separation as a guide to others.

And al-Mutanabbī said: 38.12

If not for the separation of lovers,
desires would find no way into their hearts.

The scribe Aḥmad ibn Rajā' related: "Tamīm ibn al-Muʿizz took a slave girl from me whom I loved and who loved me. One night he brought her to a drinking session and fell asleep. She took up the oud and sang for him in a voice saddened by a wounded heart: 38.13

On the day of separation
these eyes did not sleep.
When union between you and me dissolved,
what went badly for us made others happy.
People, who will unite me with a white gazelle?
Who will barter his love for me?
When people chastised me for this
I wept, and they chastised me all the more.

فأفاق المعزّمع فراغها ورأى دمعها يسيل فقال ما شأنك؟ فأمسكت هيبة له فقال لها إن صدقتني لأبلغنّك أملك فأخبرته بما كنّا عليه فأحسن إليها وردّها إليّ وألحقني بخاصّة ندمائه.

١٤،٣٨ وقال ابن ميّادة: [طويل]

أَلَا لَيْتَ شِعْرِي هَلْ يَحُلَّنَّ أَهْلُهَا وَأَهْلُكِ رَوْضَاتٍ بِبَطْنِ ٱللِّوَى خُضْرَا
وَهَلْ تَأْتِيَنَّ ٱلرِّيحُ تُدْرِجُ مُوهِنًا بِرَيَّاكِ تَعْرَوْرِي بِهَا بَلَدًا قَفْرَا
بِرِيحِ خُزَامَى ٱلرِّيحِ بَاتَ مُعَانِقًا فُرُوعَ ٱلْأَقَاحِ تَهْضِبُ ٱلطَّلَّ وَٱلْقَطْرَا
أَلَا لَيْتَنِي أَلْقَاكِ يَا أُمَّ جَحْدَرٍ قَرِيبًا فَأَمَّا ٱلصَّبْرُ عَنْكِ فَلَا صَبْرَا

١٥،٣٨ وقال أبو العتاهية: [بسيط]

أَمْسَى بِبَغْدَادَ ظَبْيٌ لَسْتُ أَذْكُرُهُ إِلَّا بَكَيْتُ إِذَا مَا ذِكْرُهُ خَطَرَا
إِنَّ ٱلْمُحِبَّ إِذَا شَطَّتْ مَنَازِلُهُ عَنِ ٱلْحَبِيبِ بَكَى أَوْ حَنَّ أَوْ ذَكَرَا

١٦،٣٨ وقال آخر: [وافر]

أَقُولُ لِصَاحِبِي وَٱلْعِيسُ تَخْدِي[١] بِنَا بَيْنَ ٱلْمُنِيفَةِ فَٱلضِّمَارِ
تَمَتَّعْ مِنْ شَمِيمِ عَرَارِ نَجْدٍ فَمَا بَعْدَ ٱلْعَشِيَّةِ مِنْ عَرَارِ
أَلَا يَا حَبَّذَا نَفَحَاتُ نَجْدٍ وَرَيَّا رَوْضِهِ بَعْدَ ٱلْقِطَارِ
وَأَهْلُكَ إِذْ يَحُلُّ ٱلْحَيُّ نَجْدًا وَأَنْتَ عَلَى زَمَانِكَ غَيْرُ زَارِ
شُهُورٌ يَنْقَضِينَ وَمَا شَعَرْنَا بِأَنْصَافٍ لَهُنَّ وَلَا سِرَارِ

١٧،٣٨ وقال الآخر: [طويل]

---

١ في معجم البلدان: "تهوي".

"As she ended, al-Muʿizz awoke, and seeing her flowing tears said, 'What is the matter?' She was shy in his presence, so he said, 'If you speak truthfully, I will give you what you hope for.' When she told him what existed between us, he was kind to her, returned her to me, and made me one of his closest drinking companions."

Ibn Mayyādah said: 38.14

I wish I knew if its people would arrive
  at green gardens in the depths of the sand dunes.
Does the wind come gently in the night,
  bringing your scent, riding bareback across desolate lands?
The lavender-scented wind spent the night
  embracing twigs of lily of the valley, drenched with dew and rain.
May I meet you soon, mother of Jaḥdar—
  I have no patience when I'm away from you.

Abū l-ʿAtāhiyah said: 38.15

A gazelle came to Baghdad whom I was not able to name
  without crying, since to mention her was perilous.
When the lover's dwelling is distant
  from the beloved, he weeps, longs for her, or remembers.

Another poet said:[243] 38.16

I said to my companion, when our reddish-white camel
  carried us between al-Munīfa and al-Ḍimār:
Enjoy the smell of the wild narcissus of Najd;
  after nightfall they are no longer fragrant.
How lovely are the scents of Najd
  and the lushness of its gardens after rain.
If your tribe visits Najd I will welcome you
  and you will have no cause for complaint.
Long months pass there without us having felt
  even the half of them, much less their last night.

Another writes: 38.17

سَقَى اللهُ أَيَّامًا لَنَا قَدْ تَتَابَعَتْ   وَسَقْيًا لِعَصْرِ ٱلْعَامِرِيَّةِ مِنْ عَصْرِ
لَيَالِي أُعْطِيتُ ٱلْبِطَالَةَ مِقْوَدِي   تَمُرُّ ٱللَّيَالِي وَٱلشُّهُورُ لَا أَدْرِي[1]

وللإمام سليمان الكلاعيّ رضي الله عنه: [طويل] ١٨،٣٨

أَحِنُّ إِلَى نَجْدٍ وَمَنْ حَلَّ فِي نَجْدِ   وَمَاذَا ٱلَّذِي يُغْنِي حَنِينِيَ أَوْ يُجْدِي
وَقَدْ أَوْطَنُوهَا وَادِعِينَ وَخَلَّفُوا   مُحِبَّهُمُ رَهْنَ ٱلصَّبَابَةِ وَٱلْوَجْدِ
وَضَاقَتْ عَلَيَّ ٱلْأَرْضُ حَتَّى كَأَنَّهَا   وِشَاحٌ بِخَصْرٍ أَوْ سِوَارٌ عَلَى زَنْدِ
إِلَى اللهِ أَشْكُو مَا أُلَاقِي مِنَ ٱلْجَوَى   وَبَعْضُ ٱلَّذِي لَاقَيْتُهُ مِنْ جَوًى يُرْدِي
فُرَاقُ أَخِلَّاءٍ وَصَدُّ أَحِبَّةٍ   كَأَنَّ صُرُوفَ ٱلدَّهْرِ كَانَتْ عَلَى وَعْدِ
لَيَالِيَ نَجْنِي ٱلْأُنْسَ مِنْ شَجَرِ ٱلْمُنَى   وَنَقْطُفُ زَهْرَ ٱلْوَصْلِ مِنْ شَجَرِ ٱلصَّدِّ

وقال الآخر: [طويل] ١٩،٣٨

إِذَا أَشْرَفَ ٱلْمَكْرُوبُ مِنْ رَأْسِ تَلْعَةٍ   عَلَى شِعْبِ بَوَّانٍ أَفَاقَ مِنَ ٱلْكَرْبِ
وَأَلْهَاهُ بَطْنٌ كَٱلْحَرِيرِ لَطَافَةً   وَمُطَّرِدٌ يَجْرِي مِنَ ٱلْبَارِدِ ٱلْعَذْبِ
فَيَا للهِ يَا رِيحَ ٱلْجَنُوبِ تَحَمَّلِي   إِلَى شِعْبِ بَوَّانٍ سَلَامَ فَتًى صَبِّ

ولا ينحصر هذا الفنّ والاشتغال به يطيل. لله الأمر من قبل ومن بعد.[2] ٢٠،٣٨

وكنت لمّا نزلت بخلفون على أمّ ربيع ذكرت من كان معنا في الزاوية الدلائيّة من المعارف والأحباب. وكانوا يومئذ قد شرّقوا لناحية تلمسان. فقلت: [طويل] ١،٣٩

١ يزيد ق: وقال أبو الطيب: لولا مفارقة الأحباب ما وجدت/ لها المنايا إلى أرواحنا سبلا. ٢ سقطت الجملة من ق.

May God grant us rain day after day,
water from the time we were with al-ʿĀmiriyyah.
When idle play was given the reins,
the nights went by but I was unaware of the month.

The exemplar Sulaymān al-Kalāʿī, God be content with him, composed these lines: 38.18

I long for Najd and for those who dwelt there;
what can soothe this longing of mine?
Departing, they took it as their home,
abandoning their lover, a hostage to love and passion.
The earth has grown narrow about me
like a sash about a waist, or an armband.
I complain to God for having afflicted me with love
—the passion that is destroying me.
With the separation from friends and the rejection of lovers,
the threat of time's vicissitudes was fulfilled.
At night we pluck intimacy from the tree of desire
and the flower of union from the tree of aversion.

Another has said:[244] 38.19

If a man burdened with sorrow looks out from a hilltop
over the canyon of Bawwān, he will awake from his grief.
The river delights him, slender like silk,
flowing ceaselessly, cold and sweet.
By God, carry the greetings, south wind,
of a young man in love to the canyon of Bawwān!

This subject is limitless and one could spend much time on it. Everything is God's to command. 38.20

When I stopped at Khalfūn by the river of Umm Rabīʿ, I remembered the companions we had known and loved at the lodge at Dilāʾ. In those days they had traveled east to the Tilimsān region. I declaimed: 39.1

سَلامٌ عَلَى ٱلْأَحْبَابِ غَيْرُ مُضِيعِ   لِذِي شَرَفٍ ذِكْرًا وَلَا لِوَضِيعِ
سَلامُ مُحِبٍّ لَا يَزَالُ أَخَا هَوًى   إِلَى جِلَّةٍ قَدْ شَرَّقُوا وَنُزُوعِ
وَمَنْ يَسْأَلِ ٱلرُّكْبَانَ عَنِّي فَإِنَّنِي   حَلَلْتُ بِبَيْتِي حَوْلَ أُمِّ رَبِيعِ
فَأَلْفَيْتُهُ يَحْكِي زَفِيرِي زَفِيرَةً   بِقَلْبٍ كَقَلْبِي بِٱلْفِرَاقِ صَدِيعِ
وَيُسْعِدُنِي فِي عَبْرَتِي غَيْرَ أَنَّهُ   يُخَالِفُنِي فِي مَهْبِطٍ وَطُلُوعِ
فَتَجْرِي إِلَى مَهْوَى ٱلْجَنُوبِ دُمُوعُهُ   وَتَجْرِي إِلَى مَهْفَى ٱلشَّمَالِ دُمُوعِي

ولمّا كنت بمدينة مراكش حرسها الله تعالى سنة ثلاث وتسعين وألف وقد بقيت ٢،٣٩
الأملاك في خلفون والكتب وما معها في مكناسة. وبقيت العلائق في جبال فازاز والقبيلة في ملويّة. قلت: [طويل]

تَشَتَّتَ قَلْبِي فِي ٱلْبِلَادِ فَقِسْمَةٌ   بِمُرَّاكُشٍ مِنْهُ عَلَى رِجْلِ طَائِرِ
وَأُخْرَى بِخَلْفُونَ وَأُخْرَى مُقِيمَةٌ   بِمِكْنَاسَةِ ٱلزَّيْتُونِ حَوْلَ ٱلدَّفَاتِرِ
وَأُخْرَى بِفَازَازَ وَأُخْرَى تَجَزَّأَتْ   بِمَلْوِيَّةِ ٱلْأَنْهَارِ بَيْنَ ٱلْعَشَائِرِ
وَأُخْرَى بِذَاكَ ٱلْغَرْبِ بَيْنَ أَحِبَّتِي   بِأَهْلِ ٱلْبَوَادِي مِنْهُمُ وَٱلْحَوَاضِرِ
فَيَا رَبِّ فَٱجْمَعْهَا فَإِنَّكَ قَادِرٌ   عَلَيْهَا وَمَا غَيْرُ ٱلْإِلٰهِ بِقَادِرِ
وَيَا رَبِّ فَٱجْعَلْهَا بِأَوْطَانِهَا فَمَا   عُبَيْدُكَ لِلْبَيْنِ ٱلْمُشَتِّ بِصَابِرِ
لَكَ ٱلْفَضْلُ وَٱلْإِحْسَانُ بَدْءًا وَآخِرًا   وَإِنِّي لِمَا أَوْلَيْتَنِي جِدُّ شَاكِرِ
فَمُنَّ بِإِنْعَامٍ وَجُدْ لِي بِحَاجَتِي   وَرِفْقٍ بِقَلْبٍ لِلْهُمُومِ مُسَامِرِ
فَمَا لِيَ إِلَّا بَابُكَ ٱلرَّحْبُ مَلْجَأً   وَمَا طَلَبُ ٱلْحَاجَاتِ مِنْكَ بِضَائِرِ

Greetings to loved ones who were not lost,
    noble ones it honors me to mention.
Greetings of a lover, still a brother to passion,
    to a group that has departed to the east.
Whoever asks the riders about me,
    know I've made my dwelling next to the Umm Rabīʿ.
I found it sighing like me
    with a heart sundered by separation, like mine.
In my grief, it brings me happiness,
    though it differs from me, rising and falling.
Its tears flow with the south wind,
    mine with the north wind.

When I went to Marrakesh, Exalted God protect it, in the year 1093 [1682], **39.2**
I had left my possessions at Khalfūn, my books and notes were in Meknes, my grazing pastures were in the mountains of Fāzāz, and the tribe was at the River Moulouyah. I recited the following:

My heart had been scattered across the country,
    part of it in Marrakesh, unsettled.
Part of it is in Khalfūn,
    another in Meknes al-Zaytūn with my notebooks.
Part is in Fāzāz, another divided
    among the tribes at the River Moulouyah.
Another among my loved ones in the west,
    among both country folk and city dwellers.
Unite them, Lord; You have the power to do so—
    none but God has such power.
Place them in their homelands, Lord,
    for your humble worshippers cannot endure separation all winter.
You are the beginning and end of virtue and benevolence,
    and I am deeply grateful for all you have bestowed.
Bless me and be generous in providing for me;
    at night accompany my worrying heart.
What refuge do I have but your welcoming door?
    No one has asked things of you and been harmed.

وَمَا لِيَ إِلَّا جُودُكَ ٱلْجَمُّ شَافِعٌ   وَحَسْبِي بَفَيْضٍ مِنْهُ أَغْزَرَ وَافِرِ
وَصَفْوَتُكَ ٱلْمَبْعُوثُ لِلنَّاسِ رَحْمَةً   بَشِيرًا شَفِيعًا مُظْهِرًا بِٱلْبَشَائِرِ
صَلَاةٌ وَتَسْلِيمٌ عَلَيْهِ مَدَى ٱلْمَدَى   وَعِتْرَتِهِ وَٱلصَّحْبِ أَهْلِ ٱلْبَصَائِرِ

٣،٣٩ وجرى يوماً ذكر البيتين اللذين أنشدهما سيّدنا بلال رضي الله عنه. وهما قوله: [طويل]

أَلَا لَيْتَ شِعْرِي هَلْ أَبِيتَنَّ لَيْلَةً   بِوَادٍ وَحَوْلِي إِذْخِرٌ وَجَلِيلُ
وَهَلْ أَرِدَنْ يَوْمًا مِيَاهَ مَجَنَّةٍ   وَهَلْ يَبْدُوَنْ لِي شَامَةٌ وَطَفِيلُ

٤،٣٩ فهاج لي إلى الأوطان اشتياق فقلت نحو هذا المساق: [طويل]

أَلَا لَيْتَ شِعْرِي هَلْ أَبِيتَنَّ لَيْلَةً   بِسَهْبِ ٱلشَّنِينِ أَوْ بِسَهْبِ بَنِي وَرَا
وَهَلْ تَعْبُرَنْ نَهْرَ ٱلْعَبِيدِ رَكَائِبِي   وَهَلْ تَتْرُكَنْ دَايَا وَأَدْوَاءَهَا وَرَا
وَهَلْ أَرِدَنْ عَسْلُوجَ يَوْمًا فَأَشْرَبَنْ   مِيَاهًا بِهِ يَحْكِي رَحِيقًا وَكَوْثَرَا
وَهَلْ تَمْرَحَنْ خَيْلِي بِذُرْوَةِ آمِنًا   وَبُطْنَانِهَا مِنْ قَبْلِ أَنْ يَحْفَرَ ٱلثَّرَى
وَهَلْ أَكْحُلَنْ يَوْمًا جُفُونِي بِنَظْرَةٍ   إِلَى ٱلْأَرْزَاتِ ٱلْفَارِعَاتِ فَتُبْصَرَا
وَهَلْ أَدْفَعَنْ جَيْشَ ٱلْهُمُومِ بِبَسْطَةٍ   مَعَ ٱلْحَيِّ فِي تِلْكَ ٱلدِّيَارِ فَتَقْصُرَا

ونهر العبيد هو وادي العبيد المعروف ومدينة داي هي المعروفة اليوم بالصومعة في تادلا. وإنّما قال أدواؤها أي أمراضها لأنها كثيرة الأمراض والوخم.

٥،٣٩ ومن غريب ما اتّفق لي في هذا البلد أنّي مررت به حين سافرت إلى ناحية مراكش في طلب العلم فأصابتني الحمّى منه. وذلك أوّل حمّى أصابتني في عمري. ثمّ بقيت في تلك النواحي عدّة سنين فلمّا رجعت ومررت به أصابتني أيضاً وكأنّها كانت تنتظرني. ولذا كان من جملة التمنّي أن أترك هذه البلدة وأمراضها ورائي بالمجاوزة إلى

What do I have but your abundant, interceding virtue,
my portion the part that amply and copiously overflows.
You sent your best delegate to the people as a mercy,
bringing good news, interceding, and spreading glad tidings!
Prayers and blessings on him for all eternity,
on his progeny, companions, and on people of insight.

One day I recalled the two verses that our leader Bilāl, God be content with him, recited: 39.3

I wish I knew if I would ever spend the night again
in a valley surrounded by sweet rushes and palm trees,
And return one day to the waters of Majannah.
Will I ever see Shāmah and Ṭafīl again?

Longing for my homeland surged up in me, and I recited the following in the same fashion: 39.4

I wish I knew if I would spend the night again
in the region of al-Shanīn or Banū Warā.
Will my steeds again cross the River al-ʿAbīd;
will they leave Dāy and its afflictions behind?
Will I one day return to the reed and drink the juice
they describe as overflowing nectar?
Will my horse prance on a peak, impregnable,
its bells jingling before trampling the soil?
Will I one day rub kohl on my eyelids,
looking toward and glimpsing the towering pines?
Will I pay off an army of anxieties amply
while living in those houses, so that my worries dwindle?

The River al-ʿAbīd refers to the well-known valley of al-ʿAbīd. The city of Dāy is in Tādlā and is known today as al-Ṣawmaʿah; the poem reads "its afflictions," that is, "its diseases," because it has many diseases and filth.

Among the curious things that happened to me in that region near the Umm Rabīʿ was that I contracted a fever on my way to Marrakesh in search of instruction. This was the first fever I had been struck with in my life. I stayed in those parts for some years, and when I returned through that region, I was 39.5

وطني. وكنّا ذات مرّة في بساتين خارج الحضرة المراكشيّة ثمّ سرينا ليلة لقصد زيارة بعض الصالحين. وركبت فرساً فما استويت عنه وبرد الليل. وكنت أستحبّ السري فانبسطت نفسي. وتمنّيت أن لو كنت على أعتق من ذلك الفرس وذكرت الأوطان. فقلت ارتجالاً أو شبه ارتجال: [كامل]

يَا سَرْيَةً لَوْكُنْتُ أَسْرِيهَا عَلَى   نَهْدٍ أَغَرَّ مُحَجَّلٍ يَعْبُوبِ
يَنْسَابُ مِنْ تَحْتِي كَأَنَّ ذَمِيلَهُ   جَرَيَانُ مَاءٍ فِي ٱلصَّفَا مَصْبُوبِ
مَا بَيْنَ خُلَّادٍ فَخُوخَاتٍ إِلَى   نَهْرِ ٱلرِّمَالِ فَمُقَطَّعٍ فَجُبُوبِ
فَإِذَا فُصِلْتُ مِنَ ٱلسَّلَامِ عَلَيْكُمُ   وَهَفَتْ صَباً فِي ٱلْجَوِّ ذَاتَ هُبُوبِ
فَهُنَاكَ تَنْشَقُنِي ٱلْحِجَازُ وَشِيحُهُ   وَتَتِمُّ عَرْفاً مِنْ شَذاً مَحْبُوبِ
صَلَّى ٱلْإِلٰهُ عَلَيْهِ مَا وَكَفَ ٱلْحَيَا   فِي ٱلرَّوْضِ مِنْ وَبْلٍ وَمِنْ شُؤْبُوبِ
وَعَلَى ٱلْأَمَاجِدِ آلِهِ وَصِحَابِهِ   مَا حَنَّ مَحْبُوبٌ إِلَى مَحْبُوبِ
يَا رَبِّ أَنْتَ رَجَاؤُنَا فِي نَيْلِ مَا   نَرْجُو فَكُنْ لِعَبِيدِكَ ٱلْمَرْبُوبِ
لَا رَبَّ نَرْجُوهُ سِوَاكَ أَمُمْكِنٌ   وِجْدَانُ آلِهَةٍ لَنَا وَرُبُوبِ؟
فَٱمْنُنْ عَلَيْهَا وَٱسْقِنَا إِنَّا لَفِي   ظَمَإٍ عَلَى شَحْطِ ٱلنَّوَى وَذُبُوبِ
وَٱجْمَعْ بِصَفْوَتِكَ ٱلْأَجِلَّةِ شَمْلَنَا   مَعْ إِخْوَةٍ وَمَعَارِفٍ وَحَبُوبِ
وَٱخْتِمْ لَنَا مَعَهُمْ بِدِينٍ قَيِّمٍ   يَتَعَلَّقُ وَتَشَوُّقٍ مَشْبُوبِ
فَٱلدِّينُ وَٱلْخَيْرَاتُ أَعْوَدُ مُقْتَنًى   أَبَداً لِكُلِّ مُشَمِّرٍ مَلْبُوبِ

again struck by a fever, as if it had been waiting for me. For this reason, it was my hope to leave that place and its diseases behind me and go to my homeland. Now, on one occasion, when we were in the gardens outside the city of Marrakesh, we set out at night to visit one of the saints. I mounted a horse, and was barely seated when the night turned cold. I enjoyed traveling at night, and my soul was at ease. I wished that I could have been on a swifter horse and I recalled my homeland. I then recited the following extemporaneously, or nearly so:

Night journey—would that I had set out upon a noble steed,
  white blazons on his forehead and legs, and swift.
Flowing beneath me as though his gallop
  were water running over smooth stones.
What lies between Khulād Fakhūkhāt
  and the river of sands is an area of hard soil.
When I left after greeting you,
  the west wind blew, gusting.
There the Hijaz revives me fully
  with the fragrance of the Beloved.
God bless this place of gardens and trickling water,
  with incessant rain downpouring.
God bless the noble people of his family and his companions,
  so long as the lover longs for the beloved.
O Lord, you are our only hope to attain our desires;
  be your slaves' Master!
We want no other lord than You:
  How could we desire multiple gods or lords?
Protect it then and grant us to drink,
  for our lips are chapped with thirst from our separation.
Reunite us with Your elect,
  with brethren, acquaintances, and loved ones.
Seal us all in a faith composed
  of affection and beautiful desire.
For faith and good deeds are the most sought acquisitions
  For those with insight and intelligence.

وجرى يوماً ذكر قصيدة ابن الخطيب التي أوّلها: [طويل] ٦،٣٩

سَـلَا هَـلْ لَدَيْهَا مِنْ مُخَبِّرَةٍ خَبَرُ وَهَلْ أَعْشَبَ ٱلْوَادِي وَنَمَّ بِهِ ٱلزَّهَرُ

فسما أيضاً شوق وحزن وعاود الفؤاد ذكر الوطن والسكن. فقلت: [كامل] ٧،٣٩

شِمْ بَرْقَهَا أَعْلَى أَجَارِعَ ذِي أَضَا وَكَفَتْ فَأَتْرَعَتِ ٱلْجَدَاوِلَ وَٱلْأَضَا
وَٱحْجُبْ عَلَيَّ وَمِيضَهُ فَلَقَدْ حَشَا وَسْطَ ٱلْحَشَا جَمْرَ ٱلْغَضَا لَمَّا أَضَا
فَكَأَنَّهُ مُذْ لَاحَ فِي تِلْكَ ٱلرُّبَا مَا بَيْنَ أَحْشَائِي حُسَامٌ مُنْتَضَى
مَا زَالَ يُذْكِرُنِي مَعَاهِدَ جِيرَتِي وَعَشِيرَتِي وَمَعَارِفِي مُذْ أَوْمَضَا
هٰذَا عَلَى أَنْ لَسْتُ قَطُّ بِمُغْفِلٍ لِعُهُودِهِمْ مَا حَانَ مِنْهَا أَوْ مَضَى
أَمْ سَاقَهَا بِجُيُوبِ ذُرْوَةٍ سُحْرَةً فَسَقَى بِهَا قَيْصُومَهَا وَٱلْعَرْمَضَا
وَأَدَارَ فَوْقَ نُجُودِهَا كَاسَ ٱلْحَيَا وَهْنًا فَأَصْبَحَ كُلُّ نَشْزٍ مُبْرِضَا
خَلَعَتْ أَكُفُّ ٱلسُّحْبِ أَرْدِيَةَ ٱلْكَلَا وَمَطَارِفَ ٱلزَّهَرِ ٱلنَّضِيرِ عَلَى ٱلْفَضَا
وَأَفَاضَتِ ٱلْغُدْرَانُ حَتَّى عَاقَرَتْ أَيْدِي ٱلرَّوَابِي ٱلشُّمِّ جِرْيَالَ ٱلْفَضَا
مَا شِئْتَ مِنْ رَوْضٍ تَرَاهُ مُذَهَّبًا فِيهَا وَمِنْ رَوْضٍ تَرَاهُ مُفَضَّضَا
بَلَدٌ صَحِبْتُ ٱلْعَيْشَ فِيهِ أَخْضَرَا نَضِرًا وَوَجْهَ ٱلدَّهْرِ أَزْهَرَ أَبْيَضَا
دَرَّتْ عَلَيَّ بِهِ ٱلْأَمَانِي حُفَّلًا وَهَمَتْ عَلَيَّ غُيُوثُ بِرٍّ فُيَّضَا
وَلَبِسْتُ فَضْفَاضَ ٱلنَّبَاهَةِ سَابِغًا وَرَكِبْتُ صَهْوَةَ كُلِّ فَضْلٍ رَيِّضَا
وَأَسَمْتُ سَرْحِي فِي ٱلْمَطَايِبِ مُمْرِعًا وَرَمَيْتُ صَيْدِي فِي ٱلْمَآرِبِ مُعْرِضَا

One day, someone recalled the poem of Ibn al-Khaṭīb, which begins: 39.6

What news of the state of Salé:
Has the valley turned green and have the flowers bloomed?

He also recalled longing and sadness, and repeatedly remembered the benefits of homeland and dwelling. So I recited: 39.7

Look to the lightning high above—
it rained and filled the streams and canals over the sandy plains of Aḍā.
Conceal from me its gleam,
for it had placed an ember in my chest.
When it flashed in those hills it was like
a drawn sword piercing my bowels.
Since glimmering, it has continued to remind me
of the haunts of my region, my family, and my acquaintances,
Though I am hardly unaware
of past and present obligations to them.
And before dawn it watered the land abundantly through its channels,
drenching its southernwood and underbrush.
It sent a cup of rain over its high plains,
and all its heights became green with vegetation.
The palms of the clouds granted green dresses,
and carelessly bestowed fringes of blossoming flowers.
Like swords, the rivers overflowed until they cut the fingers of the proud hills.
You will see some of what you wished for in the garden
covered in gold, and some in silver.
A country in which I lived a green and verdant life,
the face of time in bright bloom.
There my hopes flowed abundantly
and the rains of generosity poured over me like a flood.
I dressed myself in a flowing robe of distinction
and mounted the back of a feisty, noble horse.
I brought up my flocks to graze in the lush pastures
and shot my arrow at my desire when it turned toward me.

فِي فِـتْيَةٍ قَدْ كَانَ شُـرْبِي فِيهِـمِ   صِـفْوَ ٱلْوِدَادِ وَكُلُّ خُـلْقٍ مُـرْتَضَى
تَخِذُوا ٱلْمُرُوءَةَ وَٱلسَّمَاحَةَ وَٱلنَّدَا   وَٱلْبِرَّ وَٱلْإِكْرَامَ دِينًا مُـقْتَضَى
وَتَأَلَّفُـوا كَـٱلْمَاءِ وَٱلصَّـهْبَاءِ فِي   كَـأْسٍ وَكُلٌّ ذُو سَجَـايَا تُـرْتَضَى

لله الأمـر من قبـل ومن بعـد.

١،٤٠ حـدّثني الأخ الفاضل أبو عبد الله محمّد بن مسعود العيسويّ العرفاويّ قال سافرت إلى بلاد القبلة ذات مرّة. فمررت بالمرابط الخيّر أبي عبد الله محمّد بن أبي بكر العياشيّ فدخلت لأزوره فلمّا خرج قعد منّي قريباً ثمّ أنشدني متمثّلاً قول الشاعر: [طويل]

جَـفَوْتُ أُنَاساً كُنْتُ آلَفُ وَصْلَهُمْ   وَمَا بِٱلْجَـفَا عِنْدَ ٱلضَّرُورَةِ مِنْ بَاسِ
فَـلَا تَعْـذِلُونِي فِي ٱلْجَـفَاءِ فَـإِنَّنِي   وَجَدْتُ جَمِيعَ ٱلشَّرِّ فِي خَلْطَةِ ٱلنَّاسِ

والمراد من الشعر ومن التمثّل به الاعتزال عن الخلق طلباً للسلامة لا ما يفهم من لفظ الجفاء.

٢،٤٠ وفي الحديث خير النّاس منزلةً يوم القيامة رجل أخذ بعنان فرسه في سبيل الله يخيف العدوّ ويخيفونه. وفي رواية حتّى يموت أو يقتل. والذي يليه رجل معتزل في شِعْبٍ من الشعاب يقيم الصلاة ويؤتي الزكاة ويعتزل شرور الناس.

٣،٤٠ وعن أمير المؤمنين عمر رضي الله عنه قال الطمع فقر واليأس غنى والعزلة راحة من جليس السوء وفريق الصدق خير من الوحدة. وقال أبو الدرداء رضي الله عنه كان الناس ورقاً لا شوك فيه وهم اليوم شوك لا ورق فيه. وقال بعض الأئمّة العزلة عن الناس توفي العرض وتبقي الجلالة وترفع مئونة المكافأة في الحقوق اللازمة وتستمرّ

My drinking had been among the young men
in pure love for them—they had every good quality.
They held manliness, forgiveness, generosity,
piety, and honor to be a necessary faith.
Their affection was like water and wine
in a glass, each possessing its own pleasing traits.

Everything is God's to command.

My distinguished brother Abū ʿAbd Allāh Muḥammad ibn Masʿūd al-ʿĪsawī al-ʿIrfāwī related the following to me: "I once traveled to the south of Morocco, and passed near the admirable ascetic Abū ʿAbd Allāh Muḥammad ibn Abī Bakr al-ʿAyyāshī. I visited him, and when he emerged he sat close to me and recited the didactic words of the poet: 40.1

I turned away all with whom I had close interaction—
this turning away was not out of necessity or compulsion.
Do not rebuke me for doing so, as I discovered
all types of evil from interacting with people."

What is intended by "turning away" in these lines is not what is usually understood by the phrase but, rather, withdrawing from mankind in search of peace.

There is the hadith: "On the day of resurrection, the person with the most favored station is the man who takes the reins of his horse while on God's path, striking fear into the enemy who also terrify him." (In one version, the hadith ends with "until he dies or is killed"). The second-best station is that of the man who has withdrawn to a mountain pass, praying and giving alms, isolated from the evil of people. 40.2

It is related that ʿUmar the Commander of the Faithful, God be content with him, said, "Ambition is poverty, despair is wealth, and isolation is being spared evil company, yet the companionship of sincerity is better than being alone." Abū l-Dardāʾ, God be content with him, said, "People used to be leaves without thorns, but today they are thorns without leaves." One of the caliphs said, "Isolation from people leads to honor, maintains greatness, removes the burden of meeting the legitimate demands of others, and ensures poverty."[245] Both the ancient and modern poets have been inspired by this theme of being 40.3

الفاقة. وقد أولع الشعراء قديماً وحديثاً من هذا المعنى بالتبرّم بالناس والاستيحاش من الخلق وذمّ الزمان وأهله. فمن ذلك قول أبي العتاهية: [سريع]

بَرِمْتُ بِٱلنَّاسِ وَأَخْلَاقِهِمْ   فَصِرْتُ أَسْتَأْنِسُ بِٱلْوَحْدَةِ
مَا أَكْثَرَ ٱلنَّاسِ لَعَمْرِي وَمَا   أَقَلَّهُمْ فِي حَاصِلِ ٱلْعِدَّةِ

٤،٤٠ ونحوه قول الآخر: [بسيط]

مَا أَكْثَرَ ٱلنَّاسِ بَلْ مَا أَقَلَّهُمْ   وَٱللّٰهُ يَعْلَمُ أَنِّي لَمْ أَقُلْ فَنَدَا
إِنِّي أَفْتَحُ عَيْنِي حِينَ أَفْتَحُهَا   عَلَى كَثِيرٍ وَلٰكِنْ لَا أَرَى أَحَدَا

٥،٤٠ وقول الآخر: [بسيط]

مُخَالِطُ ٱلنَّاسِ فِي ٱلدُّنْيَا عَلَى خَطَرٍ   وَفِي بَلَاءٍ وَصَفْوٍ شِيبَ بِٱلْكَدَرِ
كَرَاكِبِ ٱلْبَحْرِ إِنْ تَسْلَمْ حُشَاشَتُهُ   فَلَيْسَ يَسْلَمُ مِنْ خَوْفٍ وَمِنْ حَذَرِ

٦،٤٠ وقول الآخر: [خفيف]

قَدْ لَزِمْتُ ٱلسُّكُونَ مِنْ غَيْرِ عِيٍّ   وَأَلْزَمْتُ ٱلْفِرَاشَ مِنْ غَيْرِ عِلَّه
وَهَجَرْتُ ٱلْإِخْوَانَ لَمَّا أَتَانِي   عَنْهُمُ كُلُّ خَصْلَةٍ مُضْمَحِلَّه

٧،٤٠ وقول الآخر: [مخلع البسيط]

إِنَّ بَنِي دَهْرِنَا أَفَاعٍ   لَيْسَ آمِنَ سَاوَرَتْ طَبِيبُ
فَلَا يَكُنْ فِيكَ بَعْدَ هٰذَا   لِوَاحِدٍ مِنْهُمُ نَصِيبُ

disaffected with people, being averse to crowds, and lamenting the age and those living in it, for instance these lines by Abū l-ʿAtāhiyah:

I am weary of people and their morals,
    and have adopted solitude as companion.
By my life! I have not cared
    if there are more or fewer people.

Similar to this are the lines of another poet:[246] 40.4

How numerous are people; rather, how few.
    God knows I do not speak falsely.
Indeed, I open my eye to the crowd
    but I see no one.

Another has said: 40.5

In this world, it is dangerous to mingle with people—
    hair turns gray with worry due to both tribulation and delight.
Like one who sails the seas—as long as he possesses a spark of life
    he will not be safe from fear and worry.

And another: 40.6

I have held fast to silence without faltering
    and have kept to my bed without being ill.
I have driven the brethren away whenever
    they had the slightest influence on me.

And another: 40.7

The people of our time are serpents;
    there is no physician to cure those they attack.
Going forward, may your fate be
    freedom from every one of them.

٨،٤٠ وقول الآخر ويعزى للإمام الشافعيّ رضي الله عنه: [بسيط]

لَيْتَ ٱلسِّبَاعَ لَنَا كَانَتْ مُجَاوِرَةً   وَلَيْتَنَا لَا نَرَى مِمَّا نَرَى أَحَدَا
إِنَّ ٱلسِّبَاعَ لَتَهْدَا فِي مَرَابِضِهَا   وَٱلنَّاسُ لَيْسَ بِهَادٍ شَرُّهُمْ أَبَدَا
فَٱهْرُبْ بِنَفْسِكَ وَٱسْتَأْنِسْ بِوِحْدَتِهَا   تَعِشْ سَلِيمًا إِذَا مَا كُنْتَ مُنْفَرِدَا

٩،٤٠ وقول طرفة بن العبد: [سريع]

كُلُّ خَلِيلٍ كُنْتُ خَالَلْتُهُ   لَا تَرَكَ ٱللهُ لَهُ وَاضِحَهْ
كُلُّهُمْ أَرْوَغُ مِنْ ثَعْلَبٍ   مَا أَشْبَهَ ٱللَّيْلَةَ بِٱلْبَارِحَهْ

١٠،٤٠ وقول امرئ القيس: [طويل]

كَذٰلِكَ جَدِّي مَا أُصَاحِبُ صَاحِبًا   مِنَ ٱلنَّاسِ إِلَّا خَانَنِي وَتَغَيَّرَا

١١،٤٠ وقول الآخر: [طويل]

وَزَهَّدَنِي فِي ٱلنَّاسِ مَعْرِفَتِي بِهِمْ   وَطُولُ ٱخْتِبَارِي صَاحِبًا بَعْدَ صَاحِبِ
فَلَمْ تُرِنِي ٱلْأَيَّامُ خِلًّا تَسُرُّنِي   مَبَادِيهِ إِلَّا خَانَنِي فِي ٱلْعَوَاقِبِ
وَلَا قُلْتُ أَرْجُوهُ لِدَفْعِ مُلِمَّةٍ   مِنَ ٱلدَّهْرِ إِلَّا كَانَ إِحْدَى ٱلْمَصَائِبِ

١٢،٤٠ وقال أبو فراس: [طويل]

بِمَنْ يَثِقُ ٱلْإِنْسَانُ فِيمَا يَنُوبُهُ   وَمِنْ أَيْنَ لِلْحُرِّ ٱلْكَرِيمِ صِحَابُ
وَقَدْ صَارَ هٰذَا ٱلنَّاسُ إِلَّا أَقَلَّهُمْ   ذِئَابًا عَلَى أَجْسَادِهِنَّ ثِيَابُ

These are the lines of a poet offering condolences to the exemplar al-Shāfiʿī, God be content with him: 40.8

Would that wild beasts were our neighbors;
we would then not see a single one of these people.
For beasts are quiet where they sleep,
but the evil of people never rests.
Flee, alone, and make solitude your companion;
you will live peacefully as long as you are on your own.

Ṭarafah ibn al-ʿAbd said: 40.9

I never had a true friend
to whom God granted sincerity.
All are more cunning than a fox—
how close to night is day.

Imruʾ al-Qays said: 40.10

It was my lot never to adopt anyone as companion
without him turning on me in betrayal.

Another said:[247] 40.11

What I knew of people led me to renounce them—
this choice was confirmed with companion after companion.
Days did not look upon me without appearing
to promise happiness, but betraying me in the end.
I did not express my hope for someone to ward off time's misfortunes
without he himself becoming a disaster.

Abū Firās said: 40.12

In whom does man trust when he is afflicted?
Where does one find companions for freeborn noblemen?
All but a few people have become jackals
dressed in men's clothing.

وقال محمّد بن تميم: [طويل] ١٣،٤٠

لَكَ ٱلْخَيرُ كَمْ صَاحَبْتُ فِي ٱلنَّاسِ صَاحِباً   فَمَا نَالَنِي مِنْهُ سِوَى ٱلْهَمِّ وَٱلْعَنَا
وَجَرَّبْتُ أَبْنَاءَ ٱلزَّمَانِ فَلَمْ أَجِدْ   فَتًى مِنْهُمُ عِنْدَ ٱلْمَضِيقِ وَلَا أَنَا

وقول الآخر: [وافر] ١٤،٤٠

دَعِ ٱلْإِخْوَانَ إِنْ لَمْ تَلْقَ مِنْهُمْ   صَفَاءً وَٱسْتَعِنْ وَٱسْتَغْنِ بِاللهْ
أَلَيْسَ ٱلْمَرْءُ مِنْ مَاءٍ وَطِينٍ   وَأَيُّ صَفاً لِهَاتِيكَ الجِبِلَّهْ

ومثله: [وافر] ١٥،٤٠

وَمَنْ يَكُ أَصْلُهُ مَاءً وَطِيناً   بَعِيدٌ مِنْ جِبِلَّتِهِ ٱلصَّفَاءُ

ونحوه: [مجزوء الرمل] ١٦،٤٠

لَا تَثِقْ مِنْ آدَمِيٍّ   فِي وِدَادٍ بِصَفَاءِ
كَيْفَ تَرْجُو مِنْهُ صَفْواً   وَهْوَ مِنْ طِينٍ وَمَاءِ

وقال أبو العلاء: [بسيط] ١٧،٤٠

جَرَّبْتُ أَهْلِي وَأَصْحَابِي فَمَا تَرَكَتْ   لِيَ ٱلتَّجَارِبُ فِي وِدِّ ٱمْرِئٍ غَرَضَا

وقول أبي الطيّب: [وافر] ١٨،٤٠

إِذَا مَا ٱلنَّاسُ جَرَّبَهُمْ لَبِيبٌ   فَإِنِّي قَدْ أَكَلْتُهُمُ وَذَاقَا
فَلَمْ أَرَ وُدَّهُمْ إِلَّا خِدَاعاً   وَلَمْ أَرَ دِينَهُمْ إِلَّا نِفَاقَا

Muḥammad ibn Tamīm said: 40.13

You might benefit from every companion you have taken;
I have received nothing from them but worry and anxiety.
I have tried the people of our time and not found a single one
to display fortitude under duress, not even myself.

Another has said: 40.14

Leave the brethren if you find they lack purity:
Seek help and be content with God alone.
Is man not made from clay and water;
what purity is there in such a nature?

Similar are these lines: 40.15

Whoever's origin is clay and water
is far indeed from a pure nature.

So too: 40.16

Do not trust that a man will be pure in his affection—
how can this be when he is made of clay and water?

Al-Maʿarrī said: 40.17

I put my family and companions to the test:
this experience left me without desire for anyone's affection.

Al-Mutanabbī said: 40.18

There was no one with any sense among the people I tested,
and I know them as well as if I had tasted and eaten them.
I found their affection only treachery,
their faith nothing but hypocrisy.

وأنشد أيضاً: [طويل] ١٩،٤٠

وَمِنْ نَكَدِ ٱلدُّنْيَا عَلَى ٱلْحُرِّ أَنْ يَرَى   عَـدُوًّا لَهُ مَا مِنْ صَـدَاقَتِهِ بُـدُّ

قيل إنّه لمّا تنبّأ قيل له ما معجزتك؟ قال قولي وأنشد البيت.

وقول الآخر: [طويل] ٢٠،٤٠

تَصَفَّحْتُ أَبْنَاءَ ٱلزَّمَانِ فَلَمْ أَجِدْ   سِوَى مَنْ غَدَا وَٱللُّؤْمُ حَشْوُ ثِيَابِهِ
فَجَرَّدْتُ مِنْ سَيْفِ ٱلْقَنَاعَةِ مُرْهَفًا   قَـطَعْتُ رَجَائِي مِنْهُمْ بِذُبَابِهِ
فَلَا ذَا يَـرَانِي وَاقِفًا فِي طَـرِيقِهِ   وَلَا ذَا يَـرَانِي وَاقِـفًا عِنْدَ بَابِهِ

وقول الآخر: [طويل] ٢١،٤٠

أَرَدْتُ مِنَ ٱلدُّنْيَا صَدِيقًا مُؤَاتِيًا   وَفِيًّا بِمَا أَرْضَاهُ يَرْضَى وَيَنْشَرِحْ
فَإِذْ لَمْ أَجِدْ أَغْضَيْتُ عَنْ كُلِّ كَائِنٍ   وَقُلْتُ لِقَلْبِي قَدْ خَلَا ٱلْكَوْنُ فَٱسْتَرِحْ

وقال غيره: [وافر] ٢٢،٤٠

أُلَامُ عَلَى ٱلتَّـفَرُّدِ كُلَّ حِينٍ   وَلِي فِيمَا أُلَامُ عَلَيْهِ عُذْرُ
وَكُلُّ أَذًى فَـمَصْبُورٌ عَـلَيْهِ   وَلَيْسَ عَلَى قَرِينِ ٱلسُّوءِ صَبْرُ

وقال محمّد بن تميم: [كامل] ٢٣،٤٠

مَنْ كَانَ يَرْغَبُ فِي حَيَاةِ فُؤَادِهِ   وَصَفَائِهِ فَلْيَنْأَ عَنْ هٰذَا ٱلْوَرَى
فَٱلْمَاءُ يَصْفُو إِنْ نَأَى فَإِذَا دَنَا   مِنْهُمْ تَغَيَّرَ لَوْنُهُ وَتَكَدَّرَا

He also said: 40.19

The distress this world provides for the noble man
includes him seeing his enemy's love has no bounds.

It is said that when al-Mutanabbī claimed to be a prophet he was asked, "What is your miracle, then?" and he said, "My line," and recited this verse.

Another poet said: 40.20

I examined the people of my time and have found none
who does not begin his day drenched in wickedness.
I drew a sharp sword of self-sufficiency from its scabbard,
and with its blade severed all hope from them.
No one shall see me standing in his path
or waiting at his door.

Another poet said: 40.21

I wanted the world to give me a loyal, upright friend
who would be content and at ease with what contents me.
Since I found no one, I will ignore all creatures
and say to my heart: Rest easy, the world is empty.

And another: 40.22

He rebuked me constantly for seeking solitude,
yet I have an excuse for what he admonished.
True, one should endure every harm,
but I have no patience for those who consort with evil.

Muḥammad ibn Tamīm said: 40.23

Whoever desires his heart to be pure in this life
let him remain aloof from mankind.
Water remains pure if it is distant;
close to people, its color changes and it becomes muddy.

وقول الآخر: [مجزوء الخفيف] ٢٤،٤٠

كُنْ مِنَ ٱلنَّاسِ جَانِبًا وَٱرْضَ بِاللهِ صَاحِبَا
قَلِّبِ ٱلنَّاسَ كَيْفَ شِئْـ ـتَ تَجِدْهُمْ عَقَارِبَا

وأمّا أبو العلاء المعرّي فقد سلى نفسه عن عماه بقوله: [مجزوء الخفيف] ٢٥،٤٠

قَالُوا ٱلْعَمَى مَنْظَرٌ قَبِيحٌ قُلْتُ بِفُقْدَانِكُمْ يَهُونُ
وَاللهِ مَا فِي ٱلْوُجُودِ شَيْءٌ تَأْسَى عَلَى فَقْدِهِ ٱلْعُيُونُ

وقال غيره: [طويل] ٢٦،٤٠

اَلنَّاسُ دَاءٌ دَفِينٌ لَا دَوَاءَ لَهُ تَحَيَّرَ ٱلْعَقْلُ فِيهِمْ فَهُوَ مُنْذَهِلُ
إِنْ كُنْتَ مُنْبَسِطًا رَأَوْكَ مَسْخَرَةً أَوْ كُنْتَ مُنْقَبِضًا قَالُوا بِهِ ثِقَلُ
وَإِنْ تُخَالِطْهُمْ قَالُوا بِهِ طَمَعٌ وَإِنْ تُجَانِبْهُمْ قَالُوا بِهِ مَلَلُ
وَإِنْ تَعَفَّفْتَ عَنْ أَبْوَابِهِمْ كَرَمًا قَالُوا غَنِيٌّ وَإِنْ تَسْأَلْهُمْ بَخِلُوا

ونحوه قول الآخر: [خفيف] ٢٧،٤٠

لَا تُعِدَّنَّ لِلزَّمَانِ صَدِيقًا وَأَعِدَّ ٱلزَّمَانَ لِلْأَصْدِقَاءِ

وقول الآخر: [طويل] ٢٨،٤٠

وَرُبَّ أَخٍ نَادَيْتَهُ لِمُلِمَّةٍ فَأَلْفَيْتَهُ مِنْهَا أَجَلَّ وَأَعْظَمَا

Another said: 40.24

Set yourself apart from people
and content yourself with God as a companion.
No matter how you examine people,
you will find them to be scorpions.

Al-Maʿarrī consoled himself for his blindness with the lines: 40.25

They said, "Blindness is a horrible sight."
I replied, "Losing my sight makes losing you easy.
By God, there's nothing in the world worth grieving
once your eyes are gone."

Another has said:[248] 40.26

People are a vile malady for which there is no cure;
stunned, one's mind is baffled by them.
When you are happy, they perceive you as ridiculous;
when you are depressed, they call you dull.
If you mingle with them, they call you ambitious.
If you avoid them, they label you boring.
If you refrain from appearing in their doorways, out of nobility,
they will say, "He is wealthy." If you beg from them, they are stingy.

There is another similar line:[249] 40.27

Do not prepare a friend for time;
let time prepare your friends for you.

Another has said:[250] 40.28

How many brothers I summoned in affliction,
only to find them a greater, more powerful affliction!

وقول الآخر: [وافر] ٢٩،٤٠

وَإِخْوَانٍ ٱتَّخَذْتَهُمُ دُرُوعًا   فَكَانُوهَا وَلٰكِنْ لِلْأَعَادِي
وَخِلْتُهُمُ سِهَامًا صَائِبَاتٍ   فَكَانُوهَا وَلٰكِنْ فِي فُؤَادِي
وَقَالُوا قَدْ صَفَتْ مِنَّا قُلُوبٌ   لَقَدْ صَدَقُوا وَلٰكِنْ مِنْ وِدَادِي
وَقَالُوا قَدْ سَعَيْنَا كُلَّ سَعْيٍ   لَقَدْ صَدَقُوا وَلٰكِنْ فِي فَسَادِي

وقال الآخر: [وافر] ٣٠،٤٠

لِقَاءُ ٱلنَّاسِ لَيْسَ يُفِيدُ شَيْئًا   سِوَى ٱلْهَذَيَانِ مِنْ قِيلٍ وَقَالِ
فَأَقْلِلْ مِنْ لِقَاءِ ٱلنَّاسِ إِلَّا   لِأَخْذِ ٱلْعِلْمِ أَوْ إِصْلَاحِ حَالِ

وقول الآخر: [كامل] ٣١،٤٠

لَا تَعْرِفَنَّ أَحَدًا فَلَسْتَ بِوَاجِدٍ   أَحَدًا أَضَرَّ عَلَيْكَ مِمَّنْ تَعْرِفُ

وقول الآخر: [طويل] ٣٢،٤٠

وَمَا زِلْتُ مُذْ لَاحَ ٱلْمَشِيبُ بِمَفْرِقِي   أُفَتِّشُ عَنْ هٰذَا ٱلْوَرَى وَأُكَشِّفُ
فَمَا إِنْ عَرَفْتَ ٱلنَّاسَ إِلَّا ذَمَمْتَهُمْ[1]   جَزَى اللّٰهُ بِٱلْخَيْرَاتِ مَنْ لَسْتُ أَعْرِفُ

ومثله قول الآخر: [طويل] ٣٣،٤٠

جَزَى اللّٰهُ بِٱلْخَيْرَاتِ مَنْ لَيْسَ بَيْنَنَا   وَلَا بَيْنَهُ وُدٌّ وَلَا مُتَعَرَّفُ
فَمَا نَالَنِي ضَيْمٌ وَلَا مَسَّنِي أَذًى   مِنَ ٱلنَّاسِ إِلَّا مِنْ فَتًى كُنْتُ أَعْرِفُ

١ ق: ضرني الا الذين عرفتم.

And another:[251] 40.29

They were brethren I took as shields,
and so they were—but for my enemies.
I imagined them to be well-aimed arrows,
and so they were—but at my heart.
They said, our hearts are purified,
and they spoke true—but they meant of affection for me.
They said, we have tried our utmost,
and they spoke true—but to corrupt me.

Another poet said:[252] 40.30

There is no benefit in meeting people,
except for the drivel of gossip.
Reduce your interaction with them,
except to learn from them or improve yourself.

Another said: 40.31

Know no one! You will not find anyone
more harmful than those you know.

Another said: 40.32

Ever since the roots of my hair turned white
I have searched mankind and studied them.
I know none in whom I have not found fault—
God reward those I do not know with blessings.

Another has similarly said: 40.33

May God reward with blessings those we do not know
and for whom we have no affection.
I have not experienced injury, nor have I been touched by harm,
by any but a young man I once knew.

٣٤،٤٠ ويقال كتب رجل من أهل الريّ على بابه جزى الله خيراً من لا يعرفنا ولا نعرفه. ولا جزى الله أصدقاءنا خيراً فإنّا لم نؤتَ إلّا منهم. وينسب للإمام الغزالي رضي الله عنه أيّام سياحته: [سريع]

قَدْ كُنْتُ عَبْداً وَٱلْهَوَى مَالِكِي فَصِرْتُ حُرًّا وَٱلْهَوَى خَادِمِي
وَصِرْتُ بِٱلْوِحْدَةِ مُسْتَأْنِساً مِنْ شَرِّ أَصْنَافِ بَنِي آدَمِ
مَا فِي ٱخْتِلَاطِ ٱلنَّاسِ خَيْرٌ وَلَا ذُو ٱلْجَهْلِ فِي ٱلْأَشْيَاءِ كَٱلْعَالِمِ
يَا لَائِمِي فِي تَرْكِهِمْ جَاهِلاً عُذْرِي مُنْقُوشٌ عَلَى خَاتِمِي

قالوا وكان نقش خاتمه: ﴿وَمَا وَجَدْنَا لِأَكْثَرِهِمْ مِنْ عَهْدٍ وَإِنْ وَجَدْنَا أَكْثَرَهُمْ لَفَاسِقِينَ﴾.

٣٥،٤٠ وقول الآخر: [سريع]

مَنْ أَحْسَنَ ٱلظَّنَّ بِأَعْدَائِهِ تَجَرَّعَ ٱلْهَمَّ بِلَا كَاسِ

قال بعضهم لوكنت ناظماً لهذا البيت لقلت من أحسن الظنّ بأحبابه ولا أقول بأعدائه.

٣٦،٤٠ واعلم أنّ تبرّم الناس بالناس واستيحاش بعضهم من بعض واستنقاص البعض للبعض هو أنّ الإنسان لما فيه من سبعيّة مؤذ بالطبع من يلقاه إمّا بيده أو بلسانه شتماً أو نميمة أو غيبة. وكلّ من يتأذّى منه يستوحش منه ويستنقصه. ولما فيه من الشهوة يتقاضى حظوظه ويضايق عليها غيره لاتّساع الشهوة وضيق الدنيا فيثور البغض والحسد وسائر الشرّ. ثمّ قد يطمع أن يستحصل حظوظه أو بعضها من الغير والغير في شغل عنه بحظوظه فيستنقصه. ومن الأوّل ينشأ العجب بالغنيّ واحتقار الفقير ومن الثاني ينشأ عدم الوفاء بالوعد والعهد وذلك أنّ الإنسان ليس له على

People say that a man from Rayy wrote on his door: "May God bless those who do not know us and whom we do not know. May God not bless our friends, as we have faced destruction from none other than them." And the following lines have been attributed to Imam al-Ghazālī from his days of wandering: 40.34

I was a slave, desire was my king;
then I became free, and desire was my servant.
I sought out solitude, being wary
of the evil of all types of humans.
No good comes from associating with people,
and the ignorant are not the same as the knowledgeable.
You who in your ignorance blame me for leaving them,
my justification is engraved on my ring.

People say: "The engraving on his ring was «We found no covenant in the greater part of them; indeed, We found the greater part of them ungodly.»"[253]

Another said: 40.35

Whoever thinks well of his enemies
gulps down worry without a glass.

And someone commented: "If I had written this verse I would have said 'his loved ones,' not 'his enemies.'"

Know that the source of people's mutual disgust, the aversion some have for others, and the fault some find with their peers lies in man's possessing something of the character of beasts that by its nature harms the one who encounters it. This harm can come at a person's hand or through his tongue, engaging in insults, gossip, or slander. Everyone thus hurt develops an aversion to him and finds fault with him. When someone has a desire, his fortune is determined: Someone else impedes it, increasing his desire and making the world oppressive so that hate, jealousy, and all other evils rise up in him. He may then desire to acquire his fortune from the other person, who is distracted from him by his own fortune and so finds fault with the former. The first of these produces a fascination with the rich and contempt for the poor. The second produces a failure to uphold promises and contracts. This is because mankind has no choice in achieving this. Inwardly, his lack of choice consists in his being in the embrace of Almighty God. For how can the worshipper experience accomplishment or conduct his affairs without his Lord? Externally, 40.36

التحقيق اختيار أمّا باطنًا فلأنّه في قبضة الله تعالى. وكيف يتأتّى وفاء أوعقد أوحلّ للعبد دون سيّده؟ وأمّا ظاهرًا فلأنّه أسير شهوته وسمير نهمته.

٣٧،٤٠ وقد قلت في وصف طباع الناس من قصيدة: [طويل]

أَلَمْ تَرَ أَنَّ ٱلدَّهْرَ حُبْلَى أَبِيَّةٌ ... وِلَادَتُهَا يَوْمًا وَإِنْ لَمْ تَكُنْ تُدْرَى
فَمِنْ مِنَحٍ تُسْلِي وَمِنْ مِحَنٍ تُسِي ... نَتَائِجُهَا صُغْرَى عَلَى ٱلْمَرْءِ أَوْ كُبْرَى
وَلَا تَأْمَنَنْ أَبْنَاءَهُ إِنْ تَحَبَّبُوا ... إِلَيْكَ فَمَنْ يُشْبِهْ أَبَاهُ فَقَدْ بَرَّا
وَكُلُّ بَنِي دَهْرٍ بِأَشْبَاهِ دَهْرِهِمْ ... عَلَى مَا قَضَى ٱللهُ ٱلْحَكِيمُ وَمَا أَجْرَى
مَتَى مَا ٱرْتَجَوْا رُغْبَاءَ مِنْكَ تَقَرَّبُوا ... إِلَيْكَ وَأَبْدَوْا خَالِصَ ٱلْوُدِّ وَٱلْبِرَّا
وَأَخْفَوْا ذَمِيمًا كَانَ فِيكَ وَأَظْهَرُوا ... جَمِيلًا وَقَالُوا ذُو مَحَاسِنَ لَا تُمْرَى
فَذٰلِكَ أَحْرَى أَنْ يَجِلُّوا وَيُنْصِتُوا ... إِلَيْكَ رَشَادًا كَانَ قَوْلُكَ أَوْ ثَبْرَا
وَإِنْ لَمْ يُرَجُّوا مِنْكَ خَيْرًا رَأَيْتَهُمْ ... جَفَاءً وَإِعْرَاضًا يُوَلُّونَكَ ٱلظَّهْرَا
وَيَنْشُونَ عَنْكَ ٱلْمُزْرِيَاتِ[١] وَإِنْ رَأَوْا ... جَمِيلًا أَعَارُوهُ ٱلْغِشَاوَةَ وَٱلْوَقْرَا
فَلَا تُصْغِ سَمْعًا لِلَّذِي ذَمَّ مِنْهُمُ ... وَلَا ٱلَّذِي أَبْدَى ٱلْجَمِيلَ وَإِنْ أَطْرَى
فَإِنَّ بَنِي ٱلدُّنْيَا عَبِيدُ هَوَاهُمُ ... عَلَى مَرْكَزِ ٱلْأَهْوَاءِ دَوْرَتُهُمْ طُرًّا
وَإِنَّ هَوَاهُمْ حَيْثُ تَرْتَقِبُ ٱلْغِنَى ... وَلَيْسَ هَوَاهُمْ حَيْثُ تَرْتَقِبُ ٱلْفَقْرَا
إِذَا مَا رَأَوْا ذَا ٱلْوَفْرِ لَاذُوا بِذَيْلِهِ ... وَإِنْ لَمْ يَنَالُوا مِنْ سَحَائِبِهِ قَطْرَا
وَإِنْ بَصُرُوا بِٱلْمُمْلَقِ ٱهْتَزَءُوا بِهِ ... وَمَدُّوا إِلَيْهِ طَرْفَهُمْ نَظَرًا شَزْرَا
وَقَالُوا بَغِيضٌ إِنْ نَأَى وَمَتَى دَنَا ... يَقُولُوا ثَقِيلٌ مُبْرِمٌ أَدْبَرَ لَفَقِيرَا

١ ق، ط: المنديات.

his lack of choice consists in his being the prisoner of his desire, accompanied by his cravings.

Describing people's nature, I have said in a poem: **40.37**

Have you not seen that time is a heavily pregnant woman,
  who will give birth one day, even if you do not know when?
You take joy in its gifts, are afflicted by its trials;
  depending on the person, these may be large or small.
Do not trust its children when they show you affection;
  they resemble their parent in their nature.
The people of every age resemble the age that produced them,
  according to what God most Wise decreed and occasioned.
Whenever they receive their desires from you
  they approach you with displays of pure affection and piety.
They downplay their sins and portray them as beautiful,
  saying: A good man's virtues do not leave!
It would be more appropriate for them to stand back and listen,
  whether your counsel offers guidance or restraint.
If they no longer seek good from you, you will find them
  useless, rebellious, turning their backs on you.
They will list what they despise about you, and if they see something beautiful
  they will conceal it, and make it a flaw.
Do not heed the one among them who slanders,
  nor the one who only displays goodness with words of praise.
For the people of this world are slaves to their desires,
  one and all—this is their turn in the center of desires.
Indeed, their desire, as you would anticipate, is wealth—
  they do not seek poverty.
If they see that it is abundant, they cling to its tail,
  even if they do not obtain a drop from its clouds.
When they see someone indigent, they mock him
  and gaze at him with mistrust.
They say he is odious when he's far away, and when he approaches
  they say he's unpleasant, disgusting, the worst of beggars.

فَـإِنْ غَابَ لَمْ يُفْقَدْ وَإِنْ عَلَّ لَمْ يُعَدْ   وَإِنْ مَاتَ لَمْ يُشْهَدْ وَإِنْ ضَافَ لَمْ يُقْرَا

وَفِي اللهِ لِلْمَـرْءِ اللَّـبِيبِ كِفَايَةٌ   عَنِ النَّاسِ وَالْمَحْرُومُ مَنْ حُرِمَ الْأَجْرَا

لله الأمـر من قبـل ومن بعـد. [١]

١،٤١ واعلـم أنّ هذا الطبع مركوز في طينة الآدميّ منذ كان غير مخصوص بأهل زمان
دون زمان. وإن كانت بعض الأزمنة يخصّها الله بغير ما يكون في غيرها من خير
أو شرّ لعارض غير أنّ الناس لمّا دهتهم هذه الداهية من تأذّي بعضهم ببعض
وعدم الظفر بالغرض من الغير جعل كلّ يستنقص أهل وقته لمشاهدة البلاء وعدم
الجدوى فيهم ويمدح من مضى. أمّا من لم يدركه فلتوهّمه أنّه على خلاف من رأى
وأمّا من أدركه فلانقطاع شرّه ووقوع الاستراحة منه مع بقاء بعض الجدوى في الوهم
ونزوع النفس إلى الإلف المألوف. فلا تسمع إلّا فسد الزمان وذهب الناس. فمن
ذلك قول بشار: [كامل]

فَسَدَ الزَّمَانُ وَسَادَ فِيهِ الْمُقْرِفُ   وَجَرَى مَعَ الطَّرْفِ الْحِمَارُ الْمَوْكَفُ

وقول الآخر: [وافر]   ٢،٤١

أَلَا ذَهَبَ التَّكَرُّمُ وَالْوَفَاءُ   وَبَادَ رِجَالُهُ وَبَقِيَ الْغُثَاءُ

وَأَسْلَمَنِي الزَّمَانُ إِلَى أُنَاسٍ   كَأَمْثَالِ الذِّئَابِ لَهُمْ عُوَاءُ

صَدِيقٌ كُلَّمَا اسْتَغْنَيْتُ عَنْهُمْ   وَأَعْدَاءٌ إِذَا نَزَلَ الْبَلَاءُ

أَقُولُ وَلَا أُلَامُ عَلَى مَقَالِي   عَلَى الْإِخْوَانِ كُلِّهِمِ الْعَفَاءُ

---

١ سقطت الجملة من ق، ط.

When he is absent, he is not missed, when sick, he is not treated,
when he dies, he is not martyred, when a guest, he gets no
hospitality.
For the man with insight, God renders people unnecessary;
he is deprived who refuses to give.

Everything is God's to command.

Man has possessed this nature in his very substance since he was created. This is not specific to people of a particular time. As much as God has distinguished some times with elements of good and evil that are not present in others, one might argue that whenever people are struck by the affliction of harming each other and failing to achieve their goal, they begin to find fault in their contemporaries' afflictions and their absence of virtue, and to praise their forefathers. As for those they never knew, let them imagine that the earlier generations were different from those they see. Concerning those they have met, let them virtuously imagine—along with the desire of the ego for what is familiar—that their evil has ceased and they are free of it. For this reason, one hears of nothing but the corruption of time and the passing of people of quality. These are Bashshār's words on the subject: 41.1

The age is corrupt, half-breeds are everywhere,
thoroughbred steeds are interbred with base donkeys.

Another said: 41.2

Have not all nobility and sincerity left—
their men gone, while only scum remain?
Time has delivered me to people
similar to howling wolves.
Friends when I have no need for them
and enemies when calamity strikes.
These lines I say without rebuking
brethren, all of whom have passed into dust.

٣،٤١ وقول الآخر: [كامل]

ذَهَبَ ٱلَّذِينَ إِذَا رَأَوْنِي مُقْبِلًا هَشُّوا وَقَالُوا مَرْحَبًا بِٱلْمُقْبِلِ
وَبَقِيتُ فِي خَلْفٍ كَأَنَّ حَدِيثَهُمْ وَلْغُ ٱلْكِلَابِ تَهَارَشَتْ فِي مَنْهَلِ

٤،٤١ وقول الآخر: [مجزوء الرمل]

ذَهَبَ ٱلَّذِينَ أُحِبُّهُمْ وَبَقِيتُ فِيمَنْ لَا أُحِبُّهْ
إِذْ لَا يَزَالُ كَرِيمُ قَوْ مٍ فِيهِمْ كَلْبٌ يَسُبُّهْ

٥،٤١ وقال منصور الفقيه: [مجزوء الرمل]

يَا زَمَانًا أَلْبَسَ ٱلْأَحْ رَارَ ذُلًّا وَمَهَانَهْ
لَسْتَ عِنْدِي بِزَمَانٍ إِنَّمَا أَنْتَ زَمَانَهْ

٦،٤١ وقول الآخر: [وافر]

مَضَى دَهْرُ ٱلسَّمَاحِ فَلَا سَمَاحُ وَلَا يُرْجَى لَدَى أَحَدٍ فَلَاحُ
رَأَيْتُ ٱلنَّاسَ قَدْ مَسَخُوا كِلَابًا فَلَيْسَ لَدَيْهِمُ إِلَّا ٱلنُّبَاحُ
وَأَضْحَى ٱلظَّرْفُ عِنْدَهُمُ قَبِيحًا وَلَا وَاللهِ إِنَّهُمُ ٱلْقِبَاحُ
سَلَامُ أَهْلِ ٱلْبَلِيدِ عَلَيْكُمْ فَإِنَّ ٱلْبَيْنَ أَوْشَكَهُ ٱلرَّوَاحُ
نَرُوحُ فَنَسْتَرِيحُ ٱلْيَوْمَ مِنْكُمْ وَمِنْ أَمْثَالِكُمْ قَدْ يُسْتَرَاحُ
إِذَا مَا ٱلْحُرُّ هَانَ بِأَرْضِ قَوْمٍ فَلَيْسَ عَلَيْهِ فِي هَرَبٍ جُنَاحُ

Another has said:[254] 41.3

Those who believed me fortunate have departed.
Once they were joyful and used to say: Welcome to the lucky one.
I remained behind—it was as if their speech
were the lapping of dogs quarreling at the pool.

Another said:[255] 41.4

Those I loved have left,
and I remain among those I do not love.
If anyone noble remains among the common folk
he is reviled by dogs.

The jurist al-Manṣūr said:[256] 41.5

Time, you have dressed noble men
in disgrace and contempt.
I have no claim over Time—
it has the power to command!

Another said: 41.6

The age of generous men has passed;
there are no longer such men, nor can anyone hope for salvation.
I have seen people transformed into dogs,
who can do nothing but bark.
Their outer form has become repulsive;
by God, they are truly vile.
The peace of the dull-witted upon you,
the first act of separation is to depart.
We leave and today find respite from you;
may others seek respite from your kind.
If the noble are few in the land of common folk,
fleeing it will not be held against them.

وقول الآخر: [طويل] ٧،٤١

مَضَى ٱلْجُودُ وَٱلْإِحْسَانُ وَٱجْتُثَّ أَهْلُهُ   وَأَخْمَدَ نِيرَانَ ٱلنَّدَى وَٱلْمَكَارِمِ
وَصِرْتُ إِلَى ضَرْبٍ مِنَ ٱلنَّاسِ آخَرٍ   يَرَوْنَ ٱلْعُلَى وَٱلْمَجْدَ جَمْعَ ٱلدَّرَاهِمِ
كَأَنَّهُمُ كَانُوا جَمِيعاً تَعَاقَدُوا   عَلَى ٱللُّؤْمِ وَٱلْإِمْسَاكِ فِي صُلْبِ آدَمِ

وللإمام الشافعيّ رضي الله عنه: [وافر] ٨،٤١

صَدِيقٌ لَيْسَ يَنْفَعُ يَوْمَ بَأْسٍ   قَرِيبٌ مِنْ عَدُوٍّ فِي ٱلْقِيَاسِ
وَمَا يَبْقَى ٱلصَّدِيقُ بِكُلِّ عَصْرٍ   وَلَا ٱلْإِخْوَانُ إِلَّا لِلتَّآسِي
عَمَرْتُ ٱلدَّهْرَ مُلْتَمِساً بِجُهْدِي   أَخَا ثِقَةٍ فَأَكْدَانِي ٱلْتِمَاسِي
تَنَكَّرَتِ ٱلْبِلَادُ عَلَيَّ حَتَّى   كَأَنَّ أُنَاسَهَا لَيْسُوا بِنَاسِ

وقال غيره: [كامل] ٩،٤١

هٰذَا زَمَانُ تَجَاهُلٍ وَتَسَامُحٍ   وَتَغَافُلٍ عَنْ أَهْلِهِ فَسَدَ ٱلْوَرَى
فَإِذَا سَمِعْتَ فَكُنْ كَأَنَّكَ مَا سَمِعْـ   ـتَ وَإِنْ رَأَيْتَ فَكُنْ كَأَنَّكَ مَا تَرَى
وَٱجْهَدْ بِنَفْسِكَ فِي ٱلتَّخَلُّصِ مِنْهُمُ   فَعَسَاكَ تَنْجُو إِنْ نَجَوْتَ وَمَا أَرَى
أَوْ لَا فَكُنْ فِي قَعْرِ بَيْتِكَ لَا تَرَى   إِنْ كُنْتَ تَرْغَبُ فِي ٱلنَّجَاةِ وَبِٱلْحَرَى

Another said: 41.7

Virtue and integrity have passed away, people have been uprooted,
the fires of liberality and generosity have gone out.
I have joined another type of people,
who deem collecting dirhams glorious and sublime.
It is as if all of them together agreed to wickedness
and resolved to crucify mankind.

The following lines are by the exemplar al-Shāfiʿī, God be content with him: 41.8

A friend sees no benefit on the day of disaster;
reason suggests he is close to an enemy.
In every age, no friends or brethren remain
except to console one another.
I lived through my life fervently seeking
a trustworthy brother, but my search was fruitless.
This country has treated me as an enemy, to such a point
that its inhabitants no longer seem like people.

Someone else said: 41.9

This is a time when people shut their eyes and are careless,
paying no attention to others, leading to the corruption of mankind.
Whatever you hear, pretend you did not hear;
whatever you see, pretend you did not see.
Do your best to be rid of them;
perhaps you will be saved if you escape, though I doubt it.
Act as though you are in the depths of your house, blind
if you actually desire salvation.

وقال أيضاً: [بسيط] ١٠،٤١

عَـمَّ ٱلْفَسَادُ جَمِيعَ ٱلنَّاسِ وَيْحَهُمُ   يَا لَيْتَ شِعْرِيَ مَـاذَا بَعْدُ يُنْتَظَرُ
إِنْ وَعِدُوا أَخْلَفُوا أَوْ حَدَّثُوا كَذَبُوا   أَوْ عَهِدُوا غَدَرُوا أَوْ خَاصَمُوا فَجَرُوا
أَوِ ٱئْتَمَنْتَهُمُ خَانُوا فَكُنْ رَجُلاً   مِنْهُمْ عَلَى حَذَرٍ قَدْ يَنْفَعُ ٱلْحَذَرُ

وقال غيره: [بسيط] ١١،٤١

مَا فِي زَمَانِكَ هٰذَا مَنْ تُصَاحِبُهُ   وَلَا صَدِيقَ إِذَا خَانَ ٱلزَّمَانُ وَفِي
فَعِشْ فَرِيدًا وَلَا تَرْكَنْ إِلَى أَحَدٍ   فَقَدْ نَصَحْتُكَ نُصْحًا بَالِغًا وَكَفِي

وقال الأرجاني: [طويل] ١٢،٤١

تَطَلَّعْتُ فِي يَوْمَيْ رَخَاءٍ وَشِدَّةٍ   وَنَادَيْتُ فِي ٱلْأَحْيَاءِ هَلْ مِنْ مُسَاعِدِ
فَلَمْ أَرَ فِيمَا سَاءَنِي غَيْرَ شَامِتٍ   وَلَمْ أَرَ فِيمَا سَرَّنِي غَيْرَ حَاسِدِ

وقال غيره: [طويل] ١٣،٤١

خُبِرْتُ بَنِي ٱلْأَيَّامِ طُرًّا فَلَمْ أَجِدْ   صَدِيقًا صَدُوقًا مُسْعِدًا فِي ٱلنَّوَائِبِ
وَأَصْفَيْتُهُمْ مِنِّي ٱلْوِدَادَ فَقَابَلُوا   صَفَاءَ وِدَادِي بِٱلْقَذَى وَٱلشَّوَائِبِ
وَمَا ٱخْتَرْتُ مِنْهُمْ صَاحِبًا وَٱرْتَضَيْتُهُ   وَأَحْمَدْتُهُ فِي فِعْلِهِ وَٱلْعَوَاقِبِ

وقال آخر: [خفيف] ١٤،٤١

نَحْنُ وَٱللهِ فِي زَمَانٍ غَشُومٍ   لَوْ رَأَيْنَاهُ فِي ٱلْمَنَامِ فَزِعْنَا
أَصْبَحَ ٱلنَّاسُ فِيهِ مِنْ سُوءِ حَالٍ   حَقُّ مَنْ مَاتَ مِنْهُمُ أَنْ يُهَنَّا

He also said: **41.10**

Corruption has spread among all the people—woe to them!
I wish I knew what there is still to expect.
When they make promises, they break them; when they speak, they lie;
if they make a pact, they betray it; if they litigate, they swear false oaths.
If you ask them for protection, they will betray you,
so be cautious among them—caution may help.

Someone else said: **41.11**

No one in your time is worthy of your companionship;
when the time comes, there is no true friend.
Live alone and rely on no one;
with this, I have given you ample and sufficient advice.

Al-Arjānī said: **41.12**

I have moved constantly between days of ease and adversity
and have called out in the neighborhoods for someone to help me.
I have experienced no misfortune without someone gloating over it
nor ever been happy without being envied.

Another said: **41.13**

I examined the people of our time
and found no true friend to help in misfortune.
I offered them the sincere gift of affection
and they met the purity of my feelings with blemishes and impurity.
I chose none of them as companion, nor was I content with or able to thank any for his deeds or for a good outcome.

Another said:[257] **41.14**

By God, we are living in a time of tyranny—
if we saw the Prophet in a dream, we would be afraid.
People have entered an evil state of affairs—
whoever dies deserves to be congratulated.

وقول الآخر: [بسيط] ١٥،٤١

أَنْعِي إِلَيْكَ خِلَالَ ٱلْخَيْرِ قَاطِبَةً لَمْ يَبْقَ مِنْهُنَّ إِلَّا دَارِسُ ٱلْعَلَمِ
أَنْعِي إِلَيْكَ مُوَاسَاةَ ٱلصَّدِيقِ وَمَا قَدْ كَانَ يَرْعَى مِنَ ٱلْأَخْلَاقِ وَٱلذِّمَمِ
أَيْنَ ٱلْوَفَاءُ ٱلَّذِي قَدْ كَانَ يَعْرِفُهُ قَوْمٌ لِقَوْمٍ وَأَيْنَ ٱلْحِفْظُ لِلْحُرَمِ
أَيْنَ ٱلْجَمِيلُ ٱلَّذِي قَدْ كَانَ يَلْبَسُهُ أَهْلُ ٱلْوَفَاءِ وَأَهْلُ ٱلْفَضْلِ وَٱلْكَرَمِ
أَيْسِرْ وَأَنْتَ صَدِيقُ ٱلنَّاسِ كُلِّهِمِ ثُمَّ ٱبْلُ سِرَّهُمْ فِي حَالَةِ ٱلْعَدَمِ
فَإِنْ وَجِدْتَ صَدِيقاً عِنْدَ نَائِبَةٍ فَلَسْتَ مِنْ طُرُقَاتِ ٱلْحَزْمِ فِي أَمَمِ
لَمَّا أَنَاخَ عَلَيَّ ٱلدَّهْرُ كَلْكَلَهُ وَخَانَنِي كُلُّ ذِي وُدٍّ وَذِي رَحِمِ
نَادَيْتُ مَا فَعَلَ ٱلْأَحْرَارُ كُلُّهُمُ أَهْلُ ٱلنَّدَى وَٱلْهُدَى وَٱلْبُعْدِ فِي ٱلْهِمَمِ
قَالُوا حَدَا بِهِمْ رَيْبُ ٱلزَّمَانِ فَسَلْ أَجْدَاثَهُمْ عَنْهُمْ تُخْبِرْكَ عَنْ رِمَمِ

وقول لبيد: [كامل] ١٦،٤١

ذَهَبَ ٱلَّذِينَ يُعَاشُ فِي أَكْنَافِهِمْ وَبَقِيتُ فِي خَلْفٍ كَجِلْدِ ٱلْأَجْرَبِ

١٧،٤١ وتمثّلت به أمّ المؤمنين عائشة رضي الله عنها ثمّ قالت وكيف لو أدرك لبيد زماننا؟ فقال عروة كيف لو أدركت عائشة زماننا؟ ولمّا بلغ ابن عباس قول عائشة هذا قال رحم الله لبيداً ورحم الله عائشة. لقد أصيب باليمن سهم في خزائن عاد كأطول ما يكون من رماحكم. هذه مفوّق مَرِيش مكتوب عليه هذا: [طويل]

أَلَا هَلْ إِلَى أَبْيَاتٍ مُنْقَطَعُ ٱللِّوَى لِوَى ٱلرَّمْلِ مِنْ قَبْلِ ٱلْمَمَاتِ مَعَادُ
بِلَادٌ بِهَا كُنَّا وَكُنَّا مِنْ أَهْلِهَا إِذِ ٱلنَّاسُ نَاسٌ وَٱلْبِلَادُ بِلَادُ

41.15 Another said:

I lament to you all the ways goodness has been undermined;
no good remains except for the aspiring student.
I lament to you the former charity of the friend,
and the morals and good conscience he used to cultivate.
Where is the sincerity people used to display to others?
Where is the protection of what is sacred?
Where is the beauty that the people of sincerity,
the people of virtue and honor once wore?
When fortune smiles on you, everyone is your friend,
but fall on hard times and they gloat over your destitution.
If you find a friend in a time of calamity,
then you proceed without prudence!
When time afflicts me with great distress,
and everyone who has shown me affection and mercy betrays me,
I enjoin on them the deeds of the noble,
the people of generosity and guidance who live at ease.
They reply that the uncertainty of the age drove them—
ask their graves to tell you of their decayed bones!

41.16 Labīd's line goes as follows:

Those who offered protection have passed on,
and I have been abandoned like a mangy skin.

41.17 ʿĀʾishah the Mother of the Believers, God be content with her, quoted this line and said, "What would Labīd have said had he reached our time?" and ʿUrwah responded, "What would ʿĀʾishah have said had she reached ours?"[258] When Ibn ʿAbbās heard what ʿĀʾishah had said, he said, "May God have mercy on both Labīd and ʿĀʾishah. In Yemen, in the storerooms of ʿĀd, I came upon an arrow as long as your lances. The feathered shaft had this written on it:

Is there an end of suffering to these lines,
a return before death to where the sand dunes curve?
Lands that we lived in and to which we belonged;
now others live there and the land remains."

١٨،٤١ أي فهذا العاديّ في زمانه يستنقص زمانه ويشير إلى أنّ الناس الأفاضل قد مضوا وأنّ الأرض تغيّرت. فكيف حال زمان لبيد ومن بعده كزمان عائشة. وقد تحصل من هذا ما قرّرنا في صدر الكلام من أنّ الدنيا لم تزل هكذا والناس هم الناس منذ خلقوا. ولقد أحسن القائل: [خفيف]

قُلْ لِمَنْ لَا يَرَى ٱلْمُعَاصِرَ شَيْئاً وَيَرَى لِلْأَوَائِلِ ٱلتَّقْدِيمَا
إِنَّ هٰذَا ٱلْقَدِيمَ كَانَ جَدِيداً وَسَيَبْقَى هٰذَا ٱلْجَدِيدُ قَدِيمَا

١٩،٤١ فالأكمل للإنسان التسليم بل الرضى بوقته. فإنّه بذلك يفوز بالأدب مع الله تعالى الحكيم العليم الذي هو ربّ الأوّلين والآخرين. ويفوز بشكره وحمده وبراحة قلبه والسلامة من التشوّف والتطلّع وسلامة الصدر لأهل زمانه والقيام بحقوقهم واعتقاد الخير في أهله والانتفاع بهم ورؤية المحاسن الوقتيّة والتغافل عن المساوي وغير ذلك. ولقد منح الله تعالى الصحابة الزمان الفاضل فكانوا يذكرون ما مضى لهم في الأزمنة السالفة من صنوف الشرّ من عبادة الأوثان وارتكاب القبائح والجهد الجهيد. فيحمدون الله تعالى ويشكرونه.

٢٠،٤١ وهكذا ينبغي للمؤمن أن ينظر إلى ما منحه الله تعالى من الخير في زمانه ديناً ودنيا وإلى ما أنجاه الله تعالى منه من الشرور الحاليّة والماضية فيحمد الله على ذلك. وقد جرت على لساني في هذا المعنى أبيات فقلت مناقضاً لما تقدّم من الأشعار: [خفيف]

نَحْمَدُ اللهَ وَقْتُنَا وَقْتُ خَيْرٍ بَذَّ مَا قَبْلَهُ مِنَ ٱلْأَوْقَاتِ
غَيْرُ وَقْتِ ٱلنَّبِيِّ صَلَّى عَلَيْهِ ٱلـ لَهُ وَٱلصَّحْبِ وَٱلثُّلَاةِ ٱلْهُدَاةِ
دِينُنَا سَالِمٌ مِنَ ٱلْبِدَعِ ٱلْعُمْـ ـيِ وَعِشْنَا بِطَيِّبِ ٱلْأَقْوَاتِ
لَمْ تَكُنْ كَٱلشُّرَاةِ نَغْشَى ٱلْمَعَاصِي لِتَفُوزَ بِٱلْخُلْدِ فِي ٱلْغُرُفَاتِ

That is to say that this was normal in his time, with which he found fault, and he alludes to the passing of noble people and the earth having changed. How then were things in the time of Labīd and after it, such as in the time of ʿĀʾishah? We can take from this what we noted at the beginning of this discussion—namely, that the world is still like this and that the people have been like this since they were created. How right was the one who said:[259] 41.18

Say to the one who thinks little of his contemporaries
and who believes that the ancients were superior,
That the ancients were once new,
and that what is new will become ancient.

The preferable course of action for man is not just to submit, but to be content with the age he is in. This is how, through proper comportment, he will achieve success with Exalted God, Wise and Knowing, Lord of the First and the Last. He will achieve success through his thanks to God and praise of Him, will find peace in his heart from hope and aspiration, and will have an open heart for the people of his time, undertaking to establish their rights, thinking well of them, and benefiting all of them. He will perceive the virtues of the age and ignore its vices and suchlike. Exalted God granted the Companions a virtuous age: They used to recount the types of evil that existed in previous times, including the worshipping of idols and the committing of vile acts, and talked about how difficult that time had been; they praised Exalted God and thanked him. 41.19

This is the attitude the believer needs to adopt toward the goodness Exalted God has granted him in his time in both religious and temporal matters, acknowledging how Exalted God has preserved him from present and past evils. Let him thank God for this. On this subject, verses have rolled off my tongue, and I have criticized earlier poetry as follows: 41.20

We give thanks to God for our time,
a time of good that surpasses those preceding
Except the time of the Prophet, God bless him,
and the Companions and the rightly guided followers.
Our faith is free from blind innovation;
we have enjoyed the best of foods.
We are not like the Kharijites who concealed sins
to win eternity in the highest heaven.

ضَيَّعُوا ٱلدِّينَ بِٱلْمُرُوقِ وَدُنْيَا هُمْ بِوَقْعِ ٱلظِّبَاتِ فِي ٱلسَّبَدَاتِ
لَا وَلَا كَٱلْجَبْرِيِّ وَٱلْقَدَرِيِّ ٱلنَّجْسِ وَلَا سَائِرِ ٱلْجُفَاةِ ٱلْغُوَاةِ
وَٱلَّذِي قَدْ نَلْقَى مِنَ ٱلْمُرِّ فِي ٱلدُّنْيَا عَسَى أَنْ نَرْقَى بِهِ دَرَجَاتِ
وَبَنُو ٱلدَّهْرِ هُمْ بَنُو ٱلدَّهْرِ قِدْماً هُمْ نَبَاتٌ يَنْمُو بِإِثْرِ نَبَاتِ
وَٱلطِّبَاعُ ٱلطِّبَاعُ لَسْتَ تَرَى فِي هَا نُبُوًّا وَلَا ٱخْتِلَافَ ٱلصِّفَاتِ
وَمَنِ ٱخْتَصَّهُ ٱلْإِلٰهُ بِخَيْرٍ فَهْوَ فِيهِ مِنْ دَارِجٍ أَوْ آتِ

٤١،٢١ نعم لا بأس بذكر الماضي من صلحاء الإخوان والحنين إلى الأوطان وإنّ ذلك يعدّ من حسن العهد. وفي الحديث أنّه صلّى الله عليه وسلّم دخلت عليه امرأة فأكرمها وقال إنها كانت تأتينا أيّام خديجة وإنّ حسن العهد من الإيمان. وكانت عائشة رضي الله عنها تقول ما غِرت على امرأة ما غرت على خديجة. وذلك من كثرة ما كان يذكرها صلّى الله عليه وسلّم.

٤١،٢٢ وقيل لبعض الحكماء بمَ تعرف وفاء الرجل وذمام عهده دون تجربة واختبار؟ فقال بحنينه إلى أوطانه وتشوّقه إلى إخوانه وتلهّفه على ما مضى من زمانه.

٤١،٢٣ وعن الأصمعي قال إذا أردت أن تعرف وفاء الرجل وذِمام عهده فانظر إلى حنينه إلى أوطانه وتشوّقه إلى إخوانه وبكائه على ما مضى من زمانه. و[١] كان سيّدنا بلال رضي الله عنه ينشد: [طويل]

أَلَا لَيْتَ شِعْرِي هَلْ أَبِيتَنَّ لَيْلَةً بِوَادٍ وَحَوْلِي إِذْخِرٌ وَجَلِيلُ
وَهَلْ أَرِدَنْ يَوْماً مِيَاهَ مَجَنَّةٍ وَهَلْ يَبْدُوَنْ لِي شَامَةٌ وَطَفِيلُ

وقد تقدّم شيء من هذا قبل.

١ يزيد ق: من هذا المعنى.

They lost their faith through apostasy, and in this transient world
they follow their blades into misfortune.
No, nor are we like believers in predetermination
or filthy believers in free will, or other deviators.
Perhaps we will experience in degrees
the bitterness we may taste of this world.
The people of the age have always been people of the age,
plants descended from plants.
Nature is nature; you will see no variance in it,
nor differing characteristics.
He whom God has chosen to experience good
could belong to either the past or future.

Truly, there is no harm in remembering the devout people of past times or in longing for one's country. Indeed, this can be considered a kind of loyal attachment. One hadith describes a woman who came to the Prophet, God bless and keep him. He honored her and said of her, "She used to visit us in the days of Khadījah, and loyal attachment is part of faith." ʿĀʾishah, God be content with her, used to say, "I never envied a woman as much as I envied Khadījah." This was because of how much the Prophet used to mention her, God bless and keep him. **41.21**

One of the philosophers was asked, "How do you know a man's sincerity and the value of his word without testing him?" To which he replied, "By his longing for his homeland, his yearning for his brethren, and his desire for what has passed of his life." **41.22**

It is related that al-Aṣmaʿī said, "If you want to know a man's sincerity and the value of his word, then consider his longing for his homeland, his yearning for his brethren, and his crying for what has passed of his life." Our leader Bilāl, God be content with him, used to recite: **41.23**

I wish I knew if I would ever spend the night again
in a valley surrounded by sweet rushes and palm trees
And return one day to the waters of Majannah.
Will I ever see Shāmah and Ṭafīl again?

(Some of this was included above.)[260]

٤١،٢٤ وقال أبو العبّاس بن العريف رضي الله عنه: [بسيط]

مَا زِلْتُ مُذْ سَكَنُوا قَلْبِي أَصُونُ لَهُمْ لَحْظِي وَسَمْعِي وَنُطْقِي إِذْ هُمُ أَنَسِي
حَلُّوا ٱلْفُؤَادَ فَمَا أَنْدَى وَلَوْ قَطَنُوا صَخْرًا لَجَادَ بِمَاءٍ مِنْهُ مُنْبَجِسِ
وَفِي ٱلْحَشَا نَزَلُوا وَٱلْوَهْمُ يَجْرَحُهُمْ فَكَيْفَ قَرُّوا عَلَى أَذْكَى مِنَ ٱلْقَبَسِ
لَأَنْهَضَنَّ إِلَى حَشْرِي بِحُبِّهِمْ لَا بَارَكَ اللهُ فِيمَنْ خَانَهُمْ فَنَسِيَ

٤١،٢٥ وقال غيره: [بسيط]

جِسْمِي مَعِي غَيْرَ أَنَّ ٱلرُّوحَ عِنْدَكُمْ فَٱلْجِسْمُ فِي غُرْبَةٍ وَٱلرُّوحُ فِي وَطَنِ
فَلْيَعْجَبِ ٱلنَّاسُ مِنِّي أَنَّ لِي بَدَنًا لَا رُوحَ فِيهِ وَلِي رُوحٌ بِلَا بَدَنِ

٤١،٢٦ وقال آخر: [كامل]

رَاحُوا فَبَاتَتْ رَاحَتِي مِنْ رَاحَتِي صِفْرًا وَأَضْحَى حُبُّهُمْ لِي رَاحَا
فَتَحُوا عَلَى قَلْبِي ٱلْهُمُومَ وَأَغْلَقُوا بَابَ ٱلسُّرُورِ وَضَيَّعُوا ٱلْمِفْتَاحَا

٤١،٢٧ وقال غيره: [بسيط]

يَا رَاحِلًا وَجَمِيلُ ٱلصَّبْرِ يَتْبَعُهُ هَلْ مِنْ سَبِيلٍ إِلَى لُقْيَاكَ يَتَّفِقُ
مَا أَنْصَفَتْكَ جُفُونِي وَهْيَ دَامِيَةٌ وَلَا وَفَى لَكَ قَلْبِي وَهْوَ يَحْتَرِقُ

Abū l-ʿAbbās ibn al-ʿArīf, God be content with him, said: 41.24

Since they inhabited my heart, I have continued to preserve for them
my sight, my hearing, and my speech.
How generous it is that they alighted in my heart;
if they settled on a rock, it would glisten with water flowing from it.
They settled in my insides—wounded by delusion;
how did they come to rest on what was brighter than a coal?
On the day of judgment, I will awaken with love for them;
may God keep his blessings from one who betrays and then forgets them.

Another said: 41.25

My body abides with me, yet my soul is with you;
the body is abroad but the soul is at home.
Let the people wonder at me: a body without a soul,
and a soul without a body.

Another said: 41.26

They left, so my courtyard was emptied of comfort
and their love became pure wine for me.[261]
They opened my heart to anxieties,
locked the gate of happiness, and lost the key.

Yet another said:[262] 41.27

Traveler pursued by beautiful forbearance,
is there a path that leads to you?
My eyelids, bloody from crying, did not treat you justly.
Nor did my burning heart keep faith with you.

٤١،٢٨ وقال غيره: [طويل]

لِيَكْفِكُمْ مَا فِيكُمْ مِنْ جَوًى أَلْقَى   فَمَهْلاً بِنَا مَهْلاً وَرِفْقًا بِنَا رِفْقَا
وَحُرْمَةُ وُدِّي لَا سَئِمْتُ هَوَاكُمُ   وَلَا رُمْتُ لِي مِنْهُ فَكَاكًا وَلَا عِتْقَا
سَأَزْجُرُ قَلْبًا رَامَ فِي ٱلْحُبِّ سَلْوَةً   وَأَهْجُرُهُ إِنْ لَمْ يَمُتْ فِيكُمْ عِشْقَا

٤١،٢٩ وقال غيره: [سريع]

مَا نَاحَ فِي أَعْلَى ٱلْغُصُونِ ٱلْهَزَارُ   إِلَّا تَشَوَّقْتُ لِتِلْكَ ٱلدِّيَار
وَلَا سَرَى مِنْ نَحْوِكُمْ بَارِقٌ   إِلَّا وَأَجْرَيْتُ ٱلدُّمُوعَ ٱلْغِزَار
وَا أَسَفِي أَيْنَ زَمَانُ ٱلْحِمَى؟   وَأَيْنَ هَاتِيكَ ٱللَّيَالِي ٱلْقِصَار؟
وَاحَرَّ قَلْبِي فَمَتَى نَلْتَقِي   وَتَنْطَفِي مِنْ دَاخِلِ ٱلْقَلْبِ نَار
وَأَنْظُرُ ٱلْأَحْبَابَ قَدْ وَاصَلُوا   وَيَأْخُذُ ٱلْوَصْلُ مِنَ ٱلْهَجْرِ ثَار
أَقُولُ لِلنَّفْسِ أَبْشِرِي بِٱللِّقَا   قَدْ وَاصَلَ ٱلْحُبُّ وَقَرَّ ٱلْقَرَار

٤١،٣٠ وذكر في التشوّف عن أبي شعيب السارية رضي الله عنه قال كان إذا وقف على قبر شيخه أبي عليّ المسطاسيّ يقول أيّ رجل دفن هاهنا! ما رأيت مثله. وأنشد: [كامل]

أَسَفًا لِأَيَّامٍ وَإِخْوَانٍ مَضَوْا   وَمَنَازِلَ فَارَقْتُهَا مَغْلُوبَا
قَلَبَتْ قَلْبِي جَمْرَةً مِنْ بَعْدِهِمْ   وَلَبِسْتُ عَيْشِي بَعْدَهُمْ مَقْلُوبَا
طَالَبْتُ بَعْدَهُمُ ٱلزَّمَانَ بِمِثْلِهِمْ   فَأَجَابَنِي هَيْهَاتَ لَا مَطْلُوبَا

٤١،٣١ وحكي أيضاً عن أبي عمران الهسكوري الأسود أنّه كان لا ترقأ له دمعة. فربّما سئل عن كثرة بكائه فيقول إنّما أبكي على فقد من أدركته من الإخوان في الله عزّ وجلّ.

Another said: 41.28

Let what passion has been placed in you suffice;
go slow with us and treat us tenderly.
My hallowed love has not turned away from your passion,
nor desired freedom or emancipation from it.
I will rebuke the heart that looks for comfort in love;
I will drive it out if it does not perish with love for you.

Another said: 41.29

In the highest branches, the nightingale does not sing
except when it longs for these habitats.
No notable such as you has ever left at night
without copious tears flowing.
Woe is me! Where are the days in the sanctuary?
Where are those too-short nights?
How my heart burns—when shall we meet
so you can extinguish the fire in my heart?
Look! Lovers maintain close relations.
Reunion takes revenge on separation.
To my soul I say, bring me news of a tryst;
love has persisted and made its home.

The following is related in *Contemplating the Sufis* regarding Abū Shuʿayb 41.30
al-Sāriyah, God be content with him: When Abū Shuʿayb al-Sāriyah stopped by the grave of his teacher Abū ʿAlī al-Masṭāsī, he said, "What a man lies buried here! I never saw his like," and declaimed:

Woe to bygone days and brethren
and to the dwellings I have left, defeated.
After them, an ember inverted my heart;
after them, I lived my life upturned.
After them, I searched time for their like.
How preposterous that I was answered by what I did not seek!

It is also related of Abū ʿImrān al-Haskūrī l-Aswad that he never ceased shed- 41.31
ding tears. He was once asked about his excessive weeping and he answered, "I weep for the loss of the brethren I knew in God, Great and Mighty."

٤١،٣٢ ويحكى أيضاً عن أبي جعفر الأسود صاحب تاغزوت أنّه كان يقول أدركت ببلاد تادلا ثلاثمائة وسبعين رجلاً صالحاً كلّهم يزارون. وأنشد: [طويل]

فَآهًا مِنَ ٱلرَّبْعِ ٱلَّذِي غَيَّرَ ٱلْبِلَى ... وَوَاهًا مِنَ ٱلْقَوْمِ ٱلَّذِينَ تَفَرَّقُوا
أَصُونُ تُرَابَ ٱلْأَرْضِ كَانُوا حُلُولَهَا ... وَأَحْذَرُ مِنْ مَرِّي عَلَيْهَا وَأُفْرِقُ
وَلَمْ يَبْقَ عِنْدِي لِلْهَوَى غَيْرَ أَنَّنِي ... إِذَا ٱلرَّكْبُ مَرُّوا بِي عَلَى ٱلدَّارِ أَشْهَقُ

٤١،٣٣ تنبيه على حكم ما وقع من استنقاص الزمان واستنقاص أهله وسبّهما بحسب النظر الشرعي أصلاً وفرعاً. فأمّا الزمان ويقال أيضاً الدهر فجرت عادة الشعراء وغيرهم قديماً وحديثاً بالتشكّي منه والتبرّم به ونسبة الإذاية والجور إليه. وقد يكون فيهم من يعتقد ظاهر ذلك وهو مشرك وقد يكون من لا يعتقد ذلك لكونه موحّداً بل إمّا غفلة وَجرياً على أسلوب من قبله من التعبير وإمّا مجازاً بطريق المقارنة لما يقع فيه من الأحداث والكوائن.

٤١،٣٤ والفاعل هو الله تعالى فلا معنى حينئذ للتشكّي منه ولا لسبّه ولا استنقاصه فإنّ ذلك سوء أدب مع الله تعالى من جهتين. إحداهما أنّه هو المتصرّف في الكلّ ولذا ورد في الخبر لا تسبّوا الدهر فإنّ الله هو الدهر. أي ما ترونه فالله تعالى هو فاعله. ثانيهما أنّه يجب على المؤمن اعتقاد كلّ ما برز في كلّ زمان من التصرّفات فذلك هو الصالح في ذلك الوقت الجاري على الحكمة سواء لاءم الطباع أو لا. ومن اعتقد خلاف ذلك فهو جاهل بالله تعالى جاهل بحكمته وقدرته. ولو ولي والٍ بلدة لم يتصرّف فيها إلّا بالحكمة والمصلحة إلّا ما خرج عن علمه وطوقه والله تبارك وتعالى عليم حكيم قاهر فوق عباده غالب على أمره لا يتعالى عن قدرته مقدور ولا يعزب عن علمه مثقال ذرّة.

٤١،٣٥ ثمّ الزمان بمعزل عن العيب والنقص فإنّما ذلك في الناس وما يقع منهم أو يقع لهم فهم أحقّ بالانتقاص كما قيل: [طويل]

It is related of Abū Jaʿfar al-Aswad, the master of Tāghzūt, that he said, “In the region of Tādlā I have known three hundred and seventy saints, all of whose graves are visited,” and he recited: 41.32

Alas for the campsite touched by destruction;
alas for the people who have left.
I guard the dust where they had stayed
and drive away those who pass it by.
I no longer have any desire but
to cry out when the riders pass my house.

Take note of the legal ruling, both fundamentally and doctrinally, when it comes to finding fault with and maligning one’s time and its people. Both the ancient and modern poets habitually complained of time, also called the age. They were distressed by it and attributed both harm and decline to it. Those who take such an attribution literally are polytheists. Others reject the attribution due to their faith in a single God but utter such sentiments either out of ignorance, aping the way those before them have expressed themselves, or metaphorically by way of comparison because of the events and matters in their own time. 41.33

The true actor is Exalted God, and there is thus no reason to complain about Him, to malign Him, or to find fault with Him. To do so is to disrespect God in two ways: First, it is He who makes everything happen as we find described in the hadith: “Do not rebuke Time, for God the Exalted is Time.” Which is to say: It is Exalted God who has fashioned what you see. Second, it is incumbent on the believer to accept that all actions, evil or not, that have taken place in every age were good for that time and took place according to God’s wisdom. Whoever reckons otherwise is ignorant of Exalted God, of His wisdom, and of His power. If He appointed a ruler over a town, that ruler did not act save with wisdom and benefit unless he departed from His knowledge and His capacity. God, Blessed and Exalted, is Knowing, Wise, imperious over His worshippers, dominant in His affairs. Nothing exceeds His power, no speck of dust escapes His knowledge. 41.34

What is more, Time is innocent of fault or defect, as these are characteristics of people. It is more appropriate to find fault with what they do or what they suffer. As has been said: 41.35

يَقُولُ أُنَاسٌ دَهْـرَ سُوءٍ لِيُعْـذَرُوا   وَهُمْ عَيْبُهُ عِنْدِي وَلَا عَيْبَ لِلدَّهْرِ

٣٦،٤١ وأمّا استنقاص أهل الزمان كما مرّ فلا شكّ أنه لا يحرّم إذ لا يدخل في الغيبة المحرّمة حيث لا يكون التعيين. وقد استشعر محيي الدين ابن العربي في رسالة القدس ذلك حيث وقع في متصوّفة زمانه. فأجاب بنحو ذلك ونزع بما وقع لعائشة رضي الله عنها من ذمّ أهل زمانها كما مرّ وغيرها من أهل الدين. ولكن الأولى الإمساك عن ذلك لما قرّرنا قبلُ ولأنّه لا يكاد يحصل من ذلك طائل غير إتعاب المرء قلبه ولسانه وتعرّضه لمثل ذلك. [متقارب]

وَمَنْ ظَنَّ مِمَّنْ يُعَانِي ٱلْحُرُوبَ   بِأَنْ لَا يُصَابَ فَقَدْ ظَنَّ عَجْزَا

٣٧،٤١ نعم ذكر ما يقع منهم من المناكر بالتنصيص بقصد الاحتراز مع الإنصاف كما فعل أبو العباس زروق في النصح الأنفع وفي عمدة المريد نافع مفيد غير أنّه صعب مفتقر إلى تحقيق في المدارك وتضلّع في العلوم وتجربة تامّة. فإنّ الأمور قليل منها ما يكون أمرًا حقيقيًا يذمّ من كلّ وجه أو يمدح وأكثرها إضافي اعتباري يختلف باختلاف الأشخاص والمقاصد والأزمنة والأمكنة والأحوال فافهم. لله الأمـر من قبـل ومن بعـد.

١،٤٢ ممّـا اتّفق لي وينتظم في سلك الملح مع تضمّن فائدة أنّي كنت خرجت من مدينة فاس حرسها الله تعالى أيّام الحصار وأتينا[1] على جبل بني زروال. ومعي جموع من الناس من طلبة وفقراء وتجّار فوافينا به رجلاً من أهل محبّتنا. فكان يتصرّف لي في أموري وفي أمور من معي من الناس بحسب تفقّدهم وإنزالهم منازلهم. وربّما نتردّد[2] فيريد أن يكشف لي عن رأيه في ذلك. فيدنو منّي ويناجيني وكان ساقط الأسنان لا يكاد يفهم كلامه. وكان مع ذلك كلام أهل تلك البلاد منغلقًا عنّا لا نكاد نفهمه.

١ ق: أتيت. ٢ ط: يتردد. ويزيد ق، ط: في أمر كيف يكون إنقاذه.

People say the age is evil as an excuse,
I hold that the people are what is evil, not the age.

As for finding fault with people of a given time, there is no doubt that this is not forbidden if it does not entail vague slander, which is prohibited (as was discussed above). Muḥyī al-Dīn ibn al-ʿArabī has referred to this in his *Jerusalem Letter* regarding the slander among the Sufis of his time. He answered in similar terms, adducing what happened to ʿĀʾishah, God be content with her, who was maligned by her contemporaries and people of the faith (as was discussed above). Yet it is preferable to abstain from doing so in accordance with what we previously explained, because there is rarely any outcome other than a person exhausting his heart and tongue and exposing himself to the same. **41.36**

Of those who have suffered in war, whoever has thought
that he will not be struck down has done so in vain.[263]

It is beneficial to mention in writing the vices people commit, while going to great lengths to be cautious and to maintain justice. This was what Abū ʿAbbās Zarrūq did in *The Most Beneficial Advice* and *The Reliance of the Disciple*, which was useful and beneficial.[264] Yet, to do so is difficult and requires a strong intellect, thorough knowledge of the sciences, and general experience. There are few issues that ought to be criticized or praised from every angle. Most are relative and subjective, differing according to the differences in people, intentions, times, places, and conditions. Understand this well! Everything is God's to command. **41.37**

One beneficial thing that happened to me, part of a series of amusing events, occurred when I left Fez, Exalted God preserve it, at the time of the siege. I came to the Banū Zirwāl Mountains accompanied by a group, including students, ascetics, and merchants. We encountered a man who belonged to the people for whom I feel affection. I employed him to attend to my affairs and those of my companions in connection with the inspection and selection of places to stay. Whenever we hesitated, he was keen to offer his opinion aboout the place. He would come close and whisper. He had lost many teeth, so he could barely be understood, never mind that the speech of the people of that region was difficult and I could hardly understand it. He also spoke **42.1**

ثمّ يخفت بصوته لئلا يسمعه من حضر فيتكلّم ولا أكاد أسمع من كلامه حرفًا واحدًا حتّى إذا فرغ من حديثه رفع رأسه إليّ وقال هكذا يكون الكلام مفصحًا بها. فكنت في هذا أباسط أصحابي فأقول لهم إنّ هذه الجملة الأخيرة من كلامه وقع فيها حكم بطريق القصر وهو موقوف على أشياء قبله لم يحصل واحد منها. الأوّل سماع اللفظ فإنّه مقدّمة الفهم. الثاني معرفة الوضع فإنّه شرط. الثالث فهم الألفاظ مفردة. الرابع فهم التركيب. الخامس فهم النسبة تصوّرًا. السادس فهم الحكم مطلقًا أي من غير قصر. السابع فهمه مقصورًا ثمّ إنّ الأخير أعني الحصر محتاج إلى دليل لأنّه بسبيل المنع. ولم يحصل شيء من ذلك كلّه وما توقّف على ما لم يحصل فهو غير حاصل. ثمّ إنّي مع ذلك أستبشر عند حديثه وربّما أحرّك رأسي موهمًا أنّي قد حصّلته وأنّي قد استصوبت رأيه وذلك أنّه لم يمكنّي في الوقت غير ذلك. فإنّي إن راجعته ليبيّن لم يبيّن إلّا بخفية كما فعل أوّلًا فلا يحصل طائل. وقد علمت أن ليس في عدم تبيّن مقاصده مهمٌّ يفوت لأنّ كلّ ما ينحو إليه من الرأي ويتشوّف إليه من المصلحة فعندي بحمد الله ما يكفي فيه. فكنت أساهله وأتركه بحاله رفقًا به وجبرًا لخاطره وتقلّلًا من الشغب. وعندي على هذا النحو مذهب وأرى كثيرًا من الناس ينْبُون عنه.

٢،٤٢ وللتنبيه عليه مع التلميح السابق سطّرت هذه القصّة. وذلك أنّي أتغافل عمّا لا حاجة إليه ولا أتتبّع ما فيه تكلّف ولا تدعو الضرورة إليه. وإنّ ذلك عندي هو أسلم وأبعد عمّا يخشى من ارتكاب الفضول أحيانًا وتجاوز الحدّ أحيانًا وإحراج الصدر أحيانًا واستثارة الشرّ أحيانًا وأقرب إلى مكارم الأخلاق وأدخل في المداراة المطلوبة وأبعد عن الملاحاة المذمومة.

٣،٤٢ وفي الحديث مداراة النّاس صدقة.[١] وفي حديث آخر رأس العقل بعد الإيمان بالله التودّد إلى النّاس.[٢] وفي خبر آخر التودّد إلى النّاس نصف العقل وحسن التدبير نصف المعيشة. وما عال من اقتصد.

---

١ يزيد ط: وفي الحديث أمرني ربي بمدارة الناس و نهاني عن ملاحاتهم. ٢ ق: أمرني ربي بمدارة الناس و نهاني عن مداجاتهم.

almost inaudibly so that anyone present could not hear him. He would speak and I would barely hear a single letter. When he was done he would incline his head toward me and say, "That is how to put it eloquently!" I often joked with my companions about this, saying, "In this last sentence of his speech there was a succinct pronouncement dependent on certain conditions that were not met. One, understanding is predicated on hearing speech. Two, it is necessary to know the context. Three, it is necessary to understand the individual words. Four, understanding of the syntax. Five, imagining what is being referred to. Six, a full, unrestricted understanding of the pronouncement is needed. Seven, understanding in a restricted sense too, and this last—that is, concision—requires some indication, as it is difficult to understand. But none of these conditions was met. What is dependent on an unfulfilled condition is itself unfulfilled." Despite this, I welcomed what he said, and may have nodded, giving the impression I had understood him and approved of his opinion. I did this because there was nothing else for me to do at the time. If I had gone back to him for clarification, he would simply have done so in the same secretive manner as the first time. There was no use. I knew that nothing important was lost by him not clarifying his intentions, since, God be thanked, I knew enough about his needs and his desires. I indulged him and left him that way, out of kindness, paying attention to his views, without stirring anything up. This is how I deal with things, although I know that many people disagree with it.

I recorded this story in order to draw attention to this matter and due to the 42.2
prior intimation to it. My way consists in my ignoring what is irrelevant, and in not occupying myself with what involves unnecessary hassle. In my opinion, this is the best way, and it keeps me at times from being overly curious, from being impertinent, from causing anxiety, and from provoking evil. This is the noblest way to behave; it is the most conducive to kindness and the furthest from reprehensible rebuke.

One hadith states: "It is a charitable act to treat people with gentleness." 42.3
Another hadith goes: "After faith in God, the greatest form of discernment is expressing affection toward people." And another: "Half of discernment is expressing affection toward people, half of living is good organization, and whoever is thrifty will not know distress."

وقال الشاعر: [طويل] ٤،٤٢

وَمَنْ لَا يُغَمِّضْ عَيْنَهُ عَنْ صَدِيقِهِ   وَعَنْ بَعْضِ مَا فِيهِ يَمُتْ وَهْوَ عَاتِبُ
وَمَنْ يَتَتَبَّعْ جَاهِدًا كُلَّ عَثْرَةٍ   يَجِدْهَا وَلَا يُسْلِمْ لَهُ ٱلدَّهْرُ صَاحِبُ

وقال الآخر: [طويل] ٥،٤٢

أُغَمِّضُ عَيْنِي عَنْ صَدِيقِي تَغَافُلًا   كَأَنِّي لِمَا يَأْتِي مِنَ ٱلأَمْرِ جَاهِلُ
وَمَا بِي جَهْلٌ غَيْرَ أَنَّ خَلِيقَتِي   تُطِيقُ ٱحْتِمَالَ ٱلْكُرْهِ فِيمَا تُحَاوِلُ

ونحوه قول الآخر: [وافر] ٦،٤٢

أُغَمِّضُ لِلصَّدِيقِ عَنِ ٱلْمَسَاوِي   مَخَافَةَ أَنْ أَعِيشَ بِلَا صَدِيقِ

وقال غيره: [طويل] ٧،٤٢

إِذَا كُنْتَ فِي كُلِّ ٱلْأُمُورِ مُعَاتِبًا   صَدِيقَكَ لَا تَلْقَى ٱلَّذِي لَا تُعَاتِبُهُ
فَعِشْ وَاحِدًا أَوْ صِلْ أَخَاكَ فَإِنَّهُ   مُقَارِفُ ذَنْبٍ مَرَّةً وَمُجَانِبُهُ
إِذَا أَنْتَ لَمْ تَشْرَبْ مِرَارًا عَلَى ٱلْقَذَى   ظَمِئْتَ وَأَيُّ ٱلنَّاسِ تَصْفُو مَشَارِبُهُ؟
وَمَنْ ذَا ٱلَّذِي تُرْضَى سَجَايَاهُ كُلُّهَا؟   كَفَى ٱلْمَرْءَ نُبْلًا أَنْ تُعَدَّ مَعَايِبُهُ

وقال غيره: [متقارب] ٨،٤٢

إِذَا مَا ٱلصَّدِيقُ أَسَا مَرَّةً   وَقَدْ كَانَ فِيمَا مَضَى مُجْمِلَا
ذَكَرْتُ ٱلْمُقَدَّمَ مِنْ فِعْلِهِ   فَلَمْ يُنْسِنِي ٱلْآخِرُ ٱلْأَوَّلَا

A poet has said:[265] **42.4**

Whoever does not close his eyes to his friend,
and to his foibles, will find fault with him until he dies.
Whoever makes every effort to pursue each lapse will find them,
and the one who committed them will never be safe.

Another poet said: **42.5**

I close my eyes to my friend's faults in feigned ignorance,
so that when he comes to me I am ignorant of the matter.
But there is nothing ignorant about me except that my disposition
is able to bear the odious aspects of his designs.

This is similar to another poet's lines: **42.6**

I overlook the evil deeds of a friend
out of fear that I will end up friendless.

Another said:[266] **42.7**

If in all affairs you rebuke your friend,
You won't find one who won't rebuke you.
Live alone or with your brother,
and if at some point he yields to sin, avoid him.
If you never drank anything impure
you would go thirsty—for what peoples' drinks are pure?
Who possesses only pleasing characteristics?
It suffices a noble person to consider his vices.

Another said: **42.8**

If a friend acted poorly once,
and in the past had acted decently,
I remember the earlier deeds.
For the last would not make me forget the first.

وقال غيره: [طويل]   ٩،٤٢

وَأَغْفِرُ عَوْرَاءَ ٱلْكَرِيمِ ٱدِّخَارَهُ   وَأُعْرِضُ عَن شَتْمِ ٱللَّئِيمِ تَكَرُّمَا

وقال غيره: [كامل]   ١٠،٤٢

اِحْرِصْ عَلَى حِفْظِ ٱلْقُلُوبِ مِنَ ٱلْأَذَى   فَرُجُوعُهَا بَعْدَ ٱلتَّنَافُرِ يَعْسُرُ

إِنَّ ٱلْقُلُوبَ إِذَا تَنَافَرَتْ وُدُّهَا   مِثْلُ ٱلزُّجَاجَةِ كَسْرُهَا لَا يُجْبَرُ

وعن أمّ المؤمنين عائشة رضي الله عنها خلال المكارم عشر تكون في الرجل ولا   ١١،٤٢
تكون في أبيه وتكون في العبد ولا تكون في سيّده. يقسمها الله لمن أحبّ صدق
الحديث ومداراة الناس وصلة الرحم وحفظ الأمانة والتذمم للجار وإعطاء السائل
والمكافأة بالصنائع وقِرى الضيف والوفاء بالعهد ورأسهنّ كلّهنّ الحياء.

وقال الشاعر: [وافر]   ١٢،٤٢

أُحِبُّ مَكَارِمَ ٱلْأَخْلَاقِ جُهْدِي   وَأَكْرَهُ أَن أُعِيبَ وَأَن أُعَابَا

وَأَصْفَحُ عَن سِبَابِ ٱلنَّاسِ حِلْمًا   وَشَرُّ ٱلنَّاسِ مَن يَهْوَى ٱلسِّبَابَا

وَمَن هَابَ ٱلرِّجَالَ تَهَيَّبُوهُ   وَمَن حَقَّرَ ٱلرِّجَالَ فَلَن يُهَابَا

وقال غيره: [كامل]   ١٣،٤٢

وَلَقَدْ أَمُرُّ عَلَى ٱللَّئِيمِ يَسُبُّنِي   فَأَجُوزُ ثُمَّ أَقُولُ: لَا يَعْنِينِي

وقال غيره: [بسيط]   ١٤،٤٢

إِنَّ ٱلْمَكَارِمَ أَخْلَاقٌ مُطَهَّرَةٌ   فَٱلْعَقْلُ أَوَّلُهَا وَٱلدِّينُ ثَانِيهَا

وَٱلْعِلْمُ ثَالِثُهَا وَٱلْحِلْمُ رَابِعُهَا   وَٱلْجُودُ خَامِسُهَا وَٱلْعُرْفُ سَادِسُهَا

Another said:[267] 42.9

The generous man's treasures compensate for his being one-eyed;
showing generosity turns away the curses of a vile person.

Another poet said: 42.10

Take care to preserve hearts from harm—
it is hard to bring them back after conflict.
Truly, if the hearts' affections descend into discord
they cannot, like glass broken, be forced together.

ʿĀʾishah, Mother of the Believers, God be content with her, related: There are ten virtues that a man does not inherit from his father, nor a slave receive from his master. God distributes these to whom He pleases: sincere speech, treating people with benevolence, ties of kinship, keeping safe what is entrusted, protecting the neighbor's rights, giving to supplicants, performing acts of kindness, being hospitable to guests, honoring pledges, and, the greatest virtue of all, having a sense of shame. 42.11

A poet has said:[268] 42.12

The most desirable moral virtue is my effort.
I hate to find fault or to have fault found with me.
I forgive out of forbearance those who insult me,
so too the evil of those who resort to abuse.
Whoever respects men will be respected;
who hates them will not.

Another poet said:[269] 42.13

He ordered a vile man to insult me.
I permitted this, saying, This does not bother me.

Another has said:[270] 42.14

Moral virtues are pure characteristics:
Discerning reason is the first, faith the second.
Knowledge is the third, forbearance the fourth,
generosity the fifth, custom the sixth.

وَٱلْبِرُّ سَابِعُهَا وَٱلصَّبْرُ ثَامِنُهَا   وَٱلشُّكْرُ تَاسِعُهَا وَٱللِّينُ عَاشِيهَا
وَٱلنَّفْسُ تَعْلَمُ أَنِّي لَا أُصَدِّقُهَا   وَلَسْتُ أَرْشُدُ إِلَّا حِينَ أَعْصِيهَا
وَٱلْعَيْنُ تَعْلَمُ فِي عَيْنَيْ مُحَدِّثِهَا   مَنْ كَانَ مِنْ حِزْبِهَا أَوْ مِنْ أَعَادِيهَا

١٥،٤٢ وقال غيره: [كامل]

اتْرُكْ مُكَاشَفَةَ ٱلصَّدِيقِ إِذَا   غَطَّى عَلَى هَفَوَاتِهِ سِتْرُ

١٦،٤٢ وفي الحكمة اللبيب العاقل هو الفطن المتغافل وفي قوله تعالى ﴿عَرَّفَ بَعْضَهُ وَأَعْرَضَ عَنْ بَعْضٍ﴾ مشرّب في هذا المعنى. ويقال ما استقصى كريم قطّ. وفي الحديث لمّا أسري بي كان أوّل ما أمرني به ربّي أن قال إيّاك وعبادة الأوثان وشرب الخمر وملاحاة الرجال. وفي حديث آخر احذروا جدال كلّ مفتون فإنّه يلقّن حجّته إلى انقطاع مدّته.

١٧،٤٢ وقال الشاعر:[1] [كامل]

إِنِّي مَحَضْتُكَ يَا كِدَامُ نَصِيحَتِي   فَٱسْمَعْ لِقَوْلِ أَبٍ عَلَيْكَ شَفِيقِ
أَمَّا ٱلْمِزَاحَةُ وَٱلْمِرَاءُ فَدَعْهُمَا   خُلُقَانِ لَا أَرْضَاهُمَا لِصَدِيقِ

١٨،٤٢ وقال الآخر: [كامل]

اتْرُكْ مُكَاشَفَةَ ٱلصَّدِيقِ إِذَا   غَطَّى عَلَى هَفَوَاتِهِ سِتْرُ

١٩،٤٢ وهذا باب واسع مشهور وفيما ذكرنا منه كفاية. لله الأمر من قبل ومن بعد.

١،٤٣ من جملة ما اتّفق لي في هذه السفرة إلى جبال الزبيب وسفرات أخرى لزيارة الشيخ عبد السلام بن مشيش رضي الله عنه أنّي سمعت لغة لأهل تلك الجبال يكسرون

١ يزيد ق: يوصى إبنه.

Piety is the seventh, endurance the eighth,
  gratitude the ninth, flexibility the tenth.
The ego knows that I do not trust it
  and that I am not guided right except when I disobey it.
The eye knows through the eyes of the one who addresses it
  who are its friends, who its foes.

Another poet has said: 42.15

Do not expose a friend when
  a veil has been thrown over his errors.

There is a maxim: "The intelligent and reasonable person is astute and ignores the faults of others." And in the words of the Almighty: «He made known part of it and ignored part of it».[271] And they say, a noble person makes no demands. A hadith goes: "When I was taken on the night journey, the first thing that my Lord commanded me was, 'Avoid idol worshippers, the consumption of wine, and the discourse of men.'" Another hadith states: "Be wary of debating anyone who is insane, for he will stick to his argument till death." 42.16

A poet has said:[272] 42.17

My advice, Kudām, urges you on,
  so listen to the words of an affectionate father:
Leave off jesting and people—
  two contrivances I would not wish for a friend.

Another has said: 42.18

Do not expose a friend when
  a veil is thrown over his errors.

This is a well-attested and vast topic; what we have mentioned suffices. Everything is God's to command. 42.19

One of the things I experienced on this trip to the Banū Zirwāl Mountains, and on other travels to visit the tomb of the teacher ʿAbd al-Salām ibn Mashīsh, God be content with him, was hearing the language of the mountain people. They place a *kasrah* at the end of a word when speaking. I looked into it and 43.1

آخر الموقوف عليه استقراء فتتبّعتها فوجدتها لها ضابط. وقد رأيت غيرهم من أهل الآفاق يسمعون عنهم ذلك فيحكونه على غير وجه وينسبون إليهم ما لا يقولون جهلاً منهم بضوابطها. فإنّهم لا يكسرون إلّا الفتحة بعدها ألف.

٢،٤٣ أمّا الألف المقصورة كالدنيا أو الممدودة كالسماء والطلباء والشرفاء والأصليّة كالماء أو المقلوبة عن هاء التأنيث في مجرى العرف كالبقرة والشجرة والصحفة فإنّ العوامّ من غيرهم يقولون في الوقف على هذه البقرا والشجرا بألف. وهؤلاء يكسرون فيقولون البقري والشجري وتنقلب الألف ياء وهذا كلّه في الوقف. فإن وصلوا نطقوا بالألف كغيرهم وإن لم يكن الفتح ولا الألف كالشجر والبقر مرادًا به الجنس وقفوا بالسكون كغيرهم. وإنّي لمّا تأمّلت ذلك من كلامهم وحقّقته في أقرب مدّة اتّضح عندي معنى الاستقراء في نحو هذا بالمشاهدة وعلمت كيف كان أئمّة العربيّة القدماء يستقرئون النحو واللغة من أفواه العرب ويضبطون لغة كلّ قبيلة في ذلك.

٣،٤٣ وتبيّن أنّ ذلك أمر صحيح بيّن وللتنبيه على هذا حكيت هذه القصّة. فلا يقل جاهل ما لنا ولهذه اللغة؟ فلتعرف أو لا تعرف هذا مع أنّ معرفة الشيء خير من جهله فالجاهل بالشيء أعمى فيه وفي ظلمة عنه والعالم به بصير به وفي نور فيه. و﴿هَلْ يَسْتَوِي ٱلْأَعْمَىٰ وَٱلْبَصِيرُ أَمْ هَلْ تَسْتَوِي ٱلظُّلُمَاتُ وَٱلنُّورُ﴾ والعلم ذخر يجده صاحبه عاجلاً أو آجلاً وحجّة ينتصر بها في الخطوب أيضاً.

لله الأمر من قبل ومن بعد.[١]

---

١ سقط من ق، ط.

found that they did this according to a rule. I had seen people from all over who had heard about this go on to talk about it in various ways, attributing to the mountain people things they did not say, out of ignorance of the dialect's rules. They only substitute with a *kasrah* the *fatḥah* followed by an *alif.*

As for the broken *alif* in a word like *dunyā*, "the world," or the elongated *alif* in words such as *al-samā'*, "the sky," *al-ṭalabā'*, "the students," and *al-shurafā'*, "the nobles," or the root *alif* in a word like *al-mā'*, "water," or the customary inverted *alif* for the feminine *hā'* in words such as *al-baqarah*, "cow," *al-shajarah*, "tree," and *al-ṣafḥah*, "page," other people pronounce them in pausal position as if with an *alif*, thus for example *al-baqarā* for "cow" and *al-shajarā* for "tree." These people insert a *kasra*, saying *al-baqarī* for "cow" and *al-shajarī* for "tree," replacing the *alif* with a *yā'*. This is only when there is a pause. If it is in the middle of the sentence, they pronounce the *alif* like other people and if there is no *fatḥa* or *alif* at the end of the word—as with the collective forms *al-shajar*, "trees," and *al-baqar*, "cows"—they end the word with a pause, as all others do. When I contemplated this aspect of their speech and had quickly verified it, I realized the importance of observing how people pronounced things. I realized then how the ancient masters of Arabic studied grammar and language closely from the mouths of the Arabs. By doing so, they set down the language of every tribe. 43.2

It became clear that this is illustrative and correct, which is why I have recounted this story, in order to draw attention to this. Do not let the ignorant say: What does this dialect have to do with us? Know this, or ignore it, though knowing something is better than not knowing. There is blindness to being ignorant of something and in the dark about it, and one who knows sees it clearly, and is aware. «Are the blind and the seeing man equal, are shadows and light equal?»[273] Knowledge is a treasure whose owner finds it sooner or later, a proof through which he will also be victorious in many matters. 43.3

Everything is God's to command.

Notes

1 In the Islamic exegetical tradition from the fourth/tenth century onward, the guardian angel of paradise was at times given the name Riḍwān.

2 A woman known for her skill in making spears. See Ibn Manẓūr, *Lisān al-ʿArab*, s.v. *r-d-n*.

3 The three names given here are those of tribes.

4 ʿUmar ibn al-Khaṭṭāb, the second caliph following the Prophet.

5 The line is from the Kufa *maqāmah* in the *Maqāmāt* of al-Ḥarīrī (d. 516/1122).

6 Al-Yūsī seems to have confused Hind bint al-Nuʿmān ibn Bashīr with Ḥumaydah bint al-Nuʿmān ibn Bashīr. Both were Umayyad poets, but it was the latter who was famous for mocking her husbands in verse, and who married al-Fayḍ ibn Muḥammad ibn al-Ḥakam ibn Abī ʿAqīl. She died in Syria at the end of the reign of ʿAbd al-Malik ibn Marwān (r. 65–86/685–705).

7 This may be a reference to God having given the prophet David the ability to work iron with his hands, with the same facility as if he were weaving with threads. See Q Saba' 34:10, and Ibn Kathīr, *Tafsīr*, 3:491.

8 A reference to the traditional account of when the Prophet Muḥammad and Abū Bakr al-Ṣiddīq were fleeing Mecca for Medina. They took refuge in a cave and a spider wove a web over its entrance, convincing his Quraysh pursuers that the cave was empty.

9 Compare this account of the Valley of Beasts with that found under *wādī al-sabāʿ* in Yāqūt, *Muʿjam al-buldān*, 5:343–44, where the valley is situated near Kufa, and where different lines of poetry regarding it are given.

10 The name Muḥammad literally means "one who is praised."

11 The speaker here is the Prophet Muḥammad. The Hadith is the body of reports relating the words and actions of the Prophet Muḥammad. The Prophet's son Abraham died while still an infant.

12 Q Maryam 19:28. I use the translation of Arberry throughout, at times making minor alterations for the sake of consistency or clarity.

13 This paragraph is at times obscure, in part because al-Yūsī is referring to concepts that he does not fully explore. The general issues raised are reminiscent of the opening of Aristotle's *Categories*. As a logician, al-Yūsī was familiar with aspects of the Aristotelian corpus.

14 This lodge, today known as the Ḥamziyyah-ʿAyyāshiyyah lodge, is located in the High Atlas south of Midelt and near the small town of al-Rish. It still contains a valuable library based around a collection of manuscripts al-ʿAyyāshī brought back from his travels east.

15 This line is attributed to both Abū l-Aswad al-Duʾalī (d. 69/689) and ʿAbd Allāh ibn ʿUmar ibn al-Khaṭṭāb (d. 73/693).

16 See Lane, *An Arabic-English Lexicon*, s.v. *s-l-m*.

17 A proverbial expression.

18 A *malḥūn*, a type of colloquial Arabic poetry specific to the Maghrib.

19 Yāsīn is one of the names of the Prophet Muḥammad (and also the title of the Qurʾan's thirty-sixth surah).

20 Q Zukhruf 43:77.

21 A reference to ʿAḍud al-Dawlah's father, Rukn al-Dawlah (d. 366/976).

22 The Arabic contains a pun here on the word *majāz*, which can mean both "bridge" and "metaphor," that I have represented in English with the dual meanings of "figure."

23 Compare sections 36–42 with Ibn Khaldūn, *The Muqaddimah*, 1:264–68.

24 This is possibly ʿAbd al-Wahhāb al-Aʿrābī (d. 250/864), who came to Baghdad from the desert and wrote works on Arabic.

25 The poet is Ibn al-Rūmī (d. 283/896).

26 This is Ibn al-Rūmī again.

27 Attributed variously to Majnūn, Yazīd ibn al-Ṭathriyyah (d. 126/744), and ʿUmar ibn Abī Rabīʿah (d. 93/712 or 103/721).

28 The poet is Abū Tammām (d. 232/846).

29 The poet is Ibn al-Khaṭīb (d. 776/1374).

30 A reference to the descendants of the Prophet through his son-in-law ʿAlī ibn Abī Ṭālib; also relevant that the dynasty that had taken power over Morocco during al-Yūsī's lifetime refers to itself by the same term (al-ʿAlawiyya).

31 Q Furqān 25:38.

32 The amount of time al-Yūsī spends discussing genealogy could be attributed solely to its general importance in Arabic literature, but two factors related to the eleventh/seventeenth century bear mentioning: first, the fierce debate between Moroccan scholars in the tenth/sixteenth and then again in the eleventh/seventeenth century on whether Muslims who were descendants from Jewish and Christian converts were equal to other Muslims; second, the increasing importance of descent from the Prophet with the ascent to power of the Saadians in the tenth/sixteenth century, and the tensions between them and the Friends of God (often referred to in the scholarship as saints or marabouts), often of Berber origin. For background on the first, see García-Arenal,

"Les *Bildiyyīn* de Fès" and Mayyārah, *Naṣīḥat al-mughtarrīn*; on the second, see Touati, "Les héritiers." For al-Yūsī himself as an example of this tension, see Geertz, *Islam Observed*, 30–35. Geertz himself notes that his depiction of al-Yūsī has much more to do with the stories that grew up around him later than with the historical person.

33 Q Sajdah 32:7.

34 Q Sajdah 32:8.

35 The poet is Abū l-ʿAtāhiyah (d. 210/825 or 211/826).

36 Variously attributed to an unnamed poet, to Ibn Bassām (d. 302–3/914–16), and to al-Ḥasan al-Baṣrī (d. 110/728).

37 Q Baqarah 2:30.

38 Q Shams 91:9–10.

39 Q Anbiyā' 21:23

40 A reference to Q Mursalāt 77:25–26.

41 Q Aḥzāb 33:43.

42 Q Āl ʿImrān 3:59, Kahf 18:37, Ḥajj 22:5, Rūm 30:20, Fāṭir 35:11, Ghāfir 40:67.

43 Q Anʿām 6:2, Aʿrāf 7:12, Ṣāffāt 37:11, Ṣād 38:76.

44 Q Ḥijr 15:26, Ḥijr 15:28, Ḥijr 15:33, Raḥmān 55:14.

45 Q Ḥijr 15:26, Ḥijr 15:28, Ḥijr 15:33.

46 The poet is al-Najāshī (d. 49/669).

47 Q Isrā' 17:70.

48 The Qur'anic verse in question had produced a great deal of discussion among exegetes as to whether humankind was superior to angels or not, with many exegetes arguing that man's free will made him superior.

49 With reference to Q Aʿrāf 7:169.

50 Q Āl ʿImrān 3:33.

51 Q Ḥujurāt 49:13.

52 Q Mā'idah 5:20.

53 Q Baqarah 2:47.

54 The pre-Islamic poet Ṣalā'ah ibn ʿAmr ibn Mālik (fl. first half of sixth century).

55 The Arabic contains a pun here on bones (*ʿiẓām*), representing one's inherited honor, and being a self-made man like ʿIṣām, a story that went on to become proverbial.

56 The editors quote the following gloss: "If ʿAmr had been the son of these two men buried in these two places, then he would have found success, would have struck whoever fought him with ill intent, and would have looked for him wherever he might be." See al-Yūsī, *al-Muḥāḍarāt*, 1:60.

57 This line references the two sons of ʿAmr Muzayqiyā', Thaʿlabah and al-Ḥārith.

58 See Lane, *Lexicon*, s.v. *ẓ-b-y*.

59 From the Karjiyyah *maqāmāh* in the *Maqāmāt* of al-Ḥarīrī.

60 From the commentary of Abū ʿAbbās Aḥmad al-Sharīshī (d. 619/1222) on the *Maqāmāt* of al-Ḥarīrī.

61 Q Kahf 18:82. I have changed the translation slightly.

62 Possibly the poet Ḥātim al-Ṭāʾī (fl. sixth century AD).

63 The poet is al-Mutawakkil al-Kinānī, a poet of the Umayyad period.

64 The poet is al-Baʿīth ibn al-Ḥurayth (d. ?).

65 The reference is to Q 106, Sūrat Quraysh.

66 As the verses are directed to one of the Banū Asad, I have departed from the Arabic syntax in my translation to preserve this meaning.

67 The poet is al-Mutanabbī (d. 354/955).

68 An allusion to Q Rūm 30:19.

69 For this line, see Lane, *Lexicon*, s.v. *s-ḥ-m*.

70 For this line, see Lane, *Lexicon*, s.v. *ʿ-n-j*.

71 Q Nūr 24:30.

72 This line is unclear, as al-Mutanabbī's family claimed to belong to the South Arabian Yamānī tribe.

73 Al-Yūsī introduces the third type of nobility here without drawing attention to that fact.

74 The poet is Ibn al-Rūmī.

75 Attributed to al-Ḥakam ibn ʿAbdal ibn Jabla al-Asdī l-Ghāḍarī (fl. Umayyad caliphate), Abū l-Aswad al-Duʾalī, and ʿAlī ibn Abī Ṭālib (d. 40/661).

76 The lines are attributed to Abū l-ʿAlāʾ al-Maʿarrī (d. 449/1058) and to Abū Tammām.

77 The poet is al-Khansāʾ (d. between AD 634 and 680).

78 The poet is Abū Tammām.

79 These lines are quoted in their original context in §6.40 above.

80 The grammatical work by Ibn Mālik (d. 672/1274). Compare with al-Yūsī's *Fahrasah*, 126.

81 Ibn al-Jawzī (d. 597/1200) describes in the *Ṣifat al-ṣafwah* how Abū l-Ḥussayn Khayr ibn ʿAbd Allāh (d. 322/933–34) broke a promise he made to God and as punishment was given the shape of a slave, who worked as a weaver for six months (see al-Yūsī, *al-Muḥāḍarāt*, 1:82).

82 With reference to Q Ḍuḥā 93:11: «And as for the blessing of thy Lord, proclaim».

83 Q Fatḥ 48:29.

84 Q Māʾidah 5:54.

85 The identity of Shuʿayb is contested among Qurʾanic exegetes, although most agree with Abū Madyan that the prophet Shuʿayb was also Moses's father-in-law, given the

name Jethro in the Bible, whom Moses met when he fled to Midian (Moses's father-in-law is not named in the Qur'an). This identification was contested by some exegetes, as in Q A'rāf 7:85 Shu'ayb is introduced immediately following the prophet Lot, and although it remained unclear when he actually lived, the time between Lot and Moses was substantial.

86 Q A'rāf 7:92.

87 In reference to the battle at Ḥunayn in 8/630, where the Prophet defeated several tribes, including the Thaqīf.

88 This is a famous hadith.

89 The poet is the first/seventh-century al-Ḥuṭay'ah.

90 I thank Maurice Pomerantz for his help in understanding these lines.

91 Al-Ghazālī's *The Revival of Religious Sciences* (*Iḥyā' 'ulūm al-dīn*).

92 Q Muḥammad 47:31.

93 Q 'Ankabūt 29:1–3.

94 Q Baqarah 2:155.

95 Q Āl 'Imrān 3:186.

96 A common Qur'anic phrase. See for example Q A'rāf 7:187, Hūd 11:21, Rūm 30:6.

97 Q Shūrā 42:19.

98 Q Ibrāhīm 14:34.

99 Q A'rāf 7:131. The verse continues: «But if any evil smote them, they would augur ill by Moses and those with him. Why, surely their ill augury was with God; but the most of them knew not».

100 The term *ma'rifah*, rendered here as "mystical knowledge," is knowledge that comes from spiritual practice, as opposed to knowledge acquired through study, or *'ilm*.

101 The name of a tree from the period before Islam on which unbelievers hung their weapons, around which they circled, and under which they sacrificed.

102 A reference to the oath alluded to in Q Fatḥ 48:18: «God was well pleased with the believers when they were swearing fealty to thee under the tree, and He knew what was in their hearts, so He sent down the Shechina upon them, and rewarded them with a nigh victory».

103 Named for the second sura of the Qur'an, "al-Baqarah," "The Cow." Vincent Cornell has discussed Abū Yi'zzā (d. 572/1177) and Tāghiyah being in the Middle Atlas in *Realm of the Saint*, 68–79, and Cornell, *The Way of Abū Madyan*, 8–10.

104 This is a possible reference to the duty of commanding the right and forbidding the wrong, which al-Yūsī is rather conservatively interpreting as being limited for scholars

to being carried out by the tongue (as opposed to the hand). On this duty, see Michael Cook, *Commanding Right and Forbidding Wrong in Islamic Thought*, 33 and passim.

105 A reference to either the *Ṣaḥīḥ* of Muslim (d. 261/875) or al-Bukhārī (d. 256/870), the two most famous collections of Hadith.

106 The poet is Kuthayyir (d. 105/723).

107 On Ribāṭ Shākir and al-Tādilī's description of Munyat bint Maymūn (d. 595/1199) see Cornell, *Realm of the Saint*, 51–53.

108 On the phenomenon of messianism in North Africa in the Middle Ages, see García-Arenal, *Messianism and Puritanical Reform*.

109 The poet is al-Ḥarīrī.

110 Compare with al-Qāḍī al-Quḍāʿī (trans. Tahera Qutbuddin), *A Treasury of Virtues*, 168–69, where the three types of people are defined quite differently.

111 In fact by Ḥātim al-Ṭāʾī (fl. second half of sixth century).

112 A reference to Ḥātim al-Ṭāʾī's wife, Māwiyya bint ʿAbd Allāh.

113 By either Nuʿaym ibn al-Ḥārith ibn Yazīd al-Saʿadī or al-Hudhlūl ibn Kaʿb al-Anbarī, both pre-Islamic poets, declaimed to their wife.

114 Ḥarāllah is the one less well-known location. It is mentioned in al-Zabīdī's *Tāj al-ʿArūs* as being either a small town near Murcia or a region named after a Berber tribe, and he noted that if it had not been for al-Ḥarāllī (d. 637/1239–40), this town would have been forgotten entirely (see al-Yūsī, *al-Muḥāḍarāt*, 1:115–16).

115 Al-Yūsī is alluding here to the *faḍāʾil* literature, in which the merits of a particular city or region were praised, and specifically to these types of works on Mecca, Medina, and Jerusalem. On the genre, with particular reference to Jerusalem, see Livne-Kafri, "The Muslim Traditions 'In Praise of Jerusalem' (*Faḍāʾil al-Quds*): Diversity and Complexity."

116 There is a play on words here. The *Sound Collections* are the collections of Hadith of al-Bukhārī and Muslim, here compared with the water and air of his home region in terms of their authority and trustworthiness.

117 The poet is either Ibn ʿAbbās al-Tilimsānī (d. 871/1467) or Ibn Marzūq (d. 781/1379).

118 Tilimsān is believed by some to be the place where the Qurʾanic figure al-Khiḍr built up the wall referred to in Q Kahf 18:77 (Yāqūt, *Muʿjam al-buldān*, 2, 44).

119 The poet is al-Ṣimmah ibn ʿAbd Allāh ibn al-Ṭufayl al-Qushayrī (d. 95/714).

120 The poet is ʿAbū ʿAbd Allāh al-Maghīlī (d. 910/1505–6).

121 Compare with §6.10 above.

122 The poem is attributed to a poet of the Banū Kilāb.

123 The poet is Ibn al-Dumaynah (fl. second/eighth century).

124 The poet is al-Ḥusayn ibn Muṭayr (fl. second/eighth century).

125 The poet is Abū l-Ṣakhr al-Hudhalī (fl. second half of first/seventh century).

126 The poet is al-Ṣimmah ibn ʿAbd Allāh.

127 These lines are attributed both to Jamīl (d. 82/701) and Jarīr (d. ca. 110/728–29).

128 The poet is Marwān al-Aṣghar (fl. third/ninth century).

129 These lines are from al-Qālī's *al-Amālī*, an anthology al-Yūsī drew upon frequently.

130 Yāqūt (*Muʿjam al-buldān*, 1:414) places Abraham's Garden in the territory of the Banū Asad, in northern Arabia, and cites these very lines, attributing them to the Seljukid poet al-Abīwardī (d. 507/1113).

131 Lines attributed to an anonymous Bedouin woman.

132 This sentence will seem obscure if it is not known that Arabic is generally written without short vowels. Because of this, when introducing obscure words, authors will often specify how they should be pronounced.

133 The phrase *ashʿār al-maʿānī*, and the more common *abyāt al-maʿānī*, refer to riddles that occur either intentionally or inadvertently in poetry (see al-Yūsī, *al-Muḥāḍarāt*, 1:127–28).

134 The poet is al-Nizār al-Asadī (d. ?).

135 A line from a poem elegizing Yazīd ibn ʿUmar ibn Hubayrah, last Umayyad governor of Iraq.

136 The poet is al-ʿAbbās ibn al-Aḥnaf (d. after 193/808).

137 The poet is al-Tūba ibn Maḍras ibn ʿAbd Allāh al-Tamīmī, known as al-Khanūt.

138 These lines are attributed to a member of the Banū Tamīm.

139 Abū ʿUbayd al-Bakrī, the fifth/eleventh-century Andalusī geographer, explains in his *Tanbīh* that al-Qālī had gotten his facts wrong concerning this story (see al-Yūsī, *al-Muḥāḍarāt*, 1:132).

140 The poet is Zarāfah ibn Sabīʿ al-Asadī, al-Khālid ibn Naḍlah al-Ḥajwānī, or al-Ḥārith ibn Saʿd ibn Thaʿlabah.

141 The poet is Abū l-Fatḥ al-Bustī (d. ca. 400/1010).

142 These lines are from the forty-seventh *maqāmah*, known as al-Ḥijriyyah.

143 I am grateful to Dris Sulaimani for help understanding these verses.

144 Q Ṭūr 52:48.

145 The translation of this line is speculative.

146 For an overview of the history of this hadith, see Stearns, *Infectious Ideas*, 28–30. Al-Yūsī will return to the subject of contagion below.

147 Q Naḥl 16:1.

148 For a nuanced discussion of marriage as a financial transaction that involves exchanging money for the right to sex, see Ali, *Marriage and Slavery in Early Islam*, 49–62.

149 The four Qur'anic quotations are Q Ṭā Hā 20:117, Fāṭir 35:6, and Yā Sīn 36:60. The last passage is found repeatedly in the Qur'an (one example is Q A'rāf 7:22). I have modified Arberry's translation, replacing "Satan" with "devil."

150 Q Baqarah 2:268.

151 Compare with al-Qāḍī al-Quḍā'ī, *A Treasury of Virtues*, 11.

152 Q Baqarah 2:25. I have altered Arberry's translation slightly.

153 The same line of Ṭarafah's was quoted above in §1.2.

154 Q Yā Sīn 36:69. Abū Bakr's quotation from the Qur'an has a double meaning that is not without humor, as it both defends God's revelation from being given the status of poetry and simultaneously notes that the Prophet was known for not being skilled as a poet.

155 The poet is Jarīr ibn 'Abd al-Masīḥ al-Mutalammis (d. ca. 569).

156 The Umayyad poet Ibn Mufarrigh (d. 64/688).

157 Khaṭṭ is an area in Oman from which arrows and swords are obtained, and for which the name Khaṭṭ can stand in metonymically. See Ibn Manẓūr, *Lisān al-'Arab* under *kh-ṭ-ṭ*, where he cites this very line.

158 The poet is Nahshal ibn Ḥarrī (d. during the reign of Mu'wiyah ibn Abī Sufyān (r. 41/661–60/680)).

159 The line is by the pre-Islamic poet 'Abīd ibn al-Abraṣ (d. during the first half of the sixth century).

160 The Tamīmī leader al-Aḥnaf ibn Qays (d. 72/691).

161 The poet is Abū Yazīd Qays ibn al-Khutaym ibn 'Udayy al-Awsī (fl. first/seventh century).

162 This line is obscure without the one following: "They do not cry for my brother, / yet I console myself for his loss through their lamenting" (see al-Yūsī, *al-Muḥāḍarāt*, 1:166).

163 The poet is Ma'n ibn Aws al-Muzanī (fl. first/seventh century).

164 This line is in Abū Tammām's *Hamāsah*.

165 The line is attributed both to Ka'b ibn Zuhayr ibn Abī Sulmā al-Muzanī and his more famous father, the first/seventh-century poet Zuhayr ibn Abī Sulmā.

166 Attributed to Dhū l-Iṣba' al-'Adwānī, who lived in the first/seventh century.

167 The line appears in the *Ḥamāsah* of Abū Tammām.

168 Tumāḍir bint 'Amr, known as al-Khansā', had gone out to greet a group of camels that had scabies. She had then taken off her clothes to wash them and Durayd had seen her while she was unaware of him. This was when he recited several lines of poetry, the last of which is given here. See al-Yūsī, *al-Muḥāḍarāt*, 1:168.

169 The poet is the pre-Islamic poet al-Akhnaṣ ibn Ka'b al-Jihnī.

170 Al-Yūsī refers here to his book *Zahr al-akam fī l-amthāl wa-l-ḥikam*, which has been edited by Muḥammad Ḥajjī and Muḥammad al-Akhḍar in 3 vols.

171 In the science of Hadith the terms *riwāya* and *dirāya* are often juxtaposed when differentiating between the transmission and assessment of a given tradition, but al-Yūsī is using the terms more broadly here.

172 This line is attributed to Abū l-Aswad al-Duʾalī.

173 I have chosen to translate *mahdī* as "savior," but cf. García-Arenal, *Messianism and Puritanical Reform*, 5: "The terms 'Messiah' and 'Messianism' have a specifically Judaeo-Christian ring and imply a whole series of non-Islamic doctrines and beliefs, but most scholars find it admissible to employ these terms in an Islamic context so long as one is clear about the sense in which they are being used, i.e. to convey the important idea of an eschatological figure, the Mahdī, who 'will rise' to launch a great social transformation in order to restore the purity of early times and place all aspects of human life under divine guidance for a period preceding the End of Time."

174 Al-Yūsī refers here in passing to the bitter debate around the permissibility of smoking that broke out at the beginning of the seventeenth century among Muslim scholars. Al-Yūsī himself held that smoking was odious if not outright forbidden.

175 This is possibly Abū l-Qāsim al-Ghāzī. See §10.4.

176 This anecdote is cryptic.

177 The poet is in fact Abū Nuwās (d. between 198/813 and 200/815).

178 A disciple of the Baghdad Sufi Junayd, al-Shiblī is famous in Sufi tradition for his states of "drunkenness," in some of which he behaved irrationally.

179 The poet is Abū l-ʿAtāhiyah.

180 In Islamic law, legal obligation to perform mandatory rituals such as prayer is predicated on the believer being of sound mind.

181 In Arabic, the letter *qāf* (q) in both "hobbled" (*maʿgūlah*) and "ties" (*ʿigāl-hā*) has been replaced with *gāf* (g), a letter that doesn't exist in formal Arabic.

182 In both the question and the answer of the Arabic, the *qāf* of the verb "to say" (*qāl*) has been replaced with *gāf* (g).

183 Likely the Djmaʿ al-Fnaʾ, where one can still find storytellers today.

184 The figure of the poison damsel or vishkanya is an old one in Indian literature, and the attempted assassination of Alexander by one goes back at least as far as the pseudo-Aristotelian *Sirr al-asrār* (*Book of Secrets*), which was most likely written in Arabic in the tenth century, and which in its Latin translation became immensely popular in the European Middle Ages.

185 The poet is al-ʿAkawwak (d. 213/828).

186 Likely Ibn Dā'ūd (d. 187/803), vizier to the third Abbasid caliph.

187 The poet is Abū l-ʿAlā' al-Maʿarrī.

188 The poet is Maḥmūd ibn Ḥasan al-Warrāq (d. ca. 230/845).

189 Al-Yūsī's collected poetry has been published as *Dīwān al-Yūsī.*

190 These lines appear in several classical anthologies without attribution.

191 Al-Khaṣīb ibn ʿAbd al-Ḥamīd administered the land tax in Egypt until 190/805–6, a period during which Abū Nuwās spent time there in exile.

192 The poet is Zuhayr ibn Abī Sulmā.

193 Q Falaq 113:5.

194 Al-Yūsī is referring here to the 1591 campaign al-Manṣūr ordered carried out against the Songhay empire in what is today Mali.

195 This region of Morocco was well-known for its Jewish population, which had a long history there.

196 Q Āl ʿImrān 3:119.

197 The poet is Ibn al-Muʿtazz (d. 296/908).

198 On al-Habṭī and the controversy surrounding him, see El-Rouayheb, *Islamic Intellectual History*, 221–23. El-Rouayheb includes in his analysis a translated passage from this section, from which my translation has benefited.

199 This book has been edited and published under the slightly different title: al-Ḥasan al-Yūsī, *Mashrab al-ʿĀmm wa-l-Khāṣṣ min Kalimat al-Ikhlāṣ.*

200 The unnamed leader here is Muḥammad ibn ʿUmar ibn ʿAbd al-ʿAzīz ibn Abī Maḥallī (fl. eleventh/seventeenth century), with whom al-Yūsī disagreed vehemently.

201 Possibly a reference to a famous tradition attributed to ʿAlī ibn Abī Ṭālib: "Speak to the people in a manner that they understand, so that they do not deny God and His Prophet."

202 A reference to ʿAlī ibn Abī Ṭālib having agreed at Ṣiffīn that his and Muʿāwiyah ibn Abī Sufyān's claims to the caliphate would be decided by arbitration.

203 Al-Yūsī is evoking Q Anfāl 8:30: «They plotted, and God plotted. And God is the best of plotters».

204 This is one of the very few times al-Yūsī mentions a legal principle, in this case *sadd al-dharīʿah,* or "preventing the means," which justified prohibiting legal actions that could be expected to lead to forbidden ones. See al-Jīdī, *al-Tashrīʿ al-islāmī*, 118–19.

205 I have cut a sentence from the English translation that addressed the vocalization of the unusual word for "tribulation" that al-Yūsī then glosses as "difficulty."

206 Q Āl ʿImrān 3:140.

207 These lines are attributed to Imru' al-Qays.

208 A quote popular among Muslim scholars and usually attributed to the pseudo-Aristotelian *Sirr al-asrār* (*Book of Secrets*). Al-Yūsī quoted the same passage in his famous letter admonishing the second ʿAlawite sultan, Moulay Ismāʿīl. See al-Nāṣirī, *Kitāb al-Istiqṣāʾ*, 6:112.

209 Throughout *The Discourses* the importance of the early political history of the Muslim community following the Prophet's death is clear, though not surprising considering that it has been a constant touchstone for Muslim scholars and political thinkers. The absence of the third caliph ʿUthmān in this paragraph, and the short shrift he is given in the next, speaks to al-Yūsī's critical evaluation of his career, though at no point does al-Yūsī depart from the general Sunni consensus on the righteousness of the Prophet's first four successors. The inclusion of ʿAmr ibn al-ʿĀṣ here—he was both the conqueror of Egypt and an important ally of the first Umayyad ruler, Muʿāwiyah ibn Abī Sufyān—instead of ʿUthmān could be read as an implicit criticism of the third caliph.

210 Al-Yūsī has taken two lines out of context from an episode preserved in the Hadith in which ʿUmar ibn al-Khaṭṭāb had a conversation with the ascetic Uways at Medina during the pilgrimage. ʿUmar offered Uways a new robe and shoes, only for Uways to discourse on the importance of renouncing this world for the next, and to tell him that the two of them would never meet again. It is at this point that ʿUmar cries out—one assumes out of frustration at meeting Uways's level of piety—wishing he had never been born.

211 See n. 171.

212 A proverbial reference to a person in an impossible military position, this phrase originated in the Arab account of the early-seventh-century battle at Dhū Qār, near Kufa, where Arab tribes defeated the Sassanid forces. In the original narration the Persians were referred to as "Red."

213 This is Abū ʿAbd Allāh Maḥammad ibn Abī Bakr al-Dilāʾī (d. 1046/1635–36), the second leader of the Dilāʾ lodge who has not, in fact, been previously mentioned. His son, Abū ʿAbd Allāh Maḥammad al-Ḥājj (d. 1082/1671), who headed the lodge during al-Yūsī's stay, is mentioned on a number of previous occasions (§§18.1, 18.12, 19.1, 23.1, 29.1).

214 Q Isrāʾ 17:37.

215 Scholars now believe that Ibn Tūmart did not in fact meet al-Ghazālī, although it was widely believed during the Almohad and subsequent periods. See Griffel, "Ibn Tūmart's Rational Proof for God's Existence and Unity."

216 Cf. Ibn Khaldun, *The Muqaddimah*, 2:202.

217 This is most likely the famous Yemeni traditionist ʿAbd al-Razzāq al-Ṣanʿānī (d. 211/827), who compiled an important collection of Hadith.

218 I am uncertain about what al-Yūsī is referring to here.

219 The poet is al-Ḥuṭay'ah.

220 The poet is al-Ṭughrā'ī (d. 513/1119).

221 The poet is al-Mutanabbī.

222 The full hadith is: "The sound vision of an upstanding man is one of the forty-six parts of prophecy."

223 A hadith.

224 In the Qur'an, the Tablet refers to the heavenly tablets of fate, where everything that has been and will be is recorded.

225 Q Ra'd 13:39.

226 A differentiation is made between miracles granted to saints (*karamāt*) and those to prophets (*mu'jizāt*), which is difficult to convey in translation. Both refer to miraculous events taking place through God's power at the hands of His chosen servants.

227 This line is attributed to 'Abd Allāh ibn Mubārak (d. 181/797).

228 This line is attributed to Sufyān al-Thawrī (d. 161/778).

229 Q Zukhruf 43:39.

230 This line contains an allusion to Q Hūd 11:114: «Good deeds compensate for bad deeds».

231 A line recited by al-Ash'ath ibn Qays (d. 40/661) at the Battle of the Camel. The Ḥa Mīm surahs, from forty through forty-six, all begin with the letters *ḥa-mīm*.

232 The poet is Abū Isḥāq Ibrāhīm al-Tujībī al-Ilbīrī (d. 459/1067).

233 A reference to the figure of the Samaritan, who in the Qur'an is responsible for the Israelites worshipping the golden calf during Moses's absence, and who was punished by being cast out of society and told to tell others not to touch him. See Q Ṭā Hā 20:97.

234 Both this and the next quote are hadiths.

235 Q Ṣāffāt 37:164.

236 On the North African Sufi custom of distributing food at *zawāyā* (sing. *zāwiyah*) and the context for these comments of al-Yūsī, see Rodriguez-Mañas, "Charity and Deceit."

237 A reference to the *ahl* or *aṣḥāb al-ṣuffah*, a group who made their home in the vestibule of the Prophet's home (and mosque) as they had nowhere else to sleep. Some later Sufis traced the origins of their practice back to this group.

238 This is a hadith.

239 Probably a reference to the Prophet refusing Gabriel's offer to turn Mount Ṣafā into gold to help convince the Quraysh to convert to Islam, so that they would instead do so out of faith.

240 Muḥammad himself belonged to Quraysh; many early converts came from Thaqīf and Daws.

241 Q Āl ʿImrān 3:14. The verse in whole reads: «People are drawn to the love of pleasures, of women, children, heaps of gold and silver, horses of mark, cattle, and tillage. That is the enjoyment of the present life; but God—with Him is the fairest resort». I have slightly altered Arberry's translation.

242 Attributed to the Umayyad poet Qays ibn Dhirīḥ (d. 68/688).

243 These lines, by al-Ṣimmah ibn ʿAbd Allāh, sometimes also attributed to Majnūn, are also quoted in §14.9.

244 These lines are attributed to a Persian youth from Bawwān.

245 This saying is often attributed to the caliph ʿUmar ibn al-Khaṭṭāb.

246 The poet is al-Diʿbil (d. 246/860).

247 The lines are attributed to both Ibn al-Rūmī and al-Muʿtaṣim ibn Ṣamādih (d. 484/1091).

248 These lines are attributed to al-Shāfiʿī.

249 The line is by Jaḥẓah al-Barmakī (d. 839/936).

250 The poet is Ibrāhīm ibn al-ʿAbbās al-Ṣūlī (d. 243/857).

251 The poet is Ibn al-Rūmī.

252 The poet is al-Ḥumaydī (d. 488/1095).

253 Q Aʿrāf 7:102.

254 The poet is Dhū l-Isbaʿ al-ʿAdwānī.

255 These lines are often attributed to the Prophet Muḥammad's grandson, al-Ḥusayn ibn ʿAlī ibn Abī Ṭālib (d. 61/680).

256 Responding to Ibn Lankak (d. 360/970).

257 The poet is Ibn Lankak.

258 This is presumably ʿUrwah ibn Zubayr (d. 93–94/711–13).

259 The poet is Ibn Sharaf al-Qayrawānī (d. 460/1067).

260 Compare with the lines quoted above in §39.3.

261 This line contains an elaborate pun in that the poet uses the same root, *r-w-ḥ*, in four different ways: *rāḥū* (they left), *rāḥatī* (my courtyard), *rāḥatī* (my comfort), and *rāḥ* (wine).

262 These lines are attributed to Ibn al-Fāriḍ (d. 632/1235).

263 The poet is al-Khansāʾ. The first hemistich is often given as "Of those who have encountered (*yulāqī*) war."

264 Aḥmad Zarrūq did not write works that are known today by these names; al-Yūsī may be referring to his *Sufficient Advice* (*al-Naṣīḥah al-kāfiyyah*) and his *Provisions for the Disciple* (*ʿUddat al-murīd*), which Aḥmad Bābā al-Tinbuktī referred to as *Reliance of the Disciple*.

265 The poet is Kuthayyir.

266 The poet is Bashshār (second/eighth century).

267 The poet is Ḥātim al-Ṭāʾī.

268 The poet is al-Ḥusayn ibn Muṭayr (fl. second/eighth century).

269 The poet is ʿUmayrah ibn Jābir al-Ḥanafī.

270 These lines are attributed to ʿAlī ibn Abī Ṭālib.

271 Q Taḥrīm 66:3.

272 The verses are by the Hadith scholar Misʿar ibn Kudām (d. 155/771–72).

273 Q Raʿd 13:16.

Glossary of Names and Terms

This glossary contains entries for names of people and places mentioned in the text, along with selected events and terms. My first references here were the *Encyclopedia of Islam* and, for geographical entries, Yāqūt's *Muʿjam al-buldān*. Yet many of the figures mentioned by al-Yūsī are Moroccan scholars whose fame did not extend beyond Morocco itself, and here the following biographical dictionaries were indispensable: Muḥammad ibn Aḥmad al-Ḥuḍaygī's (d. 1189/1775) *Ṭabaqāt al-Ḥuḍaygī*, Muḥammad ibn al-Ṭayyib al-Qādirī's (d. 1187/1773) *Nashr al-mathānī li-ahl al-qarn al-ḥādī ʿashr wa l-thānī*, and for scholars of the Darʿah Valley, Muḥammad al-Makkī ibn Mūsa ibn Nāṣir al-Darʿī's (d. after 1166/1752) *al-Durar al-murassaʿah bi-akhbār aʿyān Darʿah.*

al-ʿAbbās ibn al-Aḥnaf (d. after 193/808) Arab poet of the Ḥanīfah clan who grew up in Baghdad, known for his amatory poetry, a companion of the Abbasid caliph Hārūn al-Rashīd (d. 193/(809).

ʿAbd Allāh ibn Bassām I was not able to identify this figure.

ʿAbd Allāh ibn Hammām (d. after 96/715) Umayyad poet closely involved with the politics of the Umayyad family.

ʿAbd Allāh ibn Ḥassūn (d. 1013/1604) Sufi from Fez known for his sanctity, who settled in Salé and become one of the city's most important saints.

ʿAbd Allāh ibn Ḥusayn al-Raqqī [al-Darʿī al-Qabbāb] (d. 1045/1635) prominent Sufi of the Shādhilī order from al-Raqq, a town between Darʿah and Sijilmāsah, who died in Tamgrūt. He taught Abū ʿAbd Allāh Maḥammad ibn Nāṣir al-Darʿī and his brother Ḥusayn, and transmitted to them and others his understanding of the Shādhilī order, which he had received from Abū l-ʿAbbās Aḥmad ibn ʿAlī al-Ḥajjāj al-Darʿī, and which went back to the teachings of Aḥmad Zarrūq.

ʿAbd Allāh ibn Muʿāwiyah (d. 129/746–47) ʿAlid rebel who was executed by the Abbasid general Abū Muslim.

ʿAbd Allāh ibn Mubārak (d. 181/797) ʿAbd Allāh ibn ʿAbd al-Raḥmān al-Ḥanẓalī, merchant and scholar of Hadith. He was known for his ascetic practices and alternated years of performing the pilgrimage and carrying out jihad.

ʿAbd Allāh ibn ʿUmar ibn al-Khaṭṭāb (d. 73/693) Companion of the Prophet, the son of the second caliph, and an important figure in the politics of the early Muslim community.

ʿAbd al-ʿAzīz ibn ʿAbd al-Ḥaqq al-Ḥarrār [al-Tabbāʿ] (d. 914/1508–9) the successor to al-Jazūlī as the leader of the Jazūliyyah in Morocco.

ʿAbd al-Kabīr I was not able to identify this figure.

ʿAbd al-Khāliq ibn Yāsīn al-Daghūghī see Abū Muḥammad ʿAbd al-Khāliq ibn Yāsīn al-Daghūghī.

ʿAbd al-Malik ibn Marwān (r. 66–86/685–705) fifth Umayyad caliph, who consolidated Umayyad rule and employed al-Ḥajjāj as his loyal administrator in Iraq to crush ʿAlid resistance there.

ʿAbd Manāf a clan of the Quraysh.

ʿAbd al-Muʾmin ibn ʿAlī (d. 558/1163) a follower of Ibn Tūmart, he was the first Almohad ruler.

ʿAbd al-Muṭṭalib (d. AD 578) the Prophet Muḥammad's paternal grandfather, who cared for his grandson after Muḥammad's early death.

ʿAbd al-Qādir [al-Jīlānī] (d. 561/1166) Ḥanbalī scholar of Baghdad and eponym of the Qādiriyyah Sufi order, which subsequently spread to North Africa. He studied for some years with the enigmatic Sufi Ḥammād al-Dabbās (d. 523/1131).

ʿAbd al-Raḥmān ibn Muḥammad I was not able to identify this figure.

ʿAbd al-Raḥmān al-Thaʿālibī (d. 873/1468) Abu Zayd ʿAbd al-Raḥmān ibn Muḥammad ibn Makhlūf al-Jazāʾirī, a theologian and author of a work of Qurʾanic exegesis who also wrote on the Prophet's dreams. He died in Tunis.

ʿAbd al-Salām ibn Mashīsh (625/1227–78) famous Moroccan Shādhilī saint who was a disciple of Abū Madyan and was assassinated in his retreat on Jabal al-ʿAlam near Tetuan. Initially only known locally, his fame spread after the ninth/fifteenth century with the spread of the Shādhilī order itself.

ʿAbd al-Wahhāb al-Shaʿrānī (d. 973/1565) famous Sufi of North African origin who lived in Egypt.

ʿAbd al-Wāḥid [al-Sharīf al-Filālī] (d. 1003/1594–95) Moroccan scholar who lived and died in Marrakesh, where he taught and acted as a jurisconsult (*muftī*) and enjoyed a close relationship with the sultan Aḥmad al-Manṣūr.

al-ʿAbīd river in the Banī Milāl region of Morocco.

ʿAbīd ibn al-Abraṣ (fl. first half of the sixth century AD) pre-Islamic Arab poet of the Banū Saʿd ibn Thaʿlabah, who played an important role in the revolt against Ḥujr ibn al-Ḥārith, the king of the Banū Kindah (and father of the poet Imruʾ al-Qays), whom he killed.

Abū ʿAbbās Aḥmad ibn Abī Bakr al-Hashtūkī I have not been able to find any information on this scholar.

Abū ʿAbbās Aḥmad ibn Muḥammad ibn al-Sayyid al-Sharīf al-Ḥasanī I was not able to identify this figure.

Abū ʿAbbās Aḥmad ibn Muḥammad al-Maqqarī (d. 1041/1632) the famous author of *Nafḥ al-ṭīb* (an overview of the history of al-Andalus and of the life and works of the Granadan vizier Ibn al-Khaṭīb). He met Abū ʿAbd Allāh Maḥammad al-Ḥājj in Cairo in 1041/1631.

Abū ʿAbbās Aḥmad Zarrūq (d. 800/1493) prominent Moroccan Shādhilī Sufi, Mālikī jurist, and Ashʿarite theologian who spent much of his life in Fez and died in Misratah, Libya. He wrote a commentary on Ibn ʿAṭāʾ Allāh's *Ḥikam* and an overview of Sufism, *Principles of Sufism* (*Qawāʾid al-taṣawwuf*).

Abū l-ʿAbbās ibn al-ʿArīf (d. 536/1141) Amazigh scholar of the Ṣinhājah, he was a famous Andalusī Sufi who was persecuted at the instigation of the judge Ibn al-Aswad.

Abū l-ʿAbbās al-Mursī (d. 686/1287) originally from Murcia in al-Andalus, he settled with Abū al-Ḥasan al-Shādhilī in Alexandria, in Egypt, and was one of his main students.

Abū l-ʿAbbās al-Sabtī (d. 601/1205) Aḥmad ibn Jaʿfar al-Khazrajī, prominent Moroccan Sufi who studied with Abū ʿAbd Allāh al-Fakhkhār and died in Marrakesh.

Abū ʿAbd Allāh ibn Nāṣir see Ibn Nāṣir.

Abū ʿAbd Allāh Maḥammad al-Ḥājj [ibn Maḥammad ibn Abī Bakr al-Dilāʾī] (d. 1082/1671) grandson of the founder of Dilāʾ lodge and its third leader. He headed the lodge during al-Yūsī's stay there.

Abū ʿAbd Allāh Maḥammad ibn Abī Bakr al-Dilāʾī (d. 1046/1635–36) second leader of the Dilāʾ lodge and a prominent Sufi and scholar famed for his knowledge of Hadith and Qur'anic exegesis. He went on pilgrimage in 1005/1596–97 and studied with the famed Zayn al-ʿĀbidīn al-Munāwī (d. 1031/1621) in Egypt before returning to Morocco. He was buried in al-Dilāʾ.

Abū ʿAbd Allāh Maḥammad ibn Nāṣir [al-Darʿī] (d. 1085/1674) Abū ʿAbd Allāh Maḥammad ibn Muḥammad ibn Aḥmad ibn Muḥammad ibn Ḥusayn ibn Nāṣir ibn ʿAmr ibn ʿUthmān al-Darʿī, al-Yūsī's teacher and founder of the Nāṣirī branch of the Shādhilī Ṣūfī order in Tamgrūt in the Darʿah Valley. He gave al-Yūsī his formal introduction into the Shādhilī order.

Abū ʿAbd Allāh Mubārak ibn Muḥammad [ibn ʿAbd al-ʿAzīz] al-ʿAnbarī al-Ghurfī (d. 1090/1679–80) renowned scholar from Sijilmāsah, known also as Mubārak ibn ʿAzzī, who studied with Abū ʿAbd Allāh Maḥammad ibn Nāṣir al-Darʿī and died of the plague.

Abū ʿAbd Allāh Muḥammad al-ʿArbī ibn Abī l-Maḥāsin Yūsuf al-Fāsī (d. 1021/1642) one of the four sons of Abū l-Maḥāsin, the founder of the famous al-Fāsī family of scholars.

Abū ʿAbd Allāh Muḥammad al-Darrāq al-Fāsī (d. 1070/1659–60) the founder of a successful family of doctors, he came to Fez from the Sūs Valley in southern Morocco.

Abū ʿAbd Allāh Muḥammad ibn ʿAbd Allāh ibn ʿAlī ibn Ṭāhir al-Sharīf (al-Sijilmāsī) (d. 1089/1678–79) scholar and Sufi from Sijilmāsah, who taught, among others, Abū Muḥammad ʿAbd al-Qādir al-Fāsī, and performed the pilgrimage to Mecca, studying also in the East. He died of the plague.

Abū ʿAbd Allāh Muḥammad ibn ʿAbd al-Karīm al-Jazāʾirī (d. 1102/1691) jurist and student of al-Yūsī, died in Fez.

Abū ʿAbd Allāh Muḥammad ibn Abī Bakr al-ʿAyyāshī (d. 1067/1656–57) father of the famous traveler Abū Sālim al-ʿAyyāshī.

Abū ʿAbd Allāh Muḥammad ibn Abī Ṭāhir (d. tenth/sixteenth century) son of Abū l-Ṭayyib ibn Yaḥyā al-Maysūrī.

Abū ʿAbd Allāh Muḥammad ibn Aḥmad al-Hashtūkī (d. 1098/1687) judge who studied in Algeria and the Sūs, taught al-Yūsī grammar and jurisprudence, and was appointed judge first in Fez and then in Marrakesh, where he died.

Abū ʿAbd Allāh Muḥammad ibn Masʿūd al-ʿĪsawī al-ʿIrfāwī I was not able to identify this scholar.

Abū ʿAbd Allāh Muḥammad ibn al-Murābiṭ al-Dilāʾī (d. 1089/1678) prominent scholar known for his excellence in grammar and Arabic as well as his eloquence. He was buried in his family's garden in the Andalusī quarter of Fez.

Abū ʿAbd Allāh Muḥammad ibn Saʿīd al-Sūsī (al-Marghitī) (d. 1089/1678) prominent scholar and ascetic who excelled in many sciences, including grammar and medicine. He was born in the south of Morocco but lived for the most part in Marrakesh, where he died, and where he was buried near the grave of his teacher Abū Bakr al-Suktānī.

Abū ʿAbd Allāh Muḥammad ibn Sulaymān al-Jazūlī (d. 869/1465) famous founder of the Jazūliyyah branch of the Shādhiliyyah and author of the extraordinarily popular book of prayers *Dalāʾil al-khayrāt*. After his death, he was ultimately buried in Marrakesh as one of that city's Seven Saints. He is today popularly known in Morocco as Sīdī Ben Slīmān.

Abū ʿAbd Allāh Muḥammad ibn Tūmart al-Sūsī see Ibn Tūmart.

Abū ʿAbd Allāh Muḥammad al-Ṣaghīr ibn Abī ʿAmr al-Murrākushī I was not able to identify this scholar.

Abū ʿAbd Allāh Muḥammad al-Ṣāliḥ ibn al-Muʿṭī (al-Sharqī) (d. 1681) ascetic and Sufi of Marrakesh who studied with, among others, Abū Muḥammad ʿAbd al-Qādir al-Fāsī (with whom he read al-Ghazālī's *Revival*, as well as books on Sufism and Hadith).

Abū ʿAbd Allāh al-Sanūsī (d. 895/1490) Muḥammad ibn Yūsuf ibn ʿUmar ibn Shuʿayb, famed Algerian Ashʿari theologian, logician, and Sufi whose works on theology and logic were influential well past al-Yūsī's time, and on several of whose works al-Yūsī wrote commentaries. He died in Tlemcen.

Abū ʿAbd Allāh (Yaʿqūb ibn Dāʿūd) (d. 187/803) vizier to the third Abbasid caliph al-Mahdī from 160–66/777–82, he fell victim to court intrigue between a group of ʿAlids and their opponents, and was cast into prison.

Abū l-ʿAlāʾ al-Maʿarrī (d. 449/1058) Aḥmad ibn ʿAbd Allāh ibn Sulaymān, prodigious blind poet, prose writer, vegetarian, and skeptic, who lived and died in Maʿarrat al-Nuʿmān in northern Syria.

Abū ʿAlī al-Fāsī possibly the Andalusī scholar of the late Umayyad period, Abū ʿAlī al-Ḥasan, or al-Ḥusayn ibn ʿAlī al-Fāsī, who tutored the famed Ibn Ḥazm (d. 456/1064) when he was a boy.

Abū ʿAlī al-Ghujātī I was not able to identify this figure.

Abū ʿAlī al-Ḥātimī (d. 388/998) philologist and grammarian who wrote two treatises on the poet al-Mutanabbī.

Abū ʿAlī al-Masṭāsī I was not able to identify this figure.

Abū l-Aswad (d. ?) Abū Bakr ibn Aswad, Almoravid judge who prosecuted the Sufi Ibn al-ʿArīf along with Abū Bakr al-Mayūrqī and Ibn Barrajān (d. 536/1141), most likely for their anti-Almoravid leanings.

Abū l-ʿAtāhiyah (d. 210/825 or 211/826) Ismāʿīl ibn al-Qāsim ibn Suwayd, famous ascetic poet, known by his teknonym "father of lunacy."

Abū Bakr ibn al-ʿArabī (d. 543/1148) student of Hadith from Seville who journeyed East and studied with al-Ghazālī in Baghdad as well as with other scholars in Egypt, following which he returned to Seville, where he achieved great renown. He died while traveling between Marrakesh and Fez, as a prisoner of the Almohads.

Abū Bakr ibn al-Ḥasan al-Taṭāfī (fl. eleventh/seventeenth century) a scholar from the Maḍgharah region of the Tāfīlālt.

Abū Bakr ibn Ḥijjah al-Ḥamawī (d. 837/1434) famed poet of the Mamluk period from Ḥamāh in Syria.

Abū Bakr ibn al-Ḥusayn al-Taṭāfī I have not been able to identify this scholar.

Abū Bakr al-Shiblī (d. 334/945) famous Baghdadi Sufi and disciple of Junayd.

Abū Bakr [al-Ṣiddīq] (d. 13/634) early Companion of the Prophet and, along with the Prophet's cousin ʿAlī ibn Abī Ṭālib, one of the first converts to Islam. He was the father of Muḥammad's wife ʿĀʾishah, and the first caliph (*khalīfah*) to lead the Muslim community following the Prophet's death.

Abū l-Dardāʾ (d. 32/652) Companion of the Prophet known for his knowledge of the Qurʾan who died in Damascus after having been appointed judge there.

Abū Dhuʾayb (d. ca. 28/649) famed and prominent poet of the Hudhayl tribe.

Abū l-Faḍl ibn al-Naḥwī (d. 513/1119–20) proponent of the works of al-Ghazālī during the Almoravid rule.

Abū Faḍl al-Jawharī I was not able to identify this scholar.

Abū Firās (d. 357/968) the famous poet Abū Firās al-Ḥamdānī, who as administrator of al-Manbij took part in many raids against Byzantium with his cousin and ruler, Sayf al-Dawlah. After the latter's death, he revolted against Sayf al-Dawlah's son Abū l-Maʿālī and was killed.

Abū l-Ḥasan al-Shādhilī (d. 656/1258) the founder of Shādhilī Sufi order, who was persecuted by the scholars of Qayrawān.

Abū ʿImrān al-Hastūrī l-Aswad I was not able to identify this scholar.

Abū ʿImrān Mūsā ibn Idrāsan al-Ḥallāj (fl. sixth/twelfth century) an Amazigh disciple of Abū Madyan.

Abū Jaʿfar al-Aswad I was not able to identify this scholar.

Abū Jaʿfar al-Ḥaddād (d. second/eighth century) teacher of the prominent Baghdadi Sufi Junayd known for devotion to trusting in God.

Abū Kabīr see al-Hudhalī.

Abū Madyan (d. 89/1193 or 594/1198) Shuʿayb ibn al-Ḥusayn al-Anṣārī, Andalusī Sufi and ascetic from Seville who during the Almoravid period settled in Fez. His spiritual education was completed under Abū Yiʿzzā Yallanūr and his teachings proved influential in the following centuries on the Sufism of the Muslim West. He died near Tlemcen.

Abū l-Mahdī al-Daghdūghī (d. ca. 560/1165) prominent Sufi from near Asfī.

Abū Muḥammad ʿAbd Allāh ibn Maḥammad (al-Darʿī) (d. 1091/1680) born in 1057/1647–48, he studied with his father and with Abū Sālim al-ʿAyyāshī and distinguished himself in jurisprudence and Hadith. He died of the plague.

Abū Muḥammad ʿAbd al-Khāliq ibn Yāsīn al-Daghūghī (d. 571/1174) famed Moroccan scholar and Sufi who was later venerated as a saint. His grave is near the River Nafis close to Marrakesh.

Abū Muḥammad ʿAbd al-Qādir ibn ʿAlī al-Fāsī (d. 1091/1680) prominent Sufi of Fez who had his own lodge and was a spiritual mentor to and teacher of al-Yūsi.

Abū Muḥammad al-Ḥusayn ibn Abī Bakr (fl. eleventh/seventeenth century) one of al-Yūsī's earliest teachers, with whom he studied Ibn Abī Zayd al-Qayrawānī's (d. 386/996) *Treatise.* He impressed al-Yūsī with his devotion to study and his encouragement of his students.

Abū Muḥammad ibn ʿAbd Allāh ibn ʿAlī ibn Ṭāhir al-Ḥasanī [al-Sijilmāsī] (d. 1089/1678–79) prominent Sufi and teacher of many scholars.

Abū Nuwās (d. between 198/813 and 200/815) al-Ḥasan ibn Hāniʾ al-Ḥakamī, famous poet of the ʿAbbasid period, best known for his poems on wine and pederasty. He was born in Ahwāz and died in Baghdad.

Abū l-Qāsim al-Ghāzī (d. 981/1573) famed saint and spiritual authority from the Tāfīlālt in southern Morocco.

Abū l-Qāsim ibn Būʿtal al-Shabbānī I was not able to identify this scholar.

Abū l-Qāsim ibn Zaytūn Presumably a judge in Baghdad in the third/ninth century. I was not able to find any further details on him.

Abū Qāsim al-Junayd see Junayd.

Abū Saʿīd ʿUthmān ibn ʿAlī al-Yūsī (d. 1084/1673–74) learned relative of al-Yūsī who studied with the reputed traveler Abū Sālim al-ʿAyyāshī, among others.

Abū Salhām (d. 344/955–56) Abū Saʿīd al-Maṣrī Abū Salhāmah, a renowned saint with a famous mausoleum on the Mediterranean shore near the town named after him.

Abū Sālim ʿAbd Allāh ibn Muḥammad al-ʿAyyāshī (d. 1090/1679) famed traveler and author of a celebrated *Riḥlah* or travel account of his second pilgrimage to Mecca and return to Morocco.

Abū Ṣaqr I was not able to identify this figure.

Abū Shuʿayb al-Sāriyah (d. 541/1146–47) Sufi saint of the Sanhājah from the town of Azmour, he was a teacher of Abū Yaʿzzā. He died in Azmour and was known as "the column" (*al-sāriyah*) due to his extending the standing portion of the prayer.

Abū Sufyān [Ṣakhr ibn Ḥarb ibn Umayyah] (d. ca. 34/654) prominent early opponent of the Prophet Muḥammad among the Quraysh, and a late convert to Islam. Father of Muʿāwiyah ibn Abī Sufyān, founder of the Umayyad dynasty.

Abū Tammām (d. 232/846) famed Abbasid poet and anthologist.

Abū l-Ṭayyib ibn Yaḥyā al-Maysūrī (d. 988/1508) prominent Sufi and scholar, author of numerous works.

Abū ʿUbaydah (d. 18/639) ʿĀmir ibn ʿAbd Allāh ibn al-Jarrāḥ, an early convert to Islam and a prominent Companion of the Prophet, who praised him repeatedly alongside Abū Bakr and ʿUmar ibn al-Khaṭṭāb. His reputation for piety and closeness to the Prophet made him a plausible candidate for caliph on the Day of the Portico.

Abū ʿUmar ibn ʿAbd al-Barr (d. 463/1070) Andalusī Mālikī jurist from Cordoba who excelled in his knowledge of Hadith and served for a time as a judge in Lisbon and Santarem. He died in Játiva.

Abū Yazīd ʿAbd al-Raḥmān ibn Yūsuf al-Sharīf I was not able to identify this scholar.

Abū Yazīd (Bayazid Bisṭāmī) (d. 234/848–49 or 261/874–75) Iranian Sufi whose ecstatic sayings were much commented upon and debated by Sufis in the centuries following his death.

Abū Yiʿzzā (also Yaʿzā or Yaʿzzā) Yallanūr (d. 572/1177) Moroccan Sufi scholar and saint, who was famous for his miracles and whose tomb is in the Middle Atlas. Teacher of Abū Madyan. He died in Tāghiyā.

Abū Zakariyyā' al-Malījī (fl. sixth/twelfth century) Yaḥyā ibn Mūsā, Sufi saint from Malījah, a town sixty-eight kilometers to the west of Marrakesh, who settled in the Rijrājah region near Rabat and was known for his miracles. Teacher of the abovementioned Abū Muḥammad ʿAbd al-Khāliq ibn Yāsīn al-Daghūghī.

Abū Zayd ʿAbd al-Raḥmān al-Lajā'ī [al-Tarārī] (d. 599/1202–3) Moroccan scholar from the Lajā'iyyah Mountain north of Fez, contemporary to the founding of the Almohad empire.

ʿAdan (Aden) important port and trading city on the southern coast of Yemen, inhabited since pre-Islamic times.

ʿAdī ibn Zayd (d. ca. AD 600) Christian poet of the end of the sixth century who moved from the Sassanid to the Lakhmid court in al-Ḥīrah, where, after becoming an advisor to the ruler al-Nuʿmān III (r. AD 580–602), he was executed by him as a result of court intrigue.

ʿAdnān legendary ancestor of the Arabs of northern Arabia.

ʿAḍud al-Dawlah (d. 372/983) the honorific, meaning "the Pillar of the State," of arguably the greatest Buyid ruler, one who united his family's territories in Iraq and Iran. His father was known as Rukn al-Dawlah, or Corner of the State.

Aḥmad ibn ʿAbd Allāh ibn Mubārak al-Waqāwī I was not able to identify this scholar.

Aḥmad ibn Abī Maḥallī see Ibn Abī Maḥallī.

Aḥmad ibn Abī l-Qāsim al-Ṣūmaʿī (d. 1013/1604–5) prominent Sufi and head of a Sufi lodge in Tādlā. He collected over 1,800 volumes in his library, was known for his love of reading, and wrote works on Sufism and prayers.

Aḥmad ibn ʿAlī I was not able to identify this figure.

Aḥmad ibn Ḥanbal (d. 241/855) acclaimed scholar of Hadith and the reputed founder of the Ḥanbalī legal school, famous for his upstanding moral character and willingness to speak truth to power.

Aḥmad ibn Ibrāḥīm (al-Anṣārī) (d. 1052/1642–43) prominent Sufi and ascetic from the Darʿah Valley who studied under the spiritual authority ʿAbd Allāh ibn Ḥusayn al-Raqqī, whom he succeeded as the head of the lodge there.

Aḥmad ibn Rajāʾ I was not able to identify this scholar.

Aḥmad ibn Yūsuf [al-Rāshidī al-Malyānī] (d. in the 930s/1524–34) from the village of Malyāna near Algiers, a prominent Sufi known for his miracles.

Aḥmad al-Manṣūr (d. 1012/1603) the most powerful sultan of the Saadian dynasty, who came to power after the Battle of the Three Kings at al-Qasr al-Kabīr in northern Morocco in 1578, when he played a part in defeating the rulers of Spain and Portugal. He subsequently oversaw the Moroccan conquest of West Africa and Timbuktu in 1591 and the establishment of an army of African slave soldiers. He died of the plague.

Aḥmad Zarrūq see Abū ʿAbbās Aḥmad Zarrūq.

ʿĀʾishah (d. 58/678) daughter of the first caliph, Abū Bakr al-Ṣiddīq, married by the Prophet when quite young after the death of his first wife, Khadījah, in AD 619. She became his favorite wife and played an important role in transmitting hadiths about the Prophet's words and actions, as well as being influential in politics following Muḥammad's death.

Ajāwaz I was not able to identify this location with certainty. There are reports of a village by the name of Agauz in the Rijrājah region as well as one in Tagaost in the southwest of Morocco.

al-Akhshabayn a mountain near Mecca.

al-Akhṭal (d. before 92/710) Ghiyāth ibn Ghawth ibn al-Ṣalt, famous Arab Christian poet given the nickname "loquacious," who lived during the Umayyad period and became court poet of the Umayyad caliph ʿAbd al-Malik.

ʿAlī Abī l-Shakāwī ("owner of skins") (d. 1004/1595–96) saint who spent time in the companionship of the famous saint Abū l-Maḥāsin (d. 1013/1604) and acquired his nickname after miraculously producing from one skin numerous bowls of milk. He was buried in Salé.

ʿAlī [ibn Abī Ṭālib] (d. 40/661) cousin and son-in-law of the Prophet Muḥammad, ʿAlī was either the first or (after Abū Bakr) the second male convert to Islam and the fourth caliph following Muḥammad's death. He was killed by one of his former followers. Those Muslims who believed that he and his descendants had been chosen by God to rule over the Muslim community would later be referred to as the Partisans of ʿAlī (*Shīʿat ʿAlī*).

ʿAlī ibn Ibrāḥīm al-Būzīdī al-Tādlāwī (d. 956/1549) a prominent leader of the Jazūliyyah.

ʿAlī ibn ʿUthmān [al-Yūsī] I was not able to identify this figure.

ʿAlī ibn Yūsuf al-Darʿī (d. 1045/1635) scholar who studied with Abū ʿAbd Allāh Maḥammad ibn Abī Bakr al-Dilāʾī and then taught in the lodge of Sayyid al-Nās.

ʿAlī al-Ujḥūrī (d. 1066/1655–56) prominent Egyptian scholar of the Mālikī legal school known for his piety and asceticism, who was also one of the few scholars in the seventeenth century (along with Ibn Abī Maḥallī and Aḥmad Bābā al-Tinbuktī) who advocated for the legal permissibility of smoking. He wrote works on legal theory, theology, and the merits of ʿĀshūrāʾ (the tenth day of Muḥarram) and Ramadan. He taught a variety of Moroccan scholars who passed through Egypt, including the traveler Abū Sālim ʿAbd Allāh ibn Muḥammad al-ʿAyyāshī.

ʿAlqamah [ibn ʿAbadah al-Tamīmī] sixth-century Arab poet who was possibly a rival of Imruʾ al-Qays.

ʿAlqamah ibn ʿAlāthah (d. ca. 20/640) Companion of the Prophet whom the second caliph, ʿUmar ibn al-Khaṭṭāb, appointed to administer the Ḥawrān region of southern Syria.

ʿĀmir a branch of the Hawāzin tribal confederation.

ʿĀmir ibn al-Ṭufayl (d. 2/624) prominent leader of the Arabs in pre-Islamic times, who died on his way to convert to Islam.

al-ʿĀmiriyyah see Laylā al-ʿĀmiriyyah.

Amorium (Ar: ʿAmmūriyyah) Byzantine city of importance in Asia Minor, captured by the Abbasid caliph al-Muʿtaṣim in 223/838.

ʿAmr ibn al-ʿĀṣ (d. 42/622 or 43/664) Companion of Muḥammad famed for his role in the conquest of Egypt in 19–21/640–42, where he founded the city of Fusṭāṭ, which he subsequently administered until he was removed by the third caliph, ʿUthmān. At Ṣiffīn he sided with Muʿāwiyah ibn Abī Sufyān in outmaneuvering ʿAlī ibn Abī Ṭālib.

ʿAmr ibn Barrāqah a poet of the Hamdān tribe who lived into the early Islamic period and was sent to the caliph ʿUmar ibn al-Khaṭṭāb (r. 13–23/634–44) as the head of a delegation.

ʿAmr Muzayqiyāʾ famed Yemeni king of the pre-Islamic period, said to have been the greatest king who ruled over Maʾrib. After the dam broke, he later led his people to the valley of the ʿAkk tribe, where he died.

Aristotle the famed Greek philosopher of the fourth century BC.

al-Arjānī (d. 544/1149) Nāṣiḥ al-Dīn Abū Bakr Aḥmad ibn Muḥammad ibn al-Hussayn al-Arjānī, a poet from a village in al-Ahwāz.

al-ʿArjī al-ʿUthmānī (d. 120/737) Abū ʿUmar ʿAbd Allāh ibn ʿUmar ibn ʿAmr ibn ʿUthmān al-ʿArjī, descendant of the caliph ʿUthmān, an Umayyad poet who was imprisoned by the governor of Mecca, Muḥammad ibn Hishām, after writing love poetry about the latter's wife and mother. He died after nine years in prison.

al-Aʿshā (d. 7/629) Maymūn ibn Qays, a Jahili poet known as Abū Baṣīr (one who sees clearly).

al-Aṣmaʿī (d. 213/828) Abū Saʿīd ʿAbd al-Malik ibn Kurayb, famous Iraqi philologist who was active at the court of Hārūn al-Rashīd and counted Jāḥiẓ among his students.

Awlād al-Ḥājj I was not able to identify this place.

Axis [of the age] head of the Sufi hierarchy and site of God's manifestation.

ʿAzzah (d. 105/723) the beloved of Kuthayyir ibn ʿAbd al-Raḥmān, a chaste (*ʿUdhrī*) Umayyad poet who wrote many verses to her while she was married to an older man.

Badr small village southwest of Medina, and the site of the first major battle of the Muslim community, in 2/624, in which the Muslims defeated the Quraysh of Mecca.

Bakr ibn Wāʾil pre-Islamic tribal confederation of Central Arabia, parts of which later migrated to Iraq and Iran during the early Islamic conquests.

al-Bakrī ibn Aḥmad ibn Abī l-Qāsim ibn Mawlūd al-Jāwzī I was not able to identify this figure.

Bakriyyah lodge another name for the Dilāʾ lodge, derived from the name of its founder, Abū Bakr ibn Muḥammad (d. 1021/1612).

Banū ʿAbd al-Ḥaqq the Merinid dynasty, which ruled Morocco from the seventh/thirteenth to the ninth/fifteenth century.

Banū Mūsā Arab tribe of the Tādlā region who were descended from the Banū Hilāl.

Banū Numayr Arab tribe of the plains of Yamāmah who were generally poor, which led to their raiding neighboring tribes.

Banū Sāsān term in classical Arabic literature referring variously to groups of tricksters or beggars.

Banū Warā a place in the Middle Atlas.

Banū Zirwāl mountains north of Fez, known for their grapes.

Barghawāṭah tribe of the Maṣmūdah tribal confederation who were initially Kharijites, before converting to Sunni Islam.

Bashshār [ibn Burd] famed Iraqi poet of the second/eighth century, who was born in Basra and achieved renown under both the Umayyads and the Abbasids despite his blindness and reputed ugliness.

Baṭn al-Rummān place known as Zāwiyah al-Shaykh on the left bank of the Umm Rabīʿ River in the Fazzāz region of the Middle Atlas.

Bawwān a place famous for its beauty in Iran, between Arjān and Nūbandjān.

Bilāl [ibn Rabāḥ] (d. between 17/638 and 21/642) Abyssinian slave and early convert to Islam, who attained fame as the first muezzin of Islam and who played a part in the conquest of Syria following the Prophet's death. He was buried in either Aleppo, Damascus, or Darayyā.

al-Buḥturī (d. 284/897) Abū ʿUbādah al-Walīd ibn ʿUbayd Allāh, Arab Abbasid poet and anthologist.

Chellah a Merinid necropolis just outside the walls of Rabat, built on the ruins of a Roman settlement, where there are also numerous tombs of saints.

Commander of the Faithful traditional title for the caliph; often used by al-Yūsī to refer to the second caliph, ʿUmar ibn al-Khaṭṭāb.

al-Dabbās (d. 523/1131) Ḥammād al-Dabbās, Baghdadi mystic who was famed for his miracles; spiritual teacher of ʿAbd al-Qādir al-Jīlānī.

al-Dajjāl apocalyptic figure who plays a similar role in Islamic eschatology to that of the Antichrist in Christian accounts of the end of days. He does not appear in the Qur'an, but is vividly described in the Hadith.

dāniq a sixth of a dirham.

Darʿah refers both to the river originating in the south of the High Atlas that flows into the Atlantic Ocean south of Cape Nun, and to the valley of the same name.

Dāy city in the Middle Atlas close to today's Banī Milāl that was known for harboring many diseases.

Day of the Portico the debate held shortly following the Prophet Muḥammad's death in 11/632 between the Muslims who had migrated to Medina from Mecca (*al-muhājirūn*) and those in Medina who had converted following the Prophet's arrival (*al-Anṣār*) in AD 622 regarding who should succeed the Prophet in the role of leading the community. The debate took place on a covered porch or portico (*saqīfah*) of the Banū Sāʿida, a tribe from Medina.

Dhū l-Rummah (d. 117/735) Abū l-Ḥārith Ghaylān ibn ʿUqbah, a Bedouin Arab poet of the Umayyad period, whose nickname Dhū l-Rummah means "the one with the frayed cord," and whose beloved was Mayyah.

al-Ḍimār a valley in Central Arabia.

Dukkālah initially a reference to a Berber tribal confederation, the name refers to the region between the rivers Umm Rabīʿ and Tensift, and the Atlantic coast.

Durayd [ibn Ṣimmah] (d. ca. 8/630) born ca. AD 530 and lived to the age of one hundred. He was famed for his skill in both fighting and poetry.

Farazdaq (d. 110/728 or 112/730) Tammām ibn Ghālib, prominent Arab poet who was famous for his rivalry with Jarīr and who died in Basra.

Farkalah area in the southern Tāfīlālt region of Morocco some eighty kilometers west of Rashidiyyah.

Fāṭimah (d. 11/632) the Prophet Muḥammad's oldest daughter (with his first wife, Khadījah), the wife of ʿAlī ibn Abī Ṭālib, and the mother of the Prophet's only grandsons, al-Ḥasan and al-Ḥusayn. She died soon after Muḥammad himself.

al-Fayḍ [ibn Muḥammad ibn al-Ḥakam] ibn Abī ʿAqīl husband of Ḥumaydah bint al-Nuʿmān ibn Bashīr (d. ca. 85/704), known as a young man for being handsome and fond of wine. Once, when drunk, he is said to have struck Ḥumaydah, which occasioned her mocking him in verse.

Fāzāz mountain in the High Atlas, southwest of Midelt and west of the Ḥamziyyah-ʿAyyāshiyyah lodge.

al-Ghaḍā' valley in Najd, in the Arabian Peninsula.

Gharandal village in the south of the Sinai.

al-Ghazālī (d. 505/1111) Abū Ḥāmid Muḥammad ibn Muḥammad al-Ṭūsī al-Ghazālī, famed Iranian jurist, theologian, philosopher, and Sufi who wrote the influential and at times controversial *Revival of the Religious Sciences,* which al-Yūsī studied and cited. He died in Ṭūs.

al-Habṭī (d. 963/1556) ʿAbd Allāh ibn Muḥammad al-Habṭī, scholar and Sufi who studied in the Ghamārah Mountains and al-Habṭ before moving to Fez and studying there. He subsequently founded a lodge in the al-Ashab

Mountains and was famous for teaching the women, children, and servants in the region the theological foundations of Islam and for writing a long didactic poem on correct practice. In the mid-tenth/sixteenth century he was at the center of a bitter controversy over the meaning of the *shahādah* (profession of faith).

Hadith the body of reports related from and about the Prophet Muḥammad, second only to the Qur'an in terms of importance in the Islamic legal and ethical traditions. I use the uppercase Hadith to refer to the body as a whole, the lowercase hadith to refer to individual reports.

al-Ḥajjāj [ibn Yūsuf] (d. 95/714) famously efficient and brutal administrator of the Umayyads.

al-Ḥājj al-Dilā'ī see Abū 'Abd Allāh Maḥammad al-Ḥājj.

Ḥamzah [ibn 'Abd al-Muṭṭalib] (d. 3/625) the Prophet Muḥammad's uncle, who was killed at the battle of Uḥud by the Meccan forces.

Ḥarb Arab Yemeni tribe largely based in the Ḥijāz region; the name also means "war" in Arabic.

Harim ibn Sinān al-Murrī leader of the Murrah tribe of North Arabia, who achieved fame for making peace after the war of Dāḥis wa l-Ghabrā' in the late sixth century.

ḥarīrah chickpea stew, made with lamb, chicken, or beef. A staple of Moroccan cuisine.

al-Ḥarīrī (d. 516/1122) Arab author of the famous *Maqāmāt* or *Assemblies*, who was born in Basra and lived much of his life there.

al-Ḥārith ibn Miskīn (d. 150/864) Egyptian judge.

al-Ḥārith al-Jafnī sixth-century leader of the Jafnah tribe who allied himself at times with the Byzantines and who fought repeated wars with the Lakhmid ruler al-Mundhir III.

al-Ḥasan al-Baṣrī (d. 110/728) famed preacher, scholar, and ascetic.

al-Ḥasan ibn 'Alī (d. 49/669–70) oldest son of the Prophet's cousin and son-in-law, 'Alī ibn Abī Ṭālib.

al-Hashtūkī see Abū 'Abbās Aḥmad ibn Abī Bakr al-Hashtūkī.

Haskūrah tribal confederation as well as a town of the same name, both in the High Atlas.

Ḥassān [ibn Thābit] (d. ca. 40/659) member of the Khazraj tribe who lived in Medina, and who became famous for the poetry he wrote in support of the Prophet and Islam following his conversion.

Ḥātim [al-Ṭāʿī] sixth-century poet famed for his extraordinary acts of generosity.

Haytham I have not been able to identify this figure.

Ḥijr village where the Thamūd lived, between Syria and Medina.

Hind bint ʿUtbah (d. during the reign of either ʿUmar ibn al-Khaṭṭāb [13–23/634–44] or ʿUthmāṇ [23–35/644–55]). At the beginning of Muḥammad's prophetic career she was the wife of Abū Sufyān ibn Ḥarb, and mother of Muʿāwiyah ibn Abī Sufyān, the future founder of the Umayyad dynasty. Muḥammad's uncle Ḥamzah killed her father at Badr, and she is notorious for having Ḥamzah's liver (or heart) brought to her after he was killed at Uḥud.

al-Ḥudaybiyyah village near Mecca where the Prophet and the Meccans made a truce in 6/628.

al-Hudhalī (Abu Kabīr) poet and contemporary of the Prophet who lived in the second half of the sixth and the beginning of the seventh century.

Ḥumayd ibn Thawr first/seventh-century poet who is thought to have converted to Islam and to have died during the reign of ʿUthmān or ʿAbd al-Malik.

al-Ḥusayn ibn al-Ḍaḥḥāk (d. 250/864) poet from Basra who died at the age of around one hundred.

al-Ḥuṭayʾah (fl. first/seventh century) Jarwal ibn Aws, early Islamic poet who converted nominally to Islam, and then left the faith after the Prophet's death during the *riddah* wars. He died during Muʿāwiyah ibn Abī Sufyān's reign as caliph and was famous for his avarice and the high quality of his poetry.

Iblīs name of the devil in Muslim tradition.

Ibn ʿAbbād (al-Rundī) (d. 792/1390) prominent Sufi of the eighth/fourteenth century who was from Ronda in al-Andalus, but left for North Africa, where he studied with Ibn ʿĀshir in Salé and settled in Fez, where he served as preacher in the Qarawiyyīn mosque from 777/1375 until his death. He wrote a famous commentary on the *Ḥikam* of Ibn ʿAṭāʾ Allāh.

Ibn ʿAbbās (d. 68/686–88) famed Companion of the Prophet and reputed father of Qurʾanic exegesis, who played an important role in the politics of the early Islamic period. He died in al-Ṭāʾif.

Ibn Abī Bakr al-Dilāʾī see Abū ʿAbd Allāh Maḥammad ibn Abī Bakr al-Dilāʾī.

Ibn Abī l-Barāʾ presumably one of the scholars of Qayrawān, where Abū l-Ḥasan al-Shādhilī was persecuted.

Ibn Abī Maḥallī (d. 1022/1613) Abū l-ʿAbbās Aḥmad ibn Abī Maḥallī, the scholar and Sufi from Sijilmāsah who claimed to be the savior and who attempted to establish himself as ruler of Morocco after the fall of Larache to the Spanish in 1017/1610. After successfully conquering Marrakesh and driving out the Saadi ruler Zaydān ibn Aḥmad al-Manṣūr, he was subsequently defeated and killed by Yaḥyā ibn ʿAbd Allāh al-Ḥāḥī (d. 1035/1626), who was acting on behalf of Zaydān.

Ibn ʿĀmir al-Shāmī (d. 118/736) famous early Qurʾan reciter, whose recitation is numbered among the canonical seven. He died in Damascus.

Ibn ʿArafah (d. 803/1401) Abū ʿAbd Allāh Muḥammad al-Warghammī, prominent and influential Tunisian Mālikī jurist.

Ibn ʿAṣmah I was not able to identify this scholar.

Ibn ʿAṭāʾ Allāh (Tāj al-Dīn) (d. 709/1309) Egyptian scholar and Sufi of the Shādhilī order who studied with Abū l-ʿAbbās al-Mursī and wrote the influential and much commented-upon *Ḥikam*. He died in Cairo.

Ibn Dabbūs judge in Fez in the sixth/twelfth century who opposed the teaching of theology (*kalām*).

Ibn al-Fāriḍ (d. 632/1235) famed Sufi and author of a much praised and commented-upon collection of poetry; he died in Cairo.

Ibn al-Ḥājj eighth/fourteenth-century Mālikī jurist from Cairo who wrote a work entitled *Introduction to the Noble Revealed Law* (*Madkhal al-sharʿ al-sharīf*).

Ibn Ḥamdīs al-Ṣaqallī (d. 527/1132–33) poet born in Sicily who left for al-Andalus and later North Africa, following the Norman invasion of 451/1060.

Ibn Ḥassūn see ʿAbd Allāh ibn Ḥassūn.

Ibn Ḥāzim Abbasid poet of the late second/eighth to third/ninth century.

Ibn al-Khaṭīb (d. 776/1374) Lisān al-Dīn ibn al-Khaṭīb, famous eighth/fourteenth-century polymath of Granada who is buried outside of Fez, where he was strangled in his jail cell after having been accused of heresy for his writings on Sufism.

Ibn Masʿūd (d. 32/652–53) famous Companion of the Prophet, renowned for his transmission of Hadith and Qurʾanic exegesis.

Ibn Mayyādah (d. 136/754 or 149/766) Abū Sharāḥīl al-Rammāḥ ibn Abrad, Bedouin poet who wrote panegyrics for the Umayyads and early Abbasids.

Ibn Mubārak al-Tastāwatī (d. 1006/1597–98) illiterate Sufi saint known for his miracles, a teacher of Ibn Abī Maḥallī. He was buried in Tāsawt.

Ibn Nāṣir see Abū ʿAbd Allāh Maḥammad ibn Nāṣir.

Ibn al-Rūmī (d. 283/896) Arab poet who was the descendant of a Byzantine convert, and who lived in Baghdad.

Ibn Tūmart (d. 524/1130) Abū ʿAbd Allāh Muḥammad ibn Tūmart al-Sūsī, founder of the messianic Almohad dynasty, which overthrew the Almoravids.

Ibn ʿUmar see ʿAbd Allāh ibn ʿUmar ibn al-Khaṭṭāb.

Ibrāhīm al-Laqānī (d. 1041/1632) Egyptian Mālikī scholar who wrote a number of well-known theological works, and an influential condemnation of the practice of smoking.

ʿImrān in the Qurʾan, the father of Moses, Aaron, and Mariam.

Imruʾ al-Qays [ibn Ḥujr] legendary sixth-century pre-Islamic king of the Kindah tribe and poet, author of one of the most famous pre-Islamic Arabic poems.

al-ʿIrāqī (d. 806/1404) ʿAbd al-Raḥīm ibn al-Ḥusayn al-Kurdī, scholar of Hadith, jurisprudence, and linguistics. He spent his life between Damascus, Aleppo, Alexandria, and the Hijaz, and died in Cairo. The line quoted by al-Yūsī is from his *A Thousand Verses on the Sciences of Hadith* (*Alfiyyah fī ʿulūm al-ḥadīth*).

ʿIṣām [ibn Shahbar al-Jarmī] chamberlain of al-Nuʿmān ibn al-Mundhir (d. 602), the last Lakhmid king of al-Ḥīrah.

Isḥāq al-Mawṣilī (d. 235/850) celebrated poet and musician from Rayy who lived and died in Baghdad.

al-Ishbīlī possibly Muḥammad al-Zubaydī al-Ishbīlī (d. 389/989), author of *The Ways in Which the Commoners of al-Andalus Err Linguistically* (*Mā yalḥanu fīhi ʿawām al-Andalus*).

Jaʿfar ibn Abī Ṭālib (d. 8/629) cousin of the Prophet, older brother of ʿAlī ibn Abī Ṭālib, and an early convert and member of the early group of Muslims who took refuge in Abyssinia, where he won the negus's favor by reciting Qurʾanic verses about Jesus. He returned on the day Muḥammad captured Khaybar (7/628) and died the following year as a martyr in battle at Muʾtah.

Jafnah the tribe of Jafnids, a subdivision of the Arab tribal confederation of the Ghassanids, which had settled in southern Syria in the fifth century and had converted to Monophysite Christianity.

Jāhiliyyah "age of ignorance," before the Prophet Muḥammad received revelation and spread the message of Islam.

Jarāwah branch of the Amazigh Zanatah confederation.

Jarīr [ibn ʿAṭiyyah ibn al-Khaṭafah] (d. ca. 110/728–29) prominent Arab poet and satirist who died at eighty, not long after the death of his long-time rival Farazdaq.

Junayd (d. 298/910) Abū Qāsim al-Junayd, famed representative of "sober" mysticism and a nephew and disciple of al-Sarī. He lived and died in Baghdad.

Kaʿb ibn ʿAwf I have not been able to identify this tribal grouping.

Kaʿb ibn Juʿayl minor poet of the early Umayyad period who was a partisan of Muʿāwiyah ibn Abī Sufyān's and wrote poetry supporting him politically. It is related that he gave his contemporary al-Akhṭal his nickname.

Kamīliyyah early Shiʿah sect, which, as described by al-Yūsī, held that the rightful imam needed to advocate for his right to rule, otherwise he should be opposed. Associated with Abū Kāmil Muʿādh ibn Ḥuṣayn al-Nabhānī in Kufa in the early second/eighth century, the movement dissipated following the revolt of al-Nafs al-Zakiyyah in the middle of the second/eighth century.

Kawthar name of a river or pool in paradise.

Khadījah the Prophet's first wife, who initially employed him in her affairs. She was a widow, who was some fifteen years his elder when he married her in his early twenties. She was the first convert to Islam and comforted him after the first revelations in 610. She died in 619, the same year as Muḥammad's uncle Abū Ṭālib, later known as the Year of Despair. As long as she was alive, the Prophet took no other wives.

Khalfūn site of a lodge founded by al-Yūsī on the Umm Rabīʿ River, near what is today Khanīfrah.

Khālid ibn al-Walīd (d. 21/642) famous general who played an important role in the early Islamic conquests.

al-Khansāʾ ("the snub-nosed one" or "the gazelle") (d. between AD 13/634 and 60/680) Tumāḍir bint ʿAmr, of the Sulaym tribe, she was born around AD 575 and acquired fame for her elegies for her brothers Muʿāwiyah ibn

Abī Sufyān and Ṣakhr, who were killed fighting the Murrah and Asad tribes. She refused the marriage proposal of Durayd ibn Ṣimmah (marrying a kinsman instead) and died in the reign of either ʿUmar or Muʿāwiyah.

Khārijah ibn Sinān leader in the sixth century of the Murrah tribe and brother of Harim ibn Sinān al-Murrī.

Kharijites group of Muslims in the first/seventh century who began as supporters of the fourth caliph, ʿAlī ibn Abī Ṭālib, only to rebel against him following his agreement to submit his dispute with Muʿāwiyah ibn Abī Sufyān to arbitration at the battle of Ṣiffīn in 37/657. One of their number killed ʿAlī himself in 40/661. In later centuries, Sunni scholars used their example as one of paradigmatic heresy.

Khaybar oasis inhabited by Jewish tribes near Medina, attacked by the Prophet and a Muslim force in 7/628. During the siege, ʿAlī ibn Abī Ṭālib distinguished himself repeatedly.

al-Khayf name of a mosque at the eastern end of the valley of Minā, near Mecca.

Khayr the Weaver (al-Nassāj) (d. 322/934) Muḥammad ibn Ismāʿīl, famous Sufi of Baghdad with a study circle.

al-Khayzurān [bint ʿAṭāʾ al-Jurashiyyah] favorite wife of the third Abbasid caliph, al-Mahdī (r. 158–69/775–85), and mother of Hārūn al-Rashīd.

Khazraj along with the Aws, one of the two main Arab tribes of Medina, early converts to Islam.

Kulāb valley on the side of the mountain Thahlān, in the lands of the Banū Numayr.

Kumayl ibn Ziyād [al-Nakhaʿī al-Kūfī] (d. ca. 82/701–2) close companion and supporter of ʿAlī ibn Abī Ṭālib, he was killed by the Umayyad governor al-Ḥajjāj and buried near what is now Najaf.

al-Kumayt al-Asadī (d. 126/743) Arab poet of Kufa and fervent supporter of the ʿAlids.

Labīd [ibn Rabīʿah Abū ʿAqīl] (d. 40/660–61) poet of the Jāhiliyyah, who lived through the Prophet's mission and converted to Islam. Most of his poetry was composed in the pre-Islamic period.

Lajāiyyah I have not been able to identify the exact location of this mountain.

Laktāwah village in the Darʿah Valley.

Laylā [al-ʿĀmiriyyah] legendary Arab Bedouin poet from the first century of Islam, and the cousin and obsessive love interest of Majnūn, from whom she was separated when young.

al-Maʿarrī see Abū l-ʿAlāʾ al-Maʿarrī.

Maḍgharah (often written Maṭgharah) Amazigh tribe belonging to the Butr confederation.

Maghrib "the West" (literally "where the sun sets"), used to describe North Africa, often particularly an area roughly coterminous with the current borders of Morocco (especially when specified as *al-Maghrib al-aqṣā* "the Farthest West").

Maḥammad ibn Abī Bakr [al-Dilāʾī] see Abū ʿAbd Allāh Maḥammad ibn Abī Bakr al-Dilāʾī.

Maḥammad ibn al-Sharīf (d. 1075/1664) first ruler of the nascent Alawite state, he administered Sijilmāsah and the surrounding area from 1050/1641 to 1074/1664, when he was killed in battle by his brother Rashīd, who would continue to consolidate Alawite power over much of Morocco.

al-Mahdī (d. 169/785) Abū ʿAbd Allāh Muḥammad, the third Abbasid caliph. Al-Khayzurān was his favorite wife.

Majannah, Shāmah, and Ṭafīl three mountains in Arabia near Mecca.

Majnūn (Qays) the legendary Bedouin of the Banū ʿĀmir ibn Ṣaʿṣaʿah, sometimes given the name Qays ibn al-Mulawwaḥ, who fascinated Arab, Persian, Turkish, and Urdu authors by having gone mad (*majnūn*) after his beloved Layla was promised in marriage to another.

Mālik [ibn Anas] (d. 179/796) reputed founder of the Mālikī school of jurisprudence, which was dominant in North Africa from the third/ninth century onward. He lived most of his life in Medina.

Maʿn ibn Zāʾidah (d. 152/769–70) Umayyad military commander.

Manʿij valley and river in northern Arabia.

al-Manṣūr see Aḥmad al-Manṣūr.

Manṣūr al-Namarī Abbasid poet of the second/eighth century.

al-Marākanah I have not been able to identify this location.

Māriyah daughter of Ẓālim ibn Wahb al-Kindī and mother of the Banū Jafnah, who lived in the sixth century.

Maslamah ibn ʿAbd al-Mālik (d. 121/738) son of the Umayyad caliph ʿAbd al-Mālik by a slave, he was not a candidate for the caliphate, but had an illustrious career as a general on the Byzantine frontier.

Maṣmūdah along with the Ṣanhājah, one of the two major Amazigh tribal confederations of Morocco. In al-Yūsī's day, they were split largely into two, the northern Maṣmūdah from the Sabū River to the Mediterranean, and the southern Maṣmūdah from south of the Umm al-Rabiʿ River to the Anti-Atlas.

Maysarah I have not been able to identify this place.

Meknes [al-Zaytūn] Moroccan city in the Middle Atlas, which, along with Fez and Marrakesh, enjoys the distinction of having been the seat of rule for a dynasty, in this case that of the Alawite ruler Moulay Ismāʿīl (d. 1139/1727).

Minā area in the hills about five miles to the east of Mecca, between it and Arafah. It plays an important role in the rituals of the pilgrimage, as this is both where the pilgrims spend the night and where they carry out the sacrifice commemorating Abraham's willingness to sacrifice his son Ishmael.

Moulouyah (Malwiyyah) major river with its source in the High Atlas in the ʿAyyashī Mountains, it flows through the Fezzaz region of the Middle Atlas into the Mediterranean near Saʿīdiyya.

Muʿāwiyah [ibn Abī Sufyān] (d. 60/680) founder of the Umayyad caliphate.

al-Muḥallaq (ʿAbd al-ʿAzīz ibn Ḥantam al-Kalābī) I have not found any information on him beyond the anecdote cited by al-Yūsī.

Muḥammad ibn Abī l-Qāsim (al-Sharqī al-Tādlawī) (d. 1010/1602) prominent Sufi known for his blessings and miracles.

Muḥammad ibn Mubārak al-Tastāwalī I have not been able to identify this scholar.

Muḥammad ibn Muḥammad ibn Nāṣir I have not been able to identify this scholar.

Muḥammad ibn Tamīm (d. 333/945) Mālikī jurist and poet from Qayrawān who, after revolting against the Fatimids, died in prison.

Muḥammad ibn Umayyah (200/815–?) most prominent member of a family of scribes in third/ninth-century Baghdad, he was also a minor poet.

Muḥammad al-Sharqī al-Tādlawī see Muḥammad ibn Abī l-Qāsim.

Muḥriz al-ʿUklī I was not able to identify this poet.

Muḥyī al-Dīn ibn al-ʿArabī (d. 638/1240) famous and influential Andalusī Sufi who shaped almost all Sufi thought after him and whose legacy was fiercely debated for centuries. He died in Damascus.

al-Munīfah well of the Tamīm tribe between Najd and Yamāma.

al-Muntaṣir billāh (d. 247–48/861–62) Abū Jaʿfar Muḥammad ibn Jaʿfar, eleventh Abbasid caliph, who died after a brief rule of six months.

Munyat al-Dukkāliyyah (d. 595/1199) Munyah bint Maymūn, Arab female saint known for the mortification of the flesh who lived in Marrakesh and made repeated visits to Ribāṭ Shākir.

al-Muqannaʿ al-Kindī (d. 70/690) Muḥammad ibn Ẓafar ibn ʿUmayr al-Kindī, Umayyad poet who veiled himself because of his great beauty, which he concealed for fear of attracting the evil eye.

al-Muraqqish name of two pre-Islamic poets, both of whom were known for their tragic love affairs.

al-Mutanabbī (d. 354/955) Abū l-Ṭayyib Aḥmad ibn al-Ḥusayn, arguably the most acclaimed Arab poet of the premodern period, nicknamed "the one who claims to be a prophet." He was murdered by raiding Bedouin after an eventful life at various courts in the eastern Mediterranean.

al-Muʿtaṣim (r. 218–227/833–842) Abū Isḥāq Muḥammad ibn Hārūn al-Rashīd, eighth Abbasid caliph and son of Hārūn al-Rashīd who succeeded his brother al-Maʾmūn.

al-Nābighah (fl. AD 570–600) Ziyād ibn Muʿāwiyah, pre-Islamic poet who wrote several poems for the Ghassanid king al-Nuʿmān ibn al-Ḥārith.

Nahshal Arab branch of the Banū Tamīm that settled in Khurasan, in eastern Iran.

al-Najāshī (d. 49/669) Qays ibn ʿAmr al-Ḥārithī, poet who was imprisoned by the caliph ʿUmar ibn al-Khaṭṭāb for his satire of the Banū l-ʿAjlān.

Najd plateau region in Arabia to the east of the coastal region next to the Red Sea.

al-Nāṣir [ibn al-Sulṭān al-Ghālib billāh] (d. 1004/1595 or 1005/1596) administrator of Tādlā during the life of his father the Saadi ruler ʿAbd Allāh, Aḥmad al-Manṣūr's older brother. After his uncle al-Manṣūr came to power in 986/1578, he fled to Spanish-controlled Asila and went into exile in Spain. In 1003/1595, al-Nāṣir landed in al-Malila in northern Morocco and raised an army against al-Manṣūr, seizing Tāzā. Al-Manṣūr sent army against him, defeated him, and sent his head to Marrakesh.

Naṣr ibn Sayyār (d. 131/748) last governor of Khurasan under the Umayyads, who faced an increasingly difficult situation during the last years of his administration.

al-Nawār wife of the famed poet Farazdaq (d. 112/730) who, after he divorced her, repented and longed after her.

al-Nuʿmān [ibn al-Mundhir] (d. AD 602) was the last Lakhmid king of Hirah, the north Arabian vassal state of the Sassanians.

al-Nūrī (d. 295/907) Aḥmad ibn Muḥammad al-Baghawī, Baghdadi Sufi disciple of al-Ṣarī as-Saqaṭī known for his "ecstatic" sayings.

al-Qalʿah Qalʿat Banī Ḥammād in the Maadid Mountains in modern-day Algeria.

al-Qālī (d. 356/967) Abū ʿAlī Ismāʿīl ibn al-Qāsim ibn ʿAydhūn ibn Hārūn ibn ʿĪsā ibn Muḥammad ibn Sulaymān al-Baghdādī, philologist of Turkish origin, who after studying in Baghdad settled in Cordoba in 330/942 at the invitation of the Cordoban caliph ʿAbd al-Raḥmān III's son al-Ḥakam and was instrumental in the transfer of linguistic knowledge from Iraq to al-Andalus. He was also the author of *al-Amālī* (*The Dictations*) and *Dhayl al-amālī wa-l-nawādir* (*Supplement to the Dictations and Rare Anecdotes*), a work al-Yūsī drew on extensively.

Qays branch of the northern Arabian Mudar, whose tribal identity becomes prominent during the Umayyad period in the early garrison cities founded outside the Arabian peninsula.

Quraysh tribe inhabiting Mecca into which the Prophet Muḥammad was born. During the early years of the Muslim community, the majority of the Quraysh were opponents of Islam, but by the time the Prophet died they had converted to Islam. As close relatives of the Prophet, they would play a central role in Muslim societies in the following centuries.

al-Quṭāmī (d. 101/719–20) ʿUmayr ibn Shiyaim, Christian poet who lived in the Umayyad period.

al-Rāḍī [billāh] (d. 329/940) twentieth Abbasid caliph, during whose time the power of the caliphate declined substantially.

Rashīd ibn al-Sharīf (al-Rashīd) (d. 1082/1672) founder of the Alawite dynasty that continues to rule Morocco today. After consolidating his rule over Morocco, and in the process destroying the Dilāʾ lodge where al-Yūsī had lived and studied, he based his capital in Fez.

rawḍah hall in the Prophet's mosque in Medina where the Prophet and his first two successors, Abū Bakr al-Ṣiddīq and ʿUmar ibn al-Khaṭṭāb, are buried.

ribāṭ word used in the Maghrib both to refer to a fortified city that was the base for military operations (such as the Almohad fortress Rabat, the current capital of Morocco) and to a building or establishment used by Sufis for contemplative devotion (overlapping in meaning here with *zāwiyah* or lodge).

Rijrājah tribal confederation based next to the Tansift River near Marrakesh.

al-Ṣaghīr ibn al-Manyār (d. 1056/1646) Muḥammad al-Ṣaghīr ibn Muḥammad, Sufi scholar known for his proficiency in Qurʾanic recitation.

Saʿīd ibn ʿAbd al-Munʿim al-Mannānī al-Ḥāḥī (d. either the 940s/1530s or 953/1546) prominent scholar and Sufi, known for his asceticism and piety, who was of the Berber Ḥāḥā tribal confederation of the Maṣmūdah in the Western High Atlas.

Saʿīd ibn al-Musayyab late first/seventh-century interpreter of dreams and scholar of Hadith.

al-Ṣalatān al-ʿAbdī (d. ca. 80/700) Qutham ibn Khabiyya al-ʿAbdī, famed Umayyad poet.

Ṣāliḥ [ibn ʿAbd al-Quddūs] (fl. second/eighth century) Abbasid poet and philosopher who was put to death for heresy under al-Mahdī or al-Mahdī's son Hārun al-Rashīd.

Salmah mountain range in the Ṭayy region in northern Arabia.

Salūl branch of the Hawāzin tribal confederation.

al-Samawʾal [ibn ʿAdiyāʾ] Arab-Jewish poet of the sixth century, famed for protecting the weapons Imruʾ al-Qays had entrusted to him even at the cost of the life of his own son.

Ṣanhājah see Maṣmūdah.

al-Sanūsī see Abū ʿAbd Allāh al-Sanūsī.

al-Sarī (Sarī al-Saqaṭī) (d. 253/867) renowned Sufi who lived and taught in Baghdad. He was also the uncle and teacher of Junayd.

Ṣaʿṣaʿh ibn Ṣuḥān (d. 56/676) prominent figure in early Kufan politics who sided with ʿAlī ibn Abī Ṭālib at Ṣiffīn and later interacted repeatedly with Muʿāwiyah ibn Abī Sufyān.

Sayf al-Dīn al-Āmidī (d. 631/1221) famed theologian who was accused of heresy while teaching in Cairo and who died in Damascus.

Sayf ibn Dhī Yazan mythical figure nominally based on the Ethiopian emperor Sayf(a) Arʿad, who is the protagonist of a folk epic that was most likely composed in Mamluk Egypt in the ninth/fifteenth to tenth/sixteenth centuries.

Shabānah branch of al-Maʿqil tribe of Yemeni origin that settled in North Africa during the reign of the Almohads.

al-Shaʿbī (d. between 103/721 and 110/728) early legal expert of Kufa.

Shādhilī order (Shādhiliyyah) Sufi order that emerged among the followers of the Moroccan Sufi Abū l-Ḥasan al-Shādhilī (d. 656/1258), who moved to and died in Egypt. Neither al-Shādhilī nor his successor, Abū l-ʿAbbās al-Mursī (d. 686/1287), left any books, and the written tradition of the order was provided by al-Mursī's successor, Ibn ʿAṭāʾ Allāh. The order grew in popularity in Egypt and North Africa in the ninth/fifteeth century, aided in Morocco by the efforts of Abū ʿAbd Allāh al-Jazūlī.

al-Shādhilī see Abū l-Ḥasan al-Shādhilī.

al-Shāfiʿī (d. 204/820) Abū ʿAbd Allāh Muḥammad ibn Idrīs al-Shāfiʿī, the eponym of the legal school that his students named after him; a student of Mālik ibn Anas, he wrote an early and enormously influential work on Islamic law and legal theory titled *The Epistle* (*al-Risālah*). He grew up in Medina, and later moved to Egypt, dying in Cairo.

al-Shanīn place in the Middle Atlas.

al-Shaʿrānī see ʿAbd al-Wahhāb al-Shaʿrānī.

al-Sharqī al-Tādlawī see Muḥammad ibn Abī l-Qāsim.

Shaybān Arab tribal group that belonged to the Bakr ibn Wāʾil. It was close to the Banū Hāshim during the rise of Islam and was later allied with the Abbasids.

shaykh ("master") term of respect used to designate a scholar or spiritual authority. In the organized Sufism of the post-formative period, each branch of a Sufi order had a shaykh who directed the spiritual practice of the order's devotees.

al-Shiblī see Abū Bakr al-Shiblī.

Sībawayhi famed second/eighth-century grammarian who, according to legend, disappeared after being defeated in competition by the grammarian al-Kisāʾī (d. 189/805).

sīdī designation of respect used in North Africa for prominent saints and scholars.

Sīdī al-Ghazwānī son of Muḥammad ibn Abī l-Qāsim, he later moved to Fez and studied under the prominent scholar Aḥmad al-Manjūr (d. 994/1586–87).

Sīdī Raḥḥāl [al-Kūsh] (d. in the 950s/1540s) saint known for his miracles living near Marrakesh in Anmāy, where he died and was buried.

Sijilmāsah main city of the Tāfīlālt region in the south of Morocco, and until the tenth/sixteenth century an important stop on the trade route with sub-Saharan Africa. The ancestral home of the Alawite dynasty.

Subū large river in northern Morocco, which passes near Fez and enters the ocean at Mahdiyya.

Suhayl [ibn ʿAmr] (d. 18/639) Meccan leader of the Quraysh who converted following Muḥammad's taking of the city in 630, shortly before the conversion of Abū Sufyān. During the conquest of the Levant he died in the plague of ʿAmwās.

Sulaymān [ibn Sālim] al-Kalāʿī (d. 634/1237) Andalusī Mālikī scholar and prominent Hadith scholar who died in battle, and, aside from two short visits to North Africa, never left al-Andalus.

Sūs valley in the southern region of Morocco between the High Atlas and the Anti-Atlas mountains.

al-Suyūṭī (d. 911/1505) Abū l-Faḍl ʿAbd al-Raḥmān ibn Abī Bakr, possibly the most prolific Muslim author of all time, an Egyptian polymath of the Shāfiʿī school who wrote on virtually every subject, but especially on Hadith and the Qurʾan.

Tādlā large region in central Morocco stretching from the origins of the Umm Rabīʿ and Moulouyah rivers in the north to the High Atlas in the south. Originally Berber, the region was settled by a number of Arab tribes during the Almohad period in the sixth/twelfth century.

Tāghzūt small village in the region of Huceima in the north of Morocco.

Tāj al-Dīn ibn ʿAṭāʾ Allāh see Ibn ʿAṭāʾ Allāh.

Tāmaghrawāt I was not able to identify this location.

Tamīm ibn al-Muʿizz name of both the son of the fourth Fatimid caliph (d. 374/985), and the fifth Zīrid ruler of Ifriqiyyah (d. 501/1108).

Ṭarafah [ibn al-ʿAbd] famed sixth-century pre-Islamic poet who belonged to the Qays ibn Thaʿlaba section of the Bakr ibn Wāʾil tribe. Little is known of his life, but he is said to be related to the poets al-Muraqqish (father and son) and al-Mutalammis, as well as having a sister, Khirniq, who was also a poet.

Ṭayy name that designates both the Arab tribe that settled in the north of Arabia and the region itself.

al-Thaʿālibī see ʿAbd al-Raḥmān al-Thaʿālibī.

Thaqīf powerful Arabian tribe that opposed the Prophet Muḥammad until after the Muslims' failed siege of al-Ṭā'if in 8/630, when the Prophet convinced their Bedouin allies to abandon them and the Thaqīf came to Medina to convert to Islam.

Tilimsān city in what is today western Algeria, some sixty kilometers from the border with modern Morocco and outside of the control of the Alawite kingdom of the eleventh/seventeenth century.

Tīrā river in the Aḥwāz region of southwestern Iran.

Tuwāt collection of oases in the south of modern Algeria, conquered by Aḥmad al-Manṣūr in the tenth/sixteenth century as part of his attempt to consolidate control over the caravan trade with West Africa and in preparation of his conquest of the Songhay Empire.

'Ubayd ibn Ḥaṣīn member of the Numayr tribe satirized by Jarīr.

Uḥud mountain between Mecca and Medina, site of a battle at Mount Uḥud that took place in 3/625 or 4/626, and was the first military defeat experienced by the Muslim community; in it over seventy Muslims, including the Prophet's uncle Ḥamzah, were killed by the Meccans.

'Ukāẓ most important pre-Islamic tribal market fair in Arabic, held to the southeast of Mecca in the territory of the Hawāzin.

'Umar ibn 'Abd al-'Azīz (r. 99–101/717–720) eighth Umayyad caliph, who in later tradition became famous for his piety.

'Umar ibn al-Khaṭṭāb (r. 13/634) second caliph after the Prophet Muhammad's death, known in Sunni tradition for his moral probity and occasionally harsh nature.

Umayyah ibn Abī l-Ṣalt pre-Islamic poet who lived to see the beginnings of Islam.

Umm Rabī' one of Morocco's three major rivers, it originates in the Middle Atlas and flows west, entering the ocean near al-Jadīdah.

'Uqbah ibn Nāfi' [al-Fihrī] (d. 63/683) Companion of the Prophet and the nephew of the conqueror and then administrator of Egypt, 'Amr ibn al-'Āṣ, he led Muslim expeditions west into North Africa, founded the city of Qayrawān, and later continued farther into what is now Morocco. He later became legendary as the Muslim conqueror of North Africa.

'Urwah ibn Ḥizām (d. ca. 30/650) early Islamic poet, famous for writing poetry on chaste, unrequited love (*'Udhrī*).

ʿUrwah ibn Udhaynah Arab Umayyad poet from Medina who is known for his love poetry. He was alive during the reign of the caliph Hishām (105–25/724–43).

ʿUrwah ibn al-Ward pre-Islamic poet of the ʿAbs clan, considered a *ṣuʿlūk* or brigand poet.

ʿUrwah ibn al-Zubayr (d. 93/711–12 or 94/712–13) son of the Prophet's Companion and brother of the counter-caliph ʿAbd Allāh ibn al-Zubayr, who was twenty years his senior. He was a scholar and jurist who distinguished himself in the field of Hadith. He lived much of his life in Medina and died there.

ʿUthmān [ibn ʿAffān] (r. 23–35/644–55) third caliph after the Prophet. An early convert who belonged to the prominent Meccan clan Banū Umayya, he oversaw a dramatic period of expansion of Islamic rule, was criticized by some for nepotism and corruption, and was murdered in Medina under unclear circumstances.

Uways al-Qaranī (d. 37/657) semilegendary early Muslim said to have died at the Battle of Ṣiffīn fighting on the side of ʿAlī ibn Abī Ṭālib, and regarding whom it was later alleged that he and the Prophet communicated by telepathy (they did not meet in person).

Wāʾil see Bakr ibn Wāʾil.

al-Walīd see al-Buḥturī.

Wāsiṭ a city in central Iraq.

al-Yāfiʿī (d. 768/1367) Abū ʿAbd Allāh ibn Asʿad, Abu l-Saʿāda ʿAfīf al-Dīn, Sufi from Yemen who lived most of his life in Mecca. He founded a branch of the Qādiriyyah and as an Ashʿarite wrote against Muʿtazilism.

Yaḥyā ibn Yūnus I was not able to identify this figure.

Yaʿlā ibn Mṣlīn al-Rijrājī Berber warrior who was the third of three sent by their teacher Abū Muḥammad ibn Tīsīt from Aghmāt to fight the Barghwāṭah tribes. He was successful where the first two had failed, and at the end of the fourth/tenth century built Ribāṭ Shākir as a defense against future raids.

Yūsuf al-ʿAjamī (d. 768/1367) Sufi and scholar who is said to have revived the sober Sufism of Junayd in Egypt. He was known for his harsh disciplining of his followers.

Yusūf ibn ʿUmar [al-Thaqafī] Umayyad governor of Iraq between 120/738 and 126/744, and as such was responsible for putting down the rebellion in Kufa of Zayd ibn ʿAlī in 122/739–40.

Yūsuf al-Wafāʾī I was not able to identify this scholar.

al-Zalāmīṭ I was not able to identify this location.

Zarrūq see Abū ʿAbbās Aḥmad Zarrūq.

Zaydān ibn Aḥmad al-Manṣūr (d. 1036/1627) one of Aḥmad al-Manṣūr's three sons who fought with each other for control of Morocco following their father's death in 1012/1603. Although he never asserted himself over all Morocco, Zaydān emerged as the strongest of the three, basing himself in Marrakesh.

Zaydān ibn ʿUbayd al-Āmiri (d. 1083/1672) head of the Alawite troops in Fez during the reign of Moulay Rashīd and the beginning of the reign of Moulay Ismāʿīl, killed when the people of Fez revolted following the death of Moulay Rashīd.

Zayd ibn ʿAlī (d. 122/740) great-grandson of ʿAlī ibn Abī Ṭālib, who revolted against the Umayyads and was killed. His attempted revolt gave rise to the Zaydī branch of the Shiʿah.

Zuhayr [ibn Abī Sulmā Rabīʿa] famed pre-Islamic early seventh-century poet who composed one of the hanging odes on the figure of Harim ibn Sinān al-Murrī.

zunnār distinctive belt that was to be worn by non-Muslim monotheists living under Muslim rule to distinguish them from the Muslim population. In practice, it was only selectively enforced as an obligation.

Chronology of Major Events Relevant to *The Discourses*

974/1566	Abū Bakr ibn Muḥammad (d. 1021/1612) founds the Dilā' lodge, which has close ties with the Shādhilī Sufi order.
983/1576	Aḥmad ibn Ibrāhīm al-Anṣārī founds in Tamgrut what will later be called the Nāṣirī lodge, after one of its prominent students.
1012/1603	Death of Aḥmad al-Manṣūr, last Sa'dī to rule all Morocco.
1022/1613	Death of the messianic rebel Ibn Abī Maḥallī.
1036/1627	Death of Zaydān ibn Aḥmad al-Manṣūr, son of Aḥmad al-Manṣūr and ruler of Marrakesh.
1040/1631	Al-Yūsī is born in Tamzīzīt in the Fezāz region of the Middle Atlas of Morocco, near Sefrou.
1044/1634–35	Muḥammad ibn Abī Bakr al-'Ayyāshī (d. 1067/1657), father of the famed traveler Abū Sālim al-'Ayyāshī (d. 1090/1679) and student of Abū Bakr al-Dilā'ī and Maḥammad ibn Abī Bakr al-Dilā'ī, founds the 'Ayyāshī lodge in the High Atlas (later renamed the Sidi Ḥamza lodge after one of his descendants).
1046/1636	Death of Maḥammad ibn Abī Bakr al-Dilā'ī, second head of the Dilā' lodge, at the age of nearly eighty.
1050s/1640s	Al-Yūsī travels widely within Morocco, studying in, among other places, Sijilmāsah, Marrakesh, and Taroundant, where he is briefly appointed to teach in the Great Mosque (at not yet twenty years of age).
1060/1650	Al-Yūsī makes his first visit to the Nāṣirī lodge in Tamgrūt, where the head of the lodge, Abū 'Abd Allāh Maḥammad ibn Nāṣir, inducts him into the Shādhilī order of Sufism.
1063–79/1653–68	Al-Yūsī lives and works at the Dilā' Sufi lodge in the Middle Atlas, which during these years is the main political and intellectual center in northern Morocco, led by Abū 'Abd Allāh Maḥammad al-Ḥājj al-Dilā'ī, grandson of its founder.

1070s/1660s	Al-Yūsī witnesses a controversy in Sijilmāsah regarding the proper meaning of the *shahādah*. This controversy continued until 1090/1679, ending when the plague killed the principal participants.
1079/1668	Rashīd ibn al-Sharīf (d. 1082/1672), the first ruler of the ʿAlawite dynasty, razes the Dilāʾ lodge and brings al-Yūsī and other scholars to Fez.
1082/1671	Death of Abū ʿAbd Allāh Maḥammad ibn Nāṣir, third leader of the Dilāʾ lodge, in exile in Algeria.
1083/1672	Al-Yūsī founds a lodge at Khalfūn on the Umm Rabīʿ River, near what is today Khanīfrah. Due to his being seen as a potential political threat by Moulay Ismāʿīl (d. 1139/1722), the second ʿAlawite ruler, he spends little time here.
1085/1674	Death of Abū ʿAbd Allāh Maḥammad ibn Nāṣir, head of the Nāṣirī Shādhilī Sufi lodge in Tamgrūt.
1087–90/1676–79	Moulay Ismāʿīl sends al-Yūsī to Marrakesh, where he teaches at the Ashrāf Mosque.
1090/1679	Moulay Ismāʿīl sends al-Yūsī to Meknes, which he has chosen as the new capital for the ʿAlawite dynasty.
1090–93/1681–82	Moulay Ismāʿīl sends al-Yūsī to Marrakesh.
1095–98/1684–87	Moulay Ismāʿīl sends al-Yūsī to reside in the ruins of the Dilāʾ lodge.
1095/1683–84	Al-Yūsī begins writing *The Discourses*, which he finishes three years later.
1101/1690	Al-Yūsī performs the pilgrimage to Mecca with Moulay Ismāʿīl's son al-Muʿtaṣim.
1102/1691	Al-Yūsī dies in his hometown of Tamzīzīt near Sefrou; his body is later moved to a tomb near Sefrou.

Bibliography

Abū Tammām, Ḥabīb ibn Aws. *Diwān al-ḥamāsa*. Edited by Aḥmad Ḥasan Basaj. Beirut: Dār al-Kutub al-ʿIlmiyya, 1998.

Ali, Kecia. *Marriage and Slavery in Early Islam*. Cambridge, MA: Harvard University Press, 2010.

Berque, Jacques. *Al-Yousi: Problèmes de la culture marocaine au XVIIème siècle*. Paris: Mouton, 1958.

Cook, Michael. *Commanding Right and Forbidding Wrong in Islamic Thought*. Cambridge, UK: Cambridge University Press, 2000.

Cornell, Vincent. *Realm of the Saint: Power and Authority in Moroccan Sufism*. Austin: University of Texas Press, 1998.

———. *The Way of Abū Madyan: Doctrinal Works of Abū Madyan Shuʿayb ibn al-Ḥusayn al-Anṣārī*. Cambridge, UK: The Islamic Texts Society, 1996.

Al-Darʿī, Muḥammad al-Makkī ibn Mūsa ibn Nāṣir. *Al-Durar al-muraṣṣaʿah bi-akhbār aʿyān Darʿah*. 2 vols. Edited by Muḥammad al-Ḥabīb Nūḥī. Casablanca: al-Mu'assasah al-Nāṣiriyyah li-l-thaqāfah wa l-ʿilm, 2014.

El-Rouayheb, Khaled. *Islamic Intellectual History in the Seventeenth Century: Scholarly Currents in the Ottoman Empire and the Maghreb*. Cambridge, UK: Cambridge University Press, 2015.

———. "Opening the Gate of Verification: The Forgotten Arab-Islamic Florescence of the 17th century." *International Journal of Middle East Studies* 38 (2006): 263–81.

García-Arenal, Mercedes, and Gerard Wiegers. *A Man of Three Worlds: Samuel Pallache, a Moroccan Jew in Catholic and Protestant Europe*. Baltimore: Johns Hopkins University Press, 2003.

García-Arenal, Mercedes. *Messianism and Puritanical Reform: Mahdīs of the Muslim West*. Leiden: Brill, 2006.

———. "Les Bildiyyīn de Fès, un groupe de néo-musulmans d'origine juive." *Studia Islamica* 66 (1987): 113–44.

Geertz, Clifford. *Islam Observed: Religious Development in Morocco and Indonesia*. Chicago: University of Chicago Press, 1968.

Griffel, Frank. "Ibn Tūmart's Rational Proof for God's Existence and Unity, and His Connection to the Niẓāmiyya Madrasa in Baghdad." In *Los Almohades: Problemas y Perspectivas* edited by Patrice Cressier, María Isabel Fierro, and Luis Molina, vol. 2, 753–813. Madrid: CSIC, 2005.

Gutelius, David. "Between God and Man: The Nāṣiriyya and Economic Life in Morocco, 1640–1830." PhD diss., Johns Hopkins University, 2001.

Al-Ḥarīrī, al-Qāsim ibn ʿAlī. *Maqāmāt al-Ḥarīrī.* Beirut: Dār Ṣādr, 1980.

Hammoudi, Abdallah. "Sainteté, pouvoir et societé: Tamgrout aux XVIIe et XVIIIe siècles." *Annales* 35 (1980): 615–41.

Head, Gretchen. "Space, Identity, and Exile in Seventeenth-Century Morocco: The Case of Abū ʿAlī al-Ḥasan al-Yūsī." *Journal of Arabic Literature* 47 (2016): 231–59.

———. "Moroccan Autobiography: The Rhetorical Construction of the Self and the Development of Modern Arabic Narrative in al-Maghrib al-Aqṣā." PhD diss., University of Pennsylvania, 2011.

Honerkamp, Kenneth. "Al-Ḥasan ibn Masʿūd al-Yūsī." In *Essays in Arabic Literary Biography 1350–1850.* Edited by Joseph E. Lowry and Devin J. Stewart, 410–18. Wiesbaden: Harrassowitz Verlag, 2009.

Al-Ḥuḍaygī, Muḥammad ibn Aḥmad. *Ṭabaqāt al-Ḥuḍaygī.* 2 vols. Edited by Aḥmad Bū Mazgū. Casablanca: Maṭbaʿat al-Najāḥ, 2006.

Ibn Khaldūn. *The Muqaddimah.* Translated by Franz Rosenthal. 3 vols. Princeton: Princeton University Press, 1958.

Ibn Kathīr. *Tafsīr.* 4 vols. Beirut: Al-Maktabah al-ʿAsriyyah, 1998.

Ibn Manẓūr, Jamāl al-Dīn Muḥammad ibn Mukarram al-Ifrīqī. *Lisān al-ʿArab.* Edited by ʿAbd Allāh ʿAlī al-Kabīr, Muḥammad Aḥmad Ḥasab Allāh, and Hāshim Muḥammad al-Shādhilī. Cairo: Dār al-Maʿārif, 1981.

Ibn Zaydān. *Al-Manza al-laṭīf fī mafākhir al-mawlā Ismāʿīl ibn al-Sharīf.* Edited by ʿAbd al-Hādī al-Tāzī. Casablanca: Maṭbaʿat Idyāl, 1993.

Iḥnāna, Yūsuf. *Tatawwur al-madhhab al-ashʿarī fī l-gharb al-islāmī.* 2nd ed. Rabat: Manshūrāt Wizārat al-Awqāf, 2017.

Jacques-Meunié, Denise. *Le Maroc saharien: Des origins à 1670.* 2 vols. Paris: Librairie Klinksieck, 1989.

Al-Jīdī, ʿUmar. *Al-Tashrīʿ al-islāmī.* Rabat: Manshūrāt ʿUkāẓ, 1987.

Kugle, Scott. *Sufis and Saints' Bodies: Mysticism, Corporality, and Sacred Power in Islam.* Chapel Hill: University of North Carolina Press, 2011.

Lane, Edward. *An Arabic-English Lexicon.* 8 vols. London: Williams and Norgate, 1863 (offset edition Beirut: Librairie du Liban, 1968).

Livne-Kafri, Ofer. "The Muslim Traditions 'In Praise of Jerusalem' (Faḍā'il al-Quds): Diversity and Complexity." *Annali (Istituto universitario orientale)* 58 (1998): 165–92.

Al-Madgharī, 'Abd al-Kabīr. *Al-Faqīh Abū 'Alī al-Yūsī.* Rabat: Wizārat al-Awqāf wa-l-Shu'ūn al-Islāmiyyah, 1989.

Mayyārah, Muḥammad ibn Aḥmad ibn Muḥammad. *Naṣīḥat al-mughtarrīn wa-kifāyat al-muḍtarrīn.* Edited and introduced by Muḥammad al-Ghurāyab and Muṣtafā Bin'alah. Rabat: Rabat Net Publishing, 2013.

Maziane, Leïla. *Salé et ses corsaires (1666–1727): Un port de course marocain au XVIIe siècle.* Caen: Presse universitaires de Caen, 2007.

Munson, Henry. *Religion and Power in Morocco.* New Haven: Yale University Press, 1993.

Al-Nāṣirī, Aḥmad ibn Khālid. *Al-Istiqṣā'.* Edited by Aḥmad ibn Ja'far al-Nāṣirī. 9 vols. Casablanca: Wizārat al-Thaqāfah wa-l-Ittiṣāl, 2001.

Al-Qāḍī al-Quḍā'ī. *A Treasury of Virtues: Sayings, Sermons, and Teachings of 'Alī.* Edited and translated by Tahera Qutbuddin. New York: NYU Press, 2013.

Al-Qādirī, Muḥammad ibn al-Ṭayyib. *Nashr al-mathānī li-ahl al-qarn al-ḥādī 'ashr wa l-thānī.* 4 vols. Edited by Muḥammad Ḥajjī and Aḥmad al-Tawfīq. Rabat: Maktabah al-Ṭālib, 1982.

Rabinow, Paul. *Reflections on Fieldwork in Morocco.* Berkeley: University of California Press, 1977.

Reichmuth, Stefan. "The Praise of a Sufi Master as a Literary Event: Al-Ḥasan al-Yūsī (1631–1691), His Dāliyya (Qaṣīdat at-tahānī) and Its Commentary (Nayl al-amānī)." In *Ethics and Spirituality in Islam: Sufi Adab.* Edited by Francesco Chiabotti, Eve Feuillebois-Pierunek, Catherine Mayeur-Jaouen, and Luca Patrizi, 504–19. Leiden: Brill, 2016.

Rius Piniés, Mònica. *La alquibla en al-Andalus y al-Magrib al-Aqṣà.* Barcelona: Institut Millás Valicrosa, 2000.

Rodriguez-Mañas, Francisco. "Charity and Deceit: The Practice of the *iṭ'ām al-ṭa'ām* in Moroccan Sufism." *Studia Islamica* 91 (2000): 59–90.

Rouighi, Ramzi. "The Andalusi Origins of the Berbers?" *Journal of Medieval Iberian Studies* 2 (2010), 93–108.

Saad, Elias. *Social History of Timbuktu: The Role of Muslim Scholars and Notables 1400–1900.* Cambridge, UK: Cambridge University Press, 1983.

Sayeed, Asma. *Women and the Transmission of Religious Knowledge in Islam.* Cambridge, UK: Cambridge University Press, 2013.

Serrano Ruano, Delfina. "Later Ash'arism in the Islamic West." In *The Oxford Handbook of Islamic Theology.* Edited by Sabine Schmidtke. Oxford, UK: Oxford University Press, 2016.

Staples, Eric. "Intersections: Power, Religion, and Technology in Seventeenth-Century Sale-Rabat." PhD diss., University of California Santa Barbara, 2008.

Stearns, Justin. "'All Beneficial Knowledge is Revealed': The Rational Sciences in the Maghrib in the Age of al-Yūsī (d. 1102/1691)." *Islamic Law and Society* 21 (2014): 49–80.

———. *Infectious Ideas: Contagion in Premodern Islamic and Christian Thought in the Western Mediterranean*. Baltimore: Johns Hopkins University Press, 2011.

Touati, Houari. "Les héritiers: anthropologie des Maisons de science maghrébines aux XIe/XVIIe et XIIe/XVIIIe siècles." In *Modes de transmission de la culture religieuse en Islam*. Edited by Hassan Elboudrari, 65–92. Cairo: Institut français d'archéologie orientale du Caire, 1993.

Wiegers, Gerald. "A Life between Europe and the Maghrib: The Writings and Travels of Aḥmad b. Qâsim al-Ḥajarī al-Andalusî (Born c. 977/1569–70)." In *The Middle East and Europe: Encounters and Exchanges*. Edited by Geert Jan van Gelder and Ed de Moor, 87–115. Amsterdam: Rodopi, 1992.

Wilson, Peter Lamborn. *Pirate Utopias*. 2nd ed. New York: Autonomedia, 2003.

Yāqūt al-Ḥamawī. *Muʿjam al-buldān*. 5 vols. Beirut: Dār Ṣādir, 1977.

Al-Yūsī, al-Ḥasan. *Dīwān al-Yūsī*. Edited by ʿAbd al-Jawwād Saqqāṭ. Rabat: Maṭbaʿ Dār al-Manāhil, 2016.

———. *Fahrasat al-Yūsī*. Edited by Ḥamīd Ḥamānī al-Yūsī. Casablanca: Maṭbaʿ Dār al-Furqān, 2004.

———. *Ḥawāshī al-Yūsī ʿalā sharḥ kubrā al-Sanūsī*. Edited by Ḥamīd Ḥamānī al-Yūsī. 2 vols. Casablanca: Maṭbaʿ Dār al-Furqān, 2008–12.

———. *Mashrab al-ʿĀmm wa-l-khāṣṣ min kalimat al-ikhlāṣ*. Edited by Ḥamīd Ḥamānī al-Yūsī. 2 vols. Casablanca: Dār al-Furqān li-l-Nashr al-Ḥadīth, 2000.

———. *Al-Muḥāḍarāt fī l-adab wa-l-lughah*. Edited by Muḥammad Ḥajjī and Aḥmad al-Sharqāwī Iqbāl. Beirut: Dār al-Gharb al-Islāmī, 1982.

———. *Al-Qānūn fī aḥkām al-ʿilm wa aḥkām al-ʿālim wa aḥkām al-mutaʿallim*. Edited by Ḥamīd Ḥamānī al-Yūsī. Rabat: Maṭbaʿat Shālat al-Rabāṭ, 1998.

———. *Rasāʾil Abī ʿAlī al-Ḥasan ibn Masʿūd al-Yūsī*. Edited by Fāṭima Khalīl al-Qablī. 2 vols. Casablanca: Dār al-Thaqāfah, 1981.

———. *Zahr al-akam fī l-amthāl wa-l-ḥikam*. Edited by Muḥammad Ḥajjī and Muḥammad al-Akhḍar. 3 vols. Casablanca: Dār al-Thaqāfah, 1981.

Al-Zabīdī, Muḥammad Murtaḍ. Tāj al-ʿArūs. Edited by ʿAbd al-Munʿim Ibrāhīm and Karīm Sayyid Muḥammad Maḥmūd. Beirut: Dar al-Kotob al-Ilmiyah, 2012.

Al-Zayānī, Abū Qāsim ibn Aḥmad. *Le Maroc de 1631 à 1812: Extrait de l'ouvrage intitulé Ettordjemân almor'arib ʿan douel elmaghrib*. Edited and translated by O. Houdas. Rabat: Dar Al Amane, 2013 (1886).

Further Reading

Berque, Jacques. *L'intérieur du Maghreb: XVe – XIXe siècle*. Paris: Éditions Gallimard, 1978.

———. *Ulémas, fondateurs, insurgés du Maghreb*. Paris: Sindbad, 1982.

Boum, Aomar. *Memories of Absence: How Muslims Remember Jews in Morocco*. Stanford: Stanford University Press, 2013.

Ernst, Carl. *Words of Ecstasy in Sufism*. Albany: SUNY Press, 1984.

García-Arenal, Mercedes. *Ahmad al-Mansur: The Beginnings of Modern Morocco*. Oxford: Oneworld, 2009.

Al-Ḥajjī, Muḥammad. *Al-Ḥarakah al-fikriyyah fī 'ahd al-Sa'diyyah*. 2 vols. Rabat: Manshūrāt Dār al-Maghrib, 1976.

Harrak, Fatima. "State and Religion in Eighteenth Century Morocco: The Religious Policy of Sidi Muhammad b. 'Abd Allāh," PhD thesis. University of London, 1989.

Kilito, Abdelfattah. *Arabs and the Art of Storytelling: A Strange Familiarity*. Syracuse: Syracuse University Press, 2014.

Kister, M. J. "Call Yourself by Graceful Names." In M. J. Kister, *Society and Religion from Jāhiliyya to Islam*, 3–25. Aldershot, UK: Variorum, 1990.

Knysh, Alexander. *Sufism: A New History of Islamic Mysticism*. Princeton: Princeton University Press, 2017.

Kugle, Scott. *Rebel between Spirit and Law: Ahmad Zarruq, Sainthood, and Authority in Islam*. Bloomington: Indiana University Press, 2006.

Michon, Jean-Louis. *The Autobiography of the Moroccan Sufi Ibn 'Ajība*. Translated by David Streight. Louisville, KY: Fons Vitae, 1999.

Al-Qaddūrī, 'Abd al-Majīd. *Ibn Abī Maḥallī al-faqīh al-thā'ir wa rihlatu-hu al-iṣlīt al-kharrīt*. 2nd ed. Casablanca: Kullīyat al-Adab, 2013.

Renard, John. *Friends of God: Islamic Images of Piety, Commitment, and Servanthood*. Berkeley: University of California Press, 2008.

Sanseverino, Ruggero Vimercati. *Fès et sainteté, de la fondation à l'avènement du Protectorat (808–1912)*. Rabat: Centre Jacques Berque, 2014.

Touati, Houari. *Entre Dieu et les hommes: Lettres, saints et sorciers au Maghreb (17e siècle)*. Paris: Éditions de l'École des Hautes Études en Sciences Sociales, 1994.

Warscheid, Ismail. *Droit musulman et société au Sahara prémoderne: La justice islamique dans les oasis du Grant Touat (Algérie) aux XVIIe–XIXe siècles*. Leiden: Brill, 2017.

Index of Qur'anic Verses

Index of Hadith

§3.3 If you send me a messenger, let it be someone who has a pleasant face and an auspicious name.

§3.4 May things go well for you.

May God be reconciled with Aslam, "Soundest," and forgive Ghifār, "Forgiven," whereas 'Uṣayyah, "Disobedient," has disobeyed God and His Prophet.

§3.17 Seek goodness in pleasant faces.

§3.19 A son was born to me that evening and I named him after my ancestor Abraham.

They were named after the names of their prophets.

§5.2 Do not give people the names of angels.

§5.3 Name people after me, but do not call them by my teknonym.

In God's view, the most perfidious name is that of a man called king of kings.

§6.3 God made Medina beloved to us to the same extent as Mecca, if not more.

§6.7 Hearts are created with a disposition to love those who treat them well.

§6.9 It is a mountain that loves us as we love it.

§6.16 The genealogists lie.

§6.17 You are the sons of Adam, and Adam came from dust.

§6.18 God preserved you from the foibles of the Time of Ignorance and the vaunting of ancestors that took place then. You are the sons of Adam and Adam was made from dust.

§6.28 Honor your aunt, the palm tree.

§6.30 You are the sons of Adam . . .

§6.36 The one who is noble is the son of someone who is noble, going back three generations: Joseph, son of Jacob, son of Isaac, son of Abraham, thus a prophet who was the son of a prophet, son of a prophet, son of a prophet.

§6.39 Suhayl and Abū Sufyān. Islam elevates and is not surpassed.

§6.54 Truly, her father loved generous deeds.

§6.59 The noble is the son of the noble.

§6.60 I was sent to exemplify noble qualities.

Truly, God chose Ishmael from Abraham's sons, and chose the Banū Kanāna from Ishmael's sons, the Quraysh from the Banū Kanāna, the Banū Hāshim from the Quraysh, and me from the Banū Hāshim.

§6.62 Truly, in poetry there is wisdom.

§7.7 I am the prayer of my father Abraham, eternal peace be his, and the dream of my mother.

§8.1 Matters are best at their mean.

§8.2 God created Adam in his image.

§8.7 The angel of the mountains came to the Prophet, God bless and keep him, on the day of Thaqīf, and said to him, "What do you wish? Shall I cast the two peaks of al-Akhshabayn upon them?" He, God bless and keep him, said, "I implore you rather that God bring from their loins worshippers of God who associate none with Him."

§8.8 Whoever resembles a people is one of them.

§9.4 The Prophet, God bless and keep him, was working one day in the house, and I glanced at his face, God bless and keep him, and he was visibly happy.

I said, "Prophet of God, by God, you are the most deserving of the words of Abū Kabīr."

He set down what was in his hands and took me in his arms, kissing me on the forehead, and said, God bless and keep him, "ʿĀʾishah, I have never been happy with anyone the way I am with you."

I don't know what makes me happier, the victory at Khaybar, or the arrival of Jaʿfar.

The eye weeps, the heart grieves, we can say only what pleases our Lord. O Abraham, I grieve at your departure.

§9.6 Prophets will face the greatest trials, and yet be the most exemplary.

§9.8 Exalted God said: "Truly, my mercy has precedence over my anger."

§14.4 That is the city of my brother Jonah, peace be upon him.

§15.1 If you see a man who has been granted renunciation of the world and is of few words, draw close to him—he imparts wisdom.

§16.5 A Bedouin said to him, "What are we to think when we see camels like gazelles upon the sand, and then a mangy camel joins them and all become mangy?" The Prophet, God bless and preserve him, said, "Who infected the first one?"

§16.16 Truly, these women are ungrateful to their closest family. If you were kind to one of them for time eternal and she then took offense at something you did, she would say, "I have never seen you do anything good."

§17.1 The wise saying is the lost camel of the believer.

There is wisdom in poetry.

§17.3 Saying that there is no might or power except in God is one of the treasures of heaven.

§17.5 The truest saying spoken by a poet was that of the poet Labīd: Everything except . . .

§17.6 The world and everything in it is damned, except for the remembrance of God and what facilitates it, the scholar, and the seeker of knowledge.

§17.11 Your only true possessions are the food you have already consumed, the clothes you have already worn out, and the alms you have already given away.

§20.2 Marry a woman for her piety, her beauty, and her possessions, but most of all for her piety.

The whole world is pleasure, but the greatest pleasure is a devout woman.

A devout woman is like a white-feathered crow among crows.

§23.4 There are none in the land of my people, so you will find that I have an aversion to them.

§24.8 God will never elevate anything in this world without humbling it.

§24.15 The nursing woman is fortunate, the weaning woman unfortunate.

§28.8 There is no contagion and no evil omen.

§28.9 Flee from the leper as you flee from the lion.

Do not water the sick animals with the healthy.

§28.10 Seek good from those with beautiful faces.

§28.11 If you send me a letter, send it with someone who has a beautiful face and a beautiful name.

§28.21 Do you know what your Lord said? They said, "God and his Prophet know best." He said, "Exalted God says, 'It appears that among those

§37.16 I took care not to accept anything from anyone who was not of the Quraysh, the Thaqīf, or the Daws.

§40.2 On the day of resurrection, the person with the most favored station is the man who takes the reins of his horse while on God's path, striking fear into the enemy who also terrify him.

§41.21 She used to visit us in the days of Khadījah, and loyal attachment is part of faith.

§41.34 Do not rebuke Time, for God the Exalted is Time.

§42.3 It is a charitable act to treat people with gentleness.

After faith in God, the greatest form of discernment is expressing affection toward people.

Half of discernment is expressing affection toward people, half of living is good organization, and whoever is thrifty will not know distress.

§42.16 When I was taken on the night journey, the first thing that my Lord commanded me was, "Avoid idol worshippers, the consumption of wine, and the discourse of men."

Be wary of debating anyone who is insane, for he will stick to his argument till death.

Index

About the NYU Abu Dhabi Institute

The Library of Arabic Literature is supported by a grant from the NYU Abu Dhabi Institute, a major hub of intellectual and creative activity and advanced research. The Institute hosts academic conferences, workshops, lectures, film series, performances, and other public programs directed both to audiences within the UAE and to the worldwide academic and research community. It is a center of the scholarly community for Abu Dhabi, bringing together faculty and researchers from institutions of higher learning throughout the region.

NYU Abu Dhabi, through the NYU Abu Dhabi Institute, is a world-class center of cutting-edge research, scholarship, and cultural activity. The Institute creates singular opportunities for leading researchers from across the arts, humanities, social sciences, sciences, engineering, and the professions to carry out creative scholarship and conduct research on issues of major disciplinary, multidisciplinary, and global significance.

About the Typefaces

The Arabic body text is set in DecoType Naskh, designed by Thomas Milo and Mirjam Somers, based on an analysis of five centuries of Ottoman manuscript practice. The exceptionally legible result is the first and only typeface in a style that fully implements the principles of script grammar (*qawāʿid al-khaṭṭ*).

The Arabic footnote text is set in DecoType Emiri, drawn by Mirjam Somers, based on the metal typeface in the naskh style that was cut for the 1924 Cairo edition of the Qur'an.

Both Arabic typefaces in this series are controlled by a dedicated font layout engine. ACE, the Arabic Calligraphic Engine, invented by Peter Somers, Thomas Milo, and Mirjam Somers of DecoType, first operational in 1985, pioneered the principle followed by later smart font layout technologies such as OpenType, which is used for all other typefaces in this series.

The Arabic text was set with WinSoft Tasmeem, a sophisticated user interface for DecoType ACE inside Adobe InDesign. Tasmeem was conceived and created by Thomas Milo (DecoType) and Pascal Rubini (WinSoft) in 2005.

The English text is set in Adobe Text, a new and versatile text typeface family designed by Robert Slimbach for Western (Latin, Greek, Cyrillic) typesetting. Its workhorse qualities make it perfect for a wide variety of applications, especially for longer passages of text where legibility and economy are important. Adobe Text bridges the gap between calligraphic Renaissance types of the 15th and 16th centuries and high-contrast Modern styles of the 18th century, taking many of its design cues from early post-Renaissance Baroque transitional types cut by designers such as Christoffel van Dijck, Nicolaus Kis, and William Caslon. While grounded in classical form, Adobe Text is also a statement of contemporary utilitarian design, well suited to a wide variety of print and on-screen applications.

Titles Published by the Library of Arabic Literature

For more details on individual titles, visit www.libraryofarabicliterature.org

Classical Arabic Literature: A Library of Arabic Literature Anthology
Selected and translated by Geert Jan van Gelder (**2012**)

A Treasury of Virtues: Sayings, Sermons, and Teachings of ʿAlī, by al-Qāḍī al-Quḍāʿī, with the **One Hundred Proverbs** attributed to al-Jāḥiẓ
Edited and translated by Tahera Qutbuddin (**2013**)

The Epistle on Legal Theory, by al-Shāfiʿī
Edited and translated by Joseph E. Lowry (**2013**)

Leg over Leg, by Aḥmad Fāris al-Shidyāq
Edited and translated by Humphrey Davies (**4 volumes; 2013–14**)

Virtues of the Imām Aḥmad ibn Ḥanbal, by Ibn al-Jawzī
Edited and translated by Michael Cooperson (**2 volumes; 2013–15**)

The Epistle of Forgiveness, by Abū l-ʿAlāʾ al-Maʿarrī
Edited and translated by Geert Jan van Gelder and Gregor Schoeler (**2 volumes; 2013–14**)

The Principles of Sufism, by ʿĀʾishah al-Bāʿūniyyah
Edited and translated by Th. Emil Homerin (**2014**)

The Expeditions: An Early Biography of Muḥammad, by Maʿmar ibn Rāshid
Edited and translated by Sean W. Anthony (**2014**)

Two Arabic Travel Books
Accounts of China and India, by Abū Zayd al-Sīrāfī
Edited and translated by Tim Mackintosh-Smith (**2014**)
Mission to the Volga, by Aḥmad ibn Faḍlān
Edited and translated by James Montgomery (**2014**)

Disagreements of the Jurists: A Manual of Islamic Legal Theory, by al-Qāḍī al-Nuʿmān
Edited and translated by Devin J. Stewart (2015)

Consorts of the Caliphs: Women and the Court of Baghdad, by Ibn al-Sāʿī
Edited by Shawkat M. Toorawa and translated by the Editors of the Library of Arabic Literature (2015)

What ʿĪsā ibn Hishām Told Us, by Muḥammad al-Muwayliḥī
Edited and translated by Roger Allen (2 volumes; 2015)

The Life and Times of Abū Tammām, by Abū Bakr Muḥammad ibn Yaḥyā al-Ṣūlī
Edited and translated by Beatrice Gruendler (2015)

The Sword of Ambition: Bureaucratic Rivalry in Medieval Egypt, by ʿUthmān ibn Ibrāhīm al-Nābulusī
Edited and translated by Luke Yarbrough (2016)

Brains Confounded by the Ode of Abū Shādūf Expounded, by Yūsuf al-Shirbīnī
Edited and translated by Humphrey Davies (2 volumes; 2016)

Light in the Heavens: Sayings of the Prophet Muḥammad, by al-Qāḍī al-Quḍāʿī
Edited and translated by Tahera Qutbuddin (2016)

Risible Rhymes, by Muḥammad ibn Maḥfūẓ al-Sanhūrī
Edited and translated by Humphrey Davies (2016)

A Hundred and One Nights
Edited and translated by Bruce Fudge (2016)

The Excellence of the Arabs, by Ibn Qutaybah
Edited by James E. Montgomery and Peter Webb
Translated by Sarah Bowen Savant and Peter Webb (2017)

Scents and Flavors: A Syrian Cookbook
Edited and translated by Charles Perry (2017)

Arabian Satire: Poetry from 18th-Century Najd, by Ḥmēdān al-Shwēʿir
Edited and translated by Marcel Kurpershoek (2017)

In Darfur: An Account of the Sultanate and Its People, by Muḥammad ibn ʿUmar al-Tūnisī
Edited and translated by Humphrey Davies (**2 volumes; 2018**)

War Songs, by ʿAntarah ibn Shaddād
Edited by James E. Montgomery
Translated by James E. Montgomery with Richard Sieburth (**2018**)

Arabian Romantic: Poems on Bedouin Life and Love, by ʿAbdallah ibn Sbayyil
Edited and translated by Marcel Kurpershoek (**2018**)

Dīwān ʿAntarah ibn Shaddād: A Literary-Historical Study
By James E. Montgomery (**2018**)

Stories of Piety and Prayer: Deliverance Follows Adversity, by Muḥassin ibn ʿAlī al-Tanūkhī
Edited and translated by Julia Bray (**2019**)

The Philosopher Responds: An Intellectual Correspondence from the Tenth Century, by Abū Ḥayyān al-Tawḥīdī and Abū ʿAlī Miskawayh
Edited by Bilal Orfali and Maurice A. Pomerantz
Translated by Sophia Vasalou and James E. Montgomery (**2 volumes; 2019**)

Tajrīd sayf al-himmah li-stikhrāj mā fī dhimmat al-dhimmah: A Scholarly Edition of ʿUthmān ibn Ibrāhīm al-Nābulusī's Text
By Luke Yarbrough (**2020**)

The Discourses: Reflections on History, Sufism, Theology, and Literature—Volume One, by al-Ḥasan al-Yūsī
Edited and translated by Justin Stearns (**2020**)

English-only Paperbacks

Leg over Leg, by Aḥmad Fāris al-Shidyāq (**2 volumes; 2015**)
The Expeditions: An Early Biography of Muḥammad, by Maʿmar ibn Rāshid (**2015**)
The Epistle on Legal Theory: A Translation of al-Shāfiʿī's *Risālah*, by al-Shāfiʿī (**2015**)
The Epistle of Forgiveness, by Abū l-ʿAlāʾ al-Maʿarrī (**2016**)
The Principles of Sufism, by ʿĀʾishah al-Bāʿūniyyah (**2016**)

A Treasury of Virtues: Sayings, Sermons, and Teachings of ʿAlī, by al-Qāḍī al-Quḍāʿī with the **One Hundred Proverbs**, attributed to al-Jāḥiẓ (2016)

The Life of Ibn Ḥanbal, by Ibn al-Jawzī (2016)

Mission to the Volga, by Ibn Faḍlān (2017)

Accounts of China and India, by Abū Zayd al-Sīrāfī (2017)

A Hundred and One Nights (2017)

Disagreements of the Jurists: A Manual of Islamic Legal Theory, by al-Qāḍī al-Nuʿmān (2017)

What ʿĪsā ibn Hishām Told Us, by Muḥammad al-Muwayliḥī (2018)

War Songs, by ʿAntarah ibn Shaddād (2018)

The Life and Times of Abū Tammām, by Abū Bakr Muḥammad ibn Yaḥyā al-Ṣūlī (2018)

The Sword of Ambition, by ʿUthmān ibn Ibrāhīm al-Nābulusī (2019)

Brains Confounded by the Ode of Abū Shādūf Expounded: Volume One, by Yūsuf al-Shirbīnī (2019)

Brains Confounded by the Ode of Abū Shādūf Expounded: Volume Two, by Yūsuf al-Shirbīnī and **Risible Rhymes**, by Muḥammad ibn Maḥfūẓ al-Sanhūrī (2019)

The Excellence of the Arabs, by Ibn Qutaybah (2019)

Light in the Heavens: Sayings of the Prophet Muḥammad, by al-Qāḍī al-Quḍāʿī (2019)

About the Editor–Translator

Justin Stearns is associate professor in Arab Crossroads Studies at NYU Abu Dhabi. He is an intellectual historian of the pre-modern Muslim world, and is author of several articles on the historiography of al-Andalus and a book, *Infectious Ideas: Contagion in Premodern Islamic and Christian Thought in the Western Mediterranean*. He is preparing a book on the natural sciences in Morocco in the seventeenth century.